ORO Editions
Publishers of Architecture, Art, and Design
Gordon Goff: Publisher

www.oroeditions.com
info@oroeditions.com

Published by ORO Editions, San Francisco, CA

Copyright © 2021 Association of Collegiate Schools of Architecture, Inc. All rights reserved.

All rights reserved. No part of this book may be reproduced, stored in a retrieval system, or transmitted in any form or by any means, including electronic, mechanical, photocopying or microfilming, recording, or otherwise (except that copying permitted by Sections 107 and 108 of the U.S. Copyright Law and except by reviewers for the public press) without written permission from the publisher.

You must not circulate this book in any other binding or cover and you must impose this same condition on any acquirer.

Authors: Igor Marjanović, Marc J Neveu, Sara Stevens—editors
Preface: Marc J Neveu
Introduction: Igor Marjanović, Marc J Neveu, Sara Stevens
Book Design: Pascale Vonier
Project Manager: Alejandro Guzman-Avila
Managing Editor: Jake Anderson

10 9 8 7 6 5 4 3 2 1 First Edition

ISBN: 978-1-951541-69-9

Color Separations and Printing: ORO Group Ltd.
Printed in China.

ORO Editions makes a continuous effort to minimize the overall carbon footprint of its publications. As part of this goal, ORO Editions, in association with Global ReLeaf, arranges to plant trees to replace those used in the manufacturing of the paper produced for its books. Global ReLeaf is an international campaign run by American Forests, one of the world's oldest nonprofit conservation organizations. Global ReLeaf is American Forests' education and action program that helps individuals, organizations, agencies, and corporations improve the local and global environment by planting and caring for trees.

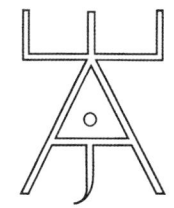

The—Evolving—Project

The·Journal of·Architectural Education·and the·Expansion of·Scholarship

Igor Marjanović, Marc J Neveu, Sara Stevens—editors

Contents

11 **Preface**	**13** **Introduction**
20 **Research**	**96** **Environment**
130 **Pedagogy**	**224** **Politics**
301 **Index**	

Chronology

Year	Issue	Title	Author	Category	Page
1947	1:1	The Architect Looks at Research	Walter A. Taylor	● Research	25
1955	10:1	A New Look at Civic Design	Kevin Lynch	● Environment	100
1955	10:1	The Architect's Role in Urban Renewal	Catherine Bauer	● Politics	228
1957	12:2	History and the Architect	Sigfried Giedion	● Pedagogy	134
1957	12:2	Research and Criticism in Architecture	Eduard Sekler	● Research	30
1959	14:2	Objectives of Architectural Education	Ralph Rapson	● Pedagogy	138
1960	15:1	Full Scale Prototype Structures	Arthur E. Burton	● Pedagogy	141
1960	15:1	How Become an Architect?	Richard J. Neutra	● Pedagogy	144
1961	15:4	Humanism and the Teaching of Architecture	Joseph Hudnut	● Research	33
1962	17:2-3	The Purpose of the City	John B. Jackson	● Environment	103
1962	17:2-3	The Ecology of the City	Ian McHarg	● Environment	105
1963	18:2	Architectural Education and Behavioral Science	Carleton Monroe Winslow Jr.	● Research	37
1967	21:3	Television as a Design Tool	Stuart W. Rose and M. Scheffel Pierce	● Pedagogy	145

Year	Issue	Title	Author	Category	Page
1967	21:5	The Environmental Design Umbrella	Lawrence B. Anderson	Pedagogy	150
1968	22:2	The Death of the Beaux-Arts: The Cal-Oregon Experiment in Design Education	Murray A. Milne and Charles W. Rusch	Pedagogy	152
1968	22:3	What Architectural Schools Expect from Sociology	Robert Gutman	Politics	230
1969	23:2	Toward a Theory of Architecture Machines	Nicholas Negroponte	Pedagogy	158
1969	23:4	The Money Problem	Daniel Solomon	Politics	232
1974	27:1	Review: Defensible Space by Oscar Newman	W. Russell Ellis	Environment	107
1974	27:1	Poetics	Louis I. Kahn	Pedagogy	162
1976	30:1	The Urban Landscape	Elizabeth Blackmar	Environment	109
1976	30:1	Messages in the Interstices: Symbols in the Urban Landscape	Marc Treib	Pedagogy	163
1977	30:3	Observations on Energy Use in Buildings	Richard Stein	Environment	113
1979	32:4	Notes of a Traveler	John Habraken	Research	39
1979	32:4	On Formal Analysis as Design Research	Denise Scott Brown	Research	45
1979	33:1	Gaming at CRS	Charles Estes	Pedagogy	168

1981	35:1	With People in Mind	Denise Scott Brown	● Research	51
1981	35:1	Commencement Address	Aldo van Eyck	● Environment	119
1982	35:2	Typology and Primary Elements	Todd Williams and Ricardo Scofidio	● Pedagogy	170
1982	36:2	Architecture as Drawing	Alberto Pérez-Gómez	● Pedagogy	173
1986	39:4	Past or Post Modern in Architectural Fashion	Diane Ghirardo	● Research	54
1987	40:2	An Open Letter to Architectural Educators and Students of Architecture	Daniel Libeskind	● Pedagogy	180
1986	40:2	Hold It (Meditations Upon a Gorgonzola Cheese)	Jennifer Bloomer	● Research	60
1987	40:3	Private Reactions to Public Criticism	Kathryn H. Anthony	● Pedagogy	182
1988	41:2	Gender Issues in Teaching Architectural History	Karen Kingsley	● Politics	234
1989	43:1	Black Architects: An Endangered Species	Robert Traynham Coles	● Politics	240
1991	44:3	The Crisis of Interdisciplinary Historiography	Mark Jarzombek	● Politics	243
1991	44:3	The Pruitt-Igoe Myth	Katharine G. Bristol	● Politics	249
1992	45:2	The Ecology Question	Richard Ingersoll	● Politics	258

Year	Issue	Title	Author	Category	Page
1993	47:1	Writing Multiculturalism into Architectural Curricula	Regina Davis	● Politics	261
1995	49:1	Contesting the Public Realm: Struggles Over Public Space in Los Angeles	Margaret Crawford	● Politics	269
1999	53:2	Boundary Studies	Lily Chi	● Pedagogy	193
2000	54:1	(W)rapped Space: The Architecture of Hip Hop	Craig Wilkins	● Research	62
2001	55:2	Bauhaus Hausfrau: Gender Formation in Design Education	Katarina Rüedi Ray	● Politics	275
2003	57:1	Imminent Domain: Pervasive Computing and the Public Realm	Dana Cuff	● Politics	283
2006	59:3	The Canon and the Void: Gender, Race, and Architectural History Texts	Kathryn H. Anthony and Meltem Ö. Gürel	● Pedagogy	200
2007	60:4	Compelling Yet Unreliable Theories of Sustainability	Kiel Moe	● Environment	122
2007	61:1	Research in Design: Planning Doing Monitoring Learning	Stephen Kieran	● Research	75
2007	61:1	Is There Research in the Studio?	Kazys Varnelis	● Research	80
2009	62:3	The Postwar Legacy of Architectural Research	Avigail Sachs	● Research	84
2011	64:2	From Model to Mashup: A Pedagogical Experiment in Thinking Historically about the Future	Ana Miljački	● Pedagogy	212
2019	73:2	Images Doing Work: Construction Photography at the Tuskegee Institute and Black Mountain College	Anna Goodman and Maura Lucking	● Politics	292

Acknowledgments

This book has been produced under the extraordinary conditions of the COVID-19 pandemic, in home offices, with interruptions by children and pets, across time zones, and with gratitude for the help, support, and contributions of many individuals. We wish to thank Michael Monti, executive director of the Association of Collegiate Schools of Architecture (ACSA) and expert scanner, and Carol Mannix, publications manager at the ACSA, for their support and efforts in realizing, producing, and finalizing this book. We also wish to thank Pascale Vonier for her excellent graphic eye and extreme patience with ever-late editors. Karen Jacobson provided invaluable editorial advice, for which we are deeply grateful. Iryna Demianiuk helped correct image scans of photocopied black-and-white images that were blurry to begin with. The editors are grateful as well for the financial support of the ACSA.

We are especially indebted to all the authors, reviewers, board members, staff, and editors who have contributed to the journal over the many decades of its existence. Without their efforts, this volume would not have been possible.

Igor Marjanović is a current board member of the *Journal of Architectural Education* and the JoAnne Stolaroff Cotsen Professor and chair of the undergraduate architecture program at Washington University in St. Louis.

Marc J Neveu is the current executive editor of the *Journal of Architectural Education* and is a professor and the architecture program head at Arizona State University.

Sara Stevens is a previous board member of the *Journal of Architectural Education* and an associate professor at the University of British Columbia's School of Architecture and Landscape Architecture.

Preface

Marc J Neveu

It is with a sense of humility that I, as the current executive editor of the *Journal of Architectural Education*, introduce a selection of essays from the journal's seventy-five-year history to readers who may not have been reading the JAE twenty-five, much less fifty, years ago. Rereading almost seventy-five years of the journal took time; narrowing down the essays to those contained in this volume was not easy. Amazing essays were left out. That said, the process was made all the more enjoyable by the help from members of the Editorial Board and, specifically, my coeditors Igor Marjanović and Sara Stevens. I am forever grateful for their attention to detail, expansive knowledge, and incredible generosity with their time.

 When I first joined the Editorial Board, the meetings were described as "the best faculty meeting you never had." Bringing together diverse perspectives from a wide variety of institutions and subfields, the board meets twice annually to debate and discuss the submissions, themes, and content to include in each issue. These discussions are intellectually rich and always collegial. I don't know who coined the "best faculty meeting" phrase, though I suspect George Dodds had something to do with it, but I do know that has been the case for my tenure on the board. My experience with and on the Editorial Board has been one of the most rewarding of my academic career.

 Over the past seventy-five years, the design of the journal; its content categories; the organizational structure of its leadership; its funding models; its digital presence; the scale of the publication; its editors, authors, readers, and staff; and the publishing context have all radically changed. That said, the mission of the journal has not. The *Journal of Architectural Education* has been published since 1947 for the purpose of enhancing architectural design education, theory, and practice. I am honored to have contributed to this effort and to have joined so many of the journal's "best faculty meetings." I look forward to its continued evolution.

Introduction

The Evolving Project

Igor Marjanović, Marc J Neveu, and Sara Stevens

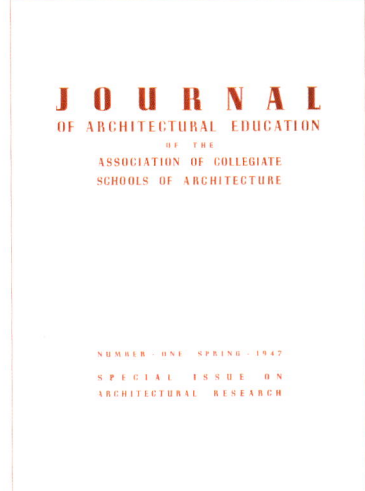 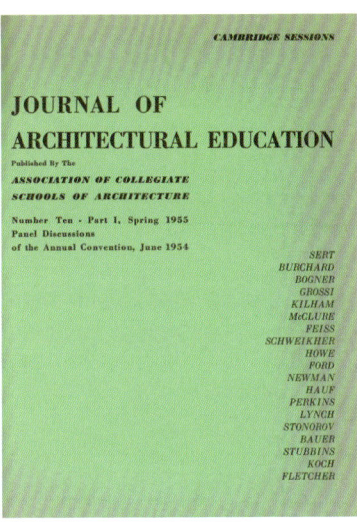 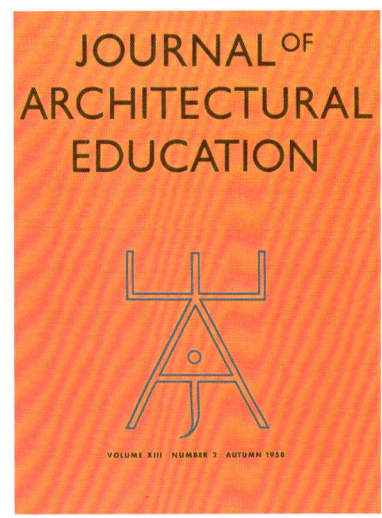

1940s **1950s**

The *Journal of Architectural Education* was first published in 1947 by the Association of Collegiate Schools of Architecture (ACSA), the oldest collateral organization for architecture schools, founded in 1912. The journal developed from a pre–World War II bulletin called *The Evolving Architect*, edited by the educator, researcher, and practitioner Walter T. Rolfe. Given the constant evolution of the journal, that name has proven to be prescient. In 1946 the prominent architectural historian Turpin Bannister, who was also influential in the formation of the *Journal of the Society of Architectural Historians*, was tapped to revive the effort, and he named the ACSA publication the *Journal of Architectural Education*. Through the journal's first decade, and through a rotating cast of editors and authors, the content consisted mostly of proceedings from annual meetings of architectural educators. As the journal evolved, it incorporated longer and more scholarly content, including design work.

The intention of collecting this scholarship in the present volume is not only to reprint important essays within the journal's history—and within the field at large—but also to bring light to the evolution of postwar architectural discourse. Over the course of its seventy-five years of publication, the journal has traced the expansion of the concept of architectural scholarship from the training of professional architects to participation in the larger research culture within universities and in society. As one reads through the issues, the pressures within and upon the field are evident, whether from internal debates between more technical or more artistic approaches or from allied fields such as engineering or planning. As the decades progress, the role of research in the field becomes more prominent, including the questions of what it constitutes and how it might be measured, paralleling the rise of the research university and the societal shift toward new knowledge production that so characterized the postwar years.

The book is organized into four major themes: research, environment, pedagogy, and politics. The themes were specifically chosen not to align with the various subcategories of discourse—such as history/theory, representation, design, or technology—or with allied fields such as landscape architecture, urban design, or interior architecture. Instead the four broader themes allow for interwoven threads and dialogues to emerge across many decades and locations. Questions also emerge: What pedagogical issues appear and then fade? How does our approach to environment change and reflect differing views of the environment and, more recently, climate change? What constitutes architectural research? How is it carried out and to what ends? Finally, how is architecture related to, and understood through, various political lenses? These questions have been germane throughout the history of the journal, and they remain

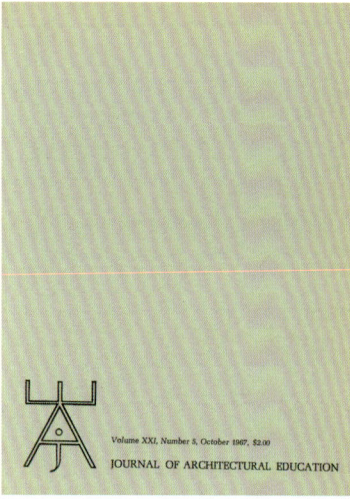

1960s

relevant today, in particular at a moment when architectural discourse is reengaging with politics and the environment with a renewed sense of urgency.

Creating this edited volume presented an interesting opportunity to frame the ebb and flow of architectural discourse as documented by one of its most significant scholarly outlets. Our intent is not to compile a "best of" volume but to highlight themes and resonances across decades, to illuminate different corners of research, and to track the evolution of architectural scholarship. The introductions and themes reframe the content. Illustrations have been refreshed, replaced by higher-quality or color versions where possible. Yet the project also presented a predicament, as the three-hundred-page limit—as generous as it might have seemed initially—posed a challenge in that we were unable to include many essays that deserve to be reprinted. None are lost to history, however, as the issues are all available online through the JAE website. We see this book as a companion to the online repository of JAE content, and we hope that readers will take advantage of both resources.

Institutional Chronicle Meets as Disciplinary History

Focus on Research: 1940s and 1950s
Building on Rolfe's prewar bulletin *The Evolving Architect*, the journal provided a platform to engage research as an emerging area of the field for both scholars and practitioners. When the decision was made in 1946 to revive the bulletin, under the title *Journal of Architectural Education*, the intent was to imagine a journal that would accommodate gradual change in the discipline. The first issue included news items, the results of a survey on research, and scholarship on research in architecture. Other early issues included reflections from prominent educators such as William Wurster and Sigfried Giedion. Reflecting participation at the ACSA Annual meetings, the authors of the journal were not diverse, in terms of either race or gender. It took almost a full decade for a female author, Catherine Bauer (1955), to be published. W. Russell Ellis's book review (1974) was, we believe, the journal's first article by a Black author. The composition of the faculty, as well as the visibility of race and gender, while perhaps typical of the time, nonetheless underscores the journal's complicity in perpetuating a largely white and male-dominated field.

The journal's contents over its first decade consisted mostly of reports and a few presentations from the annual ACSA conference. The secretary of the ACSA at the time, Buford Pickens, helped shift the emphasis to more scholarly contributions, and that change can be seen by the end of the 1950s. Discussions of pedagogy again focused on the question of how best to prepare a class of professionals in a field formerly dominated by the ideology of the École des Beaux-Arts. As American and Canadian architecture schools assimilated the apprenticeship model, the model of the École des Beaux-Arts, and, later, the Bauhaus model of education, the journal existed as a site for debating the merits of different approaches. Toward the end of the 1950s the journal began to present questions about the limits of the field: whether an architect ought to be involved in urban renewal, for example, or how humanism might influence the practice of architecture.

Limited in page count, the journal during these decades was relatively consistent in its graphic layout.

 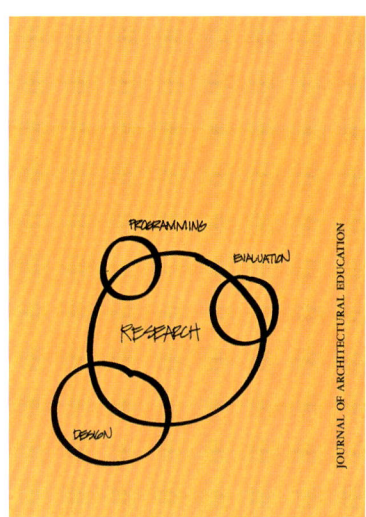 

1970s

While the covers remained sober, an icon composed of the journal's initials landed on the cover of volume 11 in 1956 and continued to appear into the late 1960s. It resembles a one-eyed totemic creature with some sort of crown that also resembles its own typographic character. It is a curious addition to what was a relatively innocuous graphic approach. Having caught our attention, it appears on the cover of this publication as well.

Focus on Environment: 1960s and 1970s
The form of the journal in the 1960s and 1970s was lively if never consistent. The content varied greatly, and new types of contributions were introduced and abandoned regularly. One constant was the publication of the presentations at the AIA-ACSA Teachers Conference at Cranbrook Academy of Art every two years. (AIA stands for American Institute of Architects.) With a focus on teaching, the mini conferences included invited speakers and had an audience of around fifty to sixty faculty members. Proceedings were published as an issue of the JAE from 1963 through the 1970s. Another oddity was the printing of the yearbook of the Environmental Experience Stipends Program, whose mimeographed reports became a journal issue for that year. Two years later the second mimeographed report was published, out of order, with the original volume number. Added to all of this was traditional scholarship, as well as new initiatives, including poetry, "place" reviews, and letters to the editor. Still, issues were typically not more than sixteen pages long, and images were limited to black-and-white photographs of people speaking at conferences.

By the 1970s the journal had grown in page count, with issues averaging around thirty pages. Book reviews were included in addition to scholarly essays. In 1975 the organizational structure of the journal was reformed. Dave Clarke, then executive director of the ACSA, assumed the role of executive editor for publications. He instituted a policy of themed issues, along with guest editors—the first being Kent Bloomer on "Humanist Issues in Architecture" (1975). For the first time, theme issues titled "Canada," "Landscape," "Preservation," "Energy," "Aging," "The Profession," "Drawing," "Symbolism," and "Gaming" appear and were mixed with open issues dedicated to a variety of topics. Also changed was the journal's title. Beginning in 1975 and for almost a decade, the full title of the journal was replaced with the three initials, rarely capitalized: *jae*.

Environment, however broadly conceived, became the driving disciplinary question of the day, even if the meaning of the term always required definition. While the design of buildings still sat at the center of concerns, with questions of energy and indoor environment paramount among them, the essays reflected the growth of scholarship as the expansion, quite literally, of the boundaries of the field. Rather than limiting their discussions to the shell of a building or site, the authors raised questions about urbanism, economics, ecology, historic preservation, game theory, and behavioral science. Through this, the term *environmental design* became the standard way to address the collection of disciplines around architecture—including landscape architecture, planning, and urban design—which together created the "built environment." As all of this publication was taking place in the context of the oil crisis, the authors were asking questions about the social responsibility and agency of architects.

1980s

Focus on Pedagogy: 1980s and 1990s
In 1982 the composition of the board again changed, and with this change came a shift in editorial direction. Under a new executive editor, Peter Papademetriou, themes and guest editors were eliminated, the Editorial Board was instituted, and a blind peer-review process was established, replacing a process that had been casual at best up to that point in the history of the journal. Driving these changes was an editorial decision to present a broader discipline of ideas rather than a specialized discipline of themes. And the journal went through a complete redesign. The yellow covers of previous issues gave way to a design featuring a grid, and a larger format was instituted. Interviews were also introduced; most bizarre, perhaps, was an interview with the Nazi architect Albert Speer, seemingly included for those interested in neoclassical design but also reflecting a complete lack of political awareness.

In 1986 executive editor David Bell introduced two major changes to the journal. First, he reintroduced Op Arch—opinion pieces that were not peer-reviewed as a way to include very current debates and polemics. Bell also proposed including design content, reflecting the aspiration to legitimize design work in a peer-reviewed form and within the larger research culture of universities. The first call for design submissions came with the architectural historian Diane Ghirardo's first issue as executive editor, which in 1989 included a design for a car wash by C. Shayne O'Neil. Ghirardo focused on including more architectural criticism as well as letters to the editor, which led to more critical and polemical material. The journal's page count also expanded significantly: by the late 1980s it had doubled in size, and in 1990 it was again completely redesigned to accommodate a variety of formats and types of content, as well as a vast increase in illustrations. Peggy Deamer was appointed as inaugural design editor (1996), which led to a greater number of peer-reviewed and scholarly submissions in the field of design. At the same time the journal evolved to be more inclusive in its authorship and diverse in its themes. An increasing number of special issues, essays, and authors, such as Karen Kingsley (1988) and Regina Davis (1993), focused on gender and race. Though these were major issues for the discipline and society at large, they still played a minor part in the larger arc of the journal.

The 1980s saw yet another shift, both cultural and disciplinary. As "late capitalism" accelerated numerous postmodern tendencies—including the critique of architecture's social mission as a myth—the discipline and profession turned to historicism and an obsession with surface. Scholarship in the journal aligned with the larger cultural shifts: the prominence of philosophy, questions of representation, and the Beaux-Arts tradition. The multiplicity of voices shifts into focus, while previous concerns, such as the reliance on social and behavioral sciences, fall into the background. In the 1990s a number of scholars poignantly questioned the lack of gender representation in the field and, certainly more timidly, the lack of racial representation and the presence of structural racism. Methodologically, some authors backed their arguments about race and gender with data, using social science tools to make visible a long-standing set of problems. Others embraced cultural theory (including feminist theory), psychology, and identity formation in their courses, asking students to read different kinds of history texts or to write new his-

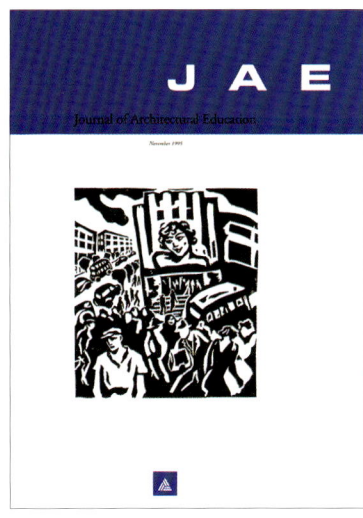  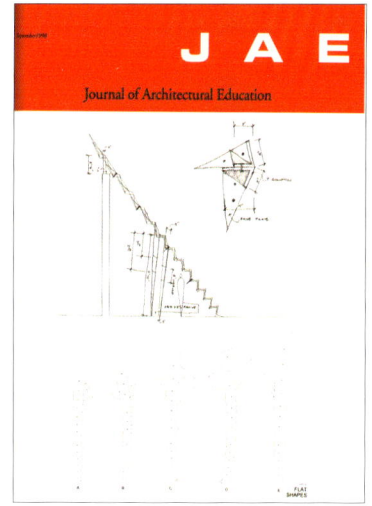

1990s

tories themselves (such as those of Black architects in the United States). Many essays report on student projects in studio that engage questions of the body, giving prominence to design and form making as effective avenues for the creation of new scholarship. This question of pedagogy as research returns to one of the original premises of the journal—namely the question of what actually constitutes research in architecture—while also providing a springboard to the next two decades, which saw an increased interest in both design scholarship and politicization.

Focus on Politics: 2000s and 2010s
In 2002 executive editor Barbara Allen, responding to the increased interest in publishing visual material, introduced a new layout that would more easily accommodate design work. Lily Chi, then design editor, proposed categories for design content such as Design as Research and Design as Critical Inquiry, reinforcing the fundamental streams of architectural research. As a result of the changes, the design content increased in page count, improved in printing quality, and deepened the scholarly engagement with design over case study–like presentations. Although limited, project images were printed in color, reflecting the saturated media landscape of the period, and the journal made its first foray into the World Wide Web, as most media expanded into new online platforms as well.

Executive editor George Dodds began his term in 2007 with a redesigned all-white cover as a nod to the journal's first issue, published in 1947—both issues looked at architecture and research. Under Dodds's leadership the two current essay categories—Design as Scholarship and Scholarship of Design—were established, and the journal shifted from four issues per year to two. In a continuing effort to carve out space in the journal for design content, the category Design as Scholarship created clearer boundaries around what constituted design as a scholarly activity and helped to construct a robust discourse around design in the journal's pages. With the continued changes in the media landscape, executive editor Marc J Neveu introduced a new website distinct from that of the ACSA that included access to the entire archive of the journal as well as a redesign of the physical journal. Under Neveu's leadership Amy Kulper and the Design Committee (established by Dodds) developed new frameworks for curated design content, selected by the editors, as well as Micro Narratives. Reviews editor Ivan Rupnik led the expansion of the Review section, which is now completely online. As such, reviews are not limited to the printed journal's production schedule or space constraints and can more quickly respond to recent publications, exhibitions, and events and support scholars on the tenure track. A consistent thread of articles continues to engage multiple identities, viewpoints, and narratives, calling for scholarly, professional, and wider political reform. Yet despite the continuous, if not dominant, presence of such critical voices in JAE—and in academia more broadly—questions remain: Why, forty years after some of these critiques were raised, does the field still embody such stark inequalities? Why is the representation of Black and Indigenous people and other people of color so lacking, both in the field and more broadly?

The nature of scholarship calls for both timely and timeless responses. As the new millennium brought significant shifts globally, including the inability of

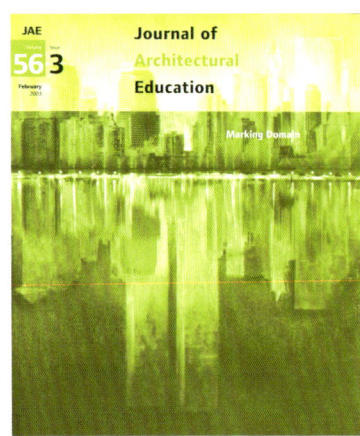

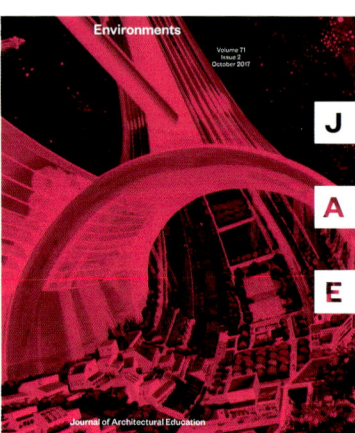

2000s **2010s**

neoliberal capitalism to address widespread climate crisis or provide a transparent platform of political engagement for all citizens, the JAE deepened its critical voice in addressing issues of diversity, equity, and inclusion in particular. This is demonstrated not only in the content of the scholarship produced but also in the constituency of the Editorial Board, theme editors, authors, and issue themes. Efforts over the previous decade to diversify the board, paired with a rigorous double-blind peer review process that selects essays regardless of author identity or affiliation, are just a beginning. While a scholarly journal is not able to address massive social and political issues with the speed of the news media, it may be able to have a more lasting effect by producing scholarship through a process that is consciously inclusive. As many authors have repeatedly reminded us on the pages of JAE, architects and scholars are not elected officials, so they should not assume such authority. Yet their responsibility as citizens and teachers remains, and that is perhaps the main lesson of the last two "politicizing" decades—to educate the new generations of architects on the basis of facts and scholarship means that the road to social change is a slow, multigenerational process. Encompassing the work of many generations of scholars, this book seeks to establish important historical arcs that trace these changes over the decades, suggesting not only lessons from the past but also pathways for the future.

Notes on Republication

The complexity of selecting essays published over a long span of time requires a few explanatory notes. We have not revised the texts but have instead maintained the authors' original voices and styles. Some images have been eliminated for legibility; many images lacked captions in the journal and here as well. Certain texts were written as short reports or op-eds, or even as a poem, and do not align with today's expectations for scholarly prose, yet their unique voices are authentic and telling of an era in which architects grappled with the fundamental question of what written scholarship in the field should be. Some references have been edited for clarity, and we have attempted to correct typographical or grammatical errors.

Assumptions about gender also do not align with today's expectations. In many historical essays the use of pronouns reflects the assumption that all architects were men; we have left these references as they were in the original, even when they contradicted themselves. For example, John Habraken's article (1979) refers throughout to the "traveling architect" as a man but illustrates the article with a photograph of two women hikers, seemingly in charge of their own destinies (see figure 1 in Habraken). Terminology has been left as in the originals, even though it may reflect an earlier political moment and not ours, for example, in the treatment of terms referring to race or ethnicity and in the oversimplified dualism of Western versus non-Western. Beyond these general notes, other problematic or unclear references, where found, have been called out in editors' notes within the individual articles.

Research

25
1947
The Architect Looks at Research
Walter A. Taylor

30
1957
Research and Criticism in Architecture
Eduard Sekler

33
1961
Humanism and the Teaching of Architecture
Joseph Hudnut

37
1963
Architectural Education and Behavioral Science
Carleton Monroe Winslow Jr.

39
1979
Notes of a Traveler
John Habraken

45
1979
On Formal Analysis as Design Research
Denise Scott Brown

51
1981
With People in Mind
Denise Scott Brown

54
1986
Past or Post Modern in Architectural Fashion
Diane Ghirardo

60
1986
Hold It (Meditations Upon a Gorgonzola Cheese)
Jennifer Bloomer

62
2000
(W)rapped Space: The Architecture of Hip Hop
Craig Wilkins

75
2007
Research in Design: Planning Doing Monitoring Learning
Stephen Kieran

80
2007
Is There Research in the Studio?
Kazys Varnelis

84
2009
The Postwar Legacy of Architectural Research
Avigail Sachs

Research

Igor Marjanović and Sara Stevens

> It is our hope that this book will be a help and inspiration to war-weary architects once more starting the joyous task of creation. We have balanced the book with technical and aesthetic information and with the sociology necessary for the modern, humanitarian architect. The aim has been to show trends and to help the forward-looking architect by giving him the necessary background of basic contemporary knowledge on which his imaginative work should be based.
>
> —Jane Drew

Reflecting on a sobering yet optimistic moment in the aftermath of World War II, Jane Drew captured a major shift in the architectural profession taking place in the United Kingdom and beyond—namely, a transition from the neoclassical Beaux-Arts tradition to active participation in postwar reconstruction through new forms of design knowledge influenced by building science, sociology, and culture. Taken together, these changes contributed to the emergence of a new professional, "the modern, humanitarian architect." Central to this shift was the alignment of architectural education and practice with the progressive social and formal agenda of modernism and the subsequent introduction of the term *research* into academia and practice. Indeed, *research* was one of the bywords of architectural modernity, often used to describe the professional work of postwar architects focusing on public housing and larger urban systems. Consequently, new books were published and new architecture programs were initiated to address this shift, so it is not surprising that the first issue of the *Journal of Architectural Education* (JAE) in 1947, edited by Turpin Bannister, was devoted to research, including Walter A. Taylor's manifesto-like "The Architect Looks at Research." Elaborating on the importance of sociology and technology and the distinctions between "Free Fundamental," "Basic Fundamental," and "Applied Research," Taylor argues for a structured approach to research in education and practice and the importance of professional and governmental entities, such as research stations, national agencies, and the recently created Department of Education and Research at the American Institute of Architects, which he led.

This line of inquiry continued into the 1960s, with authors like Carleton Monroe Winslow Jr. (1963) arguing for the importance of social and behavioral sciences in architectural research, cementing the merger of a modernist agenda and socially progressive vision that would become an important trend in the JAE and in the field more broadly—one recounted in Avigail Sachs's 2009 essay "The Postwar Legacy of Architectural Research." Sachs cannily argued that architects of this period used the term *research* in a fashion similar to the way we use the term *theory* today—namely to expand the fixed territory of practice. As Sachs recounts, despite significant intellectual and financial investments in sun labs and wind tunnels across the country, the idea of architectural research was never fully realized, as many experiments had limited impact or were short-lived. Regardless, the architects of this era "were not arguing, necessarily, for the 'scientification' of the design process" and "did not conflate research with design, but rather distinguished it as a systematic exploration to yield generalizations that could be used by architects in a range of contexts." And herein lies one of the main conundrums of architects' engagement with research as told in the pages of the JAE: can design be considered a form of research in its own right?

Theory, Criticism, and Design Research
This dilemma is evident in a shift taking place a mere decade after the first issue of JAE, with repeated calls for architects to engage a more humanistic approach. A number of essays focused on the importance of arts and humanities, such as Eduard Sekler's "Research and Criticism in Architecture" (1957), arguing for theory and criticism as the foundation of architects' design judgment. Similarly, Joseph Hudnut's text "Humanism in the Teaching of Architecture" (1961) provides an early example of the revalorization of history—but also theology and humanities—stating that students should not "rush too precipitately into the iron arms of the Bauhaus."

This would expand into a full-blown critique of modernism by a generation of authors who resorted to history and semiotics as a way to revalorize both the past and the present of architecture. Denise Scott Brown was one of the most important proponents of that criticism, channeling it into a completely new approach, which she labeled "design research." Her 1979 article "On Formal Analysis as Design Research" elaborates on her studio teaching, in which students mapped Las Vegas in many different ways in order to understand its formal and vernacular qualities—as disjointed as they were—acting not so much as scientists but as designers with formal analyses and propositions in mind. She sees studio teaching as a form of research in its own right, one that could result in new forms of knowledge. "Our research produced written descriptions, movies, video tapes, slides, photos, tapes, maps, charts, matrices, drawings, two songs, a cake, and a book," concludes Scott Brown. This wide palette speaks to the ability of architecture to stretch the notion of research to its limits, while repositioning itself as a wide, generalist discipline. Or, as Hans Hollein famously wrote in 1968, "Everything is architecture" ("Alles ist Architektur"), capturing the spirit of the entire era. In her 1987 article "Hold It (Meditations upon a Gorgonzola Cheese)"—another delicious reference—Jennifer Bloomer proclaims, "you can see the architecture wherever it is," using the metaphor of her hometown of Atlanta as "an intricate assemblage of steel, concrete, plastic, and plywood, with cranes saluting and pieces of buildings going up and down." This multiplicity of design languages, research outputs, and methodologies recalls John Habraken's (1979) metaphor of the architectural researcher as a traveler—a mapmaker, a careful observer armed with tools of analysis and intuition, all at once.

The ongoing anxiety about whether studio teaching constitutes research emphasizes a tension between the demands of professional practice and that of the university and, ultimately, the uncertainty of the methodological basis of architectural research. This question is revisited in Kazys Varnelis's article "Is There Research in the Studio?" (2007). The essay depicts a historical arc of design research based on the innovative use of visual imagery—such as drawing, photography, and film—to provide new considerations for people, spaces, and community. While they trace different protagonists in their essays—from Charles and Ray Eames to Alison and Peter Smithson—it returns to the seminal role of Scott Brown's Las Vegas studio and her practice with Robert Venturi. Such studio-based practices are not only an example of architecture's exceptionalism when it comes to research but also a potential new model of research more broadly, in which architecture's uniquely generalist voice could be meaningful beyond the field itself.

Such historical continuity of architects' engagement with visual research tools and synthetic thinking often defied the modern-postmodern divides. Scott Brown "returned" to JAE in 1981, this time as a practicing architect rather than an educator. In "With People in Mind," she argues for a generalist approach in architectural practice too, one that does not separate "people or technology, form, style, economics" but instead looks at their integration. And in doing so, she poses a larger dilemma: "Although there is indeed much to question in the nostrums evolved by architects and planners of the Great Society, we are surely wiser for their experience. . . . There must be a way to be socially concerned in the 1980s." Through these words she captures the dilemma of an entire generation of architects caught between the Great Society of the 1960s and the late capitalism of the 1980s, two moments that are loosely aligned with architectural modernism and postmodernism.

Research, Knowledge, and Society

Somewhat paradoxically, the ultimate impact of design research as a postmodern category was measured by the modernist question of architecture's social contract. This gap was widely debated in the 1980s and 1990s, including in Diane Ghirardo's 1986 essay "Past or Post Modern in Architectural Fashion." She attacks corporate postmodern architects such as Charles Jencks (whom she called a "theorist"—in quotation marks), Robert A. M. Stern, and Stanley Tigerman, criticizing them for their bland glass architecture or superficial historical pastiche and accusing them of "diverting attention from issues of substance to issues of surface." Writing during the Cold War, Ghirardo is equally critical of architects on both ends of the spectrum, arguing that "capitalist formalism denies culturally based meanings and instead promotes architecture as elitist manipulation, while Marxism defines architecture as a craft resulting from typological analyses devoid of personal expression."

In some ways Ghirardo's criticism points to the fact that at its best architecture engages cultural meaning and personal expression, which is an argument that could be expanded to the question of research too. Rather than being concerned with the exactitude of its own methodology, architectural research can be seen as a broad spectrum of activities that engage the manifold intersections of architecture and culture at many different scales. Craig Wilkins's essay from 2000 integrates a wide array of cultural references: from Russian Constructivism and Henri Lefebvre's social production of space to "specific African-American spatial practices of this cultural moment informed by transnational diaspora spatial practices." In making a case for a hip-hop architecture—based on a design proposal for a hip-hop park on Chicago's South Side—articles like this are important as they bring discourses in relationship to each other, rather than promoting scholarly specialization. Consequently, architectural research moves freely from big to small, from individual to collective, often in nonlinear ways, creating not only pedagogical but also practical openings. For Stephen Kieran (2007) there is a similar question of the relationship between architecture and its natural environment—including light and air—that is negotiated through knowledge transfer between science and design. "Research brings science to our art," Kieran wrote, recalling the ethos of postwar architects. He continued, "We need a deep research ethic to guide the art of intuition." Still, as recently as the 2000s, the tension between architectural practice, Kieran's primary profile, and research had not been put to rest (with even a harking back to the Beaux-Arts–inflected "art of intuition"!).

Kieran's words emphasize the unfinished nature of the larger project of architectural research, which, in the end, may not be a methodological predicament so much as a reflection of architecture as a tangible discipline that is at the same time constantly on the move—always repositioning itself relative to the fast-moving pace of science, technology, and society. This is *the* evolving project of architectural research—to paraphrase the source of our title—a loose springboard to generate new knowledge, often in unpredictable and opposing ways. This capacity to generate new discourses is also reflected in the structure of this book and the chapters that follow: pedagogy as a uniquely architectural territory of research studios, seminars, and publications that saw architecture as environment (spatial or ecological, described by technical or visual means) or architecture as politics (a form of spatial practice laden with questions of power, governance, and who we are, both individually and collectively). These are the questions that stem from architects' attempts to reckon with the methodological questions of their work—including research—the evolving story that is telling not only of a single journal but also of the shifting role of knowledge in our society more broadly. These questions were relevant back then in the early days of the journal, and yet they remain pertinent even today, when populist political rhetoric casts doubt on the validity of scholarly work. Venues such as JAE therefore have an even greater importance and responsibility to facilitate the production of new knowledge, even in ways that are methodologically messy and idiosyncratic, allowing architecture to embrace forms of research that are not welcomed elsewhere—inquiries that are empirical and intuitive, textual and visual, political and formal, all at once.

Note
Epigraph: Jane Drew, *Architects' Year Book*, vol. 1 (London: Paul Elek, 1945), dust jacket.

The Architect Looks at Research

Walter A. Taylor
American Institute of Architects

What is Research?
Research may be variously defined and classified. Dictionary definitions of research are "A searching for something, especially with care and diligence"; "Careful or critical examination in seeking facts or principles, diligent investigation." It may be most broadly defined as "Organized search for useful knowledge."

Classification of Research
The traditional subdivision of science and research has been as "pure" and "applied." Careful analysis suggests a three-way division:

A. *Free Fundamental* research, for which the application may be at first unknown. This kind of activity, in the words of Vannevar Bush, "extends the endless frontiers of knowledge." It is in this type of research that universities make their distinct and most important contributions. Less frequently it is carried on through endowed or industry-supported fellowships in non-academic institutions.

B. *Objective Fundamental* research. While dealing with basic concepts and data, this research attempts to provide insight and understanding relevant to some field of practical importance. Research of this general classification may be found in all types of institutions and laboratories. Many universities are well fitted to carry on this kind of research, especially problems involving two or more fields of knowledge. Some of the most important problems in architecture and the building industry are of this type, involving physiology, psychology, sociology, the physical sciences, home economics, structural engineering, etc. As in practice the architect is the coordinator in a team of specialists, so in these broad problems having to do with shelter for human activities the architecture faculty are the logical leaders in the university research.

C. *Applied Research* is concerned with determining the qualities and performance of a vast variety of materials and equipment, singly and in combination. It bulks very large in time and personnel, and is of immediate concern to industry of all kinds. It is carried on in thousands of industrial, commercial, government, and university laboratories. It is more thoroughly and systematically performed under the auspices of organizations such as the American Society for Testing Material, the Underwriters' Laboratories, the Bureau of Standards, etc.

A school of architecture related to an engineering experiment station in the same university may aid in this kind of research, perhaps most helpfully by indicating new problems and suggesting procedures and type of findings required.

Other types and classifications of research may be related to the above three-way grouping.

Universities and Research
The history of science and the history of education show an important relationship between research and the universities ever since the founding of the thirteenth century universities. Crowther notes a decline in vigor of European universities beginning in the nineteenth century because of the lack of experimental science.

Roger Bacon and Boyle, early scientists of eminence, emphasized practical applications of scientific knowledge. Bacon suggested a classification of scientists as Pioneers, Benefactors, and Interpreters. He classified experiments as "experimenta lucifera" (i.e., light-shedding, fundamental) and "experimenta fructifera" (i.e., fruitful, applied).

There is excellent historic precedent in the life and work of Count Rumford, American by birth, for the studied application of science to increasing the health, happiness, and comfort of humanity. Rumford's science was basic, but he was motivated by zeal for the use of science to improve living conditions. He began research in the fields of heating and fuel, ventilation, smoke abatement, and illumination.

The Industrial Revolution of course provided great impetus to scientific research in the universities, typified by W. Farish, appointed in 1816 at Cambridge as Professor of Natural and Experimental Philosophy.

Only since the nineteenth century have teaching laboratories been accepted as parts of universities. Now not only are they accepted, but it is a basic distinction between a college and a university that in the latter, scholars are pioneering in knowledge. In some institutions teaching is a parallel or even secondary function.

The university research worker can bring to bear on a problem a point of view different from that of the industrial research worker. The university man may have a broader and better background of fundamentals. He can also approach the problem more openly because he "doesn't know that it can't be done."

During the war years some most significant fundamental contributions were made. The greater accomplishments were in application. But by and large, we have been living off of our scientific capital, which is now in need of replenishment.

Research and Schools of Architecture
Teaching can never become secondary in schools of architecture, but the Association of Collegiate Schools of Architecture could very well promulgate a policy with regard to research that is distinctly architectural and of the "objective fundamental" type.

The thinking of schools of architecture regarding research should not be limited to the more or less routine testing of materials which is so well done by existing agencies. As part of a university, taking a broad view of the position of universities in advancing knowledge, and to the extent that he regards architecture as a science as well as an art, the teacher may share the prospect of the scientific life as one of intellectual adventure. The practical but humanitarian attitude of the architect will help to break down the artificial barrier between so-called pure and applied science, emphasizing the dual role of the scientist as discoverer and interpreter.

The broad view of research suggests another distinction. Study of building material or building elements such as roof, floors, walls, has been extended "horizontally" to the examination of a certain detail in all building types. The architect makes use of this data piecemeal, as occasion requires. The alternative is a "vertical" scientific analysis of a building type or group of buildings for a certain activity or function. This involves study of building requirements and of all materials and construction in conjunction for the particular building type. This kind of analysis may begin before there is any designing in the sense of drawings.

In research we may bear in mind another distinction between architect and engineer, namely that the architect is concerned not only with "how" to put building materials together, but also with "what" materials for "what" purpose.

The wider view of research suggests pioneer investigations in the development of uses for existing materials, and development of materials for given uses, in contrast to the routine testing of materials more or less standardized for familiar uses.

The overlapping of types of research and the need for a comprehensive approach is noted in the report of the Building Research Station of the Royal Institute of British Architects:

> There are certain natural scientific divisions—chemical, physical, and engineering—but they never were divisions in the sense of being divided from one another, and recognition of the fact that most building problems need to be studied comprehensively to get an answer that means anything in practice, has succeeded in obliterating any sense of division....

The core of their studies (Physical Division) is formed by the classic group, light, heat, and sound. The field is so large that good contacts have to be maintained with such bodies as the National Physical Laboratory and with the Medical Research Council on physiological and psychological aspects.

The essences of the light-heat-sound groups lies of course in the fact that ultimately the criteria are mostly those of the human body and, since changes in this do not lie with scope of design, the latter has to confirm to the former. New development should lead to the establishment of physiology in an important position among architectural studies.

America Research-Minded
The present increased attention to research on the part of architects and The American Institute of Architects is but a part of the surging interest shown by the public and many kinds of organizations.

Research has reached a new high in general popularity. The following blurb is from an advertisement in *Fortune*: "It (research) is the driving force of creative industry. It combats depressions, stimulates prosperity. It is America's great economic stabilizer." Journalists observe that "Science is news, as never before." Because of this wide popularity it is advisable to look for the motivation of much that is heralded as research. One may find that the real purposes are to stimulate sales, for political or other kinds of propaganda, or as a "front" for other activities, or even to corral funds to create a sinecure for the promoter of the project.

In spite of the few questionable types of research projects, the wide interest in research can be explained. In general, it is characteristic of a postwar era that fundamentals are re-examined freshly and fearlessly. The practical and social consequences of science are always evident to the thoughtful, but in wartime the very rapid progression of ideas through the successive stages of research, development, production, and use makes the average citizen more aware of the importance of research. He is more willing to see private and public funds used for research, because he believes that the wartime partnership of government, science, and industry should be extended into peacetime.

Existing Research Facilities
The Bureau of Standards, the American Society for Testing Materials, and the Underwriters' Laboratories are too well known to require more than mention. Each is somewhat limited by charter to certain areas or types of investigations within which limits they function most effectively and publish findings which are completely impartial and reliable.

A partial indication of the vast amount of research now carried on is in the report of the National Research Council on Industrial Research Laboratories of the United States.

There are 2443 laboratories engaged in industrial research located in 47 states, the District of Columbia, Alaska, and Hawaii. This figure does not include 292 colleges and universities located in all of the states and D.C., which offer research service to industry. These laboratories are staffed by 133,515 persons including 54,321 of professional rank (of which 20,637 are engineers) and 34,563 technical assistants.

Analysis of the report reveals that the non-academic laboratories include in their activities research in 55 fields related to the building industry, with 1668 listings in over a thousand laboratories.

Research Before Congress
Indication of the wide public interest in research is the bill known as the "National Science Foundation Act of 1946," H.R. 942. This bill was introduced in the present Congress by Mr. Celler. Its purpose is "to promote the progress of science and the useful arts, to secure the national defense, to advance the national health and welfare, and for other purposes." It proposes, among other things:

- to provide support for scientific research and development;
- to correlate the scientific research and development of the several government agencies;
- to achieve full dissemination of scientific and technical information to the public, and to foster the interchange of scientific and technical information in this country and abroad;
- to create a central scientific agency within the Government—"National Science Foundation," including a Division of Engineering and Technology. Advisory to the Foundation would be a National Science Board, including Divisional Science Committees.

Under this Act funds for research would be apportioned among the States, to be used in/by facilities of tax-supported colleges and universities and land-grant colleges. There are provisions for scholarships and fellowships. The existing Office of Scientific Research and Development would be transferred to the Foundation.

Also of interest to educators are the almost identical bills, H.R. 573, introduced by Mr. Harris, January 7, 1947, and S 140, introduced by Mr. Fulbright (and Taft), January 10, 1947. Provisions are for an executive department of the Government, to be known as the Department of Health, Education, and Security. This would mean that Education would share cabinet rank with two other fields of public welfare.

Proposed Non-Governmental Research
The U.S. Chamber of Commerce, sharing the concern of many other agencies for an adequate and coordinated research program for the building industry, has set up the Construction Industry Advisory Council. After due deliberation and exploration of the needs, this Council has requested the National Research Council, an adjunct of the National Academy of Science, to set up a Building Construction Research Board similar to the Highway Research Board which has successfully performed a necessary and useful function. Mr. James R. Edmunds, Jr., President of The American Institute of Architects, is a member of the C.I.A.C. and, together with Octagon staff members, has participated in the formative conferences. The National Research Council has agreed to set up the desired Board and the profession will be adequately represented on the advisory, policy-making group.

Under the new terms of renewed affiliation between the A.I.A. and The Producers' Council, there will be active collaboration between The Institute and the Council along several new lines, including notably the setting up of test projects on materials used in combination. This program is now being put into effect by the Joint Committee of The Institute and Council, with the collaboration of the Department of Education and Research and the Council's newly appointed Technical Consultant.

Financing Research
The familiar picture of the lone inventor or the zealous professor burning, and paying for, the midnight oil, is still valid but limited. With tremendous scope and complexity of problems to be solved, and the wide public interest, research is now in the big money, both private and governmental. The proposed Building Construction Research Board, non-governmental, contemplates an annual budget of approximately $100,000.

The above-mentioned Bills introduced in Congress would entail vast appropriations, including salaries of from $10,000 to $15,000 for a dozen top executives.

The Building Officials Conference of America is now seeking $900,000 to endow a research institute.

The Department of Commerce is now processing applications for aid to research projects from a fund of $150,000.

In England the government allocates $15,000,000 per year to scientific research.

The A.I.A. Department of Education and Research
The increasing complexity of building and the desire of Institute members for technical and research assistance has led to the establishment of the Department of Education and Research as part of the new structure of The Institute, incorporating the former Department of Technical Services.

The Department has studied recent proposals for a testing service to be maintained by The Institute. The following factors are noted as impediments to the full and satisfactory carrying out of such proposals:

1. In the nature of building construction, the performance of materials and equipment depends to a very large extent upon design, selection, supervision, and the quality of workmanship applied to field assembly of materials used in combination. Testing, approval, and labeling would be, at best, only a partial guarantee.
2. While The Institute should provide or assist in providing to its members the best and most reliable data regarding building materials and equipment, the Institute cannot assume for its members the responsibility of selecting and controlling the use of materials. This is a local matter of personal judgment and skill and is of the essence of professional service.
3. The range of building materials and equipment is so varied that the full development of the schemes proposed would require a larger and more complete laboratory than now exists in any one place. It does not seem possible that the Institute could find unencumbered funds sufficient to enable it to surpass or even compete with heavily endowed educational and scientific organizations or government-financed institutions of similar purpose.

For research and other indicated activities the function of the Department of Education and Research is a composite of listening post and reporting agency, clearing house and coordinating center, and instigator of needed activities. The scope is much broader than matters ordinarily termed technological and includes sociological, economic, physiological, psychological, and aesthetic aspects of architecture.

The Department will assist and stimulate the membership, and especially the educators, in continually reanalyzing human requirements for all kinds of occupancy and shelter.

In matters of research the Department will serve as liaison between the Profession and various technical, scientific, professional, and educational agencies, including those of other countries, and will endeavor to maintain the closest possible contact with such agencies. The purpose of these contacts will be to keep the Profession fully informed, to avoid duplication in research, to aid in planning coordination and collaboration.

Sources include committees and special interest groups within the profession and in other designing professions, scientific and technical societies, educational institutions and societies outside the profession, building officials and code authorities, building industry organizations, representatives of special owner groups or building types and research agencies in other fields related to living standards and human welfare.

In order to cover the field and to avoid duplication, the activities of the Department will have to be in large measure *research on research*. The Department will report findings according to their merit and immediate usefulness to the architect.

The contacts with other organizations will disclose research projects which should be undertaken jointly by groups of architects and representatives of other groups.

The wide range of subject matter of interest to the profession is indicated in the following outline, similar in parts to the program of the Building Science Board of the Royal Institute of British Architects:

A. Requirements
   1. Social or Functional
      a. Human activities; individual and family—dimensions, furniture, room sizes, etc.
      b. Human activities; group—all bldg. types
      c. City and regional planning—zoning
   2. Physiological
      Effects on human beings of temperature, humidity, heating methods, color, light, noise, smoke, other air pollution, sanitation.
   3. Psychological
      Aesthetics; optical norms of beauty, space effects, effects of light, color, noise, etc.
   4. Safety

B. Structural Theory: continuity, wind stresses, stressed skin, impact, etc.

C. Building Materials
   Customary classifications related each to:
   Physical properties including interaction in assembly.

   Chemical properties including interaction
   - Color fastness
   - Sound transmission
   - Abrasion
   - Heat transmission
   - Weather resistance
   - Electrolytic deterioration, corrosion

D. Building Equipment
   Customary subdivisions

E. Construction
   1. Costs
   2. Labor—training, jurisdiction, efficiency
   3. Prefabrication
   4. Ethical & Contractual
   5. Organization
   6. Codes

F. Professional
   1. Education
   2. Ethics
   3. Registration
   4. Legislation

Among all of these wide possibilities special emphasis will be upon that which is distinctly architectural. Matters which pertain distinctly to engineering and building technicalities can be largely covered by reporting the activities and findings of other *reliable* organizations. The areas which are distinctly basic and peculiar to architectural service are those of the human requirements for shelter, listed as Section A of the above outline.

Cross fertilization of ideas between groups within the profession and between the profession and other groups of specialists should result in findings which will enable architects to serve society most effectively in anticipating needs and trends in the designing of shelter and environment for all kinds of human activity.

The Department will advise with members and schools of architecture regarding coordination of proposed research projects and possible sources of financial assistance.

Dissemination of Findings

The products of research will be made available to the profession through publications of several types:

1. *Bulletins*—the extensive resources of research and technical information will be tapped, edited, and reported in a bulletin service which will be readable, informative, and arranged for ready clipping and filing of material of permanent value to the practitioner.
2. *Handbooks*—compilation of periodically published material, and other types of material, for professional and lay use.
3. *Teaching Material*—organization of above and other types of material in the form of outlines, lecture notes, work sheets, etc., for:
    - Short-term institutes or seminars to be given in large centers;
    - Self-teaching individuals or groups in smaller or remote centers.
4. *Public Education*—material similar to the above, in non-technical or popular form, developed in collaboration with the Department of Public and Professional Relations for public education and lay consumption.

The success of the above proposed program of research in and for the architectural profession will depend to a considerable extent upon the interest, initiative, and cooperation of the schools of architecture.

Research and Criticism in Architecture

Eduard Sekler
Harvard University

Once upon a time there was a master saddle-maker. A proficient good master. He made saddles which were shaped in such a manner that they had nothing in common with saddles of earlier centuries. Nor with Turkish or Japanese ones; in short modern saddles. But this he did not know. He only knew that he made saddles as well as he could.

Now a remarkable movement came into the city. It was called 'Secession.' It demanded that one should produce nothing but modern objects of daily use.

When the master saddle-maker learned this he took one of his best saddles and with it went to one of the leaders of the 'Secession.'

And he said to him: "Professor. . . I have heard about your demands. I am a modern man too. I should like to work in a modern manner. Tell me: is this saddle modern!"

The professor inspected the saddle and gave a long lecture to the man. . . . The balance was: no, this is not a modern saddle.

Quite ashamed the master went away. And he reflected, worked, and reflected again. But much as he tried to fulfill the professor's high demands, he brought nothing forth except his old saddle time and again.

Dejectedly he went to see the professor once more. He explained his plight. The professor looked at the master's attempts and spoke: "Dear master, patently you possess no imagination."

Yes, this was it. He obviously did not possess it. Imagination! But he had not even known that it was necessary for the craft of saddle-making. Had he had it, he certainly would have turned painter or sculptor. Or poet or composer.

The professor, however, said: "Come again tomorrow. After all we are here in order to promote the trades and to fructify them with new ideas. I will see what can be done for you."

And in his class he announced the following competition: Design for a Saddle.

Next day the master saddle-maker came again. The professor could point him out forty-nine designs for saddles. It is true he had only forty-four students but five designs he had made himself. These were to go into "The Studio." For there was mood in them.

For a long time the master gazed at the drawings and his eyes became brighter and brighter.

Finally he said: "Professor, if I understood as little about riding, about horses, about leather and about workmanship as you do, then I would also have your imagination."

And now he lives happily and content.

And he makes saddles. Modern ones? He does not know. Saddles.

It is not very encouraging to reflect more than half a century after this tale was written by Adolf Loos how applicable it still is, not only to a great deal of what in design goes under the name of "enrichment of the architectural vocabulary" but also to events in the fields of architectural criticism and research.[1] Attempts in both fields, as far as they exist at all, show an alarming tendency to make up in fantasy what they lack in comprehension of the real problems involved—a state of affairs which cannot remain without effects on the whole process of architectural education, since criticism and research are two of the most important components of any field of education.

They are mentioned together here because basically they can be considered as two aspects of one and the same activity, an activity predominantly though not entirely intellectual which has a great deal of relevance for the architect and direct bearing on design.

Places of higher learning, if we may count architectural schools among them, derive whatever genuine vitality they possess from the polar tension between the two parallel planes of teaching and research. In architectural teaching it is generally and rightly assumed that the professional activity of the teacher corresponds to research work done in other fields. This is true in all those cases where architectural work can indeed be equated with creative research and has not just become a routine operation. Otherwise the ingredient of genuine research needful in a complete educational diet has to come from elsewhere.

Too often it would seem that the architectural student acquires a completely erroneous conception of what research means in his field and he rarely finds occasion to revise it during his later career. What he remembers may well be nothing but quick trips to a library where material provided by a helpful librarian was scanned rapidly with a view to immediate usefulness for a very special purpose, with little criticism applied and even less method.

Small wonder that the student (and the professional he becomes later) does not learn to value this type of work highly, feeling that it imparts no intellectual discipline nor any spiritual values. In fact dilettantism and eclecticism may be the only lasting results of such spurious research, and the lack of humility for which architects are blamed so often in our time may well be traced back in part to an education that never gave them a chance to learn how to let things alone which they were not equipped or willing to tackle seriously.

Research is as much an ethical problem as an intellectual one. Here would seem to lie its greatest educational value. The actual results of a special research project undertaken by a teacher may not even be very relevant to his students; what matters are the honesty of effort, critical method, and clear recognition of legitimate fields of inquiry. Only when architects give up pretending to be psychologists, sociologists, economists, historians, physicists, etc., etc., can they expect to achieve useful and valid results. Doing research in their own field properly they will learn to appreciate and understand truly the meaning of results in other fields and to handle these in such a manner that the well-known drawbacks of specialization are avoided.

It may seem that I paint too gloomy a picture of the architectural research worker between the Scylla of dilettantic superficiality and the Charybdis of sterile specialization. Fortunately there are gratifying examples of research done by small groups under the guidance of outstanding personalities which not only produce important results but also give to those who participated the satisfaction of a thing well done and an orderly framework for their future thinking and acting. But it still seems necessary to consider very seriously what happens in a field that has little tradition, abounds in projects, swamps us with printed matter and yet has left so very many questions unanswered that would be open to rational inquiry and at least partial answers. This is true of all facets of architectural research, some of which are even hardly defined at the present stage.

Thus it will be necessary to delimit architectural research as strictly as possible from building and engineering research on the one hand and historical research on the other. It is true that architects can successfully embark on projects in either domain, and have done so, but only if they are willing to undergo the proper additional training. This involves considerable sacrifices and the risk of forgoing in the process things which are most proper and significant to their own profession.

Owing to architecture's special position between art and science this risk may indeed be greater than is apparent at first; the architect shares with every artist the continuous striving for a balance between emotion and order but in addition he has to reconcile the conflicting demands of the artist's and the scientist's way of working. There may be a great deal which is compatible in both as far as the creative process is concerned but the basic difference remains between the scientist's quest for objectivity and the artist's need for greatest possible intensity of a subjective interpretation of experience. If an architect gets too involved with scientific or scholarly pursuits, this may well affect his habits of work as an artist to a greater degree than is desirable.

Architecture then would appear to call for a special kind of research which in my opinion can be directed mainly in three directions. They are interrelated but have diverse affinities with non-architectural research.

One line of investigation links up most closely with the applied natural sciences and concerns itself with the architectural consequences of results achieved in building and engineering research.

Another legitimate branch of architectural research relates more closely to the social sciences and economics and can best be described as the functional analysis of building types; workability and efficiency of architectural solutions are analyzed in a manner which has been well illustrated in the more specialized field of housing research which falls under this general category.

Finally there is, hardly existing as yet, research that is nearest to art-critical and historical disciplines, including aesthetics and consequently philosophy; it deals with a clarification of architectural thinking in terms of a possible doctrine and basis for criticism.

While little need be said about the first two types of architectural research (which are well established in many countries), the third is likely to prove a controversial topic. Architects are notoriously skeptical of theory and criticism; rightly so, I think, because they have been disappointed too often. Yet they actually never give up theorizing and criticizing; without it no judgments, either of competitions or during the teaching process, would be possible nor could there be communication about those values which are most real to the architect just because they are most purely architectural.

In architectural criticism, as in the criticism of art and music, it is true there will always be widely divergent opinions among critics, since good criticism in the last resort is an act of re-creation and thus has its element of intuition related to that which is present in the work to be criticized. But no relevant criticism is possible outside a common frame of reference which in architecture is still lacking to a great degree, though it exists in other fields.

The creation of such a framework, delimiting freedom from arbitrariness without encasing the creative spirit in a stylistic cage, cannot be achieved either by research alone or by individual creative effort alone. Both must play their part in a process that to me seems the only way out of chaos.

There is no historical precedent for this because never before was there such a complete loss of spiritual background in architecture without any replacement. As long as a common spiritual denominator existed there was no difficulty in deriving architectural doctrine from this source, although a good deal of dispute might occur about individual points of interpretation—from the quarrels concerning the geometrical system to be used at Milano Cathedral to the heated arguments between *Anciens* and *Modernes* in seventeenth century France. Today architecture no longer stands on a firm ground of doctrine that stems from a generally accepted "Weltanschauung." All the architect can do therefore is to scrutinize and clarify conditions that are inherent in the process of architectural creation itself and to deduce guiding indications from this; in other words to study carefully the world of architectural forms and to derive from this whatever laws of morphology he may find valid there, all the time being aware, of course, of the pitfalls that accompany every quest for a doctrine; from abstruse esotericism to false expediency that will proffer prescriptions where only precepts are possible. It seems obvious that such a quest for doctrine is a process that can profit greatly if it is conducted along the methodical and disciplined lines of research rather than on a basis of personal idiosyncrasies and emotional reactions.

Note

1. See Adolf Loos, *Trotzdem*, 2nd ed. (Innsbruck: Brenner Verlag, 1931). This volume of essays belongs among the most important documents for the history and understanding of the modern movement and is far too little known among English-speaking readers. The story of the master saddle-maker first appeared in 1903. In its translation as well as in general criticism of the rest of this essay the author acknowledges the kind assistance of his colleagues Professor Serge Chermayeff and Professor Jacqueline Tyrwhitt.

Humanism and the Teaching of Architecture

Joseph Hudnut
Massachusetts Institute of Technology

Whenever I talk with students in architectural schools I am impressed by the universality of their thought. Their minds seem to be hospitable only to absolute ideas and everlasting standards. The principles in which they believe were true before the earth was shaped from the sidereal drift; are true today when the earth is shaken by the great wars; and will be true on that dread day when Gabriel shall blow his impertinent saxophone.

The prophet of this faith is, as we all know, Mies van der Rohe. It is he who has driven from the thought of our students all the trivial fond records of architecture—its fantasies, its accidents, its history, its poetry, its silliness—in order that his commandment all alone may stand. To his magic flute all our students are dancing.

Not only our students but all of our architects. Well, nearly all. Saarinen, it is true, dances only now and then; quite as often he is flirting with that dowdy dowager, Tradition. Rudolph and Stone, more persistent wallflowers, prefer the company of those painted ladies, Popular Opinion and Genial Prejudice. The rest of us dance. We dance sedately, in steps that are precise and prescribed, resolutely free from all gaiety and passion—and from any suspicion of humanism.

I think it unlikely that this dance will end so long as Mies van der Rohe plays his lucid, elegant, and ecumenical flute: so long as his incomparable style decorates the functional revelation and confirms our faith in its harsh moralities. Our humanism must wait at the doors of our schools until some new master shall approve its truth in a language as voluble.

It may happen nonetheless that the advent of this master is less distant than we suppose. The pride and firmness of an established creed often foretell its end. Already we hear premonitions of revolt in the conferences of architects, in the architectural press, and in the still, scornful voice of that troublesome creature, the young instructor. We must take into account also the caprices of Fortune, a lady in love with surprise—and with a well-developed sense of humor.

Certainly it is not my wish to topple Mies van der Rohe from his excellent throne as arbiter of architecture or to replace him by some present protagonist of another manner of expression. His painstaking perfection, his sure craftsmanship, his exquisite sense of materials—the fundamental virtues in all architecture—deserve the imitation of practitioner and student. And yet I think it might be occasionally a wholesome experience for our students if, having designed for the millionth time the House of Seagram and the Bacardi Rum Building, they should be confronted by a master not quite so universal in his thought, not quite so impersonal in his practice, not quite so uncharitable to that human frailty called romance. In a word, I would have them make the acquaintance of a humanist.

But there are at least three distinct species of humanists, and I shall not be understood unless you will permit me to distinguish them one from another.

The best-known humanists are the humanists of the Renaissance, some of whom still exist among us: men whose Christian faith is enlightened with the secular authority of Greece and Rome, who believe in universal truths and yet are curious of history and scientific discovery, whose ideals of human conduct comprise urbanity, tolerance, and serenity.

This kind of humanist is most favorably represented by Montaigne; less favorably by the Five Orders According to Palladio.

Somewhat less known are the New Humanists: men whose Christian faith is fortified, rather than weakened, by the upsetting revelations of modern science, who, like Saint Thomas, find a divine order in the natural order, whose ideal of conduct is aristocratic in temper, intellectual in its discipline.

This kind of humanist is most favorably represented by T. S. Eliot; less favorably by the Cathedral of Saint John the Divine.

If I had my way each of these humanists should be known—and welcomed—in our schools of architecture. I would not have my students indifferent to any idea or to any faith. And that, I think, is sufficient justification for my desire that they should know also a third type of humanist and one to which my own thought and feeling are most closely allied.

This is the humanist whose mind is adjusted to the new truths of the natural and social sciences, whose interests are centered not in the Kingdom of God but in the dignity and prestige of man in his earthly environment, who finds in the science of man a new morale of confidence and security.

This kind of humanist is most favorably represented by John Dewey; less favorably by the Air Force Academy.

My students will not applaud me when I thus suggest that there are many paths, leading through more than philosophy, to an understanding of architecture. Our students come to us eager for certainty. They will take to themselves every instruction which is framed within an assured knowledge of absolute truth, sonorously pronounced. For that the religious leader has every advantage over the humanist. It is not from reason (as they imagine) that our students draw that obscurantism of ritual and vision upon which they build their sterile castles of steel and glass.

I would dissolve these superstitions neither by formal precept nor by a special discipline arranged for that purpose; nor should I hope to overcome the oppressions of functionalist doctrine by new oppressions of liberalism. My students should encounter the great humanists in the general stream of a cultural history. They should encounter them there as individuals and not as symbols of antiquated doctrines, easily discredited. They should not be introduced to prove something or to illustrate some categorical interpretation of history such as Age of Faith, Revival of Learning, and Romantic Reaction. Their thought should be brought to the student without the mediation of critic or interpreter, their personalities unblurred by the footnotes of commentators; nor should the student be too generously supplied with the ready-made judgments of his instructor.

The course in cultural history should be continued in the courses in the history of architecture which should thus be restored to their former dignity and importance beside the courses in design. The student, having learned the grandeur of the human story, will be prepared to find that grandeur in the history of architecture. There, also, he will be companioned by great spirits.

You may teach architecture as the story of functional form, or as the random evolution of enclosed space, or as the fateful consequences of invention and technology, or as the interpreter of civilizations—and of course you may teach the history of architecture as a store of those patterns from whose interplay in the mind new patterns are subconsciously generated. I have no quarrel with those who teach in any of these ways and yet I think that no student will understand architecture until we teach it as a humanity. By this I mean that we should present all architectures as documents in the study of man, as witnesses of the invincible spirit of man.

For this purpose architectural history has evident advantages over all other courses in our curriculum. In history, buildings stand in the illuminating realm of time apart from the conflicts and confusions which blur all contemporary structures; they speak to our students of the eternal and elemental attributes of architecture. In history, buildings are participants in that endless quest for excellence which is the motivation of all art and the proof of art's maturity: the quest of which form is the eloquent symbol. In history, buildings are charged also with that promise of happiness which is called romance. In history we do not need a theory to persuade our students that a sense of time, of form, and of romance are the essentials in good architecture.

The buildings of past ages, unlike those of our day, stand in a continuum of human experience. They look backward to that which had occurred before their era and forward to that which will follow them. They hold in either hand the past and the future. Thus they are endowed by time with dynamic vitality.

In such buildings the content of architecture takes on a rhythm of occurrences in which all of architecture is unified and made into one art. A fourth dimension gives to each building a wide and human extension: the Parthenon, the Cathedral of Paris, the Garden of Versailles are wrapped in the whole of architecture. They speak to us not merely as individual and separate voices but as elements in a harmony of voices. And as they tell us together the story of architecture, they rehearse that story of mankind which is felt through them, reaffirming the splendor of that story, re-enacting its drama and its pathos.

Our new buildings, with rare exceptions, are not thus dressed. We know that our era is the best of all possible eras. We know that the achievements of our industries in league with our technologies eclipse all those of every age which has preceded our own. We are confident that our architecture could have no higher mission than to express in the language of steel that resplendent realism. And from that premise we arrive, by a series of syllogisms, at an art incompetent of beauty: proud, self-sufficient, and empty of time.

Almost all of our students—and many of our architects—do not know that time thus gives to buildings a human relevance. No doubt that is why they are unaware that form—which, like time, is a theme of history—also gives to buildings a human relevance. And of course I am speaking of form not as a reasoned or calculated unity but as a unity and harmony of visual elements, standing in space, surrounding space.

There is form, said Alberti, when all the parts of a building consent to live together. It is important, he added, that the structure and purpose of a building should be made known in its appearances, but that importance is less urgent than the achievement of form. Until our time form, thus defined, was to architecture a guiding star.

This persistent authority of form could not have arisen from academic precedent or from immediate perceptual satisfactions. It must have responded from some very deep necessity in the heart of mankind: the same necessity, I think, for completeness and peace which prompted the building of civilizations. Buildings, when they attain form, environ us as simulacra of those larger forms, attesting their validity, declaring a human part in the Great Plan unfolding around us. They are little worlds of order, near to our heart's desire.

I have noticed that this ministry is most evident in buildings revealed in the ample page of history. We see buildings in a new manner as they recede from the air of their origin; they take on new appearances and valuations. When buildings are newly built we apprehend them as utilities and structural patterns; we are curious of their purpose and the ways in which they are adapted to purpose; we perceive their materials and the ways in which these are shaped and assembled. And yet these understandings occupy us only for a moment. With the passage of time we become increasingly aware of the formal values which at first engaged our attention only casually. We become observant of proportion, of esthetic surface, of rhythmical dispositions. Our utility becomes a language. If it is eloquent we will forget its awkward adaptations to service, its failures in techniques, its stupidities.

I have no doubt but what the Parthenon was envisaged as a utilitarian building when after long anticipation it crowned at length the beautiful Acropolis. The goddess who defended the city against the dreadful wrath of the Persians had then been honored by a glittering statue of gold; a debt of honor had been paid; and the architects had built around the precious image a durable and practical shelter. It was thus that the building was understood and valued. And yet the temple was scarcely completed before a new character was stamped upon it. It became each day less a shelter, less a utility built for protection and security, and more each day a sculptured form, an exquisite balance of marble, space, and story—the very embodiment of the serene dignity of Athens.

No one can tell us how well form follows function in the Taj Mahal. Only the theologians remember the rituals of prayer for which the Cathedral of Chartres was fashioned. And if someone in the Garden of Versailles should remind us that its noble vistas are only the whims of a self-indulgent king we should find that reminder an impertinence.

How has it happened then that we have learned to think of form in buildings as an attribute inimical to their integrity?—as if form, which is integral to man, could be less integral to the art which presses most nearly upon human life!

"It must be agreed," writes Wittkower at the end of an essay on proportion, "that the quest for balance, symmetry, and proportional relationships lies deep in human nature. It can be confidently predicted that today's "organic chaos" is a passing phase and that the search for form in the arts will continue as long as art remains an endeavor of man."[1]

We must, I suppose, await a new generation before that endeavor will redeem our architecture; and perhaps we shall wait still longer, considering the present climate of cynicism, before our architects and students will learn to esteem—perhaps in the study of history—a third value in buildings quite as important to our happiness as form. I am thinking of that poetic content which when it is recognized has the power to lift us out of the dull air of our necessities.

There are buildings, when we make their acquaintance in history, which possess a power over our emotions; which tell us stories that move us; which are charged with romance—and I am mindful not only of those buildings which are wrapped in remembrances but also of that enchantment in buildings which arises from the conscious intention of an architect to inform them with poetry. There were eras in the history of civilization when a building, to be called a work of art, had to enclose a sentiment.

Our new buildings, resolute to be reasonable—to "throw out all that is unreasonable"—have thrown out Christianity, love and youthful adventure, song, fantasy, and make-believe. Impersonal, taciturn, and universal, endlessly standardized and commercially practical, easily understood and imitated, they express little else in our culture than the comfortable serviceability of our de-humanized industries. Empty of sentiment and personality, their interminable walls of glass exclude like gates of brass every humanist and poetic value—and with these all the joyousness of life.

Are these buildings, then, truly reasonable? Reasonable in their conformities to an arbitrary code of design; reasonable in their efficiencies; reasonable in their response to a commercial necessity. They speak to us in the language of business; their logic is the logic of business.

Imagine a world in which men speak only the language of business: a world in which "business English" is the only linguistic medium of communication—relieved no doubt by some alloy of political English and sporting-page English. Such a language would be completely foreign to the language of the artist and the poet; completely foreign to those radiances which the imagination draws from the world. If a sonnet by Keats or Shakespeare should survive into that grey universe there would be no man capable of the imaginative response which should make them understood.

Our students are still capable of that response. When in history they make the acquaintance of the Petit Trianon or the Garden of the Generaliffe they sometimes forget to ask the cost, the principle of engineering, or the relevance to the democratic principle. Some day—distant no doubt in time and space—they will take to their drafting boards that which history has taught them.

We ought to show our students on every occasion the promises inherent in those works of architecture which in recent months have held a plea against the rage of the functionalists. A study of such works is not inappropriate in a study of history—a field of inquiry which does not, as many suppose, end with the Bauhaus. We may, for example, show our students how the RCA Building gains an emotional power from receding planes borrowed from the cathedral; how it gains elegance from the fragment of Nancy laid at its feet; how it gains fantasy from the bronze god who brings preposterous fire to a skating rink. We may show them how Rudolph respects the towers of Wellesley and Saarinen the cloisters of Yale. And could it be that Mies van der Rohe himself may be the prophet of a new Renaissance? Is there not a hint of Michelangelo in the foyer of the House of Seagram, a remnant of Roman space in the plaza laid out in front of it? We who are the guardians of history may, I think, appear as history's champion in a modern world. A lance broken there will not deprive us of honor.

Our students should know that there are many types of excellence. They should be curious of all excellence and learn to recognize and value excellence wherever it appears. They should not close their eyes to the Jesuitical Baroque, or turn their backs on the vulgar Romans, or sigh for the common man in the nonfunctional halls of the Tuileries; neither should they rush too precipitately into the iron arms of the Bauhaus.

"The sifting of human values! That," said William James, "is what we ought to mean by the humanities; the study of things in which human effort and conquests are the prime factors."[2]

Studying in this way we learn that types of activity have stood the tests of time; we acquire standards of the good and the durable; and when we see how diverse the types of excellence may be, how flexible the adaptations, how various the tests, we gain a richer sense of what the words better and worse may signify. Our critical sensibilities grow both more acute and less fanatical. We sympathize with men's mistakes even in the act of penetrating them; we feel the pathos of lost causes and misguided efforts even while we applaud what overcame them.

"That," said William James, "is the better part of what men call wisdom."

Notes
1. Rudolf Wittkower, "The Changing Concept of Proportion," Daedalus 89, no. 1 "The Visual Arts Today" (Winter, 1960), 213. [Editors' note: Citation added.]
2. Editors' note: This text was delivered as a speech. The editors were not able to verify the source of the James quotation.

Architectural Education and Behavioral Science

Carleton Monroe Winslow Jr.
University of South Carolina

Few buildings today are brought down by structural failure; many—some would say most—are weakened by what the author of this article, an architect and educator who holds a degree in sociology, calls anthropological failure. If this state of affairs is to be remedied, Carleton Monroe Winslow Jr. maintains, there will have to be more and better courses in behavioral sciences at the undergraduate level in architectural curricula, together with an increase in empirical research into the part played by environmental factors in determining social behavior. And the latter, no less than the former, will have to be instigated by the schools.

Architects and planners constantly assert that respect for human behavior is central to their design considerations. To some extent this is true. Physical size is considered in terms of heights of doors and spaces. Sight is sometimes acknowledged by color and illumination. Hearing is sometimes reflected in noise and acoustical considerations. Despite this, more buildings fail anthropologically than structurally and these failures, I suggest, are due to 1.) inadequate courses in behavioral sciences at the undergraduate level in architectural curricula and 2.) lack of empirical research in the isolation of environmental factors as determinants of human behavior.

What is needed at the undergraduate level is a course or sequence of courses which cuts across the rather arbitrary (and frequently disputed) frontiers between the disciplines of biology, anthropology, sociology, ecology, and psychology. Such a course must be designed to accomplish two things: 1. survey the range of human behavior and 2. take the architect right to the current frontier of current research methodology, not with the idea that he will become a social scientist, but with the idea that he will be aware of the body of existing data and further that he will be able to pose the *intelligent question*. Such a course will also train the architect to think about social problems, in a scientific way. For instance, the mere observation that a high incidence of juvenile delinquency occurs in areas of sub-standard housing does not in itself mean that the poor housing conditions *cause* the delinquency. Both phenomena may be a product of some more fundamental problem related to economics or race relations. As a result of this training, then, the student will learn to distinguish between mere association and a cause and effect relationship. He will further learn to examine the criteria used to establish such factors as "incidence of delinquency" and "substandard housing." He will learn something of the nature of sampling and statistical analysis upon which so much social research relies. He will be just as able to read a sociological report as the results of a soil analysis.

We are now led to the second reason for anthropological failure in buildings. This is a lack of empirical research in the isolation of environmental factors as determinants of social behavior. This area, it seems to me, can become an important one for architectural research but it will have to be accomplished as a joint effort with various branches of the behavioral sciences. Architects and planners *talk* about the presumed benefits of well-designed environments but they really do not know how these benefits are reflected in terms of behavior. In fact, since the demise of the so-called "School of Geographic Determinism," sociologists have come to regard environment as a *limiting but not predetermining factor in social behavior*.[1] It is therefore quite natural that social scientists should be attracted to the apparently more fruitful areas of social stratification, race relations, etc.

There is, however, a growing body of information in the areas of community and urban sociology. The status of these branches is indicated by assigned categories (17 and 18) in the reference periodical, *Sociological Abstracts*. During 1961 and 1962 over two hundred articles were abstracted in these areas alone. It is true that few appear to concern themselves with isolating environmental factors for use by the architect but on close examination many of the studies may contain valuable material.

We must face the fact, too, that social research will follow encouragement. Environmental design will have to encourage environmental research in the social science field, which is another way of saying that money is needed. If the United States Navy allocates money for research in the area of leadership on a broad basis, social science will engage in research in leadership. That the sociologists stand ready to engage fully in urban and community problems is attested by the articles mentioned above. An idea of the range of interest with which these articles deal is indicated in the selected bibliography.

Ernest Manheim, in a paper entitled "Theoretical Prospects of Urban Sociology in an Urbanized Society," feels that as urbanism is becoming an increasingly dominant factor in American life, urban sociology will develop toward something approximating the study of American civilization:

Urban society is rapidly becoming American society. The majority of text books on urban sociology clearly reflect this change. There are few subjects of sociological research in any province of American life which are left out of standard textbooks and understandably so, because there are few areas of problem-oriented research which in this country are unrelated to urban society.[2]

Urban sociology, however, does not imply isolation of environmental factors as determinants of human behavior. It means that more and more social problems must be studied within the urban frame of reference because more and more (in the words of the abstract) American society is approaching a state of total urbanism.

Structurally our buildings are designed to three or four places beyond the decimal point; sociologically we design by hunch. This will only be changed when a significant body of research on the influence of the environment on human behavior is accumulated. The only place this work will be done is in the social science departments at the instigation of, and in cooperation with, the schools of architecture and planning at our universities.

Notes
1. This quotation, in essence, is taken from a personal discussion with Professor Edward McDonagh of the Department of Sociology, University of Southern California.
2. Ernest Manheim, "Theoretical Prospects of Urban Sociology in an Urbanized Society," *American Journal of Sociology*, LXVI (November, 1960): 226-229.

Bibliography
The following books and articles are selected from those reviewed in *Sociological Abstracts* in 1961 and 1962. They were selected to give some idea of the range of current social research. Few, if any, attempt to isolate environmental factors. All should be of interest to environmental designers.

Current Problems
Crawford, K. G. "Urban Growth and Boundary Readjustments." *Canadian Public Administration* III (March 1960): 51–58.

Devereux, Edward C., Jr. "Neighborhood and Community Participation." *Journal of Social Issues* XVI (1960): 64–84.

Duncan, Beverly, Georges Sabagh, and Maurice D. Van Arsdol, Jr. "Patterns of City Growth." *American Journal of Sociology* LXVII (January 1962): 418-429.

Higbee, Edward. *The Squeeze: Cities Without Space.* New York: William Morrow & Co, 1960.

Hoover, Edgar M., Jr., and Raymond Vernon. *Anatomy of a Metropolis: The Changing Distribution of People and Jobs within the New York Metropolitan Region.* Cambridge, MA: Harvard University Press, 1959.

Keyes, Fenton. "The Correlation of Social Phenomena with Community Size." *Social Forces* XXXVI (May 1958): 311–315.

Ktsanes, Thomas and Leonard Reissman. "Suburbia—New Homes for Old Values." *Social Problems* VII (1959–60): 187–195.

Kurtz, Richard A. and Joanne B. Eicher. "Fringe and Suburb: A Confusion of Concepts." *Social Forces*, XXXVII (October, 1958): 32–37.

Lynch, Kevin. *The Image of the City.* Cambridge, MA: The Technology Press & Harvard University Press, 1960.

Ogburn, William Fielding. "Technology and Cities: The Dilemma of the Modern Metropolis." *Sociological Quarterly* I (July 1960): 139–153.

Rapkin, Chester and William G. Grigsby. *Residential Renewal in the Urban Core.* Philadelphia: University of Pennsylvania Press, 1960.

Ross, H. Laurence. "The Local Community: A Survey Approach." *American Sociology Review* XXVII (February 1962): 75–84.

Smith, Joel and George L. Maddox. "The Spatial Location and Use of Selected Facilities in a Middle-sized City." *Social Forces* XXXVIII (December 1959): 119–124.

Strauss, Anselm, "Spatial Representation and the Orbits of City Life," *Sociological Quarterly* I (July 1960): 167–180.

Thomas, W., "Planning in the 1960s" *Political Quarterly* XXXI (October-December 1960): 466–476.

Historical Urban Problems
Carpenter, David B. "Urbanization and Social Change in Japan." *Sociological Quarterly* I (July 1960): 155–166.

de Dainville, François. "Grandeur et Population des Villes au XVIIIe Siècle." *Population* XIII (July-September 1958): 459–480.

Rosenau, Helen. *The Ideal City in Its Architectural Evolution.* Boston, MA: Boston Book & Art Shop, 1960.

Sjoberg, Gideon. *The Preindustrial City: Past and Present.* Glencoe, IL: The Free Press, 1960.

Notes of a Traveler

John Habraken
Massachusetts Institute of Technology

Research is an attempt to explore new territories and to add them to the map of knowledge that we maintain and revise constantly. The researcher is the traveller. After numerous adventures and hardships, doubts, anxieties, and excitements, he returns to explain to the people back home what he has seen and how it fits into what everybody already knows. Those who welcome him back want to know what he can add to the picture of the world with which they are familiar. He is expected to fill in a blank spot. Sometimes it does not fit and the map must be revised, a cause for controversy and debate. The shared view of the world is at stake!

The social connotations are obvious. A body of knowledge is something to be shared among the natives of a culture. It is to a large extent what makes them a tribe. The interpretation of the accumulated facts in a theory is what makes that culture. The map of their world holds them together, while at the same time it makes individual movement possible, as well as easy communication.

Communication (1)
In architecture today there is no map we share. We may or may not share certain skills, beliefs and attitudes—perhaps even some ideologies and languages, but there is certainly no map of the world that we share. In fact, we are not even sure that we share the same world. A commonly understood and accepted map may never be possible.

For those of us who have decided to travel anyway and try to venture beyond the compounds of friendly neighboring villages, this primitive state has its disadvantages. When we survive and come back to report, it is hard to connect. The tales of our experiences sound out of place and cannot be verified. We speak of animals no one has seen before and are at a loss to describe them. The words we choose cause confusion, while we stretch their meanings. This unavoidable breakdown of communication brings a sense of isolation. Even the exchange with other travellers is difficult at best. We are not even sure we have explored the same continent. It may be impossible to piece together the data each of us brought home. Even in the best of circumstances one's research will have accumulated a very modest structure of knowledge that is shared by relatively few individuals. Its purpose, its methods and its achievements will only be understood by a few.

Isolation
The isolation of those who do operate in what could be called a research mode in architecture must not be con-

fused with the isolation of individuals in the sciences who may be so specialized that they can only talk to a few others. For them, there is indeed a map to point out where they are. They can be reached. Their isolation exists because the body of knowledge is so vast that no one can encompass it all. Their problem is a technical one. Our problem is the opposite: it is existential. We do not know where we are. We report about different worlds. To reach each other takes an act of faith—one may never return to where one came from.

Communication (2)
These problems of communication are disconcerting. I like to believe that two researchers in different places within the physical sciences who meet on a social occasion need no more than a few minutes to connect their respective standpoints. Although it may be more difficult for them to describe what is within their specific territory of investigation, they have no problem identifying where the territory is. The rest of their conversation can be the exchange of mutually useful information.

Location

I often find myself avoiding an attempt to establish location, because I know there will be no time to work it out satisfactorily: explaining words that have several meanings and avoiding misunderstandings that only bring disorientation. What is the territory I have traveled? I am exploring design. And here I find myself explaining what I mean by it. For me, design is the formulation of decisions about what has to be made, in such a way that someone else can make it. Yes, it has to do with creation—but a creation is not a design, and a designer is not just someone who creates, but a person who documents something that did not exist before in order to allow others to act. Therefore, design is a social activity that has to do with explicit communication. Design only makes sense when we work with others or when we project our own activities. I am sure that these few sentences are not sufficient to establish rapport with others. Design, for many of my colleagues, is first of all a creative adventure. So it is to me when I design; but I can study creativity, the road to synthesis, the issues of problem solving and originality, without ever studying design or even mentioning it. The research of design, to me, must deal with the communication and formulation of a coherent set of decisions. It must tell me something about people interacting in decision making and execution.

But that is not obvious to all in "my" field. There are those who see "a design" as a product in itself, a work of art, never really meant to be executed or to trigger action by others. For some, a design is a statement about buildings, that should be appreciated—and bought—as an object of contemplation. There are those for whom "a design" is an expression of the designer's feelings and no more than that. I have no problem with that kind of preoccupation at all, but I have reached this point and have not yet fully indicated where I am when I "do research in design." We are still trying to establish location. It may take me a bit longer before I can begin to tell you what I learned in that research.

Communication (3)

I would like to compare notes with other travellers, but the very nature of our problem—the lack of a shared map of our world—must make me very careful to avoid generalizations. What may be true for the kind of expeditions that I was involved in may not be at all valid for those who move in different directions. Any advice I can give to would-be explorers can only be personal in nature. I have to talk about my own experiences and I will do so. But then those experiences may be difficult to place in a context that makes sense to others, for the reasons mentioned before.

Social Support

Stanley was sent by the *New York Herald*. Columbus had the backing of a Spanish royal couple.[1] In research, one needs supporters as well.

No research is totally separated from the "real world." Because it takes time, space and money and never produces these things itself, research is dependent on those who nourish it materially. Research, therefore, is ultimately the fruit of a social and political world that shares enough beliefs and values with those who do the research to allow them to do so, to accept the risk of their failures and claim some credit for their successes.

If this is true for all research, no matter how far removed from day-to-day concerns, no matter how "pure," it is inescapably true for research in the design of our physical environment. Design is a form of human interaction. The ultimate test for the "success" of any research results lies in the question of whether chosen results will be accepted or rejected by the social body to whom they are supposed to make sense. In design, moreover, any attempt by the researchers to test what it does, how it goes, or how it could be changed, has to be done in conjunction with those who design. Any formulation of a design theory is an attempt to describe the behavior of designers. Any introduction of a design method is, finally, an attempt to change the behavior of people who design. Research in design is therefore doubly connected to the social fabric.

Conditions (1)

In the social context, we have several conditions that must be met to make research go. One is the condition of support, the willingness of those who do not do the research to believe in the researcher's objectives enough to fund the work to be done. The second is the condition of interaction, the willingness of those who are supposed to benefit from the research to try out and use the results. It is self-evident that the willingness to interact is at the same time a form of support. It is hard to respond or even to criticize unless one is willing to believe that the attempt itself is worthwhile.

A third condition is one that protects the research done. One cannot expect everybody to be enthusiastic about unrested new ideas. There is always a hostile environment. There is always fear of new ideas. There is always competition ready to denounce another party's efforts. It may not be enough to have only support—there must also be people who actively protect the work and leave the researcher enough time to do the research.

Conditions (2)

I was very lucky as far as my working conditions were concerned. The research was paid for by a group of professional architects who were ready to interact with any results we found. At the same time, they were willing—first by their prestige, and later through their active engagement in the debate—to protect what was going on. The ideal condition is to have support, interaction, and protection from the same group. We came very close to this.

Conditions (3)
Time is another, very important, condition. Research takes time. Those who support and protect must have patience. It is here where the interaction becomes crucial. In cases where the results come slowly and failures are apparent, it is only the confidence developed through interaction that gives grounds for continued support. If someone says, "Hey! These people are onto something!" and that someone carries some weight because he knows what he is talking about, it can make all the difference. The judgment as to how long is long enough is the most difficult one to make in any research setting. It is here where the chemistry between the individuals involved is most important.

Design Research
Clearly the odds are against those who do design research. The field is unknown. There is no commonly accepted ideology to bind supporters, protectors, and interactors together. There is no commonly shared body of knowledge to explain what the research is all about and where it can bring us. There is no track record for the profession as such, to give confidence to those who are able to offer support. For the same reason, those from the profession who could interact with the researchers often find it difficult to do so (and they are usually operating in small scale organizations that don't allow them to spend much time on interactions with no immediate pay-off). In short, those who can interact have no tradition to support. Those who create research agendas offer widely different theories, are often removed from the social context to which their work must contribute, and are often not even knowledgeable about each other's work.

Ideology
The interesting issue is, of course, that protection, support, and interaction can only come if there is a common understanding about what the issues are that should be pursued. In other words, it is exactly the shared ideology that sets the intellectual, political, and social context that is missing. To create better conditions for research in design is not a matter of research management alone. It has to do with stating a belief, embracing a speculative theory that is broad and convincing enough to make people then concentrate resources and energy on the narrower issue of design.

There must be an outline that allows us to distinguish relevant from irrelevant directions. The ideology allows us to draw the first contours of the world. We put our research in. There is no research without an ideology, just as there is no science without it. We must distinguish between the two and feel free to discuss both. To stay with an ideology without applying it in our own area of knowledge and expertise is ineffective. To stay within our fields without exposing ourselves in the larger context of human concerns, where no one is an authority, is dangerous. Not to know the distinction is perhaps the most objectionable of all. All of this, of course, is not new, but it has to be repeated again and again.

My Ideology
The belief on which we started our research was that the dweller should make decisions about the physical environment in which he lived. If the user was to make decisions, while at the same time there seemed to be a role for professionals to play, the question became "who is deciding on what?" That led to the—theoretical—division of the physical world into two realms: the elements about which the user personally makes decisions and those about which he does not. From there flowed a whole series of questions: What constitutes a design decision? How do the decisions of different parties relate to each other?

It was clear that the ideology challenged vested interests and their modes of operation in the professional worlds of government, finance, and technology, in that it assumed different human relations and territorial claims.

It would be a contradiction to expect that the first objective of research must be to test and possibly refute the ideology that supports it. Ultimately we act on faith. For better or for worse, we assumed that our ideology was right. If it was not, we would find out. Our research task was to be executed within the boundaries of a narrow professional field by those who were knowledgeable in that field. But this task was defined from a much wider context that gave it a goal to pursue. This context was a belief to be accepted without proof. Even now, when it seems that the methods finally developed in the research do indeed "work," this does not mean that that philosophy was "right," although success may make it more acceptable, more likely to be "right."

Method
Our problem was the following: all right, if the user must be able to change his own physical environment, how must professional designers operate to make that possible? If the *support* is that part of the building that the user cannot individually change, how do I, as a designer, design a support? We found that the design process that we were familiar with was based on the assumption that everything was subject to professional design decisions. That is how we got into a design *method*, and decided to develop the methodological tools that would allow professionals to operate effectively in the world that the ideology demanded.

Expertise
The decision to focus specifically and exclusively on method was a decision to stay very close to where our own skills and expertise were. We were designers and design was what we were interested in. At a time when we tend to think in terms of global problems, where experts of many fields have to cooperate to deal with

the issues, it is necessary to repeat that one can only cooperate from the strength of one's own expertise. And ours was design. We decided to stay with it. If others in their own field would do the same—but within a shared ideology—cooperation would come. We were often told that our research group should have sociologists, financiers, engineers, lawyers, and others in it. Financial constraints, as much as an instinctive sense of its prematurity, saved us from making that mistake.

Vehicle
On the level of ideology, we are all amateurs. If that is what gives us direction as to where to go, our specific expertise—in this case design—is the vehicle that must bring us there. Here, we cannot accept any but the most rigid standards of clarity and logical consistency. The captain of the ship will allow the socio-political context to influence his decision as to where to sail, but he will darn well make sure that his ship is run in a strictly professional way. His life depends on it. Any amateurism, any rhetoric or public relation gimmickry, anything less than just plain skilled craftsmanship, will make the expedition vulnerable as it charts its course. The researcher who cannot distinguish social from professional responsibility is in trouble.

Architects, like other professionals, operate in the real world. Their research is constantly in danger of confusion between the two issues mentioned here. As long as we are unable to clarify the vehicle we operate—our territory of expertise, as distinct from other fields—our voyages will be difficult to plan.

Companions (1)
The crew has to be chosen to come aboard. What kind of designer do we need? Here the choice is clearly the result of the stated objectives. The remarks I can offer are therefore very much to be seen in the context of the particular research in which I was involved. Anyone in a design research operation must, of course, be a skilled designer in the narrow sense of the word. That is, someone who is visually literate, can think in three dimensions, and feels at ease with manipulating built form at a reasonable level of complexity. But, assuming that there are enough people who have the training and the talents to fulfill these minimal requirements, what else is important?

I have learned to distinguish a number of abilities that I like to think every architect should possess, but that I know every researcher in design must have. The two most essential are the ability to understand other peoples' values and the ability to understand time and change.

Values (1)
First and foremost, there is the question of values and value judgment in design. Any investigation about design should distinguish between the kinds of decisions to be made and the kinds of information to be formulated and communicated, on the one hand, and the values of these decisions and communications, on the other. In research, we want to understand design as an activity that deals with value judgments, but which therefore should be distinguished from them. The objective of research in design is not to express our own values as designers, but to understand issues of form and decision-making as they relate to different criteria, representing different values.

The subculture of architects, and the education that produces them, puts stress on the quest for the good, as distinct from the bad. We feel we are the protectors of quality, however that may be defined. Our education is largely directed by two things: that the student learns how to establish his own value system and to express it in built forms—architecture as a form of self expression, a way to set a standard, to safeguard the quality of the environment and to educate the layman; and that he is initiated into a peer group that knows what is good or bad, and is aware of those elusive and secret do's and don'ts that make one a "good" architect—the hidden agenda that makes one fit his own value system within that of the colleagues he admires.

These two educational goals may be mostly implicit, but they are strong. They can also be in conflict with each other. The ensuing stresses are enough to make a problem of any curriculum. There is preciously little in all this to prepare a person for a detached approach toward understanding how issues of form and quality interact. We do not train ourselves to understand issues of value in the built environment without immediately deciding whether or not we agree with them. Those who have never learned to observe and understand, but only to pass judgment, may or may not make good architects, but they will *never* make good researchers.

Change
As housing and residential settlement was the subject of our explorations, and adaptability to users through their intervention over time our goal, change became a crucial factor. It takes some training to be able to see the built environment as something that is in constant flux, and to discern the patterns of movement and the various rhythms of change of different methods to take account of the possible variations that may be made by others after we are done. Yet these transformations have been with us for a long time. The urban designer knows that his work should create a framework within which architects can work over time. We know that buildings tend to come and go while streets remain. We know that buildings can stand for a long time while their interiors are done over by each succeeding generation. Yet we have never absorbed this knowledge into our attitudes and methods. We tend to be defensive about issues of change. We don't want to have others change what we have done. But what is done today could be seen as an incentive for action by others who follow. As others will act anyway, the recognition of

that inevitable fact may lead us into a solution that allows for more continuity than could be arrived at in ignorance of the dimension of time. At any rate, the game becomes more interesting and less uptight if one feels at ease with change.

Time (1)
Time, and the changes it brings with it, have been the architect's enemy. The architectural creation was always a statement that had to defy time. Its function was to be a symbol of truths and powers that had to reach beyond the generations. The movements of the everyday environment could be ignored. Architecture was a stone in the waters of time.

Time (2)
The rejection of possible future change is one way to fight time. Rejection of the past is another. Understanding what might happen after our intervention is only half the picture. The other half is the acceptance of what has been done before, the recognition of what exists: the power and meaning of the site. It is no coincidence that the "modern architecture" generations hardly ever put other buildings in their presentations. They did not like the past. Is it a coincidence that restoration was invented in the same period by others in the field? It is yet another way to stop time.

Values (2)
The site and the past are constraints. Rules and regulations and constraints as well. They are invisible sites. At the same time, they are expressions of values, creating a certain value system. Architects have a hard time seeing norms and standards as anything but hostile harassment. But those who move into housing often have to live with the results of such rule systems, and the study of design cannot ignore them. No method can succeed if it does not involve the formulation of norms and the evaluation of their impacts.

Companions (2)
If you ask me what it takes to be a member of a party exploring the continent called design, you will get a description of the strange creatures one encounters on the way and the strange geographies one has to feel at home in: a story about the hostile regions of regulatory processes, the frightening herds of other people's values, the shifting sands of time, the weird animal called change, and, finally, the unknown tribes of users. It is enough to decide that architecture should leave housing alone, as it generally has done in the past.

Mapping
An expedition is not mounted to enjoy the scenery, but to map new territory. Research wants to build theory: the mapping of a body of knowledge. When the narrow goal of my involvement in research was to develop methods as design tools, a good part of the attraction was the opportunity to understand design better. Over the years, we built up a set of formally defined elements by trial and error, arriving at a description of their relations and the operations that allowed their manipulation. Slowly, an underlying logic revealed itself. The construct that eventually emerged could be gradually recognized for what it was—or rather, for what it stood for: a theory that needed explicit formulation.

In retrospect, it is almost self-evident that a preoccupation with method would lead to theory. To map our world, we first of all need the means to describe its elements and their relations. Because we were interested in design as a way to convey information, the formal means of description of the built environment became a primary occupation. But any formal way of describing implicitly contains a theory of what one wants to describe. A method of description needs a classification of elements, which must be put in their (spatial) relationships. How we choose to classify them depends again on how we see the world. The interaction is both inescapable and fascinating. To develop the means, a theory is implicit. To explicate a theory, a formal way of describing its elements is needed.

Experimentation
As theory and description relate to one another like *Yin* and *Yang*, there are two other elements of interaction as well, that seem to be common to all research: experimentation and observation. As we observe the world, the need to explain what is seen leads to theory. Its communication leads to description. Theory and the means to describe lead us to keener and renewed observation, and so on. The one balances the other. But the force that drives it all is experimentation. In design research, experimentation is done through design, the exploration of which is possible within given constraints—the observation of the impact of specific values on form, the evaluation of a given space for its capacity to hold change—all this to test the methods of design as tools for intervention.

Observation
Experiments deal with intervention into what is explored. Observation leaves the world as we find it, and is the beginning of all research. It is not just seeing: it is seeing with detachment—the suspension of knowledge and certainty. It is curiosity, before the question is asked. The answer is the end of observation and the beginning of theory. The theory leads to understanding, and understanding makes us see the world as we could not see it before. It allows us to see more, which may lead again to observation.

Observation leads to a record—a sketch, a photograph. But the record is not "an observation," but rather the beginning of an answer. The use of media can get in the way of observation. The eye that can observe is the eye that discovers.

Discoveries
The most exciting part is the act of discovery—the recognition that the concept of *position* is central to everything that design stands for, the role of *values* as the messages conveyed while we design (expressed in terms of elements and position), the concept of levels, that brings order in the vastness of the design subjects to which we turn, or the concept of *function* as a relationship of action on different levels. Discoveries are the result of theory applied to reality. They are the building blocks of new theory. The concepts we "discovered" often found their way in our operations—and proved useful—long before we could adequately define them. They emerged by observation and experimentation. The best discoveries make us recognize the self-evident as part of a theoretical construct.

Communication (4)
These notes must sound like the incoherent ramblings of a weary traveller, clutching his soiled collection of papers brought back from far away places. I am in the midst of shuffling and ordering my notes to construct the map that has to explain it all. But to whom? First of all, to oneself. But one travels to expand the world one shares with others. As our world of design is one of confusion, not much factual information can be conveyed in a short message. Lacking a shared body of knowledge, we feel that a brief exchange can perhaps only serve to convey the excitement, enthusiasm and discovery that true exploration brings as its rewards. It may still be an out-of-place kind of activity, but it surely is worthwhile once you have tried it.

Research
Does all this really have to go under the term research? While I use the term daily out of convenience, I am not sure. How does one define the term? If research is an activity that helps us understand the world by developing maps that allow others to follow the route and verify what we have seen, the answer may be yes, we do research in architecture. If research is an activity that takes place in a structured system of discourse, accepted by all participants, an activity that allows us to add knowledge and understanding like building blocks to a structure we all understand, the answer must be no. We are not there yet. We are still wandering about, comparing notes, when our paths happen to cross. But we may get there. Sometimes I am sure we will.

Editors' note: Controversial references here to Henry Morton Stanley and Christopher Columbus, both notable for their perpetration of colonial violence, are left as they were in the original.

On Formal Analysis as Design Research

Denise Scott Brown
Architect and Planner

Working hard at sightseeing one sunny afternoon in Southern California, Bob and I decided "this is no vacation, this is our research."[1] Later, planning the following year's studio at Yale, we remembered this and wondered if our brand of sightseeing research—which is entertaining, enjoyable, and enormously instructive for our own work—could not, if carefully and rigorously organized, prove enjoyable and instructive for our students as well, and help advance our personal investigations much further.

So in 1968 and 1970 we conducted two studios: "Learning from Las Vegas, or Formal Analysis as Design Research"; and "Remedial Housing for Architects, or Learning from Levittown."[2] Both dealt with the architecture of suburban sprawl. Working as a group, we tried to analyze and describe our sources in a way that would let us develop theories usable to us as architects and urbanists. What we hoped to gain from our research were:

- A new view of some scorned areas of the metropolis, and some objective information on suburbia that would let us face its problems more rationally and less emotionally than we architects have to date. Needless to say, our view wasn't new to planners or social scientists, but it was to most architects.
- Techniques for analyzing and describing suburban form—particularly new graphic techniques that could be useful to designers as communication tools (especially self-communication) while designing.
- Architectural theories and principles more useful to face the problems of late 20th century American society than those we've inherited from the early Modern Movement.

This article makes the case that our "formal analysis" is research, even though it doesn't employ computers or make use of behavioral psychologists. Furthermore, it is applied research, suited to the professional practice of

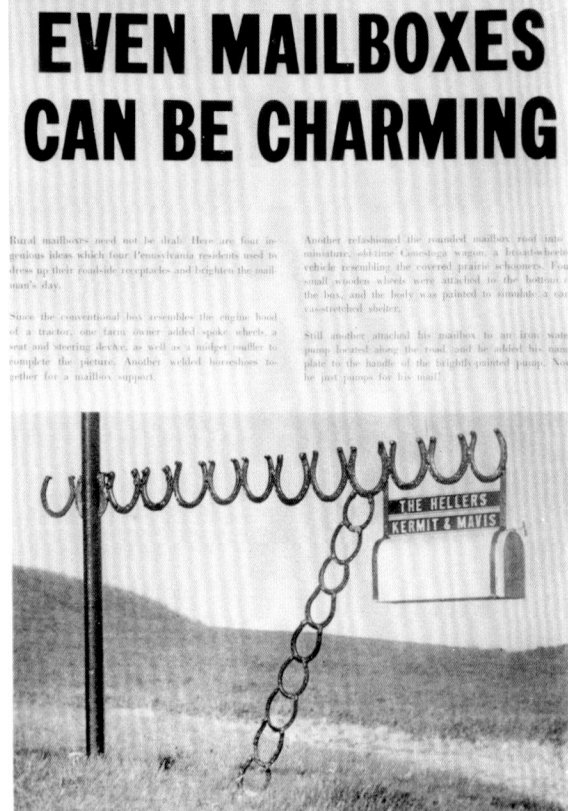

"Precedents of Suburban Symbols," Learning from Levittown studio, Yale University.

architecture, with pedagogical value—particularly in studio, where it can be the means to rehabilitate studio education.

I will define what I mean by "formal analysis" and describe its possible content. But to do so, I will need to discuss the recent history of studio education in architecture and urban planning, and describe how my thoughts on the subject developed.

Architecture Studios and Planning Studios

The studio has traditionally been the fulcrum of architectural education—equivalent to the medical student's clinic or the law student's case studies. Ideally, it is a place where professional skills are learned in practice, and where the real tools of the trade are taught. Yet in many schools, studio is underfinanced and therefore poorly planned and prepared; projects are often outlined by instructors on a napkin during lunch on the day class begins, and presented to the students verbally. Despite lip service to the contrary, there is little effort to relate studio to other coursework, and in fact the studio tends to have a negative impact on other courses during charettes. In graduate school, faculty and students consider that the liberal arts have been "gotten out of the way" and make little effort to relate architecture to any broader culture. Nor is effort typically made to plan and structure the research related to the studio project. In the least organized, worst prepared studios, the students may be still floundering around in a sea of "research" six weeks after the project has started. Research, as it was viewed by the traditional architectural schools, meant research in structures. Doctorates, when they were given at all, were given in architectural history and intended to support wholly academic careers. But when, in the 1960s, big changes came in architectural schools, these focused on research. With outside funding, research programs at some architecture departments bulged enormously, while the faculty took on an academic, university-wide orientation. The traditional orientation of architectural education toward professional practice was eroded, the new architectural scientists regarded studio as a know-nothing, archaic, authoritarian remnant of the École des Beaux-Arts—although in some schools studio found a second life as the locus of students' involvement in community projects.

In planning education, studio was seen as the place to coordinate and practice what was learned in coursework, and to gain some initial experience in professional planning work. But, during the 1960s, these studios, run by architect/planners, were criticized by social planners as anti-intellectual, physically biased, imperialist (because they took up too much student time), old-fashioned, and elitist (because they derived from architecture). In response, studio faculty turned toward third world and American ghetto problems where the emphasis was on economic and social development and on low-income, preferably self-help, housing. This wasn't enough, however, and by the mid-1960s, studio was virtually abolished for nonarchitects in planning.

Planning studios were, in general, better structured and much better prepared than architecture studios. The planning faculty, with full-time appointments and teaching assistants, could simply give more time to preparation. Planning studios were group projects, with separate work topics assigned to individuals or small

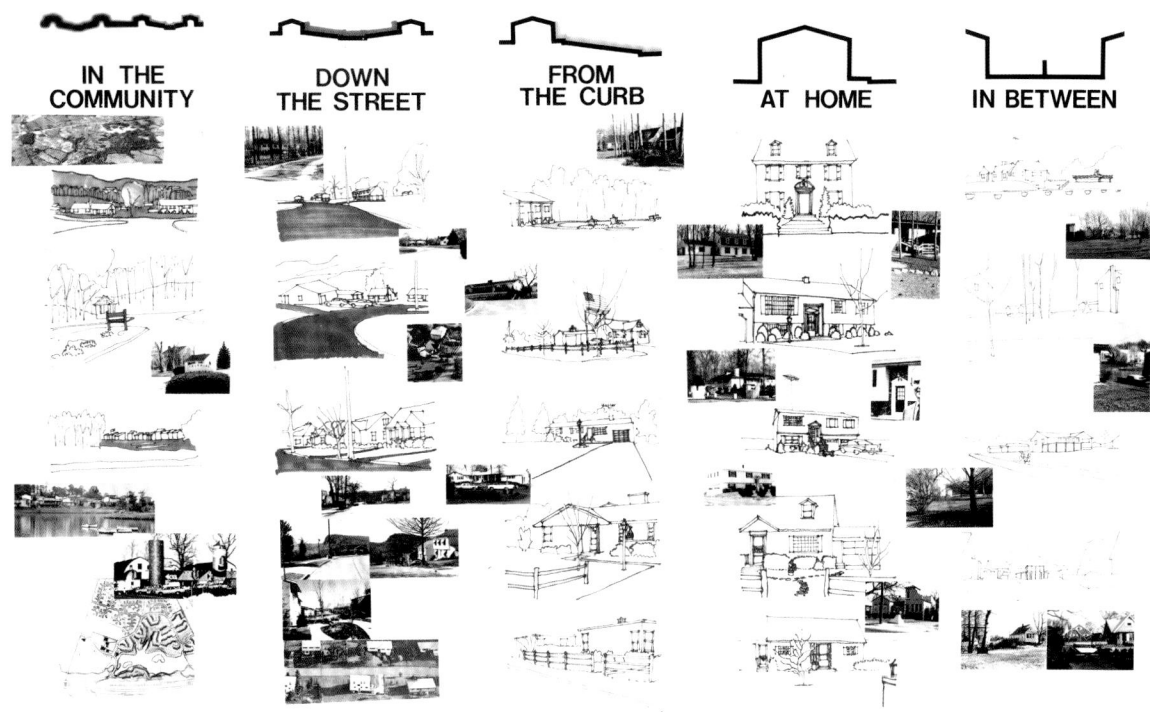

"Suburban Space, Sprawl, and Imagery," Learning from Levittown studio, Yale University.

groups. "Crits" were as much information-sharing sessions and preparation for the next phase of the project as a forum for criticism. Juries were marathon affairs in which the work of the whole semester—research and design—was presented and often heatedly discussed by economists, sociologists, and transportation engineers, as well as by the architects on the faculty. A typical criticism of planning studios was that no connection was made between the first half (research) and the second half (design). To architect-planners, research and analysis were a ritual, gratefully abandoned in favor of the preferred activity—design. In an effort to remedy this, I began to structure brief periods of analysis followed by brief periods of synthesis—policy recommendations or designs. The syllabus gave direction to the next period of analysis by revealing where more information was needed to continue the project. One benefit of this cyclical approach was that the students knew why they needed the information when they started a period of analysis, and therefore had some motivation to do it. This applies particularly to students in urban design. Holmes Perkins had admonished me to "remember design is their first love—don't lead them too far away from it," so I avoided running a totally research-oriented studio. This avoidance reached its logical conclusion on our return from Las Vegas, with all our information red-hot. I assigned a brief sketch design on what the students thought the Strip should be. They promptly described the problem as "that busywork Denise is making us do."

To introduce architects to the non-architectural subject matter of urban design and planning, I evolved a series of planning-like studios that were both interdisciplinary and strongly structured. I called them "Form, Forces, and Functions," and their theory was that the form of the city owes as much to forces within the natural environment, society and its technology as it does to "functions" as architects define them. The aim was to help architects grapple with unfamiliar material by relating it to their own task of physical form-making, and to prepare them to work with other professionals who have no understanding of architecture.

After ten years of teaching studio—and despite the debates about its validity or usefulness—I remain convinced it is an excellent pedagogical tool for a professional program in architecture or planning. Far from being abolished, it should be rehabilitated and—at least for introductory programs—made the focus around which coursework revolves. This is because people absorb unfamiliar material most readily when they need to apply it to a purpose they understand well, and when that purpose relates to something with which they are already familiar.

Many architects dislike abstractions. An architecture student once said to me in exasperation: "I'm an architect, and I think in *concrete* terms!" Such people (and, I suspect, most people) find it easier to go from the concrete to the abstract—to examine the city physical and the visible behavior of its occupants, and to derive from this a series of social and architectural insights, aided by book learning. In short, to work inductively rather than deductively.

A Schedule of Las Vegas Strip gas stations.

Studio as a research tool seems particularly suited to applied research—in our case, research for designers. Such research must lead to specifics. It may go from the concrete (i.e., documenting and analyzing the Strip) to the abstract (i.e., theories about Modern architecture), but it should help the architect at the drawing board, even if this happens unconsciously. "What did you learn from Las Vegas?" is not a question we can necessarily answer very clearly.

Formal Analysis in the Studio

The Las Vegas and Levittown studios emphasized research, with the stress of the analysis of form. This analysis was made largely in terms of societal forces and of function as architects define it. The emphasis on form stemmed in part from the growing feeling that architects, particularly urban designers, are becoming de-skilled. Surveying the subsequent professional performance of students from graduate programs in schools where I have taught, it seems that in our eagerness to provide a broad education and a lively social awareness, we have short-changed students in the area of formal knowledge, particularly in the practice of translating verbal requirements into physical form.

The main focus of the studios was on a kind of do-it-yourself cultural anthropology, an attempt to describe cultural objects as symbol systems. The initial phases of each studio were strongly structured, but every effort was made to give individual students their own choice of work topic and to structure their work with their interests in mind. By the middle of the semester we had turned most of the work of structuring over to the students. Each studio included a month-long library research phase (based on an annotated bibliography that ranged from regional science to historic iconology), a site work phase, and several analysis and descriptive phases, in which a brief design phase was interspersed.

In the Las Vegas studio, our "field work" consisted of ten intense days in Las Vegas where the students gathered information individually or in small groups, using a set work program. The students took slides and several films of the Strip and Fremont Street. They also collected base maps, aerial photographs, and publicity material about Las Vegas and the different hotels and casinos. We found early photographs of Las Vegas, to note change and permanence in the city, and made tape recordings of the memories of old-timers. We also recorded the views of planning officials on zoning and other regulations for the Strip. We interviewed at the Young Electric Sign Co., visited their plant and commissioned a detailed description of his design philosophy from the designer of the Aladdin sign.

Our attempts to find statistical information about the life of the city, its linkages and activity patterns were quite unsuccessful. Questions about land values brought forth the answer, "if you had that information, you would be the most powerful person in Las Vegas." We couldn't take photographs inside the casinos, and our one attempt to taperecord inside a casino ended with the last words on the tape: "Get that guy!" Our efforts to document how people used the Strip through tracking studies foundered on our inability to design studies we could perform. Following people by car, riding with them in buses, and attempting to hitchhike in their cars produced little information and several mishaps. Finally, we simply stationed students at the entries of several casinos, to observe which entrances cars used and where they parked in relation to the signs.

The fieldwork for the "Learning from Levittown" studio took place mainly in New Haven, but included a visit to Columbia, Reston, and Williamsburg. The bulk of the research—and our chief addition to knowledge in the field—was an analysis of people's attitudes to the physical appearance of housing. This analysis was based on questioning, looking at housing, and analyzing the housing and housing-related content of mass media. We monitored television westerns, situation comedies, and Chevy and furniture polish ads and analyzed developers' blurbs, the real estate sections of local papers, popular and professional journals, comic strips, and 18th century novels—to see what attitudes about housing were implicit in them. A parallel study investigated architects' attitudes toward housing since the turn of the century, and documented the *idées fixes* that architects of the Modern Movement have had on the subject of housing. Finally we described the symbolic decoration used by suburbanites, and analyzed its function in defining suburban residential space and enhancing its perception at the neighborhood level, from the road, and from the front yard.

The brief design periods in each studio were used to help students structure their reactions to the city and therefore organize their findings, and to get them thinking about how to use the material professionally. The "designs" weren't necessarily physical: one asked for the design of new roles for architects; another for the components of a socially-concerned, regional housing strategy for New Haven; and a third asked students to "do for housing what Oldenburg did for hamburgers."

The products of the two studios were physical descriptions of the places under study, and analyses of the physical and symbolic requirements they fulfilled. Our findings led to theoretical formulations about architecture, and, as a continuing process, to a body of work. Our research produced written descriptions, movies, video tapes, slides, photos, tapes, maps, charts, matrices, drawings, two songs, a cake, and a book.[3] A movie, entitled "Three Camera Deadpan," was made by attaching the cameras to the front of a car and driving the length of the Strip. We also made a still photograph panorama by splicing individual shots taken at regular intervals down each side of the Strip. We made time lapse movies covering 24 hours in the life of the Strip, and of the open space in a public housing project in New Haven. We also videotaped people in public housing talking about their houses.

We tried to devise mapping techniques that suited the Strip. Some were based on conventional land use mapping methods, while others used the map of Rome done by the 18th century mapmaker, Nolli, as a prototype. One map located every sign along the length of the Strip. We used charts and schedules to make a comparative analysis of different designs for vast

Nolli's Map of Rome (detail).

spaces—Versailles, Broadacre City, the Radiant City, highway interchanges, the Strip. We also compared directional spaces—the Eastern bazaar, the medieval European city, Main Street USA, and the Strip. We defined the constituent elements of the typical casino-hotel and charted each casino's particular design of these elements. We made matrices to show the stylistic sources of current developer-designed housing, and also to show variations in the use of housing imagery by socio-economic group, and in the degree to which residents produce the imagery themselves. Finally, we looked at alterations made to the same type of house by different income groups. We made taxonomies of the elements of the suburban house subject to symbolism—fences, mailboxes, garden ornaments, front doors, shutters. We analyzed the messages that viewers were given by the houses shown in movies, on television, and in merchant builders' ads.

Our experiences, and the criticism of our friends, convinced us that we were not in the design of research, but that it made good sense to isolate the variable "form" for analysis, and that "formalism" in architecture and urban design is irresponsible only when it is not conscious.

Architecture, Science, and Scientism
I have made the case elsewhere that the architect who analyzes form is not necessarily lacking in social concern, and have explained why architects must be convinced of this fact.[4] I have also pointed out that concentrating on one variable is approved scientific and humanistic behavior in analysis, but not in design. I have suggested that the distaste that some architects have shown for our studies is probably more a class-based dislike of our subject matter than a dismay with our research techniques.

But their worries probably also relate to a fear of the unmeasurable, non quantitative aspects of architecture. In our culture, the mantle of science lends respectability—or has done so until recently. Others have noted how disciplines perceived as being at the edge of academic respectability tend to acquire a spurious scientism, a physics envy or science voodoo, to which the insecure can turn for proof of their field's "rigor." Architecture and planning are no exceptions to this tendency.

Yet there are times in the development of knowledge when quantification is pre-mature, and in architecture there are intangibles that resist measurement, but that can be well handled all the same. It is irrational to resist the appropriate application of scientific method, even when it treads on sacred artistic ground. But it is equally irrational and irresponsible—not to say unscientific—to omit the unmeasurable and limit one's attention solely to that which can be handled mathematically, or "scientifically proven."

I sense a decline in scientism in architecture as architects learn more about scientific methods—particularly about what the computer can and can't do—and as the American romance with technology sours. Techniques that involve the intuition and judgment of trained observers are accepted in sociology, that high priest of physics in the social sciences. The techniques we developed could stand improvement, but they are useful to practitioners. Non-quantitative, operational, poetic, these techniques are not so much anti-scientific as pre-scientific (and pre-artistic). They define new areas for more rigorous development by both scientists and artists.

All images courtesy of The Architectural Archives, University of Pennsylvania, by the gift of Robert Venturi and Denise Scott Brown.

Notes
1. Editors' note: Bob here refers to Robert Venturi, her partner at Venturi, Scott Brown and Associates, and her husband.
2. Editors' note: Both of the studios referenced here were taught at Yale University.
3. Steven Izenour, Denise Scott Brown, and Robert Venturi, *Learning from Las Vegas: The Forgotten Symbolism of Architectural Form* (Cambridge, MA: MIT Press, 1977).
4. Denise Scott Brown, "On Architectural Formalism & Social Concern," *Oppositions* 5 (Summer, 1976): 99–112.

With People in Mind

Denise Scott Brown
Architect and Planner

I've chosen to be an architect with a second profession in urban planning. I'm an architect and a planner, or an architect/planner. To span these two fields I must range from the social sciences and law through architecture, interior design, and the arts. Within this broad field that I've assigned myself, I operate as a professional, an academic, a theoretician, a writer, and an educator. It's very difficult for me to define my focus exactly, because I seem to specialize in the linkages.

For me, teaching a small community or a group of architecture students is like a game of patty cake. I must get a rhythm going and persuade someone to join in. A child will first follow by eye and meet my hands with help, then suddenly she catches the rhythm and can do it herself. Eventually she teaches someone else.

The art of getting into people's heads something that wasn't there before has always fascinated me. Architects, because they can do harm, must learn to be open minded. As urban designers, they must be especially sensitive to social questions. But many students of architecture don't want to read. They would rather draw; and they certainly don't want to read sociology. How boring! Many urban architects, who really need to be aware of the problems of people who live in cities, think that urban sociology is not pertinent to them. How do you teach them in such a way that they'll want to find out this information? One of my ways is to set students problems that they find challenging, but that depend on the information for their solution. One such problem could be the design of housing for low-income families. In order to solve the problem—and they really want to solve it because it's something they feel strongly about—they have to know how poor families live, and, in the end, they have to read about them. To solve their creative problem, they need information.

In the early 1960s at Penn, and then at Berkeley, I taught that there are forces in the city—economic forces, technological forces, and social forces—that shape the physical form of the city much more than do the "programs" or "functions" that architects design for. Architects say form follows function, function should determine form. (They used to say it. They say it less now.) But forces also determine form. Economic forces are enormously strong in directing what kinds of buildings are built and determining where they're located. I taught several courses and studio projects that I called FFF—Form, Forces and Functions—in which we tried to analyze how the structure of society is related to the form of the city, and tried to make explicit the connections between social and physical phenomena, between people and buildings. This is a theme of both my professional work and my pedagogy. To demonstrate how one professional and practitioner who teaches has endeavored to make this connection for students (or, rather, to help them make it), I have appended an edited version of some of the material I wrote in 1963-65 for University of Pennsylvania civic design studios, where the relation between society and buildings was a major emphasis. These excerpts show some approaches that can be taken to help prepare our students to confront architectural problems with people in mind.

In this studio we try to join forces and functions to physical forms, words to pictures, the things social and natural scientists know to the things architects know; to take a broad view of the city to learn its "spirit" and where it is going; and to relate this broad view to what you, as architects, already know of built form.

. . . A city is the coming together of people to do in groups what they cannot do for themselves as individuals. This group activity is made formal in the institutions of the city, which thus represent the joining of citizens for corporate purpose (e.g., shopping, education) or for activities which, though performed by small groups, are general to all citizens (e.g., the activity involved in the institution "Home").

. . . To coordinate form, forces, and function, we try to survey in broad terms what goes into the making of a city, and to relate our findings to the knowledge and interest you, as architects, already have in built form. Our work is based on the thesis that there are forces and factors in society and in the environment which determine the physical form of the city, and a greater understanding of the interplay of forces and forms in the city will enable all involved in city planning and city form-giving to do a better job.

Part of the problem lies in the very breadth of scope that excites and challenges us. The problems and possibilities of cities are so wide and deep that it is impossible for one person to span them. But when these problems become the separate concerns of specialists, the meaning of the whole is lost, and, in a very demonstrable way, the needs, spiritual and material, of citizens go unfulfilled. Yet we need our specialists and their depth of knowledge; what we lack is connection. It could be claimed that our present problems in planning are due less to a lack of knowledge than to a lack of ability to share knowledge. We, as specialists, know a great deal, but we don't share a vocabulary, or sometimes even a common spirit. We can't communicate amongst

Venturi, Rauch and Scott Brown. "Action Plan for The Strand," Galveston, Texas, 1975. Proposed typical façade renovations with signage and canopies replaced. Drawing by Stanford Hughes.

ourselves and therefore mistrust each other more than we should, and are unable to use our skills and knowledge jointly to the best advantage. If the sociologist-planner and architect-planner can't really talk to each other, how can we expect the social implications of the physical plan or the physical implications of the social plan to be sound? And how can a profession which calls its architect-planners "designers" and "artists" and its social-scientist-planners "analysts" and "scientists" (showing thereby a misconception of the work of both and of the meaning of all these terms) expect much in the way of sound, creative thought from either?

Van Eyck says, "What you should try to accomplish is built meaning. So get close to the meaning and build!" This is the same as saying the form of the city should be "art" expressing and interpreting, in the manner of art, through form, content and symbol, the aspirations of its people. "Art." This most abused and least definable of terms, denigrated as much by those who speak in its name as by those who cry out against it, is nevertheless one which we cannot in the end escape. The path of rationality will take us far, but not all the way. We come at last to a gap. The implications of creativity—the need to "jump"—cannot be avoided. The art of the city has, in the past, been born of confusion, created in trial, made by the many and over the years. There is no avoiding this situation. Ideal cities, even when built, are not real cities, challenging the loyalty and aspirations of the citizenry. The real artist can deal with the non-rational, and knows that doubt and confusion can be fertile to the creative mind. The artist in the city is a person of faith and dedication who acts with conviction in the presence of doubt.

. . . The single building, if it is to satisfy on the deepest level, must itself inflect toward the city, serving its clients as citizens as well as individuals, setting them within the society.

The vaults of knowledge of the specialists could be pure treasure to the civic designer. Few creators live entirely on their own; much less so those who aim to serve their society through "building its meaning." Civic designers' inspiration must come from the reality of the world around them, sometimes from its hard reality. They must be, if they are to succeed, temperamentally inclined to view the constraints and limitations of the real world not as impediments to inspiration, but as challenge and opportunity for greater creativity through their very bindingness. If not, if civic designers continue to find the world of the sociologist "very dull" because "they deal in 2.5 people"; if the mystery and joy of numbers and their uncertainty, or the mechanics of decision-making processes, or the concept of maximizing, remain foreign ground to them; if they believe ecology is only concerned with plants and flowers, and climate is something we have overcome though mechanical systems, then I'm afraid they are the ones who are stuffy and dull—and they will lose the job.

In 1968 and 1970, Robert Venturi and I taught several studios at Yale where we again tried to make explicit the connections between social and physical phenomena. In the 1960s and early 1970s students were very responsive to the social questions we raised, and "people" and "community" received more attention in studio than they do today. This has something to do with the times and changes within the culture around the students. Owing to economic worries, students and others are turning toward saleable skills and traditional modes of practice. Students want to draw, know about structures, and be able to "design."

But students vary. In some schools they have been very responsive to my approach and in others less so. And I find the designs of students also vary immensely from school to school. In general, architects and architectural educators, and therefore students, don't

Venturi, Rauch and Scott Brown with BRW, Inc. and Williams/O'Brien Associates, Inc. "Urban Design Plan," Hennepin Avenue, Minneapolis, 1981. Drawing by James Timberlake.

set a high priority on satisfying people in design. Where they do, it is sometimes a pietism and an escape used by students and architects who feel they can't handle all of architecture's problems. We saw a lot of this in the 1960s: poor designs with a social rhetoric used to cover inability. Even where architects' hearts are in the right place, their ideas are often highly unsophisticated and not above the preliminary level of wanting to "do good."

In response to this, Robert Venturi and I taught a studio called "Remedial Housing for Architects," in which we examined the housing field from an action-oriented and architectural point of view, designed to make subsequent study of housing deeper and more meaningful. We didn't get involved in civic or community action in that course, but in learning what is needed to make our professional contribution to this action more relevant.

Part of the problem seems to be that graduate education puts "cultural preparation" first in undergraduate pre-architecture or liberal arts degrees, and presumes that the architecture student will perform the integration of this cultural knowledge with subsequent graduate architectural training on his or her own. In my experience this doesn't happen. The students take a "gut" course in "Sosh" because it is required and is easy, but do not see the relevance of its subject matter to the problem in housing design that is tackled in the second year of graduate architectural study. Somehow sociology should become part of that second-year housing studio.

When confronted with students' questions about what takes precedence in the design process—people or technology, form, style, economics, etcetera, my answer is that all of these are inextricably intertwined. The question remains, however, how to teach, particularly beginning students, about this mixture in a way that they can handle. Architecture and urban design students must assimilate knowledge of people in a useful and sophisticated way, and retain their interest in this information not as amateur sociologists but as *designers*.

Since I no longer teach, the problem of practicing what I teach or teaching what I practice has become that of designing according to my own philosophy, and of practicing with these same concerns in mind. It is hard for both students and architects to find an effective focus for social concern in the 1980s, and this again mirrors conditions within the larger society. In some schools such interests are considered "old hang-ups of the 1960s." In schools and in the profession, Post-Modernist architectural philosophies and stringent economic conditions are too often seen as adequate reasons for architects to turn away from social problems.

Although there is indeed much to question in the nostrums evolved by architects and planners of the Great Society, we are surely wiser for their experience. And I can find no justification in either the state of our art or our economy for ignoring social responsibility. There must be a way to be socially concerned in the 1980s. It is good that someone is again looking for it.

Editors' note: This present essay is excerpted from the original.

All images courtesy of The Architectural Archives, University of Pennsylvania, by the gift of Robert Venturi and Denise Scott Brown.

Past or Post Modern in Architectural Fashion

Diane Ghirardo
University of Southern California

The phenomenon of Post Modern culture has manifested itself primarily in two ways in contemporary architectural production and discourse. One, which is almost exclusively stylistic, has attempted to seek a renewal in architecture through the rejection of all aspects of Modernism in favor of a picturesque and superficial Classicism. This version of Post Modernism accepts de facto the pluralist worldview of contemporary capitalist development and avoids the larger questions of architecture's place within the complexities of today's socio-political universe. The other manifestation of Post Modernism in architecture is theoretical. It seeks a critical reading of architecture within the complex labyrinth of contemporary culture. It tries to understand how meaning has come to have a tenuous existence in the artifacts and life of our time. It has proposed, both through theory and practice, various possibilities as to how we might negotiate this situation. This paper engages in discussion and critique of both of these orientations, their implications and ramifications.

If the historian has difficulty assessing events in the past, so much the worse are matters for the contemporary critic who attempts to explore events *in medias res*. The contemporary discourse about Post Modernism in architecture does not lend itself to a neat taxonomy, not least because the participants sometimes term themselves Post Modernists, and other times reject that label. For the purpose of this essay, two very general categories of Post Modernism seem to emerge: what I shall call stylistic Post Modernism (SPM) and theoretical Post Modernism (TPM).

Stylistic Post Modernism is that of the popular press, an architecture characterized by a departure from the stylistic canons of the Modern Movement. Its leading practitioners claim that the architecture of Modernism eschewed ornament, emphasized the expressive potential of functionalism only, and denied both history and the human element in architecture, while Post Modernist buildings celebrate ornament, historical allusions, color, and humanity. To this extent, stylistic Post Modernism helped relax the stranglehold of a perceived Modernist orthodoxy, but this primarily affected the lesser architectural talents who mindlessly repeated the dogmas articulated by Henry-Russell Hitchcock and Philip Johnson in *The International Style*.[1] Even Robert Venturi, in the earliest text which Post Modernists claim as their own, *Complexity and Contradiction in Architecture*, repeatedly referred to the masters of the Modern Movement—Le Corbusier, Mies van der Rohe, Gropius—as having achieved the kind of complexity and interest which he argued should replace the boring boxes of modern architecture.[2]

SPM found an early expression in the Venice Biennale of 1980 organized by Paolo Portoghesi, which included the work of leading Post Modernists as well as that of younger architects. To the extent that it is possible to apply this term, Charles Jencks is the leading "theorist" of this particular stream of Post Modernism.[3] Jencks argues that Modern Movement architecture shed its "plural traditions," but that Post Modernism, by being more "inclusivist" (that is, allowing the architect eclectic use of elements from the past), fulfills the primary goal of heightened communication. Of course, if communication is to be other than mindless babble, it must be conveying some message, but Jencks is silent on this score. Architecture has languages and conventions, says Jencks, and he suggests that these should be open to all architects to use according to their fancies.[4]

The leading practitioners of SPM—Robert A. M. Stern, Michael Graves, Paolo Portoghesi, Stanley Tigerman—are unable to offer a richer definition of their version of Post Modernism. Their architecture constitutes a rebellion against the stylistic constraints of international Modernism, as well as a return to domestic architectural practice of the late-nineteenth century. Although they argue for a greater stylistic diversity, their architecture tends toward pastiche, and at that, a pastiche comprehensible only to the cognoscenti. One must know Boullée's fantastic designs in order to comprehend Helmut Jahn's and C. F. Murphy Associates' Argonne National Laboratories Support Facility (1979), or Raphael in order to comprehend Stanley Tigerman's A House Done in the Intention of the Villa Madama (1980). The populist surface conceals a highly patrician substance.

At bottom, stylistic Post Modernism hinges on the belief that architecture is simply style, Post Modernism being the successor style of Modernism. A "classical language" of architecture, known and shared throughout the western world, provided the secure elements for architectural composition until the twentieth-century Modern Movement. From the preformulated elements of this language, architects since the Renaissance had been able to devise endless variations—but however they manipulated, distorted, or played with it, they never abandoned that classical language. Modern Movement architects responded to the issue of style with the argument that since the materials, fabrication techniques, and production conditions of building had been profoundly altered, the old styles were no longer relevant or valid. A modern architecture, they believed, must come to terms with the reality of the new conditions of production as well as those of changed social circumstances.[5] SPM ignores all of these concerns and retreats to the security of the pre-Modern, preformulated elements of the architectural language, taking a secure place as a consumer oriented enterprise in the cycle of consumption and production.

From this narrow conception of architecture as style emerges an architecture of picturesque effects aimed largely at a fashion conscious well-to-do audience. Clients from this class can afford the elaborate and expensive decorations devised by their architects to "personalize" their houses. By its very association with the world of fashion, this is an architecture of consumption; as a plaything of the cultural Cosa Nostra, it represents a comforting retreat to the fanciful but nonetheless stable cultural images of the past. One need hardly add that these images are unblushingly aristocratic: rarely does this architecture allude to the peasant or working-class past. Robert Stern argues for the recovery of the old because, as he recently remarked, he distrusts the revolutionary in both art and in politics.[6]

Apart from the attack on the aesthetics of the Modern Movement, stylistic Post Modernists also explicitly divorce themselves from the political, social, and utopian goals of the Modern Movement, such as the plans of Le Corbusier for the Radiant City or the Plan Voisin. Although such utopian visions have been largely discredited in the last half century (the suburbs of most major European cities are their worst progeny), the baby and the bathwater go down the drain together for Post Modernists. Architecture should have no political or social agenda, they argue; it is an art and a personal expression. Stylistic Post Modernists elect not to talk about ideas, or theories, but about aesthetic experiences and styles.[7]

Emblematic of this tendency is a recent symposium at the University of Texas at Austin.[8] The symposium aimed to explore the future of the natural and urban environment in America. Although such symposia are notoriously inconclusive, this one began promisingly enough with lawyer Henry Diamond raising the issue of land use legislation, Ian McHarg proposing environmental information laboratories to enable citizens to make informed decisions about issues which affect their communities, William K. Reilly exploring the tension between homogenization and the conservation of place in the shaping of American cities, and William Ruckleshaus urging a change from the ethos of produce and profit to one of preserve and protect. But when the architects came on the panel, the level of discussion sank to embarrassing lows: Robert Stern argued for cities more like Disneyland than Lubbock, Texas; Nathaniel Owings (whose firm Skidmore Owings and Merrill has largely been responsible for the glass-box skyscraperization of American cities) demanded height limitations on buildings which he characterized as nothing more than expressions of ego; and Denise Scott Brown, Charles Moore and Bernardo Fort-Brescia concluded the conference with squabbles about infringements on their aesthetic freedom enforced by local Design Review Boards. As in most of their in-house debates, the architects were able to divert attention from issues of substance to issues of surface. Questions about appropriate land use, the direction of urban change, and social priorities do not figure in the discourse of stylistic Post Modernists: only narrow aesthetic issues concern them. Even worse, quality of construction often plays second fiddle to questions of image, as in Graves's Portland Public Office Building and Charles Moore's Piazza d'Italia in New Orleans. The position adopted by Post Modernists is as thin as their architecture; only rarely does any of their work yield sufficient substance to generate serious discussion. I have elsewhere drawn a comparison with junk food—easily digestible, cheap, lots of fat and little nutritional value—which still seems an accurate characterization of stylistic Post Modernism.

In the end, this brand of Post Modernism offers nothing more than flashy new packaging for the same old Modernist box which these same architects vigorously opposed. Part of the packaging, it would appear, is that of the architects themselves. Tom Wolfe immortalized them in *From Bauhaus to Our House*, *Time* featured Philip Johnson on its cover, and both *Time* and *Newsweek* regularly devote space to the latest antics of contemporary architects.[9] Architectural fashion magazines have exploded throughout the country, from the in-house *Progressive Architecture* to *Architectural Digest*, followed by *Metropolitan Home*, *Houston Home and Garden*, *Texas Homes*, and many others. Each regularly turns the spotlight on leading local or national architects, but nowhere was this accomplished with the *chiaroscuro* of *Vanity Fair's* portrayal of four leading American architects as contemporary Howard Roarks for a remake of *The Fountainhead*.[10]

Although at first blush it seems as if architects have finally arrived, in fact the profession is in crisis, a crisis which stylistic Post Modernism only thinly masks. The hoopla surrounding stylistic Post Modernism is compensatory: the architect has become a media darling just as the profession's significance dwindles. For nearly every project, the architect in a sense arrives last on the scene. Contemporary practice shrinks the role of the architect from that of an active agent in the construction of the community and its structures to that of an exterior designer or an interiors specialist. Leasing agents, developers, commercial loan officers, planning and zoning commissions make the important decisions, leaving for the emarginated architect the trivial task of selecting finishes and glosses inside and out.[11] The utopian aspirations, social and political commitments, philosophical rigor, and lofty self-confidence of the Modern Movement recede even further into the distance. Stylistic Post Modernism's exclusive preoccupation with style can be seen as a pathetic acceptance of the trivialization of the profession.

Vague uneasiness and a sense of crisis in the profession becomes, for the theoretical Post Modernists, almost total despair. This second branch of Post Modernism is as diverse as stylistic Post Modernism is blandly homogenized, as rich with theory as the latter is bereft of it. One strand in TPM takes its cue from Italian architectural criticism and theory of the last twenty years, represented in this country primarily by Manfredo Tafuri, but which in Italy includes Massimo Cacciari, Francesco Dal Co, and others. Two major works by Tafuri have been translated into English: *Theories and History of Architecture* (1976, translated 1980), and *Architecture and Utopia* (1973, translated 1976), in addition to several articles which appeared in the now defunct journal *Oppositions*.[12] Following the strategy proposed by Roland Barthes, Tafuri's texts are assemblages of paragraphs loosely strung together which cannot be comprehended as a continuous, linear discourse. It is impossible to review here the complexities of his arguments or even to do justice to all of his ideas; but a few points are central for understanding his perception of architecture's place in contemporary society.

The opening words of *Architecture and Utopia* are as instructive as were those of an earlier discussion of utopia: Socrates opened *The Republic* with the words "I went down...", by which he signaled the duty of the philosopher to engage in the life of the polis. Tafuri begins with the words "Allontanare l'angoscia..." (To ward off anguish...), and far from engagement, Tafuri proposes detachment. Tafuri returns repeatedly to this anguish, an anguish which involves the intellectual's response to the confrontation with capitalist rationality, the motivation for bourgeois ideology, and indeed, despair at the loss of purpose for architecture. A tension exists between architecture's demand for order and the city's will to formlessness. Architecture is "a stable structure which gives form to permanent values and consolidates the urban morphology," but with the city fully open, Tafuri deems any attempt to seek equilibrium within it utopian.[13] In the wake of the Enlightenment, architecture renounced its symbolic role as well as its task of forming "objects"; it became instead the technique of organizing preformed materials, only one link among many in a chain of production in the city. Both utopia and architectural ideas were instrumentalized by "capitalist rationality" in its early stages of development; and architectural ideology, contaminated by capitalism, could no longer hold out any hope for design:

The entire cycle of modern architecture . . . came into being, developed, and entered into crisis as an enormous attempt—the last to be made by the great bourgeois artistic culture—to resolve, on the always more outdated level of ideology, the imbalances, contradictions, and retardations characteristic of the capitalist reorganization of the world market and productive development.[14]

Tafuri also recognizes the crisis of the profession which I outlined above, and he insists that it is pointless "to propose purely architectural alternatives" within the (capitalist) "structures that condition the very character of architectural design."[15] Since capitalist rationality has robbed architecture of its historical tasks, Tafuri concludes that all that remains for architecture is to return to "pure form, to forms without utopia; in the best cases, to sublime uselessness." The profession, in Tafuri's words, now "navigates in empty space."[16]

Although he later denied that he had thus declared architecture dead, his book was widely understood as such in Italy and America; if nothing else, he had certainly established the groundwork for such an interpretation. In a sense Tafuri has turned the tables: where Modernism vested too much power in the architect to alter and redeem society, Tafuri grants none at all. Whether one must accept his either/or characterization of architecture is yet another point: must it be utopia or silence, redemption or loss, emptiness or meaning, with no possible navigation in a quieter arena somewhere between the extremes?

A more coherent, readable, and carefully explored position is offered by Alberto Pérez-Gómez in *Architecture and the Crisis of Modern Science*.[17] He too discerns the death of architecture, but in very different terms. Tafuri identifies the origins of architecture's crisis in the corruption by capitalism since the Enlightenment, while Pérez-Gómez finds that the crisis took shape after the Galilean revolution, and especially after 1800, with the functionalization of architectural theory. Mathematical certainty became the goal in architecture as in other areas of human conduct. The dominant assumption over the last two centuries has been that meaning in architecture derived from "functionalism, formal games of combinations, the coherence or rationality of style understood as ornamental language, or the use of type as a generative structure."[18] Pérez-Gómez follows Husserl in detecting a split between two dimensions of meaning: the formal, or syntactic, and the transcendental, or semantic; it is the latter which architecture rejected. Scientific thought claimed the distinction of offering the only legitimate interpretation of reality, and when architecture accepted this primacy, it was "... deprived of a legitimate poetic content ... reduced to either a prosaic technological process or mere decoration."[19] But, observes Pérez-Gómez, the sciences fail to address the most important and real issues of human behavior, although modern humanity nonetheless operates under the "illusion of the infinite power of reason" and is therefore bereft of the "capacity for wonder."[20]

Pérez-Gómez, like Tafuri and even like stylistic Post Modernists, comments upon the sterile and dehumanizing character of the modern city and its vacuous architecture. But Pérez-Gómez also indicts the two major contemporary schools of thought for asserting the separation of structure and meaning. Capitalist formalism denies culturally based meanings and instead promotes architecture as elitist manipulation, while Marxism defines architecture as a craft resulting from typological analyses devoid of personal expression.

The one bright spot in the last 200 years has been theoretical projects, such as those of Piranesi, which gave expression to a highly personal vision but which also criticized the dominance of scientific thought and the loss of poetry. Indeed, for Pérez-Gómez, the way out is disarmingly simple: contemporary architecture must seek a "new metaphysical justification in the human world . . . the reconciliatory mission of the architect is poetic."[21] He concludes with the observation that while construction as a technological process is prosaic—deriving directly from a mathematical equation, a functional diagram, or a rule of formal combinations—architecture is poetic, necessarily an abstract order but in itself a metaphor emerging from a vision of the world and Being.[22]

Pérez-Gómez and Tafuri represent two of the most important and perceptive architectural theorists today, but they are hardly the first to detect this loss of meaning, or even to declare the death of architecture. In some respects their conclusions echo those of Victor Hugo when he argued that since the Renaissance, architecture had irredeemably yielded its communicative role to the written word.[23] Tafuri and Pérez-Gómez, then, articulate unspoken perceptions that have underlain architectural discourse for some time.

Despite obvious differences in their theories and their intellectual sources, their conclusions—that is, the consequences for the concerned practitioner—turn out to be parallel. Both confront the loss of meaning in architecture and marginalization of the profession, in a sense, by retreating from engagement. Thwarted by the modern conditions of production, architecture for Tafuri must return to pure formalism, uselessness, and succumb to its own emptiness. For the architect who does build, each structure can only be a blank gesture of despair, a monument to the "pastness" of architecture and to its futility in the modern world. For Pérez-Gómez, on the other hand, the architect can recover meaning only through a retreat into a private world of "personal expression and reference to the totality."[24] And indeed, he asserts that it is in "theoretical projects, rather than in building, that symbolic intentionality has been best embodied after the Industrial Revolution."[25] Although Pérez-Gómez carefully avoids advocating that the architect draw rather than build, the conclusion is almost inescapable, and Daniel Libeskind and his Cranbrook students indeed draw it.[26] The reification of abstract personal visions occurs not in structures but on paper and in books, which for them is the only possible architecture. It is as if, having lost the redemptive promise so integral to the utopian aspects of the Modern Movement, and having been cast adrift from secure cultural values in the post-Enlightenment world, architecture has lost everything. For the architect who wants to construct, the news is disquieting.

One cannot avoid detecting a certain nostalgia in the comments of both Tafuri and Pérez-Gómez, although it is a far more considered one than that which appears in SPM: a nostalgia for an earlier time when an architecture rich with meaning was intimately bound to cultural values and institutions. Both Tafuri and Pérez-Gómez correctly identify major changes in architectural practice since the Industrial Revolution, but I wonder whether the current crisis is itself as much one of perception as anything else. Distance obscures details, and so it is with history. So little of the constructions of the past millennia remain for us to examine that it is impossible to gain a sense of the building production of past ages, and what little does remain largely consists of the most symbol-laden public or private (often commemorative) structures. Although houses, barns, and chicken coops carried a symbolic charge in a world dominated by *mythos*, it hardly matched the weight of symbolism embodied in public or religious structures. Likewise a solitary Medieval or Renaissance house (even a palazzo for the wealthy) rarely expressed broad cultural and religious values with the same riches, complexity, and power as a cathedral or a town hall. The point is simply that perhaps Tafuri and Pérez-Gómez demand a symbolic weight of structures incapable of supporting it, and certainly not on a mass basis. At the same time, they refuse to accept what may be painful but true: the "banal box" skyscraper of a bank, an oil company, a communications company, or a multinational conglomerate may, for the future archeologist, express the values of our society quite well: production, profit, and waste.

Some of the most interesting architects—Aldo Rossi, Peter Eisenman—have found a way out of the dilemmas outlined by Tafuri and Pérez-Gómez without succumbing to formalism, refusal to build, or mindless games of style. Rossi has never lost the "sense of wonder" which Pérez-Gómez correctly identifies as crucial for an architect. Rossi's *Scientific Autobiography*, in fact, is a sustained account of his *meraviglia*, and his architecture apportions symbolic meaning where it belongs: more in the cemetery, the school, the monument, less in other constructions.[27] And the symbolism is rooted specifically in his awareness of his culture and his sense of wonder at the world. Rossi manages to accomplish this despite a full recognition of the current "crisis."[28] Other architects seem to pursue rather different but equally valid tectonic realizations of personal vision: Steven Holl, Mario Botta, the erstwhile partnership of Batey and Mack, Agrest and Gandelsonas, Stirling and Wilford.

Peter Eisenman, on the other hand, is consumed by an apocalyptic vision of the post-Holocaust, post-atomic bomb world. Intellectually indebted to Foucault, Derrida and post-structuralism, Eisenman argues that post-fifteenth-century architecture—including Modernism—operated under the influence of three fictions: representation (a billboard for a message), reason (a rational source for design), and history (a mirror for the

Zeitgeist). Ensnared in a wider crisis of value, architecture ended up bereft of legitimacy. So far, Eisenman concurs with Pérez-Gómez's assessment, but he cannot accept a refusal to build as an answer. A "not-classical" architecture, in Eisenman's view, attempts only "to be a representation of itself, of its own values and internal experience."[29] Elsewhere he describes this "negative of the classical" as the idea of decomposition, "which becomes in a particular building, such as Giuseppe Terragni's Giuliani Frigerio apartments, a series of fragments."[30] Eisenman successfully implemented his understanding of contemporary architecture in his design for the Visual Arts Center at the Ohio State University (1983). A series of fragments—traces of the past and current context—which hover between significance and arbitrariness renders a structure at once rooted in a specific sense of place, but also engaged with the "loss of center" which Eisenman so keenly perceives in the contemporary world.[31]

Beyond their specific contributions, Eisenman and Libeskind play important roles in contemporary architecture: both challenge accepted beliefs, provoke thought and discussion. Such theoreticians are crucial to the health of the profession precisely because of their provocative critiques. This does not mean that it is wise to gather schools and disciples around them; instead of posing challenging new questions, all too often disciples tend to repeat answers. One Libeskind disciple sniffs at those who want to discuss the future prospects for architecture: "There's no point in talking with you until you've read Heidegger." There is a danger that TPM disciples—who typically lack the broad vision of their mentors—will attempt to tyrannize with their theories in a manner parallel to that exercised by the disciples of scientific rigor and rationality in the eighteenth and nineteenth centuries. Frank Lloyd Wright long ago observed that disciples tended to bastardize their master's work, an observation which still holds.[32]

Despite vast qualitative differences, in some respects SPM and TPM are quite similar. They share a nostalgia for architecture's ability to represent, to have meaning. Stylistic Post Modernists paper over the loss with representational kitsch derived from earlier times; theoretical Post Modernists either reject building in favor of drawing, attempt to embody the loss of meaning in construction, or retreat to a formalist architecture of "uselessness." It is as if, having ushered representation out, theoretical Post Modernists sneak it in again through the back door: the absence of external validation becomes the source of new representation, whether in drawings or buildings. In each case, representation remains the key element.

Both SPM and TPM likewise selectively misread history. Except for Tafuri, they reduce Modern Movement architecture to style, functionalism, the machine aesthetic, and so forth. To read their analyses, one would never know that for many European Modernists, architectural style was the handmaiden of political and social programs. Indeed, notably absent from both SPM and TPM (as well as the work of the architects mentioned above) is any sense of political, ecological, or social responsibility, let alone utopian hopes. Both also tend to dismiss the efforts of architects who attempt to address these more pragmatic concerns.

A related problem concerns the recent trend in architectural theory to raid contemporary philosophical and literary theories: during the 1970s linguistics and semiotics were in vogue, today post-structuralism dominates. The impetus toward scientific rigor which Pérez-Gómez identified has been supplanted by an attempt to endow architecture with an intellectually rigorous metaphysical content parallel to that found in philosophical and literary criticism. It is difficult to explain why this happens, but architects and critics who perceive themselves as members of an intellectual community seem to find architecture validated only by reference to theories current in other disciplines. But the influence seems not to run the other way: literary critics and philosophers do not avail themselves of constructs derived from architectural theory. Architectural texts fashioned in this manner are often tortured or incomprehensible, partly because the authors sometimes fail to understand the models, but also because the distinctive subject matter of architecture does not lend itself to such Procrustean beds. The less comfortable the fit between architecture and the borrowed finery of another discipline, the more unreadable and obscure the relevant texts: but instead of dooming them to failure, incomprehensibility seems to guarantee their success until a new fad emerges, usually to be picked up with a lag-time of five to ten years after its original appearance. Insights derived from other disciplines may usefully serve as springboards for creative activity or for theoretical analysis, to be sure, or they might serve as private intellectual exercises. But the more or less rigorous imposition of rigid systems from literary theory means that often the most important issues are not even addressed, that architecture's unique character remains unexamined.

Those who engage in such enterprises seem to ignore that architecture's impact upon our daily lives, even upon our intellect, differs quite substantially from the impact of literature, for example—and we are unlikely to learn much about the nature of that impact by forcing the models of literary theory and criticism upon architecture. Even the poetic content of the greatest architecture resists explanation or codification by reference to these theories, and the designs of someone like John Hejduk, for example, are hardly enhanced, let alone explained, by the mystification which seems endemic to the current fads in architectural theory. Such enterprises, though perhaps more erudite than those of stylistic Post Modernism, seem equally compensatory and evasive.

My purpose is not to advocate a particular style or approach, but rather to examine contemporary trends and identify weaknesses and omissions. Of all the possible approaches today, the least rewarded are serious attempts to improve the quality of life in cities and towns. While the arrogance of early Modernists about the prospect of fabricating a brave new world through architecture exploded with World War II, for many architects this signals neither a refusal to build nor total capitulation to the cycle of production and consumption. For them, architecture may involve representation, but it also has many other aspects. Architecture, building, construction: they shape our environment and embody our relationship with the world. Some architects are more concerned about the way this occurs. Like Tafuri and Rossi, Jaquelin Robertson identifies the city as the locus of investigation, and like Socrates he advocates engagement.[33] If America does not alter its processes of city building, he argues, we will be condemned to a world of Mexico Cities. Propelled by greed and laziness, building campaigns since 1945 have violated ecological laws that hold our fragile system together. Architects cannot single-handedly save the world, but as Robertson argues, they can operate in their arena of competence with a sensitive awareness of larger concerns; they can help build more healthful cities.

Time and human efforts quelled the ecstatic utopian aspirations of early Modernists: perhaps the limited, sober position articulated by Robertson constitutes another, more modest Post Modernism. It argues for architects to take seriously the well-being of the cities. Nothing could be further removed from stylistic Post Modernism, nothing could be less glamorous, less fashionable. As Victor Hugo observed, however, "Fashion has committed more crimes than revolution."[34]

Notes

1. Alfred Barr, Henry-Russell Hitchcock, Jr., Philip Johnson, and Lewis Mumford, *Modern Architecture: International Exhibition* (New York: Museum of Modern Art, 1932).
2. Robert Venturi, *Complexity and Contradiction in Architecture* (New York: Museum of Modern Art, 1966).
3. Charles Jencks, ed,. *Free Style Classicism: The Wider Tradition*, AD Profiles 39 (London: Architectural Design, 1982); Charles Jencks, *The Language of Post Modern Architecture*, 2nd edition (New York: Rizzoli, 1977). See also my review essay, Diane Ghirardo, "Imitation as the Sincerest Form," *Design Book Review* 2 (Summer 1983): 34–39.
4. Jencks, *Free Style Classicism*, 5, 14.
5. For a sound discussion of the Modern Movement see Kenneth Frampton, *Modern Architecture: A Critical History* (New York: Thames & Hudson, 1980), 123–191, 210 223.
6. "The Land, The City, and the Human Spirit," a symposium at the LBJ Library, Austin, Texas, April 12–13, 1984.
7. See Robert A. M. Stern, "Review of *Modern Architecture: A Critical History* by Kenneth Frampton," *Skyline* (October 1981): 22–25.
8. "The Land, the City, and the Human Spirit."
9. Tom Wolfe, *From Bauhaus to Our House* (New York: Farrar Strauss Giroux, 1981). See my review, Diane Ghirardo, "Review of *From Bauhaus to Our House*," *Archetype* 11, no. 4 (Fall 1982): 30–31.
10. Suzanne Stephens, "The Fountainhead Syndrome," *Vanity Fair* (March 1984): 40–45. The four architects celebrated in macabre black and white photographs were Peter Eisenman, Michael Graves, Richard Meier, and Robert A. M. Stern.
11. See Diane Ghirardo, "Architecture of Deceit," *Perspecta* 21 (1984): 110–115.
12. Manfredo Tafuri, *Architecture and Utopia: Design and Capitalist Development* (Cambridge, MA: MIT Press, 1976); and Manfredo Tafuri, *Theories and History of Architecture* (New York: Harper & Row, 1980).
13. Tafuri, *Architecture and Utopia*, 42.
14. Tafuri, *Architecture and Utopia*, 178. Another problem in reading Tafuri is his unsystematic terminology. "Capitalist rationality" and "architectural ideology" are particularly difficult to pin down to a precise meaning in his text.
15. Tafuri, *Architecture and Utopia*, 181.
16. Tafuri, *Architecture and Utopia*, ix–x.
17. Alberto Pérez-Gómez, *Architecture and the Crisis of Modern Science* (Cambridge, MA: MIT Press, 1983).
18. Pérez-Gómez, 4.
19. Pérez-Gómez, 11.
20. Pérez-Gómez, 6.
21. Pérez-Gómez, 325.
22. Pérez-Gómez, 326.
23. Victor Hugo, *Notre Dame de Paris,* trans. Jessie Haynes (New York: Heritage Press, 1955).
24. Pérez-Gómez, 325.
25. Pérez-Gómez, 324.
26. Daniel Libeskind, *Between Zero and Infinity* (New York: Rizzoli, 1981); and Daniel Libeskind, *Chamber Works: Architectural Meditations on Themes from Heraclitus* (London: Architectural Association, 1983).
27. Aldo Rossi, *A Scientific Autobiography,* trans. Lawrence Venuti (Cambridge, MA: MIT Press, 1982).
28. Aldo Rossi, "Semplicemente un percorso" in Daniel Libeskind, *Chamber Works.*
29. Peter Eisenman, "A Non-classical Architecture: The End of the Beginning, The End of the End," *Perspecta* 21 (1984): 154–73.
30. Peter Eisenman, Peter "The Futility of Objects: Decomposition and the Processes of Difference," *Harvard Architecture Review* 3 (1984) 65–81.
31. Kurt Forster, "Traces and Treason of a Tradition" in *A Center for the Visual Arts: The Ohio State University Competition* (New York: Rizzoli, 1984).
32. Frank Lloyd Wright, *Genius and Mobocracy* (New York: Duell, Sloan and Pearce, 1949).
33. Jaquelin T. Robertson, "In Search of an American Urban Order, Part I: The Nagasaki Syndrome," *Modulus: The University of Virginia Architecture Review* 16 (1984), 2–15; Aldo Rossi, *The Architecture of the City*, trans. Diane Ghirardo and Joan Ockman (Cambridge, MA: MIT Press, 1981). Of course, Robertson is neither the first nor the only one to argue such a position. Among those who have argued along similar lines are Lewis Mumford in many books, Jane Jacobs in *The Death and Life of Great American Cities* (New York: Random House, 1961) and Peter Blake in *Form Follows Fiasco: Why Modern Architecture Hasn't Worked* (Boston, MA, and Toronto, ON: Little, Brown, & Co., 1977).
34. Hugo, 68.

Hold It (Meditations Upon a Gorgonzola Cheese)

Jennifer Bloomer
Georgia Institute of Technology

Architecture has always been about holding things. Even before it was sheltering, it was holding: recall two of the constructions of the mythical first architect—the labyrinth and the *daidalon*, holding respectively the monster bullman and his progenetrix, who was for a while architecture herself, containing. Architecture: holding secrets, the spirits of the dead, the bodies of the living, but also holding down. Holding down the transient in the knowledge that it cannot be made permanent. Holding the culture, containing it, keeping, preserving it. Architecture has performed the same function as the Pythagoreans, the mystic priests, medieval monks, books. It is the writing of culture.

It is the making of a distinction between nature and culture which has gotten us into trouble. We split off parts—the machine becomes an entity which does things (draws drawings, for instance). And, although we are vaguely aware that it is we who made the machine, we tend to view it as Other, not really of us, not "natural." As Frederick Turner has so poignantly observed, the manufacture of nuclear weapons and the activity of strip mining are as "natural" as the making of honey by bees or the indifferent bubbling of anaerobic bacteria lying about in murky places, waiting to reclaim this place.[1] Of course, what it comes down to is that same old twentieth-century bugaboo: language. We, the natural language makers, define—make the end, the edge, the boundary (the place of being bound)—that which is nature and that which is culture. So here we are, bags of protoplasm (what really defines the boundary between the world and me, the surface of my skin and the air, my protoplasm and your protoplasm?), making distinctions between somethings we have decided to call nature and somethings we have called culture, both inventions borne out of the nature of our uniquely endowed (or so we say) protoplasm—soup of carbon, hydrogen, oxygen, and some other stuff—our Mobile Homes. And now every one of us, every bit of us, seems to be about little tiny strings hiding away in dimensions we will never measure—strings, but no lines.

The line which some of us struggle to draw between theory and practice is as indefinite, as troublesome, and as unnecessary as the nature/culture distinction. We must stop drawing lines and start saving string. Theory—or practice—is saving string, "piling up fragments ceaselessly," as the blind Irishman did, making a dumping ground.[2] Allegory. We must pile up—make our soup—with passion. That which we make, whether it is theory or observation or speculative office buildings, must hold the object(s) of our passion—which is "always already" culture. Or is it nature?

Historically, theory in architecture has been assembled from parts of bodies of theory in other disciplines, notably philosophy and science. The focus of twentieth century theorizing across many "disciplines" has been language, the grand universal, the mother of reflexivity. With this has come the disappearance of distinct boundary lines among disciplines traditionally deemed distinct.

American architectural production of the past twenty years has been informed predominantly by linguistic and literary theory. The work ranges from Robert Venturi's production of architectural theory out of William Empson's *Seven Types of Ambiguity* to Peter Eisenman's exercises upon Chomskian linguistic theory, from Jencks and Baird to Agrest and Gandelsonas, from the fascination of Michael Graves *et al.* with "figurative" architecture to Eisenman's more recent flirtations with Derridean thought, from the mainstream preoccupation with "narrative" architecture to Robert Segrest's theory of the carnivalesque as presented in the Perimeter Projects, with its multiple, partial connections to the grand complex of contemporary French post-structuralism.[3]

There are two broad fields in which we can locate (however uncomfortably and tentatively) most of these ideas about architecture. On the one hand, we can make a field constelled by the terms, "symbol," "form-oriented," "*architecture parlante*"; on the other, a field of "sign," "process-oriented," "*architecture de l'écriture*." We might also underlay each with an appropriate figure of speech: metaphor for the former, metonymy for the latter.

The field designated *architecture de l'écriture* challenges the often simplistic relationships (both literary and architectural) of the architectural activity of the other category. It unfolds the potential for an architecture which is etymologically "true," an architecture more concerned with materials (whether physical or intellectual), connections, and patterns of possibilities than with image, expression, and representation. However, it is difficult to deny that there is something compelling about the work in the other category, despite its shaky or murky intellectual bases. One involves an intelligence, the other an understanding based in a leap of faith; one is about inquiry and exploration, the other about mumbo-jumbo. Both involve wonder.

What are the possibilities in the space of opposition? I am interested in the possibilities of textual architecture resulting from the projection of one field upon the other, the metaphorical upon the metonymical. We are talking allegory here: constructions which are fragmented, hieroglyphic, palimpsestic, incomplete; the piling up of fragments, a "dumping ground," dissemination upon a fuzzy plot.[4] Soane and Borromini did it; and Tschumi and, lately, Eisenman, operate to a certain extent in this space. But Joyce was the master. *Finnegans Wake* is the model. (If the book could cause the demise of the building, might it not also resurrect it?)

The book is a construction of innumerable fragments of culture spattered, disseminated, upon a fuzzy symbolic armature, an armature of overlappings, tears and holes, strange loops. "How To Build" instructions are embedded in the walls of this museum, this river building: THE SECTION IS THE GENERATOR. BOG IS IN THE DETAILS.

[Consider a section through the human heart: four collapsing and expanding rooms, valves flep!ping [sic] crazily like some silly cartoon's rubber swinging doors, aorta winking away. Bits and pieces of us flowing through. (Hold me in your heart, in your mobile home.)]

The section is a text which can drive an allegorical process. It works like the linguistic device of Raymond Roussel. The section is the machine element of allegory, setting the allegorical process (theory) in motion, generating the allegorical form (theory again). It is static in structure, dynamic in operation. Compare it to Kafka's writing machine. Think biology.

Is it in the premise that architecture is a solid?

In my city, the sky is spotted with construction too-fast becoming buildings. Although they are all destined to be smooth-skinned phalluses enrobed in colored glass and slices of stone (with the exception of Mr. Johnson's, which will come with buttresses flying) with various types of tops, at the moment each is an intricate assemblage of steel, concrete, plastic, and plywood, with cranes saluting and pieces of buildings going up and down. They are bony, brittle things which call to mind the prehistoric house recently unearthed in Siberia: walls of woven bones and roof of arcing tusks. You can see the architecture wherever it is. At Christmas time, the cranes had gaily lighted trees on their tips, hundreds of feet above the ground. (Léger may have known, but so do construction workers . . .)

Let us attend the stringy plot of Deleuze and Guattari: Toward a Minor Architecture. We must construct like dogs digging holes, rats digging burrows, like Calvino making his imploding holey home. Dig in.

"Since the language is arid, make it vibrate with a new intensity. Oppose a purely intensive usage to all symbolic or even significant or simply signifying usages. Arrive at a perfect and unformed expression, a materially intense expression."[5]

Make an architecture of assemblage, minor constructions within the major language.

The architecture of the mainstream holds the culture of late capitalism, but tentatively, distractedly, like the good night embrace of people on a blind date, or of those married too long. An unsatisfactory *status quo*. But things are not so bad. We can grab it, clutch it, hold on to it, hold it. Hold it. Think what Joyce would have done with a *Sweet's Catalogue*, the *National Building Code*, and *Architectural Graphic Standards*, and the most mundane (in every sense of the word) survey of architectural history. Not to mention the whole business of representation. He certainly would have left the cranes on.

Notes

1. Frederick Turner, "Cultivating the American Garden: Toward a Secular View of Nature," *Harper's* 272, no. 1623 (August 1985): 45–52.
2. The construct of allegory used here is taken from Walter Benjamin, "Allegory and Trauerspiel," in *The Origin of German Tragic Drama*, trans. John Osborne (London: New Left Books, 1977), 178.
3. See *Assemblage* 1 (October 1986).
4. Craig Owens, "The Allegorical Impulse: Toward a Theory of Postmodernism," *October* 12 (Spring 1980): 67–86; and Craig Owens, "The Allegorical Impulse: Toward a Theory of Postmodernism, Part 2" *October* 13 (Summer 1980): 58–80.
5. Gilles Deleuze and Felix Guattari, *Kafka: Toward a Minor Literature*, trans. Dana Polan (Minneapolis, MN: University of Minnesota Press, 1986), 19.

(W)rapped Space: The Architecture of Hip Hop

Craig L. Wilkins
University of Minnesota

My research work is broadly framed around the confluence of contemporary and historical-spatial-theoretical understandings, architecture, the progressive self-defining energy of African-American culture, and the historical legacy of urban spaces in current society. A preeminent principle of this confluence focuses on questions of identity. "(W)rapped Space: The Architecture of Hip Hop" theorizes the development of an African-American spatial paradigm that at once recalls, creates, and deploys a new space of diasporian origin that is predicated on a response to spaces that represent an erasure of identity and, concomitantly, the presence of repressive power.

> A revolution that does not produce a new space has not realized its full potential.
>
> —Henri Lefebvre[1]

I read somewhere that writing about music is like dancing about architecture. In this composition, I will illustrate the truth of those words—although I trust, not in the way the author intended—as I identify and analyze the space produced by the hip hop revolution. I plan to argue that hip hop produces a (w)rapped space that is, one, a phenomenon of sonic organization and use, created in and by a distinct social context, two, dependent on experience and memory, and linked to time in the form of the past, present, and future, three, defined and communicated by people through *patterns of use in the built environment*.

I will also address a specific spatial understanding of hip hop culture as it reverberates from rap music into the built environment, identifying four primary spatial principles evident in the physical manifestations of hip hop architecture—palimpsestic, anthropomorphic, performative, and adaptive—that are generated in response to spaces that represent the power of oppression. This hip hop spatial paradigm at once recalls, creates, and deploys new spaces that speak to the Africentric Diasporian project of identity embedded in rap music.

Ready for a little sumpin' sumpin' special? I'm 'bout to break you off some. (Meaning: give you something to consider.)

Social Formations of Sound

Music both creates and is created by a distinct social context essential to the development of identity and subjectivity. This reciprocal relationship anchors my view of sonic foundations of hip hop that is reinforced by several theoretical claims below and forms the basis of the music/space relationship.

Some Writings about Music...

Simon Frith and Angela McRobbie in their essay "Rock and Sexuality" position rock and pop music as the place where "boys and girls learn their repertoire of public sexual behavior."[2] By drawing on theories that posit sexual subjectivity as a primary element of defining an individual's or a group's identity, and by focusing on music's capacity to construct male and female identities among teenagers through socially sanctioned public sexual expression, they reject the notion of rock music liberating a long-repressed sexuality and instead posit that "the most important ideological work done by rock is the construction of sexuality."[3] They further argue that this construction is controlled by the "'gatekeepers' of the industry, who determine how people listen to [music]."[4] This suggests that those who control the choices and forms of music that become available to listeners have an over-determined influence on the construction of sexuality and identity of those listeners.

George Lipsitz, in his book *Time Passages*, directly links the (sexual) identity produced by music to the notion of time by applying the concept of dialogical criticism developed by literary critic Mikhail Bakhtin. That concept is defined here as a dialogue with history—critically dependent upon memory—and with the study of music.[5] It is his position that: "one reason for popular music's powerful affect is its ability to conflate music and lived experience, to make both the past and present zones of choice serve distinct social and political interests."[6]

In his analysis, Lipsitz posits that the socially defined public arena—that place where the everyday interactions of society takes place—"is the matrix of production and reception of popular music" and memory is central to the construction of that public arena.[7] In his analysis, Lipsitz argues that not only is memory necessary for the construction of music, it is also central to the construction of social context and thus necessary for the construction of identity.

Finally, in the essay, "The Sound of Music in the Era of its Electronic Reproducibility," John Mowitt takes Lipsitz's position a step further and argues that current technology has separated the production and reception of music, and it has "privileged the moment of reception in cultural experience," further illustrating the social context of music's construction and its influence on subjectivity and identity.[8] Key to this argument is Mowitt's assertion that subjectivity is heavily influenced by the fact that experience "takes place within a cultural context organized by institutions and practices," which in this case are the institution and practices of the music studio. He argues that the experience of hearing—and its concomitant effects on memory—is less influenced by initial production than by technical reproduction done in the studio and this phenomenon positions memory as both "fundamental to music and profoundly social."[9] Mowitt posits that a primary, if not the primary, reason for music's social importance is precisely this organization of sound (noise) around socially sanctioned public structures of listening that define normal, or "proper" ways of making sense of what you hear; it is a "standard of normalcy" that helps to define a social order, or to use a better word, community. "All music, any organization of sounds, is then a tool for the creation or consolidation of a community, of a totality."[10] What is critical to understand from Mowitt's argument is the idea that music can create and be created by a community.

To summarize, my project focuses on these central themes: a., that music creates, and is created by, a distinct social context through experience (interaction with others) and memory (of that interaction and past interactions), and also, b., that musical experience and memory play an important role in constructing specific identities and, with that, communities. Sound in space creates identity. These sonically constructed communities are linked to time through an interactive, reciprocal conversation with history that shapes the socially defined public arena in which music is produced, reproduced, and received. Music, then, becomes integral to a way of life. We live in sound-defined spaces. Albert Murray says as much when, writing on the painting influences of Romare Bearden, he states: "and not only was impeccable musical taste an absolute requirement for growing up hip, urbane, or streetwise, but so was the ability to stylize your actions—indeed, your whole being—in terms of the most sophisticated extensions and refinements of jazz music and dance."[11]

Understanding sound in this fashion is useful in positing the notion of music as an element of individual and collective identity that is:

1. a phenomenon of sonic organization and use created in a distinct social context,
2. dependent on experience and memory, linked to the time—past, present, and future, and
3. defined and communicated by people through patterns of use.

Below, we will see similar themes emerge as foundational elements of not only a notion of music, but also for a particular notion of space.

Social Formations of Space

Henri Lefebvre in his book *The Production of Space* posits that space is a social product. He argues against the dominant Western notion of space as posited by Enlightenment figures such as John Locke—that space is pre-existing—and instead proposes that "spaces are produced."[12] For Lefebvre, space is experienced, or more accurately, "lived" by bodies—or people—in motion that constantly intersect, interact, produce, and reproduce, a phenomenon that he refers to as "social space." Social space, as defined by Lefebvre, is both "*work* [the interaction] and *product* [what is created by the interaction]," and can be understood as the social activities that occur in a particular time and place that constitute—and are *specific* to—the establishment of a distinct social context.[13] These social activities—referred to by Lefebvre as the group's *spatial practices*—facilitate the production and reproduction of both the place of, and the characteristics of, the spatial relationships of any particularly defined group of people.

Lefebvre's space is reciprocal; it at once recognizes, shapes, and affirms the identity and subjectivity of the people who shape, produce, and reproduce it. According to Lefebvre, because social space is dependent upon people for its (re)production and people are (with apologies to Ralph Ellison's *Invisible Man*) ever-present in the socially defined public arena, he concludes that "no space disappears in the course of growth and development: *the worldwide does not abolish the local.*"[14] For Lefebvre, there exists at any given moment, a multiplicity of distinctive social contexts, all of which produce spaces which, as opposed to Foucault's heterotopias, "interpenetrate one another and/or superimpose themselves upon one another."[15]

Furthering this spatial theory, Michel de Certeau, in his book *The Practice of Everyday Life*, theorizes the communication and navigation of these multiple, simultaneously socially constructed spaces and demonstrates how Lefebvre's social space becomes legible. De Certeau sees the movement through space as a way of communication with others, consisting of both experience and memory. He posits that movement through space and the memory of experience (movement through the world) constructs a language we use to spatially communicate. He calls this language of movements, "pedestrian speech acts," that, in fact, "secretly structure the determining conditions of social life" by implying interaction between a speaker and observer that communicates meaning.[16] Within a framework of communication that is reciprocally transformed and transforms the elements of language (musical, verbal, and pedestrian) are words consistently chosen, appropriated, adapted, and employed by people to communicate meaning that is unique to that particular group, space, and time.[17] In other words, sometimes "bad" is bad, sometimes "bad" is good. De Certeau describes what this analysis means to the understanding of space: "Thus space is composed of intersections of mobile elements. It is in a sense actuated by the ensemble of movements deployed within it. Space occurs as the effect produced by the operations that orient it, situate it, temporalize it, and make it function. . . . In short, *space is a practiced place*. Thus the street geometrically defined by urban planning is *transformed into a space* by walkers."[18]

In sum, what is vital to understand from Lefebvre's spatial theory is the notion that bodies (people) interacting produce space. This interaction is specific to a time, place, and social formation, but is also historical—it has a memory, a past. Space—like music—cannot be static; it is dynamic, adapted by its user for the communication of specific meanings as illustrated by de Certeau's "pedestrian speech acts." For Lefebvre and de Certeau, the formation of space is dependent on the interaction, the understanding of the interaction in a dialogically critical (reciprocal) way, and the memory of interaction (experience) communicated through the language of the pedestrian speech act. At its very essence, space, for them, is a "performed communication." Lefebvre, de Certeau and others have allowed me to posit the notion of space as reciprocal and as:

1. a phenomenon of spatial organization and use, realized in a distinct social context (people interacting),
2. dependent on experience and memory, linked to time—past, present, and future, and
3. defined and communicated by people through patterns of use.

Bet! (Meaning: definitely a sure thing.) *Check that!* (Meaning: read again.) This hypothesis is almost identical to the previously outlined notion of music and, as such, uncovers a heretofore hidden opportunity for further critical spatial inquiry. If space is derived from experience and memory, whose communication is performed, and music is derived from experience and memory, whose form of communication is performance, then might we not look at sound and space as a similar occurrence, constitutive of each other? If so, then space might be defined more specifically as a:

1. socially constructed phenomenon of sonic organization and use,
2. dependent on experience and memory, linked to time—past, present, and future, and
3. defined and communicated by people through their patterns of use.

Rap Formations of Space

More Writings about Music…
So, peep that. (Meaning: look closer / listen harder.) Sound-mediated or performed space becomes the key to understanding hip hop's cultural creation—rap music—as the principal foundational element of Hip Hop Architecture.[19] *How, you say? Bust it!* (Meaning to follow.)

Space is
1. socially constructed phenomenon of sonic organization and use . . .

"Rap music is a technological form that relies on the reformation of the recorded sound in conjunction with rhymed lyrics to create its distinctive sound."[20] Rap music is unquestionably a music born of technology and is, as Mowitt has concluded previously, socially constructed. The core of rap music lies in the ability of the musical production (DJ, producer, engineer) to manipulate particular sounds, breaks, ruptures in continuity and flow—recalling their existence by their absence—and in the ability to mix several disparate sources of sonic pleasure into the listening experience. With the use of what is termed "sampling"—the digitally enhanced process of transferring a sound, or series of sounds (the sample), from one source to another source—"rap technicians employ digital technology as instruments, revising black musical styles and priorities through the manipulation of technology."[21] The primacy of studio/tech production has been key to the development of the rap genre and the epitome of a musical phenomenon created in a distinct social context—the studio.[22]

Space is
1. dependent on experience and memory, linked to time—past, present, and future . . .

"Music is nothing but organized noise. You can take anything—street sounds, us talking, whatever you want—and make it music by organizing it."[23] As Mowitt has previously touched upon, music's social importance is precisely this organization of noise around socially defined structures of listening. It is our shared understanding of the "correct" way to listen that is embedded in our memory and creates community. What becomes important to discern is: "Which community is forming in the musical technologies of the collective memory, and what is its relation to those technologies that facilitate the exact reproduction of the musician's actions for listeners?"[24]

Black music in general, but rap music's historical connection with the collective memory of the African diasporic community in particular, is complex and varied, and the hierarchy of its components is not at all universally agreed upon.[25] What is generally acknowledged as important, essential, and historical about Black music are: a. its nature (rhythm, repetition, layering, flow, rupture), which recalls the link to its African origin; b. its orality (toast, call and response, storytelling griot), which descends from specific African, Caribbean, and American influences; and c. its content (oppression, segregation, self-determination, self-naming), which is constituted in part by the postmodern condition of fragmentation and the project of reclaiming the Black *subject* from the "*Negro*" *object*.[26] These elements help to link the African diaspora over distance and time to a collective memory that is Africentric in origin and nature, but is—and this is key—specific to its current locale and defines a particular type of spatial practice, a principal tenet of Lefebvre's social space.

Space is
1. defined and communicated by people through their patterns of use . . .

The identity created by sound is best illustrated and understood by studying the use/influence of music on the lifestyles of the diaspora. As alluded to earlier in this essay by Albert Murray's discussion of Romare Bearden, Black music is really an integral part of the way Blacks live and communicate.[27] At its most basic level, music is for the diaspora an unconscious way of being that informs both the physical and mental response to its call and is acted out in all variety of ways, subtle and not. At its most heightened, it is a recognition and celebration of an Africentric life force. But at all levels, it is important, even essential, to the *performance of life*—Gilroy's "enhanced mode of communication"—for diasporic members.[28] This performance of life manifests itself in a variety of ways in the diaspora, but all are inexorably linked by the project of reclaiming the Black subject from the "Negro" object.

Rap music is clearly a tool to use in the process of redefining self. Whereas Dick Hebdige's analysis of punk culture and music revealed as a central theme punk's desire for an escape from the principle of identity, in hip hop culture and music, identity is paramount. Primary to rap music's significance is that it produces, as Rose phrases it, a style that nobody can deal with, one that is "bigga and deffa."[29] With and within the music, producers express their individual and collective identity—the "who" we are—and, in a confluence of structuralist and Africentric discourses, the music calls upon the listener to express their identity—Are you "who" too? Thus an Africentric spatial practice, and a corresponding community, is at once recalled, produced, and enhanced in the music of the hip hop culture.

Rap Formation of Hip Hop Architecture

Some Dancing about Architecture . . .
So, *G* (meaning: partner in common or specific project), what does all this have to do with space, or for that matter, architecture? This next section will specifically address a spatial understanding of hip hop culture that employs this confluence of space and music as a paradigm that recalls, creates, and deploys new spaces that speak to the Africentric diasporian project of identity in the built environment. Hip hop architecture creates spaces that are constructed by the intersections of mobile elements—people (bodies)—but often includes objects of material culture (debris, monster speakers, cars) as well. Hip hop space is made readable by the ensemble and interaction of people and elements engaged in the performance of everyday life. These particular performances are a function of diasporian spatial practices that have survived the Middle Passage and are specifically recalled and enhanced by the music of rap.[30] It is the recognition of, and participation in, specific "pedestrian speech acts" or "performances of communication" that makes the space function and communicate. As such, hip hop architecture is a stage for Africentric identity emergence. The space of hip hop invites us to ask whether it is logical to expect a culture that has been placed on the margin of society's concerns to employ the same language (pedestrian speech patterns or performances) used by those responsible for such marginalization, thereby reinforcing the very practice that is repressing them? Is it logical to expect the response of this community to spaces that represent the power of their oppression to be the same as of those who developed such spaces? The answer that the paradigm of hip hop space provides to these two critical questions, so central to the validity of the discipline and profession of architecture, is a resounding, emphatic, and unequivocal *no*.

Physical Manifestations of Hip Hop Space

More Dancing about Architecture . . .
Below I will outline four primary principles necessary for the physical manifestations of hip hop space. I am certainly not the first to recognize the power for spatial change that rap music provides. Houston Baker, Jr., states:

> It would be salutary...if the 'grim neighborhoods' of public housing were to reap the benefits of the type of hearing provided by the Central Park moment....We might also find in our new public concern both exacting and effective ways to channel the transnational capital of everyday rap into a spirited refiguration of African-American urban territories.[31]

I posit that strategies can be adapted from this transnational capital and manifested in built form. The accompanying images are part of a 1994 proposal to develop a Hip Hop Park on the near south side of Chicago. The site is a debris-laden vacant lot in the midst of one-to-three-story warehouses. The most prominent features of the actual site are the two partial facades that remain from the former building—a faux classical coliseum. The project demonstrates the application the following primary principles of (W)rapped space found below.

Hip Hop Architecture: Palimpsestic. "The power and promise of rap music rests in the bosom of urban America. . . . Years of degradation, welfare handouts, institutional racism, and discrimination have created a community where little hope, low self-esteem, and frequent failure translates into drugs, teen pregnancy, and gang violence."[32]

The architecture of hip hop is linked to the urban context in which it was born. This is where the call and response for the physical manifestation of this space is strongest. Part of the social context of the inner city—

Figure 1. Typical condition at site and various other sites in urban areas.

particularly in predominantly poorer African-American communities—is one of disarray and decay. Everyday, intentionally unclaimed, naturally deconstructivist structures are allowed to fall away piece by piece in unattended lots that are typically appropriated by the local residents as places for sundry and nefarious activities. These are the available—and appropriate—sites for the construction of hip hop spaces. The charge here is to remake and reclaim the Black subject from the "Negro" object, and this calls for a remaking of these places, the erasure of the dominant "proper," and the repositioning of these urban spaces as empowering.

Thus, the first, and most basic principle of the physical manifestations of hip hop architecture is that it be *palimpsestic* in nature and intent. It is an erasure of both dominant spatial understandings of "proper" and its hegemonic physical manifestations, while simultaneously—in the same location—the construction of a hip hop spatial consciousness and its physical manifestations. Essential to this consciousness is the recognition that hip hop space flows, ruptures, and intersects with bodies. In hegemonic spatial structures, these things are viewed as discontinuations, accidents that were not planned (both in the architectural and the organizational sense). This spatial perspective is antithetical to the spatial organization inherent in hip hop. As a space formed by sound, such "accidents" are designed and ex-

pected, and they are considered not only as continuous, but as invitations to perform.

Hip hop architecture is palimpsestic in the fact that it is engaged in reclaiming the subject from the object. Consistent with the foundations of hip hop's flow, layering, and rupture, the palimpsestic nature of hip hop architecture reorganizes and rewrites the "visible boundaries [of architecture], such as walls or enclosures in general, [that] give rise for their part to an appearance of separation between spaces where in fact what exists is an ambiguous continuity" *in the same location* of the dominant culture's hegemonic definition of "proper" spatial use.[33] This reorganization's primary objective is to recapture the Black subject from the "Negro" object and affirm the body's identity in spaces that have historically done just the opposite.

Palimpsestic Application. A specific application of the palimpsestic principle in the Hip Hop Park project is evidenced by the appropriation of space by the local youth as a place of recreation, due to the lack of available open space in their community in the manner of de Certeau. This park would authorize a place for the typical outdoor performances that occur regularly in this community, provide staging space for hip hop dancing, present wall space for graffiti artwork (tagging), and provide portable vendor booths along a "street and corner" within the park to serve as a hip hop community flea market. Providing for the specific spatial practices of this community assists in erasing the notion of this space as a place of vandalism and degradation, and it rewrites it—in the same place—as a place of validation and desire. The object was to approach the design of this space from a hip hop perspective that focuses on the (re)affirmation of identity, incorporating principles of appropriation and adaptation to palimpsestically create spaces specific to the needs of the user—the hip hop community (see Figure 1).

Hip Hop Architecture: Anthropomorphic. A principal purpose of hip hop architecture is to create a "home place" (as bell hooks has referred to it) or, for the purposes of this essay, a space that engages and employs similar identity (re)construction strategies that take place at various sites within the diaspora. Therefore, another primary principle of hip hop architecture, as it concerns reconstructing a positive Black identity, is that it be *anthropomorphic*, which is "*in many respects, one of architecture's universals . . .* [and] *is also a frequently expressed feature of architectural traditions in Africa.*"[34]

The anthropomorphism in hip hop space is not concerned with typical Western understandings of the concept that focuses centrally on the physical attributes or appendages of the body. It is instead concerned with a holistic understanding of the place the body inhabits. It is similar to the DJ/producers' call of "who we are" and as such, is intimately connected with the identity of the body *within* space. Unlike in the West, where "architec-

Figure 2. Park entrance walls allow for neighborhood graffiti artists to express themselves.

tural anthropomorphism had its primary basis in the *valuation* of the human body as an expression of God's creative perfection, African architects more characteristically see in the human a model of life and vitality and an expression of social relationships and values."[35]

Anthropomorphic Application. As a space that is constructed by the bodies of its users, it is critical to consider the body in space and provide for its interaction in various forms and with various objects. The park provides for the specific spatial practices of the hip hop community as these individuals define their space through pedestrian speech acts. Providing for cultural and communal use in this space in terms such as "pleasurable" and "desirable" is what brings the space of hip hop—and its subsequent architectural manifestation—into being. Thus the spaces provide not only for the tangible interaction in various forms of creating and viewing the performance of everyday life (the economic, political, communal, and physical exchanges) by people in motion, but also for the tactile interaction with (im)mobile objects (graffiti walls, speaker stands, and vending booths) as well. The park is designed to facilitate this interaction, with the understanding that the more tangible and substantive the interaction, the more valuable and legitimate the architecture becomes (see Figure 2).

Hip Hop Architecture: Performative. To paraphrase Shakespeare, if "all the world's a stage, and we are merely actors," then the physical manifestation of a hip hop spatial understanding is this phrase's most recent—and important—connotation. The notion of *simultaneity*— the intersection of body and stage around the construction of identity—communicated through performance is a primary element of the diaspora and must be a part of hip hop space.[36]

The organization of hip hop spatial understanding can be found in the deep call of the diaspora in rhythm and repetition. Hip hop architecture is the emergence— in form—of the base and the beat, the flow and the rupture, the call and response. Consequently, an additional primary principle of hip hop architecture is that it is *performative*. It is about both providing the stage (backdrop) and privileging (inviting) the performance, where space is produced through the conjunction of people within it. The importance of performance—both the everyday and the ceremonial—in the creation of space in the diaspora, underscores the centrality of architecture itself both as a setting for everyday life and ceremonial action and as a theater for the presentation of dramas for the community as a whole. Through these performances, key aspects of architectural meaning are given expression.[37]

Performative Application. The design of the Hip Hop Park can be viewed as one large stage, a stage for the performance of life for diasporic members—in this case, the hip hop community—that recalls historical spatial practices that are specific to this particular location. Hip hop architecture is concerned primarily with identity, and central to the creation of that identity are patterns of performance that are created by the music, by the musicians, and by the listeners. Each of these activities is suggested (invited) in the design by their location, but they are not fossilized in these locations. Like the transformative nature of the hip hop culture, these spaces are easily changed (and most likely will be continuously transformed) by the users to meet the complex performance of spatial and identity construction. The spaces suggested for the performance by the musicians (the central stage) and by the listeners (passively in the center grass knolls and actively in the hip hop dance spots and the bazaar area) are designed to encourage their use

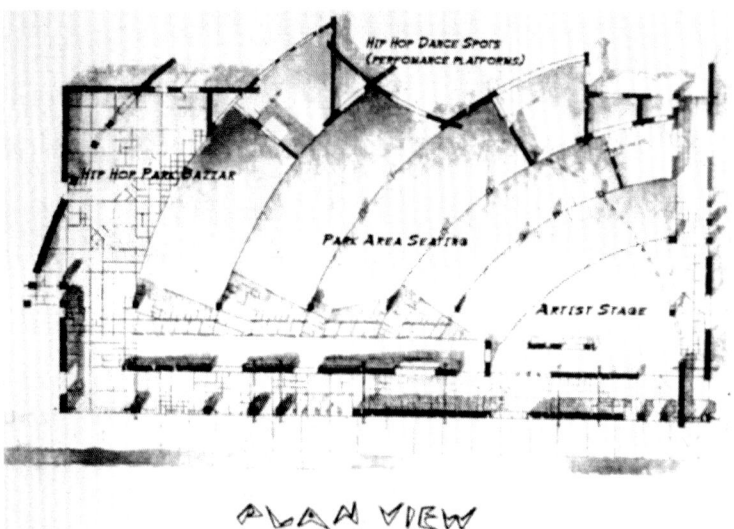

Figure 3. Park plan.

as currently designed, but also to encourage their reorganization in other ways by the users, as the community continues to write and rewrite its identity in and on this space (see Figure 3).

Hip Hop Architecture: Adaptive. Finally, hip hop architecture is *adaptive*. It has to be. The sites that are available for the emergence of hip hop forms necessitate it; the people for whom the structures will be built will demand it; the availability of materials for this (these) project(s) requires it; the assemblage of these structures compels it. Hip hop architecture's diasporic dialectic is inescapable. From its vegetal and mud and clay site-specific African origins, to the design of "shotgun homes" of the late eighteenth-century Caribbean and early nineteenth-century America, to the late nineteenth-century Tuskegee Institute/University project, to the thatched roofs of the early twentieth-century "critter houses" of South Carolina, hip hop architecture is also committed to using and reusing materials transformatively and creatively, removing the hegemonic "proper" not only from spatial communication but from symbol and material communication also. The architecture of hip hop embodies the spirit that architectural professor Laverne Wells-Bowie describes as "architecture as a cultural practice . . . [the] sense of architecture acknowledging diversity of location, that wherever folks are dwelling in space, they can think creatively about the transformation and reinvention of that space."[38]

Adaptive Application. The current material culture available in the community has been adapted in the hip hop bazaar. Behind the concept of the bazaar is the desire to facilitate the entrepreneurial spirit of hip hop culture and to build on its "power from powerlessness" theme. This space is designed to facilitate young entrepreneurs, street vendors, and small community enterprises that would like to reach a larger and repeat clientele, but who do not have the initial capital investment for renting space for commercial needs, inventory, or storage. These enterprises provide a vital service—the underground economy that sustains many marginalized communities—but live a transient existence within the community.[39]

As such, the hip hop booths are a principal component of the bazaar/marketplace in this design and are designed to be easily assembled, disassembled, and transported. Made from wood, metal, wire, and canvas, they blend perfectly with the materials used in the park design, as the walls, flooring, and booths utilize the materials discarded in the neighborhood everyday—at once cleaning the areas of debris and adapting the discarded into the useful. The canvas covers of differing colors are intended to be utilized by neighborhood graffiti artists to simultaneously display their skills and to announce the various vendors in the bazaar, giving the market a particularly community flavor, creating an "'architecture of the site' as opposed to the architectural ideal of 'an architecture on the site'" and adding yet another layer to the construction of individual and communal identity (see Figures 4 and 5).[40]

Conclusion

Writing about Music Is Like Dancing about Architecture . . .
In this essay, I have explored a particular relationship between rap music, space, and architecture. Rejecting previous investigative essays that focus on music, space, and architecture as being inadequately probative, I have employed a counterquest for an aesthetic paradigm of architectural and sonic production, one that approaches the question of music and architecture from the inside out. In this investigation I have

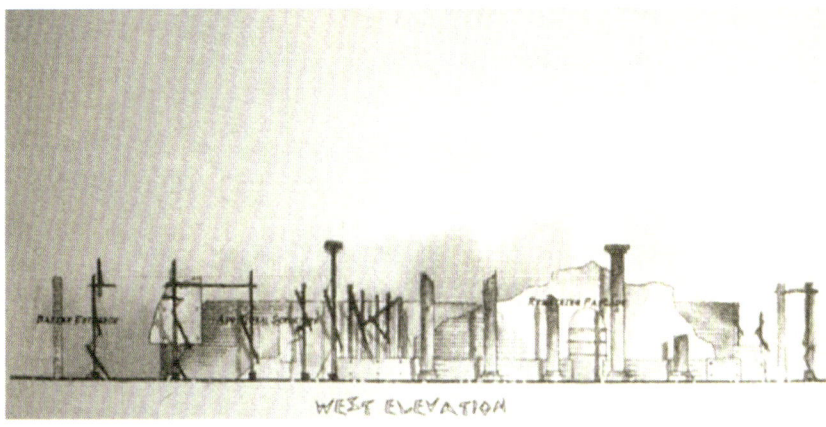

Figure 4. East elevation showing the community bazaar entrance and tagging wall made from a combination of new construction with existing walls and site materials.

Figure 5. Aerial view looking southeast toward downtown Chicago showing the integration of existing and new (appropriated) materials.

positioned rap music as the womb from which hip hop space and architecture are born.

Theory in architecture is all too often discussed only in terms of form. The ideology in architecture that permeates the profession and discipline is rarely analyzed. This piece attempts to open up that discussion on a number of levels. My primary purpose in engaging in this examination of music, space, and architecture is to begin to explore new paradigms of architectural spatial theory and manifestations that are initiated from the marginalized citizenry—specifically, the African-American community. This search is for a spatial paradigm that resists the power of dominant hegemonic understandings of space embedded and accepted in architecture and creates power for the marginalized from their built environment, primarily by identifying ways they can and do express their spatial practice in physical form to affirm their validity. The revolutionary production of hip hop space—a phenomenon of sonic organization and use created in a distinct social context, dependent on experience and memory, linked to time (past, present, and future), defined and communicated by people through their patterns of use in the built environment—has clearly been identified as a prototype demonstrative of an African-American spatial practice and available for physical expression. In this theorizing, the production of hip hop architecture is an attempt to "recover a sense of community outside the state-regulated and commodified universe" dependent on "a systematic reorganization of space to enlarge the realm of public discourse and physical freedom . . . a new code of space," and it is an attempt to build upon the foundations of "expressive rather than instrumental (institutional) social relations."[41] Hip hop architecture takes as its point of departure a phenomenologist understanding of subjective/substitute images, and combines it with the notion of spatial construction through interrelations, into this "new code of space." And here, you thought that it was only noise.

The preeminent principle in hip hop culture and its music is one of identity. Rap music employs various specific, identity (re)defining strategies developed by the African diaspora as a result of its Black subject from "Negro" object reclamation project. The specific spatial understanding of hip hop culture, embodied in the physical manifestations of hip hop architecture is predicated on the response to those spaces that represent an erasure of identity and, concomitantly, the presence of oppressive power. A hip hop spatial paradigm at once recalls, creates, and deploys a new space of diasporian origin and produces an architectural manifestation that is at once palimpsestic, anthropomorphic, performative, and adaptive. Hip hop architecture is engaged in taking existing architecture and transforming it into something that expresses the spatial practices of the residents of marginalized communities, an object that makes sense to them. By making architecture an artifact that is "owned" by reason of individual, community, and/or cultural relevance and reaffirms their identity as a people, the architecture of hip hop strives to make the built environment something desirable and therefore valuable to those inside and outside the community. Le Corbusier recognized the necessity of transformation when he argued that "if we challenge the past, we shall learn that 'styles' no longer exist for us, that a style belonging to our own period has come about."[42] *Snap!* (Meaning: stop, something just clicked.) *Check that.* (Meaning: read again.) Le Corbusier is (subconsciously?) stating that the discipline of architecture *flows*, with periodic *breaks* in its continuity. That it is, in effect, breakdancing. Architecture: hip hop(ping) through history. And all this time you thought you couldn't dance.

We are in one of those moments in time where a "pop" or "rupture" in the performance is necessary. The old solutions (styles) no longer apply. Our concerns, our problems at this time, are different. Architecture should be about that, about responding to society now, with an eye always toward the future. When Bones, Thugs, and Harmony rap about *It's The First of The Month* or Luniz raps that *I Got Five on It*, this speaks to the concerns of a broad spectrum of the populace and suggests modes of aesthetic solutions. Where are the structures that reflect these modes? Where is the building about which I can say: *I Got Five on It*? Inner-city design strategies to date primarily have been developed outside of the affected community. Strategies developed by "experts"—that look at the architecture of survival, of identity, of erasure and that determine that it is nothing more than vandalism—have emerged. But these strategies have emerged out of a) a failure to understand what that architecture is really saying about the community that produced it and, b) a willingness to impose narrowly defined spatial theories that masquerade as "universal" aesthetics upon an "other." Historically, design in these marginalized communities from a universal (read: Euro-American) spatial understanding has not been "universally" successful. I live in a "Boogie-Woogie Bugle Boy" building, but I'd much rather live in a Boogie Down Productions space. Hip hop architecture calls on the architectural "flow" to develop a space, that nobody can deal with—a [space] that cannot be easily understood or erased, a [space] that has the reflexivity to create counter-dominant narratives against a mobile and shifting enemy. . . . In the post-industrial urban context of dwindling low-income housing, a trickle of meaningless jobs for young people, mounting police brutality, and increasingly draconian depictions of young inner-city residences, hip hop style is black urban renewal.[43]

As such, hip hop architecture is one model for halting the destruction and deterioration of African-American urban communities and the best hope to restore their viability as sustainable communities. The architectural entities that evolve from a hip hop spatial paradigm draw on the best of the past and the present. Employed in communities where there is a need and cry for an environment that does not repress but relieves, hip hop architecture replaces the constrictive with the supportive. It defines and asseverates an African-American identity. Like rap music, hip hop architecture reuses and renames space and in the process "renders visible 'black' meanings, *precisely because of*, and not in spite of, its industrial forms of production, distribution, and consumption."[44] It nurtures a place where African-Americans can see a positive portrait of themselves in their environment.

To that end, I should mention that I am challenged in my thinking by the theoretical work of the Russian Constructivists in the early part of this century, whose essential task, as argued by one of its leading theorists Moisei Ginzburg, was the: "creation of 'social contenders': buildings, complexes, or even whole cities that could not only perform their immediate functions but also motivate users (or, if necessary, constrain them) to new actions, new habits—and thereby new ways of living."[45]

What the Constructivists identified above as *new ways of living* is more accurately identified in my hypothesis as the specific African-American spatial practices of this cultural moment informed by transnational diaspora spatial practices. I am most intellectually stimulated by their notion of the "new urban design—the purposive production of urban meaning—[as being] productivist (and activist), mobile and demountable and diffuse in its forms and media" that enables structures where "all the accessories that a metropolitan street imposes on a building—illustrations, publicity, clock, loudspeaker, even the lifts inside—are drawn into the design as equally important parts and brought to unity" by "transforming mediating signs, to add new signification to that already existing."[46]

The Hip Hop Park project is an example of this type of effort, an effort to listen to what's on the street and—literally—read the writing on the wall. As Gil Scott-Heron, anticipating Lefebvre while paving the way for this hip hop moment, has so eloquently said: "The revolution will not be televised. . . . It will be live."[47]

Notes
1. Henri Lefebvre, *The Production of Space* (Oxford: Blackwell, 1995), 36.
2. Simon Frith and Andrew Ross, *On Record: Pop, Rock and the Written Word* (New York: Pantheon Books, 1990).

3. Frith and Ross, *On Record*.
4. Simon Frith and Angela McRobbie, "Rock and Sexuality," in *On Record*, eds. Simon Frith and Andrew Roth (New York: Pantheon Books, 1990), 317–332. Frith and McRobbie further argue that while music is responsible for constructing gendered identities, rock is essentially a male form that offers a variety of male sexual poses to young males, but for women in rock "to become hard aggressive performers, it was necessary for them, as Jerry Garcia commented on Janis Joplin, to become 'one of the boys.'" (322) They summarize their position with the assertion that: "both in its presentation and its use, rock has confirmed traditional definitions of what constitutes masculinity and femininity, and reinforces their expression in leisure pursuits." (330) Frith and McRobbie's argument demonstrates music's ability to form subjectivity/ identity—in this instance, defining sexual positions by way of public activity.
5. George Lipsitz, *Time Passages: Collective Memory and Popular Culture* (Minneapolis, MN: University of Minnesota, 1990). Lipsitz posits that every instance of cultural production "is the product of an ongoing historical conversation in which no one has the first or the last word." He asserts that music is produced through, reflects, and affects the social and political context in which it evolves, making it inherently social and its meaning emerges from within the socio/historical context around its production and its reception. In other words, Mozart would have written differently had he lived in modern-day Brooklyn with access to a tape player, MIDI machine, and a microphone—products of this time, this history—and not only might Mozart have produced a different music, music would have greatly contributed to producing a different Mozart.
6. Lipsitz, *Time Passages*, 104.
7. Lipsitz, *Time Passages*, 105.
8. John Mowitt, "The Sound of Music in the Era of Its Electronic Reproducibility," in *Music and Society: The Politics of Composition, Performance and Reception*, eds. Richard Leppert and Susan McClary (Cambridge: University Press, 1977), 173.
9. Mowitt, "Sound of Music," 181. To illustrate memory's fundamental and social influence on music, Mowitt gives an example from Maurice Halbwachs's "The Collective Memory of Musicians," in *The Collective Memory*, trans. Francis J. Ditter and Vita Yazdi Ditter (New York: Harper & Row, 1980), 158–86, that posits that when performing, many musicians find referring to the score frequently unnecessary because they know their pieces "by heart," due to many hours practicing, often with other musicians. This event "by heart" is a moment that is "exerted on a performer's brain by the 'colony' of other brains," those "other brains" belonging to fellow musicians. In other words, musicians play what they "remember" having heard being played previously, highlighting "a particular history and technology of reproduction [that] supplements the musician's memory." The sound is memorized by many players until a convention, a "normative" collective memory of the sound is realized. Thus, a collective "memory" defines the proper or "normative" way to listen and a community is produced.
10. Mowittt, "Sound of Music," 179. Jaques Attali, as quoted by Mowitt. Emphasis mine.
11. Albert Murray, *The Blue Devils of Nada: A Contemporary American Approach to Aesthetic Statement* (New York: Pantheon Books, 1989), 123.
12. Lefebvre, *The Production of Space*, 84. Locke's construction of space and place is crucial to the following discussion about Lefebvre because all other modern notions of space in Western civilization flow as either an acceptance of; a reaction to; or a modification or rejection of Locke's perspective. This is particularly true of Lefebvre's hypothesis of social—and other—spatial production. Locke argues that space "exists" prior to our knowledge—it is "out there" (essentialized)—discernible only by the relationship (position) of bodies within it. The spot where a body is at rest is called place, discernible only by its relationship (mathematically) to two or more reference bodies (points). Lockean notions of space are held in definitive terms—distance, capacity, extension, and so on—available through the mind by sight and touch and apportionable on an abstracted and mathematical scale (for example, *this* piece is *this* distance from *that* piece and is *this* long, *this* wide).
13. Lefebvre, *The Production of Space*, 102.
14. Lefebvre posits that social space is quite different than Lockean space. It is a relationship between nature and "activities which involves the economic and technical realms but extends well beyond them," and is built upon a triad of spatial concepts: spatial practice, representations of space, and representational spaces that require intersecting bodies to be produced. In brief: *Spatial practices* are understood as the social activities that occur in a particular time and place that constitute—and are *specific* to—the establishment of a distinctive social order. Spatial practices in Lefebvre's conceptual triad are observed or "perceived." Spatial practice "presupposes the use of the body" and presupposes, then, an identity for the body that is being used. *Representations of space* are theorized, rational, logical, or "conceived" spatial understandings, informed by a particular world perspective and the place of the subject within it. Representations of space therefore grant a level of reflectiveness to the identity spatial practices presuppose, and in effect recognize, if not bestow, *subjectivity* to the body. *Representational spaces* are "space[s] as directly *lived* through its associated images and symbols, and hence the space of 'inhabitants' and 'users.'" As "lived" experience, representational spaces "have their source in history—in the history of a people as well as in the history of each individual belonging to that people." Representational space, which "is alive; [and] speaks," then, *affirms* the body's identity/subjectivity in speaking. This bodily triad of social space conflates to create a dialogue with history and memory that indicates a spatial application of Lipsitz's earlier posited notion of dialectical criticism.
15. Michel Foucault, "Of Other Spaces," *Diacritics* 16, no. 1 (Winter, 1986): 23. In this essay, Foucault argues that "our epoch is one in which space takes for us the form of relations among sites" and that "we live inside a set of relations that delineate sites which are irreducible to one another and absolutely not superimposable upon one another." Lefebvre's social space challenges that position by positing that the perceived, conceived, and lived that make up the space of home, and that intersects with the space of yard, penetrates into the space of neighborhood, that integrates into the space of city and so forth, ad infinitum, into the space of the everyday. He likens this spatial interpenetration to the principle of superimposition—the phenomenon of motion found in hydrodynamics—where "great movements, vast rhythms, immense waves—these all collide and 'interfere' with one another; [but] lesser movements, on the other hand, interpenetrate." Lefebvre, *The Production of Space*, 86.

16. Michel de Certeau, *The Practice of Everyday Life* (Berkeley, CA: University of California Press, 1984), 96. To de Certeau, the pedestrian speech act is homologous to the verbal speech act in three ways: as "a process of appropriation" of an existing framework of meaning; as "a spatial acting-out of the place" from the existing framework in order to communicate meaning; and "it implies relations among differentiated positions" by implying interaction between a speaker and listener to communicate meaning. His initial notion of the "process of appropriation"—*the adaptation of an existing framework of meaning to a heretofore nonenvisioned specific purpose*—has applications in both the sonic and the spatial. As he suggests, language is the framework for speech, without which, speaking to communicate cannot occur. Similarly, sound is the framework necessary for music to communicate, and space is the framework for the pedestrian to communicate. Vocal, musical, and spatial frameworks are consistently employed, discarded, manipulated, and ultimately redefined for the purposes of the ever-changing communication of meaning. His second notion, concerning the "spatial acting-out of the place"—*the choosing of a series of enunciations (from that existing framework) to communicate meaning*—also incorporates a sonic/spatial correlation. In the sonic, producers of music choose a set of enunciations of music to communicate; similarly, in the spatial, pedestrians choose a set of movements through space to communicate a meaning of space. Finally, de Certeau's "relations among differentiated positions"—*the communication of meaning in the social through interaction with another*—also holds true for the sonic and spatial. In the sonic, communication of meaning socially through interaction with another through sound occurs between producers and receivers of the music (in terms of it being pleasurable, dangerous, subversive, interesting). Similarly, in the spatial, movement through these spaces constitutes communication with others, as our conscious and unconscious movements are read and interpreted by others (in terms of being pleasurable, dangerous, subversive, interesting), even if no reception is intended.

17. De Certeau, *Practice of Everyday Life*. De Certeau further asserts that memory of experience (social interaction/historical dialogue) constructs not only the language we use to communicate but its rhetoric—the way we use the language to communicate: "It is assumed that practices of space also correspond to manipulations of the basic elements of a constructed order [and] it is assumed that they are, like the tropes in rhetoric, deviations relative to a sort of 'literal meaning' defined by the [constructed order]." (100) For example, in verbal speech there is "proper" English, and all other uses are a derivative of that proper form, from dialect to slang. He notes on page 100 that space also lays claim to a "proper" form: "It is assumed that [other uses] are, like tropes in rhetoric, deviations relative to a sort of 'literal meaning' defined by the urbanistic system. There would thus be a homology between verbal figures and the figures of walking (a stylized selection among the latter is already found in dancing) insofar as both consist in 'treatments' or operations bearing isolatable units, and in 'ambiguous dispositions' that divert and displace meaning in the direction of equivocalness... In reality, this faceless 'proper' meaning (i.e., 'proper' sans figure) cannot be found in current use, whether verbal or pedestrian." (100) Implied here is that the "proper" pedestrian speech act in space is the one intended by the spatial organizer (be it architect, landscape architect, interior designer, or others) and all other uses, from shortcuts to avoidance, are derivatives of the "proper" use.

18. De Certeau, *Practice of Everyday Life*, 117.

19. 19. Tricia Rose, *Black Noise: Rap Music and Black Cultural Expression* (Hanover, CT: Wesleyan University Press, 1994), 2. "Rap music is a black cultural expression that prioritizes black voices from the margins of urban America. Rap music is a form of rhymed storytelling accompanied by highly rhythmic, electronically based music.... From the outset, rap music has articulated the pleasures and problems of black urban life in contemporary America." (2)

20. Rose, *Black Noise*, 65.

21. Rose, *Black Noise*, 96.

22. Rose, *Black Noise*, 94. Tricia Rose presents a particularly rap version that builds on Mowitt's theory of the social construction of music through technology. In discussing the musical piece "Paid in Full" by the rap duo of Eric B. and Rakim, Rose illustrates the primacy of Mowitt's studio in the production of the music by highlighting the lyrical acknowledgment by the duo of their location in the studio. Also, during the recorded "conversation" between Eric B. (the producer) and Rakim (the rapper), there are specific, identifiable directions to the studio engineer as to the technical manipulation of the music for "effect," now that they have completed the lyrical "performance" portion of the piece. This acknowledgment of the power of studio technology over the music produced in the reproduction of the music itself, "demystifies technology and its production.... Eric B. and Rakim suggest that they are *in control* of what technology produces—including its on-site manager, Ely, the engineer," (94) thereby confirming the primacy of the technology and its studio location.

23. Rose, *Black Noise*, 82.

24. Mowitt, "Sound of Music," 182.

25. For instance, Paul Gilroy in the *Black Atlantic* argues that it is difficult, if not impossible, to consider the musical traditions of African Diaspora as unbroken and universally traceable while also positing that in their difference, these various strains of diasporic musics still recall a collective memory. Similarly, Tricia Rose in *Black Noise* argues—particularly with rap—that any focus on the possible legacy of the oral traditions of Africa to African-American expressions in diasporic music is to ignore the music itself. Gerald Early in *One Nation Under a Groove* argues that the development of R & B/Soul music—with Motown at its head—was a uniquely Black American experience. There are many more perspectives that at once question and reinforce a direct continuous historical link in the sonic traditions of Black music, but my point here is that there is a common point of departure from which these critics—and others—begin their investigations. Paul Gilroy, *The Black Atlantic: Modernity and Double Consciousness* (London: Verso, 1993); Rose, *Black Noise*; Gerald Lyn Early, *One Nation Under a Groove: Motown and American Culture* (Ann Arbor, MI: University of Michigan Press, 2004).

26. The nature of Black music is demonstrated through the music's focus on rhythm and repetition. As it concerns rap music, this focus has much to do with performance. I should make it clear that, in this instance, I am using performance to refer to three individual, but wholly dependent, instances: the performance of the music itself (the production of the sound), the performance of the musicians (when producing the sounds), and the performance of the listeners (the reception of the sounds, as depicted in movement or

dance). Paul Gilroy in the *Black Atlantic* argues for a position where performance is a primary necessity for the emergence of memory in the African diaspora: "This orientation to the specific dynamics of performance has a wider significance in the analysis of black cultural forms than has so far been supposed. Its strengths are evident when it is contrasted with approaches to black culture that have been premised exclusively on textuality and narrative rather than dramaturgy, enunciation and gesture—the pre-and anti-discursive constituents of black metacommunication." Gilroy, *Black Atlantic*, 75. The rhythm and repetition of African music facilitates an invitation to performance. An invitation meant to be extended out in time, to flow beyond its immediate location. As music meant to be performed, it is cognizant of the limitations of the body and, so, calls to many performers to participate, creating an additional layer of flow and rupture—sometimes consistent, other times contradictory—to the music itself. These instances of performance illustrate not only the social aspect of music as it relates to the African diaspora, but also the *construction of space by music*, through the performances that are part of the music itself. As described by Lerone Bennett in *Before the Mayflower: a History of Black America* (Chicago, IL: Johnson Pub. Co, 1969), 26–27: "Before the coming of the white man, music and rhythm were everyday things in Africa. Music was everywhere and it was grounded in two techniques which survived in the New World: polyrhythmic percussive technique and the call-and-response pattern (leader and chorus alternating). The poetry of tom-toms, the symphonies of synchronized bodies: these ebbed and flowed with the rhythm of life. Men and women danced because dancing had a social and religious meaning and because dancing was meaning, was life itself." The technical nature of the (re)production of rap music, in particular the use of sampling, allows for an overamplification of the musical focus on performance facilitators, the break or the back beat, to become primary. In rap music, the beat is the king (or queen), and whether it is the beat/rhythm of the music or the voice is, for all intents and purposes, unimportant. The fact that the rapper Guru of Gang Starr has alternately said, *If the beat were a princess, I'd marry it* and *It must be the voice, that gets you up* with equal conviction, illustrates this point. What is important is the memory that this use of rhythm awakens. It awakens the desire to perform—in answer to the call of the music. It is at once, immediate and historical, local and global, American and Diasporic. As to the Black music's orality, it too, has its presence in the memory of the Diasporian community. Many black cultural critics and historians posit that the vocalese of rap descends directly from the tradition of the storyteller/tribal historian—the griot—in African societies. This perspective rests in the understanding of the primacy in traditional African cultures of the spoken word and all of its communicative allies—dramaturgy and gesture (performance). Others trace the orality of rap to a type of sonic phenomenon deeply embedded in the African tradition known as antiphony—call and response. Adapted to a specific interaction between two subjects, its appearance in African-American culture as toasting, also known as *crackin', boastin', playin' the dozens, snappin',* or *signifyin'* is designed to come to a resolution only when one cannot answer the call of another. This position suggests that the development of the vocal pattern of toasting is, if not constituted by, certainly runs parallel to, the development of similar diasporic musical patterns in Africa and America. Others still, like Paul Gilroy quoting Cornel West from *Re-Making History*, proposes yet another possibility, positioning rap music as "borrowing from the linguistic innovations of Jamaica's distinct modes of 'kinetic orality.'" This further suggests an interesting *flip[pin'] of the script,* that instead of lyrical patterns being either separate from, or influenced by, music patterns, that the vocal framework actually influences the musical patterns. The fact that the Jamaican *patta*—patterns of rapid vocalese bathed in distinct rhythmic tones, inflections, and enunciations—has heavily influenced Caribbean music, supports such a position and suggests further investigation. However, for the purposes of this essay, it is not necessary—even if it were possible—to discern the truth of one perspective over the other. What is important is the acknowledgment by each perspective of its African diasporic foundation and the development of vocal historical frameworks and patterns as independent from the music itself. Cornel West, "Black Culture and Postmodernism," in *Remaking History*, eds. Barbara Kruger and Phil Mariani (Seattle, WA: Bay Press, 1989), 87–98. The final segment of rap music's historical dialectic with the collective memory of the African diasporic social order is its objective content; it highlights rap music's connection with the diasporic collective memory, which is largely influenced by the postmodern condition of fragmentation that has characterized diasporian struggles for identity. The author/poet David Muria has said that marginalized cultures encounter an almost perpetually deafening silence about their condition and position in the world from the dominant culture. He believes the reason for this is that dominant culture allows only atomized, randomized bits and pieces of marginalized cultures' histories to be heard/told. The hegemonic aggressiveness of the dominant culture works not only to silence the dominant culture, but the marginalized culture as well, as its members, in acknowledgment of hegemony, chose those fragments of their culture and history that will facilitate advancement/acceptance within the dominant culture. I would argue that for the African diasporic experience, and for African-Americans in particular, this fragmentation is much worse simply because, unlike many marginalized cultures here in America, there has been a continued negation by the dominant culture of any cultural origin—a critical location of historical memory—for African-Americans. In this passage from *Color and Democracy: Colonies and Peace* (New York: Harcourt & Brace, 1945), 91–2, W. E. B. DuBois illustrates two aspects of the dominant culture's negation: "In the Immigration and Naturalization Service of the United States Department of Justice passengers arriving on aircraft are to be labeled according to 'race,' and are determined by the stock from which aliens spring and the language they speak, and to some degree nationality. But 'Negroes' apparently can belong to no nation: 'Cuban,' for instance, refers to Cuban people 'but not to Cubans who are 'Negroes'; 'West Indians' refers to the people of the West Indies 'except Cubans or Negroes'; 'Spanish American' refers to peoples of Central and South America and of Spanish descent; but 'Negro' refers to the 'black African whether from Cuba, the West Indies, North or South America, Europe or Africa' and moreover any alien with a mixture of blood of the African (black) should be classified under this [Negro] heading." This passage points not only to the negation of Africa(n) by replacing it with the all encompassing term "Negro"—not a nation or even a place, but an object; a thing—but also to the erasure of the cultural specificity of each of the diasporic strains now placed under the inadequate term "Negro." It at once removes a culture from its original location, violently strips away the subjectivity of its members, and relocates the objects according to a set of strategic hegemonic rules defined by the dominant culture. "Negroes" now belong to "no-place." At its most basic level, the lyrical content of rap music engages in the dialectic concerning marginality, location, agency, and the subject/object imbroglio. The lyrics of rap music are a form of aggressive agency, a reinterpretation of those conditions and locations that were stripped away in an effort to reclaim the Black subject (the *person*) from the "Negro" object (the thing). This distinctive Africentric *social practice* is at once recalled, produced and enhanced in the music of the hip hop culture. As Tricia Rose points out in *Black Noise*, "Hip hop has styles and themes that share striking similarities with many past and contiguous Afrodiasporic musical and cultural expressions. These themes and styles, for the most part, are revised and reinterpreted, using contemporary cultural and technological elements. Hip hop's central forms—graffiti, breakdancing, and rap music—developed in relation to one another and in relation to the larger society." (27)

27. Gilroy, *Black Atlantic*, 76: "Music, the grudging gift that supposedly compensated slaves not only for their exile from the ambiguous legacies of practical reason but for their complete exclusion from modern political society, has been refined and developed so that it provides an enhanced mode of communication beyond the petty power of words—spoken or written." Also see Bennett, *Before the Mayflower*.
28. Ann Daly, "Conversations About Race In the Language of Dance," *New York Times*, December 7, 1997, 44. "Choreographers are increasingly exploring the limits and possibilities of existing dance forms to address African-American [identity], as Mr. Lemon is doing with post-modern dance in 'Geography.'"
29. The title of LL Cool J's 1987 album on Def Jam records.
30. Mike Steele, "Bring It In," *Star Tribune, Entertainment*, December 14, 1997, 18. "That beat has hung on from minstrel shows to the blues, jazz to rock to rap, ragtime to "Shuffle Along." It all began more than 250 years ago in the feet of [enslaved Africans] who created something out of nothing. Their drums were outlawed after [enslaved African] rebellions, but [they] found other ways to keep the rhythm flowing: They turned their feet into drums, conversing in rhythmic codes. . . . That's history in street rhythm carried by dancing feet."
31. Houston A. Baker Jr., *Black Studies, Rap and the Academy*, (Chicago, IL: University of Chicago Press, 1993), 58–59.
32. Venise Berry, "Redeeming the Rap Music Experience," *Speculations*, eds. Charles I. Schuster and William V. Van Pelt. (Upper Saddle River, NJ: Simon & Schuster, 1996), 191.
33. Lefebvre, *The Production of Space*, 87.
34. Suzanne Preston Blier, *The Anatomy of Architecture: Ontology and Metaphor in Batammaliba Architectural Expression* (Chicago, IL: University of Chicago Press, 1994), 118.
35. Blier, *Anatomy of Architecture*, 119. Emphasis mine.
36. The intersection of several subject positions that are part of the world of people of color is discussed by Paul Gilroy when he speaks about the double consciousness of the diasporic experience, while W. E. B. DuBois speaks of a "twoness" and James Baldwin about duality. For simplicity's sake, I have referred to these similar themes as "simultaneity." Gilroy, *Black Atlantic*.
37. Suzanne Preston Blier, *The Anatomy of Architecture*, 200.
38. bell hooks, *Art on my Mind: Visual Politics* (New York: New Press, 1995), 157.
39. Margaret Crawford, "Contesting the Public Realm: Struggles over Public Space in Los Angeles," *Journal of Architectural Education* 49, no. 1 (1995), 7. Due to the historical and continued obstacles hindering full scale access to mainstream capital markets in marginalized communities, there has always been a need for a secondary economy. In the African-American community, this economy has essentially become institutionalized on the streets of many neighborhoods and in some ways understood as a communal right. As Crawford notes: "Defending their livelihood, vendors are becoming a political as well as an economic presence in the city. . . . In Baldwin Hills, a middle-class African-American neighborhood, a parking lot between a gas station and a supermarket has become a scene of intense, if fluctuating, social and commercial activity. On most days, a van parks in the lot, offering car detailing services. The operators, two local men who are now retired, set out chairs, providing a social magnet for the neighborhood men who pass by. On weekends, a portable barbecue is set up nearby, selling 'home-cooked' ribs and links. On holidays and weekends, a group of middle-aged women joins them, setting up tables to sell homemade crafts and gifts. Mostly grandmothers who work at home, their products represent both hobbies and an income supplement. Replicating the domestic order of the surrounding neighborhood and expanding the private roles of grandparents into the public realm, their local activities provide a focus for the community that is also accessible to anyone driving by. Simultaneously local and public, the activities in this parking lot strengthen the neighborhood while they visibly represent its culture to outsiders." (7)
40. Ismail Serageldin, ed., *Architecture of Empowerment* (Lantham, MD: Academy Editions, 1997), 43.
41. Carl Boggs, *Social Movements and Political Power* (Philadelphia, PA: Temple University Press, 1986), 49.
42. Le Corbusier, *Towards a New Architecture*, trans. Frederick Etchells (New York: Praeger Publishers, 1982), 251.
43. Tricia Rose, *Black Noise*, 61.
44. Tricia Rose, *Black Noise*, 17, as quoted from Andrew Ross.
45. Ross King, *Emancipating Space: Geography, Architecture and Urban Design* (New York: Guilford Press, 1996), 64.
46. King, *Emancipating Space*, 61, 62, 69.
47. The title of Gil Scott-Heron's 1974 album on the Flying Dutchman label.

Research in Design: Planning Doing Monitoring Learning

Stephen Kieran
KieranTimberlake Associates

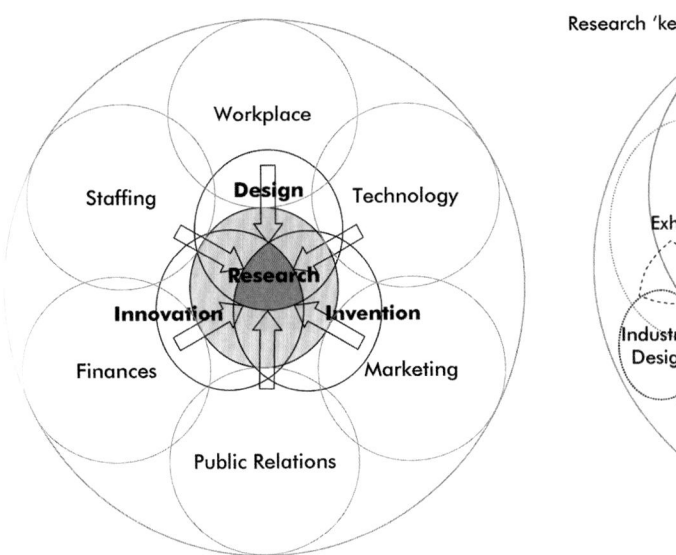
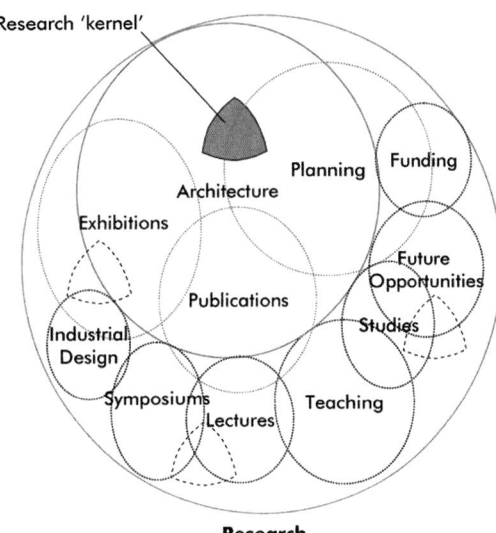

Figure 1. Research strategy. KieranTimberlake Associates LLP.

To develop an ethical architecture that unifies the art of design with the science of performance; a research ethic is a necessary prerequisite.

Architects tend to see most acts of design as unique. Site and program together give rise to circumstance. Circumstance inspires intention. Design organizes intention into instruction. Builders construct from what we instruct. And we all move on to the next set of circumstances and program, none the wiser. Architecture exists in a world where all we ever do is design and build prototypes, with little real reflection and informed improvement from one act of design to the next.

This view contrasts sharply with product design. Products are not fixed to place, and they are designed for replication, sometimes in vast quantities. Because of the intention to replicate, good products are subjected to a relentless cycle of improvement. This cycle begins with a plan, then moves to doing, monitoring, and learning—then, it repeats itself with an improved plan and more doing, monitoring, and learning—and so on. At its best, product design is an enduring flywheel that insists upon improving prior acts. It is a flywheel driven by criticism and reflection, underpinned by a research ethic that is not content to just plan and do but rather insists upon measuring performance and learning as the precursors to further planning and doing.

As educators of architects, we focus nearly all our efforts on the planning side of the flywheel. The bulk of our curriculum remains embedded in the nineteenth-century design studio where we plan, then we plan again and again, with little real growth in the quality and productivity of what we do either artistically or technically. While an ever-increasing number of schools have included the second part of the flywheel—building—in the curriculum, few schools of architecture teach research skills and fewer yet insist upon critical reflection and learning based upon research findings. In 2000, James Timberlake and I resolved that we were no longer going to teach design studio at the University of Pennsylvania. Instead, we began a design research laboratory that is now in its seventh year. One year later, with the impetus of an inaugural grant from the Latrobe Fellowship through the American Institute of Architecture College of Fellows, we reorganized our practice about a research core (Figure 1). This research core is a culture that we continue to nurture and build. It requires discipline and skill. The discipline is in the ceaseless inquiry about how we can do what we have just done better. The skill is in knowing how to frame questions and seek out measurable data that we can act upon to improve what we have done. We embrace an International Standards Organization (ISO)-certified

Figure 2. Curtain wall construction, Levine Hall, University of Pennsylvania. KieranTimberlake Associates LLP.

process in our firm as one way to instill a research culture in our practice. ISO requires embedding reflection and learning into the process of planning and doing. Research is a central part of how we reflect and learn. Our research core is funded both internally through firm operations and externally through occasional corporate, foundation, and government grants. We have full-time staff dedicated to this enterprise. While our design research laboratory at Pennsylvania has been focused on speculative research with only occasional prototyping, the research efforts in our office are more broadly based, ranging from highly speculative projects to applied research that grows from our design commissions.

A recent series of glass building envelopes provides a window into our evolving effort to establish a deeply ingrained research ethic as part of the design process at KieranTimberlake Associates. There are many reasons why large areas of glazing are increasingly employed not only in our work but also in that of many other architects. Environmental factors including daylight and view into and out of buildings are important but they need to be balanced against overall energy use and carbon footprint. Given how important environmental obligations are to architecture, it is alarming how little performance-based research exists on these systems. While we and other architects, engineers, and university-based researchers can and do develop virtual performance models to test our designs, there is little actual verification of those projections after construction. If we are to have a truly performance-based architecture that addresses environmental issues in a verifiable way, then we need to introduce monitoring into our practice. We have an ethical obligation as architects to own the consequences of what we design. We can no longer just complete the project and walk away, exhausted from the effort, looking forward to the next opportunity. Our obligation is to reflect and look back, monitoring, researching, and learning from what we have just done so that we can move forward, however incrementally, aspiring toward a cycle of continuous improvement derived from a performance-based design ethic and aesthetic.

In three projects developed over the past few years, we have introduced the process of monitoring what we have planned and built. Most glass curtain walls suffer from both temperature discomfort for occupants along their perimeter and high energy use to overcome this discomfort. At Levine Hall, a research and teaching facility for the School of Engineering at the University of Pennsylvania, we employed the first active curtain wall in the United States (Figure 2). This wall is glazed with an exterior insulated glass unit (IGU) and an interior glazed panel set about four inches from the exterior glazing. The chamber between these panels is the return air plenum for the building, drawing air in at its base and extracting air out at the ceiling through ductwork into remote air handlers. Because the space between the glass layers is filled with air drawn out of the building interior, the interior glazed surface temperature is similar to the desired interior temperature. Despite the seemingly obvious advantages of this system, little performance monitoring existed. Ali Malkawi, the director of the T.C. Chan Center at the University of Pennsylvania School of Design, introduced monitoring devices to measure temperature and air flow (Figure 3). The results of this monitoring verify the comfort of the interior spaces in a variety of environmental conditions. Data produced by these monitoring devices show that temperatures adjacent to the window and at the work surface remain close to seventy-two degrees despite the drop in exterior temperatures. This occurs because the temperature differential between the cavity and the room is negligible, damping conductive heat loss across the interior layer of glass. A further benefit of the active wall system is that the surface temperature of the window remains close to the room temperature for the same reasons, minimizing radiative heat loss from the body to the cold glass as often happens even with facades constructed using insulated glazing units.

At Yale University, we are now completing construction of a new Sculpture Building for the School of Art (Figure 4). The vision lights at all four floors, each eight foot eight inches high, are triple glazed with low-E glass. The five foot four inch-high spandrels, including a three and one-half foot-high sill, are double glazed and have a third glazed layer composed of translucent aerogel in a fiberglass panel. Although still translucent, this portion of the curtain wall has an R-value in excess of twenty, significantly increasing the overall thermal performance of the building envelope. The south and parts of the east facade also incorporate a louvered shading system that reduces solar loads through the vision light and improves lighting conditions in spaces designed for artists and architects. Owing to concerns over heat buildup in the cavity between the clear glazing and the aerogel panels, our research team introduced monitoring devices into the wall assembly. The goal was to determine if the cavity space between the IGU and the aerogel panel required ventilation. To this end, two adjacent panels on the east and south walls are being monitored, one being vented to the interior and the other remaining sealed. The preliminary data suggest that the heat buildup does not exceed the material tolerances of the fiberglass and will not compromise the integrity of the translucent panels in either the vented or the unvented configuration—although the vented configuration does not reach as high an internal temperature as the unvented. The data also suggest that the size of the ventilation apertures (which are essentially just holes drilled in the upper and lower angle stops that secure the translucent panels) is too small to allow for enough air circulation between the cavity and the interior to maintain a temperature equilibrium. Further monitoring and testing will continue throughout the first year of occupancy to determine if cavity temperatures can be maintained at appropriate levels throughout the year.

At the same time, these data suggested a further line of development for this curtain wall system. Even on extremely cold days in February with outside temperatures in the low teens, the heat in the cavity approaches

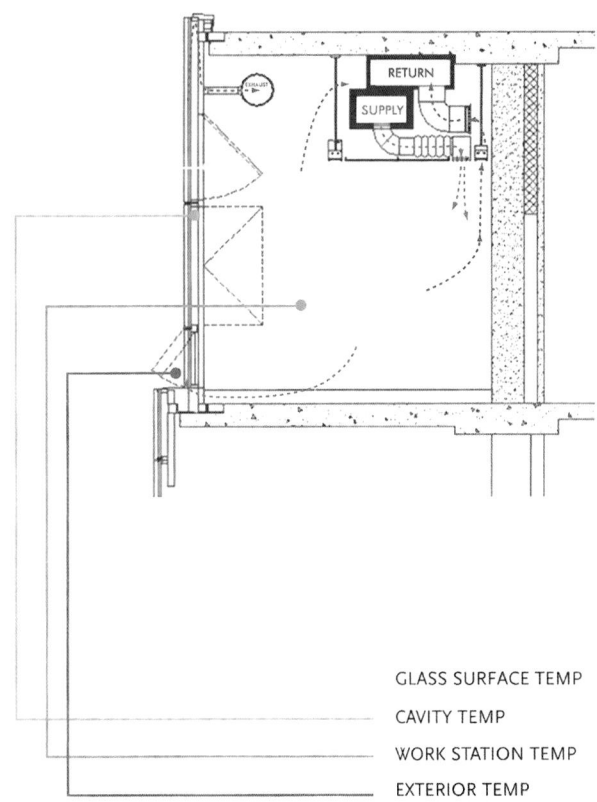

Figure 3. Monitoring device locations, Levine Hall. KieranTimberlake Associates LLP.

140 degrees during the day on the south facade. However obvious this information now seems, its existence suggests the potential to use this double-layer system as a solar thermal heating device. Why leave this free very warm air outside the building envelope on such a cold day when it could provide significant passive solar heating if we could introduce it to the building interior? Conversely, on very warm summer days, how might we vent air in this cavity back to the exterior rather than wrap the structure in a heated thermal blanket? The presence of the performance-monitoring information has spurred a new line of inquiry by our research team toward an even higher performing solution. Planning and doing are monitored. From the monitoring, we gain insight into a new line of inquiry. We learn from the research and move forward toward even more beautiful and high-performing solutions.

Last, we have just completed a new home on the eastern shore of Maryland. The west elevation of this home faces the Chesapeake Bay and is glazed. To take advantage of the prevailing offshore breeze and the extraordinary site, we developed the home so the entire west wall opens through accordion-style glass doors that fold against the end walls (Figure 5). In essence, the entire house can become a porch, extending the range of natural ventilation well beyond that of conven-

Figure 4. View, Sculpture Building, Yale University. KieranTimberlake Associates LLP.

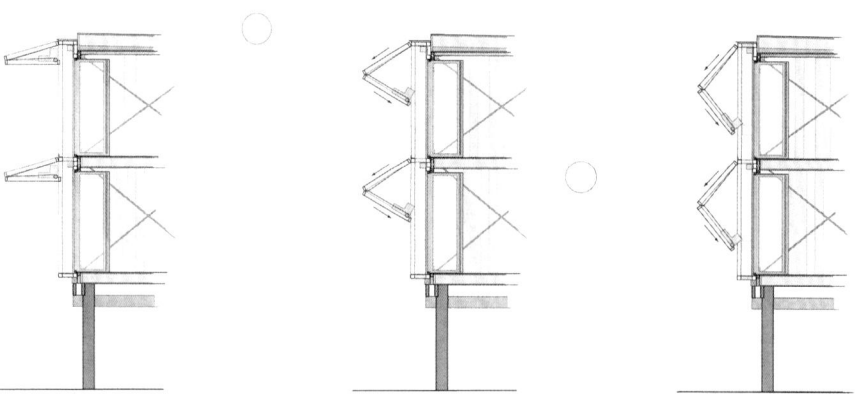

Figure 5. From left, west wall positioning at noon, mid-afternoon, and early evening, Loblolly House. KieranTimberlake Associates LLP.

TEST AREAS
SENSOR LOCATIONS

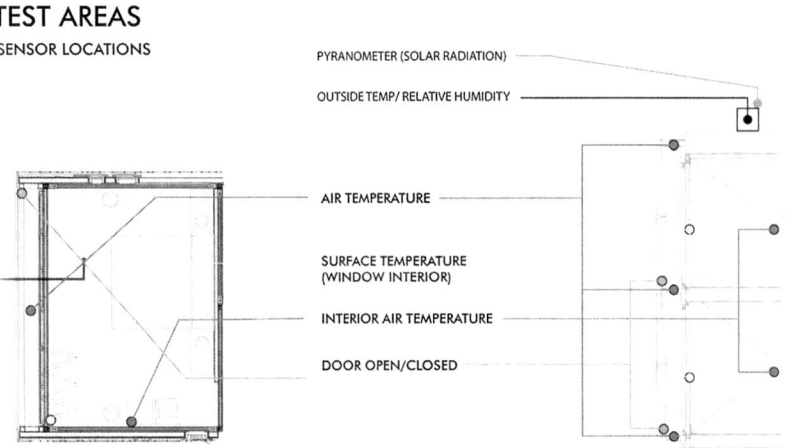

PYRANOMETER (SOLAR RADIATION)
OUTSIDE TEMP/ RELATIVE HUMIDITY
AIR TEMPERATURE
SURFACE TEMPERATURE (WINDOW INTERIOR)
INTERIOR AIR TEMPERATURE
DOOR OPEN/CLOSED

Figure 6. Monitoring device locations, Loblolly House. KieranTimberlake Associates LLP.

tional structures. To secure the home in bad weather and to provide an adjustable solar shading system, however, we developed a second layer to this facade. The second layer is a lateral bifolding polycarbonate clad hanger door. It provides protection against excessive wind, and when lowered in the winter months, it introduces a thermal pocket against the glazed western wall. To study the performance of this operable double wall, we introduced temperature and motion sensors to the assembly (Figure 6). We measured and continue to measure temperature inside the cavity and the room against exterior temperature, taking into account the position of bifold hanger doors. The preliminary results suggest a temperature differential during the day that is up to 30 percent warmer in the cavity than the outside air, reducing conductive losses and maintaining higher surface temperatures on the glazed portions of the interior folding doors. Obviously, the system is dependent on incident solar radiation and does not offer significant insulating capabilities on cloudy days. Since the facade faces west and receives radiation in the afternoon on sunny days, however, this temperature differential persists into the evening after the sun has gone down, even though the cavity is open at the base and the polycarbonate and non-gasketed hanger door has little insulating value. These data suggest further lines of development, including separating the open two-story cavity into two single-story cavities to enhance the thermal stacking effect and introducing thermal mass into the cavity to store heat for the evening hours. In addition, we will experiment with drawing heated air out of the top of this cavity into the house interior, using the facade as a type of Trombe wall.

Research brings science to our art. Responses to place and program provide intuition to guide form. Research provides information and insight that enhances the performance of our intuitions. Architectural education rightly focuses on developing design intuition. To move the art of architecture forward, however, we need to supplement intuition with science. Research skills need to be brought to the center of the architectural curriculum, providing the basis for a cycle of continuous reflection, learning, and improvement. We need a deep research ethic to guide the art of intuition.

Is There Research in the Studio?

Kazys Varnelis
Columbia University and University of Limerick

This article surveys the development of the "research studio" in architectural education and examines its relationship to research, scholarship, and criticism.

Over the last decade, "research studios" have become common in schools of architecture. Investigating clothing, logistics networks, favelas, malls, airports, and cities worldwide, such studios invoke analysis rather than design as their method and aim for publication or exhibition as end products. But, as is often the case in architectural education, this pedagogical model has thus far has been little theorized.

Running from 1996 to 2000, Rem Koolhaas's Harvard *Project on the City* is the most well-known of these. Over the course of an academic year, teams of architecture students led by Koolhaas explored shopping, Lagos, the Pearl River Delta, and Rome (Figure 4).[1] Although Project is no exception to the prevailing lack of explicit methodological statements in research studios, by looking at its product, we can deduce a method. Research in these kinds of studios is architectural in so far as it draws on the processes of information gathering, analysis, and synthesis that an architect undertakes in the early phases of design, utilizing the architect's skills in structuring visual and verbal communication into a coherent whole.

But just where did the research studio come from?
In search of an answer, we might turn back to founding editor Turpin Bannister's "The Research Heritage of the Architectural Profession," in the first issue of the *Journal of Architectural Education*. Bannister traces a long tradition of research in architecture to the Renaissance, a lineage that he observes flourishing in the academies of the eighteenth and nineteenth centuries. Like scientists, Bannister notes, architects once came together in professional meetings and publications to share their discoveries and to receive input from others. But to Bannister's lament, in the latter part of the nineteenth century architects gave up their leadership in structural and technological innovation to engineers in favor of pursuing a purified art of design. With remarkable optimism, Bannister envisions the JAE as a key institution in renewing the role of the architect as researcher, capable of sustaining and encouraging such dialogue among architects.[2] Regrettably, Bannister's hope for the JAE is hardly borne out by the evidence of subsequent years. The agenda set out in Bannister's first issue of the Journal was immediately replaced by the publication of the proceedings of the annual meeting.

When articles began a decade later, they were largely polemics about where architecture should go rather than specific accounts of research projects.[3] Research and scholarship, as such, remained in the purview of the history of architecture, largely a subfield of the history of art or, alternatively, in the realm of architectural technology.[4] The sort of research studio that we are now familiar with would be absent in the academy for a considerable time.

By this point, however, two collaborative practices, that of Charles and Ray Eames and that of Peter and Alison Smithson, began to pioneer early forms of architectural research. The former gained experience in design research through their wartime experimentation with plywood and their work on mass production of plywood splints and plywood. Starting in 1953, the Eameses undertook a series of documentary films such as *A Communications Primer* (Figure 1) or *Powers of Ten*, sometimes for clients, sometimes for their own purposes. Often constituted as a rapid succession of images, these films produced what film critic Paul Schrader called "information overload" as a means of delivering one fundamental idea.[5] Ideas were central to the Eameses' films. Charles explained: "They are not really films at all, just ways to get across an idea." By contrast, Eames felt that more traditional architectural design had no hope as a medium for ideas since intermediaries such as the bankers, contractors, engineers, and politicians would "cause the concept to degenerate."[6]

Similarly, in Britain the Smithsons took the world "as found" as a point of exploration, exploring both the city around them and an equally compelling landscape of commodities and advertisements emerging out of postwar rationing. Influenced by Marcel Duchamp's practice of found objects, the use of photographs of industrial objects in early modern texts by Le Corbusier and Walter Gropius, the photographs of East London working class neighborhoods taken by Nigel Henderson, as well as the pioneering work of the Eameses, the Smithsons set out toward "a new seeing of the ordinary, an openness as to how prosaic 'things' could re-energise [their] inventive activity."[7]

The Smithsons' interest in the everyday life of the East End of London, together with their fascination with commercial images, was influential on a key architectural research project, Denise Scott Brown, Steven Izenour, and Robert Venturi's *Learning from Las Vegas* (Figure 3). According to Scott Brown, for a studio method she drew upon urban planning studios that she

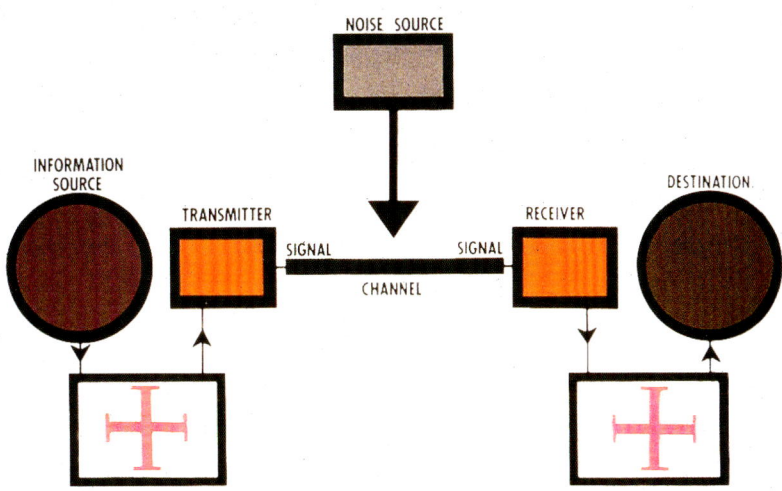

Figure 1. Still from Charles and Ray Eames, A Communications Primer, 1953. © 1953 Eames Office.

had taken at the University of Pennsylvania: "structured research, conducted in teams, with a teaching aim but also aims for research and artistic discovery."[8] Unlike the work of the Eameses and the Smithsons, *Learning from Las Vegas* was developed within an architecture studio and maintained a more systematic process of investigation into the city. If *Learning from Las Vegas* was a key moment in architectural research, it spawned relatively few followers, with the notable exception of Rem Koolhaas's own investigation, *Delirious New York: A Retroactive Manifesto for Manhattan*. In this work, Koolhaas drew upon the work of Scott Brown, Izenour, and Venturi, together with urban research studios run by O. M. Ungers into various aspects of Berlin, and used the "Paranoid Critical Method," which he appropriated from Salvador Dali, to blur the boundaries between research and fiction.[9] But like *Learning from Las Vegas*, which remained important mainly in urban planning studios, *Delirious New York* inspired few immediate followers in architecture.[10] Both texts would have to wait a generation for their impact to be felt.

Instead, the discipline turned the lens of architectural research in on itself, taking form as its subject of investigation. More compelling at the time than the work of Scott Brown, Izenour, and Venturi or Koolhaas, architectural historians such as Vincent Scully and Colin Rowe offered influential lessons in design pedagogy elaborating more specifically architectural methods of researching form.[11] "The Formal Basis of Modern Architecture," Peter Eisenman's dissertation under Rowe, undertaken in Cambridge and finished in 1963, is the epitome of this sort of work and, had it been published earlier, might have offered a certain kind of model to the discipline.[12] Driven by these early forms of research and by the impact of history and criticism in the studio, architecture began to adopt the trappings of reflexivity. In response, architects began to pose themselves as historians and even as theorists. Some, like Eisenman, went on to get doctorates, but as that demanded a considerable time commitment and generally required that architects study in history of art programs rather than in design studios, most did not. Under postmodernism, which reached its heyday in American architectural education in the mid-1980s, research into historical form and typology began to emerge as a significant aspect of design studios.

Apart from finding a home in the university, research—or at least more speculative production—was made easier in the postwar era by new granting organizations. The Graham Foundation, founded in 1956, and the National Endowment for the Arts, established by the U.S. Congress in 1965, encouraged research-oriented and speculative projects. For example, the Graham Foundation funded Archigram's *Instant City*, Robert Venturi's *Complexity and Contradiction in Architecture*, and Reyner Banham's *Los Angeles: Architecture of Four Ecologies*. The Institute of Architecture and Urban Studies in New York, which Eisenman directed, served as a key institution during this period, operating from both tuition and grants, supporting a variety of forms of architectural research such as Stanford Anderson's study of the street, funded by the U.S. Department of Housing and Urban Development, as well as Koolhaas's *Delirious New York*.[13]

By the 1980s, as interest in critical theory spread in the field—in large part through the Institute for Architecture and Urban Studies' journal *Oppositions*—architects began to identify the most advanced sites of architectural thinking with theoretical investigation instead of with urbanism or formal research.[14] As a result, by the late 1980s and early 1990s, studios that were largely textual in nature or that produced only representations began to proliferate in schools. If administrators and practitioners sometimes worried that such studios led to inaction or paralysis in the design studio and soon sought alternatives, these studios laid the groundwork for research studios in the vein of *Project on the City*.

To this incomplete narrative of the research studio's late emergence, we need to add the dimension of the critical. In a "theory backlash" in the pages of journals

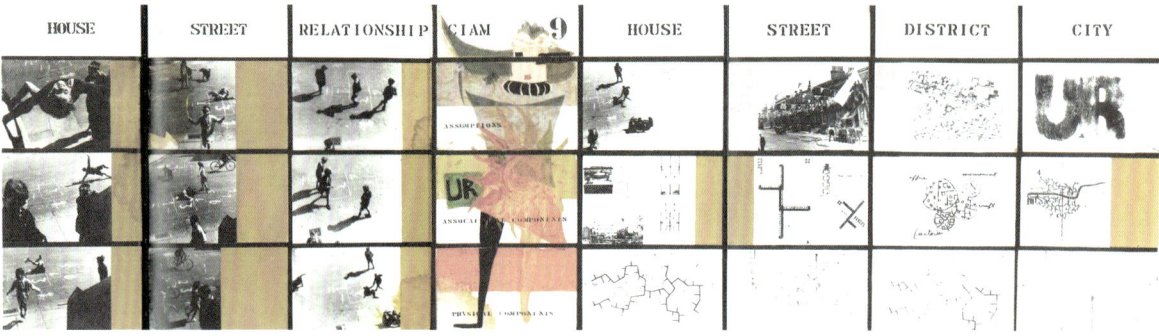

Figure 2. Peter and Alison Smithson, CIAM Grille. © 1953 Peter and Alison Smithson.

Figure 3. Robert Venturi, Denise Scott Brown, and Steven Izenour, Cover, Learning from Las Vegas. © 1972 The MIT Press.

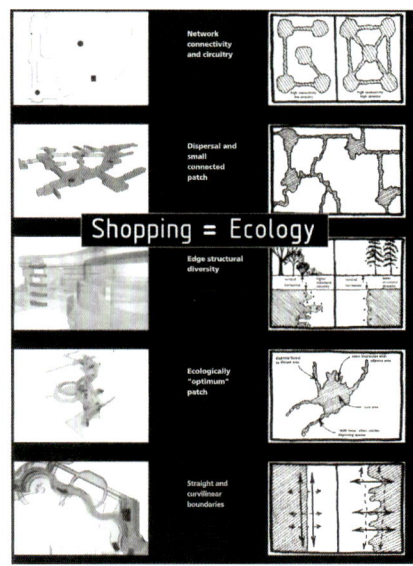

Figure 4. Harvard Project on the City, Shopping = Ecology from "Shopping" Mutations. © 2001 ACTAR.

such as *Praxis* and *Log*, as well as in a recent rash of symposia at schools around the world, criticality and theory have come under attack by the proponents of "post-critical" thought, or, as it has been more recently refigured, "projective architecture."[15]

To address post-criticism in a broader sense is beyond the scope of this article and even superfluous. Nevertheless, it is worth pointing to a certain alliance between post-criticism and the research studio in its origins in taking the world as found, be it in the relentless collecting of imagery by the Eameses or the Smithsons' appropriation of Duchamp. If historically derived from processes of appropriation, many research studios do eschew criticism in favor of information gathering. To some degree, *Project on the City* suffers from this, as Hal Foster has observed when he asked of the work, "great poetry can come of this ambivalence, but that may be all?"[16]

Scholarship in the research studio is, unquestionably, different from what we might expect in the classroom. Often, footnotes disappear in favor of images, and inhabiting the archive is replaced by surfing the web. But does the research studio merely co-opt processes of the history and theory seminar while abandoning methodology? Should we be hasty in dismissing its products as uncritical?

To be sure, any broader notion of scholarship in the university is hard to come by. Disciplines as radically disparate as dance, physics, English, sociology, public policy, law, mathematics, journalism, nanotechnology engineering, and Japanese language do not come together easily, most especially in cases of tenure review. When interdisciplinary interaction happens, it is against the grain of the university. Nevertheless, if we can identify a shared idea of what scholarship is in the university, it would be in terms of systematic research that produces a "contribution to knowledge."

But what sort of space does the research studio inhabit in the university? To be clear, a studio is a room in which an architect, an artist, a photographer, or dancer works. In other words, it is a place for the arts. Nor is "studio" an innocent term in the discipline as a whole.

Most architects work in offices. Only recent graduates and the self-styled avant-garde (generally those who teach in universities) work in studios. A research studio, then, aspires to systematic research, but of the sort that the avant-garde might undertake, not applied, or, if applied, promising radical results. Based on this, works of architectural research aspire not just to represent the world but to help us look at the world in a fundamentally new way.

Perhaps the best analogy we might have for the research studio is a return to the Eameses and the emergence of the architectural research out of film, in particular the documentary. To take some of the examples we invoked: *Powers of Ten*, to a degree approached by precious few works in any discipline, helps us reimagine the world anew from atom to the furthest reaches of the universe. The "as found" work of the Smithsons on the East End of London is a contribution to knowledge in that they used visual means to present something that was otherwise ignored and forgotten (Figure 2). No texts could be as compelling as the simple photographs and analyses they showed. *Learning from Las Vegas* and *Delirious New York* allowed us to see their respective cities, and indeed, the world, in fundamentally new ways.

This, then, is the question that research studios need to address, indeed it is a broader litmus test for architecture, be it postcritical, critical, or otherwise: How does it help us to re-envision the world anew? By this, architecture should not just add to the existing condition, either through replication of data, through nonlinear geometries, or exotic materials and structures, but rather it should make a contribution to knowledge. By its nature, this suggests that we should not go with the flow but rather redirect it utterly, remaking the terrain through which flows travel. If such a goal is somewhat immodest, I would nevertheless argue that the promise of such radical architecture is precisely what drives great architecture and great architectural research. To do any less would be irresponsible.

Notes

1. Pearl River Delta ran during the 1996–1997 academic year and Shopping from 1997 to 1998. In 1998–1999, teams were split between Rome and West Africa, and in 1999–2000 the dual-track investigation continued, the latter being narrowed to Lagos. Koolhaas has continued to teach various research studios, such as a project on Communism. Project, however, had a delimited run, four years to culminate in four books. Jeffrey Inaba lays out the history of the project and some of the thinking behind it—albeit without explaining the methodology involved—in "Maybe. The Harvard *Project on the City* asks 'Has the City Outgrown Architecture?'" in AMOMA/Rem Koolhaas, *Content* (Köln: Taschen, 2004), 256–257. It is worth observing that the Project publications were extensively reworked after the studios concluded.
2. Turpin C. Bannister, "The Research Heritage of the Architectural Profession," *Journal of Architectural Education* 1, no. 1 (1947): 5–12.
3. Literature on this period in pedagogy is still largely lacking, however; see Klaus Herdeg, *The Decorated Diagram* (Cambridge, MA: MIT Press, 1983).
4. The Society of Architectural Historians was founded in 1947 but only split its annual meeting from the College Art Association in 1973. See Osmund Overby, "From 1947: The Society of Architectural Historians," *The Journal of the Society of Architectural Historians* 49 (1990): 9–14.
5. Paul Schrader, "Poetry of Ideas: The Films of Charles Eames," *Film Quarterly* 23 (1970): 10. See also Beatriz Colomina's crucial work on the Eameses, largely collected in *Domesticity at War* (Cambridge, MA: MIT Press, 2007).
6. Charles Eames quoted in "Films as Essays" in Eames Demetrios, ed., *An Eames Primer* (New York: Universe, 2001), 143–44.
7. Alison and Peter Smithson, "The 'As Found' and the 'Found,'" in David Robbins, ed., *The Independent Group: Postwar Britain and the Aesthetics of Plenty* (Cambridge, MA: MIT Press, 1990), 201–202.
8. Denise Scott Brown in "Relearning from Las Vegas," interview with Hans Ulrich Obrist and Rem Koolhaas, *The Harvard Design School Guide to Shopping: Project on the City 2*, eds. Chuihua Judy Chung, Jeffrey Inaba, Rem Koolhaas, and Sze Tsung Leong (Köln: Taschen, 2001), 599.
9. Rem Koolhaas, *Delirious New York: A Retroactive Manifesto for Manhattan* (London: Academy Editions, 1978; republished by Monacelli Press, 1994). Koolhaas acknowledges the influence of *Learning from Las Vegas* on *Delirious New York* in "Relearning from Las Vegas," *Harvard Guide to Shopping*, 593.
10. See, for example, the work in John Colter and Mark Skiles, eds., *Off-Ramp* 6, especially Margaret Crawford as told to Mark Skiles, "My Daily Trip Down La Brea" *Off-Ramp* 6 (Los Angeles, CA: Southern California Institute of Architecture, 1996): 42–63, and Roger Sherman and Harrison Higgins, "Out of Order," *Off-Ramp* 6 (Los Angeles, CA: Southern California Institute of Architecture, 1996): 64–79.
11. Stanley Tigerman, "Has Theory Displaced History as a Generator of Ideas for Use in the Architectural Studio, or (More Importantly), Why Do Studio Critics Continuously Displace Service Course Specialists?," *Journal of Architectural Education* 46, no. 1 (1992): 48–50. This brief article is still crucial for understanding the recent trajectory of architectural pedagogy.
12. Peter Eisenman, *The Formal Basis of Modern Architecture* (Baden: Lars Müller, 2006).
13. Stanford Anderson, ed., *On Streets* (Cambridge, MA: MIT Press, 1986).
14. Jean-Louis Cohen, "L'architettura intellettualizzata: 1970–1990," *Casabella* 586–87 (January–February 1992): [100]–105, 125–26.
15. See *Praxis* 5 (2003), "Architecture After Capitalism," eds. Amanda Schafer and Amanda Reeser, and *Log* 5, (Spring/Summer 2005), "Postcriticality," guest editors Sarah Whiting and Robert E. Somol.
16. Hal Foster, "Bigness," *London Review of Books* 23, no. 23 (November, 2001), http://www.lrb.co.uk/v23/n23/fost01_.html (accessed November 29, 2001).

The Postwar Legacy of Architectural Research

Avigail Sachs
University of California, Berkeley

This article contributes to the current discussion of design as research by examining the ideological basis for the enthusiastic pursuit of scientific research in architecture in the postwar period. The concept of "research" was steeped in theory and ideology, but the research itself was shaped by the research economy—its policies and its institutions. Three very different case studies illustrate this phenomenon and demonstrate the importance of considering the research economy as a factor shaping the direction of architectural research.

Research, Idea, and Reality
How does design research contribute to architecture in theory and in practice? In September 2007, the *Journal of Architectural Education* (JAE) published an issue devoted to exploring that question: *Architectural Design as Research, Scholarship, and Inquiry*.[1] This collection of articles seeks to define a mode of scholarship and inquiry that is special to architecture—and one that is not adequately described in terms of "the scientific method." The editors, George Dodds and Jori Erdman, reject the "relatively narrow" understanding of the architect's role that is reflected in an "instrumental" approach to architectural research. This approach, they observe, "still commands much of the discourse, curriculum, research agendas, and funding initiatives at many architecture programs in both North America and abroad."[2] And they specifically cite the articles in the first issue of the JAE as instances of this narrow attitude (see Figure 1).

This article offers a different reading of the first issue of the JAE. Based on an examination of post–World War II archival material—at the American Institute of Architects (AIA) and the schools of architecture at Michigan and Berkeley— I conclude that the term research was used in the postwar period much as we might use the term "theory" today. The argument for scientific research in that period was in fact part of a wider argument about the nature of modern architectural practice and the future of the architectural profession in the United States. The ideal, in William W. Wurster's phrase, was to "broaden the base of the profession" by creating knowledge solidly based in science—that is, objective, impartial, and rigorous.[3] This knowledge, when disseminated and shared by members of the profession, would form a solid foundation for creative and even individualistic design processes.

Reginald Issacs, who taught landscape architecture at Harvard, clearly stated this point of view:

I do not believe that landscape architecture, city planning or architecture can call themselves professions unless there is a rapid increase from practically zero in the number of scholars in these professions. . . . Only through original research will there be a systematic and consistent contribution to knowledge in our professions. There are few self-made scientists in any field. The chance accomplishments of individual discovery is far too hit-and-miss to assure needed improvement of our professions. I hope to see half of the present faculty of the Graduate School of Design replaced by scholars—not by practitioners such as myself.[4]

Why then do we so often identify this work as narrow and practical? Part of the reason has to do with the fundamental changes that have taken place since the 1950s in the broader field of the philosophy of science. The postwar concept of scholarly research was firmly rooted in contemporary ideologies relating to scientific management, behaviorism, technological progress, and basic research. With the dismantling of "big science," especially in the social sciences, many of the underlying beliefs were discarded or openly attacked, leaving only a residue of methods that today seem alien and narrow.

Another reason—and this is the topic of this article— is that the idea of an architecture based on research—like any other human idea—was never realized in its entirety. The *idea of research* was never associated with a definite definition of research. But in order to create the necessary institutions to channel the new profusion of research resources that flowed through the postwar military-industrial complex, the nebulous term research had to be defined and molded into fundable projects. Architects adopted research methods originally developed in engineering, psychology, sociology, and other fields to lend credibility to their work. Architectural research came to be defined in terms of product development, building systems design, environment-behavior studies, and so forth. The case studies described in this article—the research programs at the AIA and at the Universities of California, Berkeley and Michigan, Ann Arbor—are but three of many examples selected to illustrate the extensive range of meanings that the ideal notion of research took on in the postwar years.

This process of institutionalization and its consequences has special relevance for us today. As the

September 2007 issue clearly illustrates, we are today once again in the process of defining and refining the *idea* of architectural research. Today's concept is very different from the postwar definition and in many ways is constituted in opposition to it. We also no longer work in the research economy of the postwar years, with its particular policies and funding opportunities. But in making our ideas of research a reality, and institutionalizing them in schools and firms, we operate within the research economy of today. As in the 1950s, this research economy will impose its particular methodological and ethical choices. By examining the dilemmas and choices of our predecessors, we can better recognize and understand some of the problems we will have to address as well.

"An Architecture Based on Research"

When Turpin Bannister, the editor of the first issue of the JAE—and like-minded colleagues, architects, and educators throughout the United States—called for the inclusion of research in architectural practice, they were not arguing, necessarily, for the "scientification" of the design process. They did not conflate research with design but rather distinguished it as a systematic exploration to yield generalizations that could be used by architects in a range of contexts (see Figures 2 and 3). The products of research, they argued, would place architectural practice on a shared and *proven* basis from which a truly modern architecture could emerge. Walter A. Taylor, director of the Department of Education and Research (E&R) at the AIA, wrote in the JAE, no. 1:

> Research, therefore, can supply the practitioner with a fundamental approach to his problem, and can either replace or confirm the intuitive and rule-of-thumb process that so besets us today. Research cannot reduce design to a formula, for design by its very nature is the final creative integration. Research could give the designer new resources that might conceivably sharpen and stimulate creative integration to a new height of clarity and effectiveness. We do not know positively, of course, because we have never had an architecture based on research, but it would be exciting to attempt it.[5]

The proponents of an architecture based on research conceived of research as a collective project, and they did not expect every architect to undertake research on his/her own. Instead, they advocated that the profession as a whole should pool resources to amass new and systematic knowledge and disseminate it widely. The schools of architecture were specifically charged with training future researchers who would undertake research for the entire profession. This ambitious vision bears all the hallmarks of a modernist project: it was based on the positivist assumption that the knowledge

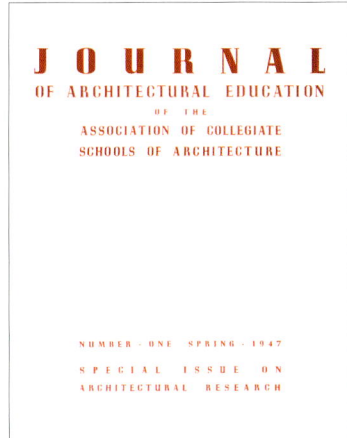

Figure 1. The first issue of the JAE, published in 1947, was devoted to research in architecture and advocated the introduction of the "scientific method" into professional practice. Courtesy Wiley-Blackwell Publishing.

produced in research was objective and widely applicable and therefore superior to knowledge derived from other pursuits. Robert McLaughlin, Dean at Princeton University in the 1950s, summed up this position well:

> It is not enough for the architect to attack each problem as an artist. He needs to have the knowledge of scientists, and no single architect can have that. The world of knowledge underlying architecture is too vast for the individual to encompass. How does the profession meet this problem? The method of science is the method of research: research for principles of architecture that, once encompassed, become the basis for rational design decisions.[6]

As Magali Sarfatti Larson argues, professions are social entities whose power can fluctuate: professions can both gain and lose their autonomy.[7] This means that professionals can make conscious (and unconscious) attempts to direct this process. In the postwar years, American architects were acutely aware of a professional crisis. The Great Depression and the wartime economy, when most construction all but ceased, had done more than deprive architects of work. Organized in small private offices, most architects were ill prepared to contract with public agencies. Working on New Deal and defense projects, architects found themselves collaborating more than before (work was divvied up so that more architects would be paid) as well as engaging in new types of building assignments, particularly housing and community planning. Although the postwar building boom alleviated the architects' most pressing problem—finding work—it was clear that it would not reverse the new social and economic conditions of practice. Many advocates of research, moreover, were

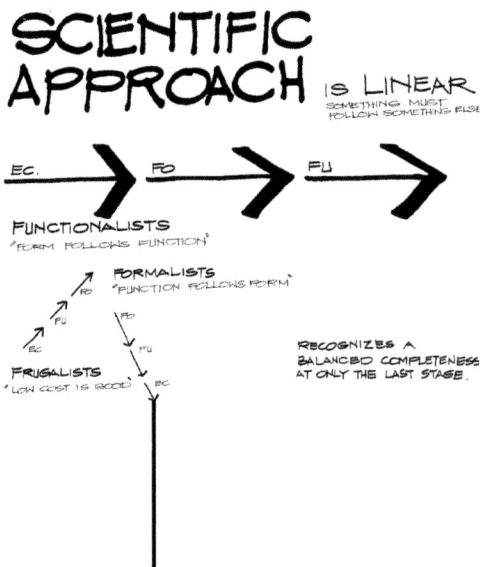
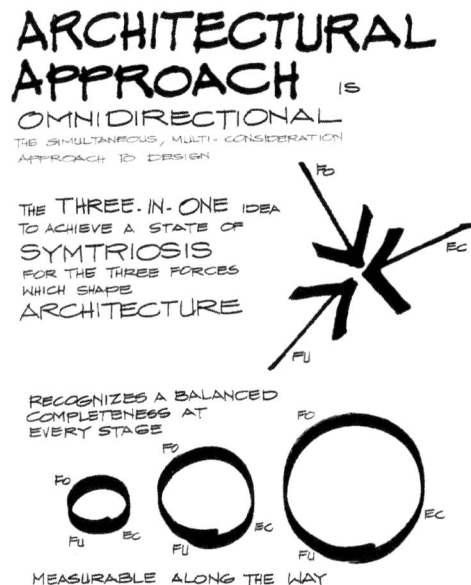

Figures 2 and 3. The Texan architect, William W. Caudill, was a founding partner of the firm CRS and strongly supported "research" in the firm and at TAMU. He did not, however, conflate research with design but rather saw them as distinct and complementary professional practices. Courtesy of the CRS Center, TAMU.

committed, ideologically and politically, to the continued involvement of architects in public work. The call for a research-based architecture was clearly connected to a call for a new (research-based) *architect* and a re-professionalization of the profession.

Subscribing to research, however nebulously defined, was the most expedient way to place architecture firmly within the American culture of professionalism.[8] Science, broadly defined, has always played a crucial role in the American professions' struggles over power, since—unlike their counterparts in Europe—American professions could not rely on guild traditions as a source of authority.[9] And now military victory, the product in part of the American technological superiority, served to consolidate and intensify a widespread American consensus in which scientific investigation was seen as crucial for further progress and a better societal order. This consensus was the basis for widespread investment in research throughout what Oliver Zunz has called an "institutional matrix of inquiry" that linked scientists in research universities, institutes of technology, corporate laboratories, and private and public foundations.[10] Often, it was enough to describe something as research to be able to command resources. Architecture schools, moreover, especially those located in the growing research universities, had to conform to some degree to the restructuring in their parent institutions.

Advocating a research-based profession was also a way to make a statement about the importance of housing as a topic for the profession. Housing, conceived as both a social and a technical problem, was a topic of research and fact finding as early as the late nineteenth century, and the connection between good housing and scientific (or quasi scientific) knowledge was further consolidated in the twentieth century. Architects had not ignored this development: as early as 1927, the *Architectural Record* advised its readers to adopt "the research method of science—observation, hypothesis, education, experimental verification."[11] Housing, however, remained on the periphery of the profession's interest, and only a few (albeit prominent) academic programs included the topic in their curriculum. The Depression and especially the New Deal forced architects to reframe their relation to the problem. Emphasizing research as a general field of inquiry over the more specific *housing* research was a way to further appropriate and "gentrify" the problem and place it squarely within architecture.

This focus on the social and community aspects of housing also reconnected architects with the postwar scientific disciplines of city and regional planning and landscape architecture. Similarly, the emphasis on the technical aspects of housing as a topic for research in architecture affirmed a connection between the architects and the building industry—the amalgamation of producers of materials, building systems, and prefabricated components. Research, particularly the development of new materials and systems, played a key role in advances in the building industry from the early twentieth century, and several of the more progressive industrialists were quick to establish research units dedicated to the development of new and more efficient building materials and systems.[12] Many individual architects were involved in this development as both employees and entrepreneurs. In 1933, for example, the aforementioned Robert McLaughlin established a company named American Houses, Inc.,

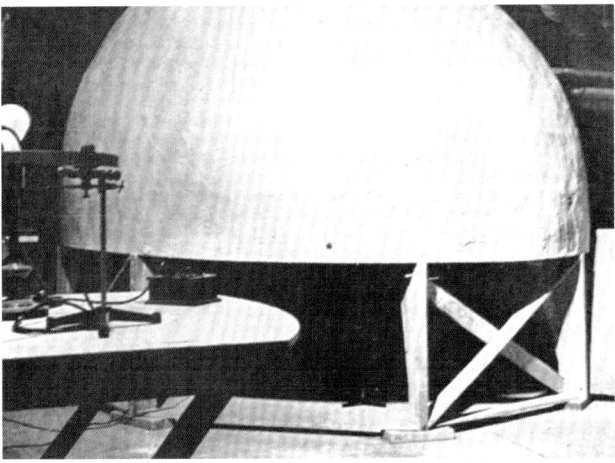

SKY LAB SHOWN HERE IS A PHOTOGRAPH OF THE 10-FOOT LIGHTING HEMISPHERE. MODELS APPROXIMATELY 20 FEET WIDE CAN BE TESTED IN THIS DOME WITH THE TESTING RESULTS BEING VERY SIMILAR TO THE NATURAL LIGHTING EFFECTS OF A FULL SCALE STRUCTURE.

WIND LAB PROFESSOR McCUTCHAN WITH STUDENTS STANS. BURY (LEFT) AND HINTON (RIGHT) ARE PREPARING THE TESTING SETUP WITHIN THE WIND LAB—AN OPEN THROAT WIND TUNNEL. THE CYLINDERS IN THE BACKGROUND THROUGH WHICH THE AIR FLOWS INTO THE TUNNEL FACILITATE LAMINAR AIR FLOW.

Figures 4 and 5. The Sky Lab and the Wind Lab at the TEES at the TAMU had an Architecture Division directed by Caudill in the 1950s. One of the projects undertaken in this division was a research studio in which the students tested their models of a classroom and documented the results of their "experiments." Gordon McCutchan and William W. Caudill, *Research Report Number 32: An Experiment in Architectural Education through Research* (College Station, TX: TEES, The Texas A&M. College System, 1951). Courtesy of Roland Chatham (photographer) and CRS Center, TAMU.

which became one of the leading prefabricators in the United States.[13]

Finally, for many of the proponents of an architecture based on research (and its corollary, collaborative practice), research was a way to signify their preference for adaptive pragmatic experiments over radical avant-garde innovations—in other words, a resistance to formalism.[14] As the proponents of research in architecture often made clear, they were worried that American architecture would fall back into the prewar pattern of eclecticism. They also feared that the codification and academization of European Modernism in the United States would lead to an eclectic rather than creative interpretation of International Style architecture. In their view, eclecticism was a characteristic of an individual artistic approach to architecture, the very practice they were working to replace in the re-professionalization project. William W. Caudill, a Texan architect and founding partner of the firm Caudill Rowlett Scott (CRS), was forthright on this issue: "I firmly believe that the greatest advancement in architecture will be made through research much more than through reading the Wright Bible or the Corbu Bible."[15]

Basic Architectural Research

The wartime Federal research policy was, by necessity, a top-down and centralized project in which the military set the priorities for new and continuing research projects. After the war ended, many Americans, Senator Harley Kilgore among them, felt that this centralized approach should be maintained.[16] If the products of research were to benefit the nation at large, Kilgore argued, the patents that resulted from Federally funded projects should belong to the agency that funded them, and those agencies should also have the authority to direct future research for the benefit of the entire nation. Kilgore was opposed by a powerful lobby led by the scientist Vannevar Bush, which advocated a decentralized and autonomous policy. Bush's postwar report, *Science the Endless Frontier,* outlined a system in which scientists (as experts in science) were given full responsibility to determine the scope of research projects and also retained the legal rights to their discoveries.[17] This position, with its emphasis on basic as opposed to applied research, prevailed, becoming a powerful part of federal research policy and setting priorities for many researchers.[18] This political and economic climate was the first to shape the argument for architectural research. In this research economy, there were both theoretical and practical values in defining *architectural* research that could be categorized as basic research and that was distinct from housing research. Much of the postwar discourse on research in architecture pertains to this ideological and pragmatic problem, but reaching a definition that would be both broad and precise proved as difficult then as it is now.

In order to define architectural research as basic research, it was first necessary to distinguish it from technical and fact-finding inquiries. The distinction between the two types of research problems was

Fig. 5. CONTRAST BETWEEN HOUSE BUILDING AND MOTOR-CAR MAKING
The disorderliness of a typical house assembly and the order of the production line of a motor-car assembly plant

Figure 6. A drawing comparing the building industry with the manufacturing of cars. Published in 1933, this drawing anticipated the central preoccupation of people in the building industry in the postwar period. Albert Farwell Bemis, and John E. Burchard, *The Evolving House* (Cambridge, MA: Technology Press of the Massachusetts Institute of Technology, 1933), 31. Courtesy of MIT Press.

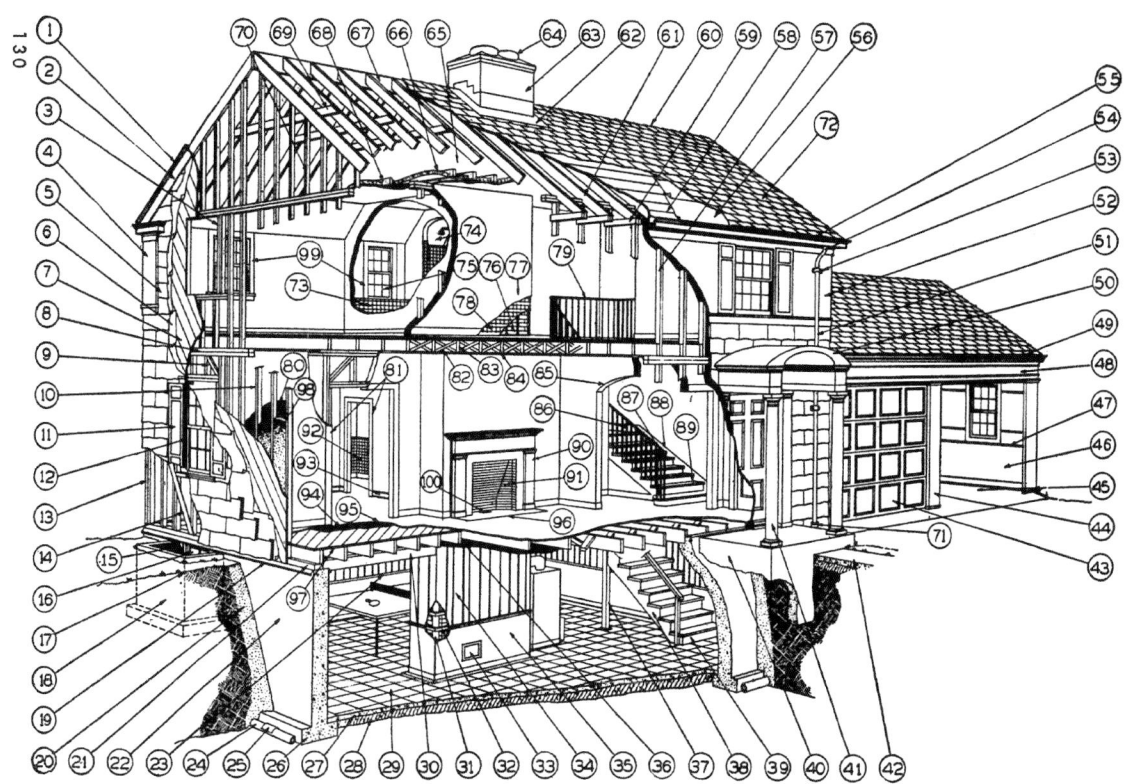

Figure 7. A guide to small houses that shows the range of building materials and systems that were being marketed to consumers. The Department of Education and Research at the AIA worked to direct the research and development in this field. Harold E. Group, ed., *House-of-the-Month Book of Small Houses* (Garden City, NY: Garden City, 1946), 130.

reflected in research proposals. In 1946, Caudill (who taught and engaged in research at Texas A&M University [TAMU] in addition to his work in the firm CRS) submitted a proposal for a project, promising that the results would be "exemplified in the actual construction of a LOW COST RURAL SCHOOL as a practical application of the ideas and recommendations formulated through this proposed research project."[19] Eight years later, however, he described his work in much broader terms as a project to define the parameters of "man's comfort," to use his term.[20] Caudill published the results of this work in the form of research reports under the auspices of the Texas Engineering Experiment Station (TEES) at TAMU, creating pioneer publications in the field of environmental studies in architecture (see Figures 4 and 5).[21]

This is the context for Taylor's preoccupation, in the first issue of the JAE, with the distinctions between "Free Fundamental," "Objective Fundamental," and "Applied Research."[22] In an attempt to create a unique position for architects, Taylor argued that architectural research is often of a composite nature: even though it included pragmatic solutions, it was "more"

than merely applied research. Taylor also defined the architect as "a technologist who specializes in the human aspects of the problem," and he added, "I believe that this is broad enough to include everything from aesthetics to air conditioning and city planning."[23] Taylor's discussion of research was made available to a large audience when it was included in the 1954 report, *The Architect at Mid-Century*, written and edited by Bannister.[24]

In 1956, the E&R published its own report on architectural research and gave this definition:

> Architectural Research encompasses areas of building research for which the architectural profession is best qualified to accept responsibility. Architectural Research deals primarily with problems of function and form in buildings and their surroundings. It thereby includes research in planning and research in esthetics.[25]

As this example suggests, many definitions of architectural research remained tautological and contributed little to a better understanding of its nature. But by the 1950s, the idea of architectural research had gained enough support that a common definition of architectural research was not essential. Even without clear disciplinary boundaries (few disciplines are clearly defined after all), architects could draw on postwar resources to build a disciplinary apparatus—a

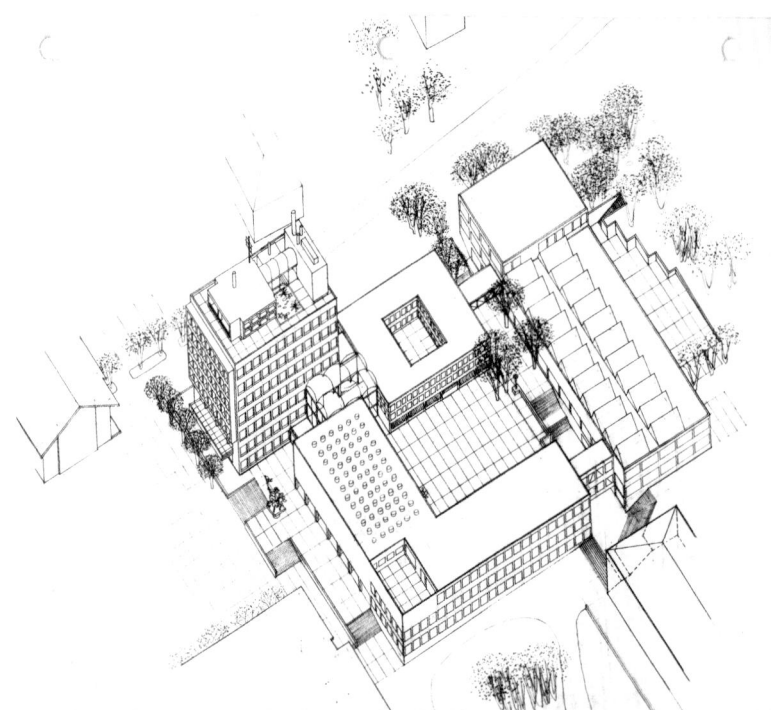

Figure 8. Proposal for Wurster Hall completed in 1964 for the CED at University of California, Berkeley. Architects: Esherick, Olsen, and DeMars. (Source: Joseph Esherick Collection (1974-1), Environmental Design Archives, University of California, Berkeley.)

set of institutions that could receive money, materials, and equipment and distribute them to individual researchers. Architects had a choice between setting up a professional organization and making use of existing institutions—the schools of architecture—and shaping them to suit their needs. In the postwar years, architects did both. A third route was to collaborate with other researchers especially city and regional planners, social scientists, and engineers—and partake in their disciplinary power. Architects followed this route as well, hiring social scientists in architectural firms and linking departments of architecture with planning and landscape architecture. In each of these routes, architectural research took on different, specific and practical, meanings.

The Department of E&R at the AIA

The AIA established the Department of E&R in 1946 as part of a larger reorganization of the Institute. Taylor, the appointed director, had (as we have seen) an ambitious vision for architectural research, and he was a staunch supporter of a research-based practice. His goal was to establish architects as the leaders of the factory-based building industry. In a memo written circa 1946, Taylor wrote optimistically: "It appears that many members of the profession and many interests outside of the profession look to The Institute, and particularly to the Department of E&R to create an active program of reporting, investigating and research."[26] The AIA did provide some support for the Department's initiatives, but Taylor and his colleagues relied on the building industry for major funding. They even lobbied the Producers Council (one of the representatives of industrialists) to pay the director's salary![27] More than this, Taylor and his colleagues saw their work as a service to society and argued that "because society as a whole will benefit through research for better shelter and environment, it should contribute major support through foundations, government agencies and elements of the building industry that are dependent upon the public for markets."[28]

Measured against these ambitious plans, the E&R achievements were very few, mainly due to a shortage of funds. In 1949, the Department set up an advisory service to act as a "listening post and reporting agency, clearing house and coordinating center, and the instigator of needed activities."[29] The AIA service, however, did not endorse the products developed through the research conducted under its auspices. Without such an endorsement from the AIA, corporate businesses in the building industry looked elsewhere for a safer return on their investment, either within their own research departments or in the academy. Moreover, the Advisory Service was rapidly dwarfed by the work of the Building Research Advisory Board, a private, nongovernmental, nonprofit organization under the auspices of the National Academy of Sciences. In 1954, Taylor and his staff conceded to this larger entity and discontinued their own service.

In its heyday, the Department of E&R launched a project to gather knowledge in a field in which it could claim some monopoly: architects' assessments of new building materials and processes. The Department plan called for this information (or "findings") to be filtered through "publications" as well as the AIA standing committees to the Department itself, where it would be organized and systematized before being disseminated to AIA members and the general public. The AIA had expanded considerably in the immediate postwar years, and it had not only the voluntary work of AIA committee members but also full-time personnel to assign to the project. In the 1950s, the Department published in the AIA Bulletin such documents as technical or "building type" reference guides, bibliographies, and special technical articles. Though the scheme was neither efficient nor systematic, it did reflect the organization of knowledge in many architectural firms and was firmly rooted in the profession's norms and needs. Caudill, for example, was an enthusiastic supporter of this plan:

> We believe that if the architects can in some way carry out a continuous research program within their own offices, if only on a very small scale, good advancement can be made. We also believe that if architects will exchange ideas, and will unselfishly work towards improving our architecture, the profession will be much better off.[30]

Caudill and his partners made serious efforts to incorporate research into the work of their own firm, CRS.[31] Their scheme, in fact, bears a strong resemblance to Stephen Kieran's description of a profession structured around a kernel of research.[32] But, as Caudill complained, this project was supported, and therefore also controlled, by the design work done in the firm: "when we are busy we cannot spare the personnel; when we are not busy we cannot afford research."[33] Caudill's comment also points to the snag in the AIA program. Although cooperation and collaboration were seminal ideals in the profession projected to emerge from the reprofessionalization project, the existing profession was based on *competition* between private practitioners—and the AIA apparatus was not strong enough to overcome these internal differences. The AIA continued with its efforts to collect practical knowledge, but as early as 1973 the authors of the AIA Research Survey acknowledged that architects, both in schools and in firms, did not recognize the need to share information and that there was a gap between the two realms.[34]

The AIA project, based as it was on outside resources, was also thwarted by a circumstance beyond its control. The project relied on continued growth in the demand for factory-made homes—but by 1948, revised lending policies limited the buying power of many home consumers. Industrialists and builders were faced with an array of problems, in production and distribution and from local building codes and zoning laws, and they were unable to develop the industry to the level envisioned at the end of the war. Moreover, standardized housing was often rejected by members of the building trade unions and by banks which refused to finance experimental ideas. Prefabrication also became associated with impermanence, and as the success of Levittown, New Jersey, made clear, Americans wanted mass-produced houses that did not look as if they had been made in a factory. With the market uninterested in the E&R project and the AIA unable to provide full financial support, the goal of creating a central research agency within the profession was stalled and never realized in its entirety.

The School of Architecture at Berkeley

If the AIA favored a centralized policy that focused on applied research, the School of Architecture at Berkeley represents the opposite extreme. (The School later became the College, and it is now an academic Department.) Wurster, appointed dean of the school in 1950, was emphatic in his interpretation of research as a decentralized project. In 1959, for example, he wrote this in response to the proposal of establishing a position of director of architectural research at the AIA:

> I feel that the appointment of such a Director might well be contrary to the very idea of research and would do more harm than good. … The appointment of a Director would lead Foundations to believe that architects were primarily interested in the development work rather than basic research. A true research approach is based upon the freedom of dedicated individuals to pursue their particular research interests and not in a directed program.[35]

At Berkeley, Wurster and his colleagues were supported by a generous university policy and were free to devise a research program on the model outlined by Vannevar Bush. Postwar Berkeley was in many ways an ideal institution in which to experiment with such research projects and policies. The University of California, benefiting from the enrollment of numerous students funded by the GI Bill, had deep reserves that allowed for long-term planning.[36] The Berkeley campus was also able to draw on considerable federal funding for research projects. Though the natural sciences, especially nuclear physics, attracted most of the federal and military investment, the top administration at Berkeley, led first by President Sproul and later by President Kerr, made and adhered to a policy of sharing the money throughout the university to benefit the less lucrative departments. Both presidents also warmly backed the fundamental changes in the School of Architecture.

The first major change was to create the College of Environmental Design (CED), an umbrella institution that combined the School of Architecture with two planning and research departments: Landscape Architecture and City and Regional Planning. Wurster and Catherine Bauer, his wife and colleague at Berkeley, had begun advocating the combined school soon after they joined the faculty, but the CED came into being only in

Figure 9. A Youtz Nine Unit House, developed at the University of Michigan as illustrated in a report written for the War Production Board, Washington, DC, in 1944. George G. Brigham, Final Progress Report on Experimental Investigation in Connection with a Study of the Youtz System of Construction, Washington, DC, Ann Arbor, MI: Office of Production, Research and Development, The War Production Board, Washington, DC. Department of Engineering Research University of Michigan, Ann Arbor. Submitted to Industrial and Consumer Products Branch, Office of Production, Research and Development, War Production Board, 1944. Foldout illustration.

1959. The proposed college, and even more so its name, had become the focus of protracted debate over modern architecture, design, planning, and the connection between them. The Planning and Landscape faculty feared that aligning with architecture, a *design* field, would undercut the special position of *planning* and would undermine the connection between the Department of Planning and the Social Sciences and between Landscape and Agriculture and Forestry.[37] Wurster and others worked hard to convince the majority of the faculty to support the new institution and to bring architecture closer to these related research traditions, and they were ultimately successful (see Figures 8).

The second major change was the development of a comprehensive research policy. The departmental research committee, which was staffed in rotation so that almost all faculty members had a say, adapted the university research regulations to architecture to produce a sixty-page policy manual outlining how research was to be encouraged and supported. The committee recommended that faculty seek extramural funds, but it also worked to secure funding from the university, to provide incentives for researchers, to protect their freedom of choice of topics for research, and to support the collection of data (especially through collaborative projects) so as to avoid duplication. The emphasis on individual responsibility, however, precluded writing a concise definition of architectural research. Instead the policy includes several pages of discussion of what is and what is not included in "systematic and deliberate investigation seeking to add to the body of knowledge of architecture."[38]

Wurster and his colleagues also made the appointments needed to support the new research policy, particularly the position of assistant research architect. Ezra Ehrenkrantz, the inaugural appointee, combined teaching and research with the administrative work of setting up the program. In 1960, the department research committee processed and approved eight research proposals that were then forwarded to the University Committee on Research.[39] In the same year, Ehrenkrantz and others sought to expand the research program beyond the borders of the United States by preparing a program for research in India and applying for grant money from the Ford Foundation and the Government of India. The faculty at Berkeley also initiated the first graduate program based on research rather than design. A 1956 draft proposal for the program was explicit: "The graduate program and the research activity will be very closely related although not synonymous. Graduate students and faculty in all options will be encouraged to participate in research connected with their main effort."[40]

The architectural research program at Berkeley in the 1960s, thriving in the climate of continued investment in research, contributed widely to the discussion of architecture. As an institution, it fared far better than its AIA counterpart, but this continuity came with a price. As the research program developed, so did a *discipline* of architecture that is separate from the *profession*. On the one hand, many sources of academic funding lie outside the purview of the profession, and on the other, the discipline is organized by the priorities of academic life at least as much as by professional requirements.

Figure 10. The Unistrut building system on the cover of the University of Michigan Research News. C. Theodore Larson Papers 1930–1985 [bulk 1951–1974], Bentley Historical Library, University of Michigan.

Figure 11. The Unistrut building system featured on the cover of a Unistrut Products Company brochure. C. Theodore Larson Papers 1930–1985 [bulk 1951–1974], Bentley Historical Library, University of Michigan.

This outside dependency has exacerbated the distinction between research and design as separate intellectual processes and contributes to the larger concern about the gap between the architecture schools and the profession. The original plan for the CED called for inter- and intra-professional collaboration that would counterbalance such divisions, but as with the profession as a whole, such collaboration has proved to be easier to project than to accomplish.

The Architectural Research Laboratory at Michigan

The architectural research program at the University of Michigan, unlike the programs at the AIA and Berkeley, was rooted in prewar housing research undertaken in the department. Michigan began offering courses on housing during the Great Depression when it established the Home Planners Institutes to help Michigan citizens build affordable housing. During the war years, the school collaborated with the Engineering department to conduct two projects sponsored by the National Housing Agency and implemented through the Office of Production, Research and Development of the War Production Board. After the war ended, Dean Wells Bennet appointed C. Theodore Larson as a faculty member charged with overseeing and directing research initiatives in the department. At the same time, the architecture faculty updated the school's bylaws to reflect the importance of research.[41] In 1949, the department went further and established the Michigan Architectural Research Laboratory (ARL) so as to provide individual research projects with central organization including clerical and accounting services.[42]

The ARL was one of the centers that attracted projects originating in the building industry. A notable example was the Unistrut School Construction research completed under Larson's direction and initiated by Charles W. Attwood, an alumnus and the president of Unistrut Inc., a company specializing in building systems. Attwood asked Larson to research the application of the Unistrut modular housing system in the construction of school buildings, a market he (like Caudill) wanted to penetrate. Larson explained: "The object in research has been the development of a standardized system of low-cost schoolhouse construction offering a high degree of durability, flexibility, expansibility, demountability and reusability."[43] Thus, the project was in reality a hybrid between a design project and a more generalized research project, though it was completed on the university campus. The products of this project—construction drawing and specifications—were published as research, and the building itself housed the Lab until it was dismantled in the 1970s when the School of Architecture moved to another campus (see Figures 10 and 11).[44]

The Unistrut project, like other research undertaken at Michigan, exemplified work that benefited all the participants. Attwood received the information he needed to further his business, and the university acquired a building at base cost, while gaining practical experience for faculty members and students. Such projects allowed the school to sustain a vigorous and diverse research program, albeit often responding to needs outside the profession. Its diversity is evident in the 1957 research policy: "Architectural research can be defined as comprising all those studies that are aimed at discovering new factors that should be considered in the planning and design of buildings and communities."[45] In 1961, Dean Philip Youtz concurred stating: "I don't think that it is an either-or matter but rather a question of emphasis."[46] This diversity of goals as well as means is not a problem in itself, but it does raise questions about the scope and nature of *architectural* research, as compared, for example, with housing research.

In Retrospect

Each of the institutions discussed in this article—the Department of E&R at the AIA and the schools of architecture at the University of California and the University of Michigan—were headed by avid supporters of the idea of an architecture and architectural practice based on research. These academic leaders worked hard, along with their colleagues, to implement and institutionalize those ideas. As the case studies demonstrate, the meaning, nature, and scope of architectural research was shaped not only by the research policy adopted but also by the research economy of each of the institutions. In each case, the source of funding for research projects—with whatever "strings" were attached to it—together with the means chosen to disseminate research findings shaped a different conception of what architectural research should encompass and how it should be undertaken.

But what of the future? As the "Architectural Design as Research, Scholarship, and Inquiry" issue of the *Journal of Architectural Education* (2007) demonstrated, architectural research is today once more a topic of discussion and consideration. As such discussions become more elaborate and concrete, we need to remember the experience of the postwar research program. Most importantly, we must recognize and understand the research policy and economy in which we practice and include this understanding in our consideration of goals and objectives. A definition that does not take these realities into consideration will produce an "ideal" research program that is just that—ideal but unreal. This is a difficult problem, since an apparatus for architectural research must balance between centralized and decentralized models of research, between individual and group goals, and between competing policies, methods, and types of knowledge. A system that balances all these considerations is perhaps beyond our reach, but we should surely inquire into the nature of such a system and the implications of the inevitable trade-offs that reality requires. Such a collaborative system must depend on discourse. It is well, then, that the JAE has opened the door to a sustained discussion.

Notes

1. The issue was an extension of a Special Focus Session at the 2007 ACSA Conference. The issue was co-edited and the session co-moderated by JAE Executive Editor George Dodds and JAE Design Editor Jori Erdman.
2. George Dodds and Jori Erdman, "Introduction," *Journal of Architectural Education* 61, no. 1 (2007): 4–6.
3. "President's Report Issues, 1944–1945," *MIT Bulletin* 81, no.1 (1945): 138.
4. *Landscape Architecture in Practice and Education Discussion for the American Society of Landscape Architects' Annual Meeting June 28, 1954.* Institute Archives and Special Collections, Hayden Library, MIT Collection, Architecture Dean Papers AC 400 Box 3 Folder School of Architecture and Planning Policy 3/3, Cambridge, MA, 1 (emphasis added).
5. Walter A. Taylor, "The Schools and Architecture Research," *Journal of Architectural Education* 1, no. 1 (1947): 25–39.
6. Robert W. McLaughlin, *Architect: Creating Man's Environment* (New York: McMilllan Company, 1962), 118.
7. Magali Sarfatti Larson, *The Rise of Professionalism: A Sociological Analysis* (Berkeley, CA: University of California Press, 1977), XV.
8. Burton J. Bledstein, *The Culture of Professionalism: The Middle Class and the Development of Higher Education in America* (New York: Norton, 1976), 80–128.
9. Elliott A. Krause, *Death of the Guilds: Professions, States, and the Advance of Capitalism, 1930 to the Present* (New Haven, CT: Yale University Press, 1996), 29–36.
10. Olivier Zunz, *Why the American Century?* (Chicago, IL: University of Chicago Press, 1998), 5–23.
11. Gwendolyn Wright, *USA*, Modern Architectures in History, edited by Vivian Constantinopoulos (London: Reaktion Books, 2008), 82.
12. Burnham Kelly, *The Prefabrication of Houses: A Study by the Albert Farwell Bemis Foundation of the Prefabrication Industry in the United States* (Cambridge, MA, and New York: Technology Press of the Massachusetts Institute of Technology and John Wiley and Sons, 1951), 21–25.
13. Colin Davies, *The Prefabricated Home* (London: Reaktion Books, 2005), 54.
14. Wright, *USA*, 152.
15. Letter to Mr. Walter A. Taylor, Director, Department of Education and Research, AIA from William W. Caudill, dated June 19, 1952. The AIA Archives Box 431S, Washington, DC, 1.
16. Daniel Lee Kleinman, *Politics on the Endless Frontier: Postwar Research Policy in the United States* (Durham, NC: Duke University Press, 1995), 6–7.
17. Vannevar Bush, *Science the Endless Frontier: A Report to the President on a Program for Postwar Scientific Research* (Washington, DC: United States Government Printing Office, 1945).
18. Roger L. Geiger, *Research and Relevant Knowledge: American Research Universities Since World War II* (New York: Oxford University Press, 1993), 19–29.
19. Letter to Dr. A. A. Jakkula, Acting Head, Engineering Experiment Station, A&M College of Texas, from:

William W. Caudill Re: Request for Research Project dated 1946. Caudill Papers, CRS Archives, CRS Center, Texas A&M University, College Station, TX.
20. Letter to Mr. Bartlett Cocke, Secretary-Treasurer, Texas Board of Architectural Examiners, from: William W. Caudill Re: Interpretation of Practical Experience dated September 27, 1952. Caudill Papers, CRS Archives, CRS Center, Texas A&M University, College Station, TX.
21. For example: William W. Caudill, Sherman E. Crites, and Elmer G. Smith, *Some General Considerations in the Natural Ventilation of Buildings* (College Station, TX: Texas Engineering Experiment Station, 1951), 1–43.
22. Walter A. Taylor,"The Architect Looks at Research," *Journal of Architectural Education* 1, no. 1 (1947): 13–24.
23. *The Continuing Educational Process: Remarks at the Southeastern Regional Meeting of the Association of Collegiate Schools, Atlanta, Georgia, Saturday, April 24, 1948*. The AIA Archives Box 478S, Washington, DC, 5.
24. Turpin C. Bannister, *The Architect at Mid-Century: Report* (New York: Reinhold, 1954), 408–413.
25. *Special Report #4: A Statement on Architectural Research by the AIA Committee of Research*. The AIA Archives, Box 311S, Washington, DC, 1.
26. *Expanded Program*. The AIA Archives Box 199S, Washington, DC, 12.
27. AIA, Committee on the Structure of the Institute, "Foreword Concerning Facts of Report of the Committee on the Structure of the Institute," *The AIA Bulletin* (January 1946): 1–2.
28. *The Plan of Research for the American Institute of Architects* (September 8, 1959). The AIA Archives, Box 410S, Washington, DC, 4–5.
29. Memorandum Re: Organization and Functioning of Department of Education and Research, AIA. The AIA Archives Box 442S, Washington, DC, 1 (February 1, 1947).
30. Letter to Mr. Walter A.Taylor, Director, Department of Education and Research, AIA from William W. Caudill, 1.
31. Avigail Sachs, "Marketing through Research: William Caudill and Caudill Rowlett Scott (CRS)," *Journal of Architecture* 14, no. 1 (2009): 737–52; Paolo, Tombesi, "Capital Gains and Architectural Losses: The Transformative Journey of Caudill Rowlett Scott (1948–1994)," *The Journal of Architecture* 11, no. 2 (2006): 145–68; *Research as a Competitive Positioning Strategy: A Case Study of CRS*, 85th Annual Conference Meeting of the Association of Collegiate Schools of Architecture, March 15–18, 1997.
32. Stephen Kieran, "Research in Design: Planning Doing Monitoring Learning," *Journal of Architectural Education* 61, no. 1 (2007): 27–31.
33. CRS Memorandum to Tom Bullock and William Pena from William W. Caudill, dated October 9, 1959 Re: Research Program. Caudill Papers, CRS Archives, CRS Center, Texas A&M University, College Station, TX.
34. AIA, *The American Institute of Architects Research Survey* (Washington, DC: American Institute of Architects, 1973): 1.
35. Letter to Mr. Walter Campbell, Chairman, AIA Research Committee, dated February 26, 1959. Records of the College of Environmental Design. Office of the Dean William W. Wurster Collection, Environmental Design Archives, University of California, Berkeley, CA.
36. See Geiger, *Research and Relevant Knowledge*.
37. Only one architecture faculty member went on record with outright opposition, but many of the practicing architects in the Bay Area raised their voices. Minutes of Faculty Meeting February, 10 1959, at 8:15 AM, Cork Room. Records of the College of Environmental Design, Dept. of Architecture Faculty Minutes 1957–1981 Collection, Environmental Design Archives, University of California, Berkeley, CA.
38. *Policy Statement on Architectural Research for the Department of Architecture of the University of California, January 1959*. Records of the College of Environmental Design, Office of the Dean William W. Wurster Collection, Environmental Design Archives University of California, Berkeley, CA, 7.
39. Memo to: Faculty, Department of Architecture, From: Sami Hassid, Chairman, Research Committee, Ezra Ehrenkrantz, Research Coordinator, Subject: Yearly Report to Faculty, dated May 20, 1960. Records of the College of Environmental Design, Office of the Dean William W. Wurster Collection, Environmental Design Archives University of California, Berkeley, CA.
40. *The Graduate Program in Architecture A Report to the Faculty of the College of Architecture by the Graduate Program Committee*, Environmental Design Archives, University of California, Berkeley. Records of the College of Environmental Design, Office of the Dean William W. Wurster Collection, Berkeley, CA.
41. *College of Architecture and Design Memorandum (The Research Laboratory)*. A. Alfred Taubman College of Architecture + Urban Planning (University of Michigan), Records 1878–1999, Bentley Historical Library, University of Michigan, Ann Arbor, MI.
42. *The Architectural Research Laboratory and its Future Development*. A. Alfred Taubman College of Architecture + Urban Planning (University of Michigan), Records 1878–1999, Bentley Historical Library, University of Michigan, Ann Arbor, MI.
43. *Research Project: Unistrut School Construction Project M811*. C. Theodore Larson Papers, 1930–1985 (bulk 1951–1974), Bentley Historical Library, University of Michigan, Ann Arbor, MI.
44. Nancy Ruth, Bartlett, *More than a Handsome Box: Education in Architecture at the University of Michigan 1876-1986* (Ann Arbor, MI: University of Michigan College of Architecture and Urban Planning, 1995), 81–83.
45. *Report for October 1957*. A. Alfred Taubman College of Architecture + Urban Planning (University of Michigan), Records 1878–1999, Bentley Historical Library, University of Michigan, Ann Arbor, MI.
46. Letter to the Members of the ACSA Research and Graduate Studies Committee: Professors Gourley, Hanson, Nichols and Wurster dated December 18, 1950. Records of the College of Environmental Design. Office of the Dean William W. Wurster Collection, Environmental Design Archives University of California, Berkeley, CA.

Environment

100
1955
A New Look at Civic Design
Kevin Lynch

103
1962
The Purpose of the City
John B. Jackson

105
1962
The Ecology of the City
Ian McHarg

107
1974
Review: Defensible Space by Oscar Newman
W. Russell Ellis

109
1976
The Urban Landscapes
Elizabeth Blackmar

113
1977
Observations on Energy Use in Buildings
Richard Stein

119
1981
Commencement Address
Aldo van Eyck

121
2007
Compelling Yet Unreliable Theories of Sustainability
Kiel Moe

Environment
Sara Stevens

There is nothing stable about the word *environment*. Over the course of the journal's first seventy-five years, authors used the term to convey a variety of meanings. While from our contemporary position we perhaps regard the term as a dated or awkward reference to the climate crisis or the Anthropocene, it also reminds us of the politics of the environmental movement of the 1970s. The term *sustainability* later came into vogue in architecture and has been joined by *resilience* more recently. But as a lens to study the shifts in the field of architecture and architectural education over the course of the last eight decades, *environment* has a depth and richness that involves and also cuts across questions of urbanism, technology, ecology, building energy performance, and most tellingly, the use of the social sciences in architecture and the very nature of what it is to design. The eight essays that follow elucidate the changing meanings of the term, collectively attempting to draw boundaries around the discipline of architecture, testing the limits of what are, and what are not, its methodologies, its allies, and most importantly, its expertise.

The weightiness (arguably the clunkiness) of the term *built environment* is also at stake in this theme. But before *built environment* became a normalized term, Kevin Lynch wrote about the human environment, suggesting something like a nineteenth-century biologist's use of the word, synonymous with *milieu*—the biological material within a proximate zone. For Lynch, writing in 1955, the task at hand was "humanizing the city," which for him meant creating "a sensuous environment for human beings so that one feels at ease, is adequately stimulated—so that there is a sense of mutual adjustment and response between the individual and the urban environment in which he [sic] lives." This soft approach to understanding urban conditions reflects, in part, a reckoning with the functionalist-driven approach of modernist design that was typical of the time. Seven years after Lynch's piece, a special issue on urbanism contained the articles by J. B. Jackson and Ian McHarg included here. Lynch's ideas were refined as part of an attempt to broaden the idea of city to emphasize the vernacular as a counter to any overemphasis on high design. Still relying on the milieu-like meaning of *environment*, these articles reflect a shift in concerns. In his article "The Purpose of the City," Jackson presents a catholic interpretation of what constitutes urbanism through an accessible rendering of wide historical swaths: Baroque, Romantic, contemporary. For McHarg, in contrast, in his article "Ecology of the City," the biological is even more present: dissecting different landscape types, pulling them apart to layer them up like slides under a microscope.

By the 1960s environmental design came into favor as a way to broaden the field of architectural design to also include landscape architecture, planning, and urban design. It also served to broaden methodologies that aligned design fields with social science. Environmental design's expansive capacity was tested in the 1950s and early 1960s, and by the mid- to late 1960s, it began to express a more political positioning of the role of the discipline of architecture, enlarging its territory of expertise. While architecture was seen as a *designed* object, the environment was instead presented as a thoroughly *researched* phenomenon that could be "defended" by architects' social and technological expertise. As evident in the "Research" section of this book, the use of social science to bolster the research agenda of architectural scholars grew quickly from that impulse to legitimize and expand the field and, in one high-profile case, backfired. W. Russell Ellis's biting review of Oscar Newman's book *Defensible Space*, which fanned interest in a new subfield of the discipline and aligned with the efforts of the Environmental Design Research Association (EDRA), heavily critiqued Newman's poor application of social science to the built environment, questioning the biological determinism that some social science applications in the field tended toward. As fast and as totalizing as the rise of social science was in the discipline, those who questioned it managed to stay only a few paces behind.

By the 1970s the term *environment* denoted a pluralism of meanings: environment as the urbanism around a building, environment as the biological milieu, and environment as the psychosocial conditions of human existence. Another aspect joined these: the (interior) environment as a set of measurable physical conditions, which, when suboptimal to human comfort, should be probed for technical solutions. Representative of this thread is Richard G. Stein's article "Observations on Energy Use in Buildings" (1977), which called for a focus on improving environmental performance through systems management but already began to question whether the most cutting-edge technological fixes were the right approach. Inherent to this conception of environment is the idea that interdisciplinary approaches sit at the core of architecture: even a pure engineering solution is insufficient without tempering through a synthesis of lenses. Here too is the alignment of technical/engineering solutions to the perceived conflict between weather (rain, water, sun, heat, cold), architectural materials and assemblies, and human comfort that would form the foundation of the ideology of sustainability that would so dominate later decades. More humanistic approaches, especially as related to urbanism, run throughout the journal, where Elizabeth Blackmar in "The Urban Landscape" (1976) echoes J. B. Jackson's call a dozen years earlier for consideration of synthetic and historical approaches to understand the dynamics of urban change and spatial analysis.

Despite the repeated calls for synthetic and interdisciplinary approaches to research and a consistent interest in the term *environment*, the journal seems to reflect a lack of awareness of the biggest threat to the environment yet: human-caused climate change. The word Anthropocene appears only very recently. Sustainability, despite being a leading area of research in allied technical fields, has always been viewed askance in the JAE. Kiel Moe's article "Compelling Yet Unreliable Theories of Sustainability" (2007) both typifies and overcomes this interpretation. In it, he critiques typical narratives of sustainability, intending to remove the limitations—by reintroducing the milieu—they set to approaches to environmental problems in architectural research. Elsewhere in the JAE published design proposals seem far from sufficient to the challenge and engage more at a rhetorical level. Measured by what has been published in the journal, the discipline's response to the challenge is incommensurate. And yet some surprisingly early pieces raised enduring questions. For example, Aldo Van Eyck's commencement speech at New Jersey Institute of Technology, published in 1981, called for deeper thinking about the planet. Van Eyck relied on an expansive definition of environment, as "the great and only place in which we all live," describing humankind's deplorable treatment of the planet as resulting in a "pathology of landscape," which most saw fit to ignore. Despite unmatched "technological and scientific ability," the world he saw seemed unable to solve "the problems survival in any given environment posed," and unlike previous societies, people of his day were unable to find balance with the environment. Nor were they able to "extend collective behavior into adequate, often beautiful, built form." The problem of environment was as overwhelming then as it is now. Yet Van Eyck ends with an undeniably political call for "solidarity," one that perhaps still holds promise today.

A New Look at Civic Design

Kevin Lynch
Massachusetts Institute of Technology

The city is a very ancient kind of human environment. It has a history of five or six thousand years, perhaps longer, and in almost all that time the city has been the center of civilization. But, nevertheless, it is only very recently that the city has, in a new way, become the dominant type of human environment. It has become, in some of the more advanced countries, the typical environment, the one in which it is most common that people live and work. It is only very recently that it has become not only a center of consumption, a center of control, but also a center of production—the major part of production.

It is only very recently that it has set the style for almost everyone in the ways of life, in the products used, in the scale of things which seem most important. Two-thirds of the population in this country now live in cities, and we estimate, whether you like the prospect or not, that perhaps by the end of the century ninety per cent of the population of this country will live in urban areas.

Then, as all know, there have been tremendous technological and social changes which have brought an entirely new form to the city, have made it entirely different from what it has been for a long time in the past. This city has many kinds of important effects. It has economic effects. It has social effects. It has biological effects. But I only mean to speak this afternoon about one particular effect: the sensuous impact of the city on the individual—in other words, the look, the sound, the smell, the feel of the modern city.

This impact certainly is a very complicated one, one that we don't know a great deal about. Sometimes it almost eludes analysis, but we have a good deal of evidence that it has a powerful effect and, moreover, that this effect has a certain amount of regularity and similarity between many people of widely varying backgrounds. For that you only have to note how often in conversation and in literature the reference to the physical city comes up, and also, I think, to note the surprising consensus as to what particular cities in this country people find pleasant, what cities people would choose to live in if they had a choice.

I think that most people will characterize the city, in large part, as ugly, inhuman, exhausting as a place to live in, and so on. This is rather strange, rather peculiar, because the city, after all, is our most artificial environment. It is the one which is to the greatest extent man-made, and, therefore, one would assume most suited to men and most pleasant to men. Obviously, something has gone wrong.

The whole city, the physical city, has many analogies with architecture, taken in the more usual sense—with the individual building or a small group of buildings. But it has certain differences that I think must be understood first if you are going to talk about it. The city environment is a very complicated one, made up of different parts—its buildings, its roads, utilities, transportation ways and so forth—and it is encompassing in time and space. It completely surrounds the person to a great depth so that he only experiences it over time; it is also an environment very likely associated with his whole life, and thus his associations color each thing he sees.

It is seen generally as a complicated thing, made up of many parts. It is seen generally in a fragmentary way, in a succession of pulses, perhaps connected together, perhaps disconnected. And perhaps one of the most salient facts about it is that it is most often seen by a moving observer, so that time sequence is one of the key characteristics of the way in which we perceive the city.

Furthermore, it is not the work of any one man but the product of a great number of people, whether they work in a coordinated fashion or not: a product of many wills, many decisions, constantly in change, constantly in process.

I think most of us at one time or another, when we were not so occupied with other things, have had the experience—the rather disturbing experience—of actually seeing the city, of actually looking at it and sensing the disturbed and chaotic forms out of which it is made. Luckily or not, this, I think, is a rather rare occurrence. More generally, the city is experienced as a subconscious irritation or perhaps a drain on nervous energy and only infrequently as a meaningful or pleasant experience.

We have perhaps a few hints of the great delights that a fine city can bring. These appear fragmentarily in our contemporary cities or, more likely, in half-alive museum towns left over from an earlier time. That these are great delights cannot be denied: the great city which has one character and one feeling, the possibility of meaning or fitness in urban forms, the thrill of contrast and vitality in the city, all of these things which we so rarely experience and only have a hint of in our present day cities.

It seemed to me then that we are faced with the job of humanizing the city. By that I mean to adapt it as a sensuous environment for human beings so that one feels at ease, is adequately stimulated—so that there is a sense of mutual adjustment and response between the individual and the urban environment in which he lives.

Architecture has some of the responsibility for carrying out this job. As Professor Perkins has mentioned, there are other groups that have an important part to play, but certainly the architect has a most important role. One of the first steps is that both the designer and the general citizen must begin to see the city, to actually look at it. And this usually comes only when we begin to do something to it, when we begin to enter into some kind of active relation with it.

In our case the active relation may vary from just a simple attempt to describe it graphically or verbally, all the way to a major rebuilding job. It is only when a person begins to think, to do something about the city, that you begin to appreciate what kind of environment it is. Indeed, I think it is very likely that one of the principal reasons that the city is felt to be an inhuman place is not so much because of any particular color or forms or surfaces that it happens to contain—it is the fact that there is very little active relation between the inhabitant and the city he lives in.

The forms that make up our city, the ordinary buildings, the streets and so on, are, in great majority, forms that no one ever intended, imagined or conceived, no one ever thought through. This is immediately revealed in the kind of forms that come into being.

The next step is that the citizen, in order to survive in this kind of an environment, has to shut his eyes to it. The environment gets more and more out of control in the visual sense, and finally, the inhabitant simply despairs of any control at all. He cannot in any way manage this chaotic setting into something that really fits his own life. It is probably symptomatic that we concentrate on the interior of the house, as though we are lining our nests in an alien world. So many Americans spend their time and their care on the interior of the house rather than on the city street.

It is an interesting fact that when we do come to design the city consciously as professionals, we are likely to feel a certain poverty of the imagination. The range of forms we work with, the range of forms we choose from in making a piece of civic design is quite limited in comparison with the wealth of forms that the designer uses, thinks about and works with when he comes to a single building. And I suspect that this poverty of form is also a result of the fact that we so rarely really look at a city or rarely do anything to it, that only with an active attempt to work on the city will we come to a richer vocabulary, if you wish, of what city forms could be.

Clearly this subject above all cries out for attention and study. What we know about it, I think, is quite limited. A great number of individuals, a number of schools, a number of practicing architects have become extremely interested in the subject of the sensuous form of the city and are beginning to think about it and are beginning to work on it. Perhaps you know that at M.I.T. we have just begun a three-year study on the visual form of the city and we hope that this may be one start in this direction, among many others.

The subject has an immediate meaning for the architect even when he is putting a single building in the city. He has to know that his building takes effect not as a single impact but is part of a whole. The building he puts in will exist in time and will become part of a continuous process of change. Very likely it will have many unintended effects due to the setting in which it is placed. It is important that we try to understand and try to predict what those effects will be.

For example, take the sense of what I call warmth in the city. This is a subjective feeling of a citizen toward his environment that it is comfortable, that it is human, that it almost talks or responds to him.

In this sense, in our modern cities, we fail with rather monotonous regularity. Or in an attempt to correct it we very often turn to using superficial variety or try to turn back to primitive forms or "cozy" forms. And sometimes, in despair, we romanticize decay itself. It seems to me that real warmth in the physical environment comes from several things. In the first place, and this is speaking in a general sense, it rises from forms that show human care and adaptation, and which have been worked out so that they fit the human activities and functions that are going on within them. This is the kind of pleasure that we get from a well-kept garden, for example.

Warmth comes from the signs of life in the city, things which we intimately associate with human action—perhaps laundry, perhaps benches, perhaps curtains on the windows, many things of this sort—and comes particularly, I think, in an environment which allows the individual to make his own mark, his own impress on the physical surroundings. Mind you, I don't say that this means that every person must have a totally different house. You can show your individuality either by a new or entirely different kind of house or perhaps by a different doorknob. Most people can identify their own car very quickly and very readily despite the standardization of the general shape.

I think that warmth also comes in the city from the use of distinctive forms. In other words, forms around which association can gather, a door which has a particular color, a house a peculiar shape, so that you can identify your own life and make your own associations with a distinct physical form. It comes certainly from the proper use of scale; it may come from many other things. But these are the things that occur to me. This quality of attachment and warmth, then, which is so important in our urban environment, seems to arise in a setting which makes human activity both apparent and significant. It is then important for us to try to find out, and we must try to analyze, what it is that will give this quality, what it is that can be done by physical means.

These physical means, of course, are neither the only nor the most important method for creating this quality of warmth. Indeed, in general if I want the general citizen to participate in the city environment, participate in the making of it and in the enjoyment of it, I must use both physical and social means. Incidentally, the process of doing this, the process of participation, may be equally as important and perhaps sometimes more important than the physical end result.

It seems to me that it is up to the architect to begin to grasp the pervasive effect of the city, to begin to operate on it consciously, to see how it colors his own work, and, in reverse, to see how his own work colors the entire setting. I should like to repeat that I have been talking only about the sensuous impact. There are many other impacts of the city, economic and social, of which the architect must also be aware.

In teaching architecture, then, there must be a constant stimulus to the student to become aware of the city and of his responsibility toward it. We must encourage the architectural student to actually look at the city—and this may be for the first time in his life. It can be done by getting him to do a job of simple observation or recording, graphic or written. Or you make more careful studies of the total physiognomy of an area, taking one area and studying all its sensuous aspects and how they interrelate with its functions.

In design you would give problems which emphasize the setting of a building or of a group of buildings in an urban scene. And in particular, I should think it would be important to make clear that it is just as senseless to make a perspective or a model or a study or drawing of any kind of a building which doesn't show the surrounding works of man and doesn't take into account their probable changes. It is just as senseless to do that as to make a model that doesn't show the contour of the ground, the topography on which the building will be set.

I think the students can be set to analyses of their own subjective reaction to the visual scene of the city and perhaps to developing kinds of techniques, techniques of representation and special study which will emphasize those effects and bring them under control in the process of design itself.

Certainly the student has to be made to look on the form of the total physical environment as a continuous process, which, being a process, involves time effects, is strongly influenced by the way in which a thing is built or created, and which involves interaction of many different people.

So then it seems to me that we need to understand the complicated and dynamic nature of the sensuous environment in the city, and to draw as many people as we can into the process of making it and of using it. Perhaps thereby we may be able to do something which has only very rarely been achieved in history: that is, the production of a city which as a whole will be a delightful, human environment, which will be a great collective work of art.

The Purpose of the City

John B. Jackson
Landscape (magazine)

By contrasting the Baroque, the Romantic and the Contemporary city landscapes, it is possible to approach some understanding of the urban landscape which is evolving around us and the role which every urban landscape plays in our lives. For each landscape, urban or rural, represents a unique way of organizing space and activity in order to achieve a desirable purpose.

The Baroque City Landscape
It is customary to define the Baroque Age as the years between 1550 and 1750 corresponding to the rebirth of Rome the city. In the middle of the sixteenth century, Rome was fast coming to life after generations of neglect and decay. The new cathedral of St Peter was at last being built. The popes took pains to beautify and enlarge the city, and in the older quarters as well as on the surrounding hills splendid palaces, churches, villas and monuments were rising. Noble families came to live in Rome and in their wake came countless artists and architects, painters and sculptors, actors and writers and musicians, and, of course, a vast horde of tourists, adventurers and students.

By the end of the century the population had tripled to become one hundred thousand. Everyone in Europe who wanted to acquire polish, and at the same time enjoy himself, found his way to Rome during the winter season where probably the most entertaining aspect of Rome was Rome itself.

From early in the morning until dark the city resounded with a bewildering assortment of activities, engaged in by people of every class and age and origin: vendors of fruit and cold drinks and sausages, marionette players, beggars, fashionable sightseers, and constant processions of priests, soldiers, visiting celebrities, weddings, funerals and the carriages and sedan chairs of the rich.

Pageantry of this sort must have been fascinating to watch, but a rich and varied street life, like that of any European city of the period, means that there was actually no other place for these activities. The Baroque city did not provide its citizens with small private or specialized areas. All but the very rich lived in crowded and promiscuous quarters, and even the rich lacked the secluded living rooms, patios and studies our houses possess. When a Roman of the Baroque Age wanted to converse with friends, or when he had business to transact, the street was the best place to go.

The street scene in Rome also constantly reminded the citizen that he lived in a strictly ordered, hierarchical society, a society organized according to rank or class or grade or birth. Much of the Baroque landscape was designed to dramatize this principle. The Baroque parade, like the Baroque public spectacle, was a visible demonstration of social purpose and order: the succession of participants, building up to a climax, was not only a matter of art but of a social hierarchy. A pope's birthday celebration, the funeral of a cardinal, the anniversary of a saint, an important wedding or funeral were very intricate organizations of precedence and rank. Wherever the citizen looked, wherever he went, he was reminded of a permanent order behind an apparent confusion.

In theory this strong sense of a social order means that the city itself should have been divided according to classes, but in the Baroque city there were, strictly speaking, no specialized quarters for the rich or for the poor; they were all together. The Baroque city was looked upon as a society of buildings, and perhaps it was the appearance, the design of the buildings, which indicated their social standing, rather than their location or function.

Many traits of the Baroque Age seem to be coming back to life and are being deliberately fostered. I myself happen to admire its formality, its vigor, its humanism, but I think we should take a second look at its shortcomings. The emphasis on a hierarchical rather than a functional organization of society was hostile to any easy growth or change.

Secondly, the disregard for private life reflected little or no understanding of the importance of interior existence, speaking psychologically as well as architecturally, with the result that the age which came after it went to the other extreme and emphasized the individual experience, the individual environment, at the expense of the whole city landscape.

The Romantic City Landscape
We are familiar with the usual textbook explanations for the rise of the Romantic city: the beginnings of democracy, the rise of capitalism, the dawn of the industrial revolution, the introduction of sentiment and emotion into art and the rediscovery of nature. I myself feel that beneath all these changes was a change in the way men defined themselves. They were disenchanted with their identity as social beings and began to see themselves as more or less unique individuals, each privileged or obliged to make his own adjustment to the surrounding world. People lost interest in traditional man-made public areas and started, very tentatively at first, to create a whole series of small individual worlds for one specific purpose only.

The most obvious instance of an urge to create and control a small private environment is the rise of the suburb with its freestanding house. In the middle of the eighteenth century this became a noticeable movement; and Paris was among the first cities where it occurred. Hitherto that city had been typically Baroque. Then, with comparative suddenness, the well-to-do middle class and the aristocracy decided to desert their palaces and mansions in the crowded downtown section cheek by jowl with tenements, taverns, workshops, stables, lodging houses, and began to build houses in the new western section where the Etoile and the Champs Elysees and the Parc Monceau are now located. The older part of Paris abandoned by the wealthy became a slum, which much of it still is.

The result of the migration to the suburbs was a division of the city for the well-to-do into two distinct parts: a residential part and a business part; and when railroads and large industrial installations came to Paris the working class experienced the same division. As we all know, these divisions in the city multiplied in the course of the nineteenth century.

A characteristic of the Romantic city was its cult of nature which we have to thank for our parks and public gardens and for the introduction of greenery into our cities. We can also thank that phase of the cult for much of our finest painting and poetry and music, but the cult of nature had another, less fortunate aspect; the nation and the city were looked upon as spontaneous organisms which men were to respect and admire but not seek to control, for nature was working toward her own inscrutable ends.

It is not hard to point out the faults of the Romantic city landscape. The period is still too near to have acquired the charm of antiquity. Because we are now in the midst of seeking a new form for our cities, we are particularly aware of the obstacles presented by our Romantic heritage: slums, decaying downtowns, congested streets, the formlessness and immensity of every contemporary city.

The city landscape we have inherited is far uglier than the one inherited by our Romantic forebears; but we should in fairness observe that today's modern city is also incomparably rich in diversity of experience. Whatever its horrors, it is capable of producing self-awareness and a more intense individual existence.

The Contemporary City Landscape
The beginning of the Contemporary city was sometime immediately after World War II. It is far too early to distinguish the form it will take, but since I happen to be one of that old-fashioned breed that believes there is a meaning to history, I will not hesitate to say that the future will be in many ways a continuation and amplification of the past. Let me mention two characteristics which seem to me to be typical of the Contemporary city landscape.

Certain traits of the Baroque city seem to be reappearing in a twentieth century guise. The most obvious of these is a renewed interest in planning with its heightened awareness of esthetic factors in the city landscape, a coming together of architecture and urbanism and a realization that planning is very much involved with how people work and live and enjoy themselves.

Another aspect of our Contemporary city landscape that resembles the Baroque is a fresh emphasis on the spectacular, the representational. The impact of advertising is by no means confined to the printed word; it not only lines our highways with billboards, it lines our streets with elaborate commercial or promotional architecture institutionalizing commercial firms and humanizing public institutions.

Finally, there is a growing revival of mass pageantry—world's fairs, monster rallies, and sporting events. I question the possibility of reviving the Baroque street scene in the USA because the public is no longer the same. For better or for worse, the average European or American has become largely independent of the street. The notion that we can lead any significant part of our lives in public is an agreeable one but unrealistic. This is not to say that public gathering places are not needed, but they must be adapted to our less extrovert society.

The solution as I see it is not a series of pedestrian malls or more parks or sidewalk cafes or shopping centers or any neo-Baroque revival but a totally new kind of public gathering place. We are not a homogeneous group; we do not derive pleasure from people as such, but rather we tend instinctively to form groups of compatible persons. I strongly suspect that the new kind of public gathering place will be highly specialized, enclosed, well-defined areas, excluding by some kind of psychological barrier the enormous heterogeneous public.

There are two aspects of our Romantic tradition which show few signs of disappearing. The modern city remains divided into many distinct quarters, each with its own type of activity. There are many critics of the urban landscape who deplore this compartmentalization, but it seems to be strongly entrenched in the modern city scheme.

The other is the feeling for the sanctity of the individual and the individual environment expressed in the fact that half of the population of this country now owns its own home.

It remains for the future to reconcile these two very different tendencies: the neo-Baroque desire for public amenities and socially directed design and the Romantic desire for the isolated experience in the isolated environment.

An analogy to the biological theory of differentiated and integrated animal societies suggests at least two of the choices in urban philosophy which confront us now. The virtue of the differentiated society is order and beauty and power; the chief virtue of the integrated society is simply that it produces more and better individuals. It exists not as an end in itself but to improve the conditions of life and the possibilities of self-fulfillment.

There is nothing new in this concept of a society of specialized beings. This has been the one increasing purpose of our history: to grow in self awareness and to acquire a richer identity. It is the role of the contemporary city to carry the process one step further: to show that it is only within a humane social order that the individual can achieve self-fulfillment, not in Romantic solitude, not in Baroque subjugation to the common will, but through an active relatedness to others.

The Ecology of the City

Ian McHarg
University of Pennsylvania

Cities are probably the most inhumane environments ever made by man for man. It is taking the best efforts of modern medicine and social legislation to ameliorate the abuses which the physical environment imposes upon us.

With all the improvements which have occurred during the last century in the social environment, the physical environment has not proportionally improved but has absolutely retrogressed. We plan with a surfeit of economic and social determinism and not enough other criteria. I would not diminish them as determinants, but certainly they have to be qualified by others as well. In looking for other determinants of urban form, I have found the views of the natural scientist, particularly the ecologist, most illuminating.

The ecologist is concerned with ecosystems: functioning interacting systems composed of organisms and their environment. The ecologist has developed the conception that we are covered by a web of life, a biosphere, with all life on the planet interacting. One can think of the entire world as a world-life body in which all organisms, all species, have a role, which is comparable to the cell and to the organ within the human body. The minute one takes a view of this sort, one is immediately proscribed from gouging, hacking and destroying because the conception of the whole world-life body as being interacting somehow induces some restraint in self-mutilation.

Such restraint is supported by the knowledge that all organic systems are by themselves depletive. Any single organic system would simply deplete the resources of the world and be extinguished. Man, of course, is a depletive organic system. In order for organic systems to work, there must be reciprocity. Somebody's waste is that which you consume, that which you dispose of as waste is that which something else consumes. This is called symbiosis.

The ecologist is further concerned with succession, i.e., a development and adaptation in time. The ecologist has the possibility, as an inheritor of the Darwinian-Wallace tradition of evolutionary biology, to see the relationship between process and form in a clearer way than anyone else. Architects used to say "Form follows function." This was a kind of a manifesto, always illustrated by inorganic systems like utensils and planes and rockets. This was all right as far as it went, but if one notes that this was being proclaimed at a time when Darwin had existed for almost a century, and sciences like morphology and zoology and biology and botany had been well advanced, it was, in retrospect, a kind of infantilism.

If one looks at organic systems, I think one would have to adapt the statement and say "Form expresses process" or better still, "Process is expressive." Zoology, morphology, botany and biology are all based on the presumption that the adaptation of the species, the role of the species and the location in terms of the environment can be determined from the aspect of the species and its adaptation to the environment.

One of the most beautiful examples is a simple deciduous forest. The distribution of the plants, the shape of the plants, the relative size of the plants, the periodism at which they flower and fruit is vastly expressive. Indeed one could determine almost all the important things about the distribution and flowering periods of the plants by their actual shape. That which tends to be seen as a sort of undifferentiated green has specificity and is an extraordinarily expressive statement of a highly ordered system.

A compressed example where process is expressed very clearly in form is the formation of a sand dune. The entire process from beginning to mature dune covers only about twenty-five years. When the beach has an inclination of five to ten per cent, wave action will deposit particles of sand. A sand bank, or island, is gradually formed and when it reaches a height of nine or ten feet, marram grass volunteers. The dune is progressively stabilized by a succession of vegetation, sometimes including live oak and pine. The ecologist can identify all the elements of vegetation in terms of the limitations within which they can exist (salinity, brackish water, exposure, etc.) the environments to which they have adapted, the association of these plants, and also their succession. Here is something which seems to me has absolutely enormous relevance. One can see in the function of all of these variables, a form which is totally expressive.

Examination of a Region
There is one larger process which is less complete than the examination of the dunes, i.e., the examination of a region. Confronted with the necessity of land-use planning for the Delaware River basin, our study group selected the cycle of water as a device for examination. Besides the cycle of evaporation and precipitation, one can specify places where horizontal movement of the water occurs. The intrinsic functions of the forested upland sponge, the agriculture piedmont, the estuary marsh, the underground aquafer, the aquafer recharge area, the rivers, the streams, the flood plains and the riparian land can be identified, their areas can be demarked. Each is expressive of its particular role or process. One could immediately conclude something about the degree of

permissiveness or nonpermissiveness of these particular functions, relative to other functions.

If you take an area like the Delaware River basin and locate all of these areas, suddenly you find that you have covered something in the nature of fifty or sixty per cent of the whole region and you also find that you have produced something like a negative development map. Before you locate new towns and developments anywhere you like on the basis of some economic determinism, let's add this parameter to your planning! Look and see what intrinsic functions actually occur in this supposedly undifferentiated green space and see the degree to which these intrinsic functions can co-exist with the development which you propose.

I have a sense that if the best common knowledge of biology, ecology, and oceanography, which has permeated landscape architects like myself, had been operative on the Jersey shore, there would have been no catastrophe in March 1962 at all. It was only the gross stupidity of breaching the dunes, destroying the vegetation and building on top of the dunes which produced the catastrophe. In the Delaware River basin some conception about the demarcation and the intrinsic functions of open space will tell you the degree to which it is permissible to alter the existing balanced environment.

But coming to the city is another problem. I am thoroughly scornful of that which proposes to be city planning and spend the best part of my time indicating that which is supposed to be the highest and best good of civilized man and his fine transformation of nature toward his own ends, but I'm not certain how to do any better. I have only little bits and pieces taken from several scientists which I believe are worthy of our consideration.

Pathologists doing studies with rats in extensive environments have produced some quite astonishing information. They place breeding couples in a superabundant environment in which they produce big, healthy litters and they're happy, and they eat and they populate and everything is fine. Then, as the population begins to reach half its maximum (there is a maximum determined not by available food and water but by density and social pressure) "pathological togetherness" occurs. A whole lot of subordinate animals emerge which just cower in corners and are bitten by other rats. The size of litters diminishes really quite startlingly. There is cannibalism, intrauterine resorption, and the birth rate falls down dramatically.

Diminution of Population
Hardly has this been recorded when something else happens. One finds the adult animals start being prey to all sorts of diseases. This is what really gives one pause, because the diseases they get are absolutely identical in kind and in number and distribution to those of twentieth-century urban man. As a result there is such a diminution of the population as to frequently lead to extinction.

Now man, in cities, has devices by which he can ameliorate social pressure, but, nonetheless, I think the correspondence between the kind of diseases and the distribution of diseases in these rats (they're not dying from TB, or pneumonia, or dysentery; they're dying from cancer, lung disease, kidney disease, heart disease and they are prey to neurosis) and twentieth century man is startling. As density increases, stress increases; from that the susceptibility to disease increases; and reproductive capacity falls.

The next bit is atmospheric ionization. All combustive processes produce positive ionization. In normal countryside it tends to be about 70/30 negative/positive and in the cities almost the opposite, 70/30 positive/negative. There is no doubt at all that this positive ionization has physiological and psychological effects. It inhibits the capacity of the organism to reject the carcinogenic elements which combustion also produces among others.

Sensory Overload
Then there's sensory overload. Lynch and Luckashoff showed that there are so many stimuli in the city that most people simply disdain them all. Studies at Eastern Psychiatric Hospital in Philadelphia show that many people confronted with sensory overload respond by filtering out this sensory overload to a point of suffering hallucinations from sensory underload. If our physical environment is so anarchic, so disordered, that people have to filter out in order to survive, this is an extraordinary castigation of the form of the city.

Then there are such things as smog, temperature inversion and the carbon dioxide cloud. We may all be increasing our tolerance to these, but honestly, I don't know that there are so many compensating advantages to justify it. Why don't we get rid of carbon monoxide?

The simple idea of South Sea Islanders, that you should plant ten trees when every child is born, makes awfully good sense for people who depend on oxygen. The knowledge that a fountain produces negative ionization is a wonderful bit of knowledge when one realizes we tend to suffer from too much positive ionization. If stress is a basis for susceptibility to disease and the instance of many diseases, then we must seek the form of the city which will reduce stress, with the possibility of maximum tranquility and introspection.

We mustn't subscribe to life-inhibiting processes. By accepting the form of the city and the processes of the city that do exist today, we are, indeed, doing this. I don't think it's the proper fulfillment of our own role that the city can only exist because of the best advances of medicine and social legislation. We must be certain that architecture and landscape architecture and planning don't subscribe to perpetuating and increasing that which is life-inhibiting. We must find a modern city that is not an eighteenth-century city with gouges and additions and unacceptable grafts, but truly a modern city.

I suggest that there may be some analogy, some insight and, perhaps, even the possibility of finding form from process, through the perceptions of the ecologist.

Review: Defensible Space by Oscar Newman

W. Russell Ellis
University of California, Berkeley

Oscar Newman, *Defensible Space: Crime Prevention Through Urban Design* (New York: The MacMillan Co., 1972)

This is a preliminary review resulting from work on a larger critical review. If you have read the book, I welcome your response.

For some time now serious architects have proposed to improve their works by bringing them closer to the facts of social life rather than to their fantasies about it. The enthusiasm for this possibility has persisted over the last decade but has been vulnerable to the architect's first love—designing buildings which get built and noticed.

Having fished in a shallow pond of social science concepts and methods, many architects have found their catch highly suggestive but of little practical use when confronting the immediate necessity of designing a particular thing for a particular someone. So, while the literature exploring potential relationships between the built environment and patterns of human association expands, the profession impatiently awaits studies and findings with direct applicability to architectural practice.

Oscar Newman's *Defensible Space* appears to have met a felt need among some architects as well as among professional law enforcement agents. It is already a majestic hit, has been gloriously reviewed in the *Wall Street Journal* and the *New York Times* and has inspired the Law Enforcement Assistance Administration "to give a university or private corporation $2 million to formulate new architectural designs to reduce crime."[1] In fact, the study was itself funded by an arm of the Justice Department.

The book is an ideologically corrupt but meticulous and thorough empirical study of crime and design in public housing projects and urban apartment complexes. The study is based in an argument announced by its sub-title:

> Design can make it possible for both inhabitant and stranger to perceive that an area is under the undisputed influence of a particular group, that they dictate the activity taking place within it, and who its users are to be. This can be made so clearly evident that the residents will not only feel confident, but that it is incumbent upon them to question the comings and goings of people to ensure the continued safety of the defined areas. Any intruder will be made to anticipate that his presence will be under question and open to challenge; so much so that a criminal can be deterred from even contemplating entry.

With exemplary statistical care Newman demonstrates that the frequency of various common crimes in New York public housing varies with things like height of building, size of project and population, etc. He argues, less convincingly, from police statistics on the location of criminal incidents that certain existing spaces defining entries to buildings and apartments are, by their physical layout, more "defensible" than others.

This because of the feelings of territoriality they inspire in the residents and because of their outstanding "surveillance capacity" ("the ability to observe the public areas of one's residential environment and to feel continually that one is under observation by other residents while on the grounds of projects and within the public areas of building interiors").

Newman describes some interesting examples of housing projects by current architectural "practitioners of defensible space." He also describes the results of the unique opportunity he had to test some of his ideas by redesigning certain features of outdoor areas in existing situations, and includes for our delectation his proposals for radio and television monitoring of existing projects without defensible spaces or good surveillance capacity.

As an architectural study the book is interesting and well put together. As social science it is terribly weak. The ostensible argument for defensible spaces relies on the manner in which they "catalyze natural impulses of residents," increasing sentiments of communality, proprietorship, belonging, "reinforce existing societal values," and the like. Absolutely none of the systematically assembled data bear on this heart of the argument. Despite an impressive array of crime statistics, his hypothesis is ultimately defended with comments like "police express ... ", "management informs us . . . ", "we have found ... ", "interviews indicate ... " etc. The book will take some very heavy shots on this count.

But as a human, political, and moral affair the study, the book, is profoundly reprehensible. One hardly knows where to begin. We have our models. C. Wright Mills articulated an extreme characterization of designers as workers in the "cultural apparatus," standing powerlessly in the midst of a commercial vortex of production and distribution planning "the appearance of things." Robert Goodman (*After the Planners*) massively documents his understanding of urban planners and architects as "the soft cops," realizing in built form the political goals of the powerful. Correct as both these views are in their necessary partialness, neither analysis anticipates the rank opportunism, the political and moral paralysis of Newman's work.

Let us grant that an architect who wishes to practice and is not independently wealthy can do so only if chosen by clients with the wherewithal to build. If "all the money is in poverty" or only the "Fed" and the Catholic church are buying designs this year, one estimates the degree of moral compromise involved, chooses, does or does not design the appropriate thing, does or does not eat well this year. But what is it to search for, design, and sell the shape of the shell which will protect us from the excreta of power's abuses?

I have said that the ostensible argument of the book is that defensible spaces inspire and catalyze the natural sentiments of community, mutual aid and the like. But upon closer inspection, reviewing the book's examples and projected scenarios in such spaces, it emerges that *suspicion* is being catalyzed. Over and over again we encounter the image of the unwanted "intruder" warned by the symbolic (?) effects of a physical layout not to try his funny stuff inside its boundaries. He is thrown into frightened relief, and, if he "tries anything" his visibility renders him a "hardened target" (which Newman acknowledges). The target's intrusion fairly glows in the dark since the physical layout has encouraged folks to get on with the "communal" business of keeping a weather eye out for monkey business.

The scheme of "defensible space" and its motivating conception manipulate mistrust. Of the several conceptions of territoriality which have been exported from biology and ethology and applied with such murky results to human communities, Newman has in effect adopted that linked to exclusion and aggression. The "criminal" is anonymous in this book, not the son, daughter or father of anyone living nearby, perhaps in degradation similar to that of his victim. In Newman's mysterious anthropology, the communities facilitated into existence by defensible spaces form up without them, since they live only in crime statistics. Finally, the double police locks are nobly removed from apartment doors (the dust jacket tells us this is "An Alternative to the Fortress Apartment") and are placed on men's hearts. This is the humane accommodation to an undeniable daily evil in the lives of vulnerable urban people.

There is the sound of political surrender and the stench of moral death in "Crime Prevention Through Urban Design." Why must this accommodation to degraded urban life be confirmed in concrete, six-foot cast iron fences and closed circuit monitoring systems? Gerald Suttles concludes from his studies that "many of our slum communities in large cities come to approximate warrior societies because they must perform so much of their own policing and other functions which are ostensibly the responsibility of public institutions." This does not change when those slums are transferred to new containers. The relevant public institutions and social programs are still being starved or dismembered by the same agencies which now feed the Justice Department which, in turn, buys the skills and talents of the country's Newmans to rationalize and design euphemized retreats from the continuing daily terror which results.

The flower in this book's germinal idea is despair. The book assumes crime, assumes its causes and consequences for our attitude toward daily life. Its genius is to move "it" next door and next door again until we are an agglomeration of defensible spaces and militarily encysted suburbs. And then what? An outer layer of welfare cages and humane prisons on some gradient from Pruitt Igoe to Attica where all "crime," "intruders," and "hardened targets" retreat to be collected?

There is a logic somewhere which accounts for the simultaneous emergence of a Richard Nixon at the apex of his evil and this ambitious proposal which assumes the evil and aims to get it all together "through design."

Editors' note: Appeared in *The Daily Californian*, U. C. Berkeley Student Newspaper (Spring, 1973). Reprinted again with permission.

Note

1. *San Francisco Chronicle* (March 12, 1973).

The Urban Landscape

Elizabeth Blackmar
Harvard University

Cities are the most complex and the least understood of man-made environments. Though social scientists and professionals have established special fields for urban studies, they have failed to provide an integrated view of the urban landscape, one which relates its physical forms to cultural activity over time. One way to understand space and change in the city is through the study of urban history.

Traditional geographical and sociological theorists of urban growth have tried to find patterns which allow them to abstract the physical environment of individual cities to a "general rule" of stages of urbanization. In emphasizing models, they have sacrificed understanding either the history or the space of cities to the satisfaction of neat classification and explanation. Indeed, they have created an entire literature of debate over not only the configuration of city growth (from concentric circles to sectors and clusters) but also the proper metaphor to represent the process (organic or atomistic).[1] The question is, what do these approaches tell the architect or planner about the actual processes of city building, the adaptation of space to new use, the modification of preexisting structures or the creation of new solutions? Theorists might argue that out of models of past patterns will come information pertinent to designs for new growth, but urban innovations seldom replicate the forms of prior experience. The value of urban history is not in prediction, but in reminding architects and planners of the complex variables and pressures involved in changes in the man-made environment, and in stretching their imaginations as to the range of possibilities and alternatives in the uses of space.

In the last decade, social and urban historians have begun to look beyond the accomplishments of individuals and elite groups to the experiences of whole populations.[2] This recognition of the importance of reconstructing the "vernacular" dimension of average lives has implications for architects and planners as well. Yet for all the heightened interest in the larger social arena of the past, these historians have failed to effectively translate demographic and economic trends into a spatial dimension. On the other hand, historical geographers studying cities appreciate the importance of space; but in concentrating on analysis of generalized land use and residential patterns, they have neglected its visible social dynamics.[3] These trends in social and geographic history provide the essential larger framework of change against which to set the landscape of the city. But to have full meaning, the data of social history must be located in that physical environment which is itself an element of history. Thus architects and planners looking for the historical context of buildings and cities must base their perspective on reconstruction of both social fact and material artifact. Furthermore, they must analyze changing attitudes and values which are given expression in space, in social criticism of the environment and in planning.

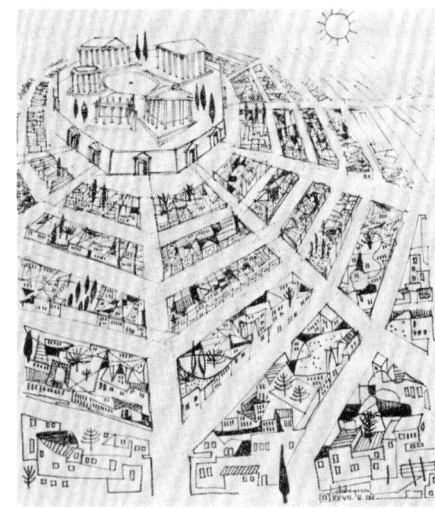

The City of the "Laws" of Plato, drawing by L. Durigeon.

What kinds of demographic factors affected, and continue to affect, the shape of cities? Studies of American urban history have focused on European immigration as the most significant aspect of nineteenth century city growth, even though natural increase and rural migration contributed substantial numbers of new urban dwellers.[4] The concentration and interaction of different ethnic, regional, and class groups created a distinctly urban culture of contrasting—and often conflicting—styles and living arrangements. Recent work in family history has further alerted historians to issues of age, life cycle, family composition, and kinship networks which assume a spatial form and hence enter into patterns of urban living.[5] Finally, social historians relying on census manuscripts and city directories have followed historical populations in, out, and through the city to uncover tremendous geographic mobility in both the nineteenth and twentieth centuries.[6] To understand the physical accommodation of the city to the growth, variety, and mobility of its people, environmental historians must consider such spatial dimensions as the improvement or deterioration of individual living environments, the options of residential location in proximity to work, the clustering of kin and ethnic groups, the organization of neighborhoods, the existence of urban areas catering to transients, and the emergence of a counter-urban environment in the suburbs.

The city is more than the sum and motion of its people; it contains their productive activity as well. Nineteenth-century industrialization and twentieth-century technology reorganized both the space and the social structure of the American urban environment. Geographical historians such as David Ward have explored the transformation of the preindustrial mercantile city into a complex center of marketing, finance, and industry by investigating the emergence of key internal structures and specialized districts, particularly the central business district and adjacent immigrant ghettos. Ward's work, however, shows some of the limitations of viewing space exclusively in terms of its economic functions. City growth is not an impersonal process, and yet we have little understanding of how decisions are made and initiated, or of how spatial "trends" get set.

In order to adequately "explain" change in the landscape, interpretations of urban history must be informed by contemporary concerns over the questions of power and policy—who controls and who shapes the environment? To look at the problem historically raises the problem not only of the succession of urban forms, but of the practical process of development: who was responsible for making decisions regarding land use and how did they act to adapt land to their own best interests and needs? Who received the profits from early speculative building; what assumptions, aspirations and materials influenced design solutions; at what point did an owner of inner city property cease to feel personal responsibility for its condition and use and begin to regard it more as an investment or commodity than as a possession or an emblem of identity? When did middlemen and agents assume their roles as the brokers of public space? Most importantly, what options were open to an expanding urban population with respect to their own housing, neighborhoods, or the total design and use of their cities?

Industrialization affected much more than the efficient organization of the productive sector of the city; it altered the very social structure, a change which is most dramatically revealed in the relation of different classes to property, and hence the urban landscape as a whole. James Vance and others have found that the preindustrial city was spatially integrated with respect to residence and place of work. Class separation arose with the establishment of differentiated employment districts and the appearance of a "generalized housing market."[7] The segregation of economic groups was reinforced by internal urban transportation systems, the activity of speculators, and ultimately by overt discrimination

The New Atlantis of Bacon, drawing by L. Durigeon.

in the form of restrictive covenants. Clearly the most important determinant of class segregation was the economic power to own, select, or control property.

Studies of nineteenth-century social mobility show that workers attached a high priority to owning their own property.[8] Such social aspiration became manifest in stable working class neighborhoods. It also was incorporated into a public ideology which designated home ownership an indication of success. But many nineteenth-century workers never had the option of ownership; their city was either the cast-off of a migrating middle class or the product of speculative builders and developers. To understand the relation of class to the urban environment requires looking beyond issues of control and ownership to those of expression as well. City residents have made inherited space distinctly their own, giving neighborhoods unique visible, cultural, and organizational characteristics that defy the notion of ownership as the only mark of identity or status in relation to the landscape. Though historians have begun to study the place of neighborhoods in different urban experiences, they need to go deeper into the shapes and the activities within these distinct areas of the city.

Sam Bass Warner offers a useful model for environmental historians seeking to integrate the physical development of the city with social and economic change, and to address larger questions of class and control. In revealing the relation of Boston's street-car system to the growth of suburbs Warner transforms what is so often treated as a mechanical set of stages in urban development into a vivid process of amateur entrepreneurial promotion and eager homeowner response. Not only does he establish the direct connection of transportation routes to settlement patterns, and the relation of the shape of suburban subdivisions to the tradition and economy of the grid street and frontage lot; he also is able to pursue middle class ideology into house plans, landscaping, and community government. Middle class homeowners sought to identify with a rural ideal and abandoned their city row houses for detached individualized houses. Meanwhile large segments of Boston's population remained restricted to dense neighborhoods that only in the twentieth century would be celebrated for their preservation of public values.[9]

Besides studying the formation and activity of neighborhoods and special districts, another approach to understanding the urban landscape is to examine the history of specific features of the city—its buildings, streets, open spaces and parks. These physical forms offer an index to collective social purposes. With respect to parks, some recent work in landscape architecture has taken a historical turn, but too often with only tangential reference to broader social issues. Albert Fein, for example, in placing Frederick Law Olmsted at the head of the democratic environmental planning tradition, outlines the social context of Olmsted's ideas and plans; but his analysis fails to illuminate either the extent to which Olmsted was reacting against the industrial or immigrant city, or the practical effect of his plans in design and in use.[10] An 1861 article in *Harper's Magazine* was more direct in relating Central Park to the social, sanitary, and spatial tensions of New York City. The history of parks involves not only their design, but their intent, control, use, and impact. The landscape of urban recreation—be it streets or playgrounds—may represent a battleground between reformers advocating forms of "moral uplift" and urban dwellers seeking space for self expression. Design in urban landscaping has had other implications besides nostalgia for the country or interest in engineering social harmony through space. The crafted landscape functions symbolically; it is the physical incarnation of social priorities—from civic pride to private consumption.

The environmental historian looking at the many changes in street or highway design, paving, or regulation can discover the role of innovation and experimentation in forming the urban landscape. At the same time, that historian may encounter the limits of society's flexibility and willingness to adapt to new conditions. It is important to remember that even the most prosaic features—from sewers to utilities—involve the relation of different groups to the city. Throughout the nineteenth century, such basic "urban" amenities as internal plumbing, electric lighting, or paving and curbing were distributed according to the ability of their consumers to pay. These commonplace urban features can also assume meaning beyond their practical functions as seen in the multiple uses of streets throughout history for marketing, play, public tributes, and confrontations.

Perhaps the most obvious features of the urban landscape are its buildings and structures. They are constructed with deliberate attention to market and materials, economy and efficiency, taste and status, and external regulations. Viewing the history of architecture merely as a progression of styles and vocabularies abstracts it from history and the landscape.

What models exist for architectural history that looks beyond the aesthetic source of design elements or identification of particular schools of architectural style? Charles Lockwood in an illuminating study of New York row houses balances an appreciation of the design of these buildings against a recognition of the social forces behind their repeated modifications.[11] Similarly, Alan Trachtenberg's history of the Brooklyn Bridge sets that dramatic feature in both its practical and symbolic context of a dynamic expanding New York City, touching on a range of issues in city building from engineering problems to politics.[12] Carl Condit in his study of American building art also suggests how urban history can be rendered concrete through the examination of the building industry itself and the engineering implications, requirements and possibilities of particular materials.[13] To appreciate the urban landscape we must learn to identify all types of structures through their practical history and use.

If the history of the city begins with new pressures on space and the ad hoc reorganization of that space in response, it must end with the efforts to plan and control the process of change. City planning began with the mobilization of reformers against the problems of the city, as seen in Roy Lubove's valuable study of Progressive tenement reform at the turn of the century.[14] Recognition that part of the solution to urban decay lay in its prevention; the rise of a class of trained specialists (engineers and managers); and a desire to retain qualities of open space in the over-built city contributed to the acceptance of city planning. But its form is best explained by the domination of middle class urban dwellers who were as concerned with their own protection, status, and power as they were with the face and fate of the city as a whole. Mel Scott, in his history of urban planning, written for the American Institute of Planners, provides a comprehensive survey of experiments in planning and design in the twentieth century with the insight, and the bias, of a professional planner.[15]

I have argued that the best way to understand the forms and activity of the city landscape is through an awareness of their history. Though there are models of urban history that address the issues of what forces shaped the city, appreciation of the evolution of urban space cannot be left solely to professional historians. Nor can this awareness be achieved merely by sitting in a library reading about the past. To understand the urban landscape we must begin by participating in it. Architects, planners, historians, and city dwellers must learn to observe the space around them, to see what is there and inquire where it came from. By walking the city, we can start to think about the spatial impact of social forces such as population growth and mobility; or the practical problems of traffic; or the cultural expression of different urban groups through their use of space. Where historical forms of the city have been permanently lost, the "environmental historians" must turn to the visual and descriptive record of archives—maps, drawings, photographs, personal accounts, and documents. Once we have observed the landscape closely, we can ask deeper questions about the process of its formation.

Leaving behind pre-existing debates and categories of either traditional architectural history or sociological urban theorists, these questions must inquire into the urban experience at its most immediate level—what kinds of physical environments have cities provided, what are the "internal structural" as well as surface features? How and why has the urban experience differed for different groups? Whose needs, interests, or customs has the organization of urban space served; how have those "needs" been determined, asserted, and acted upon; and equally important, what has been the resistance to new shapes within the city? How did people in the past view their own environment—what were the contemporary comments, criticisms, and proposals for changes?

There are many unexplored sources for answers to these questions. Besides the essential visual and impressionistic records of the past, there are public records—from deeds, tax assessment books, landlord-tenant court hearings—that offer hard-core information about the relation of city dwellers to their property. There are other documents that reveal the process of city building—construction and inspection permits, insurance records, public hearings, reform legislation, zoning ordinance. In addition there are the records of policy making, the discussions of professionals in journals, and plans and designs both implemented and rejected. Finally there are accounts, public and private, that reveal not only how the city was planned or constructed, but how it has been "used" over time, the activity that renders space dynamic. With a broad range of sources and social data, historians of the city can begin to reconstruct the forms, the process and the activity of the urban landscape.

Notes

1. David Herbert, *Urban Geography* (New York: Praeger, 1973); Peter Goheen, *Victorian Toronto 1850-1900: Pattern and Process of Growth* (Chicago, IL: University of Chicago Research Papers, 1970); David Harvey, *Social Justice and the City* (Baltimore, MD: Johns Hopkins University Press, 1973).
2. Herbert Gutman and Gregory S. Kealey, eds., *Many Pasts: Readings in American Social History* (Englewood, NJ: Prentice Hall, 1973); Kenneth T. Jackson and Stanley Schultz, eds., *Cities in American History* (New York: Knopf, 1972); Leo F. Schnore, ed., *The New Urban History: Quantitative Explorations by American Historians* (Princeton, NJ: Princeton University Press, 1975); Stephen Thernstrom and Richard Sennett, eds., *Nineteenth Century Cities: Essays in the New Urban History* (New Haven, CT: Yale University Press, 1969).
3. Martyn J. Bowden, ed., *Historical Geography Newsletter* 1, no. 1 (December 1971); Alan Pred, *Urban Growth and the Circulation of Information* (Cambridge, MA: Harvard University Press, 1973); David Ward, *Cities and Immigrants* (New York: Oxford University Press, 1971). [Editor's note: The original source did not cite any particular issue or year for *Historical Geography Newsletter*.]
4. Oscar Handlin, *Boston's Immigrants: A Study in Acculturation* (Cambridge, MA: Harvard University Press, 1959); Josef Barton, *Peasants and Strangers: Italians, Rumanians, and Slavs in an American City, 1890-1950* (Cambridge, MA: Harvard University Press, 1975); Kathleen N. Conzen, *The German Athens: Milwaukee and the Accommodation of Its Immigrants 1836-1860* (Cambridge, MA: Harvard University Press, 1976).
5. *Journal of Urban History* 1, no. 3 on "The History of the Family in American Urban Society," Tamara K. Hareven, ed. (May 1975); Michael Gordon, ed., *The American Family in Social-Historical Perspective* (New York: St Martin's Press, 1973); Theodore K. Rabb and Robert I. Rothberg, eds., *The Family in History: Interdisciplinary Essays* (New York: Octagon Books, 1971).
6. Stephen Thernstrom, *The Other Bostonians: Poverty and Progress in the American Metropolis 1880-1970* (Cambridge, MA: Harvard University Press, 1973); Peter R. Knights, *Plain People of Boston 1830-1860: A Study in City Growth* (New York: Oxford University Press, 1971); Peter R. Knights and Stephen Thernstrom, "Men in Motion: Some Data and Speculations about Urban Population Mobility in Nineteenth Century America," *Journal of Interdisciplinary History* 1 (Autumn 1970); Kenneth T. Jackson, "The Crabgrass Frontier: One Hundred Years of Suburban Growth in America" in *The Urban Experience: Themes in American History,* eds. R.A. Mohl and James F. Richardson, (Belmont, CA: Wadsworth Publishing Co., 1973).
7. James E. Vance, "Housing the Worker: the Employment Linkage as a Force in Urban Structure," *Economic Geography* XLII (1966); Sam Bass Warner, *The Private City: Philadelphia in Three Periods of Its Growth* (Philadelphia, PA: University of Philadelphia Press, 1968).
8. Stephen Thernstrom, *Poverty and Progress: Social Mobility in a Nineteenth Century City* (Cambridge, MA: Harvard University Press, 1975).
9. Sam Bass Warner, *Streetcar Suburbs: The Process of Growth in Boston 1870-1900* (New York: Atheneum Press, 1969).
10. Albert Fein, *Frederick Law Olmsted and the American Environmental Tradition* (New York: George Braziller, 1972); Roy Lubove, "Social History and the History of Landscape Architecture," *Journal of Social History* 9, no. 2 (Winter 1975).
11. Charles Lockwood, *Bricks and Brownstones: New York Row Houses 1783-1929* (New York: McGraw-Hill, 1972).
12. Alan Trachtenberg, *Brooklyn Bridge: Fact and Symbol* (New York: Oxford University Press, 1965).
13. Carl W. Condit, *American Building Art: The Nineteenth Century* (New York: Oxford University Press, 1960) and *American Building Art: The Twentieth Century* (New York: Oxford University Press, 1961).
14. Roy Lubove, *The Progressives and The Slums: Tenement House Reform in New York City 1890-1917* (Pittsburgh, PA: University of Pittsburgh Press, 1962).
15. Mel Scott, *American City Planning* (Berkeley, CA: University of California Press, 1971).

Observations on Energy Use in Buildings

Richard Stein
Architect

The idea propagated at the end of World War II—that we were on the threshold of a period in which humankind would be set free from traditional restraints imposed by natural systems—was a very heady idea, the Icarus legend brought up to date. It has resulted in the last twenty five years in a decided divergence in the path that architects were to follow. The architectural press, the critics, the schools, all encouraged an architecture that was different for its own sake and in most ways diametrically opposite to the view that had shaped the new architecture of the 1920s, 30s and 40s. Brought with it was a marked difference in the energy performance of buildings—in the amount of heating, cooling, lighting, ventilation, and other mechanically controlled environmental conditions on which the buildings depended to achieve human comfort. The figures that resulted from this approach to building design are indeed alarming, particularly in view of their implications in terms of depletable resources, an increasingly polluted environment, the exhaustion of vast acreage of land for coal mountains and of seabeds and ocean front for oil and gas exploration and depots, all in order to have energy to operate our buildings.

This article will point out the misuse and overuse of energy in all areas of building construction to demonstrate that there are options available for across-the-board reduction in energy use through building design and operation that far exceed, in cost effectiveness, the potential of new energy technologies that might be developed during the next quarter century. More importantly, these options apply as much to existing buildings as to new ones.

To understand the problem, consider high-rise office buildings, probably the most characteristic building form of the post World War II era. In the past decades, the average requirement for energy use within these buildings has more than doubled, while there has been no fundamental change in the way business is carried on inside. In fact, in New York and other large cities the same kinds of activities are carried on equally effectively or ineffectively in buildings that may have been built 50 years apart. In New York City Rockefeller Center was first begun in the late twenties and early thirties, more than 40 years ago. The oldest building has the same kind of corporate tenant as its recently completed neighbors.

When New York City was faced with continuing brown-outs and limited electricity to supply its buildings, Mayor John Lindsay established a bureau to look

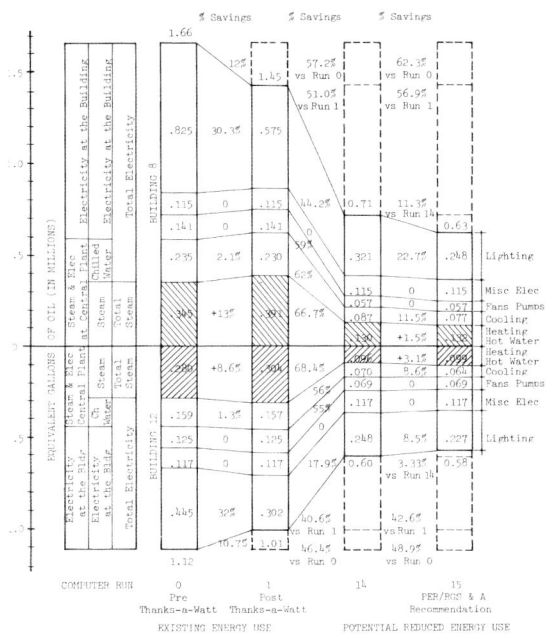

Annual energy use and potential energy savings in million gallons of source energy fuel oil (shaded areas represent anticipated savings).

into the energy problems in the city's buildings, and Dr. Charles Lawrence, an engineer and conscientious student of energy use in buildings, was appointed public utility specialist. With the assistance of New York City Real Estate Board, questionnaires were sent to the owners of 180 buildings built since World War II, primarily in the two decades from 1950 to 1970.[1] The owners were requested to indicate the amount of energy from electricity and other sources, such as steam, oil, or coal that went into the heating and cooling of their buildings. These figures were related to the square feet of rentable space and the total square feet within the building and then compared on the basis of energy per gross square foot. The results give an indication of how buildings really function and what the range is in their energy demand.

Eighty-six questionnaires were returned, which formed the basis for the study. The figures were all end-use figures, and it is necessary to apply certain conversion factors to understand their true source energy use. (All of the studies conducted by my office have gone back to source use, since ultimately, if the same end-use energy can be provided by several interchangeable

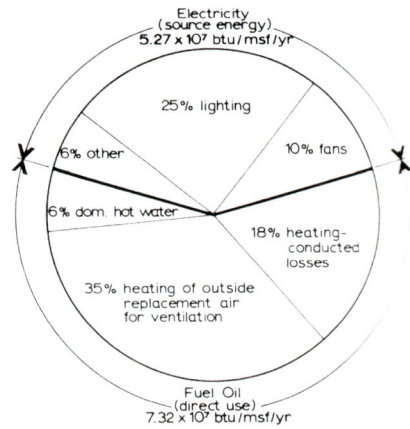

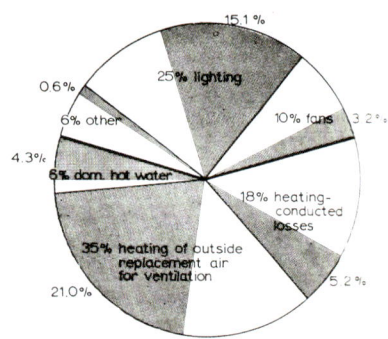

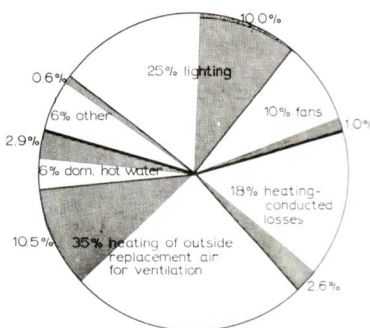

Current energy use in school buildings and anticipated savings. 2a. Present energy use pattern. 2b. Project savings (new building) 49.4 percent total. 2c. Projected savings (retrofit) 27.7 percent total.

means, the efficiency of the energy *producer* is decisive. This is particularly true when applied to electric heating as opposed to heating with other sources. After a building's heat load has been determined, electric heat requires almost four times that amount at the generating plant, while a fossil fuel burner may require one and one-half to two times that amount.)

In the study of New York City office buildings, the results are as follows (with kilowatt hours tabulated at 3,412 Btu per kilowatt hour). In the first five years covered in the survey, 1950 through 1954, converting figures back to Btu per square foot per year, there was an average of 50,500 Btu of electricity and 78,400 Btu in steam for heating—for a total energy use of 128.9 thousand Btu per square foot. In the subsequent five-year period from 1955 to 1959, electricity required 56,300 Btu and steam, 108,100 Btu, for a total of 164,400 Btu—an increase of 40,000 Btu per square foot over the previous five years. In the third five-year period there was a further jump. Electricity now consumed 60,400 Btu, steam 154,100 Btu for a total of 214,500 Btu. In the fourth five-year period, from 1965 through 1969, electricity had gone up to 78,400 Btu per square foot and steam 188,000 for a total of 266,400, making it obvious that the total energy use in this period had more than doubled.

If we consider the source energy necessary for the electricity, the figures are even more startling. (The figures are based on Con Edison's heat rate of about 12,500 Btu/kWh with no added factor for transmission losses.) Of the four five-year periods, the first used a total of 263,400 Btu per square foot; 1955 to 1959 required 314,400; and 1965 through 1969, 553,900 Btu per square foot. The last figure is the equivalent of 3.8 gallons of oil per square foot per year. With these figures and oil costs somewhere in the neighborhood of 40¢ a gallon and rising, it is not surprising that there is concern about the cost of energy use in these buildings, not to speak of the moral question of why such extravagance has entered the building process itself and why it is tolerated. What is more disturbing, however, is that the figures given are averages. By no means are they the most extreme examples of excessive energy use.

Of all the buildings considered in the Lawrence study, the greatest energy use reported was 403,000 Btu per square foot per year of on-site energy use. The lowest was 72,000 Btu. Thus, the highest energy use is 5½ times the lowest. It must be remembered that these are office buildings that serve approximately the same kinds of use and a common building type in the same climate area. The difference in energy use could be considered to result from the physical design solutions and the methods of using the buildings. If one uses the figure for source energy for electricity, the total energy requirement for the building approximately doubles. Applying that rule of thumb to the figures in the published reports (since these figures are not broken down into steam and electricity, nor is the source of the steam identified), one can assume that the high energy user uses 800,000 Btu per square foot or 5½ gallons of oil per square foot per year.

To understand these statistics it is necessary to specify the ways in which buildings use energy. Each building type has a characteristic pattern, but each building varies within it. Diagram 1 summarizes the findings of a detailed study commissioned by New York State Office of General Services to see what could be done to reduce energy use in two existing state-owned office buildings.[2] Typical of many buildings built in the

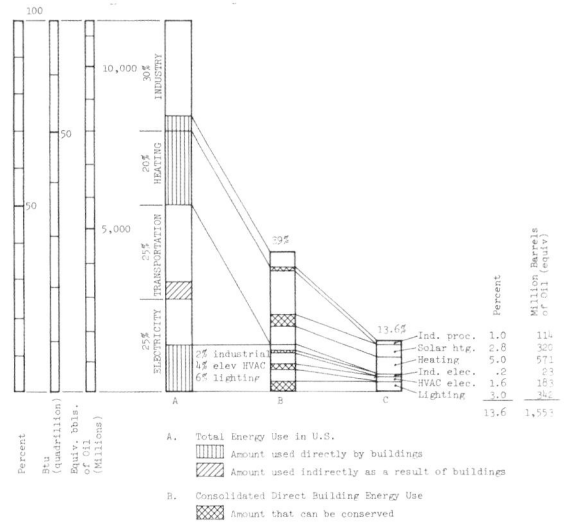

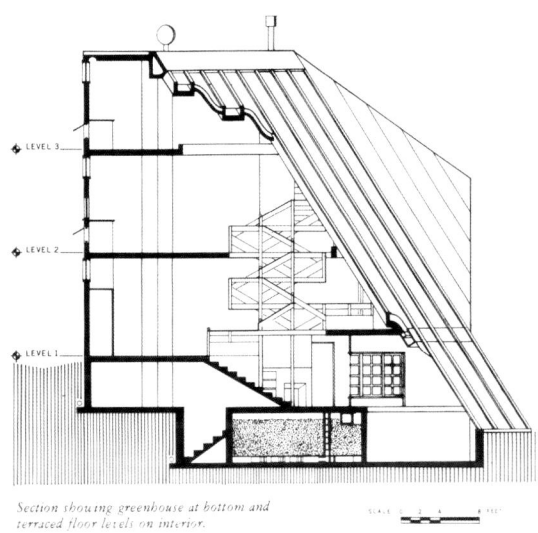

Section showing greenhouse at bottom and terraced floor levels on interior.

Available energy reduction in buildings.

1960s they have undifferentiated facades, regardless of orientation. One building has a glass and aluminum curtainwall skin, the other a glass, aluminum, and face-brick facade. The glazing in each case is tinted, single-thickness glass in inoperative windows (opened only for window cleaning). Both have about 100 to 110 footcandles of uniform distributed light produced by lighting installations that vary around four watts per square foot. Both buildings have terminal reheat systems—that is, systems that add heat to superchilled air in order to modify it to the varying temperature requirements in different parts of the building. Each building contains about 600,000 square feet in total area. One building has a square plan with about an acre of floor space per floor and a height of 12 stories; the other has about 100,000 square feet per floor for five stories. Both have additional usable space below grade.

Diagram 1 gives their energy use in millions of gallons of oil equivalent. The source energy to generate the electricity is computed in Btu which is then converted to equivalent gallons of oil at 146,000 Btu per gallon, whether the electricity is used directly in the building or in the central boiler plant which also houses the central electric chillers. This is added to the actual oil burned in the boiler plant to produce steam, prorated to the two buildings.

Both buildings operate within the energy use limits of the typical office buildings built in New York City during a comparable five-year period as described in the Lawrence study. Both buildings are located in Albany, which has a slightly colder winter but a comparable summer temperature to New York City. They are representative of neither the most efficient nor the most extravagant of the buildings built. In other words, they can be considered typical, average buildings of their type.

Electricity is by far the largest energy user when one goes back to source energy. Chilled water is provided by electric compressors at the central mechanical plant. The rest of the electricity is utilized at the building. Of all of the electricity, well over half of it (in fact, half of all the energy) goes into the lighting in one building; in the other about 40 percent of total energy is in the lighting system.

The state instituted energy conservation programs on its own—turning off some of the lights, being more disciplined in the way the systems were used—with the result of a 12 percent energy saving in one case and 10 percent in the other. However, in analyzing the buildings more closely, it was found that even this significant savings is but the tip of the iceberg. With a time of less than two years to pay back the capital costs with savings, one of them could have a further reduction of 57 percent and the other an additional reduction of 42 percent. With a longer payback time, there are other things that can be done to further reduce conventional energy requirements by an additional 7 percent or 8 percent, such as introducing double glazing, adding solar collectors and removing the ballasts in the lamps that have been deactivated.

When one looks to see how energy is used one finds that, as the building systems now operate, the skin of the building is not the greatest consumer but is responsible only for a little less than a quarter of the total requirements as represented by the heating load (which also includes heating for the terminal reheat systems). Cooling requires about 14 percent, mostly to remove internally generated heat. Thus, the improvement of the thermal performance of the wall alone does not produce the largest savings.

Before proposing a more rational energy use, one must understand what has become characteristic in this kind of building. Over the last 20 years the mechanical systems have required a constantly increasing share of the total building dollar. As architects have *simplified* the facade of the building, complex mechanical systems have increasingly become more *extensive* and expensive, to compensate for the less selective performance of the skin. If one designs a building with a more sophisticated and differentiated skin, based on its orientation and climatic performance, the additional cost in architectural work and construction work is often far less than the savings achieved by being able to reduce the size of the mechanical system. From our recent office experience, with only a slight increase in cost for the skin of college buildings, the mechanical plant—the size of the steam boilers, electrical generating capacity and number of tons of refrigeration required—was reduced by 20 percent to 40 percent below those normally estimated, based on previous experience of buildings with similar area and volume.

Further, if only the thermal performance of the skin is considered to be the determinant of energy use in the buildings, the assumption commonly is made that the minimum surface building, which has the least area for energy transfer, will be the most energy efficient. But of these two buildings, Building 12, which has a considerably larger surface area, starts out with about two-thirds the energy use of the building that more nearly resembles a cube, the difference attributable in part to reduced electric lighting energy required with proper use of natural illumination.

After all the easily available energy reductions have been made, they will both use about the same amount of energy per square foot—in source energy almost exactly the equivalent of one gallon of oil, or roughly 150,000 Btu, per square foot per year, including electricity. If one converts back to end-use on-site energy, this is in the neighborhood of 70 to 75 thousand Btu.

Now let us look at the statistics on household electrical use. Starting with 1959 USA figures there were about 180 billion kilowatt hours sold for residential use by about 50,400,000 customers. This means that each residential customer bought an average of 3,570 kWh of electricity a year. In 15 years the amount of electricity sold for residential use has tripled. The number of families served has increased 40 percent, but the use per family has increased by 100 percent, bringing the current total to about 555 billion kWh per year.

Investigations of other building types—stores, hospitals, recreational facilities, schools—all demonstrate similar increases in energy dependency in the short periods bound by the last two decades.

In a recent study our office analyzed in detail the energy use in some thousand schools in the New York City school system.[3] General statistics were studied and a number of buildings examined extensively. The standards and the educational requirements that determined the level of services were reexamined to ascertain whether the kinds of installations called for were required for effective performance of the school function.

There were some significant results of this study (Diagram 2). First, school buildings in New York City have a characteristic energy use and distribution of energy requirements different from either the typical office building or schools in other areas, particularly those dependent on air conditioning. Second, the New York City schools operate on a lower use of energy per square foot than do schools in any other area we examined. The average in source energy for all the schools was approximately 125,000 Btu per square foot for all purposes. This figure, based on present operation, is a little less than a gallon of oil per square foot per year.

In Diagram 2, showing the distribution of uses, it can be seen that lighting represents about 65 percent of electrical usage, but in this case it is only about 40 percent of total usage. Of the remaining 60 percent, which is used for heating directly, more than half is used to heat outside air to replace the air that is exhausted for ventilation code requirements. About half as much is expended to make up the heat lost through the walls and roof of the building and, of course, from infiltration at doors and other openings. About 6 percent in total is used for domestic hot water. Half of this energy use is unnecessary in new buildings and at least a quarter can be readily eliminated in existing buildings.

These specific findings may have general implications: in investigating lighting we found that the lighting that was specified and provided did not perform as designated. In the newer schools uniform lighting levels of 60 to 70 footcandles were designed. In actuality, the contribution of outside light through the windows creates enormous light level variations, in some cases as high as 1,500 footcandles near the windows to 12 footcandles at the far corner of the room. This more than 100 to 1 light level differential was not noticed by the people in the room nor was it found to be disturbing to them.

The schools had a typical oil and electrical use curve that was characteristic of almost all the schools. The only school that varied sharply was a windowless school, presumably with very efficient mechanical systems and high thermal performance in the walls and roof. Yet, it required more than twice the average electrical requirement because of the necessity for using mechanical systems and lighting at all times during building use. This underscores an important point that runs counter to a good deal of current practice; a building that uses its mechanical systems only when natural methods are inadequate will, in general, be more economical in energy use than a building that is always completely dependent on mechanical systems for its light, air, heating, and cooling.

We examined the success of the schools' education when light levels were increased by checking some 30,000 reading achievement scores over a period of six years in schools that had their light levels increased and in schools that were unchanged through the six-year period. The results indicated a lack of correlation between increased light levels and academic performance. This agrees with observed information from England on light levels, and is consistent with pre-fluorescent standards that recommended 20 to 30 footcandles as being adequate for classroom work.

Using existing buildings as laboratories is particularly instructive since so much of our overuse of energy has been institutionalized in codes, recommendations and high technology solutions to what are in fact low-technology or no-technology problems.

Since what we are seeking is a realistic basis for evaluating the alternatives available for energy conservation in buildings, we must understand the potential contribution and limitations of new solar technology, such as the flat-plate collector, which in the public mind has become the most visible and attractive symbol of good ecological intentions and of the way to solve our energy problems. To gauge its potential, our office carried out a study wherein a number of assumptions were made for the most optimistic "scenario" that one could expect for the implementation of solar technology for buildings.[4] These included incentives of government support, funding, and compatibility with existing construction and mechanical systems, all of which might result in the maximum possible use of solar collector technology within a 10-year period.

The assumptions of this optimistic scenario were as follows. Solar collectors will be installed on single family and low-rise residences including 25 percent of existing houses and 50 percent of new houses. They will provide 75 percent of the total heat requirement of these houses and have on the average a collector area equal to 50 percent of the heated floor space. The total installed cost for new residences is assumed to be $20 per square foot of collector for new residences and $25 per square foot for existing structures; this price includes all piping, storage, and controls. At the end of 10 years, 25 million out of 75 million housing units will be so equipped. The total installation cost required is $345 billion for the 15 billion square feet of collectors, assuming constant 1976 dollars.

Now, what will the results be? Approximately 20 percent of our total national energy use is used directly for fossil fuel heating and hot water, about 60 percent of this for residential purposes. Thus, 12 percent of our total energy use becomes the target for the solar substitute that we have just described, which if used on one-third of all residential units ends up to be one-third of 12 percent or 4 percent. If 75 percent of the energy requirements of these units will be provided by the solar installations, the potential fossil fuel energy reduction becomes 3 percent of the total.

Let us project a very low figure for the estimated increase in national energy use—10 percent in the next 10 years. We can then conclude that if the introduction of solar collector technology is the only energy shift we achieve and if we do not make some drastic changes in the basic way we use energy in buildings, we would only be 7 percent worse off at that time than we are now, instead of 10 percent.

Diagram 3 indicates other possibilities that are readily available for energy savings in building and in that part of industry that serves it. As shown in Bar Graph A of the diagram, basic divisions of total energy use in the United States are: source energy for electrical generation 25 percent, transportation 25 percent, heating and hot water 20 percent, and direct use of fossil fuel in industry 30 percent. In addition, a part of the electrical figure represents industrial use of electricity; approximately 40 percent of electric energy generation sold is in a category listed as *Commercial and Industrial Large Light and Power*; there is an additional use of electricity, generated by industry for its own use.

This summary describes only the energy use that results from the systems that are built into buildings and does not include optional energy uses resulting from electrical accessories, gadgets, television sets, or even such necessities as refrigerators and ranges. The statistics refer only to systems that are incorporated into building construction—heating systems, cooling systems, ventilating systems, vertical transportation systems, and pumps and motors that operate such features as water supply and sewage. Included, of course, are the lighting systems which are very large energy users. Our investigations indicate further that of the total industrial energy use, 6.25 percent is the energy used by the new building construction industry.

A certain amount in each category is also committed either through the construction of buildings or through their operation and maintenance: over 15 percent of industrial, all of the heating, about 50 percent of electrical and possibly a fifth of the transportation (which may be considered to result from the way buildings are built and located making necessary an excessive use of the automobile in order for people to take care of their shopping needs, their travel to and from business, jobs, schools, and such).

Bar Graph B in Diagram 3 consolidates all of these building related energy uses together, not including the secondary energy use for transportation. We find that almost 40 percent of the total national energy budget is committed through the building process. Shown hatched in each of the categories is the amount that can be eliminated through readily available conservation techniques and through the widespread introduction of solar heating. Solar heating must be considered as having a considerably longer lead time for installation; nevertheless, we are now grouping these together and we find that 13.6 percent of the entire present energy use can be eliminated rapidly, assuming a desire to do it and the cooperation of the American people.

Over one-third of the energy now directly used through the building process can be dispensed with, as evidenced by all of the studies described above. This is the equivalent of 9.5 quadrillion Btu of national energy use. If this amount of end-use energy were produced electrically, it would require 520 thousand-megawatt electrical plants. In other words, if we produced a new thousand-megawatt electrical plant every two weeks for the next 20 years, we would achieve the same end result, except that the amount of site damage, resource exhaustion and environmental degradation that would go with the production of electricity would be entirely eliminated simply by pursuing the course of energy use reduction that is available to us in the building design and use.

To reestablish perspective, we must look at USA figures in their global context. There are about 210 million people in the United States. The accepted world population in 1970 was 3¾ percent billion. Of these, 210 million people use 70 million billion Btu (or 70 quads). The rest of the 3¾ billion use 130 quads. Individually, on the average, the people in the United States each use about 333 million Btu per year compared with an average per capita in the rest of the world of about 39 million Btu, about 1/9th as much. Our measure of one million Btu does not represent much energy. It will produce and deliver only about 90 kWh of electricity, for instance, and 90 kWh of electricity is less than 1/50th of the average American's yearly electrical purchase and less than 1/250th of the average heating bill of an electrically heated house.

After the US has used 35 percent of the world's energy, not everyone who is left participates equally in the remaining 65 percent. For example, let us disregard the developed countries—US, Japan, Europe, Soviet Union, Canada, Australia, New Zealand and temperate Latin America—and consider the underdeveloped countries with their population of 2¾ billion. Their combined total energy use is 34 quads—about half of the total energy that is used in the United States—and the per capita energy use based on 1969 figures is about 12 million Btu per year compared with about 333 million—about 1/30th as much. These are average figures which means, of course, that many countries and millions of families are operating with considerably less energy per capita.

This is not energy that is expended by the individual. It includes all of the manufacturing uses, all of the non-personal transport uses, all of the energy lost in the generation of electricity, all of the energy to maintain and keep military and governmental apparatuses operating. After these uses have been prorated to the individuals and subtracted from the average of the 12 million Btu per person per year, the remainder can be considered available for personal use—light, heat, transportation, cooling, hot water, refrigeration, and such.

Moreover, we know that the prevailing pattern in all the countries that are experiencing the most rapid growth is that virtually all of the new population settles in cities or forms new cities, that problems of housing and building are compounded by the greater complexity of services required in the first shift from rural living to urban living. The rural dwelling can provide basic shelter through the use of available local materials.

If there is a potable water supply—a spring or a clean stream—and enough distance between structures, the primary sanitary provisions will have been met. While lighting systems, refrigeration and sewage disposal are desirable, they are not absolutely essential for survival. However, when an individual or family moves to a city or becomes part of a new, closely integrated community, a number of additional necessities will have to be provided—a central water and sewage system, some means of transportation, fuel for cooking, a method of disposing of solid waste and desirably, an access to electricity. All of these requirements increase the base amount of energy per capita so that even more is required for new populations than for the stabilized population in these areas of the world.

Realizing this, what is imperative is not the further development of gadgetry, but a fundamental reassessment of how we can live, how we can develop a lifestyle that will not be based on the deprivations of vast areas of the rest of the world where, as in the United States, there are still enormous building requirements which must be provided for simply and beautifully.

We must now address the problem as one requiring a different method and scale of building. I think the ultimate result will be a subtle enrichment of the quality and texture of our lives, a reintroduction into the cities of the desirable characteristics being lost through our over-scaled construction and energy profligacy. Redirecting our architectural objectives to solve these new problems is our major task today.

Notes

1. "Energy Conservation: Implications for Building Design and Operation," *ASHRAE Conference Proceedings*, eds. D.E. Abrahamson and S. Emmings, University of Minnesota (May 1973). [Editor's note: ASHRAE refers to The American Society of Heating, Refrigerating and Air-Conditioning Engineers.]
2. Pope, Evans, and Robbins, Inc. with Richard G. Stein and Associates, "Energy Conservation Study: State Office Building Campus, Buildings 8 and 12" (1975).
3. Richard G. Stein and Carl Stein, "Research, Phase 1: Low Energy Utilization School," *Report for Board of Education*, City of New York, NSF-RANN Grant GI-39612 (1974).
4. Richard G. Stein and Associates and Center for Advanced Computation, University of Illinois "Energy in Building Construction," Report of Study under ERDA Contract E(11-1)-2791 (December 1976). [Editor's note: ERDA refers to Energy Research and Development Administration, which is now part of the Department of Energy.]

Commencement Address

Aldo van Eyck
Architect

This article was originally the key address of the sixty-third commencement of the New Jersey Institute of Technology, 1979, on the occasion of Aldo van Eyck, Professor at the Delft Institute of Technology, and Paul Philippe Cret Professor at the University of Pennsylvania, receiving an honorary doctorate.

Man's scope spans disquieting extremes. The same can be said of his tools. Maid or master, technology assists all our doings at every level of intention. Constructive or destructive, it is always by our side—a kind and malicious companion, both.

The evidence of this companionship can be read off the face of the globe, for the environment reveals whatever occurs there—like a tell-tale mirror. What we see (if we dare to look) reflected in that mirror—the evidence—is becoming more and more harrowing—pathological. Indeed, it is befitting today to speak of the pathology of landscape. Ladies and gentlemen, you can nod and say, "Yes, we know!" But do you know, has it really penetrated your consciousness, or are you willing to acknowledge that, whilst in the past, societies responded more or less successfully to the problems survival in any given environment posed, *ours*—those to which you and I belong, the magnanimous ones—are no longer able to. This in spite of bewildering technological and scientific ability—their familiar trademark.

But it is another trademark—a less familiar one now edging in on us—which I want to put before you. I mean our pitiful inability to come to terms with—cope with—vast multiplicity and great quanta, no matter of what—and behave with sanity towards the environment, that great and only place there is in which we all live.

No previous society has made quite so little of the experience, knowledge, and technology available or fell so far short of what imaginative, concerted action could bring about. Of course, as of old, there are still imaginative and constructive efforts by individuals from which all could benefit if listened to and applied. But minimal use is made of them. In fact, a blind eye and a deaf ear is turned to what is being done on the periphery—to what is occasionally smuggled in like contraband—only to be misunderstood and misused—twisted into yet another negative.

Whatever gain is made is soon counteracted by another gain; for ours, yours and mine—the presumptuous kind—is a society of wasted gain. Just think of it. It would be funny if it weren't so awful. Ten years ago, when war was still waging beyond the Pacific, I wrote some lines in large letters on an exhibition wall in Milan.

Here they are:

> *Disturb the delicate intricacies of the* limitless microcosm. *Trespass into the* limited macrocosm *and frighten the angels. In between, mess up the Mississippi and the Mekong. If that is what we desire, it will soon be here, for there is a limit even to the limitless. Man falling in line with entropy after all. We have already turned the theory of relativity and quantum physics against ourselves. We now split atoms—we split and split. Soon it will be the stars. Mourn also for all butterflies.*

Since then, ten years have passed. What is true of the whole is also true of each part, so what is true—painfully true—of environment is also true—painfully so—of most buildings. Now if making a *good* building (one that is not a *bad* building) has become too difficult, the dilemma is indeed complete. But is it really all that difficult? Does it really require a genius to avoid the mean and meaningless—or a sage to bypass foolishness? Is there nothing between a fool and a genius—nobody in between to do the job nicely—well?

If behaving with sanity towards the environment on whatever level is no longer within our reach, then surely the societies to which we belong—our kind—thus reasonably measured—are of a very low, primitive order.

I have, ladies and gentlemen, on this special occasion, just confronted you with a fact which, alas, points towards the only definition of a primitive society that makes sense. A definition which removes the burden from all those *other* societies that never deserved to be called primitive by that magnanimous kind of ours, the behavior of which towards the landscapes of the world is like that of a half-wit with two left hands.

Whether in Greenland, Africa, America-long-ago, or the South Seas, people dealt with limited numbers both accurately and gracefully, extending collective behavior into adequate, and often beautiful, built form. Taking from the environment as much as they gave, a gratifying balance was sustained. This *we* are no longer able to do, not in the same way, nor, as yet, in any other way.

But is it really all that difficult or beyond our reach? Are we not human beings too, like those in Greenland, Africa, America-long-ago, and the South Seas? Is our

Aldo van Eyck, Sonsbeek Sculpture Pavilion, Arnhem, 1967. "The site is an old asphalt tennis court in an old park with tall trees all around. ... In order to, as it were, 'isolate' the world of art from the world of nature (coax them into opposition through juxtaposition), the large circle's counterform is to be painted silver (new large aluminum pieces of sculpture by Shinkichi Tajiri will be placed on it): the circle itself will be painted grey-black. ... A translucent (not transparent) vellum over the six walls will give the diffused light that should bring out the physical—tangible—reality of the sculpture (I want hollows to be hollows not just black shadow patches). ... The walls are 2.3m apart so that an immediate 'confrontation' with the sculpture placed along the 'streets' will be ensured—people will be physically close to one another and also close to the sculpture: intentional crowding causing intentional conflicts (city-like). Plans from *Domus* (March, 1968). "Per Tajiri: Un Ambiente di Carta," *Domus* no. 460 (March 1968): 10–13. "Il Padiglione Sonsbeek," *Domus* no. 460 (March 1968): 2–9. [Editor's note: The original did not include the article title or page numbers; these two articles are likely the source.]

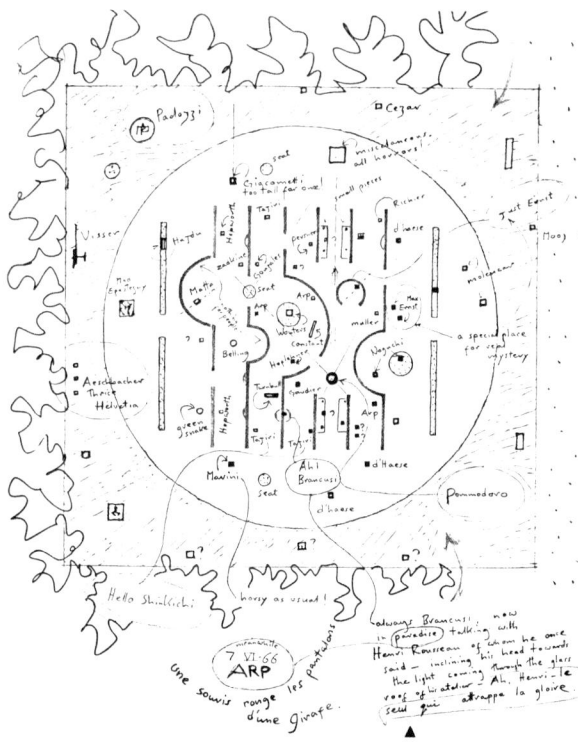

mental equipment not similar? Are we not endowed equally well? Surely we can accomplish what they accomplished in so many different ways. Believe it or not, ladies and gentlemen, those little societies, their inspiring but disappearing cultures, can still give us by their example what we took away from them: confidence.

It is in the nature of the human species, you see, to be able to deal with environment, hence also to fashion the spaces they require adequately and beautifully—the way all people are given to communicate both adequately and beautifully through language—*that other gift*, which, like making spaces, belongs to our primordial equipment.

It is painfully true of architecture that it is not just good quality that counts but a sufficient quantity of that quality. A good school elsewhere, you see, is no use to a child that needs one here. If I have a nice house (a house at all), that doesn't mean millions of others also have. So let's get moving and start with this: persuade those narrow borderlines—the hard and harsh ones—between inside and outside, between this space here and that space there—to loop generously and gracefully into articulated in-between places and give each space the right interior horizon for the gratifying sense of reference it provides.

Never cease to identify whatever you construct with the people you are constructing it for—for those it will accommodate. Identify a building with that same building entered, and hence with those it shelters, and define space—each space built—simply as the appreciation of it. This circular definition has a purpose. You see, whilst excluding all abstract academic abracadabra, *it includes* what should never be excluded but paradoxically generally is: I mean those *entering* it, appreciating it—PEOPLE.

Architecture can do no more, nor should it ever do less, than accommodate people well; assist their homecoming. The rest—those signs and symbols one

Aldo van Eyck, Children's Home, Amsterdam, 1956–60. Discovering yourself in the floor (extracting laughter from it because the mirrors distort). Can—should—architecture reflect the firmament? Why? Why rubbish beyond reach? The children stood over the mirrors and made secret discoveries they didn't keep secret, so they lost the mirrors.

is worrying about too much—will either take care of themselves or they just don't matter.

Meanwhile, let us not forget, blight has crept over our field. Let me urge each student not to fall for the new array of whimsy trends. Don't let them nestle in your mind. And let me urge whomever it concerns not to be tricked into actually building the incompetent absurdities that fill most architectural reviews from cover to cover. Architecture does *not* mean, nor has it ever meant, nor can it ever come to pass that it will one day mean, what the loathsome fives, sixes, and sevens of New York, Minnesota, and Chicago are trying to make you believe it means. So beware especially of New York—so very near—where they are bending over backwards trying to twist our profession into something it simply is not. Not even in the sense that an apple is not a pear, but still a fruit. That architecture—buildings—should no longer help mitigate inner stress, but should, instead, provoke it, is hardly a conceivable objective. But here it is, flourishing on both sides of both great oceans, allied to similar flirtations with absurdity, irony, banality, inconsistency, and, of course, with—Rome, Rome and Rome again—the most obnoxious pests afflicting architecture since fascist gigantism and Nazi blood-and-earth regionalism in Europe one-quarter of a century ago. It is worth noting that the new historicists and eclectics whose habit it is to misquote the past, instead of coming up with a large variety of cocktails, produce—all of them together—little more than a single, standard watery monomix. *But never mind the Minnesota Six.* What is needed is better functioning—on far more levels this time. Just that—just better functionalism. For

there is no such thing as a solid teapot that also pours tea. Such an object might be a penetrating statement about something (and thus perhaps still a work of art), but it is simply NOT A TEAPOT since it CANNOT POUR TEA. Nor is there—nor will there ever be—such a thing as a building which is *intentionally* either absurd, trivial, incoherent, or disconcerting, that is still a building. As for history, that wonderful body of gathering experience is there to help—NOT BE SPILT—abused—thrown away.

It will not be long before the earth's face will be like a network of scars. Energy is spilt and ebbing. Time is ticking faster. Millions have no place to go. What *can* we do less ambitious than saving the world?! What could this Institute of Technology do as soon as it is ready to do so? Well, this first: start disassociating technology—setting it free—from that ruthless and naive notion of progress to which it has been falsely tied for so long. For progress means nothing on this side of evil it if does not mean moving towards well-being for *all* people—and all people means simply that: *all* people—and away from waste, pollution, discrimination, and unnecessary poverty.

I am aware of the fact that many of those present this morning have, over the years, no doubt, sacrificed much in order that a limited number could study here and achieve what was still out of reach in their time: scope and space in which to move forward—upwards (whatever that may mean). It would be satisfying, ladies and gentlemen, would it not, if more than a few of those graduating this morning would wish to share that space and that scope with others less fortunate so that they, too, can follow and move forward? Move without changing face.

It would, I hasten to add, also be gratifying if, in a future not very distant, those graduating on a morning such as this, would represent the wonderful diversity of your country's population more accurately.

I can think of no single word as appropriate, significant, and sparkling as the one with which I shall now end: *solidarity*. Thank you.

Journal of Architectural Education, 60:4, 2007

Compelling Yet Unreliable Theories of Sustainability

Kiel Moe
Northeastern University

Theories of sustainability in American architecture are contingent upon a number of compelling yet unreliable claims that condition the discourse and practice of sustainability. This article identifies illustrative examples of these claims and discusses their importance today. The intent is to emphasize the cogent aspects of these claims while also discerning other approaches to sustainability. The major conclusion is that teaching technics and the expansion of the concept of context constitutes the most productive means for the advancement of sustainable practices.

> There is an ecology of bad ideas, just as there is an ecology of weeds, and it is characteristic that basic error propagates itself.
>
> —Gregory Bateson[1]

In the case of the unreliable narrator in fiction, the compromised credibility of a narrator becomes evident through narration that is at once compelling yet fallacious, biased, misguided, or otherwise misleading.[2] As a device within fiction, this type of narration slowly compromises its reliability and thereby alters the reader's interpretation of a text. In doing so, such narration opens up new perspectives on previous events and ideas in a text. Consequently, the reader comprehends previous content in new ways.

In what follows, I contend that the discourse on sustainability unwittingly follows the logic of an unreliable narrator. Some of its assumptions are biased, misguided, or misleading. These claims include what I describe as the *Energy Crisis* and the *Construction Industry Waste* claims. I also discuss the claims central to *Technological Determinism* and *Vernacular/Regional Determinism*. Over the years, these claims have compelled policy and action, but they contain limitations.[3] To be clear, I do not contend that the protagonists of sustainable architecture are themselves personally unreliable. Rather, the claims at the base of common approaches to sustainability prove unreliable. The aim here is to reconsider this basis. In doing so, I intend to amplify sound aspects of these claims while also proposing other approaches to sustainability engendered by a more thorough understanding of technics and context.[4]

Claim 1: Energy Crisis

Prior to the oil shortage in the early 1970s, issues pertinent to current sustainability in architecture were pragmatic topics devoid of rhetorical exaggeration. Researchers such as James Marston Fitch and Victor Olgyay developed environmental issues primarily as technical, albeit provocative, advancements of modern architecture.[5] After the oil embargo, this attitude changed. The temperament of topics related to the sustainability of architecture shifted from the literal and actual to the rhetorical.

Since then, claims about the scarcity of energy resources have routinely been used to warn of an impending energy crisis. These claims have become pervasive in our culture, reestablished by periodic spikes in the price of oil. In time, these claims have become a core component of sustainability. Introductions to several books on sustainability in architecture base aspects of their arguments for sustainable practices on statistical claims about potential energy shortages.[6] In the context of certain resources such as petroleum or coal, such claims are valid. But when considered broadly, the claims can be shown to be rhetorical escalations designed to incite awareness and urgency rather than foster reflective and intelligent practice. As Figure 1 demonstrates, there is in fact no real energy shortage. There is only a crisis of human choices in respect to our energy practices.[7] Every building site—every milieu—is a vortex of surplus solar-induced energy. As George Bataille noted,

> On the surface of the globe, for *living matter in general*, energy is always in excess; the question is always posed in terms of extravagance. The choice is always limited to how the wealth can be squandered. . . . Hence the real excess does not begin until the growth of the individual or group has reached its limits.[8]

Architects compelled by the *Energy Crisis* claim underutilize this excess.

In architecture, one response to the *Energy Crisis* claim has been the paradigm of conservation. In this paradigm, the aim of the good is to do less bad. While conservation is well intended, it is a thermodynamically pessimistic paradigm and ultimately a futile pursuit. By focusing on reduction rather than production, conservation conditions architects to work on the wrong problem. It diverts architects from a more optimistic approach grounded in the surplus and excess described by Bataille. In contrast to the conservation paradigm, the aim for architects should shift from using less

Solar energy received by the sun each day	1
Melting of an average winter's snow during the spring	10/100
A monsoon circulation between ocean and continent	10/100
Use of energy by all mankind in a year	10/100
A mid-latitude cyclone	1/1,000
A tropical cyclone	1/10,000
Kinetic energy motion in earth's general circulation	1/100,000
The first H-bomb	1/100,000
A squall line containing thunderstorms and perhaps tornados	1/1,000,000
A thunderstorm	1/1,000,000,000
The first A bomb	1/1,000,000,000
The daily output of Boulder Dam	1/1,000,000,000
A typical local rain shower	1/10,000,000,000
A tornado	1/100,000,000,000
Lighting New York City for one night	1/100,000,000,000

Daily arrival of solar energy on earth compared to other energy quantities. Based on William P. Lowry, *Atmospheric Ecology for Designers and Planners* (New York: Van Nostrand Reinhold, 1991), 317.

energy toward the means of *capturing, channeling,* and *producing* energy available in the milieu of a project.[9] For example, current building physics consultants such as Transsolar, Atelier Ten, or Peter Meierhans work to maximize the thermodynamic potential of a building in its physical milieu and demonstrate a more optimistic mode of practice. The paradigm of conservation, on the other hand, remains focused on mitigating the problem of what Reyner Banham described negatively as "power operated solutions."[10] The building physics consultants seek the integrated "structural solutions" that Banham sought. The claims and techniques of conservation limit an architect's conception of a project's milieu.

The energy in the milieu is maximal, not minimal. As such, architects need a more imaginative yet real conception of the physical milieu of architecture. A pedagogy that exposes architects to the full vitality of this milieu would focus not only on maximizing available energy resources but would consider the relationship between energy and our technics as well.[11] Technics refers to the broader context of technologies, as embedded within a historical, social, economic, ecological, and intellectual framework. Regrettably, architecture tends to teach its technical practices as isolated and technologically determined rather than socially constructed. Technology in other disciplines is a variable of social practice and progress, not its determinant. As Gilles Deleuze has stated, "Tools always presuppose a machine, and the machine is always social before it is technical. There is always a social machine which selects or assigns the technical elements used."[12] Social needs and desires predetermine any technical system. For example, the social, economic, marketing, and physiological history of air conditioning technology is central to the conditioning of spaces, people, and energy practices in the twentieth century. As Gail Cooper demonstrated, the marketing and social choices of air conditioning determined as much about the development of air conditioning as its engineers.[13] As such, the somewhat irrational history of air conditioning marketing is more central to its widespread use than its efficacy as a means of achieving human comfort. As these systems developed over time, the habitual conditioning of spaces, people, and energy practices with air conditioning systems became a prime factor in the perception of an energy crisis. The relationship between air conditioning and energy use has been determined socially rather than scientifically *and so will its alternatives.* When presented as socially constructed, architects can understand the positive and insidious possibilities of conditioning and develop alternate modes. Such instruction belongs alongside conventional pedagogical approaches to the technical descriptions of "environmental control systems." Merely teaching architects the technical components, systems, conservation strategies, and their integration in "environmental control" courses limits the horizon of sustainability.[14]

Claim 2: Construction Yields Half of the Landfill Waste and Buildings Consume Half of the Energy in the United States

A litany of statistics about the material and energy wastes of buildings is a common rhetorical device in American sustainability. These statistics are central to the introductory arguments for numerous books, articles, and websites on the subject.[15] The statistics draw attention to the role of the construction industry in a context of increasing consumption and diminishing resources.[16] Yet, one must also keep in mind another statistic that should temper responses to these statistics: all architecture firms represent about three percent of the total construction economy in the United States.[17] The other 97 percent comprises everything from road construction, bridges, and other infrastructure in addition to buildings not designed by architects. Consequently, architects are directly in control of three percent of the waste flow so often cited. While architects clearly need to provide leadership through example and affiliation, architects in conventional practice are not as immediately empowered to alter these industry-wide statistics as the claims suggest. In the arguments about material and energy waste, these statistics routinely overstate architecture's direct ability to affect waste flows.[18] Architecture is one among several culpable industrial parties. Our technics contain energy and material flows unimaginable to many architects trained

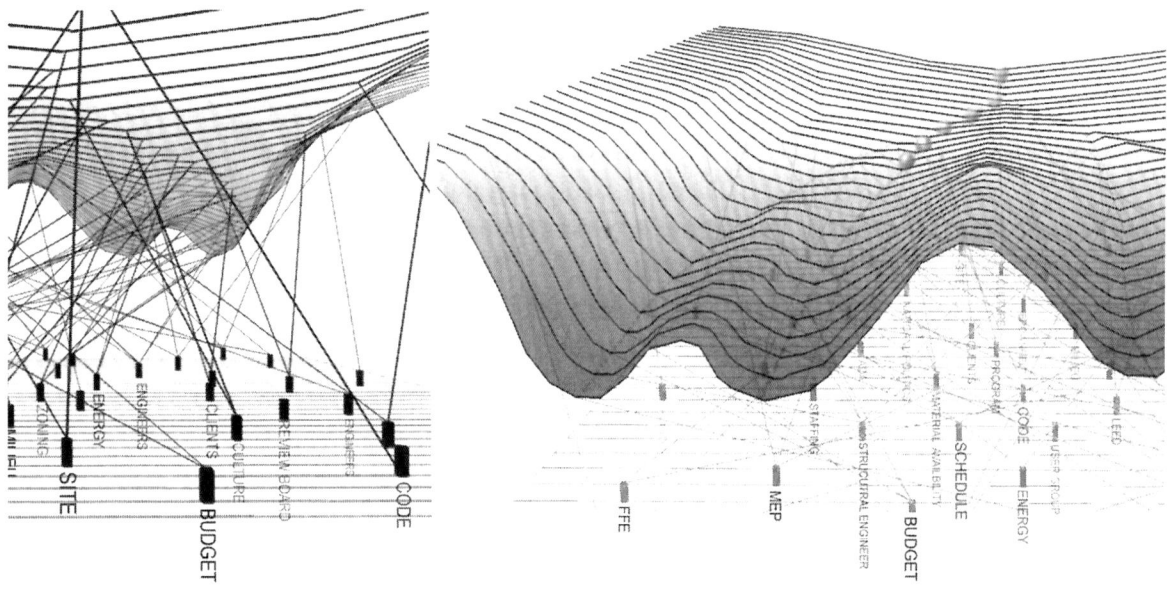

This is the epigenetic landscape of an architecture project, as seen from below and above. The multiple shaping factors of a project constantly tug on the surface from below, altering the course of a project. The resultant surface directs a project in specific directions and toward particular ends. Based upon C. H. Waddington, *Tools for Thought: How to Understand and Apply the Latest Scientific Techniques of Problem Solving* (London: Jonathan Cape, 1977), 29, 36.

to view buildings as autonomous objects rather than extensive systems. Effective strategies for construction waste must address the reality of larger, more systemic problems. Architects certainly have a role here. However, the rhetorical escalation of our role in conventional practice obfuscates cogent strategies.

One response to these statistics has been recycling. Recycled steel, reclaimed wood, and leased carpet are obvious and necessary choices in building production. However, it remains an open question whether recycling reduces consumption or merely engenders ever-increasing consumption.[19] While the habit of recycling has increased, so have more depleting forms of consumption. These larger consumptive habits dwarf recycled content.[20] In terms of electrical illumination, Michelle Addington has demonstrated that increased square footage in construction negates the gains made in energy efficiency over the same period, resulting in a net consumption of resources.[21] This logic of negated efficiencies applies to recycling as well.[22] By recycling, we often consume slightly less as we consume more and more overall. Once again, the aim of the good is to do less bad. Recycling, like conservation, distracts architects from identifying and working on the right problem. Beyond the common sense impulse to specify materials with recycled content, architecture should develop much deeper knowledge about the material effects of the construction industry.

All material produces profound effects that exceed the aesthetic or technical ends that determine most specifications for construction. The specification of material in architecture immediately implicates a vast network of effects.[23] These effects range from the molecular to the territorial and include social, economic, and ecological implications.[24] Architects are disproportionately aware of the constructions they propose and woefully unaware of the inverse architecture of material extraction, production, and transportation. Material knowledge should not focus merely on the properties and performance of materials in building assemblies. Rather, architects should grasp the way materials fundamentally organize, animate, and transform life. The production and application of materials alter unseen ecologies, sway local and distant economies, amplify or inhibit social progress, and even engender the rise and fall of cultures. Only architects with an operational sense of the history, processes, and distribution of materials will sufficiently comprehend and thus alter material usage toward sustainable ends. This suggests a pedagogical approach to material knowledge more closely aligned with the Annales School than materials and methods alone.[25] For Fernand Braudel, the material exchanges in the commerce, geography, and climate of everyday people and habits were the focus of his pan-disciplinary approach to history. In his view, these practices accumulated into a more consequential history than more prevalent narratives of major historical figures and events. Similarly, architecture must extensively consider the material effects of our practices in order to amend the material flows within the construction industry. Then, *along with the construction industry,* architects would thereby realize what Ulrich Beck describes as "reflexive modernization" and practice effective material sustainability.[26]

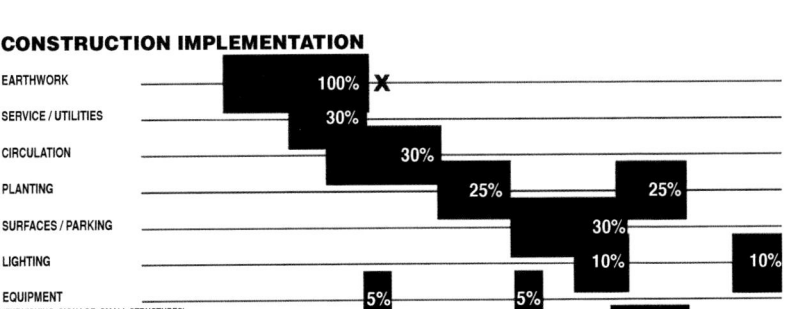

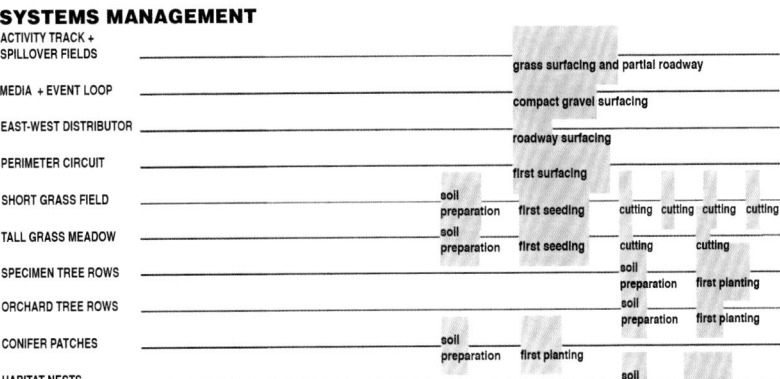

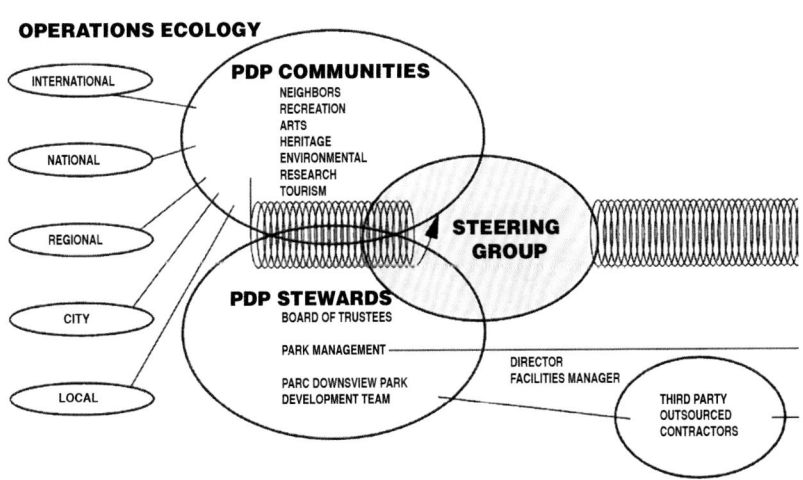

Construction Implementation, Systems Management, and Operations Ecology by the office of Field Operations for their entry to the Downsview Park Competition, Toronto, 1999. Courtesy James Corner/Field Operations.

Claim 3: Technological Determinism

Our culture frequently perceives technology as a compelling approach to sustainability. For many, new technology is the key to sustainable practices. This approach is evident in a building such as Renzo Piano's project for the *New York Times* Headquarters as well as the battery of engineering consultants, computational hardware and software, and technocratic programs such as LEED that engenders such a building. The success of technologically determined practices imparts the impression that technology and its quantitative authority guarantee a degree of sustainability. This is what David Noble describes as the "machine mentality" of our culture: no matter what the problem, technology is the solution.[27] Commenting on this approach, George Grant stated, "We can hold in our minds the enormous benefits of technological society, but we cannot so easily hold the ways it may have deprived us, because technique is ourselves."[28] If technique and technology are ourselves, we should temper our assumptions about its role in sustainable practices because technology, by itself, is unreliable.

While technological developments often amplify prospects for sustainability, we never cultivate proper technological management practices that would account for the constituent by-products of a technological world. Three Mile Island, Chernobyl, and Hurricane Katrina represent large-scale examples of failed technological management. In these cases, society unduly demands of technology what it cannot reliably provide: assured protection from hazard. Today, the difference between vibrant life and utter destruction increasingly becomes a problem of risk management based upon calculations of what is just less than hazardous. We manage the risks of technology with outmoded methods that assign culpability to individuals and individual causes. However, broader personal, political, and industrial choices actually produce this context of risk, *not individuals or individual technologies.* Hazard increasingly characterizes our world, what Ulrich Beck calls a "Risk Society."[29] The threats, sources, and effects of these hazards can no longer be isolated to any single culprit or cause. In our age, the sources, sites, and effects of catastrophe approach the continental and the global. Risk now leaves no life, and no aspect of life, untouched.

In our culture, there is precarious asymmetry between technology's *capabilities* and its *culpabilities*. While technology may engender and accelerate progress, it will minimally manage its associated risks. Technology offers no automatic security or promise on its own. Only the agency of personal and collective choices will determine sustainability. As David Noble stated, "There are no technological promises, only human ones, and social progress must not be reduced to, or confused with, mere technological progress."[30]

Without critical reflection, technology is as likely to engender, as it is to annihilate unintentionally, sustainable possibilities. In this view, sustainability is principally a subject of our technics, what Lewis Mumford called "The Machine."[31] "The Machine" represents not only the apparatus of technical production—its tools, machines, and networks—but also the agencies, histories, and habits of mind that comprise the substrate of technical production. Thus, to work on sustainability is to understand the problem of "The Machine." To understand the problem of "The Machine" is to study the social, economic, political, ecological, and intellectual substrate of technical practices. Rather than perpetuate the determinist trap and perpetual rush toward new technologies, architecture should situate technics at the core of sustainability. Presenting the culpabilities of technology alongside its capabilities would establish a more robust, albeit less euphoric, connection between technology and sustainability.

Claim 4: Vernacular and Regional Determinism

The Vernacular and Regional Determinisms each contain claims regarding sustainability.[32] In the Vernacular approach, architects perceive indigenous patterns of development as inherently sustainable responses to their respective sites and contexts of production. Similarly, Regionalism pursues sustainability by focusing on local conditions and resisting globalization. Each is pertinent because they observe established ecological and social conditions. In doing so, they seek sensible adaptations to climatic, resource, and building problems.

It is difficult, however, to imagine a reliable form of sustainability that does not engage previous *and* current technics.[33] Today, every region is a mongrel of local and global conditions. In his own way, Lewis Mumford developed such a concept of the region. According to Liane Lefaivre, Mumford merged his interests in technics with idiosyncratic aspects of regionalism.[34] Together they yielded a productive and non-sentimental approach to regionalism. For Mumford, "regionalism is indissociable from the universal or global."[35] Mumford cannot conceive of a region or a site without the global and historical substrate that presupposes it. He never intends to resuscitate prior artifacts. Rather, he studies a region to discern its technics. This expands the concept of a region from a place-only concept to the broader technics that now comprise any place.

What is fundamentally at stake in any vernacular or regional approach is a definition of context. Increasingly, context must include a broader set of agencies in its definition. A project's actual context exceeds the predominant conception of context as either that evident in figure-ground analysis, the style of a building's adjacent real estate, or its spatial region as understood in a variety of ways. To grasp the complexities of context in contemporary buildings adequately, these agencies must include political, economic, temporal, technical, ecological, social, cultural, and material parameters.

Ultimately, context is anything that may engender a decision, building, or practice. This could be too vast a pool of potential agencies, but the only context that matters is the specific context responsible for a particular decision, building, or practice. This expanded definition of context can become so extensive that a key problem is the means to visualize the integration of its multiple factors. Architects must expand their concept of context yet also be able to visualize the process of material and immaterial integration in a context in order to engender sustainability.

Currently, architecture has few, if any, theories of integration that are instructive in this way. Sanford Kwinter has developed an observation about integration that applies to this problem. In his understanding of Michel Foucault's "materialism of the incorporeal," Kwinter discusses the problems of organization, integration, and coordination in design.[36] His approach relies upon ideas from developmental biology and his discussion of these scientific theories in respect of architecture points to a more comprehensive definition of context. While prevalent architectural definitions confine context to adjacent spatial and material conditions, Kwinter's observations connect a much broader explication of context with one means to visualize it.

To guide his reader into an understanding of context, D'Arcy Thompson wrote in *On Growth and Form*: "The form of an object is a 'diagram of forces,' in this sense we can deduce the forces that are acting or have acted upon it."[37] Thompson views present form in terms of its shaping forces, the pattern of its historical development. Developmental biologist C. H. Waddington visualized this pattern of development occurring in an abstract, multidimensional space called an "epigenetic landscape."[38] An epigenetic landscape is a virtual topography of developmental pathways that determine the development of a physical entity. All the shaping forces—political, economic, historical, technical, ecological, social, cultural, material—perpetually tug on this virtual topography. The epigenetic landscape negotiates this sport of forces and ultimately accounts for the characteristics of a developing entity. A developing entity inevitably encounters events that shift development toward new ends. As Figure 2 shows, such transformations are the task of architects: strategic alterations to a project's developmental pathway. At times, these developmental transformations produce only minor inflections. At other times, these transformations produce more radical changes even if the inflecting force is the same. Such radical inflections occur when the entire system is poised, ready for qualitative change. Biologists identify this poised state as a "period of competence."[39] This is the most opportune time to inflect a system toward a desired end. Intervening outside the period of competence requires a greater effort to bring the epigenetic landscape back into a state of competence. This discussion applies literally to architecture because *context is the epigenetic landscape of architecture.*

One recent example of such thinking is a board submitted by Field Operations for the 1999 Downsview Park Competition in Toronto. Figure 3 shows how this board organizes many of the factors and agencies—administrative, ecological, economic, political, cultural, social—that ultimately frame the development and design of the project. The diagram organizes the factors in time, not space. The designers included everything from government and user groups, to construction and systems management, to biota introduction and the "Operations Ecology." This visualization attempts to envision the context of implementation. Here, design is understood in terms of its shaping forces. Rather than the design of isolated objects, these designers identify strategic spatial and temporal interventions given a particular context as a pretext for design.

My point here is that architects can no longer understand context as spatial and material configurations alone. Rather, architects must understand and design the multiple immaterial agencies that constitute any actual context. The vital, if not delirious, constitution of contexts can instigate more effective approaches to sustainability. As stated above, such approaches will require greater knowledge, better representation, and the integration of the immaterial agencies of architecture. Without an extensive concept of context, architecture will not be able to identify and integrate these larger dynamics of sustainability.

Compelling Yet Reliable Sustainability
Each of the claims presented above contribute to our assumptions about sustainability. The claims are unreliable, ultimately, because they contain a limited conception of architecture's context and technics. As such, they limit the practices of sustainability and preclude approaches that would engage architects in the much larger dynamics of sustainability. The shift in approach suggested here is not more statistics, checklists, or technologies but the development of deeper knowledge with regard to the actual context and technics of any architectural project. The most significant adjustments to the discourse and practice of sustainability will involve a shift to more literal and extensive conceptions of context and technics. Our technics are pervasive; technology is by now our nature. It dominates our practices and our lives; yet, as a discipline, we know relatively little about it. Technics, as taught through the history and philosophy of technology, should be core content for architectural education. This will prompt a radical immersion into architecture's complicated contexts. To teach architects about the systemic agencies of our technics and contexts already teaches a more potent understanding of sustainability. Architects need an operational understanding of the physical milieu of their work, expanded knowledge of material ecologies and effects, the capabilities and culpabilities of technology, the social basis of technology, the actual situation of architects in our industries, and a more vital conception of its time-imbued context. Only then will architecture practice what David Harvey has described as the "advancement of more socially just, politically emancipating and ecologically sane mix of spatiotemporal processes."[40]

Notes

1. Gregory Bateson, *Steps to an Ecology of Mind* (New York: Ballantine Books, 1972), 484.
2. Wayne Booth, *Rhetoric of Fiction* (Chicago, IL: University of Press, 1961), 158–59, 274.
3. For a more general discussion of common approaches to sustainability, see John S. Dryzek, *The Politics of the Earth: Environmental Discourses* (New York: Oxford University Press, 1997).
4. The elusive concept of sustainability here includes, in principle, the accepted definitions of sustainability such as the 1987 Brundtland Report's definition as human development that "meets the needs of the present generation without compromising the ability of future generations to meet their needs." However, I am more interested in the means and outcomes of the topic than its congested title. In many ways, the topic's title seems to confine the imagination and polemically segregate the profession. What constitutes sustainability is a commonsense set of decisions that should be at the core of any design practice, a basic fiduciary assumption. It no longer makes sense to differentiate sustainable practices from presumably unsustainable, yet taught, practices but rather to integrate these theories and practices directly into pedagogy and practice.
5. Amongst the two authors' books, two in particular are pertinent here: James Marston Fitch, *American Building and the Environmental Forces that Shaped It* (Boston, MA: Houghton Mifflin, 1972); Victor Olgyay, *Design with Climate: Bioclimatic Approach to Architectural Regionalism* (Princeton, NJ: Princeton University Press, 1963).
6. Such introductions occur in each of the following books on this topic: Brenda and Robert Vale, *Towards a Green Architecture* (London: RIBA Publications Ltd., 1991): 15–68; Richard L. Crowther, *Ecologic Architecture* (Boston, MA: Butterworth Architecture, 1992), 1–31; Rocky Mountain Institute, *A Primer on Sustainable Building* (Aspen, CO: Rocky Mountain Institute, 1995); Laura C. Zeiher, *The Ecology of Architecture: A Complete Guide to Creating the Environmentally Conscious Building* (New York: Whitney Library of Design, 1996), 1–24; Klaus Daniels, *The Technology of Ecological Building: Basic Principles and Measures, Examples and Ideas,* trans. Elizabeth Schwaiger (Boston, MA: Birkhauser Verlag, 1997), 7–44; and Sandra Mendler and William Odell, *The HOK Guidebook to Sustainable Design* (New York: John Wiley & Sons Inc., 2000), 1–13.
7. David Nye, *Consuming Power: A Social History of American Energies* (Cambridge, MA: MIT Press, 1998), 217–64.
8. Georges Bataille, "The Meaning of General Economy," in *The Bataille Reader,* eds., Fred Botting and Scott Wilson (Oxford: Blackwell, 1997), 184–9. Emphasis his.
9. I use the term "milieu" throughout in contrast to terms such as "environment." "Environment" has many cultural and historical associations, which I seek to avoid. "Milieu" retains a more focused view of the energy and materials systems that surround and constitute architecture.
10. Reyner Banham, *The Architecture of the Well-Tempered Environment* (London: The Architectural Press, 1969), 18–20.
11. This is a recurrent topic for Lewis Mumford and is the topic of his most comprehensive book on technics: Lewis Mumford, *Technics and Civilization* (New York: Harcourt, Brace & World, 1934).
12. Gilles Deleuze and Claire Parnet, *Dialogues II* (New York: Columbia University Press, 1987), 70.
13. Gail Cooper, *Air Conditioning America: Engineers and the Controlled Environment, 1900-1960* (Baltimore, MD: Johns Hopkins University Press, 1998), 183–90.
14. One example is the Solar Decathlon Competition. This well-intentioned event requires the research, design, development, coordination, and construction of a solar powered house located on the National Mall. The dramatic irony of its broader technics, however, is that the houses often require more energy in their transportation from remote locations to the National Mall than the house itself either conserves or produces. For instance, to transport the Cal-Poly, San Luis Obispo house in two trucks 2400 miles each way requires nearly 1.5 billion British Thermal Units of energy, dwarfing the energy saved or produced by the house itself.
15. James Steele, *Sustainable Architecture: Principles, Paradigms, and Case Studies* (New York: McGraw-Hill, New York. 1998); Mendler, Sandra F., and William Odell, *The HOK Guidebook to Sustainable Design* (New York: John Wiley & Sons Inc., 2000), 1–13; www.architecture2030.org (accessed July 14, 2006).
16. This article uses the U.S. Energy Information Administration data. The most current forecast on energy demand is http://www.eia.doe.gov/oiaf/aeo/demand.html, based upon the following assumptions: http://www.eia.doe.gov/oiaf/aeo/assumption/pdf/residential.pdf, http://www.eia.doe.gov/oiaf/aeo/assumption/pdf/commercial.pdf, http://www.eia.doe.gov/oiaf/aeo/assumption/pdf/industrial.pdf (all accessed July 10, 2006).
17. James Cramer, Presentation to the AIA Chicago Board Members, 2005; as quoted in Daniel S. Friedman, "Architectural Education and Practice on the Verge," *AIA Report on Integrated Practice,* adapted from the forthcoming chapter in *Designing for Designers, eds.,* T. Fisher, J. L. Nasar, and W. F. E. Preiser (New York: Fairchild, 2007).
18. Recent reorganizations of energy consumption data from earnest protagonists such as Ed Mazria in *Architecture 2030* serve as a current example. Edward Mazria, www.architecture2030.org (accessed July 14, 2006). It should be noted that in certain arguments, it proves difficult to cleanly distinguish process energy loads from architectural energy loads in a laboratory, light industrial facility, and some factories.
19. John Tierney, "Recycling is Garbage," *New York Times Magazine,* June 30, 1996, 24–29, 44, 48, 51, 53.
20. Ironically, even initially opposing positions on the issues now agree on this contested issue. Both the Worldwatch Institute and Bjorn Lomberg have stated that the actual merits of recycling are in doubt: "ultimately, recycling simply results in the manufacture of more things." Worldwatch Institute, *Good Stuff? A Behind-the-Scenes Guide to the Things We Buy,* from Worldwatch Institute, *State of the World 2004* (New York: W. W. Norton & Co., 2004), 1; Lomberg: ". . .the current recycling level is reasonable, but that we perhaps should not aim to recycle much more." Bjorn Lomberg, *The Skeptical Environmentalist* (Cambridge: Cambridge University Press, 2001), 209.
21. Michelle Addington, "Energy, Body, and Building," *Harvard Design Magazine* 18 (Spring/Summer 2003): 18–21.
22. By far, the most sustainable building is the one not built. These facts prove difficult for a program, such as LEED, that measures its success in the increasing square footage of LEED certified new construction in the United States.
23. John Fernandez, *Material Architecture: Emergent Materials for Innovative Buildings and Ecological Construction* (Oxford: Architectural Press, 2006), 299–305; Charles Kilbert, Jan Sendzimir, and G. Bradley Guy, eds., *Construction Ecology: Nature as the Basis for Green Buildings* (New York: Spon Press, 2002), 7–28.

24. Examples of this material agency saturate the history of technology. A few examples include Lynn Whyte, *Medieval Technology and Social Change* (London: Oxford University Press, 1980); Gilles Deleuze, *Treatise on Nomadology: The War Machine* [A Thousand Plateaus: Capitalism and Schizophrenia], trans. Brian Massumi (Minneapolis, MN: University of Minnesota Press, 1987), 394–415; Cecil D. Elliott, *Technics and Architecture: The Development of Materials and Systems for Buildings* (Cambridge, MA: MIT Press, 1992). More recently, popular books on the history of materials have also emerged: Mark Kurlansky, *Salt: A World History* (New York: Walker and Co., 2002); and Jared Diamond, *Guns, Germs, and Steel: The Fates of Human Societies* (New York: W. W. Norton, 1997).
25. Most of Fernand Braudel's work is pertinent here; however, the cycle on *Civilization and Capitalism* is particularly useful for our technics: Fernand Braudel, *Civilization and Capitalism, 15th-18th Century*. 3 vols: v. 1. *The Structure of Everyday Life*. v. 2. *The Wheels of Commerce*. v. 3. *The Perspective of the World* (New York: Harper & Row, 1982–1984).
26. Ulrich Beck, "Reflexive Modernization" in Ulrich Beck, Anthony Giddens, and Scott Lash, *Reflexive Modernization: Politics, Tradition and Aesthetics in the Modern Social Order* (Stanford, CA: Stanford University Press, 1994), 1–55.
27. David F. Noble, "Statement of David F. Noble at Hearings on Industrial Sub-Committee of the 98th U.S. Congress," in David F. Noble, *Progress Without People* (Chicago, IL: Charles H. Kerr Publishing, 1993), 100.
28. George Grant, "A Platitude," in *Technology and Empire* (Toronto, ON: Anansi 1969), 137–43.
29. Ulrich Beck, *Ecological Politics in the Age of Risk* (Cambridge, MA: Polity Press, 1995).
30. Noble, *Forces of Production: A Social History of Industrial Automation* (New York: Alfred A. Knopf, 1984), 351.
31. Mumford, 9–12
32. Bernard Rudofsky, *Architecture without Architects: An Introduction to Non-Pedigreed Architecture* (New York: Museum of Modern Art, 1964); Peter Calthorpe, *The Next American Metropolis: Ecology, Community, and the American Dream* (New York: Princeton Architectural Press, 1993); and Kenneth Frampton, "Towards a Critical Regionalism: Six Points for an Architecture of Resistance," in *The Anti-Aesthetic: Essays in Postmodern Culture*, ed. Hal Foster (Port Townsend, WA: Bay Press, 1983), 16–30.
33. See Steven Moore, "Technology, Place and the Nonmodern Thesis," *Journal of Architectural Education* 54, no. 3 (Spring 2001): 130–139, for an elaboration of this point in the form of a critique of Critical Regionalism.
34. Liane Lefaivre and Alexander Tzonis, *Critical Regionalism: Architecture and Identity in a Globalized World* (Munich: Prestel, 2003), 33–39. Lefaivre is careful to emphasize that Mumford's work in the 1930s in particular is relevant here. In this period, Mumford's work in technics is combined with communication with Patrick Geddes and work with Benton MacKaye produces an idiosyncratic but potent approach to regionalism.
35. Lefaivre and Tzonis, 35.
36. Sanford Kwinter, "The Materialism of the Incorporeal," *Columbia Documents in Architecture and Theory* 6 (1995): 85–89.
37. D'Arcy W. Thompson, *On Growth and Form* (Cambridge: Cambridge University Press, 1951), 16.
38. Biologist C. H. Waddington uses the terms *Chreod* (Greek for necessary path) and epigenetic landscape to describe this virtual developmental landscape and these terms have become standard. See C. H. Waddington, *Tools for Thought: How to Understand and Apply the Latest Scientific Techniques of Problem Solving* (London: Jonathan Cape, 1977), 103–29; C. H. Waddington, "Tools of Thought about Complex Systems," *Ekistics* 37, no. 218 (January 1974): 16.
39. Waddington, 111.
40. David Harvey, "The New Urbanism and the Communitarian Trap," *Harvard Design Magazine: Changing Cities* 1 (Winter/Spring 1997): 68–69.

Pedagogy

134
1957
History and the Architect
Sigfried Giedion

138
1959
Objectives of Architectural Education
Ralph Rapson

141
1960
Full Scale Prototype Structures
Arthur Burton

144
1960
How Become an Architect?
Richard J. Neutra

145
1967
Television as a Design Tool
Stuart W. Rose and M. Scheffel Pierce

150
1967
The Environmental Design Umbrella
Lawrence B. Anderson

152
1968
The Death of the Beaux-Arts
Murray A. Milne and Charles W. Rusch

158
1969
Toward a Theory of Architecture Machines
Nicholas Negroponte

162
1974
Poetics
Louis I. Kahn

163
1976
Messages in the Interstices
Marc Treib

168
1979
Gaming at CRS
Charles Estes

170
1982
Typology and Primary Elements
Todd Williams and Ricardo Scofidio

173
1982
Architecture as Drawing
Alberto Pérez-Gómez

180
1987
An Open Letter to Architectural Educators and Students of Architecture
Daniel Libeskind

182
1987
Private Reactions to Public Criticism
Kathryn H. Anthony

193
1999
Boundary Studies
Lily Chi

200
2006
The Canon and the Void
Kathryn H. Anthony and Metlem Ö. Gürel

212
2011
From Model to Mashup
Ana Miljački

Pedagogy

Marc J Neveu

> Teaching is to present the yet not said the yet not made
>
> —Louis I. Kahn

It might seem obvious that over the course of seventy-five years a publication titled *Journal of Architectural Education* would include an abundance of scholarship around pedagogy. The content of the journal evolved over that time and, yes, did include scholarship around pedagogy, but as we see in this current publication, not exclusively. This section contains eighteen essays on architectural education, spanning seventy-five volume years. The type, scope, and topics are varied. Themes ebb and flow; influences emerge and recede. Over the course of the decades, case studies are presented, reflected upon, and discursively situated. Fundamental questions—What does the architect need to know? And how does one teach such knowledge?—are addressed in a variety of ways.

What Does the Architect Need to Know?

The content of what students are to be taught is a constant question throughout the journal. Lawrence Anderson (1967) argues that the design of the physical environment is inherently interdisciplinary, but to be interdisciplinary requires the existence of the disciplines. What makes up the discipline of architecture, of course, is a big question. The notion of the banal aspects of architecture appears in an essay written years later by Tod Williams and Ricardo Scofidio (1982). The second year "passage problem" at the Cooper Union introduced students to "primary elements" and typology. In distinction to Burchard (and later, Williams and Scofidio), Ralph Rapson (1959) argues for Architecture—capital *A*—not mere building. Rapson, who goes out of his way to make sure we know that he is an architect and not an educator, goes on to explain why architects, not educators, have the knowledge that students need. Richard Neutra (1960), who traveled across the continent to study under Frank Lloyd Wright, goes even further and argues for an apprentice model in a somewhat grammatically challenged address to the Association of Collegiate Schools of Architecture. Alberto Pérez-Gómez (1982) reminds us of the distance between drawing and building. Rejecting the reductionist view of drawing as building, he argues that drawing may reveal the truth of reality. This is a good reminder for architecture students who rarely, if ever, build studio projects. None of this seems to matter for Daniel Libeskind (1987), whose open letter castigates all of architectural education. Just before Libeskind concludes the essay by stating that he is opening his own architecture school, he explains, with a nod to *Hamlet*, "The school has become a device which prevents students of Architecture from acquiring the knowledge that would enable them to articulate the fundamental question of Architecture: being or not."

How to Learn?

Throughout the history of the JAE and in this volume, the studio model is rarely if ever questioned. What happens in the studio and how students learn has, of course, varied greatly. Beyond questions of theory versus practice, the role of technology in the studio is an undercurrent in these discussions. In 1967 Stuart W. Rose and M. Scheffel Pierce utilized the then mainstream technology of the television in the studio. Students developed novel model-building techniques to create multiple iterations of formal relationships that could be televised and then broadcast for review. The media was limited only by the scale of equipment needed to film the models. Nicholas Negroponte (1969) went even further as he proposed "architecture machines" as a means for architects, ironically, to have more impact on the built environment. Early experiments with machine learning were intended to make complex and banal decisions so that designers would not have to. Negroponte predicted a bright future, with machines wandering about the city seeing and learning "good design."

A series of essays deal with design methodology, such as the curious "Cal-Oregon Experiment" (1968) based on the writings of Christopher Alexander. The essay, written by Murray A. Milne and Charles W. Rusch, is a fictitious interview that simultaneously proposed and then critiqued the methodological approaches and outcomes of two actual studios—one based in Oregon and the other in Berkeley. It is a playful poke at discourse that can seem pompous and stuffy. While not strictly pedagogic in nature, Charles Estes's essay (1979) on gaming at Caudill Rowlett Scott far predates more recent interest in gaming and education. Used only in certain situations, the methodology was an active approach to client and architect interaction that was also playful.

While a lot of ink was spilled about studio education, it was not until the 1990s that actual studio work began to be published with a consistent frequency. Notably, Lily Chi (1999) published work from a studio on the topic of boundaries that developed drawings and full-scale mock-ups that have a theater-like quality to them. Another example from Design as Scholarship is Ana Miljački's article (2011), which discursively situates student projects. Even if some critics were worried that postmodernity had returned, the essay shows a range of visual approaches. Still, there is space to be critical of the studio. Kathryn Anthony's essay (1987) on the pedagogical value of reviews is striking in a number of ways. Her research demonstrates what many of us know: there is little evidence to support the value of a final review in its traditional format of one student presenting to a row of critics. In her documented surveys, everyone involved in final reviews—students, faculty, critics, and alumni—all thought final reviews needed improvement. The essay ends with a series of recommendations that are still useful more than thirty years after they were written.

While a number of the essays in the journal seem dated, others seem outside of time. Arthur Burton's (1960) full-scale prototypes of structural forms that were constructed and tested by students look like work performed in a studio today, even though that work was completed in the 1950s. Other issues—such as the relationship between theory and practice, the influence of technology, and a focus on either disciplinary or interdisciplinary work—continually resurface in essays on pedagogy. Oddly enough, so does the criticism that our teaching methodologies have not changed much since the emergence of the École des Beaux-Arts. (See Libeskind's essay from 1987 for a more visceral critique.) One massive rift across the years of the journal is in the discussion around history. Writing in 1957, Sigfried Giedion gives an overview of how history had been conceptualized previously. The essay is full of gendered language—students and historians are all men—and is really concerned with issues of how much we should teach history, when to teach it, and how issues of "space" and "space conception" differ. Fifty years later Kathryn Anthony and Meltem Ö. Gürel (2006) question the very canon that we teach and demonstrate the utter lack of diversity in the textbooks we use to teach history, especially with regard to race and gender. They make a strong case, and it is only in the subsequent fifteen years that historians and faculty have truly begun to listen.

Note
Epigraph: Louis I. Kahn, "Poetics," *Journal of Architectural Education* 27, no. 1 (1974): 10.

History and the Architect

Sigfried Giedion
Harvard University

Uncertainty and hesitancy are noticeable in the attitude of many universities and institutes of technology as to the relations between history and the architect. The importance, or the unimportance, of the study of history has repercussions upon the whole training of the architect.

There are many opinions in the profession about this relationship, and there are also many who have not made up their mind.

One, perhaps over-simplified, attitude is that of the practitioner: "History! An architect has to build. He must be taught the necessary know-how for this. That's what his training is for. What has history to do with this job? History courses are only a waste of precious time in an already overloaded curriculum."

Another familiar attitude held in the profession is the belief that a study of the historical merely intimidates the young architectural student, and that history—if taught at all—should be given only towards the end of his studies.

Others hold that the study of history produces eclectics and that students will be seduced by the past to become copyists instead of inventors.

These and other opinions are trying to eliminate contact with the past, considering it as something useless, and even obstructive, to present-day development.

Now suddenly an interest in history has reawakened and we find discussions on this subject taking place in professional circles and in the Architectural Magazines—and more are scheduled.

How is this to be explained?

Undoubtedly it stems from the period when the vocabulary of contemporary architecture was being formulated—above all in the 1920s—following all the harm that had been done to architecture by the nineteenth-century plundering of historical forms.

At that time those who were framing the new architecture had to search within themselves and in the life around them to produce an architectural language equivalent to their own period.

Today this first step has been accomplished and contemporary architecture has become a universal language: a language capable of being adapted to meet the needs of different conditions and different idioms in the varied regions of the world. This is something quite different from an "international style"—a misnomer that should be carefully avoided.

The horizon today has been considerably widened. Closer relations between Eastern and Western civilizations, and their consequences, are in the forefront of the field. Not only this: there hovers in the background the demand for a wider range of inner relationships, and, to a certain degree, even a feeling for what is common in human existence: a new demand for continuity.

This may be the real reason why, from all sides, an interest in history has again revived. But our approach to history is, of course, quite different from that of the nineteenth century.

The Nineteenth Century

In the nineteenth century the architectural historian stood upon firm ground. An encyclopedic treatment of architectural history presented the student with a sort of inventory of the acknowledged masterpieces of architecture. There was a second inventory consisting of the classical orders and Gothic structural features which was accompanied by all the details of entablatures, friezes, and other ornamental accessories. This presented the young architect with a history of styles that proved very useful to him in the design of Classical, Romanesque, Gothic, or Renaissance banks, city halls, and law courts.

In the nineteenth century one stood upon firm ground. The study of history certainly fulfilled a useful purpose.

Banister Fletcher's *History of Architecture on the Comparative Method*, which is in some respects still useful today in the exactness of its descriptive material, is significant in that it is an epitome of all the history that was then considered necessary and useful to the young architect.

But when, early in this century, the collapse of eclectic architecture finally came about, this materialistic way of approach slowly began to be regarded as insufficient, and even detrimental, for the training of the student.

The Twentieth Century

During the formative period of contemporary architecture, in the '20s and '30s, universities and institutes of technology still clung to their former comparative, descriptive methods of teaching the history of the styles of building. And when contemporary architecture—after many long and often deceptive battles—finally won the day, there was an immense backlog of mistrust which, coupled with a deep inner uncertainty, caused the teaching of history to be banished altogether from many architectural curricula—thus throwing out the baby with the bathwater.

This is still to some extent the situation.

How do we regard history today?

We have ceased to regard history as a static process, in which past, present, and future are listed in separate columns—as in a bookkeeper's ledger. The result is that the past is no longer seen as something dim and fusty, dead as dust, but as an inseparable part of our living human destiny.

This brings us to our main problem: *how can the history of architecture be taught today?* Not old-fashioned history, but one that takes account of our changed viewpoint—that history is not static but dynamic, that history is an ever-changing process, depending upon the point of view of each succeeding generation.

This was already implicit in Jacob Burckhardt's *Reflections on History*, written nearly a hundred years ago. In this book he stated: "We shall start out from the one point accessible to us; the one eternal center of all things—Man. Man, suffering, striving, doing. Man as he is and was and ever shall be. We shall study the recurrent, the constant and the typical, as echoing in us and intelligible through us... and now let us remember all that we owe to the past as a spiritual *continuum*, which forms part of our supreme spiritual heritage."

We have now to find where the key lies to our problem today, and in this connection we have to ask whether there are any phenomena that clearly run through the whole of historical development, and upon which the history of architecture, as taught today, can be basically founded. Such phenomena—such notions—must be extracted from the innermost heart of architectural concepts.

The Objectivity of the Historian

Before going further into this, however, there is a certain prejudice that must be cleared out of the way. This is the fiction that the historian is a man who stands above the turmoil of the milling crowd and, from an ivory tower, surveys the scene with a dispassionate eye, interpreting it with a timeless rightness.

This so-called objectivity of the historian is a product of the last century, which somehow believed itself able to erect buildings of a timeless quality by piecing together a sort of photomontage of the ornamentations of bygone periods.

There is, in fact, no such thing as an objective historian. His seeming objectivity usually consists in a regurgitation of beliefs of the former generation which have become generally accepted truths and thus give an appearance of impartiality.

All great historians have been creatures of their own period, the more so the better. The historian should find inspiration in the same creative forces that animate what Paul Klee has called the "real artist."

The historian has to give insight into what is happening in the changing structure of his own time. His observations must always run parallel with those specialists of optical vision whom we call artists, because it is they who set down the symbols for what is going on in the innermost life of the period before the rest of us are aware of it.

The problems of the past are as innumerable as the trees of a forest, but there are certain problems especially related to the strivings of each particular period. In order to recognize these, the historian must himself be a real creature of his own time. He must know where the urgent problems are lying which have to be solved, and must be able to develop his own research out of them. For this the historian must have an understanding of his own period in its relation to the past and maybe also some inkling of those trends leading into the future.

History is a mirror which always reflects the face of the onlooker. The historian has to show the trends of development as clearly and as strongly as he is able. But the so-called objectivity of the historian is nothing but a fiction.

How should the historical past of architecture be presented to students of architecture?

The method of presenting history should not be different from the methods of presenting any other subject considered necessary in the formation of the architects, such as, for instance, statics or the theory of structures.

In many schools of higher learning, there has been, and still is, a tendency to try to teach the architect to undertake the sort of calculations of structures that are required of the civil engineer. The result has been to turn the architect into some kind of dilettantic engineer with no understanding of what 'statics' really means. Some time ago I asked Ove Arup, the English structural engineer who works in closest contact with architects, what place he considered statics should play in the education of the architect. He told me that from his experience in working with young architects in the London Architectural Association School, he had become convinced that it was far more important to give them a certain *sense for statics* than to teach them the techniques of complicated calculations. The great structural engineer, Luigi Nervi, once complained to me that the plans he gets from architects often reveal an astonishing lack of structural understanding. It seems therefore, that the aim when teaching statics to architects should be to develop in them a sense of the potentialities of structural materials so that the architect's own spatial imagination may be kindled, and, second, that he may know what he can and what he cannot demand from his best helper, the structural engineer.

In other words, the architect needs to be given a methodological approach, or, to remember the statement of Walter Gropius, "In an age of specialization, method is more important than information."

History should be in the same way based on a method, rather than specialization. The student should be helped, so as to widen his outlook. But this outlook should be widened not by a host of facts or purely historical knowledge. His outlook should be widened in strengthening in him a certain faculty: the sense for space.

As a by-product, he can acquire a method for encompassing architectural history today.

The Role of Space in Architecture Around 1900
From our present outlook, the innermost heart of architectural development is based upon two inseparably connected concepts: *space* and *space conception*.

During the end of the last century, three great scholars, Heinrich Wölfflin, Alois Riegl, and August Schmarsow, were the first to undermine the factual and materialistic approach. The analysis of formal shapes appeared to them too coarse to apprehend the spirit of a period.

We think of Heinrich Wölfflin's *Renaissance and Baroque*, 1888; Alois Riegl's *Late Roman Arts and Crafts*, 1901 and 1927 (unfortunately not translated into English); August Schmarsow's *Principles of the Science of Art*, 1905 (also this book is as far as I know not available in an English version).

Despite their differences, Wölfflin, Riegl, and Schmarsow all recognized that the formation of space is fundamental to architecture and that it is the changes which occur continuously in the formation of space that provide the unquestionable basis of the history of architecture.

History and Curriculum
Finally the practical question must be raised: how can the history of architecture be built into the general curriculum? This can be solved in many different ways according to the purposes of different types of schools, yet there are some constant leading principles.

In many universities an introductory survey course in the history of art is offered as part of the general undergraduate program. It would be as well if such courses were made mandatory for all students wishing to enter the architectural schools, and considered just as important as the usual requirement for a basic knowledge of mathematics. These general courses provide the student with a certain foundation and some points of reference in regard to the development of art which serves as a basis for his specialized studies of architecture.

In cases where such courses are not at present available to the young architect, one must consider in what form a first general introduction to architecture, painting, and sculpture can best be given.

The whole question of incorporating the teaching of history within the architectural curriculum circles around three problems:
How should history be taught? *How much? When?*

How?
From the moment the student enters the school of architecture, history should be presented to him from a point of view that corresponds to our present-day demands and our present-day attitude towards the past.

In my opinion this means that the history of architecture should be taught from the very beginning to the present day on the basis of space conception. This is an all-embracing postulate intimately related to the demand for spatial imagination which is so urgent to day. The widespread nature of this demand for knowledge of the historical development of space conception in many fields is instanced by the recent appearance of a book entitled *Concepts of Space: the History of Theories of Space in Physics* by Max Jammer, which opens with the statement, "It is the history of scientific thought in its broadest-perspective against the cultural background of the period which has decisive importance for the modern mind. The concept of space, in spite of its fundamental role in physics and philosophy, has never been treated from such a historical point of view. . ." The same must indeed be said of space conception in architecture.

How Much?
If history of architecture is taught on the basis of space conception, then it can incorporate much of the material that is often now handled in separate courses such as Theory of Architecture, Architectural Philosophy, and others.

A one-term course about Visual Arts at the outset of architectural studies, destined as a kind of eye-opener to arouse a visual excitement in the student, can be based upon first-rate visual material (color slides, etc.) without historical amplification. This course can and should be handled by an architect.

But the courses of Space Conception need to be the responsibility of a fully trained Art Historian. History is as much a full-time job as architecture or planning, and the frame of reference within which courses on space conception have to be set must be rather comprehensive if misleading dilettantism is to be avoided.

Care should however be taken that these courses do not stand in isolation. Apart from the courses themselves, history should be brought into coordination with design problems in the workshops. When for instance there is a design problem such as a museum, a church, an assembly building, or a shopping center, the historian should be required to give an introduction, whose length would be dependent upon the importance of the problem. The purpose is to give the students a greater oversight into the nature of the problem and the ways it has been tackled in the past, so that they can approach it with a wider outlook and be less seduced to imitate the latest fashionable examples in the current magazines.

History should be as closely connected with the workshop problems as is structural design.

The whole development of architecture today leads us towards a greater attention to the long-neglected study of proportions. We know of course that a knowledge of proportions alone can no more produce a good architect than the rules of writing a sonnet can produce a poet such as Petrarch; but in a period like our own, which is slowly beginning to demand a coherence of parts in relation to the whole, whether in a single building or in a larger complex, the study of proportions can provide a necessary backbone.

This cannot be successfully handled in lecture courses, but only in seminar work and discussions, as I have found since I first started to work on these lines in 1951.

Such studies are another way in which theoretical orientation can be brought into contact with the workshops, and I have had occasion to note how these kinds of study have a direct impact upon the practical work of the students.

Finally, how much space can really be given to history in our already overcrowded curriculum, which needs to be curtailed rather than extended in time? Courses on space conception demand at least two hours weekly throughout four terms. The time required can be found only if one avoids any kind of repetition and overlapping, and if one accepts that the history of space conception can include much that is now being studied under such other names as the theory or philosophy of architecture or the history of landscape or urban design.

When?

If taught in this way, the contact with the past should accompany the student from the beginning to the end of his architectural training, as has been done for instance in the Architectural Association School in London.

In this event, the question whether history should be taught at the beginning or at the end of the total program of studies falls aside. History walks beside the student as a friendly guide, liberating but not inhibiting his spatial imagination.

Objectives of Architectural Education

Ralph Rapson
University of Minnesota

John Burchard has sketched several directions that this seminar may well profitably investigate. He has likewise indicated a number of possible solutions for some of the knotty problems facing teachers of architecture and architects themselves.

As a preliminary remark I would like to say that although I am head of a school of architecture being involved in administration, I do not consider myself primarily an educator. I am interested in teaching—it is a vital and necessary job—but I am primarily an architect, a person who likes to design and see things built. And there is one further point that I should like to make clear; I am not interested in teaching men to become teachers of architecture, but rather teaching men to become architects.

It is difficult, if not impossible, to speak intelligently about architectural education until we have settled—to some degree at least—what the practice of architecture really is. Let me read to you what might be described as the general public's concept of the architect: "A fascinatingly frustrated creative longhair passing as an artistic, aesthetic virtuoso, yet possessing exhaustingly inaccurate technical know-all while posing as a practical builder expert on the basis of being able to develop, in an impossibly short interval of time and after innumerable changes, an infinite series of incomprehensive answers calculated with slide rule inaccuracy from vague assumptions based on debatably documented data, taken from ill-formed apprehensions and painstakingly produced with instruments of problematical precision, by a pleasant peasant of dubious reliability, indeterminate integrity, but of monumental mentality, for the avowed purpose of beautifying, amazingly confounding a defenseless and unsuspecting citizenry who was unfortunate enough to have asked for the conclusions in the wrong fashion in the first place."

We all might agree that Walter Gropius has given a fairly comprehensive definition of architecture when he defined it thus: "Good architecture I conceive to be both a science and an art. As a science it analyzes human relationships; as an art it coordinates human activities into a cultural synthesis."

In other words, it is the process of organizing and ordering, of coordinating, controlling, and creating the entire physical environment into an expressive, efficient, and aesthetically pleasing setting for man's comfort and pleasure.

It has been said many times, but bears repeating, that since the goal of our work is the calculated effect and reaction on man, that the yardstick is man himself. Architecture which has always reflected a specific social pattern cannot be divorced from man and his life. Its physical forms are the visible statements of human relations upon which happiness depends. It is obvious that the architect must seek an understanding of human psychology; he must be sensitive to the emotional needs of society; he must understand the shifting social patterns.

If this be true, knowledge of the mind and its operation, how it is motivated, stimulated, and influenced is important for an architect's success in getting the design accepted, in achieving reality. Truly distinguished architecture results from this greater understanding and appreciation of humanity and the return to moral standards. It is this insistence upon a properly understood moral and social program, honestly employing the science and technology of today, that is one of the keys of significant architecture.

In addition, the architect of today must gain understanding and knowledge in many fields—from large-scale planning to minute architectural details. He is faced with a bewildering variety of structural systems and construction methods. The building of today is a veritable network of conduits, pipes, and ducts. The architect must know the potentials and limitations of countless materials and their possibilities of aesthetic expression. The architect must understand how materials are fabricated and assembled. Maintenance, weathering, and durability may make or break his little babies, his original creations, not to mention his client and possibly himself since he has professional liability.

If building is to become architecture, it must go beyond mere shelter as language must go beyond its use as a primitive means of communication before it becomes literature. Architecture goes beyond necessity. Buildings, streets, spaces influence our thinking and deeply affect our lives. Their sincerity or superficiality creates, in turn, sincerity or superficiality in those who live in them. "First we shape our buildings and then our buildings shape us," as Winston Churchill phrased it.

Apart from satisfaction derived from the utilitarian solution, it is the purely aesthetic experience of a beautiful environment wherein architects usually fail. One can point to innumerable recent buildings where utilitarian and social needs as well as structural, engineering, and economical requirements are met. However, to a considerably less degree do we find truly inspired buildings. Beauty is an elusive thing, difficult to define and more difficult to teach, let alone achieve.

Here we take leave of logic and rationalism and enter the shaky realm of human emotions, human frailties and human aspirations.

The demands on the architect as planner, organizer, psychologist, artist, engineer, and business man raises a very provocative point in his formal education. Is it possible for an individual, however brilliant, to be specifically trained in every dimension of this expanding social and physical art? Or are we in danger of being dilettantes both in practice and education, knowing little about everything and little about anything?

In practice such a specification is seldom in any one individual. The demand is met in varying degrees by co-ordinated group effort, by architects of different talents, abilities, and interests. But to fill this comprehensive specification in education, the formal training of the architect, is quite another thing.

How are we to program these far-too-short academic years of the young man's life? With each innovation and vogue, there is constant pressure at the educational level to follow, to add more courses. I do not argue against flexibility and change, but I will not panic either. I am always reminded of Mies' statement that he is primarily concerned with basic principles rather than different solutions, that he is not worried about being interesting but that he wants to be good. It might be well to enunciate what Alfred North Whitehead has labeled two educational commandments: "Do not teach too many subjects;" and, "What you teach, teach thoroughly." In addition I feel that architectural education should be guided by able practitioners, men with strong architectural convictions founded on building experience.

I should prefer to speak about the broad aspects of architectural education, more of the qualities desired of the student and the program rather than the detailed curriculum. Admitting that the practice of architecture is an almost infinite range of talent, ability, and interest—and a high degree of specialization necessary—it follows that the educational system cannot mould all its products to the same specifications. This does not imply vagueness of purpose.

We often speak of general education versus specialized training. We should be careful since it seems that general educational subjects are really specific subjects specifically studied. Together as a group they may give a more generalized training, but it is a mistake to think of any one or two subjects giving a general education. The important thing is that each subject studied be related to the entire process.

None will deny that it is the total man we are interested in, as it is the total environment. Essentially we must be concerned with the graduation of well-rounded citizens soundly equipped with fundamental knowledge rather than highly trained specialists.

To quote Whitehead: "Culture is activity of thought and receptiveness to beauty and humane feeling. Scraps of information have nothing to do with it. A merely well informed man is the most useless bore on God's earth.

What we should aim at producing is men who possess both culture and expert knowledge in some special direction. Their expert knowledge will give them the ground to start from and their culture will lead them as deep as philosophy and as high as art."

Formal education of the architect is a two-fold process. On the one hand, it is necessary to have the broad, mature philosophy—an architectural concept and conviction worthy of the aspirations and capacities of our times; while on the other hand, it is necessary to develop the skills and tools—the detailed and technical knowledge—necessary to achieve the coordinated whole product. He must be able to cope with the many problems of actual construction.

And I think along with this direction and knowledge we must develop men with "guts." Youth tends to be arrogant, disdainful of tradition and the normal way of doing things. I am not concerned with this. I do think one of our failures is turning out too many who compromise easily. We need to turn out architects who can say "no," who will not compromise on vital issues. Direction in teaching does not mean any narrow, dogmatic approach. One of history's positive lessons is the lesson that any dogmatic solution, whether political or technological or aesthetic, gives way because it results in more and greater problems than it solves. Concerned as it is with problems of humanity, there is seldom a black and white solution to any given architectural problem—rather there is the great richness of the entire palette basically limited only by the architect's inherent and developed qualities.

Fundamentally, education is concerned with the individual—it must develop the man's initiative and intellectual powers. There are three broad phases to this process: first, the mind must learn to analyze clearly and logically—or to think creatively; second, the mind must develop the ability to employ knowledge with judgment—or to apply creatively; and third, the mind must forever remain alert and fluid, to continue the ability to learn.

Complete understanding of this learning process is essential. Creative thinking is not a mystical or an isolated phenomenon; it can only be the result of orderly acquisition of factual knowledge basic to the broad objective. This discipline is fundamental to education although just how much factual knowledge and of what quality that would be selected is most difficult.

As one acquires more and more information and knowledge of previously successful solutions, there is always the danger of stultifying the imagination. Normal habits, accepted practice, and known answers often eliminate doubt, and without doubt, one of the strong reasons or inducements for inquiry is no longer present.

The ability to apply acquired knowledge with imagination and judgment is fundamentally necessary to every creative architect. Creative synthesis is pre-eminently the life blood of architectural education and architectural practice. It is in this phase of the training and practice of architecture—the realization and integration of the many, cutup, specialized pieces unto a unified whole and total expression—that most of us fail.

Finally, if education does no more than instill a desire to continue to learn throughout life—to encourage an active and alert mind—then it has perhaps achieved its purpose. Too many have the misguided impression that education stops upon graduation; rather it is the beginning, the foundations of continued growth. Passively obtained knowledge, under rigid direction, fails to develop or stimulate the mind and does not develop individual resourcefulness and integrity.

Certain things may be best taught in school; other things may be best learned in practice. A university is not a trade school. To me, it is far more important that the man be given a sound philosophy, direction, and convictions about architecture and life; that he learn how to analyze his work and himself; and that he acquire the ability to apply himself creatively.

Robert M. Hutchins put it this way: "Education is not to teach men facts, theories, or laws. It is not to inform them or amuse them, or to make them expert technicians. Rather it is to unsettle their minds, widen their horizons, inflame their intellects, teach them to think straight—if possible—but to think, nevertheless."

In conclusion, let me say that our architectural education must remain fluid and dynamic, geared to the individual man, to our society, and to the technology of our times. We hope to give the student a broad philosophy that will aid in his search for a lasting and truthful architecture. If we can give him not only a thorough foundation in the social and technological sciences but also open his mind to orderly and creative thinking, teach him how to evaluate and apply knowledge, and to retain always an alert mind—then we shall turn out well-rounded human beings who will one day take their places as mature architects with understanding of the aspirations of humanity.

There is a short prescription found in Buddhism that succinctly sums this up: "Develop an infallible technique and then place yourself at the mercy of inspiration."

Full Scale Prototype Structures

Arthur E. Burton
Iowa State University

The following observations are based upon our experiences with the development and construction of full-scale prototype structures by students in architecture and architectural engineering at Iowa State University. Beginning with the construction of four concrete umbrellas in the spring of 1957, the projects, completed or underway, are as follows:

1. Hyperbolic paraboloids (umbrella) concrete thin shells. These were four units each ten feet square and approximately one inch thick.
2. Tetrahedron stressed-skin roof built of corrugated paper.
3. Glued, laminated wood beams assembled into a roof frame and covered by plastic. Use of glue-laminated construction made possible the unusual shapes which students in architectural design had developed.
4. A frameless building designed on the diaphragm principle and constructed of sandwich panels.
5. Arch-catenary, cable-suspended roof in reinforced concrete. This is patterned after the Berlin Exposition Hall.
6. Structural working models of barrel-type concrete shells. This project terminated in the model stage as adequate data is available on barrel shells.

How the Projects Are Developed
The success of a project always depends upon how thoroughly and carefully the structure is analyzed and the design phases are developed. The instructional value of the development phase is considerable in that the students learn that hard work and perseverance in design pays off in construction.

Models have become an indispensable part of the development phase. A clear distinction is made between various types of models which are classed as follows: architectural study, structural, and scale exhibition.

The students are required to build study and structural models individually, using a minimum of time and materials for each model, but building several if needed to solve the immediate problems. More elaborate structural models and the scale-exhibition models evolve from team effort. A high point is reached when the students discover that it is feasible to construct a model of almost any type of structure which will simulate the structural behavior of full-scale construction. With their interest aroused, some students then elect courses in advanced strength of materials and in similitude.

Nervi uses models and the techniques of similitude in developing his structures. While rigorous mathematical analysis generally lies beyond the undergraduate's training and experience, students gain much in making approximations. Each class discovers that reasonable mathematical assumptions, applied with discretion, help produce workable structures. They also discover that good workmanship in the construction phase is a vital factor.

Model test data support the mathematical assumptions made in the preliminary analysis. Quantitative results obtained from simple models of paper, balsa wood, string, and wire, costing only a few cents to build, have proved extremely helpful. The surface analysis for the arch-catenary structure was aided considerably by the use of a piano wire model over which a soap film was drawn. It is important that each student demonstrate his ability to observe and record his findings in an acceptable report while working with the small study models. Larger models help verify the facts and aid in the development of the design. More refined models are deemed necessary only for more nearly expert analyses by advanced students and graduate students.

Instrumentation for the testing of the models and the full-scale prototype structure provides an educational opportunity in forcing the student to recall basic fundamentals which they studied in physics classes. Mention of the Wheatstone bridge principle and the wire strain gauge encourages students to search for text material.

Present classes, well versed in electronics, are willing to work extra hours with the instruments. Several instrument kits, purchased by the University, were assembled by students. A kit for a laboratory oscilloscope was purchased at nominal cost. Under construction at present is a pulsed waveform generator for making strain measurements on the oscilloscope. Use of this device makes it possible to apply 150 volts A.C. on the SR4 strain gauge without producing excessive temperature changes in the gauge.

Other departments in the College of Engineering permit our students to use testing machines when the need arises.

Constructing the Full-Scale Prototype

Careful organization of the class is needed for the construction of the full-scale prototype structure. A work schedule is developed. Those who have manual skills are elected by the class to be lead men in the production work. Occasionally a student is found who is a capable organizer, fine leader, and has sufficient drive to be chosen as overall project manager. Such students, especially those having high mental ability, are hard to find.

Funds for the projects come from many sources and are always in short supply. The ingenuity of students and staff is challenged by the problems of building the components cheaper and more efficiently. In this there is a close parallel to professional practice.

The response obtained from the University departments, interested business organizations, and alumni is most gratifying. A new case is made in favor of adequate design development and documentation when the cost of a project is underwritten on the basis of its credibility and because a group of students are convinced that they can produce a workable structure. Credit should be given here to Professor Leonard Wolf for his ability to find sources of funds when funds are needed most.

Getting the approval of the Engineering Experiment Station is the most important step in beginning construction. In this several departments of the Engineering College become involved, and consultation with their staff specialists helps in guiding the project toward useful research in the areas of structural engineering and building construction. One master's degree has been granted in connection with these projects and more are planned including several in the category of architectural research. In the future, a building may be constructed for the Engineering College at the Iowa State University which will house the classrooms and laboratories needed for teaching design in the fields of architecture and engineering. Equipment for this building will be selected in advance of the construction date and included will be some equipment for small-scale construction work. In the construction of the full-scale prototypes, which are the creations of students in architecture, and in the teaching of current techniques of building erection to the students in the building construction curriculum, several pieces of materials handling equipment are required. Included will be a three-ton pendant-operated overhead crane, several types of testing machines, batching bins, and concrete and mortar mixers. Available from the University's Physical Plant Department are a front-loading tractor, a mobile crane of about two tons capacity, and trucks as needed. Since quality control of both workmanship and materials is a teaching objective in the construction of the full-scale prototypes, ways must be found of maintaining quality control during construction. The students have already obtained a fine background in the design and control of concrete mixers, and generally several students in the class have been trained in the masonry, carpentry, and welding trades and even in shipfitting.

For one project, the students completed the batching of the concrete by charging the transit mixer with the coarse material after it had arrived on the site. The sand and cement portions of the mix had been charged into the mixer at the ready-mix plant. From these batches, concrete test cylinders were made which performed exceedingly well. The design called for 4800 p.s.i. twenty-eight-day strength, and these cylinders tested over 3400 p.s.i. in seven days. The mix, incidentally, was based on a 5.63 gal. per sack water-to-cement ratio and was composed of Type I white portland cement and sand and gravel with a maximum aggregate size of ½ inch.

When an experimental structure is completed there is an interval of time during which it may be placed on public display before the testing program begins. Generally this period coincides with the University's VEISHEA celebration. Because the structure is to be placed on public display, extra care is taken by the students to make it attractive and an example of good workmanship.

Displaying the finished product in this way has produced interesting results. Occasionally there is some ridicule by spectators, but usually everyone seems to enjoy looking at the things which are being done by students in the architectural school. A name is found for each of the projects in order to describe them easily in common terms. For example, the umbrellas were also called "quadruple bird baths," the stressed-skin tetrahedron became the "flying mattress," and the glued laminated beams were called "ox bows."

Use of the Structures as Subjects of Research

If the full-scale prototypes have been reasonably developed and the judgment of the staff specialists has been incorporated during the development and construction phases, the completed structures are ready for testing.

Comprehensive testing is done by the Engineering College personnel in the Engineering Experiment Station.

These professors teach structures and mathematics to undergraduate students in architecture and architectural engineering. They deserve much credit for their continued interest in the student projects.

In testing umbrella structures, two of the concrete paraboloidal shells were tested simultaneously by a single loading mechanism which produced the effect of a concentrated load. The load was placed at each of sixty load points, and surface strains were measured with SE-4 strain gauges. By superposition the behavior of the shells under a uniformly distributed load was obtained.

Publication of Results
Results of the tests on the concrete umbrellas can be obtained from the bulletins of the Iowa State University Engineering Experiment Station and from proceedings of the meeting of the American Concrete Institute held at Mexico City, November 1959.

Facilities for publication of the work of the Engineering Experiment Station are available within the Engineering College. Publication work is under the direction of Professor John H. Bolton. Experiment Station bulletins may be obtained from him.

Conclusions
In my opinion, the class projects in the construction of full-scale prototype structures are basically a creative activity. Experience has shown that it is sometimes difficult to determine in advance which students will do outstanding work. Excellence in academic work is, of course, very important, but it has been found that skill and patience and even a well-rounded personality are almost equally important qualities for a student working in the area of creative structures. For the student who presents a successful design, there is the additional problem of his gaining acceptance for his ideas from his fellow students.

A complete rational analysis in mathematical terms is not necessary before the prototype is constructed, but much effort is needed in solving phases of the problem which can be rationalized. The problems of geometry such as true length, true shape, and clearance must be solved so that adequate detailing and layout information is obtained before construction begins.

Before any one project is selected for development, a number of models and drawings must be made from which only one or two have some merit as construction projects. We have found that on occasion a design by a student in another class is worthy of being developed. In this case, the discipline of creating a structure of the intended scale and character is an added factor which gives the class worthwhile experience. This closely resembles requirements found in professional practice. The faculty of the architectural school agreed that the results obtained with the projects thus far justify additional work in the area of creative structures.

Recommendations
Some modifications will be made in the way in which the classwork is organized as new projects are developed. First of these changes may well be increasing the scope of certain projects. A worthwhile project need not be complicated or expensive to be useful in instruction, but the opportunity is presented for original research as well as for creative design in architecture. It should be mentioned here that the University of Kansas and the University of Oklahoma are doing similar work in building full-scale structures on campus. Other schools are doing this work in summer camps.

With the five-year program in Architectural Engineering now in effect at Iowa State, the more advanced students will be assigned the analysis and development work. Of course the creative side of the problem will not be assigned and advantage will be taken of every new idea developed by the student body. Electronic means will be used at every opportunity to assist in the work, especially in strain gauge work. Since students in architecture are especially skilled in making models, more attention can be given to structural models. As is true with esthetic design, structural design requires proper joining of members and materials. In model building the joints must be both solid and strong. Imperfections which seem small in a structural model are greatly magnified when the stress is correlated to that of a prototype. Thus far sophisticated structural models have not been used in the School of Architecture.

How Become an Architect?

Richard J. Neutra
Architect

I have seen many wonderful educators scattered through architectural schools around the globe, splendid human beings in a struggle with complex resistance. Together with their students, they know, they cannot but must remain removed from the real study object, the flesh and blood client. Later in actual life he will loom. He will trust and suddenly withdraw trust.

If any client develops doubts, a crack in his initial confidence, and gets again and again into the worry about these coming thirty years of his buildings which spell his future, such worry can never be laughed off as foolish. The student early must be made to warm-heartedly feel with him. Such anxiety and "depressive' mood is rather more justified than a prospect's primary optimism and "manic" good spirit.

The young architect must learn to see with his own penetrating eyes a real, anxious, often childlike *counsel seeker*, who hopefully, very innocently approaches him, and in moments of exuberance, even cockily claims he "knows what he wants." Later he will collapse again into a lay person"s helplessness. Let us admit from the start he is entitled by human nature to his erratic inconsistency. He who learns faces still other persons who are not fully in balance—not just the client.

An "apprentice" with me and my men, contrary to a "student" in a school, probably never receives a theoretical assignment and a self-assured or downright authoritarian teaching talk. His elder is more seen by him than heard. I am seen on closest range in my own jittery strife, and in the often anxious activity of an older, much more experienced and therefore much more worried-in-detail fellow worker. This is a fascinating mode of transferring "a productive nervous and endocrine pattern," from the one who started years earlier to the one who is to get under way now.

Right or wrong, the old-fashioned teacher at least was too often looked at as pontificating; a "talking book," which has it all statically between its benign, or formidable, covers. The "master" of the shop is surely a dynamically emotionally, troublesomely engaged man with job responsibility. The apprentice learns from this reality the anxieties of the master, from step to step how to overcome difficulties, do his own necessary research, and invest the effort to coordinate experts and get a team into swing. Nothing is here theoretical. The apprentice learns from *sharing* with an admired doer man's nervous processes which never can occur in a classroom quite in this fashion.

This process is not a new invention, but a practice of the last 10,000 years, unfortunately too much discarded for the formal school, itself a fairly new, still incompletely developed, and casually endowed invention. I say this looking at our country, in spite of the billions spent on it officially here in America, and in spite of the occasional wonderful people caught in the system.

The schoolmaster is a real master of a different kind, not like you and me in the class—good boys as we may be! The master of a trade in action is a human being visibly suffering and sometimes or often triumphing, technically and economically, under a specific pressure which we boys want to learn to master, ourselves. He is the "example." Often you don"t want too much to become a teacher or imitate him or his career. You commiserate with him, and his trouble with the students, in a very different way.

The difficulty in "learning" from a schoolteacher and the success in learning from a trade or craftmaster is explained, when we understand that what we learn in the second case, but not so well in the first, are nervous processes, acquiring an organic pattern of behavior all around, which we watch in the practitioner in his long trained and still ever problematic and demanding action of grappling with his task. We learn his "sets" of fused activation, as the experimental psychologist says.

The apprentice by participating and sharing does never quite get into the inferiority feelings and remoteness of a student who with awe or with very unjustified resentment might listen to what to him seem "lectures" of the teacher (who has been granted the title *magister* and disciplinarian these long centuries!). The apprentice, like "the sorcerer's apprentice," on the contrary, may over-optimistically soon think he knows it all, and get out of hand, but as a whole, his optimism propels better than inferiority feelings. It is a doubtful state of our civilization which has given up the apprenticeship system, perhaps for an over-credulous overindulgence in schools. Fortunately, the schools get better, I believe, every year generally speaking, and the supplementation by apprenticeship has found some favor.

I have lectured, but I am never safely convinced that anyone ever got anything out of it. Young men who saw me suffer at my daily work, not merely lecture, learned most.

The pressing and unavoidable mass transaction in training may be the cause of all this mischievous abandonment of a long proven practice. We must train myriads, and still huge sectors of mankind—from the deep South to the far North, from the far East to the farthest West—remain remarkably unserviced.

Editor's note: the title, idiosyncratic as it is, is taken from the original, as is the language in the text.

Journal of Architectural Education, 21:3, 1967

Television as a Design Tool

Stuart W. Rose
University of Nebraska

M. Scheffel Pierce
University of Nebraska

Television is not only the most powerful medium of communication that our age has produced; it is also the most flexible. Yet its common role in education is that of a mere substitute, called in to mitigate the effects of the shortage of teachers or (to look at the matter historically) the excess of students. That it can be more than that is shown by two University of Nebraska faculty members, describing an experiment in the creative use of television as a tool in the development of that awareness of the characteristics of space which is among the architect's indispensable qualifications.

The study of architecture, in common with the body of fine arts and in contrast to the remainder of academia, demands that the student develop an esthetic sensitivity to the medium in which he works. In architectural design, the creation of satisfying spaces for the accommodation and enrichment of human activity is the principal esthetic objective; therefore, in architectural education, one of the chief aims should be the development of an acute awareness by the student of the characteristics of space.

The Simulation of Space
The general method by which the architectural student studies space is simulation: the representation of reality. At the outset of his studies at the university, the student is instructed in the methods of drawing and interpreting plans, elevations, sections, isometrics, perspective, etc., which are, in fact, simulations of a reality. The pencil, the pen and brush are, perhaps, the most immediate tools for preparing those types of simulations. Two specific assumptions are necessary for the further analysis of simulation methods:

1. The more immediate the tool for creating the simulation, the more valuable and useful that method becomes to the student. As a result, the pencil (and the eraser) are, perhaps, the most immediate tools architectural students have for the rapid process of simulation indication, evaluation, and alteration or refinement of spaces and forms.
2. The nearer the simulation can come to portraying the real experience, the more valuable that method becomes to the student. For this reason, rendered perspectives or constructed scale models of refined quality are normal architectural design presentation media. Because of the construction time involved, however, they are not immediate simulation methods and are not used nearly as often for study purposes as are the quick plan, elevation, and perspective sketches. Certain computer-aided developments, such as Perspective Incorporated's Illustromat 1100 or various light-pen consoles similar to that which IBM includes as a component in their System 360, are aimed at making the perspective simulation considerably more immediate.

Scanning and Motion
The purpose of the study was the preliminary development of a method which simulates space in a more realistic and efficient manner than is presently employed by the student of architecture and which is as immediate and flexible as his pencil and eraser.

Man visually perceives the world around him by scanning and, often, while in motion. A space may be considered as an entity in itself and may thereby be experienced visually by the scanning method. It may also be viewed as an element, or component, within a sequence of spaces wherein the impact of the space is critically dependent upon the relationship the space maintains with its neighboring spaces. The method for experiencing the latter would be a combination of motion plus scanning. If a method could be developed for simulating the scanning of space and the motion through a sequence of spaces, and if that method were immediate in its application, it would appear likely that the architectural student could develop a considerably greater awareness of spatial characteristics and space relationships than is possible within the scope of present methods of instruction.

The Choice of Technique
The decision to explore the potentials of closed circuit television in space simulation study was neither casual nor haphazard, although most present simulation techniques commonly employed in architectural design studies are two-dimensional reality. Contemporary technology has provided several possible methods for the four-dimensional simulation of space. These, however, are not particularly immediate to the architectural student. Three contemporary methods were initially examined in relation to their potential as realistic and

immediate simulation tools: motion pictures, computer graphics and closed-circuit television.

Motion picture techniques have been developed and utilized by the commercial moviemakers in portraying the spaces involved in various dramatic and documentary productions. Full-scale sets, scale models and animation represent the most successful devices and have been employed by the motion picture industry with distinction. Initial tests conducted in the School of Architecture of Nebraska have shown that motion picture techniques can be, with refinement, effectively employed in the design process as a realistic simulation tool. However, the necessary delay for required film processing, editing, etc. causes the process to be too slow for use in evaluation, alteration, or refinement of space and repetition. It is, therefore, not considered to be as immediate a method as would be required for optimum student benefit in the study process.

Computer graphics was, on the other hand, found to be very immediate as a simulation technique. The simulation can be performed instantly, mathematically, by a computer, thereby relieving the student of any necessity whatsoever for construction of even simple study models. Although input was, as the system was originally developed, in card form, the development of the lightpen console facilitates direct graphic input. The student may, at will, sketch with the light-pen, producing whatever orthographic views he desires. The perspective is simultaneously constructed by the computer and displayed to the student.

The reverse process is also true. The perspective may be sketched and the orthographic views constructed instantly by the computer. Thus the student may work back and forth among the different views. He may also set the perspective into motion when desired, facilitating simulation of the fourth dimension. At the present stage of computer graphics development, however, the reality of the simulation is not equal to that of either the motion picture or television media. Light establishes and qualifies our visual perception of space. Light values, surface texture and color are presently unavailable in computer graphic systems. It was, therefore, not considered to be as realistic a simulation medium as the other two investigated.

The Advantages of Television
The television medium presented the possibilities of both realistic simulation qualities and immediacy. The image-producing equipment was found to be no less effective than that of the motion picture medium, and the simulation was certainly more realistic than could be presently obtained by means of computer graphics. The immediacy of the television medium was found to be immeasurably greater than that of the motion picture process although it was, admittedly, far less immediate than the computerized technique in which no simulation models whatever were required.

One particularly desirable feature associated with the television medium was the video tape recording, which offered immediate playback to the student for purposes of evaluation, adjustment, and re-evaluation. The simulated spaces were found to be very adaptable to rapid alteration and refinement. Additional revised simulations could be recorded and evaluated for as many repetitions as necessary to achieve the quality desired. Also, several simulated schemes could be re-evaluated on a comparison basis, either consecutively or (when more than one video recorder is available) simultaneously on separate monitors. For the above reasons, therefore, the television medium was hypothesized to be more worthwhile for a thorough investigation.

An experiment for the purpose of exploring the potentials of the television medium as an effective and immediate tool for the simulation of space was consequently proposed jointly by personnel from Nebraska's School of Architecture and University Television with the faculty from both participating. The proposal involved the full participation of an entire class of architectural students; graduate students from the department of music; a sizable television production team involving closed-circuit production staff and crew, engineers and graphic artists; and a perceptual psychologist from the department of psychology. The proposal was received, accepted, and financed by the College of Engineering and Architecture.

Preliminaries
Employing methods of observation and evaluation as suggested and outlined by the perceptual psychologist, the architectural students conducted an exploratory study relative to the nature of four predetermined spatial types: rectangular spaces; angular spaces (i.e., spaces with canted surfaces); curvilinear spaces; and rhythmic, undulating spaces. After recording certain impressionistic characteristics of a variety of individual spaces within each spatial type, four individual sequences of intended visual experiences were outlined. Guided by the above preliminary study, each visual experience sequence was translated into a sequence of spatial configurations employing one of the four spatial types.

The architectural students visited the television studios and were shown the facility and available equipment. They were briefed on the exact nature of the television equipment with which they were to be directly involved in the project in order to enable the students to understand the operation and limitations of the equipment so that they could more readily adapt to the medium. The constructed sequential space simulation models were then adjusted and refined in their construction to provide whatever accommodation possible without altering, in any way, the original space configurations. In order to facilitate the continuous sense of scale throughout each sequence of spaces, scale figures were located along the designated path of movement.

As the experience of space involves much more than just visual qualities, simulations of space in total silence or with whatever random noises may have occurred in the viewing situation were thought to be an unnatural condition. Graduate students from the department of music were therefore asked to prepare a sequence of sound which would reinforce the qualities of the visual experiences intended in the simulation sequence. The simulations would then be evaluated on the basis of two viewings, one with the musical reinforcement and one without.

The Models
In preparation for the actual simulation test, the architectural students employed three basic methods for altering the construction of their space sequence models: the foldaway, the breakaway and the duplicate segment. The first method involved the location of applied hinges at certain points in which the path of movement was to change. It facilitated smooth removal of elements which would have otherwise blocked the changing line of sight of the television camera, while allowing the simulation model to remain intact.

The breakaway method was employed in the few instances in which the television camera was actually to move into the simulation spaces, some of which were smaller in one or two dimensions than the diameter of the zoom lens on one of the cameras. The simulation model was carefully segmented at the breakaway points, employing removable fastening devices which facilitated simple replacement of the segment at the conclusion of each of the recordings.

The duplicate segment technique was employed when it was necessary to transfer the image from one camera to another (usually due to a vertical or horizontal change in movement along the designated path). The simulation model was segmented, and an element common to both segments was provided, such that the final image on the first camera was identical to the initial image on the second camera. By utilizing the three basic construction techniques, the various methods of simulating motion (including zoom and focus techniques; camera movement pan and tilt; and model motion, tilt, and rotation) could be successfully employed.

Production Problems
Within the television studio, the production team faced problems of a different order. This initial study was intended to concentrate principally on variations in spatial configurations. As a result, an attempt was made to eliminate the other independent variables, one of which was lighting. But since all simulation model material was of the same value and texture, the camera had no way to convey the perception of depth or to differentiate one surface from another except by the utilization of highlight and shadow.

The problem was resolved by flooding the television studio with diffuse illumination and letting the shapes of the interior space respond with whatever shading the models provided without specific light direction. For this purpose banks of "scoops" were hung above the working area with all illumination directed upward toward a white matte paneling suspended from the lighting grid, thereby bouncing a shadowless illumination onto, and into, the space simulation models. This technique enabled the models to provide their own shading and catchlights. It was additionally necessary to use a lamp beside the camera paralleling the axis of the lens and as close to it as possible because many of the spaces in the sequences were totally enclosed, and the intensity of the general illumination was insufficient for the electronic requirements of camera operation.

A second production problem was perspective. It was desired to view the spaces from the simulated eye level of a viewer. This effect was realistically conveyed by panning, tilting, and sweeping the space, except when the space was fully enclosed such as in a tower or well. Since the camera could not get into the space to probe, the enclosed space was rotated off its base in front of the lens, which thereby produced the same effect as would be experienced if the eye looked up to the apex of the tower or, conversely, down to the base of the well. The height of the station point was set at eye-level position by raising or lowering the base on which the models rested until the axis of the lens was at a height representative of eye level for the scale being employed.

A third problem in production was the turning of corners where the nature of the sequence of interior spaces did not favor employment of the breakaway method. To accomplish this, two cameras in conjunction with the duplicate segment method were employed. As the first camera reached the end of its line of movement, a slow "match dissolve" to the second camera produced the effect of continuous movement around the turn and along the new direction of travel.

A combination of several techniques was employed when a change in levels was required. The cameras involved were mounted on field tripods and dollies rather than pedestals, thus preventing the adjustment of camera height during the simulation production. However, by being originally set at the different levels required for a given sequence model, the match-dissolve technique after a camera "tilt-up" or "tilt-down" created the effect of moving from level to level. In other cases, such as ramps and stairways, the model was prepared by either the foldaway or the duplicate segment method. The model segment, providing access to the new level (i.e., the ramp or stair), was tipped or rotated in front of the television camera lens, which produced the same effect as movement up or down the stair or ramp.

The major problem of production was the communication of a sense of movement through the spaces, especially the long, confined ones. Preliminary experimentation revealed that the use of a zoom lens to narrow progressively the angle of view through the length of a confined space effectively conveyed the sense of movement. With either fixed focus or the zoom lens a sense of movement could also be attained by means of focusing progressively from the initial to the distant point of observation. For this effect, the studio light levels were kept purposely low, and the camera worked close to the sequence models in order to provide a limited optical depth of field so that the progressive center of focus produced the sense of movement. Because the illumination, value, and texture of the model were held as constant as possible, the scale figures placed throughout the spaces were found to play an important role in reinforcing the sense of depth and movement, while also providing a point of reference for the cameraman as he focused along the designated path.

This particular experiment employed two image orthicon cameras which proved effective under the conditions provided. Many closed-circuit television studios employ vidicon-type camera equipment, but it is doubtful if they would have conveyed in as satisfactory a manner the visual impression of movement within the interior spaces. Also, the vidicon camera is subject to "lag," which makes panning (or scanning of space) jerky. This fault would destroy the empathy of the viewer by calling attention to technique. Further limitations of vidicon equipment are the requirements for higher light levels and the shorter focal length lenses which would have resulted in less flexibility for the procedures employed in this pilot study. The compactness of the vidicon camera would serve as an advantage, however, and economy is also significantly in favor of vidicon.

Presentation Procedures

The four spatial types were presented in separate units. The order of the presentation of each sequence began with pre-program information for the first two minutes. Such data, consisting of a test pattern and an identification slide for the program, normally precedes each closed-circuit television recording at Nebraska. The procedure permits the preparation of the audience for viewing and listening to television presentation (i.e., it is a transitionary element) and also allows adjustment of receiving sets without interfering with the reception of the program substance.

A series of slides was next presented, identifying the spatial type about to be viewed, the names of the students involved in the project, the class title and instructor, and the College of Engineering and Architecture. The studio production then faded in on the first viewpoint as the television cameras began their movement to represent the visual impressions of an observer seeing the spaces in sequence for the first time. Identification slides were also employed to terminate each presentation and to provide a transition from the empathetic experience of viewing designed sequences of spaces to the reality of the television viewing environment.

Each unit required approximately five minutes from beginning to end of the studio production. No predetermined elapsed time for movement through a given sequence was established. The spaces themselves required varying lengths of time for the scanning process. This depended upon the size of the volume, surface or edge characteristics, and depth of the volume through which the observer must move. Either to hurry or to drag through the spaces would create an artificiality in the movement.

Pacing was deliberately slow, approximating the speed of a leisurely walk. This was done, in part, to facilitate scanning of the spaces but also to allow time for the establishment of a psychological reaction to each space so that the progression into the next space would become even more meaningful. One of the key features of the television medium as a simulation tool is the ability to emphasize, through time and motion, the relationship between the spaces to allow the student to sharpen his awareness of the sequential experience of space.

In the playback, each segment of the video tape (representing a particular spatial type in sequence) was presented separately, after which the machine was stopped. The first playback was presented without the audio signal so that only the video portion would be displayed to the viewing panel. The tape was rewound and the segment repeated, after an appropriate interval. The second playback utilized both the video and the audio tracks, which allowed the musical impressions to reinforce the visual impressions sought for each of the spatial sequences.

The Experiment Evaluated

Evaluation of the project was accomplished in a three-step process. First, the student groups estimated the psychological effects of each space in each spatial type and in the progression from one space to the next in sequence. Second, a profile of the observed and evaluated characteristics of the various individual spaces within each of the designated spatial types was prepared by the student groups and presented, for review, to a panel of judges. The panel was comprised of professional architects, architectural educators and certain non-architectural university faculty. Third, the panel of judges and the students were shown the two videotape playbacks of each sequence to determine the degree of conformity between the expectation and the actual production.

From this type of original research in the application of television cameras and videotape as an architectural design tool in the "simulation of the visual experience of scanning and motion through a designed sequence of spaces," certain conclusions can be cited. In this pilot study, student observations, while done with certain accepted analytic methods and procedures, could not be used as a reliable basis for predicting human behavior or reaction to a space. Sampling was insufficient in both quantity and randomness.

Positively, this procedure did provide the student with an exposure to a procedure requiring a more exacting methodology than that to which he was before accustomed; it allowed him to gain an understanding of the effects that could be possible in the design of architectural space by variation of the spatial configuration; and he may, one hopes, be made aware of the means by which spaces are experienced to the point of considering these factors of scanning and motion sequences in his design work.

The common agreement among the viewing panel that evaluated the spatial simulations was, however, that a spatial experience was provided which could not, perhaps, have been made in any other way. In addition, all critiques of the simulation playbacks, despite the anticipated flaws attributed principally to lack of precedent and resulting inexperience in the execution of a television production of this nature, were expressed in terms of spatial qualities, smoothness of motion through space, etc. At no time was reference made in terms of the simulation model.

Refinement and development of this design tool is required before it can become an integral part of the design studio and the architectural design process. The television medium must be examined for its capacities to simulate accurately various designed illumination and color conditions. Special television accessory equipment may have to be developed to adapt the medium to this architectural application. The subject invites the challenge of architectural research.

The Environmental Design Umbrella

Lawrence B. Anderson
Massachusetts Institute of Technology

Ever since *The Architect at Mid-Century* there has been a ferment of self-examination in the profession of architecture, as shown by the Committee on the Profession and still later by the Special Committee on Education (known also as the Three-Man Commission) whose report dated April 1963 has been the subject of continuing studies by a new Committee on Academic Training.

The general trend of thinking within these AIA groups may be summarized as follows: 1. Architecture in our time must assume leadership for the full range of activities leading to a more humane physical environment; 2. Professional education must be redesigned so that all contributors to these activities will receive a common or similar basic education setting the goals and describing the methods to be used, followed by opportunities for specialization toward the many different disciplines that contribute to environmental design. To quote from the Special Committee: "A single group of professionals must be educated and qualified to assume central responsibility for the increasing present and future needs of the expanded urban planning concept."

It will be my thesis to suggest that part 2 of this consensus is undesirable, unrealistic, and unrealizable, that it is out of step with the accelerating development of professional expertise in the United States and inconsistent with the structure of organized knowledge.

That the profession itself should devote so much effort toward re-examination of its role in our culture is healthy indeed. We may well believe that this sustained concern is not entirely self-interested and that it reflects a real commitment to confront the very troublesome environmental problems which increasingly present themselves in a world of exploding population, incredible productivity, technological revolution, and depletion of many of our most valued resources.

In its assessment of the challenges and its proposals of reorientation to meet them, the profession needs to study the situation not only from the perspective of its own thought patterns but also in the broader context of the total knowledge available, the organization of professional disciplines that has developed over the years, and priorities of achievement that are likely to be set by society generally and by its most responsible leadership.

Universities are good places to study these forces; they are becoming increasingly important not only as general purveyors of knowledge but as forcing-beds for the growth of new specializations and as arenas where specializations interact and form new groupings.

Let me now summarize my argument. I believe that the design of the physical environment is an interdisciplinary problem; the disciplines required are too diverse to emerge from a common basic professional or pre-professional education. What is needed is exactly the reverse—each expert is first formed in his own discipline and afterward orients this discipline toward the task.

Let us distinguish between the terms *discipline* and *task*. A man who wishes to exploit knowledge (i.e., to apply it rather than discover it) first needs a discipline, a body of knowledge so organized that it can be applied. Examples: statistics, biochemistry, acoustics, structures. Second, he selects a task (or several tasks) where he can make the application of his discipline yield valuable results, say, in diplomacy, medicine, industrial development, or environmental design.

To acquire the discipline he must invest several years of hard work, during which time most of his studies are slanted toward mastery of the knowledge within his chosen field. For example, the modern engineer must seriously study physics and mathematics, then proceed to basic engineering sciences such as solid and particulate mechanics, fluid dynamics, materials, thermodynamics, geophysics, circuit theory, and heat transfer before he really begins to specialize.

Similarly, the modern doctor of medicine has to study the basic sciences applicable to curing the sick: anatomy, bacteriology, biochemistry, histology, physiology, pathology, immunology, and pharmacology. Until he has been oriented in these fields, he is not in a position to begin clinical activity.

And so it is in all the professions, especially those most influenced by the growth of scientific knowledge. Unfortunately, the human cortex is limited in extent, and once its patterns have been preempted by one system of knowledge, empty paths are no longer available for new systems ad infinitum. To put it colloquially, you can't teach an old dog new tricks.

One may also note that under present conditions the major professions each require three or four years of special-track academic programs plus internship or job training before licensure, and this is in addition to any general education the candidate may indulge in at the college level to make himself a better citizen of the culture in which he finds himself.

It is true that in spite of the great diversification of specialized professions, by and large the great traditional areas—law, medicine, engineering—have held together; especially the latter two are now great clusters of specialties with a shared common base of scientific discipline and much interchange and transfer among the subfields.

Why then should not environmental design broaden its scope while still remaining under a single educational umbrella, its handle firmly in the grip of architecture?

To a certain extent it can, but only to a certain extent. The design professions, as we ought to understand the term, are those whose three-four year discipline revolves around the design studio. Here the mind of the designer is formed by a planned sequence of experiences that enable him to develop a synthesizing approach to the solution of complex problems, wherein the design which results must withstand scrutiny at many levels, not least that of being visually coherent.

This educational formation is unique; it confers insights and powers for dealing with the environment that are not shared by other professions or groups of professions. So long as we are talking about architects, urban designers, landscape architects, or even industrial designers and graphic artists, we can see how these somewhat different tasks would be amenable to the same disciplines (allowing for some differences in tools and materials). They could all depart from the same basic preparation. Indeed, schools like the Graduate School of Design at Harvard show the value of a common basis for architecture, landscape, and urban design.

However, you will not produce a social scientist by this curriculum, and you cannot exclude social science from city planning. Neither will you produce an engineer, yet engineering is a necessary part of building.

These distinctions are what the Special Committee considers to be "attitudes" that must be transformed to fit a new concept. On the contrary, they are facts of life with which any proposed policies must reckon.

The fact is that making a suitable physical environment is interdisciplinary in a far broader way than either medicine or engineering.

Medicine is, after all, straight applied science. It is humane, it is noble, it calls forth the highest qualities of intellect and character, yet its goal is rather easily defined: to promote health. This clarity of objective makes it possible to mobilize disparate elements and hold them in a common academic and professional discipline. (Only the problems of mental health, not so readily subject to scientific diagnosis and treatment, now threaten the unity of the medical grouping.)

Engineering is applied science par excellence. Its goals are more diffuse, but they center on the benefits that can accrue from increasing control over energy and materials. Its products are meant to do their job efficiently and to be sociologically acceptable. At their best they open great new vistas of experience.

The realm of design introduces another dimension. Besides being convenient, efficient, economical, salubrious, socially suitable, and extensive of man's power and control, we are asked to speak to his mind through his vision, appealing to his sense of order and conveying emotionally charged messages comparable to those we expect to find in the best books, music, and painting. The man-made environment, besides, is more than a symbolic communication: it is reality itself and impinges on everyone. It is to emphasize this dimension that we have design education.

Social science and engineering, each a broad area in itself, are the two principal disciplines that must be joined to the design team in order to man the task of making the urban environment. It is my belief that we need true and good social scientists and engineers for this task and that we can produce only inferior ones through a design education.

The real problem, then, is not to educate them in their own discipline but to recruit them, to make them feel the same dedication to the task that we do.

Whether this is possible depends on the priorities society sets for itself. It has been objected that "the trend of the engineering profession's attitudes, interests and education is being influenced more by the challenge of technology than the needs of the building field." But the building field is a challenge of technology; it has never ceased to be, though many other tasks have been added. The head of the department of mechanical engineering of the Technical University of Berlin designed the air-conditioning system of the new Opera House. We may look forward to a time when similar events will occur in the US. In any case, we should spend our efforts attracting gifted engineers in preference to producing inferior captive technicians and labeling them engineers.

The Death of the Beaux-Arts: The Cal-Oregon Experiment in Design Education

Murray A. Milne
Yale University

Charles W. Rusch
University of Illinois, Urbana–Champaign

Four years have passed since the publication of Christopher Alexander's *Notes on the Synthesis of Form*. And already the book has gone through two printings and been translated into Italian and Japanese. In its most basic form, it presents a method for aiding the designer in systematically structuring physical design problems. Interestingly enough, it has been criticized both by what might be called the "traditional right" and the "new left" of architectural education. The former accuses the method of being partial in that it addresses itself primarily to the functional side of the problem and neglects the esthetic and culturally symbolic aspects of architectural solutions—an aspect to which the traditional right gives primary emphasis. From the other side, the "new left" attacks the method as systematically unreliable since it does not contain the rigor of scientific method. In fact, it is said that Alexander's method cannot deal objectively with the "true" complexity of design problems. Subjective judgments still must be made in the face of uncertain or incomplete information.

Perhaps most interesting is the criticism that comes from within, from those that are experienced in the method's use. The method is described as "too tedious," "too time-consuming" and "incapable of sustaining motivation over long periods of required analysis." These criticisms have led to the situation where many who are experienced with the method are moving away from it to less rigorous approaches (including Alexander himself). At the same time, interest is high among others who are undergoing their first exposure to the original approach.

In practice, the method encompasses six phases. First, the problem is defined by an explicit list of boundaries or constraints. Second, the intended behavior of all systems (including human) within the problem space is defined by a list of requirements. Third, a judgment is made about each pair of requirements to determine whether the solution to one relates in any way to the solution to the other. Fourth, the resulting interaction matrix is analyzed by computer decomposition programs into a hierarchy of reasonably independent subsystems which, in theory, constitute small coherent design problems. Fifth, a diagrammatic solution is found for the requirements in each subsystem. Finally, the diagrams are developed into architectural schematics and preliminary drawings.

In the fall of 1965, Charles Rusch, teaching a third-year class at the University of California at Berkeley, and Murray Milne, teaching a fifth-year class at the University of Oregon, used this method on the same year-long design problem. This study was financed in part by a grant from the graduate section of the University of Oregon and by the AIA Education Research Project and became known as the "Cal-Oregon Experiment." A full report on the results of the experiment is now in preparation, but the following fictional interview was contrived by the *Journal of Architectural Education* to answer some of the questions which often arise at this time.

JAE: How can you claim this is a valid teaching tool if, as many critics say, it does not result in "good design"?

Cal: First, it should be stated that there have been no projects actually built using this method, so this criticism must have been leveled at either incomplete "research" projects or at student work. I suspect that in the hands of a competent designer the results would be quite acceptable.

Oregon: It should be pointed out that unlike "traditional" designing, most of the effort is spent at a stage of analysis which occurs well before the solution has any physical form. But it is encouraging to find that when we evaluated my students' final architectural solutions, they had one thing in common: They all "worked," i.e., they all solved the initial requirements. True, some of the designs were judged elegant and some were judged ugly, but this was mainly a function of the student's previously acquired ability to handle the visual or graphic aspects of design. I happen to believe this is a facility that all of these students should have "acquired" before they reached fifth-year design.

Cal: I think supposed lack of "good design" reflects the fact that the products of this approach have been unconventional by normal architectural standards.

The functional reasons for the form to be one way or another are so strong that they have so far overridden the more traditional visual criteria, massing, balance, proportion etc.

Oregon: I would disagree slightly. I think the architectural forms which my students produced appeared to be fairly ordinary and conventional. I believe this is a result of all the time that was spent on the more salient analytical issues which tended to re-order the student's values away from the zap-pow-giggle school of architectural form making.

JAE: Your answers so far have been directed at criticism from the right. The critics on the left are not concerned with the way buildings look. They are saying that the results produced are functionally inadequate or naive. I remember hearing the remark that one study for which you had listed 160 requirements probably needed 3,000-5,000 to "cover" it adequately. Would you characterize your solutions so far as being functionally or behaviorally inadequate?

Oregon: Yes, I think it's fair to say that all the student work produced to date has faults. We're not happy with any phase of the method, especially that concerning requirement writing.

Cal: The number of requirements by itself is not reflective of coverage. You also have to look at the level of generality of the statements. For example, I could write one requirement that would cover the whole functional realm merely by stating, "Everything in the building should function correctly." Obviously, this is not too useful. On the other hand, we could write 6,000 requirements at the level of door closures, but the problem becomes unwieldy. Instead, we write at the level we think makes a difference to the form.

Oregon: In retrospect it seems obvious, but it took us a long time to realize both that it would be impossible to write all the requirements for any problem and that it is unnecessary to do so. This is because information is added at every phase of the process and need not all be stated at the beginning. The information which must be stated is that which makes this particular problem non-typical and that which could later be used as a criterion for evaluating the success of the final architectural solution.

JAE: Another general criticism is that the solutions produced are overspecified, that the forms tend to become almost inflexible in their attempt to fit the behavior precisely.

Oregon: That's a valid criticism insofar as we are living in the midst of change. When the behavior patterns change, the form is then obsolete. I agree there have been times when we have become too cute and too highly particularized, but the opposite approach dodges the issue by settling on completely unspecified spaces that can be used for any purpose, such as Mies' "absolute space." Lack of flexibility is not a fatal flaw of the method but simply indicates that up to now we have not been able to deal with this issue at the requirement phase.

Cal: I'm not against flexible spaces or absolute spaces when they are called for, as they would be in a production plant layout, for example. But remember, our job is specifying form to fit behavior patterns. We try to do this by determining the range of behavior patterns, which underlie desired or anticipated activities, and design quite specifically for them.

JAE: Let's turn to criticism from within the method. On September 30, 1966, at the Massachusetts Institute of Technology Building Design Conference, you made a joint statement in which you asserted that everyone you knew who had worked with this method had decided that he would just as soon never work another problem. You said that this occurred even among those who believed the approach was essentially sound. In your statement you mentioned tedium as being the principal culprit.

Oregon: First, let me say that I think this is really serious. If you have a great method for solving problems and no one will use it more than once, it's not going to be very effective. Problem-solving techniques must be equally suited to the problem solvers as to the problems. But to answer your questions, I think the difficulty is as much a function of architectural temperament and educational expectations as anything else. Architects have not been trained as scientists, and they don't expect their work to have that character. They have been trained to start designing near the end of a problem, and their first preliminary designs offer motivational satisfaction to keep going.

Cal: Contrast that situation with working for three or four solid months on analysis with no "on the board design" work to show for your efforts. Three or four months of analysis may not seem like much to a scientist, but it can be deadly to an architect. However, this situation is changing in two ways. The method is being changed to fit the man, and architectural education is more and more training students in scientific techniques. Because of the latter change we will probably draw a somewhat different type of student into our schools in the future, and he will have a different image or expectation of what an architect does. But this is a little beside the point; boredom and tediousness should be cut out of scientific work as well.

JAE: How is the method being changed to be less tedious?

Oregon: In general, the more we understand about the method, the less tedious it will seem because there will be fewer blind alleys and less wasted effort. I have found that the more confidence the students have in the instructor and his material, the higher will be their motivation. We have also made some obvious improvements such as writing computer programs with better man-machine communication.

JAE: All right, let's turn to the so-called Cal-Oregon Experiment. Did you have any particular difficulties getting the problem underway?

Oregon: In most design courses, the problem is stated in terms of the expected solution type. But in problems which have no prototypical solutions, we came up with the idea of defining the problem by means of a set of boundaries. They specify arbitrarily what is beyond the scope of the problem—the things the designer cannot modify. In this experiment the problem was initially defined in terms of the same boundaries at both schools. As additional boundaries were added to the list of each school, the two problems began to change slightly in character, and, in fact, the two problem spaces began to migrate away from each other. Fortunately there was enough initial commonality to keep the two problems from becoming completely disengaged, but this did indicate to us that architects, without the influence of a client's arbitrary decisions, will attempt to redefine the problem in line with their preferences.

Cal: I think the issue of boundary migration is an artifact of the classroom situation. Classroom problems can be initiated either by tightly constraining them or by leaving them open and unstructured. It is hard to present problems that represent a compromise between these extremes because either you're willing to accept someone else's categories and definitions, or you're not. If existing categories and constraints are accepted, the danger is run of unwittingly accepting existing preconceptions and being unable to break free of existing stereotypes. If no boundaries are established, then—because the classroom is an artificial situation—the problem can keep expanding almost without limit in a desperate search for "natural boundaries."

Oregon: The educational aspect of this paradox is that on one hand, the method purports to encourage innovation by not accepting a priori assumptions about the solution, but, on the other hand, it must ultimately constrain the solution space in some way in order to avoid the ever-expanding nature of the boundaries of artificial problems. The only way to resolve this conflict is to establish at the beginning of the problem a few fixed, and admittedly arbitrary, boundaries. Then, as the problem runs its course, further insight is gained and the full complement of boundaries begins to emerge by agreement among those who are involved with the problem.

Cal: In fact, there is some educational value in defining a problem in initially vague terms. This forces the student to spend some time redefining and clarifying the problem, making it more likely that he will recognize and challenge its fundamental assumptions and limitations. In this way, he exposes to observation many of his own preconceptions. But you can't dwell very long in this vagueness without slipping into the expanding boundary situation. We found it best to encourage the student to move beyond problem definition soon after he became involved in it and begin requirement writing instead. The list of requirements will help to clarify further the boundaries of the problem.

JAE: Are there other phases of the method that you found inherently troublesome?

Oregon: Diagramming is the phase which is most difficult to make rigorous or systematic. A diagram is supposed to be a graphic representation of the solution to a small, reasonably isolated subset of requirements. We realized too late that very few solutions can be represented in a purely graphic mode, and those that can are usually at different levels of scale, which makes it extremely difficult to combine subsolutions. Fortunately the students find this the most satisfying stage because it fits most closely their image of what architectural design is.

Cal: The problem is that there is just no adequate diagrammatic language or, more importantly, there is no set of diagrammatic symbols which have been agreed upon or standardized. So each student develops his own notation, and he is the only person who completely understands what he means when he uses it. At present, diagrams don't work as communication, but they are useful as a personal record of the student's decisions.

Oregon: Both of our classes began with a partial list of crude symbols which they had internally agreed upon. The problem was to find symbols which were rich enough in meaning—yet precise enough to avoid ambiguity. We were only able to develop a tiny symbol vocabulary. You can imagine how frustrating it would be to try to communicate a subtle and complex idea if you only had a 10-word language. This is the major reason why we are having so much difficulty with diagrams.

Cal: The best solution we can recommend for this dilemma is to include a verbal solution-statement as a part of each diagram.

Oregon: Incidentally, an article in the December *Journal of Architectural Education* suggested a way of selecting an appropriate mode of representation or a symbol system for any given content. It pretty well summarizes the dilemma we're describing.

JAE: What do you think are the skills acquired in this course as compared to a more conventional architectural design course?

Cal: Two kinds of skills are acquired: problem-solving skills the individual uses when working alone and skills the individual uses when working with groups. The individual skills are mostly connected with precision of one sort or another. The beginning phases demand precision in defining the problem and its boundaries, precision stating what is required of the solution, precision regarding those statements themselves. The last is essentially a verbal skill, demanding that the problem requirements be precise in several ways. For example, each statement must be made at the proper level of abstractness, it must be independent of the other statements in its physical implications, it must avoid including the specification of solution elements in the statement itself, and it must consist of the proper balance between fact and judgment. The next phase, the interaction phase, develops an ability to make fairly exact judgments. When he is required to make thousands of interaction judgments within a few days, the student becomes familiar with the various categories or levels of judgment, and the difficulties inherent in making judgments consistent with established criteria. It has been our experience that the student emerges from the course as a much more disciplined thinker than he was when he entered it. This is one of the main reasons why we are so impressed with this method as a teaching tool.

Oregon: As for group skills, the method itself does not demand group effort, but the course was taught that way primarily to make more efficient use of student time and effort, although we don't know whether such efficiency was really accomplished. Working together forced the students to a level of clarity of communication that is not demanded of students working alone. It also forced them to accept and consider other points of view and thus to expand and clarify or even compromise their own. The group effort in general was more successful in the analytic phases of the problem than in the final architectural development phase. Information gathering and analysis are fairly objective, and consensus as to what is right or important to do comes relatively easily. When the decisions become more and more judgmental and subjective, however, the group effort begins to break down and becomes quite difficult and frustrating. Much time and effort is wasted arguing questions of judgment or opinion, and leadership becomes concentrated in the hands of a few rather than many. So at the final architectural development phase each student was allowed to develop his own solution, which reduced, but in no way eliminated, some of the problems of group work.

Cal: There are good reasons why students, especially architectural students, dislike group work, but nevertheless this appeared to be one of the most valuable aspects of the total learning experience. It demonstrated to us the fact that group effort breaks down only when objective decision criteria disappear.

Oregon: In the end, the complaints about group work were infrequent, and in my class's final report, there appeared such comments as "The group work was a valuable part of the course. It is the only time I've examined every item in a design problem in such exacting detail." Or another: "The output of our group was of better quantity and quality than that of any other group I've worked in. Part of the credit for this goes to the strict analytic aspect of Alexander's method." These comments illustrate that one reason why the group effort was successful was because of the apparent or implied objectivity of the process. It is doubtful that group work would have been nearly as successful if a more subjective product had been permissible.

Cal: Do you always carry those quotes around with you?

Oregon: They comfort me in moments of doubt.

JAE: Apart from these skills you say the students acquired, what concepts do you think are more extensively covered in this type of course than in others?

Cal: In addition to the issues of problem definition and boundary migration mentioned earlier, the students in this course must come to grips with the nature of environmental structure and the nature of the design process which attempts to create that structure. We found that the method provides an excellent framework for learning about the environment and design. For example, just by being forced to state explicitly the functional and behavioral requirements of the problem and then to derive physical form from them, the student cannot help but achieve some understanding of the relation between environmental structure and function. He begins to see the environment as a network of physical relations.

Oregon: Another issue the student must face in the course concerns the concept of multiple levels of organization. This method gives him a procedure for decomposing a huge complex problem into a number of small, reasonably independent subproblems. Because all the issues involved in these subproblems are explicitly stated, he can deal with them fairly efficiently. The method then gives him a strategy for combining these subsolutions. It is an exciting moment when the student

BOUNDARIES

Overall boundaries for problems need to be established to identify the limits of possible changes in the system.

• Face-to-face communication is essential among students and between students and faculty.

• The university shall exist as an organizational (i.e., administrative) as well as physical (i.e., architectural) reality.

• Faculty will continue to conduct most classes in conventional forms (i.e., large lectures, discussion classes, seminars, laboratories, etc.).

• Most classes will meet at scheduled times for specific duration.

ELEMENTS

These elements represent some of many subsets of requirements as established by the computer decomposition of the program.

(26) Students who can observe good studiers may pick up good study habits.

(31) Students study in small groups or seminars for effective information exchange on a specific topic.

(33) Socializing presents a valuable opportunity for idea exchange between students.

(39) A greater number and diversity of people are brought together in public places that are located near to or are noticable from a thoroughfare.

(41) Spontaneous discussions between students with similar interests and problems provide an invaluable learning experience.

(46) When students have specific questions about course work, they would like to be able to reach their instructor quickly for clarification.

(48) Students believe they would study between classes more often if they could find convenient locations.

CLUSTER

The relationship of elements is shown first in an interaction matrix and second in a cluster of requirements.

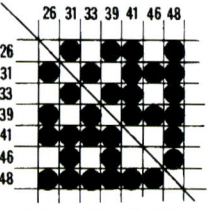

Interaction Matrix

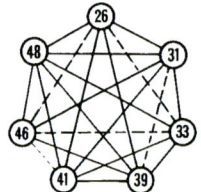
Requirement Cluster

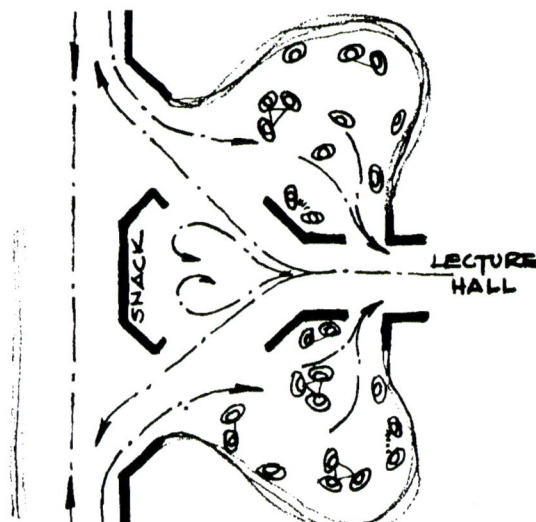

SOLUTION DIAGRAM

This is an example of the type of form proposals made as a result of the interaction study. This subset is defining a kind of "forecourt" located between the entrances to the large lecture halls and the main circulation routes of the campus (halls or walkways) the inner half of which contains the kind of furniture that will encourage informal discussion or casual study, and outer half contains vending machines and open space in which groups can stand or through which large numbers of people can move easily. The entrances to the lecture hall are arranged to provide rapid egress of the class in session, encouraging them to move to the outer half of the forecourt, with sufficient space so that stationary stand-up conversation cliques do not block the flow of traffic. Students arriving early for the next class will find it convenient to move to the inner half of the space and wait there to enter the lecture hall through the small side doors as soon as the flow of outgoing traffic subsides sufficiently. It is assumed that students would take advantage of free time before their class begins to come to this study space, have a cup of coffee and engage in social or class-related discussions with other students who are taking the same course, perhaps even having the opportunity of clarifying a point which was confusing in the previous day's assignment. The professor would be obliged to use this same means of entry and egress and so could be 'trapped' by students who have specific questions. Undoubtedly the more enthusiastic professors will be found here talking with a circle of students long after his lecture is over. It is also assumed that other students (and possibly instructors) who pass this space would be drawn in for relaxation or refreshment and might even become involved in social conversations or some other form of idea exchange. This solution reduces (but does not eliminate) the need for large study halls in places like the general library. The way this space will be utilized when lectures are not in session in the evening, remains to be considered (it is assumed that this issue will be resolved when this form-tendency diagram is combined with others as it works its way up the design tree).

first grasps the concept of the relational structure of an environmental design problem.

Cal: By grappling with issues such as these, the student begins to develop an understanding of design itself, both as a general concept and as a process composed of specific phases. Design problems are by their very nature on the frontier of problem solving. Many, if not most, of the variables in any particular design problem are not clearly understood. Because of this frontier aspect, attempts to become more systematic about design can only make the process more explicit, the character of the problems will not change.

JAE: You seem to be implying that students are not concerned with these issues in more conventional design courses.

Cal: I don't mean to be. The point is just that this method seems to require an explicitness of procedure that leads to a depth of thought on these and other general design issues which we have not observed in other courses. But they are important issues to every designer because if he can't resolve them, they can lead to confusion and wasted effort in his work.

JAE: You mentioned what you consider some of the benefits of such a course. Are there also costs? Were there learning experiences that your students missed by not taking the corresponding normal design course?

Cal: The most significant trade-off the students made in taking this course was in giving up a semester of on-the-board design for a solid semester of analysis. Thus, while there was an overall gain in analytic experience, there was a corresponding loss in traditional design experience. Our feeling is that at worst this was a temporary set back that will be made up—not a true loss. Naturally, the course need not be taught the way we did it nor placed in the curriculum the way it was.

Oregon: Also, most students come out of the course with an extremely strong functional bias. On the positive side, a concern for function promotes disciplined thought, the search for objectivity of evaluation criteria, insight into the form/function relation, etc. But on the negative side, some of my students were left with the impression that functional analysis and organization is all there is to architecture. To use Norberg-Schulz's categories of architectural responsibility—physical control, functional frame, social milieu and cultural symbolization—most of the effort is spent on the functional aspects of the problem with the social aspects partially mixed in. Physical control was tacked on toward the end with little opportunity to affect the functional relations of the solution. Cultural symbolization is almost totally ignored (only because we have not yet learned how to write requirements for it) and consequently just "happens" at the end in an often visually disastrous way. Most of the students eventually realized that, in spite of all the analysis, many details of the architecture form are not determined by the analysis. In fact, the requirements and the final form diagram are silent or indifferent to many of these aspects of form. This whole approach can go only so far in producing architectural reality. It is for this reason that we recommend that the course be process- rather than product-oriented, at least until ways are found to broaden the scope of the approach.

JAE: We've talked about many of the general criticisms leveled at the method, about the difficulties you've had in teaching it, about the skills and concepts it helps develop within the student, about some of the costs and benefits of its use in a design course. What impact do you think the teaching tool will have on the future of architectural education?

Cal: I think we have shown that this particular approach to design can have great value as an educational tool. We think that it demands, and hence develops, in the student a rigor of thought process, a disciplined approach to thinking, that is extremely beneficial to the student's education. Further, this rigor is developed particularly in regard to the design process, and the student becomes quite self-conscious about that process. He is required to clearly separate and distinguish among the various phases of the design, and he must articulate the issues on which design decisions are based, exposing them to rational consideration. I think that such self-consciousness of process is essential to the student's developing ability to design.

Oregon: The question which remains is whether there are people on the faculties of schools of architecture who are disenchanted with the present system of design education and who are capable of making a meaningful change in that system. For those people, the Cal-Oregon Experiment has shown that there is at least one other alternative that is more meaningful and more efficient than the old Beaux-Arts apprenticeship method of design education which really has not changed since the nineteenth century.

Cal: Don't you think such an antagonistic statement will upset a lot of fine old teachers?

Oregon: I hope so.

Toward a Theory of Architecture Machines

Nicholas Negroponte
Massachusetts Institute of Technology

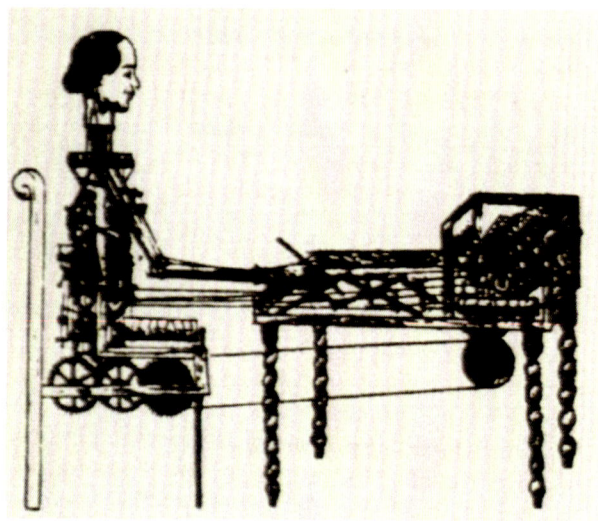

When a designer supplies a machine with step-by-step instructions for solving a specific problem, the resulting solution is unquestionably attributed to the designer's ingenuity and labors. As soon as the designer furnishes the machine with instructions for finding a method of solution, the authorship of the results becomes ambiguous. Whenever a mechanism is equipped with a processor capable of finding a method *of finding a method of solution*, the authorship of the answer probably belongs to the machine.

If we extrapolate this argument, eventually the machine's creativity will be as separable from the designer's initiative as our designs and actions are from the pedagogy of our grandparents.

The Evolutionary Machine
This discussion is not about machines that necessarily can do architecture; it is a preface to machines that can learn about architecture and perhaps even learn about learning about architecture. Let us call such machines *architecture machines*; the partnership of an architect with such a device is a dialogue between two intelligent systems—the man and the machine—which are capable of producing an evolutionary system.[1]

Certainly computers are formidable clerks. They perform well when told exactly how to do something and they can remove drudgery by doing the dull repetitive design tasks. Is that not enough? Why ask a machine to learn, to associate courses with goals, to be self-improving and to be ethical?[2]

The answer is embedded in the question. If a machine can be a self-improving evolutionary species, it sports a better chance of making its computational and informational abilities relevant. Most computer-aided design studies are irrelevant inasmuch as they only present more fashionable and faster (though rarely cheaper) ways of doing what designers already do. And, since what designers already do does not seem to work, we will get inbred modus operandi that could make bad architecture even more prolific.

The general concern of machine-assisted architecture is twofold: first, architects cannot handle large scale problems, for they are too complex; second, architects ignore small scale problems, for they are too particular and individual (and, to them, trivial). As a result of both realities, "less than 5 percent of the housing built in the United States and less than 1 percent of the urban environment is exposed to the skills of the design professions."[3] In trying to combat these deficiencies, researchers are developing information systems, computer graphics and computing services that liberate the designer and allow him more time to do that which he really loves.

Such efforts would be meaningful only in a context where machines can learn to be adaptable and learn to be relevant. (And then these efforts might be unnecessary.) Ironically, an environmental humanism might only be attainable in cooperation with machines that have been thought to be inhuman devices—devices that can intelligently respond to the tiny, individual, constantly changing bits of information that reflect the identity of each urbanite as well as the coherence of the city. If this is true, then the first issue is: can a machine deduce responses from a host of environmental data?

The Learning Machine
A 1943 theorem of McCulloch and Pitts states that a robot constructed with regenerative loops of a certain formal character is capable of deducing any legitimate conclusion from a finite set of premises.[4] One approach to such a faculty is to increase the probability of meaningfulness of the output (the design) generated from random or disorderly input (the criteria). Ross Ashby stated, "It has been often remarked that any random sequence, if long enough, will contain all answers; nothing prevents a child from doodling: $\cos^2 x + \sin^2 x = 1$."[5] In the same spirit, to paraphrase the British Museum / chimpanzee argument, a group of monkeys, while randomly doodling, can draw plans, sections, and

elevations of all the great works of architecture and do this in a finite period of time. As the limiting case, we would have a *tabula rasa* realized as a network of uncommitted design components (or uncommitted primates). Unfortunately, in this process, our protagonists will have built Levittown, Lincoln Center and the New York Port Authority Towers.

Surely some constraint and discrimination is necessary if the components are to converge on solutions with reasonable time. Components must assume some original commitment. As examples, five particular subassemblies would be part of an architecture machine: 1.) a heuristic mechanism, 2.) a rote apparatus, 3.) a conditioning device, 4.) a reward selector, and 5.) a forgetting convenience.

A heuristic is a method based on rules of thumb (or strategies) which drastically limit the search for a solution. A heuristic method does not guarantee a solution, let alone an optimal one. The payoff is in time and in the reduction of search for alternatives. Heuristic learning is particularly relevant to evolutionary machines, since it lends itself to personalization and change via talking to one specific designer or overviewing many designers. In an architecture machine, this heuristic element would probably be void of specific commitment when the package arrived at your office. Through architect-sponsored maturation, a resident mechanism would acquire broad rules to handle the exceptional information. The first time a problem is encountered, the machine would attempt to apply procedures relevant to apparently similar problems (or contexts). Heuristics gained from analogous situations would be the machine's first source of contribution to the solution of a new problem.

After repeated encounters, a rote apparatus would take charge. Rote learning is the elementary storing of an event or a basic part of an event and associating it with a response. When a situation is repeatedly encountered, a rote mechanism can retain the circumstance for usage when similar situations are next encountered. In architecture, such repetition of subproblems is extremely frequent: parking, elevators, plumbing, etc. Again, a rote mechanism lends itself to personalization. But, unlike the heuristic mechanism, this device would probably arrive originally with a small repertoire of situations it can readily handle.

Eventually, simple repetitious responses become habits (some good habits and some bad habits). More specifically acclimatized than a rote apparatus, a conditioning mechanism is an enforcement device that handles all the non-exceptional information. Habits, not thought, assist humans to surmount daily obstacles. Similarly, in a machine, beyond rote learning, design habitudes can respond to the standard events generated by the problem, by the heuristic mechanism or by the rote apparatus. Each robot would develop its own conditioned reflexes.[6] As with Pavlov's dog, the presence of habitual events will trigger predefined responses

with little effort (no conscious memory recall) until the prediction fails; whereupon the response is faded out by frustration (evolution) and is handled elsewhere in the system.

A reward selector initiates no activities. In a Skinnerian fashion, the reward mechanism selects from any action that which the "teacher" likes.[7] The teacher (the designer, an overviewing apparatus, the inhabitants) must exhibit happiness or disappointment for the reward mechanism to operate. Or, to furnish this mechanism with direction, simulation techniques must evolve that implicitly (without the knowledge of the designer) test any environment. The design of this device is crucial; bad architecture could escalate as easily as good design. A reward selector must not make a machine the minion or bootlicker of bad design. It probably must evaluate, or at least observe, goals as well as results.

Finally, unlearning is as important as learning. A remark "its (the computer's) inability to forget anything that has been put into it..." is simply untrue. Information can assume less significance over time and eventually disappear—exponential forgetting. Obsolescence occurs over time or through irrelevance. A technological innovation in the construction industry, for example, can make entire bodies of knowledge obsolete (which, as humans, we often hate surrendering).[8] Or past procedures might not satisfy environmental conditions that have changed over time, thus invalidating a heuristic, rote response, or conditioned reflex.

These five items are only pieces; the entire body will be an ever-changing group of mechanisms that will undergo structural mutations, bear offspring,[9] and evolve, all under the direction of a steersman. Though this is not the place to describe monitoring devices or hardware configurations in detail, it is important to understand the general placement of parts. Located in residence with the architect would be the architecture machine with these five subassemblies. The machine

would have local computing power and local memory and it would work 24 hours a day for a specific designer.

Away from the designer would be a parent machine to which all architecture machines could talk via telephone lines. This mechanism would have powerful processors and extensive memory (in the spirit of Sweets Catalogue, Graphics Standards, zoning laws, or all the demographic figures of the world). The architecture machines would talk to this parent device for three reasons: 1. to acquire large bursts of computing power, 2. to acquire stored information, 3. to communicate with other architects and other architecture machines. In other words, the configuration is one where many parts, human and mechanical, are communicating with themselves and with each other, while the consortium as a whole is somehow communicating with the real world.

The Seeing Machine
Communication is the discriminatory response of an organism to a stimulus.[10] If we are to reckon with communication, beyond formal rhetoric or syntax (be it English or computer graphics), we must address ourselves to the versatility of the discriminating mechanism—the interface.[11] In this case, the interface is the point of contact and interaction between a machine and the "information environment." The observation channel in which we are interested is where the processors become tangent to the real world by directly sensing it or by communicating with a human (who senses it).

For a machine to have an image of a designer, a design problem, or even a so-called design solution, three properties are necessary: an event, a manifestation, a representation. The event can be visual, auditory, olfactory, tactile, extrasensory, or a motor command. The manifestation measures the event with the appropriate parameters (luminance, frequency, brain-wave-length, angle of rotation, etc.). The representation is the act of mapping the information into a receptacle that is compatible with the receiving organism's processing characeristics.[12] These three properties—event, manifestation, representation—form the interface.

In an architect-machine partnership perhaps the most relevant sensory interfaces are visual. Computer graphics techniques have become the paradigm for computer-aided architecture systems but beyond inputting and outputting lines, points, characters, and even halftones, architecture machines must have eyes (and ears and ...).[13] Setting aside the phantasmagoria of robot-designers, consider speaking with a machine that sees you. In our present culture the thought is foolish or frightening. To our children it will be an ordinary occurrence. To Mortimer Taube it is offensive.[14] To Marvin Minsky it is obvious.[15]

Oliver Selfridge is credited with the founding works in machine-vision.[16] His machine, "Pandemonium," observed many localized visual characteristics. Each local verdict as to what was seen would be voiced (thus pandemonium) and with enough pieces of local evidence from these demons, the pattern could be recognized. The more recent work of Seymour Papert and Marvin Minsky has extensively shown that such local information is not enough; certain general (or global) observations are necessary in order to achieve complete visual discrimination.[17]

Applying the Minsky-Papert eye, it is possible to build an architectural Seeing Machine by developing a simple device that will observe simple models.[18] Such a mechanism is the prelude to machines that someday will wander about the city seeing the city. In such a manner, architecture machines could acquire information beyond that which they are given and therefore would have the potential to challenge and to question. Furthermore, such data-acquisition avoids the mutations of transfer from real world to designer's sensors to designer's brain to designer's effectors to machine's sensors and so on. For this kind of data, the consequent losses of information at each transfer point are bypassed.

Such research is an exercise in learning through seeing (learning only those aspects which are indeed visually representable). The Machine looks at a simple block-model, attempts to recognize what it has seen (using many layers of heuristics) and then extrapolates certain characteristics (probabilities, commonalities, intents, patterns, etc.). After the first model is recognized, the Machine asks for a second and then a third, until it has seen 10 block-model solutions to 10 simple problem statements. Following the 10th solution, the Machine will be given an 11th problem statement and asked to generate its own solution. In this experiment, the solution will be in the vernacular of forms presented in the original 10.

Even though such a machine is more of a mannerist than a student, the exercise is relevant inasmuch as it reverses the fashionable role of computers. Currently, a great deal of concern and research effort is placed on the machine-generation of form from a given statement of criteria (a statement that usually narrows the range of goals by being a solution-oriented verbal phrasing). For the eyes of an architecture machine, the problem is the opposite; given a form, generate the criteria...learn from the criteria and someday generate new forms.

Notes

1. This issue will be discussed at length in Nicholas Negroponte, *The Architecture Machine* (Cambridge, MA: MIT Press, 1989). The preparation of the manuscript has been sponsored by Joint Center for Urban Studies of Harvard University and MIT. The reader should also refer to Warren M. Brodey and Nilo Lindgren, "Human Enhancement Through Evolutionary Technology," *IEEE Spectrum* (September 1967): 87.
2. Warren McCulloch, *Embodiments of Mind* (Cambridge, MA: MIT Press, 1965). The reader should particularly look at the essay, "Towards Some Circuitry of Ethical Robots," in that volume.
3. John Eberhard, "A Humanist Case for the Systems Approach," *AIA Journal* (July 1968).
4. Warren McCulloch and Walter Pitts, "A Logical Calculus for Ideas Immanent in Nervous Activity," *Bulletin of Mathematical Biophysics* 5 (1943): 115-133.
5. Ross Ashby, "The Design of an Intelligence Amplifier," *Automata Studies*, eds. Claude Shannon and J. McCarthy (Princeton, NJ: Princeton University Press, 1956).
6. Albert Uttley, "Conditional Probability and Conditioned Reflexes," *Automata Studies*, eds. Claude Shannon and J. McCarthy (Princeton, NJ: Princeton University Press, 1956).
7. B. F. Skinner, *Science of Human Behavior* (New York: Macmillan Co., 1953).
8. Arthur R. Miller, "The National Data Center and Personal Privacy," *The Atlantic Monthly* 220 (November 1967).
9. The concept of simulated evolution through bearing offspring is covered at great length in Lawrence J. Fogel, Alvin J. Owens, and Michael J. Wash, *Artificial Intelligence Through Simulated Evolution* (New York: John Wiley & Sons, 1956).
10. Colin Cherry, *On Human Communication* (Cambridge, MA: MIT Press, 1957).
11. Extensive research has been undertaken to establish congenial architect-machine interfaces. URBAN5 is a computer system that illustrates some of the conveniences of graphical and natural language discourse. This has been reported in Nicholas Negroponte and Leon Groisser, "URBAN5," *Ekistics* 24 (September 1967). URBAN5 is discussed at greater length in a forthcoming publication, Gary Moore, ed., *Proceedings of the First International DMG Conference* (June, 1968).
12. Stuart M. Silverstone, *Information Manipulation for the Evolution of Physical Environments* (Cambridge, MA: Urban Systems Laboratory), MIT Research Report (forthcoming [sic]).
13. Murray Milne, ed., *Proceedings of Computer Graphics in Architecture Conference* (Spring 1966).
14. Views that oppose the concept of machine-intelligence are extensively presented by Mortimer Taube, *Computers and Common Sense* (New York: McGraw-Hill, 1961). For further material, Hubert L, Dreyfus, "Alchemy and Artificial Intelligence," *Rand Corporation Paper*, (1966): 3244.
15. Marvin Minsky, "Artificial Intelligence," *Scientific American* 215 (September 1966). The entire issue provides material on the use of computers.
16. Oliver Selfridge and Ulric Neisser, "Pattern Recognition by Machine," in *Computers and Thought*, eds. Edward A. Feigenbaum and Julian Feldman (New York: McGraw-Hill, 1963).
17. Marvin Minsky and Seymour Papert, *The Perceptron* (Cambridge, MA: MIT Press, 1969). The book further expands on some of the myths of parallel processing.
18. Such work is being carried out by Anthony Platt, in cooperation with Seymour Papert, Leon Groisser, and the author. The research is being conducted in Project MAC's Artificial Intelligence Laboratory under Ford Foundation sponsorship through MIT's Urban Systems Laboratory. The work is one of four experiments directed toward the actual construction of an architecture machine.

Poetics

Louis I. Kahn

I have taught self rewarded.
School is my chapel.
I write Psalms.
When I teach well, what I have
done is never mentioned.
Teaching is to present the yet
not said the yet not made.
It is self inspiring The inspired
finds only himself.
Singularity to Singularity.
Human agreement without example.
To make present is an offering
to criticism.
Not to judgement.
A man is greater than his works.
To judge or be judged is to
presume Eternity.
Eternity the prevailing Spirit.
Art aspires to Eternity.
Religion is its Art.

Reprinted from *Utah Architect* (Summer, 1973).
Reprinted again with permission.

Journal of Architectural Education, 30:1, 1976

Messages in the Interstices: Symbols in the Urban Landscape

Marc Treib
University of California, Berkeley

There are many landscapes, if we interpret loosely, the natural landscape being but one. Townscapes, cityscapes, urbanscapes and even fire escapes are all landscapes: "a portion of the land that the eye can see in one glance." To those of us who grew up in urban environments, negotiating with nature often proves somewhat problematic. When we leave the familiar realm of the hard city surfaces, the clues of use and habitation, the structures of circulation, there is a sense of unease. We see the forest or the field as an expanse of incomprehensible data whose order and communicative possibilities elude us. The forms, the smells, or the directional winds which yield so much information to the experienced hunter or farmer are meaningless without study. But the rural dweller immersed in the city suffers a similar feeling of loss. The intervening planes between him and the natural world destroy his connection to the rural reality.

The same might also be said of an urban American abroad in a strange city—how does one "read" signs (as opposed to reading them)? Where do we find goods and services? Who sells the salt? (It may be sold, as in Italy, with tobacco and stamps, unlikely as it seems to Americans unfamiliar with Italy's history of taxation.) Where do you get gasoline for your car when there's no service station at the intersection of two main streets, the American piazza? Where is a bus stop? What does a market look like? Every country has its system of urban elements. This system organizes by function, tradition or both so that the location of services and products will appear in the same kind of places in each town. If you come across a men's room in an American building you can usually find the women's room without difficulty because both are positioned by the same logic which operates at urban scale. Logic, or at least habit, also dictates the location of a gas station. Or a shopping center. In short, we "read" a city or learn to "read" urban elements and learn how to comprehend the levels of symbolization and the layers of meaning, overtly intended or unintentionally included in built form and conglomeration. In short, we acquire "street smarts" which we could perhaps refer to as urban visual literacy.

Visual literacy, a relatively recent term, is the concern of the International Visual Literacy Association dedicated to the development of a certain faculty. Visual Literacy refers to a group of vision-competencies a human being can develop by seeing and at the same time having and integrating other sensory experiences. The development of these competencies is fundamental to normal human learning. When developed, they enable a visually literate person to *discriminate* and *interpret* the visible actions, objects, and/or symbols, natural or manmade, that he encounters in his environment. Through the creative use of these competencies, he is able to communicate with others. Through the appreciative use of these competencies, he is able to comprehend and enjoy the masterworks of visual communication.

The intent seems to be a good one, though difficult to pin down or define precisely.

A language is a system of sounds which, by the common agreement of a linguistic group, functions to symbolically convey meaning. One enters into language either by default, i.e., being born into it; or by acceptance, i.e., by study and acquisition. Writing, and consequently literacy, are byproducts of oral language which removes temporal speech from time as a mnemonic device, or as a means for increased range of communication.

Vision is a rather different matter. Although each individual has varying perceptual capabilities, and each perception is certainly modified or colored by an individual's history and experience, there are characteristics of human perception which are universal. We all can hear certain frequencies, can withstand a certain range of temperatures, and can see in a certain spread of wavelengths. Thus, vision, unlike language, is not entered into willingly or even by choice. It is a given, excluding the occurrence of physical infirmity.

Of course, we *learn* to see. We flip right-side-up the upside-down image we actually receive on the retina, as we in the western world, aided by continued exposure to photographs, cinema and television, "see" in perspective. But the amount of variation within this perceptual field is rather broad, and to suppose the existence of a ritual visual code, rather like language, closed and defined with certain rules, seems to be straining the analogy. This is not to say that codes do not exist in our visual world—they do. But a code and its elements always exist within a specific context, and the relationship between element and context is, perhaps, the most critical for signification, and in turn, meaning.

When we speak of a code, we are in fact speaking about a corpus. The corpus is defined as the elements used for communication, whether intended or not, which exist in a syntactic relationship, i.e., which are interdependent and affect the meaning of each other by their combination. In most cases, these codes overlap so that one person's corpus may appear in fragments in those of others. If we are to speak of visual literacy we must be careful to define the corpus involved, the elements and their syntax. Without this careful definition, there can be no testing for achievement of comprehension—or literacy.

The urban environment provides a wealth of material for investigations into the nature of visual communication. One of the reasons for this richness and probably the most important raison d'etre of American materialism and capitalism in general is the profit motive. And since the product of design follows the intent or "consciousness" of a society, we can see and read the value system behind the forms. As Louis Sullivan pointed out: "... every building you see is the image of a man whom you do not see"; and at the larger scale architecture is "a clear view of its social basis as an art of expression." We have more or less what we deserve as a society. There are but few bits of signage which escape the profit motive, such as directional signing, house and building numbering, vehicle classification, and the like. A shop, on the other hand, must sell. And to sell it must sign. For all but the smallest enterprises where relations are personal and the clientele local, the sign must help locate the store and make its products known (if not for the moment, perhaps for future reference): its hours of opening, its services offered, the credit card accepted, and so forth. Obviously *all* the information is not needed *all* the time—but there will be some times when it will be. The profit motive places the most stringent functional demands on architecture, storefronts, and signing. In most instances it accepts no superfluity. "Unneeded" information costs; unlike advertising, it doesn't pay.

In the past decade, there have been numerous attempts to "clean up the environment" and to "end visual pollution." The programs have been vague because the formulation of the problem has been vague. What is visual pollution? Is it a given, or does it vary? The difficulty lies in the relativity of the problem; what is OK in one place can be bad in another. We cannot consider elements without dealing with the context. There is the ever-present danger that the application of one value system to many situations could lead to an inappropriate homogeneity of image and information, thereby throwing out the baby with the bath water.

Most attempts or crusades to "clean up the environment" and "end visual pollution" fail to take into account the hieratic nature of information in the environment. Each person establishes his or her own order of critical information, an order which changes with place and time. Thus "Bankamericard valid here" is of minor significance to most people who continually pass a certain hotel, but critical to others travelling late on a Sunday night with little or no cash. In fact, there are very few areas, again most likely in directional or identification signing, where just about everyone's ranking of importance actually coincides. But the structuring of all urban

information along these lines, i.e., within one or few design formats, would make for an informationally poor rather than rich environment in spite of its apparent visual order.

Another approach to "eliminating visual pollution," other than the wholesale elimination of information, is symbolization. Members of the designer professions seem to maintain an ongoing love affair, both conceptually and formally, with non-verbal symbols. To be "universal" we strive to develop symbolic systems using pictographic material. The Department of Transportation symbols of 1975 are perhaps the best to date; probably because the designers, unlike most, were not afraid to actually look at precedents and see what needed to be developed and what could be reused with or without modification. But even in the DOT proposal the same problems rear their ugly head, namely: (1) at what point does a word-as-a-symbol, "change" for example, really function better than a complex graphic configuration, and (2) when is an abstract symbol like the dollar sign or "no entry," which must include a period of education, better than masses of graphic contrivance?

Transportation signing is actually a highly specialized field of symbolic representation which can, if necessary, assume an educated constituent group. Although its spill-off will affect other areas of society

Oblique symbolic function: although difficult to discern in black and white, the red swirl of the Coca-Cola logo is visible before the name of the maker. The advertisement oblique tells us that the location is usually a market or eatery.

An intended independent symbol: the intention of the designer and/or client is to make a representation of the form which will be "read" regardless of context.

(on doors, for example: "no entry" or "enter here"), its major impact must focus on situations where large groups of people must read and react quickly to a limited set of messages.

From observations of the American urban vernacular environment, three areas of symbolic function can be noted. These are termed: *intended* symbols subdivided into *independent* and *dependent*, symbols whose meanings are intended by their makers and only modified by position or constraint; *implied* symbols whose meanings are less specific and more generic; and *oblique* symbols, which possess a secondary set of meanings on another level. The list is not conclusive, nor is it complete. What it presents are some preliminary thoughts on classification of symbolic sets which refer to their use within a particular context, and hence function a certain way—either with the knowledge of the original designer or after his or her disappearance from the scene.

The intended independent symbol is the form with which the designer is most familiar since this is the most common design task. Here the attempt is to create a symbol, emblem, logotype, whatever, which in character and form represents a product or parent company. Its goal is to be independent, i.e., a constant meaning unmodified by any particular context: wherever a red disc or swirl is seen one thinks of CocaCola; or at least wherever one sees its white script. Automotive symbols, such as Mercedes-Benz, Cadillac, Citröen, Ford, Chevrolet, all strive for this autonomy. But none are as familiar as Coca-Cola—in fact, few abstract symbols are compared to logotypes. Geometric shapes used as corporate symbols, for example, Chevron or Arco gasolines, fall into this category since they have no meaning without their accompanying text—though they might be quite handsome as graphic patterns. The extent to which a design can actually be independent is the product of the designer's skill, the identifiability of the goods or services involved and the success of the current design style to single out the symbol as one to

be recalled. At any one time there will be a predominant designer's "look": these days the combination of business (read: corporate) attitude and coeval design esthetic. Our most recent cresting wave has been the Swiss-style: clean, simple, often geometric symbols paired with Helvetica or another san-serif type face and a healthy dose of white space. Certain type faces—Helvetica is one, Avant Garde Gothic another—are seen as being *au courant* by the layman through exposure to designer-designed graphics. These are often utilized by the public to give the impression of all items having been "designed," trying to get a credence and independence to designs which are not the product of the schooled designer.

Although total comprehension is the goal of the corporation, even an independent symbol design is rarely successful outside a limited context without extensive advertising and media exposure. A shell represents an oil company only in and around a service station context—rein forced by a consistent red and yellow color scheme. But it need be successful only within that specific automotive context to be functional. And in this sense an average of only fifty percent total comprehension might be a good one indeed. Although this group of

Gas crisis symbol: stuffage—cars used to sell stuff spaces adjacent to gasoline pumps. Raised hoods distinguish in-service from out-of-service pumps.

intended symbols is subdivided into two subjects, the exact point at which an independent symbol becomes dependent and vice-versa would certainly vary with the specific design.

Dependent symbols require more than one element of a group for clear identification of meaning. Two figures—one male, one female—rely on the presence of each other to refer to signing for rest rooms. One male alone, used more universally perhaps with sexist bias, might indicate "human being" generically or "person." In a similar vein, the hen needs the rooster, the knight, the dame. These function only by secondary reference to male/female and beyond that to two rooms in which the sexes are separated, i.e., rest-rooms. There may also be a dependence on education, i.e., on a particular constituent group. "Do Not Enter," now adopted as an international symbol, is dependent on a constituency which has been educated to the intended meaning of the white bar on a circular red field. Without education and/or indoctrination the shape has no meaning. Once familiarity is universally achieved, however, the symbol can be removed from its original context and take its significance with it to a new home. "Do Not Enter" can leave the road and enter a hotel, or to be more precise, can stop pedestrian entrance into a hotel and distinguish "in" from "out" doors. In the end these symbols may actually be the most clearly non-ambiguous since through exposure and education meaning is attached to the clearest reading and floats free of a particular context. As a result, symbols which were made dependent by a birth in abstraction can be granted total independence.

Many structures or signs have a symbolic component which was not the intention of their maker. There are numerous elements in the urban milieu which serve to symbolize commercial buildings without words or pictorial devices. A sea of cars around a group of buildings or a certain parking/building pattern will usually be read as shopping center before the signs of any store can be seen. A structure set back on an intersection with a free-standing sign will conjure a service station, and oil stains on the parking area could in turn show signs of

Information hierarchy and the strip. A motel is more important than which motel.

use. All are urban tracks and their meanings can be read as such although there was no communicative intention.

A relatively recent example of standard elements given new meaning by a new situation was shown during the gas crisis. Service stations were often at a loss to use formal means to communicate their gasoline supply situation. At first crude signs were used, but hampered by wind and limited in size, they didn't work too well. Shortly thereafter garbage cans and stacks of tires were employed to show that the station was open but without gas or to indicate which pumps were open. Trucks or cars were also used in this capacity of blockage, usually with their hoods raised to distinguish their being read as vehicles waiting for gasoline. By this time there had been a corporate response: clean graphics, usually too small, accepted only as a partial solution by station owners. In the end, a formal system with a green flag for "gas available," red flag for "no gas—but open for your other driving needs" was adopted. But the driver bypassed all of these message symbols for the most obvious one: a line of cars inching toward a corner location was taken as an open station with gasoline for sale.

Symbols can also signify more than one referent, or possess more than one level of reference, in an oblique way. The well-known Coca-Cola sign on a storefront, of course, advertises Coke, but it indirectly tells us that the establishment is usually either an eatery of some type

The intended independent symbol, the shell, in yellow and red, on a corner site will usually be regarded as a sign for a gasoline station.

or a grocery where the beverage is sold. A smog-control inspection station also serves to identify a service station or a garage—and the shell tells more about the facility than just the brand of the gas. A marquee identifies a cinema first, as well as a particular movie. In each the stimulus of the sign triggers a response which brings all our associations through experience to that building type, in addition to the specific identification.

In actuality, we experience a good deal of the city symbolically through implication. We develop a sort of sixth sense as to where things like cleaning, food, restaurants, garages, and the like *should* be. Of course, much is determined by the economic laws of the entrepreneur. Zoning laws, a by-product, formalize and determine even more. In general there is a logic to position and location, tested on the cash register, which helps form cities. Signs advertise a product but they also infer or imply what is where. Our knowledge of the city is acquired by means of cumulative cognition at several levels.

How universal are symbols? All are ultimately culturally linked. We can assume that a gas pump could be a viable symbol for all drivers because the formation of the constituent group depends on a knowledge of the object upon which the symbol is based. But what about the cocktail glass as a sign for a bar? Or a "2/39¢" for a supermarket or grocery? These last two are more cultural than universal and could only be used in the United States, or perhaps a few other western countries, without any expectation of some difficulty in comprehension. Without careful consideration of the context of any design, its situation or its user group, non-verbal communication can be as limited and ambiguous as speech. But it is actually the ambiguity, the meanings in the interstices, that makes the urban landscape the fascinating and informationally rich place that it is. It is fortunate that we are not yet at that point where we can predict and determine with exact precision what messages are to be extracted from groups of structures. Structures can be conceived and executed in a fixed period of time. But the day of occupation is the beginning, not the end, of any project, and the beginning, not the end, of the generation of meaning particular to the individual and the context.

Bibliography

American Institute of Graphic Arts. *Symbol Signs.* Washington: Department of Transportation, 1975.

Barthes, Roland. *Mythologies.* New York: Hill and Wang, 1972.

Blake, Peter. *God's Own Junkyard.* New York: Holt, Rinehart and Winston, 1964.

Boudon, Phillipe. *Lived-in Architecture.* Cambridge, MA: MIT Press, 1972.

Carr, Stephen et al. *City Signs and Lights.* Boston: Boston Redevelopment Authority, 1971.

Dondis, Donis A. *A Primer of Visual Literacy.* Cambridge, MA: MIT Press, 1973.

Langhacker, Ronald W. *Language and Its Structure.* New York: Harcourt, Brace & World, Inc., 1968.

Maldonado, Tomas. *Design, Nature and Revolution.* New York: Harper & Row, 1972.

Potter, Simeon. *Language in the Modern World.* Baltimore, MD: Penguin Books, 1960.

Reich, Charles. *The Greening of America.* Baltimore, MD: Penguin Books, 1970.

Ruscha, Ed. *Thirty-four Parking Lots.* Los Angeles, 1967.

Sennett, Richard. *The Uses of Disorder.* New York: Vintage, 1970.

Sullivan, Louis. *Kindergarten Chats.* New York: Wittenborn, Schultz, Inc., 1947.

Treib, Marc. "Signing in the Commercial Environment: Eyekonism Part II." Print, March-April, 1973.

—"Buildings as Signs as Buildings: Eyekonism Part II." Print, May-June, 1973.

—"The Word as Image: Eyekonism Part III." Print, July-August, 1973.

—"Cocktales." Print, January-February, 1974.

—"The Urban Spectacle." Print, March-April, 1976.

Venturi, Robert. *Complexity and Contradiction in Architecture.* New York: Museum of Modern Art, 1967.

Whorf, Benjamin Lee. *Language, Thought and Reality.* Cambridge, MA: MIT Press, 1956.

Wollen, Peter. *Signs and Meaning in the Cinema.* Bloomington, IN: Indiana University Press, 1969.

Gaming at CRS

Charles Estes
Caudill Rowlett Scott

At Caudill Rowlett Scott (CRS, Houston), gaming is not a standard design activity; it is a technique to be used when the conditions of team composition and project type indicate the need for consensus in decision-making. In practice, it is a design activity aiming to develop and evaluate a variety of options for arranging building space and site facilities. It is accomplished by a team or teams made up of people from the client's organization and CRS, working in the context provided by an approved design program. The design program, in effect, sets the rules for the game and a reasonable understanding of the program by all participants is essential to success.

The gaming technique is used frequently at three levels of architectural planning and design: site planning (large scale), master zoning (building scale), and departmental arrangement (sub-building scale).

Site Planning
These projects typically involve complex organizations, such as a medical center or university and a wide range of activities requiring large land areas, multiple buildings, and extensive networks for the movement of vehicles, people, and material.

In this type of large scale gaming, the team arranges scaled and color-coded paper rectangles to examine planning concepts for proximity, flow, open space, growth, or change with time, image, security, etc. The modeling usually is three-dimensional, focusing principally upon the several layers of activity and building space adjacent to the ground plan.

Master Zoning
This term refers to the study of the functional and physical relationships among the major organizational components to be located in a building.

Here, the gaming is three-dimensional, and scaled color-coded paper shapes are used to represent organizational components. Paper circles, arrows, and strips are used to represent other important requirements, such as corridors, elevators, and points of access.

Departmental Arrangement
With the knowledge obtained from master zoning of the project, the gaming task at this level is to study the arrangement of space within the departments or organizational components. The game is played on a board using room-scaled paper squares. These are moved about to form arrangements which have the potential for handling the work of the department and supporting concepts for image, status, privacy, security, etc.

The advance work required for gaming includes distribution of the approved design program (or an abstract of it) to the people in the client organization expected to take part in gaming sessions, constructing gaming models and materials, and preparing one or more "starter" schemes for the team to consider at the outset of sessions. The gaming model should be designed so that its pieces can be shuffled and rearranged easily to form new schemes. For a three-dimensional model with levels formed of clear plastic, there should be at least three inches of space between levels to allow a person to reach into the model and move a paper symbol by hand. A plastic foam coffee cup makes a more than adequate spacer. At the start of a gaming session, the important aspects of programming and prior planning should be reviewed to provide a fresh, focused view of the work for the team. The gaming model and materials should be explained so that everyone understands the symbols used, the scale of the pieces, color codes indicating function or organization, distinctions made between existing and proposed features, etc.

State the objective of the session. Make it short and to the point, i.e., "our objective this morning is to develop at least one good layout of departmental space." Give the ground rules:

- Look for arrangements that support concepts of operation, image, privacy, flow, etc.
- Try not to be concerned with shape or looks.
- Avoid spending time on details such as those related to equipment, hardware, dimensions, etc. These will come at a later stage of work.

Explain the schemes prepared in advance of the session. As discussion of variations begins, encourage the talkers to rearrange the pieces, thus "starting the game." As gaming progresses, important comments should be noted and promising schemes documented by photography or sketches.

The principal limitations of the gaming technique are those associated with group dynamics and professional maturity and ability. As might be expected, gaming sessions involving small client groups of ten persons or less are much more successful in terms of individual participation than those with larger groups. In part, this is a natural result of the physical scale of gaming where participation depends to a large extent

Tripler Army Medical Center, Honolulu—nurses studying space arrangement in gaming session.

The major benefits of the gaming technique are:

1. Knowledge and study are required, not skill; the staff member who would not dare draw a plan to convey his thought to the architect is generally eager to do this with gaming pieces.
2. The gaming pieces are the common media of exchange. Everyone shares the same understanding of physical scale and number of units.
3. Understanding of the design process, its complexity and compromise, is increased.
4. Greater support of the project and its planning is achieved.
5. Consensus upon basic arrangements is obtained more readily than with the traditional review of drawings method.

CRS planner presents master zoning concepts for expansion and renovation of a military hospital as developed in on-site gaming sessions.

on having a front-row seat next to the model. With groups of more than ten persons, sessions are very likely to be gaming exercises actively involving only a small core of people with the others being passive observers, or presentation events where the architecture-engineering team displays the model and reviews schemes prepared earlier. The process (and product) of gaming can be very unsatisfactory if members of the group fall back upon their professional prerogatives. A client member may stiffen if his operational procedures are questioned; an architect may blanch at a case of runaway aesthetics.

Typology and Primary Events

Tod Williams
The Cooper Union

Ricardo Scofidio
The Cooper Union

In the recent past, programs in architectural education have shown themselves to be sharply divided by seemingly contradictory tendencies between "theoretical" and "practical" architecture. Reflecting a similar schism among practitioners, this conflict has become a cause of serious concern among educators and has brought into question traditional pedagogical methods. Usual practice in first-year design education at The Cooper Union has been to expose beginning students to basic design principles via a consideration of abstracted architectonic elements. Particularly successful in this regard has been the 'nine-square' problem developed by John Hedjuk and Robert Slutsky. Here, through drawing and model building, the student manipulates simple geometric elements while beginning to explore their three-dimensional implications.

It is the second year, however, that has remained the focus of our attention at The Cooper Union—a critical time neither at the beginning nor near the end of the curriculum. The second year is a period when the student is required to sustain the theoretical investigations of the previous year while for the first time attempting to integrate the growing complexities of programmatic and site requirements. Traditionally, the strategy in second year has been to introduce the students to a variety of building and site types, with a gradual and calculated increase in their complexity. However, there remain a number of difficulties with this approach. In emphasizing the derivation of forms from buildings of similar functions, the focus on building types can become too reductivist, impairing the student's ability to work inventively within a newly acquired architectonic vocabulary. Further, in moving to more complex programs and sites, issues of architectural quality are often bypassed by what seem to be overwhelming demands of programmatic concern. In the end, the abstract problems on the one hand, and the programmatic problems on the other, are often seen in an opposing manner. Does form follow function or function follow form?

The Typological Model Exercise

In actual facts, both are interrelated. Therefore, our primary task in second year education is to provide a framework for exploring the interrelation of issues of form and function. Our approach to this problem, and to the general one of bridging these concerns with issues

Figure 1: Passage—cast plaster model.

Figure 2: Passage—plaster and stone model.

Figure 3: Passage—wood & lacquer model.

taught in the first year, has been to introduce the notion of the "typological model." Our basis for developing this second-year program has been to synthesize the abstract with the pragmatic. The second year is therefore structured as a series of exercises which dissect and isolate primary architectural elements to be analyzed and explored. The separate exercises are intended to culminate in a single building. The nature of these exercises helps the student maintain a clear goal in mind. The elements proposed to the students are architectonic in a formal sense while also underscored by functional, or programmatic, ends. "Column," "wall," and "window," for example, are each in themselves elemental and generic architectural figures made more specific when placed or seen *in context*. As with teaching someone to speak, one begins with the words and builds up to the larger structure of the sentence, only after demonstrating the power and potential of the words themselves and their interrelations.

To exemplify this idea, one of the exercises we require from students is the "Passage" problem. The task is to design a passage through a volume which is four feet deep by 30 feet wide by 30 feet high. This simple exercise provides an opportunity for each student to deal with the fundamental, abstract, architectural notions of *plan* and *penetration*. The student must address the formal, architectonic, and functional aspects of 'passage' and must determine the particular context for the volume itself by giving formal definition to its two sides. In so doing, the student must also develop a knowledge of construction and detail befitting the material with which he has elected to work. The required model is at a scale of one-half inch (Figures 1, 2, 3). The size of the architectural element in question and the special nature of its function, forces the student to consider the issue of scale and its physiological impact. This exercise and the pedagogical theory behind it, however, do not preclude the use of historically-derived forms; rather, they encourage a widening of the scope of applicable precedents to be considered.

The Object-Prototype Exercise
A second exercise is the "Utilitarian Object" problem, in which the student is asked to design and construct, at full scale, a working prototype of a chosen object. By inventing an object, or redesigning an existing one, the student gives precise definition to a highly specific program. The objects considered have varied in scale from a teaspoon to a two-passenger, 'folding' electric vehicle. The development of any working prototype necessitates much analysis, and therefore the student gains a comprehensive understanding of the object in question and its relationship to the human body.

Interesting permutations of long-standing approaches to physical problems associated with certain archetypal objects, for example, have included a shovel with a curved handle (Figure 4), allowing the foot to be placed centrally above the blade for greater efficiency

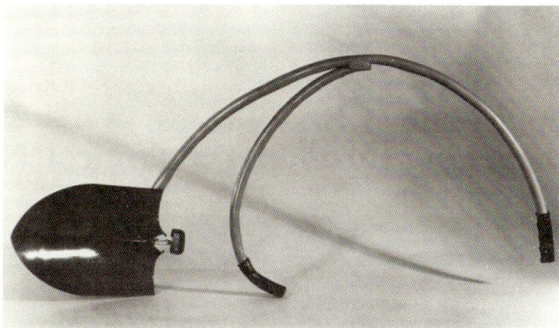

Figure 4: Utilitarian object—"utopian space."

Figure 5: Utilitarian object—fold-out chess set.

Figure 6: Utilitarian object—fold-out chess set.

in digging, and an umbrella with an off-center shaft (allowing the user to fully occupy the space directly under the center of protection). We put an emphasis on constructing such objects from raw materials. Because the requirement is to translate a thought into a drawing, a drawing into a model, and a model into a three-dimensional reality, the student is continually testing the validity of the design against the reality of production and use. Here, more than in any other problem given during the course of the year, the student directly confronts the problems of scale, material, detail, and craftsmanship (Figures 5, 6).

Explorations of "Column," "Window," "Room," and "Furniture" are subsequent exercises intended to further the student's understanding of the elements of architecture. Our intent is to use these exercises, as with the two already described, as a cumulative pedagogical base leading to a comprehensive project: the building itself. For this final project only the materials of construction and overall requirements are specified. Context and function are to be determined by the student. The complex program and site requirements of the traditional building-design problem tend to force the student to reduce these requirements to a palatable form before proceeding. The elemental approach, on the other hand, requires an additive (rather than the usual reductive) process of problem investigation.

Our emphasis on a typology of primary elements, together with our parallel concern for largely unspecified program conditions, is not intended as a manifesto for anarchy. In allowing the particulars to remain undefined at first, the student must therefore react in uncompromised ways to sets of criteria whose hierarchy of importance (and there *is* a hierarchy) must be *self*-determined. This focus on a distillation of the problem to irreducible ideas, and the process of design it engenders on the part of the student, results in a student's accommodation to the complexity of architecture: learning to make a line, to effect passage, to know and build a utilitarian object, to make a building.

Architecture as Drawing

Alberto Pérez-Gómez
University of Houston

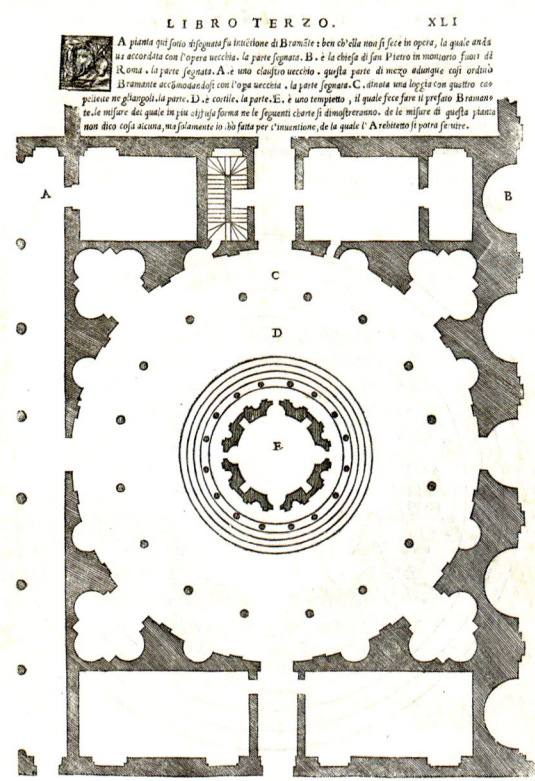

The plan of Bramante's *Tempietto* in the courtyard of S. Pietro in Montorio, Rome. Serlio reproduced this original "idea" in his treatise *Architettura et Prospettiva* (1519), in spite of the fact that only the central structure (E) was actually built.

The distance between architectural drawing and building has always been opaque and ambiguous. Indeed, much of the confusion faced by contemporary architects and educators seems to be linked to a misunderstanding of drawing as a tool of reduction. This article is an attempt to cast some light upon this problem, examining historical evidence that will lead to a discussion of prevalent prejudices which hamper our perception of modern architecture's true potential.

Vitruvius understood drawing, at best, as a minor part of the practice of architecture, while "theory" explained "the productions of architecture on the principles of proportion."[1] Alberti, as we know, was the first to distinguish between design and structure as the two constituent parts of architecture.[2] The opening pages of *De Re Aedificatoria* contend that design consists "in a right and exact adapting and joining together the lines and angles which compose and form the face of the building."[3] The role of design was "to appoint to the edifice and all its parts their proper places, determinate number, just proportion and beautiful order."[4] Design, however, was in Alberti's mind "inseparable from matter," so that drawing was perceived as the embodiment of architectural ideas, distinct from perspectives that represented (in painting), the reality of a building.[5]

During the Renaissance, architecture became a liberal art because it was perceived to be an activity of the intellect, akin to geometry and mathematics. *Disegno* was a "graceful pre ordering of the lines and angles, conceived in the mind."[6] "Image" entailed imitation (*mimesis*), thought, and conception, and was usually associated with the newly discovered powers of man as a *magus*.[7] The "image" was the architectural *idea* (from the root *Iδ*, to see) in the strict etymological sense, implying "look," "semblance," and "form." The "image" was also analogous in derivation and original sense to "species" (from *spec-ĕre*, to behold), which alludes to the original perception of the a *priori* order of reality. Thus the architect used images to embody a transcendental, abstract (geometrical) order, in accordance with the traditional Aristotelian hierarchy of places.

While the traditional builder, a primaeval poet (from the Greek *poesis*, to make), made his thoughts into building through the implementation of an operational geometry (in the original sense of giving human dimensions to external reality), the Renaissance architect articulated the necessarily "abstract language" of walls, openings, and columns in architectural drawing, by means of plans (*ichnographia*), elevations (*orthographia*), and profiles or sections. In defining the urban context and its institutions through "images," the architect enhanced the traditional sense of *place*, adding meanings that spoke to man about himself, about a new understanding of life as valuable experience, beyond medieval determinism, but that was never in contradiction to, or defied, the order of Creation.

Renaissance architectural drawing was perceived as a symbolic intention to be fulfilled in the building, while remaining an autonomous realm of expression. Hence, the building, i.e., meaning given in the immediacy of embodied perception, was always accepted as primary. Instead of dictating a set of instructions that were to be actualized by implementing neutral technological processes, the architect, still primarily a builder, knew that the "distance" between idea and matter, between

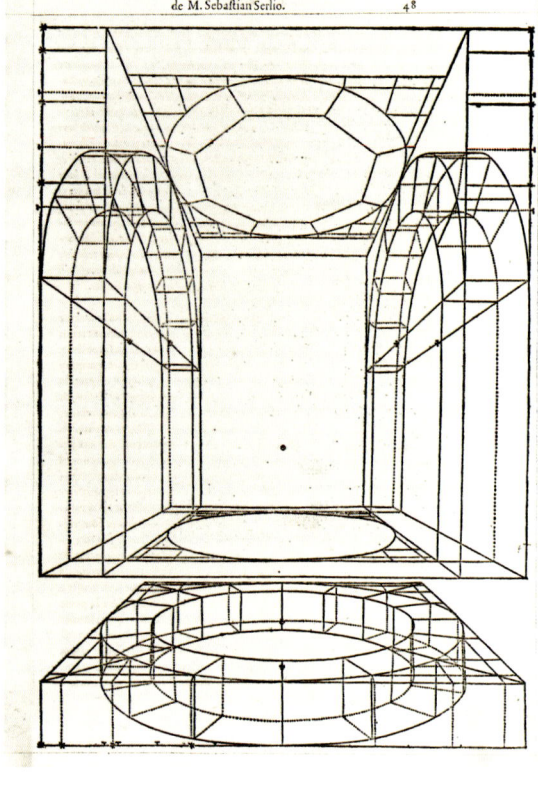

Serlio's illustration for a perspective construction. His treatise, *Architettura et Prospettiva* (1519), was the first book on architectural theory to include a chapter on perspective.

design and construction, would be reconciled through his own involvement in building. In Filarete's *Trattato*, for example, Platonic overtones notwithstanding, the architect was well aware that the building would change in the course of construction, and that it could be enriched and even improved.[8] The primacy of synesthetic, embodied perception was recognized. Nothing can replace the meaning of experiencing a building, regardless of how sophisticated the reduction of a building into other mediums might appear. Phenomenological psychology teaches us that such embodied experience is the ground for all other perceptions of meaning.

In *La Pratica della Perspettiva* (1569), Daniele Barbaro, the philosopher and mathematician, friend and patron of Palladio, made some interesting comments about Vitruvius's architectural "ideas." Barbaro emphatically disagreed with the claim that linear perspective (*perspectiva artificialis*), along with plan (*ichnographia*) and elevation (*orthographia*), was one of the architectural ideas referred to by Vitruvius in the second chapter of his Book One.[9] The interpretation of Vitruvius's *sciographia* remains problematic, and the most sensible commentators and translators of the text have always struggled with the passage.[10] It is clear that Vitruvius was not referring to linear perspective, but rather to a perception of the building's totality in depth, a view which reconciled the internal and external orders, the plan and the elevation. Vitruvius had posited his three "ideas" as the means of expression of architectural order or disposition, and Barbaro contended that *sciographia* should not be misunderstood as *scenographia*, or stage design, which was the true province of perspective. Instead, he proposed adding the section or profile to the plan and to the elevation that had been recommended by Vitruvius.

For the most part, seventeenth century architects continued to distinguish between architecture, which depended upon geometrical operations and combinations, and perspective, which acted as a tool of illusionism.[11] Perhaps only in the early eighteenth century treatise of Ferdinando Galli Bibiena was the task of the architect identified with that of the stage designer.[12] The ambiguity concerning the use of perspective as a means to embody an architectural intention is extremely revealing. During the Renaissance drawing could be more or less precise, making sometimes use of tools like grids or scales,[13] but the drawing was evidently not perceived as a "picture" of the building, as its reduction, or as a neutral collection of information for its construction. The road was certainly open for the transformation of the builder into an efficient designer, capable of controlling practice through prescriptive methods and precise drawings. But the transformation did not happen overnight. Perhaps more importantly, this historical evidence shows that the perception of theory as method, and of drawing as its tool of reduction, should not be taken for granted. Only modern architects after Durand have assumed such a role of drawing as primary and unquestionable.

Toward the end of the eighteenth century Gaspard Monge developed his descriptive geometry, which became a basic discipline of Durand's school, the École Polytechnique. The problem of describing an object through its projections on three planes had been a concern of architects before Monge, but the invention of descriptive geometry was more than a systematization of known methods. Descriptive geometry opened the way for a functionalization of the "lived world," i.e., for the inception of nonEuclidean geometries. It became an effective instrument of power, and an absolutely essential tool of precision during the Industrial Revolution. The original architectural *ideas* were transformed into universal projections that could then, and only then, be perceived as reductions of buildings, creating the illusion of drawing as a neutral tool that communicates unambiguous information, like scientific prose. Don't we even today see architectural educators stand in front of projects in a review and ignore architectural ideas, pretending instead to criticize "buildings," assuming that it is possible to predict their objective meaning?[14]

Although seemingly reacting against the "engineers" of the École Polytechnique, professors and students at the École des Beaux Arts regarded drawing as

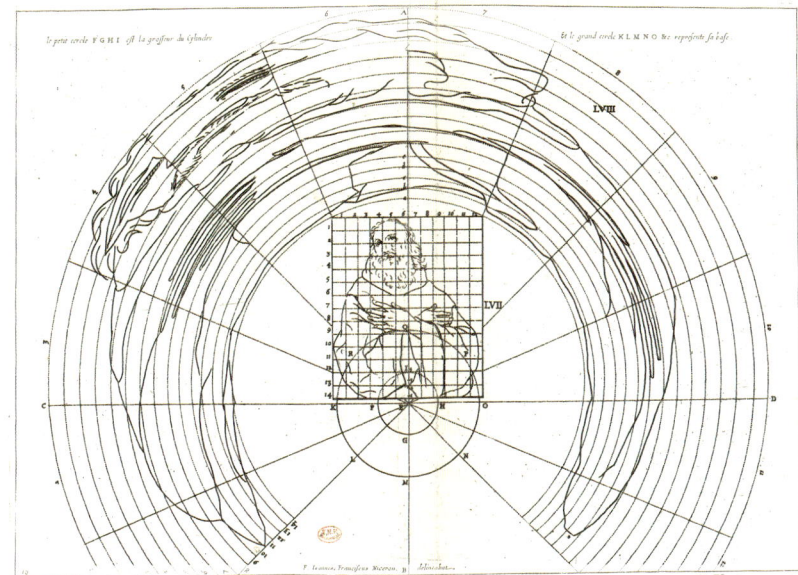

Cylindrical anamorphosis of S. Francis, from F. Niceron's *Curious Perspective* (1638), showing the use of geometrical perspective as a tool of illusionism.

an implicit manifestation of descriptive geometry. This understanding has always been taken for granted and makes for a crucial and extremely complex problem. The depth and extension of its ramifications can be grasped by remarking its connection to what Edmund Husserl described as the crisis of European science,[15] and to the inception of non-Euclidean geometries in the early nineteenth century.

Euclidean geometry, as both Ortega y Gasset and Cassirer have pointed out, rests upon intuition.[16] It is "precise" because its origins are imprecise, because its laws reside in the realm of experience. The substitution of a purely optical reality for the primary synesthetic reality of our being in the world (i.e., the substitution of *perspectiva naturalis*, the Euclidean laws of optics, for *perspectiva artificialis*) may have started during the Renaissance, but was not fully accomplished until Victor Poncelet, drawing on Monge's work, wrote his treatise on projective geometry in 1822. For Euclid each "figure" had its own properties and was perceived as irreducible. Geometry worked precisely because parallel lines never met.[17] Even during the "Age of Reason," the embodied, tactile perception of a transcendental Nature had primacy over visual reduction or perspectivism as a source of truth and meaning.

When perspective had lost its symbolic content to become the "truth of reality," the architects of the Enlightenment abandoned it as an "idea": the Baroque vista gave way to the English garden. Almost a century later, Poncelet used perspective theory to refute the postulate of parallel lines and give geometry the "generality of algebra."[18] Poncelet declared that systems of parallel and converging lines were identical, and that the lived world was homologous with the infinite geometrical universe of homogeneous space.[19] Thus all Euclidean figures lost their specificity and the world (i.e., its geometry) was reduced to a formal system of transformations.

The modern belief that drawing is simply a reduction of a building has, therefore, enormous implications. Descriptive geometry made building science possible. For the first time the architect was able to dictate to a mason or carpenter a series of operations through working drawings or precise detail designs, without having to be involved in the "craft" of "building" itself.[20] This is, of course, a precondition of contemporary methods of production in architecture and civil engineering. But this modern prejudice is also shared by most architects who regard design as obliquely related to art.

Durand was the first to advocate the methods of descriptive geometry in architectural design. In his lectures at the École Polytechnique, he declared that no building could fail to please as long as it fulfilled in an efficient and economic manner the pragmatic requirements for shelter. This amounted to a denial of symbolic order as the crux of architecture. For Durand, the building had to provide maximum pleasure with minimum means. In his *Précis*, myth and metaphysical concerns were excluded from architectural theory, and architecture became a game of formal combinations facilitated by the grid of his "mechanism of composition."[21] Thus, design was, in essence, a logic devoid of absolute meaning, in which only the syntax of style could be controlled by reason.

Modern "professional architects" have taken for granted Durand's understanding of "design" as reduction. Consequently, they continue to create mute and uninteresting functional buildings. One follows from the other: the *means* are *not* neutral. What is inessential, in fact, is whether the material skin of a building is gothic, classical, a *mélange* of styles, or a denial of styles. The Beaux Arts tradition was as rooted in functionalism as the Bauhaus, if one understands functionalism as a reductionistic attitude, whereby architecture is the function of a combination of variables, i.e., the mathematization of human needs and values.[22] This issue

Section of Guarini's church of S. Lorenzo in Turin, from his treatise *Architettura Civile* (1737). Guarini's architecture depended on the combination of Euclidean figures for its beauty and its stability.

is more profound than "post-modern" architects seem to suspect. And although the belief in a one-to-one correspondence between the drawing and the building is ludicrous, confusion has prevailed.

The true architect's concern for meaning cannot be properly embodied in a drawing whose explicit or implicit role is the reduction or "picture" of a building. Drawing must serve as the expression of a symbolic intention in the form of architectural ideas. Because very few architects in the last 200 years have made their own buildings, the importance of drawing has been emphasized. Architects have been either unable to build a symbolic order, or have intentionally avoided building because a) they did not comprehend their primordial role as makers of a symbolic order, hence their willingness to accept the irrelevant task of filling the world with sterile and inhuman structures dictated by consumerism or economics; and b) because society is apparently not interested in a symbolic order. Individuals

seem capable of postponing *ad infinitum* their pressing existential problems, living instead under the illusion of absolute rationality, without sight of objectives, and focusing only on the efficiency of means.

The rejection of reductionism in architecture must bring about a recognition of the value of theoretical projects as drawing (or model): projects which, by definition, question the possibility of their execution in a prosaic world. Prior to Piranesi, Boullée, and Ledoux, this notion of a theoretical project would not have made sense. During the eighteenth century, reason became powerful but never excluded myth. The natural philosophy of Newton, prototype of all knowledge, was ultimately motivated by the possibility of the revelation of God through a better understanding of His works.[23] Art, poetry, and science therefore, were not contradictory. All disciplines were envisioned against the same epistemological horizon dependent on a belief in a harmonious, rational cosmos, revealed to man through the perception of Nature.

After Durand, the reconciliation between form and content became the paradigmatic problem for architects concerned with meaning. Absolute validity of any one style was questioned and architecture was reduced to its pragmatic function, that is, the making of material commodities. The architect was thus forced to choose between art and science, between the false extreme of an absolute objectivity (universal mathematical reason) or that of an absolute subjectivity (personal poetic myth). The history of Western architecture in the last 200 years is thus a description of how architects have tried to come to terms with this issue. Clearly, an architecture gnawed down to its bones, one that speaks only about technological process and not about human values has often been deemed unacceptable, by both architects and society at large. True, architects have often added "referential" ornament to their buildings, trying to make their utilitarian and deterministic structures more "human," but the success of such buildings has been, at best, partial: witness the irreconcilable contradictions evident from Labrouste's Bibliothèque Ste. Geneviève to post-modernism. If the solution is not the abstract order of technology, it is also *not* embellishment.

Meaning, we must remember, is *given* in perception; it is not a product of "association." Phenomenological studies have shown that meaning is not primarily or solely an intellectual construct.[24] Architecture is an order that addresses our ambiguous, finite, human reality, it is not merely a vehicle for scientific "truths."

The paradox here is that architecture, by definition, is both abstract, *and* a mimesis of a transcendental reality. But modern man has generally denied myth and poetry as the primordial revelation of reality. We have become insensitive and blind, preferring the logical explanation of science simply because it is the source of technological power. Durand, for one, ridiculed the traditional concept of the column as the body of man, pointing out that it was nothing more than a cylinder of

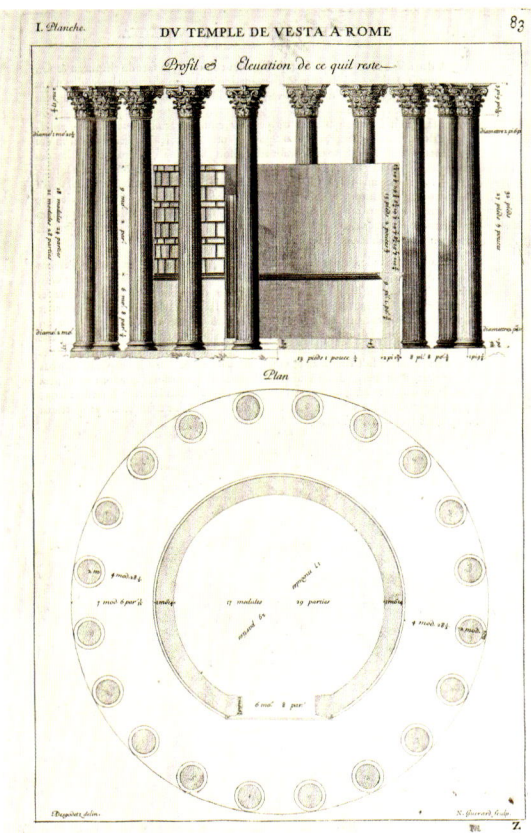

A typical plate from A. Desgodetz's *Les Edifices Antiques de Rome* (1682) illustrating the lull architectural "idea" of a Roman building.

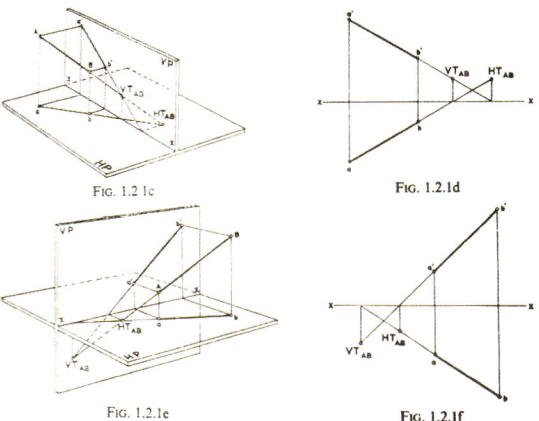

The orthogonal planes and quadrants of descriptive geometry which allow for a reduction of three-dimensional reality into a system of coordinates and their manipulation independently from intuition, from R.G. Robertson's *Descriptive Geometry* (by courtesy of Sir Isaac Pitman and Sons Ltd.).

matter. Our modern world is superficially rational and deterministic, embodying technological utopia; it constitutes *no place* for humanity. Our cities represent chaos rather than order, our structures restrict freedom rather than enhance it.

In view of all this it is crucial to recognize the role of drawing as the embodiment of architectural ideas. In a manner of speaking, particularly after Durand, the drawing *is* the architecture, a privileged vehicle for expressing architectural intentions: intentions that are poetic in a profound traditional sense, as *poesis*, as symbol making. Such architectural drawings may assume the character of poetic images generated by a metaphor, by a program that embodies an understanding of dwelling, like John Hejduk's projects for Venice. Or they may criticize architectural ideas and the abstract elements of architecture (e.g., plans, sections, elevations, or projections). This is the point of Daniel Libeskind's *Micromegas*. The perception of such theoretical projects as self-referential can only occur if the reality of architecture past and present is assumed to be the banal reductionism and pragmatic materialism that I have criticized.

The Vitruvian "ideas" cannot be implemented today as if they had always been anonymous projections in a conceptual space, as if descriptive geometry and our perspective world had always existed. Nor can the modern architect deny the power of abstraction or ignore the end of the traditional world. This paradoxical power has led the modern "architect" to an effective technological domination of building, to irrelevant formal manipulations and to city planning. Nonetheless, our rationality is also part of our humanity, as well as the paradigm of modern art: the necessary means for revealing a truly modern architecture.

The technological world-view can easily deny the necessity of architecture as a symbolic order. But human reality is ambiguous. Irrespective of how long modern man may wish to postpone coming to terms with Being, with the meaning of his existence, and regardless of how long he may wish to conceal emptiness with the illusion of progress, he must ultimately confront his limits: the dilemma of his finite life and his power to embody divinity. The perception of meaning remains universal, and man's humanity endures through the crisis. What then must the architect's attitude be?

Traditionally, the abstract Euclidean order put forward by the architect possessed an inter subjective dimension. Today, however, abstraction in art is often identified with hermetic, solipsistic intentions. Although it is true that even numbers (the epitome of the ideal) are necessarily "colored," and that most specific phenomena are taken in perception within a framework of categories, in the last 200 years architects concerned with meaning have had to take to the extremes. This is, indeed, a condition derived from the crisis itself, and carries with it the dangers implied in excessive abstraction (art for artists, excessive originality, criticism rather than poetry) or in its denial (art for society, excessive referentiality, communication rather than poetry). The traditional middle ground where the ideal and the real, the intellectual and the bodily articulations were

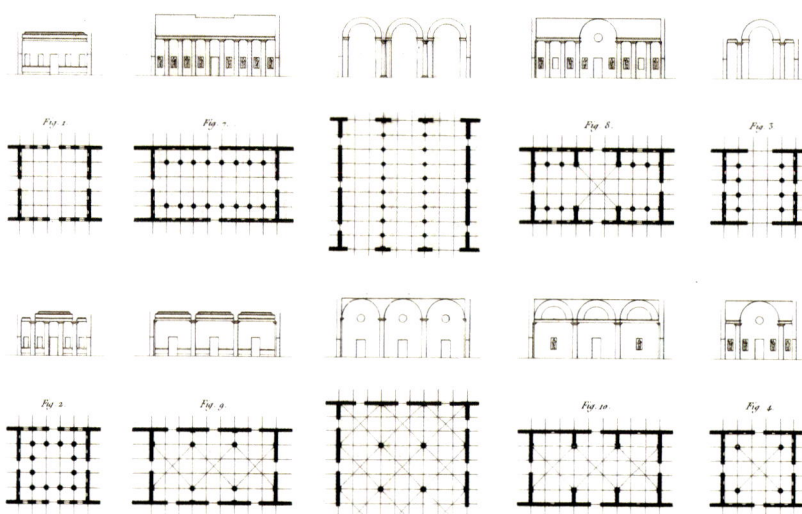

Plate from Durand's *Précis* showing the grid of his "mechanism of composition" and his method of combinations.

reconciled, seems today incapable of being the source and origin of architectural symbolic intentions. Man is either too insensitive or too humane.

The architect seems condemned to make either poetic (perhaps romantic) drawings or critical (perhaps senseless) ones. The risk is the production of either screaming, an excessive dependence on context (the embodied world of man), and an unwarranted faith in the possibility of meaning-in-the-world, *or* babbling, an excessive independence from context and an unwarranted faith in the impossibility of meaningless abstraction. When a romantic or surreal project is imagined *in* the world, often its intended meaning is lost. Does "collage" make sense in our contradictory urban environments? Is poetry, in fact, still possible after Hiroshima? Isn't metaphor anachronistic or, at best, irrelevant now that the ultimate referential ground, the *cosmos*, has been eliminated? By the same token, a drawing about ideas runs the risk of becoming a hermetic language, like much serial music or abstract painting, which is removed from the primary realm of experience, from the shared world in which meaning is grounded.

Regardless of such boundaries, these two alternatives seem to be the only way of making architecture. Ironically, these are the very alternatives explored by modern art, but which are seldom understood by architects. By accepting the *status quo* of the architectural practitioner and the "reality" of drawing as a referential tool, one rejects architecture's place as a primordial cultural institution, as the embodiment of a pre-intellectual order whose task is nothing more and nothing less than the perpetuation of culture and its coherence.

Our collective illusion is a reality that we take for granted, a Platonic world devoid of mystical connotations that Plato himself would have repudiated. Can reality simply be our technological non-sense? This was the question already addressed by Piranesi, Boullée, and Ledoux during the 18th century. Particularly the two French architects were explicit in their rejection of mathematical reason as the structure of architectural theory.[25] Betraying an authentic existential anguish, they struggled to transform theory into an explicit metaphysics that explained the meaning of architecture through a poetic discourse. Their drawings constituted a set of theoretical projects that they assumed to be true architecture, in opposition to their actual buildings. Not surprisingly, both architects felt that architecture was deeply akin to painting. Thus architecture became primarily the *making* of the drawing (or the model), the same poetic act that has always *magically* revealed the truth of reality: a process similar to the gnostic search for truth by the enlightened architect. The true architect must pursue either of two parallel alternatives in the hope of finding a point of reconciliation: he must be a born gnostic or a born phenomenologist. And when the architecture of the modern world is built, it will be (as it has been in exceptional cases) founded upon the convergence of these two perspectives: a future overlapping of poetry and criticism.

Notes

1. Marcus Vitruvius Pollio, *The Ten Books on Architecture*, trans. Morris Hicky Morgan (New York: Dover Publications, 1960), 5.
2. Leone Battista Alberti, *De Re Aedificatoria (Ten Books on Architecture)*, trans. Cosimo Bartoli and James Leoni, ed. Joseph Rykwert (London: Alec Tiranti Ltd., 1955), 2.
3. Alberti, 2.
4. Alberti, 2.
5. Compare *De Re Aedificatoria* with Leon Battista Alberti, *On Painting and On Sculpture* (London: Phaidon, 1972).
6. Alberti, 2.
7. See, for example, Agrippa Cornelius *De Occulta Philosophia* (Antwerp: J. Grapheus, 1531).
8. Antonio Averlino (Il Filarete), *Tratatto di Architettura* Il Polifilo (Milan: Il Polifilo, 1972), 504.

9. Daniele Barbaro, *La Pratica della Perspettiva* (Sala Bolognese: Arnaldo Forni, 1980), 129–130.
10. See, for example, Fabio Calvo Ravennate's manuscript, printed in *Vitruvio e Raffaello* (Rome: Officina Edizioni 1975), 78–79.
11. See Guarino Guarini, *Architettura Civile* (Milan: Il Polifilo, 1968), 242 ff. The first edition of this work was published in Turin, 1737.
12. Ferdinando Galli-Bibiena, *L'Architettura Civile* (New York: Benjamin Blom, 1971). First published in Parma, 1711.
13. This is clear in Filarete's treatise and in some of Antonio da Sangallo's drawings for St. Peter's. See Christof Thoenes, "St. Peter's: First Sketches," *Daidalos* 5 (September 1982): 81.
14. I discuss this extensively in Part IV of Alberto Pérez-Gómez, *Architecture and the Crisis of Modern Science* (Cambridge, MA: MIT Press, 1983).
15. Edmund Husserl, *The Crisis of European Sciences and Transcendental Phenomenology* (Evanston, IL: Northwestern University Press, 1970); and Edmund Husserl, *L'Origine de la Géometrie* (Paris: Presses Universitaires de France, 1974).
16. José Ortega y Gasset, *La Idea de Principio en Leibniz*, vol. 1 (Madrid: Revista de Occidente, 1967), Volume 1, and Ernst Cassirer, *The Philosophy of Symbolic Forms*, vol. 2 (New Haven, CT: Yale University Press, 1972), Part II.
17. Even geometricians found it impossible to prove the limitations of Euclid's postulate during the eighteenth century. See Girolamo Saccheri, *Euclides ab omni naevo*, trans. George B. Halsted (Chicago and London: Open Court, 1920).
18. The basic principle of Poncelet's projective geometry had been discovered in the seventeenth century by Girard Desargues. See Girard Desargues, *Les Oeuvres de Girard Desargues*, 2 vols., (Paris: Lieber, 1864). Desargues's work was never understood by his contemporaries.
19. Jean-Victor Poncelet, *Traité des Propriétés Projectives des Figures* (Paris: Bachelier, Libraire, 1822).
20. This is very clear in Jean Rondelet, *Traité Théorique et Pratique de l'Art de Batir,* 3 vols. (Paris: Chez M. A. Rondelet Fils, 1830).
21. Jacques-Nicolas-Louis Durand, *Précis de Leçons d'Architecture,* 2 vols. (Paris: the author, 1819).
22. This understanding of functionalism as an exclusive characteristic of modern architecture is discussed extensively in my forthcoming book. Toward the mid-nineteenth century, Gottfried Semper would actually use the analogy of an equation to illustrate the process of solving an architectural problem.
23. See Peter Gay, *The Enlightenment An Interpretation*, 2 vols. (London: Wildwood House, 1973), vol. 2, 126-166.
24. Maurice Merleau-Ponty, *Phenomenology of Perception* (London: Routledge and Kegan Paul, 1970), see especially parts I and II.
25. Etienne-Louis Boullée, ed. Jean-Marie Pérouse de Montclos, *Architecture. Essai sur l'Art,* series Miroirs de L'Art (Paris: Hermann, 1968); and Claude-Nicolas Ledoux, *L'Architecture Considérée sous le Rapport de L'Art des Moeurs et de la Législation*, vol. I (Paris: H. L. Perronneau, 1804).

Bibliography

Bannan, John. *The Philosophy of Merleau-Ponty*. New York: Harcourt, Brace and World, 1967.

Gadamer, Hans-Georg. *Reason in the Age of Science*. Cambridge, MA: MIT Press, 1981.

Holt, Elizabeth. *A Documentary History of Art.* New York: Doubleday, 1957. Volume III. This volume contains translated excerpts from the primary sources quoted in the article.

Ivins, William. *Art and Geometry* Dover (New York) 1964.

Heidegger, Martin. *Basic Writings.* New York: Harper and Row, 1977. Chapters 6, 7, and 8.

Merleau-Ponty, Maurice. *The Primacy of Perception*. Evanston, IL: Northwestern University Press, 1964. Chapters 2 and 5.

Merleau-Ponty, Maurice. *Sense and Non-Sense.* Evanston, IL: Northwestern University Press, 1964. Chapters 1 and 4.

Vycinas, Vincent. *Greatness and Philosophy*. The Hague: Martinus Nijhoff, 1966.

An Open Letter to Architectural Educators and Students of Architecture

Daniel Libeskind
Architecture Intermundium

Why spend time tediously applying gold-leaf unto a pinnacle of a tower (impressive!) whose foundations are rotten? Before that delicate task will have been completed, the entire edifice will collapse destroying both the work and the worker. Invisible disasters precede those that can be seen...

No amount of research, discussions on 'relevance' or compiled information can disguise one obvious fact: Architecture as taught and practiced today is but a grammatical fiction. Enough to see the gulf which separates what is taught (and how!) and what is built (and why!) to understand that somewhere a lie is being perpetrated. Only a sophistic method could mask a situation where so many spend so much to do so little—with such damaging results.

Here will resound a chorus of protests. Have we not introduced new teaching methods and up-to-date theories? Have we not retrieved lost precedents? Are we not producing a great new generation of educators and the educated? A success story, in short. Precisely. It is this "success" which has transformed a realm where "angels once feared to tread" into a supermarket of commodities, or worse, a whorehouse of opinions about them. Students are corrupted early into believing that only that which succeeds is a paradigm. They are prepared within simulated frameworks where future success can be insured. This constitutes a precondition for the school's ability to rob systematically each student of his or her problem. By the time they have become 'professionals' the process has indeed succeeded in brainwashing them so that they are no longer even able to remember that there *is* a problem: the problem of Architecture's existence in a corrupt society, and how to resist this corruption.

But the problem of Architecture just won't go away by manipulating history, scavenging through other fields, contemplating techniques of action. For Architecture can solve no problems—it itself is inherently problematical and questionable.

Having relinquished love of the divine *episteme* in favor of opinion, the architect has become a purveyor of opinions; has lost participation in *Sophia*—that wondrous dimension of Architecture which Alberti called angelic. Architecture becomes everybody's (the managers', renovators', interior designers', space planners'—a "good profession") and no one's. School becomes a pluralistic cover under which attention toward the nonexistent basis of Architecture is converted into each person's opinion as to how to supply it, and thus diffused in its potentially explosive content. "Problem solving" is simply another term for transforming the nowhere-to-be found ground of Architecture into a piece of "real estate" in order to sell it. ("Start with the site...")

Neither teachers nor students are today encouraged to undertake an adventure: dangerous, risky—perhaps hopeful?—which understands itself as a search for the whence, the whereto, and the why of Architecture's condition: a quest for the miracle, or at least the abyss which illuminates it. And if someone is still bothered by a problem to which no curriculum answer can be given then he or she should refrain from raising it, because that to which technicized thinking can give no answer is irrelevant—a "pseudo problem." (A few history courses, some humanities—and hocus-pocus—Architecture's meaningful once again!)

I believe that the atmosphere of unease which is today felt in Architecture cannot be eliminated, though the climate in which it is taught and practiced can be regulated by sophisticated control systems.

The experiential core of Architecture has sunk below the horizon of visibility so that even when it appears it is unrecognized. The process of de-culturation called education and practice has eclipsed Architecture so far and so thoroughly by the fictions of "common sense" and the "real world" that one hesitates even to speak of indifference toward it. By simply being silent the educational establishment has eliminated questioning; "practice" has developed a blind spot for that which threatens its success.

But the de-centering of being toward non-existent grounds is actually felt as reality. Indeed it is this very groundlessness which moves the participant in Architecture toward the void. This void has become the mover: the seeker the moved. Reflection upon this process of participation constitutes the true literacy of the Architect.

Education as the art of turning around toward reality—the truly revolutionary art—has become a technique of adjusting students so completely to the times that they no longer feel a desire to know anything else. The school has become a device which prevents students of Architecture from acquiring the knowledge that would enable them to articulate the fundamental question of Architecture: being or not. Pressed into a state of quiet despair or aggressive alienation, students abandon the mystery of Architecture. But this kind of attitude and reason is not reasonable. There are other ways to think and do Architecture: non-instrumental reason, non-manipulated architecture.

Architecture—that divine luxury of faith, highest crystallization of the material liberty of humanity, its imagination and spirit, must never succumb to being the degraded product of necessity provided by the technicians of educational and monetary utopias.

This is why I started *Architecture Intermundium*.

Private Reactions to Public Criticism: Students, Faculty, and Practicing Architects State Their Views on Design Juries in Architectural Education

Kathryn H. Anthony
University of Illinois, Urbana–Champaign

This article reports the results of research about the effectiveness of design juries in architectural education, a topic which scholars have seriously overlooked. Most important is a conspicuous absence of information from what is our most valuable resource: our students. This research examines the educational value of juries, both interim and final, how design students cope with public criticism, and a comparison of the architecture student "subculture" with that of other students. The study consists of two phases. Phase I is a case study at a mid-sized university. This study relied on systematic behavioral observations, interviews, questionnaires, and diaries. Students, faculty, and alumni in architecture, urban planning, landscape architecture, and outside environmental design participated in the research. Phase II is a follow-up study of other schools, based on questionnaires of architecture faculty at the Cranbrook Teachers' Seminar. Results strikingly document that the vast majority of all those questioned—faculty, students, and practicing architects—believe architectural juries need improvement. Architecture students surveyed learn very little from juries, but learn more from interim than final juries. Most students respond defensively and nervously to juries, and the high degree of tension and sheer "burnout" that architecture students experience greatly interferes with the learning process. Finally, this research documents that the architecture student "subculture" differs substantially from that of other students, and that it may well be harmful to students' health. Implications of these findings are discussed, and suggestions for improving design juries are offered.

Introduction
The purpose of this research was to study the jury systems as a method of architectural education. Although generations of architectural educators have relied on juries as the primary vehicle to evaluate their students' work, very few have taken a serious look at the jury system itself and its educational value to students in the design studio. In this respect, architectural education is almost light years behind most other academic fields where professionals have systematically evaluated and often modified traditional teaching techniques on a regular basis. The teaching of mathematics, for example, underwent a tremendous change in the 1960s with the advent of new math and more recently, in the late 1970s to 1980s with the introduction of courses on "math anxiety." Foreign language education has been transformed through language laboratories and through the "total immersion" approach. Computerized programs have substantially altered several fields of instruction in recent years. Even art education has been revolutionized in many institutions, from elementary through university levels, by applying new knowledge about split-brain theory. Courses and workshops on "drawing on the right side of the brain" have sprung up like wildflowers across the country, posing a serious challenge to traditional teaching techniques.

The teaching of architectural design, however, has remained relatively constant since the French Ècole des Beaux-Arts was established in the nineteenth century. The architectural jury came into vogue in the United States around the turn of the century, with the studio as the center of training.[1] Since that time, the process has typically included a fixed curriculum where design study begins upon entering school, the division of students into studios or ateliers led by a *patron* or master, the use of sketch projects or the *esquisse*, the tradition of older students or *anciens* helping younger ones, the teaching of design by practicing architects and the evaluation of projects by a trained jury.[2] The students' fate ultimately rests in the hands of the jury who decides whether they pass or fail. It is worth noting, however, that the design juries of the Ecole des Beaux-Arts were conducted behind closed doors. Students' design work was judged on the basis of their graphic submissions alone; no oral presentation was made. By contrast, most juries or reviews held in today's architecture schools involve both verbal and graphic presentation of students' work.

Some assumptions of this paper ought to be pointed out. They center around the notion that the jury is intended to be a learning experience. Ideally, after participating in a jury, students learn how to improve their design concepts. They also improve their ability to evaluate critically design work. The information gained from each jury experience, ideally, has a cumulative effect so that the design of subsequent work is at least partly influenced and improved as a result of the criticism received on previous design projects. This is the accomplishment of what some scholars have called "double-loop" learning, a deep level of understanding which allows one to reexamine values and assumptions.[3]

Naturally other lessons can be gleaned from the jury experience as well, but these concepts seem to be central. These assumptions form the underlying framework with which most schools of architecture operate. They are reflected in the strong emphasis on design studios (which usually constitute the largest portion of the architecture curriculum, are awarded the highest amount of course credits, and occupy the most space—compared to other classroom facilities—in architecture school buildings) and on design juries as a primary way of measuring and evaluating students' progress in design. But are these assumptions really true?

Scholars have virtually ignored the study of design juries. A literature search revealed virtually no empirical research on the educational value of the jury system. Most closely related work, however, includes the research by Hassid, who developed a system of classifying criticism, the two-volume report produced by the Consortium of East Coast Schools of Architecture, and an account of a clinical psychologist who has treated architecture students.[4] However, none of these sources deals directly with juries.

One of the most useful concepts which can be gleaned from the scant literature available was developed by Argyris, who coined the term "Mystery—Mastery" to explain how students are taught about architecture.[5] The notion here is that somehow the critic has mastered the art of design, but the process through which he or she arrived at this mastery remains a mystery to the student. R. D. Laing has called such a dilemma a "knot," a concept well articulated in the following quote:

> There is something I don't know
>   that I am supposed to know.
> I don't know what it is I don't know,
>   and yet am supposed to know,
> And I feel I look stupid
>   if I seem both not to know it
>   and not know what it is I don't know.
> Therefore, I pretend I know it.
>   This is nerve-racking
>   since I don't know what I must
>   pretend to know.
>
> Therefore I pretend to know everything.
>
> I feel you know what I am supposed to know
>   but you can't tell me what it is
>   because you don't know that I don't
>   know what it is.
>
> You may know what I don't know, but not
>   that I don't know it,
> and I can't tell you. So you will have to
> tell me everything.[6]

Donald Schön's work takes a more indepth look at the experiential nature of the design studio, however it falls short of focusing especially on design juries.[7] The recent heated debate in *Architectural Record* over the efficacy of the design studio, too, did not discuss juries in any depth.[8] The notion of criticism has been discussed over and over again in JAE, but primarily in essay form or through isolated examples from case studies, and design juries are seldom mentioned.[9] More importantly, perhaps, is a conspicuous absence of information about the educational value of design juries from what is probably our most valuable source of information: our students.

In light of this situation, this research sought to make a critical, systematic inquiry into the architectural jury system, particularly from a social and psychological perspective, while including students as a primary source of information. The following issues were addressed: 1. How educationally valuable is the jury system and for whom? How do faculty, students, and former students of architecture (practicing architects) compare on their opinions of the jury system? (One hypothesis is that current students would probably be more critical of juries than would alumni or faculty, since the students are on the "receiving end" of the criticism and since the jury experience is most immediate to them.) How do juries in school compare with client presentations in practice? (One of the common rationales for juries is that they help prepare future architects for professional presentations. Do they?) Are any changes needed in the jury system, and if so, what are some suggestions for improvement? 2. Are interim and final juries equally effective teaching and learning techniques, or is one more effective than the other? 3. How do design students cope with public criticism? 4. How do the behavior patterns (especially with regard to sleeping and eating) of architecture students compare with those in other environmental design fields, and with those outside design?

Methods

To attempt to answer these questions, a study was conducted during the course of one academic year, with a follow-up comparative portion a year later, ending in June 1985. The first and major component of the study was completed at a mid-sized western university with a relatively large Department of Architecture (approximately 550 students in a five-year Bachelor of Architecture program and forty in a Master of Architecture program). Architecture students collected most of the data under close instructional supervision as part of two courses entitled "Behavioral Factors in Architecture" and "Directed Research." Based upon feedback from students, faculty, and school administrators, various phases of the study were refined and further developed to help address issues which arose as the research progressed. Data from the second phase of research, the faculty questionnaire at the Cranbrook Teachers' Seminar, were collected by the author.

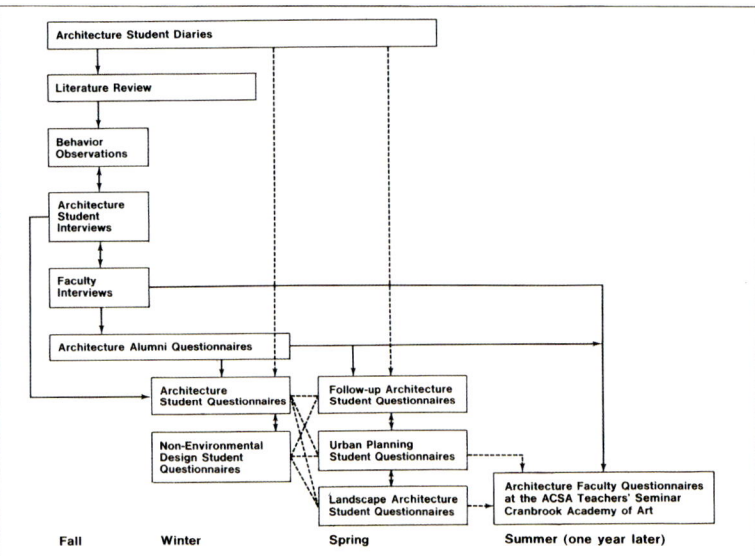

Research Process.

Phase I: Case Study

The purpose of Phase I of this research was to document certain attitudes and behaviors of architecture students and faculty in the context of design juries at a case-study school. Issues addressed included the overall educational value of juries, a comparison of the educational value of interim vs. final juries, methods of delivering and responding to criticism, and students' personal eating and sleeping habits.

To attempt to answer various questions about the jury system, a variety of research techniques was used.[10] The sequence of research is reported in Figure 1. These techniques included:

1. Systematic behavioral observations at nine architectural jury sessions, some recorded on videotape, of a total of 130 student presentations.
2. Interviews of: a) forty-three architecture students immediately after receiving criticism from jurors; b) forty architecture students on an ongoing basis throughout the term; c) nineteen environmental design faculty (eleven architecture faculty, and five landscape/planning faculty at the case-study school and three other architectural educators in the same geographic region).
3. Diaries of twenty-seven architecture students.
4. Questionnaires of: a) 189 architecture students; and as a comparison b) thirty-two landscape architecture students; c) thirty urban and regional planning students; d) eighty-one non-environmental design students (enrolled in a "General Psychology" course for non-psychology majors); and e) thirty-four architecture alumni (practicing architects) questionnaires.
5. A brief follow-up questionnaire of eighty-five architecture students.

Phase II: Follow-up Study of Other Schools

A year after all the data had been collected at the case-study school, a followup study, the second phase of this research, was conducted at the ACSA Teachers' Seminar, held at the Cranbrook Academy of Art. The seminar brought together a relatively small group of faculty and administrators from architecture programs across the country and a few from abroad. Enclosed with the on-site registration materials was a questionnaire about the jury system which participants were asked to complete and return to a lecture presentation delivered by this author. At the lecture the results of the case study were presented and a discussion session followed.

The purpose of this questionnaire was two-fold: 1) to compare how other faculty and architecture alumni (from schools other than the case study) evaluated the jury system, and 2) to try to ascertain whether or not specific features of the jury process at the case-study institution were typical, i.e., to begin to determine to a limited extent which findings might be generalizable elsewhere.

The questionnaire was based upon those administered at the case-study school to the architecture students and alumni, and to planning, landscape, and non-environmental design students. In addition, a number of items were added specifically for this group.

A total of sixteen questionnaires was returned. The results reflect responses from faculty and administrators at fourteen different institutions; twelve American and two foreign representatives from the following schools participated:

Foreign: University of Manitoba, Winnipeg, Canada; Royal Institute of Technology, Sweden.

U.S.: Andrews University; Auburn University; Ball State University; California Polytechnic State University, San Luis Obispo; Louisiana State University; Tulane University; University of California, Berkeley; Univer-

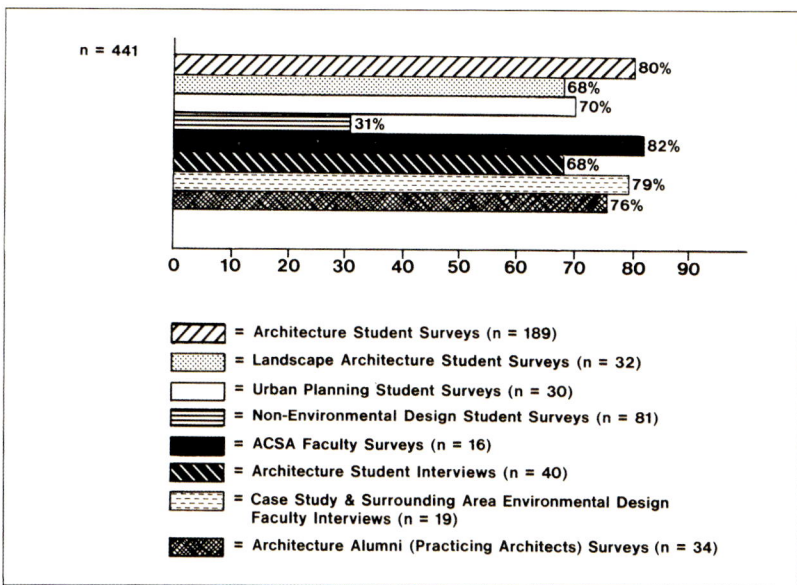

Comparisons between architecture students, faculty, and alumni and students in related and other disciplines with regard to their opinions of the jury system or ways their work was judged. Percentage indicates those who believe the system needs improvement.

sity of Illinois at Urbana–Champaign; University of Miami; University of Oregon; University of Washington; Washington State University.

These faculty and administrators were alumni of twenty-one different institutions, including Princeton, MIT, Yale, Cornell, Berkeley, Michigan, Illinois, and several others. Most had received Master and Bachelor degrees of architecture. Half had received their last degrees less than ten years ago, while a few had graduated over twenty-five years ago. The majority of those who responded (69 percent) were over thirty-five years of age. Thirteen males and three females returned the questionnaire.

Data Analysis
Qualitative data were analyzed through a content analysis. A series of statistical tests was used to analyze the quantitative data. For the behavior observations, an observation sheet was used to record behavior for each presentation at each jury session. Students presenting their work, faculty (including jurors), and the rest of the class were observed. Nonverbal and verbal behavior were noted. Based on two books on body language, specific behavior patterns were placed into particular categories (offensive, defensive, and nervous) and recorded on observation sheets.[11] Selected presentations were videotaped.

Results
Following is a summary of the major findings from this research.[12] They center around a number of themes which are explained in detail below.

The Educational Value of the Jury System
In sum, the results of all phases of this research—interviews, questionnaires, observations, and diaries—indicate that *the vast majority of those questioned believe that today's architectural jury system is inadequate and needs improvement*. (See Figure 2) This sentiment is echoed by environmental design students, faculty, and alumni at the case-study school as well as by faculty and administrators at other institutions. Ironically, the only group sampled who is satisfied with the way in which their work is judged is the sample of non-environmental design students; they have no juries at all. Since this research was not limited exclusively to the case-study campus, but includes data from other campuses, the results appear to be somewhat generalizable to other schools of architecture.

The hypothesis that alumni would be less critical of juries than current students was not borne out. Instead, it appears that compared to other groups, architecture faculty, students, and alumni are about equally critical of the system.

The advantages of the jury system, according to some respondents, is the interchange of ideas, the fact that it sets a deadline for students to work towards, and that it is a broadening and learning experience. For those who feel the system needs improvement, suggestions for students are to participate more actively, to be better prepared, more confident, to have a positive attitude, and to perceive the jury as a learning experience. Some of the recommendations for the faculty are to set clearly the format and procedures, address issues specifically and focus on problem objectives, and to schedule the jury after the project is due. Suggestions for visiting critics are to become more familiar with the problem, to speak to the issues rather than assuming a role, to examine all work seriously before beginning comments and to know the program and educational objectives of the course.

Furthermore, when the forty-three students were interviewed soon after making their design presentations, it was found that roughly two-thirds (63 percent)

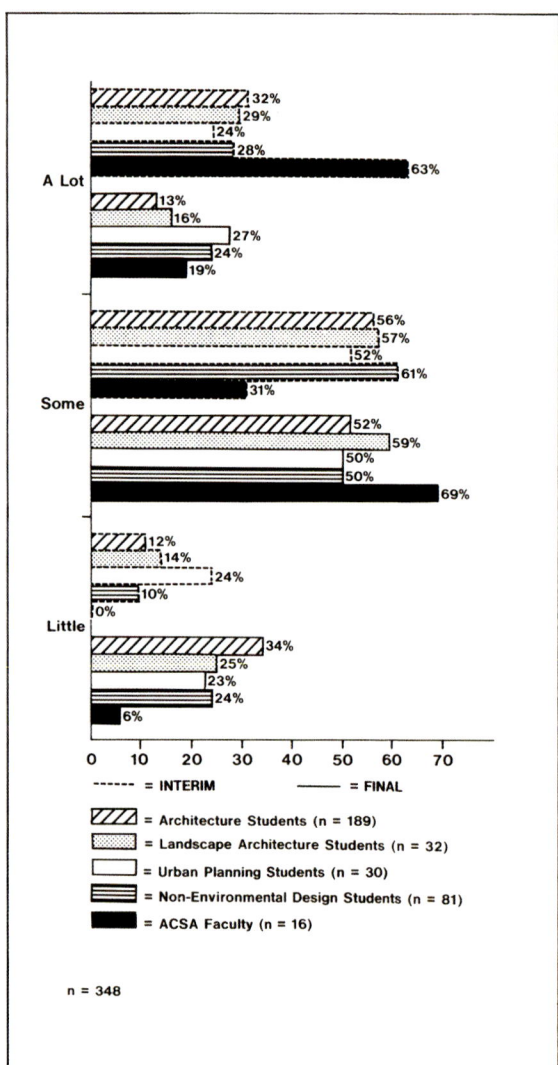

Amount learned from Interim vs. Final juries. Comparisons among students in Architecture, related and other disciplines and ACSA faculty (from questionnaires).

do not think that they had learned much from the jury comments they had just heard. Only slightly over a quarter (28 percent) believe they had performed well, citing confidence and preparation. Poor verbal presentation, nervousness, and exhaustion are the reasons cited among those who think they did only fairly. Those who think they did poorly blame their inexperience, poor verbal presentation, and lack of enthusiasm.

When asked how much they remember about projects of classmates who presented work before their own, most of those architecture students interviewed say they remember some or a lot. About half (53 percent) are able to give two correct examples describing previous projects and the jury's reaction to them. However, over one-quarter (28 percent) cannot remember anything. Most (72 percent) cannot remember anything about those projects presented after their own.

The analysis of the twenty-seven student diaries revealed that students do not seem to learn much from public criticism. After a jury, only a few students were able to answer the question "What did I learn?" even though they were very articulate in describing their own thoughts and feelings about the criticism they received. Only a handful specifically stated that they digested the criticism, rectified any problems, and incorporated these criticisms into their subsequent design work. One student learned about structures, another learned to view things beyond one's personal experience and "loosen up." These were about the only substantive comments to be found. Desk crits seemed to be most valuable. Final crits, given at the conclusion of a project or in jury format seemed to be of *least* educational value.

More often than not, however, what students claimed to have learned from design juries has more to do with presentation style, or how to "play the game," than with design. For instance, after the first crit of the term, one fourth-year student learned "to be patient, modest, courteous, to keep my talking to the bare minimum, not to be 'braggish' or unduly 'meek', and to dress effectively." After the final crit, this student learned "to speak softly but carry a gargantuan stick."

Another student said:

"What did I learn? I learned that third year (design) is no more organized than second year was last year. I learned that . . . the teachers don't agree on methodology. The most important thing I learned . . . is what *I* need to concentrate on if I want to be a good architect and the separation (between) that and what I need . . . to be an 'A' student."

In a similar vein, a third-year student designing a beach house related:

"They talked only briefly about my general design when they hit on my southern, beach front elevation. Very open. They took off on a debate over energy conservation versus ocean views, and when they realized that they had gotten carried away on that one issue, they stopped and went on to the next project . . . The instructors were too preoccupied with their own egos. They began attacking each other rather than the project . . ."

In sum, most students in our sample of diaries and interviews appear to learn little from their final juries. Furthermore, what they do learn has little to do with design.

Three-quarters of those faculty surveyed at the ACSA Teachers' Seminar believe that student presentations to a jury are either somewhat or very different from presentations to professional clients. Of the architecture alumni (practicing architects) sampled from the case-study school, most (82 percent) also concur that the two processes are quite *different*. Reasons for this are that a designer's professional presentation usually commands more respect from the client than students typically received from the jurors, that the

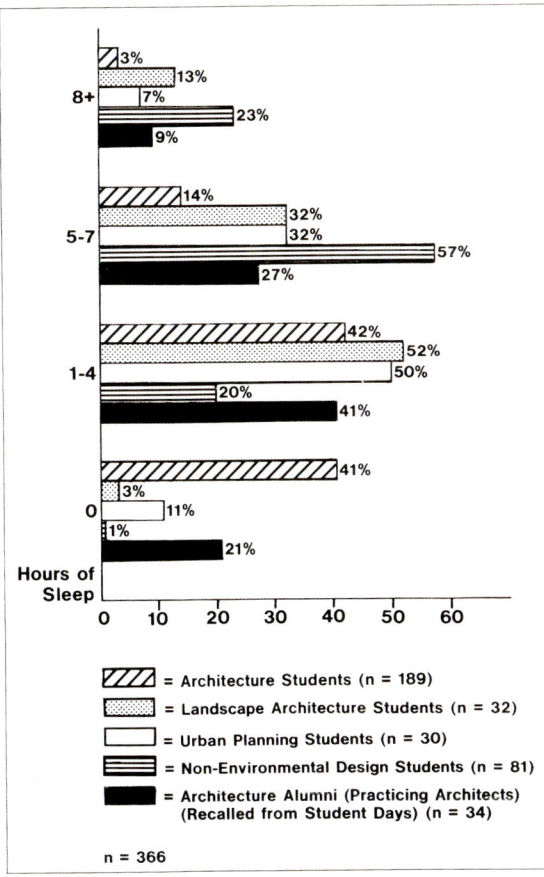

Comparison of Environmental Design, nonEnvironmental Design students', and Architecture alumni's sleeping habits the night before juries or project due date (from questionnaires).

professional presentation is a more informal process than are juries in school, and that clients are much more involved throughout the entire design process than are jurors at the university. Here are some examples of the practitioners' comments:

"I don't believe the comparison to be a relevant one. Both situations are pressure-filled, yet . . . client presentations involve much more dialog about the problem throughout the process than did the jury system at school . . ."

"Often, professionally speaking, the design presentation is a product of a team effort. In school, I don't recall working as a team on any project, which I think was and is a great detriment. The emphasis at school was on *individual creativity* throughout the design process. As a professional, I see a lot of people who carry that attitude into an office, and are almost incapable of exchanging ideas and working creatively on a team basis."

"The jury system is much more difficult to handle than client presentations. Your ego and self-esteem are much more exposed and you must deal with a larger audience. If you can handle a jury, you can handle a client. I think it's a good training ground."

"The most difficult, abusive school jury is but a comedy when compared with the indecisive, budget-conscious, critical corporate client! (not to mention the developer, the building department, or various other entities an architect must deal with)."

"Totally different. Clients tend to confine their comments to the satisfaction of the program requirements. The school jury is closer to the in-office reviews of principals and other staff."

"I believe they are worlds apart in terms of importance. The jury in school turns into a joke at the last minute, becoming merely a means of securing a grade in a class, but a professional presentation is a means of relaying your most sacred design theories in a way that may eventually become part of the built environment. It is wholly more of an exciting and real-life experience, where the school jury is merely a competition of your peers and you."

The Educational Value of Interim vs. Final Juries

Most of those questioned agree that *compared to final juries, interim juries are a more effective learning technique. While interim juries seem to serve many useful purposes, the value of final juries appears to be minimal at best*. Of all groups sampled, architecture students say they learn *least* from final juries. (See Figure 3.) Views of faculty and students on the amount learned from each format seem to differ substantially.

Generally speaking, students think they learn less than faculty think they do.

Many faculty sampled at the case-study school and neighboring institutions believe that because interim juries allow for adjustment and fine-tuning of concepts, they result in more learning than final juries. Several architecture students feel that final juries, as opposed to interim juries, do not help them very much because it is really too late to alter the project. Others feel that interim juries are not as useful as studio critiques. However, still others believe that final juries are more beneficial by offering diverse opinions, opportunities for dialog, and insights. And many students believe that it is only at final juries where their design is complete enough for others to comment intelligently on the solution. In sum, faculty and students believe that interim and final juries accomplish different goals.

Methods of Delivering and Responding to Public Criticism

Methods of delivering criticism at both the case-study school and other universities questioned appear to be similar. *Most criticism is oral and delivered in public, on-the-spot*; very little criticism is written. As a result, design students are under a great deal of stress during the jury. Unfortunately, this tension interferes with their ability to recall correctly the criticism they are given about their own work. Furthermore, their sheer exhaustion after presenting their work prevents many of them from even listening to any jury comments about other students' projects. Criticism literally seems to go in one ear and out the other.

For instance, observations revealed that while receiving the jury's comments, *most architecture students display defensive and nervous behavior.* Most of this behavior was non-verbal. Most common student behavior patterns observed were crossing arms and legs, avoiding eye contact, and covering up the mouth or chin. Twiddling fingers, tapping feet, pacing, scratching various parts of the body, and biting fingernails are other signs of nervous behavior. Most faculty behaved nervously too, as did some onlookers from the rest of the class.

The tension observed during these sessions is mirrored in the students' private diaries. Students find the design process, and especially crit sessions, to be a highly emotionally charged experience. The intensity of emotions described in the diaries is astounding. As one student summarized, going through a crit is like "riding on a rollercoaster with no seatbelt." Emotions run high and range the full gamut from high to low. However, the vast majority of emotions narrated by the design students about juries was strikingly negative. *The most commonly felt emotions are anxiety, fear, frustration, anger, embarrassment, disappointment, guilt, and disgust.*

For the most part, students' feelings of anxiety centered around feeling unprepared. A few days before his preliminary jury, one fifth-year student wrote:

"I can see it now, the gallery full of other students and aggressive words exchanged between us and the jurors. My knees are literally shaking just thinking about it. The muscles in my stomach feel tense and tied up in knots."

Before his final jury, this same student wrote:

"I feel a deep sense of futility. I have spent at least eight hours a day on my drawings, staying up until 3 a.m., getting up at 8 a.m., and my drawings don't show it. . . . As I was driving home from school today, I suddenly realized that . . . all my life was concentrated on that fateful Wednesday. Life beyond Wednesday was not important."

Another fearful student narrated: "I do not want to present my work. It is very superficial and unsubstantial. I do not want to be yelled at by my instructor."

Feelings of fear are often accompanied by visions of dreadful consequences. Often these fears are cloaked in very harsh language. As one student put it, "Undoubtedly, the jury members will crucify me . . . my instructor is famous for tearing students up." Another student, before the final jury, made this diary entry:

"The whole weekend I have been worried sick that I'm not going to get done. I had very little sleep and am coming down with a cold and a cough. I feel awful and hate architecture at this moment. I stayed up all night last night and feel miserable. I would do anything to get out of [the jury] right now. I wish I had an accident—just anything so that I wouldn't have to face the jury."

Frustration was another emotion shared by several students. Several students complained of being cut off during their presentation to the jury. As one individual put it:

"I was the second one to present, though I must admit I wasn't as nervous as I usually am (I guess 3 x 5 note cards, a nice outfit, and good drawings go a long way towards making one feel prepared). However, Visiting Juror X never let me finish my presentation (I guess he gets nervous if he doesn't get his two-cents worth in). He cut me short . . . so basically I heard him out and I tried to finish my presentation but then he interrupted me again. So I just thought, 'Well, I guess I'm through here.'"

Others were frustrated during the jury by contradictions among professors, by their own professors contradicting previous advice they had given throughout the term, or by their professors "tuning out" to their presentations altogether. A rather dramatic account went like this:

"Presentation Day — Do I feel like shit . . . . The only teacher who gave me an excellent crit was Professor X. Gave me all positive, then all negative points. Can you beat this? [My professor] walks out at the beginning of my crit and comes back in when they're criticizing all my work. Real fair."

Another student had this to say about presentation day:

"One minute before I began to speak Mr. X walked in. He was the reason for my crit going downhill . . . . It seemed as though he talked and talked and talked and everything he said . . . came out bad. What upset me is that some of the issues he brought up [contradicted] what I had been 'critted' on by [my professor], and I did not want to say, 'Well, Professor Y didn't tell me that.'"

One student entered reactions to a preliminary jury, which was held in front of faculty and a professional audience knowledgeable about the project's site.

"I was so embarrassed that they didn't say anything about [my project] or even question it. I guess they did not see what I drew—it was on an 8 ½" x 11" sheet. I was so embarrassed that after my presentation I just walked out of the class. The whole day I felt like scum of the earth.

Even worse, when I came home, the whole night I resented myself."

The next week, following another jury presentation, this same student stated:

"They asked a lot of technical stuff but nothing of architecture. I feel disappointed and depressed. I don't feel like I learned anything from this class. I just walked out full of confusion and depression. My days as an 'A' student are over."

A graduate student, whose team made a poor presentation of a group project, expressed disappointment and explained:

"Later I found out that our team was just bluffing by displaying some ideas which were scrounged together at the last minute. I felt sad and . . .embarrassed."

Those who expressed positive feelings about their jury experience were clearly a minority (ten out of twenty-seven students). Most commonly cited pleasant emotions were surprise, relief, happiness, a sense of accomplishment, and on rare occasions, euphoria. Students tended to feel this way after a favorable crit. One student entered:

"After crit—feeling fantastic—I finally have got the idea of developing a concept through the entire design. The guest critic said 'I'm happy to be here' after looking at my project . . . I also got congratulated by other students . . . will now go home and sleep for a couple days."

A student whose final jury went well explained:

"I feel satisfied, peaceful, proud to know I was productive and recognized. I won't forget the smile of my instructor, his arm around me, and his words, 'You're great!' At that moment, they meant so much to me."

Another student, while writing about favorable feedback from the jury, exclaimed, "Miracles never cease!"

The diaries also revealed that students highly regard positive criticism—but they don't get enough of it. Most of the accounts in the diaries centered around the psychological impacts of negative criticism. In fact, students' negative emotions were often directly linked to harsh, negative critiques from their professors. Stories about negative criticisms far outweigh those of positive critiques.

Students used powerful expressions to describe their negative reviews. Among some of the stronger phrases were "we got completely shot down," "the jury was ripping me apart," "the instructor came down on us," "they jumped on me," "I was crucified," or "we were massacred," "he's damn sarcastic," and "it was the ultimate slap in the face."

Accounts of positive criticism, though rare, were just as touching. Some students praised their instructor for speaking up on their behalf to the rest of the jury. One student expressed: "Professor X was a real lifesaver . . . he jumped in and bailed us out . . . He is like our father and we are his children, and he stands up for us."

Another said:

"The thing that has 'made my day,' however, is that Professor X himself came by and took a look and said, 'You have a great project here.' I felt that this was the first positive thing he ever said about my work and it made me feel a lot better."

Perhaps the saddest case was the following: "After class I ran into my professor. I told him I felt as if I didn't really get much feedback during my review and he said that it was because I had a good project." Had the student not confronted the instructor directly, there would have been no way of knowing if the instructor's evaluation was positive or negative except through the course grade.

Several students said that they felt more highly motivated to continue working after hearing positive criticism at a jury. By contrast, an entirely negative review often led to their feeling sullen and depressed and unwilling to pursue their project.

The Studio Subculture: Eating and Sleeping Habits of Design Students

Questionnaire results indicate that sleeping and eating patterns of environmental design students—especially those in architecture—dramatically differ from those outside the design professions. Architecture students constitute the largest group of those who *do not sleep at all* the night before a project is due. (See Figure 4) Most architecture students do not sleep at all or sleep very little; altogether the vast majority (83 percent) sleep less than four hours.

Most students sampled—including the non-environmental design majors—eat less than usual the day a project is due. However, almost all the environmental design students eat poorly. As a whole, substantially more of the environmental design students eat junk food than do the non-majors.

Architecture student diaries revealed that a combination of poor sleeping patterns—usually little or no sleep before the jury day itself—and poor eating habits—often junk food from vending machines or no food at all—accompanied by a consistently high level of stress contribute to many students experiencing a sense of "burnout," or complete mental and physical exhaustion.[13] One student's account was typical of others: "Today is our final presentation. I have been up all night and the night before and before . . . . Now I am too tired even to care. I just want to have it over and done with." Several were so fatigued that they reached a similar stage of apathy, feeling like they would be better off giving up altogether.

Some tried to prevent this tendency by undergoing a type of "catharsis," a cleansing of the mind and body, prior to their jury presentation. A few students purposely went home, showered, and put on clean clothes. As a result, they were out for a "fresh start," ready to begin on a clean slate.

To counteract burnout after the jury, most students reward themselves by rushing off to bed for their much needed sleep. Others feast on a delicious meal while trying to return their bodies and their minds to normal working order.

Conclusions

Several conclusions are drawn from this research: 1. The vast majority of all those questioned—faculty, students, and practicing architects—believe the jury system is inadequate and needs improvement. A minimal level of learning about design occurs at best. Most of those questioned believe that academic juries and professional practice presentations are substantially different, so the argument that school design juries help prepare future practitioners for such presentations is questionable. 2. Compared to final juries, interim juries are a more effective learning technique. 3. Most criticism at juries is oral and delivered on the spot; consequently most students respond defensively and nervously. The energy spent defending their egos and masking their emotions interferes substantially with the learning process. Students highly regard positive criticism—but they don't hear it often enough. Psychologists and learning theorists have long demonstrated the educational value of positive reinforcement; in this regard we architectural educators have a lot to learn.[14] In addition, skills such as time management and oral presentation techniques are not taught adequately and yet they have a major impact on students' grades. 4. The studio subculture differs significantly from the lifestyle of non-design students, and, although this subculture can foster a sense of belonging, some aspects of it may be detrimental to students' mental and physical health. The importance of proper sleep and diet should not be overemphasized.

An optimal level of stress may be needed to educate future architects, but the present level of stress is too high to be of maximum educational benefit. Nevertheless, juries do have some positive qualities and, with substantial refinement, they can continue to play an important role in design education.

Of course, one should not dismiss the value of juries entirely based on this study alone. As one colleague has suggested, preparing for a jury might be comparable to practicing for a musical recital. In both instances, the preparation and practice may well be an even greater learning experience than the final presentation itself. In addition, the jury may well accomplish other goals besides learning about design—for instance to socialize and sensitize students into the subculture of architecture, and to learn to negotiate with clients. Furthermore, juries can sometimes be the only place in which the various subdisciplines of architecture—such as structures, history, energy concerns, environment, and behavior issues, for instance—are integrated. In some cases, it is *only* through the juries that students view the field as a true Gestalt, where the whole is actually greater than the sum of its parts. This important aspect of juries should not be overlooked.

The conclusion here, however, is that the amount of stress produced by public criticism at juries is a key to understanding their effectiveness as a way of learning about design. *Stress can be a positive pedagogical tool, provided it is used in moderation.* In the case of the jury system, an optimal level of stress is high enough to motivate and discipline students to "put their best foot forward," so to speak, but not so high that it interferes with students' ability to function normally. It appears from all sources of information that the "ideal" feedback cycle discussed earlier, is not working properly, largely because stress gets in the way. Similarly, "double-loop" learning is not achieved, and what learning does take place remains at a relatively low level.[15] Systematic experimentation with a variety of presentation and feedback techniques, including juries—and measuring students' responses to them—would help architectural educators to fine-tune this process.

Suggestions for Further Research
Any study has its limitations which can be mitigated by further research. More specifically, further refinement of the questionnaire, larger samples, and replication of various research methods across several university campuses would undoubtedly yield more far-reaching results. A nation-wide survey of architecture faculty, perhaps administered through the ACSA, would be highly illuminating.

In addition, further research could use other methods to study the jury system and its impact on architecture students. University medical facilities could be contacted to find out the number of school related injuries suffered by architecture students around jury time; some have said that design students are accident-prone, cutting fingers while building models at 3 a.m. Counselors could also be contacted to ascertain the numbers of architecture students who sign up for therapy. Perhaps a critical issue for further study concerns the definition of the "jury" itself. Although the results of the Cranbrook Teachers' Seminar questionnaire confirm that juries at the case-study school tend to typify those of the fourteen universities represented, other institutions may conduct their jury sessions differently. For instance, at some universities the term "jury" has been replaced by "review," which in itself implies a less adversarial situation. However, the name change may well be euphemistic rather than truly symbolic of a radically new approach to evaluating students' work.

Recommendations
Based on this research here are a few recommendations to help make the architectural jury system more effective as a learning technique:

1. At the outset of a design project, have students and faculty (ideally the instructor and those who will later serve as jurors) help establish the criteria for a "successful" outcome: i.e., what types of design features or spatial qualities will help make this an "A" project. If the criteria are spelled out clearly and commonly agreed upon, the "mystery" component of the mastery-mystery phenomenon will be removed.[16]
2. Consider scheduling a final jury or review session about a week or two prior to the actual conclusion of a project. In this manner, students can incorporate some of the revisions suggested by the faculty into their final designs.
3. Require students to have special training in oral presentation techniques, either through public

speaking courses or through special sessions during studio time. Consider inviting faculty from academic departments such as speech and communication to help students learn verbal presentation skills. Another option is to have students videotaped during a "practice jury," and then play back the tape so students can see themselves.

4. Consider the purpose of an oral presentation simply to gain practice with public speaking. Invite other faculty and students to hear the presentation but not to judge the projects in public. Resort to private methods of delivering criticism (i.e. strictly in writing).

5. Ensure that all jurors, including guests, have written copies of the design programs well before the jury session.

6. Insist that students submit their design work at least one full day before their oral presentations. This will allow them time to rest up and prepare better psychologically for their jury and should help minimize burnout.

7. Require that written criticism be given to each student. (The University of Illinois at Urbana–Champaign School of Architecture encourages faculty to provide written criticism to students at design juries.) Either ask all jurors to write their criticisms down on paper and submit them to the students (via the professor, who can use the feedback to help determine the students' grade), or else assign each student a "buddy," i.e., a fellow class member to take notes on the criticism received during the presentation. Students are more likely to remember what they both hear and see in writing, rather than simply what they hear.

8. Encourage faculty and guest jurors to deliver more specific, constructive and impersonal criticism. Vague statements (like "This is a great project" or "This is an example of bad design"), unless they are part of a much more substantive commentary, can be damaging and certainly pedagogically ineffective.

9. Rather than reviewing each project individually, use a jury to evaluate critically all projects together—seeing them en masse in a large pin-up or exhibit—and comment on general trends and themes. Certain examples can be brought up to illustrate points, but names of students will not be mentioned. This removes both the public defense and the emphasis on knowledge and comprehension at the individual level, thus sparking discussion at higher levels of learning.[17] It also removes the advantages or disadvantages from being the first or last to present a project.

10. Finally, design instructors might try experimenting with a variety of formats for judging student work, and ask the students which ones help them learn the most. This might appear the most logical approach of all.

Acknowledgments

The author thanks Margaret Goglia, Jose Navarro, Ray Luna, Cynthia Cornfield, James Anderson, and Sue Weidemann for their assistance with this paper. She also thanks Marvin Malecha, Dean of the School of Environmental Design at the California Polytechnic State University, Pomona, for his support of Phase I of this research. Finally, thanks to Donlyn Lyndon and the ACSA for inviting me to present this work and allowing me to collect additional data at the Cranbrook Teachers' Seminar, and to R. Alan Forrester, Director, and the University of Illinois at Urbana–Champaign School of Architecture for its financial and secretarial support.

Notes

1. Spiro Kostoff, ed., *The Architect: Chapters in the History of the Profession* (New York: Oxford University Press, 1977).
2. John Aguirre, "The École des Beaux-Arts: A Light-Hearted View," *AIA Journal* (July 1960): 23–26; Jean Paul Carlhian, "Beaux-Arts or 'Bozarts'?," *Architectural Record* (January 1976): 131–134; Jean Paul Carlhian, "The École des Beaux-Arts: Modes and Manners," *Journal of Architectural Education* 33, no. 2 (November 1979): 7–17; Marvin J. Malecha, "The Design Critique Experience," *Orange County Architect* 4, no. 3 (1983): 18; John C. B. Moore, "The École des Beaux Arts: A Serious Study," *AIA Journal* (July 1960): 27–31; Richard Chafee, "The Teaching of Architecture at the École des Beaux-Arts" in *The Architecture of the École des Beaux-Arts*, ed. Arthur Drexler (Cambridge, MA: MIT Press, 1977), 61–109; Joan Draper, "The École des Beaux-Arts and the Architectural Profession in the United States: The Case of John Galen Howard," in Kostoff, 209–237.
3. W. Ross Ashby, *Design for a Brain* (New York: John Wiley & Sons, 1952); Chris Argyris, "Theories of Action that Inhibit Individual Learning," *American Psychologist* (September 1976): 638-654.
4. Sarni Hassid, "Development and Application of a System for Recording Critical Evaluations of Architectural Works" (unpublished manuscript) (Berkeley, CA: Department of Architecture, University of California, Berkeley, 1960); Sarni Hassid, "Interest Distribution in the Evaluation of Architectural Design" (paper presented at the Faculty Seminar on Architectural Research) (Berkeley, CA: Department of Architecture, University of California, Berkeley, 1960); Consortium of East Coast Schools of Architecture, *Architecture Education Study, Vol. II: The Cases* (1981); Leif J. Braaten, "A Psychologist Looks at the Teaching of Architecture" *AIA Journal* (June 1964): 91–95, also published as Leif J. Braaten, "A Psychologist Looks at the Teaching of Architecture" *Journal of Architectural Education* 19, no. 1 (1964): 5–9; Wayne Attoe, *Architecture and Critical Imagination* (New York: John Wiley & Sons, 1978).
5. Chris Argyris, "Teaching and Learning in Design Settings," in *Architecture Education Study*, vol. 1, ed. Consortium of East Coast Schools of Architecture, 2. vols., (New York: Andrew W. Mellon Foundation, 1981), 551–860; Chris Argyris and Donald A. Schön, *Theory in Practice: Increasing Professional Effectiveness* (San Francisco: Jossey-Bass Publishers, 1974).
6. R. D. Laing, *Knots* (New York: Pantheon, 1970), 56.

7. Donald A Schön,. "The Architecture Studio as an Exemplar of Education for Reflection-in-Action," *Journal of Architectural Education* 38, no. 1 (Fall 1984): 2-9; Donald A. Schön, *The Reflective Practitioner: How Professionals Think in Action* (New York: Basic Books, 1983).
8. Amos Rapoport, "Architectural Education: 'There is an Urgent Need to Reduce or Eliminate the Dominance of the Studio,'" *Architectural Record* 172, no. 11 (October 1984), 100, 103; Robert M. Beckley, "The Studio is Where a Professional Architect Learns to Make Judgments," *Architectural Record* 172, no. 11 (October 1984), 101, 105; Steven Hurtt, "Architectural Education: The Design Studio—Another Opinion in Defense of the Obvious and Not So Obvious," *Architectural Record* 173, no. 1 (January 1985), 49, 51, 53, 55.
9. See for example Stefani Ledewitz, "Models of Design in Studio Teaching," *Journal of Architectural Education* 38, no. 2 (Winter 1985): 2–8; and Wayland Bowser, "Reforming Design Education," *Journal of Architectural Education* 37, no. 2 (Winter 1983): 12–14.
10. These techniques are described in Robert Sommer and Barbara A. Sommer, *Practical Guide to Behavioral Research: Tools and Techniques* (New York: Oxford University Press, 1980); John Zeisel, *Inquiry by Design: Tools for EnvironmentBehavior Research* (Monterey, CA: Brooks/Cole, 1981); William Michelson and Paul Reed, "The Time Budget," *Behavioral Research Methods in Environmental Design*, ed. William Michelson (Stroudsburg, PA: Dowden, Hutchinson and Ross, 1975), 180–234; and Fred N. Kerlinger, *Foundations of Behavioral Research* (third edition) (New York: Holt, Rinehart and Winston, 1986); Louise H. Kidder and Charles M. Judd, *Research Methods in Social Relations* (fifth edition) (New York: Holt, Rinehart and Winston, 1986).
11. Julius Fast, *Body Language* (New York: M. Evans, 1970); Gerard Nierenberg, *How to Read a Person Like a Book* (New York: Cornerstone Library, 1973).
12. For a more complete version of the results of this research, consult Kathryn H. Anthony, *An Inquiry into the Architectural Jury System*. Monograph submitted for publication, 1986.
13. Recent studies on burnout can be found in Ayalla M. Pines, Elliot Aronson and Ditsa Kafry, *Burnout: From Tedium to Personal Growth* (New York: The Free Press, 1981); Herbert J. Freudenberger and Geraldine Richelson, *Burnout and Anxiety: Causes and Consequences* (New York: Bantam, 1981); Herbert Freudenberger and Geraldine Richelson, *Burnout: The High Cost of High Achievement* (New York: Anchor Press, 1980); and Michael Lauderdale, *Burnout: Strategies for Personal and Organizational Life: Speculations on Evolving Paradigms* (San Diego, CA: University Associates, Inc., 1982).
14. R. D. Parke and R. H. Walters, "Some Factors Influencing the Efficacy of Punishment Training for Inducing Response Inhibition," *Monographs of the Society for Research in Child Development* 32 (1, Serial no. 109, 1967); N. H. Azrin and W. C. Holz, *Operant Behavior: Areas of Research and Application*, ed. W. K. Honig, (New York: Appleton-Century-Crofts, 1966); B. F. Skinner, *The Behavior of Organisms* (New York: Appleton-Century-Crofts, 1961); John B. Watson, *Behaviorism* (New York: W. W. Norton and Co, Inc., 1930).
15. Ashby, *Design for a Brain*; Benjamin Bloom, *Taxonomy of Educational Objectives: Handbook I: Cognitive Domain* (New York: David McKay Co., 1956).
16. Argyris, "Teaching and Learning in Design Settings."
17. Bloom, *Taxonomy of Educational Objectives*.

Boundary Studies

Lily Chi
Cornell University

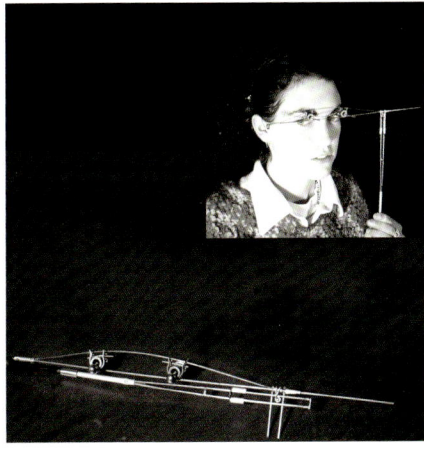
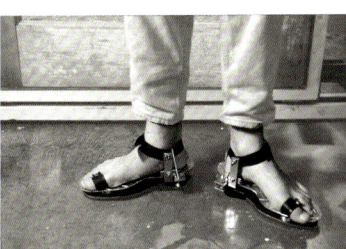

"Body-Masque" constructions; Portia Elmer, Chris King, Lelia Scheu.

The design exercises presented here were developed to open critical and creative perception of occupied and populated spatiality. The studio worked with two tactics: a focal theme that asked students to consider boundary conditions in temporal, situational, and social terms; and the use of full-scale installations as speculative devices. As experiments to raise questions about what constitutes form, site, and program, the exercises also aimed at initiating inquiry into architecture's effects, limits, and accountability.

Pedagogical Intents

The idea that the closest-at-hand is often the least examined and sometimes the ripest for such examination is an ancient one. In the context of design teaching, it suggests that pedagogy sometimes involves working in uncustomary ways in order to return to the customary more perceptively. One could argue that the critical attitude presupposes a certain measure of alienation, and that the stimulation of inquiry begins with a crisis in the familiar. These premises are common in beginning design education, where the opening of spatial perception, for example, relies on exposing the students to the world beyond preconceived object-categories. In the sequence of projects that follows, this philosophy was adopted not for first-year instruction, but for a junior-level studio. It served to investigate not tectonic or phenomenal form but "programmatic form."

The context is a third-year studio in Cornell's five-year B. Arch. program. As the last of the core studios, it occupies a Janus-like position in having a reflective as well as anticipatory function with respect to eventual thesis inquiry. Projects in this year typically explore questions of institutions and urbanism, foregrounding sociocultural issues and emphasizing programming and planning.

The exercises I present here posed a scale of inquiry to enter these concerns. They probed, in varying ways, moments of intersection and exchange between the programmatic and the architectonic in habituated experiences of built space. "Habituated" is used here provisionally to refer to experiences of architecture wherein the spectacular and visual has given way, in repetition, to other experiences of form—that is, architecture occupied over time; as background situation; as temporally conditioned; and as populated by gendered, cultured bodies. The exercises thus investigated how site and form might be inflected by and reconsidered in terms of states of cohabitation. Conversely, they made issue of the ways, overt and tacit, that built space gives finite situation to human doings and dealings. Programming, planning, and form were considered in mutual reference to the actions or interactions carried out, framed, and illuminated; and to the agents and subjects producing and produced by such action and interaction.

Construction and Polity

The studio experimented with two strategies for working this scale: a thematic focus that asked students to consider boundary conditions as mediators of interpersonal relations, and the use of full-scale installations as speculative devices. The latter were key to the critical interest of the studio.

"Studio Screen" 2, Chair; Luben Dimcheff and Selin Maner.

"Studio Screen" installation between two studio sections; Javier Arbona, Chris King.

Orthographic drawing and scaled modeling present the work of architecture as a synchronous entity. They are thus relevant tools for examining the ordering or artifactual integrity of a work. The pedagogical question here was whether experiences of built space as use-situations and as inflected by the presence of others adequately appear in these representational frameworks. The use of full-scale construction sought to force this issue in two ways: by making the students' own bodies and quotidian environments the sites and programs of analysis and design; and more surreptitiously, by having the students live with their completed projects as the term proceeded with drawn, scaled works.

In beginning with studio bodies and habitats, the constructional exercises served as focusing tools to slow the speed and scale of design perception to issues and concepts embedded in the mundane. They also offered opportunities for making issue of the students' own assumptions. Occupying their own designs within a critical context made the students visible to themselves as actors in the world and as acted upon by the world. Finally, questions of how to represent works that had multiple dimensions presented opportunities for renewed vision of terms and tools of architectural work that had become second nature.

The Exercises

The first exercise, *Body-Masque*, was a four-day study that asked students to consider the operation of sight in the negotiation of interpersonal space. The project called for the construction of a body apparel that would intercept a privileged use of sight in a particular social milieu. What constituted this privileged mode of looking or seeing, its context, and its ultimate deviation, was to be defined by the students. The project sought to unpack assumptions about the neutrality, stasis, or monolithic character of both sight and spatiality. Its value was that of a thought experiment—an exercise in self-consciousness. The interest was to make issue of the students' own occupation of space as visible *and* seeing subjects; to articulate spatial experiences in terms of relations to others, or more specifically, in terms of acts and exchanges of vision; and conversely, to consider the visibility of things in relation to subject conditions. To reinforce the critical orientation of the exercise, students were asked to reflect upon their inquiries in writing.

Despite the brevity of the assignment, the responses were inventive and surprisingly adept at moving between the mechanics and the sociality of sight. Portia Elmer's construction, for example, began as an observation on the dynamism of sight and developed into a study on dynamic acts of furtive vision. The interest in stolen glances and surreptitious looks led to the design of an adjustable eye-accessory or, in her words, "a pair of opera glasses for the voyeur." The construction consisted of a collapsible frame ("for discreet handling") supporting two ball bearings that rest on the eyelids and "roll with every subtle and discriminating movement." Pins soldered on the front of these surrogate eyeballs amplify in reverse the track of each movement, exaggerating their visibility. The anti-prosthesis, in effect, "turns voyeur into exhibitionist, exposing a socially inappropriate desire." In temporalizing vision, and in situating it with respect to acts and intentions,

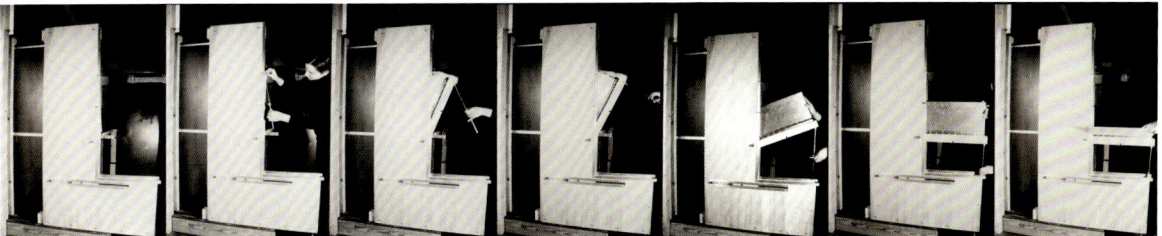

"Studio Screen" 2; Table; Luben Dimcheff and Selin Maner.

"Studio Screen" installation in Rand Hall stairway; Eugene Colberg and Jordi Mack.

Elmer's project found reverberation in a number of subsequent constructions in the studio.

Chris King explored social measures of visual space. His study began with observations on prosthetic devices as cultural signifiers that objectify and encode the body in terms of norms and capacities. Reflections on the wheelchair occupant's sitting position led to consideration of how visual space itself may be marked and encoded socially. His device focused on the nuancing of vertical, occupied space: Adjustable attachments for the feet allow wearers to change their visual horizon—and spatial authority. This reflection led King to a critical investigation of site, circumstance, and spatial contestation in the exercise that followed.

For Lelia Scheu, "a prosthesis fills the gap created or assumed by a deficiency, physical or social." Interested in its operation as a cultural instrument, she explored the possibility of an anti-prosthesis that would reveal the "seam by which flesh is inscribed, sexualized, moralized." Scheu conceived of a mechanism that would describe its own attachment to the face and its demarcation of sight. "When worn, the device bores into the skin, creating pressure points where the face moves in sympathy with the eyes. These points and their connecting lines form a grid of viewing. The rationalized function of the device, mapping sight according to the physical properties of the eye itself, is fully manifest only upon its removal. The pressure points are pulled away from contact with the skin at different rates, some drawing themselves across the face." Lelia's reflections on the seam by which both instrument and subject are constructed evolved, in later exercises, into a study of the "dissimulating membrane" as a "facade" condition—a kind of interplay between inside and outside, occupant and observer.

Studio Screen, the second exercise, was worked on by pairs of students for a period of three weeks. The exercise required students to extrapolate aspects of a selected Prosthesis into a proposal for a boundary condition within the studio building. Students were encouraged to consider boundaries not only in terms of division and limit but, in that very delimitation, as mediators, connectors, dialogical mechanisms. It was suggested that boundaries, like clothing, collude in the construction of identities and relationships, and can be considered stages of a sort.

Chris King and Javier Arbona's screen consisted of a salvaged door hung to slide horizontally within a frame, which itself was hung on tracks to

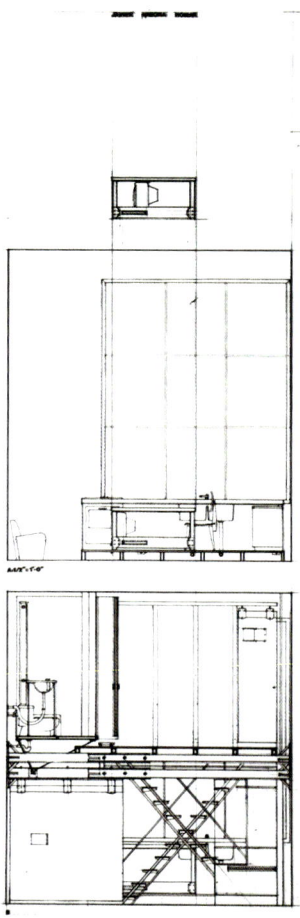

"Domestic Encounters" exercise, wall-membrane detail; Selin Maner.

Domestic Encounters" exercise; John Skillern.

move in a path perpendicular to that of the door. Together, these formed an adjustable mask/threshold that made manifest implicit and informal uses of a loosely defined corridor between two studio sections. The project was ultimately a study on the nuances and contestations of visibility and intimacy, public and private, neighborhood and community in the studio environment. In developing their installation, the students also raised questions about the assumed status of architectural interventions. With its multiple possibilities of door/mask and frame/threshold relations for defining boundary, the screen could be alternately an object of amelioration for the dynamics of studio society and an agitator of the very forces that it claimed to ameliorate.

Selin Maner and Luben Dimcheff developed a two-panel screen. The first negotiated an inside/outside, public/private relationship between their own studio section and a shared studio corridor. The second mediated between the two partners. The first panel played the role of threshold and facade to the studio section, oscillating between conflicting desires for concealment and privacy (screen to Maner's work area), and that for display and ostentation (screen to studio section). Issues of gender in experiences of visibility, public and private were pertinent to the development of this screen. The second panel articulated a wider and more complex range of boundary conditions between the two partners. If vision played a predominant role in the first, use articulated the modulations of the second. Simultaneously wall and very thin closet (a "Swiss-Army-knife-wall"), the second panel housed implements for the day-to-day needs of the partners. These implements co-opted circumstance, sitting positions, usages, and even the professor's body during desk reviews to establish conditions of privacy and exchange between the two partners.

Jordi Mack and Eugene Colberg's common interest in the tension between frontal and peripheral vision led them to an overlooked but visually powerful space in the school stairwell. A space normally occupied by a garbage can and a perpetually propped-open fire door was discovered to be one of the most "scenic" spots in the building: an effectively invisible place for observing sunsets, and goings-on in stairwell traffic.

The students' intervention, a Duchampian door-screen, formalized the latent panoptic pleasure of the site while preserving—through timing—its incongruous privacy.[1] The richness of this project lay not only in its mechanical wit, but in the attunement to habitual assumptions, visual practices, and temporal circumstance that informed the initial perception of site. The project also challenged common student assumptions about public and private.

Domestic Encounters, the third exercise, reversed the order between program and construct in asking students to read a selected Screen to develop its spatial and programmatic consequences. The exercise also returned the students to an ostensibly more familiar studio format: drawing board, scaled representation, fictional scenarios.

The scenario involved a loft-share between two relative strangers: two single, twenty-something business acquaintances who have decided, for strictly economic reasons, to share a 500-square-foot loft on a five-year lease. One works at home, keeping his own hours on the computer; the other maintains regular hours in her Wall Street office. The students were asked to analyze their chosen Screen and draw out its consequences for a number of questions. To what extent, for example, could the autonomy of the occupants as individuals be perpetuated spatially? How would their need for privacy and discretion be accommodated? What are the shared spaces and how would these be elaborated to facilitate the negotiations of two domestic strangers? How and where might frictions arise? How and where might a friendship arise? How might architecture aid in extending the initial balance of familiarity and distance between the occupants for the full five-year term? Or will architecture aid in a mutual seduction, or a conquest— of love, or real estate?

The scenario functioned on one level as a context for playing out the implications of the students' specific explorations on boundary, visibility, and spatiality. On the other hand, the fiction of an untried relationship in an impossibly small space underlined questions of architecture's role, limits, and accountability in defining—by delimiting— the terms and conditions of interpersonal encounter.

A number of students worked with the two approaches to boundary explored by Maner and Dimcheff: that of wall as mask, as strategies of visual deflection; and that of the porous wall, thickened with program, as venues for mediated engagement—formal, incidental, or provocative. Arbona's loft, for instance, was a study in visual choreography orchestrated through strategic placement not only of screens and apertures, but also settings of daily life: television area, dining table, workstation, and so on. These settings, some working with nuances of vertical space along the lines of King's prosthetic shoes, aimed at conditions of privacy *in* proximity and, conversely, communality without intimacy. The settings for daily life could thus

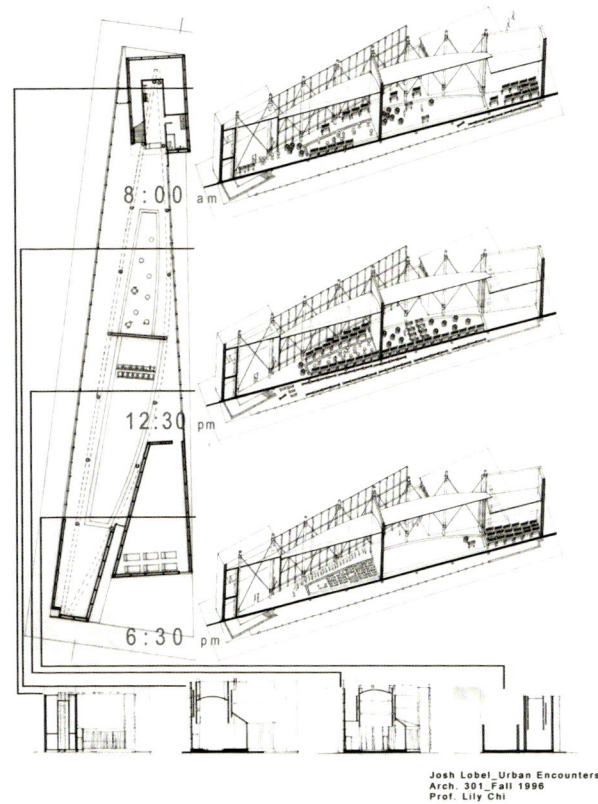

"Urban Encounters" exercise; Josh Lobel.

be engaged alternately to maintain avoidance without affront, or to venture encounter without apparent intention. On a critical level, the implied role of architecture in Arbona's project could be said to be that of a *social* prosthesis: making up alternately for absent spatial distance and emotional intimacy; mediating between the "urban" distance of the share relationship and the incongruously intimate scale of the domestic setting.

One student, John Skillern, confronted the critical undertow of the exercise directly. The loft-share scenario had a time limit. At the end of the five-year lease, one or both of the occupants had the option to purchase it outright. The time frame opened another dimension of accountability for the architecture in raising the specter of an *outcome* to the untried and therefore unpredictable cohabitational relationship. The implied proximity raised in the project between programming and plotting was a dilemma for the student. His eventual loft consisted of a marionette-like structure of ceiling tracks that accommodated (anticipated?) variations in the emotional and physical relationship of the two inhabitants. A design hypothesis about the dynamics of cohabitation from Day 1 to Day 662, the project both responded to and indefinitely postponed questions about duration, change, authorship, and architectural work.

The fourth exercise, *Urban Encounters,* magnified the scale of inquiry once again. The project made overt use of a Van Alen competition brief for a "Temporary Cultural Information Exchange." Ostensibly a call for the design of a temporary building on New York's Wall Street, the brief ultimately challenged designers to articulate new directions for the evolution of this area through proposals of new temporal occupancies, uses, and users. The project thus served the studio pedagogically in raising the question of program in the context of issues about civic roles, relations, and institutions. It was run as a thesis inquiry, involving more independent research and development.

The students' earlier preoccupation with operable parts gave way to broader investigations of urban and cultural processes in this project. Research into Manhattan's history and the changing face of what would become Wall Street seemed influential, as issues of social and cultural representation became decisive for many students. The project thus quickly acquired a critical imperative for most students, raising implicit questions about how architecture could play such a role. The projects I illustrate here exemplify two very different approaches in this respect. As did many others in the studio, however, both explored temporal and situational change for critical effect.

King's project, for example, operated at one level as a two-faced service station: a ramped promenade lined with "essential services" for the demands of nine-to-five life. It is two-faced because the accessories for daytime efficiency—dry cleaner, newspaper stand, lunch counter, shoe-shine stalls—transform in the evenings into afterwork destinations: lounge, public theater, exotic dance venue. On a more speculative level, the project was an exploration of the mechanisms—architectural and otherwise—by which cultural roles are constructed. Themes of dressing, undressing, and redressing in the design reflected King's interest in revealing the processes by which one (supposedly genderless) identity is produced, disassembled, and exchanged for another in daily rituals of use. The programming and tectonics of the project played on the juxtaposition of mechanical production and theatrical self-presentation. In a sense, the student claimed a revelatory dimension for the use of architecture by making a spectacle of what is invested in those usages.

Josh Lobel, by contrast, began with questions about the evolution of the Wall Street area as vacated finance offices are converted into luxury condominiums. The project explored the implications of this development for the question of a "cultural exchange" in a city of great socioeconomic diversity. Working on the idea of Salvation ("the saving, rescue, or salvaging of an object, form, or idea"), Lobel developed a nomadic structure: a reusable frame, clad in salvaged materials that varied according to site conditions. The frame opens upon installation into a layered arrangement of spaces to accommodate, by day, a café and "vintage" (not "secondhand") clothing shop and, by night, a discreet shelter/mission; revenue from the former went to the latter. The day–night, center–periphery organization of the project developed out of critical reflections that, in retrospect, seemed to have their beginnings in Lobel's *Body-Masque* project. A device that blocked frontal vision, his Prosthesis probed the limits imposed upon social intercourse when direct vision is limited. In considering the prospect of a "cultural information exchange" on Wall street, Lobel became interested in a dynamic between margin and center that seemed to characterize globalized, consumerist society.[2] His inquiry focused on the question of how to maintain critical effect for the margin position in this context. Sidestepping possibilities of direct encounter and its assumed benefits, the final project explored the critical potential of a *provocative* relation of *proximity:* that akin to the two sides of the proverbial coin—or two perspectives on value. In contrast to the above project, this approach claimed critical effect for architecture at a systemic level, rather than something to be consummated in the experience of any one user.

Destinations
The studio theme and pedagogy showed their impact in ways both overt and tacit. Many students explored possibilities for an operational architecture, working with moving or adjustable parts that responded to varying or changes in use and inhabitational situations. These ideas were not in themselves the goal of the studio, which aimed rather at perception and consciousness. It was thus more significant that even when the students worked with static architectures, they conceived of them as *multiphenomenal* in derivation and destination. Most important to me, however, were the questions raised for the students by their own work: questions about what constitutes form, site, and program; about architecture's effects and limits; and about the architect's role and accountability. Beyond being of critical interest, such deliberations were welcomed as initiatory efforts, however tentative or youthful, toward further independent thesis inquiry.

In retrospect, the studio could have better incorporated another intriguing potential of the full-scale construction project: the possibility of learning from having to live in one's designs over time. This quotidian engagement with architecture—a process whereby a spectacular, aestheticized, and concept-burdened project fades into background, reemerges in unforeseen ways, or simply becomes a source of irritation—seems to promise, indeed, some of the most valuable instruction.

Acknowledgments
Many thanks to Javier Arbona, Eugene Colberg, Chris King, Josh Lobel, and John Skillern for their efforts in excavating work for this article. Thanks also to Josh Lobel and Chris King for their aid in preparing prints.

Notes

1. The students were, in fact, unaware of artist Marcel Duchamp's Door: 11 Rue Larrey, 1927, while developing their installation.
2. Lobel drew from two works in particular for these observations: Janeen Costa and Gary Bamossy, eds., *Marketing in a Multicultural World: Ethnicity, Nationalism, and Cultural Identity* (Thousand Oaks, CA: Sage Publications, 1995); and Andrew King, *Postmodern Political Communication: The Fringe Challenges the Center* (Westport, CT: Praeger, 1992). The student summarized his own understanding of the issues in his thesis statement: "The center describes a condition of a society preoccupied with the here-and-now of image and fashion. That which is new/stylish today one day, is normative/mere convention the next. This creates an ironic opportunity for the marginal. If and when the marginal is identified as fashionable, it gains access to mass media, and the global forum it initially lacks—thereby becoming the center. Then, under the terms of the postmodernist transitional, it is either incorporated into mass culture, or remains on the margin as something that cannot be had by all—that cannot be fully consumed, and therefore remains 'the thing' to have. Conversely, that which aims at the center, and is born of the center, is doomed to a temporal existence and may quickly be forgotten."

The Canon and the Void: Gender, Race, and Architectural History Texts

Kathryn H. Anthony
University of Illinois at Urbana–Champaign

Metlem Ö. Gürel
Bilkent University

Architectural history books play a significant role in conveying the culture, norms, and values of the architectural discipline to newcomers. In recent years, numerous publications have spotlighted the importance of women and African Americans as critics, creators, and consumers of the built environment. Yet, to what extent is this recent discourse on gender and racial issues included in architectural history texts? And how gender or racially inclusive are they? Are twenty-first-century architectural educators presenting newly uncovered architectural histories from the nineteenth and twentieth centuries? Building upon prior research, this article seeks to address these issues by examining history texts currently assigned at fourteen leading architectural schools accredited by the National Architectural Accrediting Board (NAAB). In textbooks with multiple editions, we compared relevant information in both earlier and later versions. Our analysis of these history texts revealed that contributions of women remain only marginally represented in the grand narrative of architecture. And for the most part, African Americans are omitted altogether. We challenge authors to reassess the next generation of architectural history texts and suggest ways to do so.

Architectural history books play a significant role in conveying the culture, norms, and values of the architectural discipline to newcomers. In recent years, numerous publications have spotlighted the importance of women and African Americans as critics, creators, and consumers of the built environment. Yet, to what extent is this recent discourse on gender and racial issues included in architectural history texts? And how gender or racially inclusive are they? Architectural history relies upon the analysis of great monuments to explain the development of the built environment.[1] Whether interpreted primarily within formalistic, stylistic, or aesthetic concerns or, more recently, sociocultural contexts, buildings encompassing the traditional boundaries of the canon reflect traditional Eurocentric patriarchal perspectives. Inevitably, this provides only a partial view since the built environment in its totality is shaped by diverse groups of people. If buildings are to be interpreted as sociocultural objects and architecture as an artifact of social, cultural, economic, and political phenomena that mirror societies at certain points in time, architectural history must recognize how diverse groups of people contribute to the built environment.

In this spirit, this paper examines how gender and racial issues are addressed in architectural history survey textbooks. The study focuses on twentieth century architecture, spilling marginally into the late nineteenth and early twenty-first centuries, as this period coincides with the entry of women and African Americans into the field. Within this framework, we conducted a comparative content analysis of "popular" architectural history survey texts required in architectural history classes in several American architectural schools accredited by the National Architectural Accrediting Board. We used a chronological analysis, comparing earlier and later editions, to chart the influence of gender and racial research on architectural history survey books over the past twenty years.

Architectural history textbooks are a primary part of survey courses that introduce students to the canonical premises of the discipline. Not only do they transmit the culture and normative precepts of architecture to newcomers but they also "offer a case by which to explore how to sustain communication among different branches of knowledge and to allow the possibility of larger historical reflection."[2] Recent architectural survey courses taught in the United States have been modified to accommodate additional perspectives such as non-Western experiences. Through the adoption of more inclusive textbooks, the content in these history courses has widened the traditional boundaries of the canon, shifting from an exclusive focus on Eurocentric histories to a broader view. For example, Sir Banister Fletcher's *The History of Architecture* has long been replaced by more "inclusive" texts, such as Spiro Kostof's *A History of Architecture*. To encourage such practices, the NAAB has recently introduced an accreditation criterion requiring the restructuring of mandatory survey courses to include non-Western architecture at an "understanding" level.[3] Arguably, these changes, in turn, will increase interest of non-Western architectural research in American universities.

In fact, the NAAB has played a critical role in the gradual transformation of architectural history courses. The 2004 NAAB Student Performance Criterion 8, Western traditions, calls for "*Understanding of* the Western architectural canons and traditions in architecture, landscape, and urban design, as well as the climatic, technological, socioeconomic, and other cultural factors that have shaped and sustained them." Criterion 9, Non-Western Traditions, calls for "*Understanding of* the parallel and divergent canons and traditions of architecture and urban design in the non-Western world." Criterion 13, Human Diversity, calls for "*Understanding of* the diverse needs, values, behavioral norms, physical ability, and social and spatial patterns that characterize different cultures and individuals, and the implication of this diversity for the societal roles and responsibilities of architects."[4] Note that the 1998 NAAB Student Performance Criteria called for only an awareness of both non-Western traditions and human diversity.[5] This increase from awareness to understanding, a shift to a desired higher level of learning, reflects NAAB's will to strengthen this aspect of the architectural curriculum.

The last two decades have also witnessed a body of creative research on women, African Americans, and the built environment, which attempts to integrate them into a broadened view of history as well as more enlightened general education courses. Gender and racial issues have entered into the field of architectural history, theory, and criticism. However, has this research made its way into mainstream architectural history textbooks that expose students to the world of architecture? In other words, has the grand narrative of architecture responded to the dynamism of this recent body of research? If so, to what extent do current architectural history texts reflect this trend? To what extent have they kept pace with recent research? Moreover, can architectural history survey courses be gender and racially inclusive? And why is this important?

Next we will provide an overview of research and criticism of the canon. Then, we will analyze some major architectural history textbooks to assess the extent to which they include gender and racial research that expand upon the existing canon.

Rethinking Architectural History in Terms of Gender, Race, and Space
Ever since the late 1970s, the architectural discipline has witnessed an increased interest in feminist research. *Women in American Architecture: A Historic and Contemporary Perspective* (1977), a publication and exhibition organized by the Architectural League of New York through its Archive of Women in Architecture, was one of the earliest attempts to document women's architectural history.[6] Edited and curated by Susana Torre, this pioneering project assembled a collection of work exploring the accomplishments of women practitioners in American architecture. While early feminist work, in the tradition of radical feminism, offered critical insights on women's experience of "man-made environments,"[7] the ensuing approaches have addressed postmodern thought by questioning the traditional premises of the male canon through introducing new objects of study—"the actual material which historians chose to look at"—and reevaluating "the intellectual criteria by which historians interpret those objects of study."[8] According to Jane Rendell, drawing upon psychoanalysis, poststructuralism, philosophy, and gender theory, this interdisciplinary research has embraced theory, history, and criticism, promoting a fundamental rethinking of architectural history.[9]

Although scholastic contributions vary in focus, content, approach, and method, they all reflect the common stance that women's contributions should be given appropriate representation. In this regard, some feminist historians have pursued research to expose contributions of "prolific" women architects who left a mark on the architectural landscape yet did not receive the recognition that they deserved. Among these are biographies, essays, and exhibitions on Julia Morgan, Eileen Gray, Lilly Reich, Charlotte Perriand, and others.[10]

One avenue through which unacknowledged contributions of women architects/designers have been illuminated has entailed exploring architectural collaborations of now famous historical pairs such as Mies van der Rohe and Lilly Reich, Le Corbusier and Charlotte Perriand, Edwin Lutyens and Gertrude Jekyll, Charles Rennie Mackintosh and Margaret Macdonald, Walter Burley Griffin and Marion Mahony Griffin, Louis Kahn and Anne Tyng, Alvar Aalto and Aino Marsio-Aalto, Alison and Peter Smithson, and Ray and Charles Eames. More recent partnerships, such as Robert Venturi and Denise Scott Brown, Margaret McCurry and Stanley Tigerman, Tod Williams and Billie Tsien, Frances Halsband and Robert Kliment, Elizabeth Diller and Ricardo Scofidio, and Laurinda Spear and Bernardo Fort-Brescia, have also sparked the interest of feminist historians and critics.[11] In this spirit, women architects such as Denise Scott Brown who denounced sexism and the star system had a major impact in promoting scholarly interest in this area.[12] Gwendolyn Wright's "A Partnership: Catherine Bauer and William Wurster" presented yet another model of collaboration by showing how Catherine Bauer, a social historian, 'metamorphosed' the practice of the architect William Wurster, whom she met and married in 1940, by 'politicizing' him, infusing his domestic designs with her social and political ideas, just as he helped her to become aware of the needs of middle-class American families.[13]

Other historians have examined the contributions of women to the built environment by shifting the focus from the individual architect/designer to the client. The capacity of patronage to illuminate women's influence as clients and consumers in the design of the built environment has been intriguing to many historians. They reassessed the role of the architect, portraying the client as collaborator in the design and the development of spaces, and the architect as operator in this collaboration, rather than as genius solely responsible for the creation of a building. Research on female patronage has been broad in scope ranging from the Western modern to Islamic architecture. Alice T. Friedman's *Women and the Making of the Modern House* is among the most significant scholarly works on this topic.[14]

In search of an alternative architectural history, feminist historians proposed a paradigm shift from the "monumental" to the "residential" to explore the links between domestic architecture and feminist theories. In this arena, the seminal work of Dolores Hayden and Gwendolyn Wright aimed to clarify "relationships between house design, urban growth, cultural and economic factors, and work structures."[15] Hayden's *The Grand Domestic Revolution: A History of Feminist Designs for American Homes, Neighborhoods, and Cities* (1981) explored the history of feminist ideas and theories of nineteenth century figures such as Catharine and Harriet Beecher, Melusina Fay Pierce, and Charlotte Perkins Gilman in the development of housing.[16]

Other scholars focusing on the built environment traditionally considered as peripheral to the domain of architecture, such as interior design, landscape architecture, and urban history, have perpetuated "a view of architecture as part of a continuum of space which extends from a consideration of objects and interiors at the macro scale to regional and local planning processes at the macro level."[17] Material culture studies and vernacular architecture constitute two major areas of exploration.[18] Numerous books and articles examine the history of female interior designers and their role in shaping the built environment starting at the turn of the twentieth century.[19] Isabelle Anscombe's *A Woman's Touch* (1984) is considered to be a pioneer in this area.[20] Pat Kirkham and Penny Sparke's study of "Women Designers in the USA 1900–2000" is an example of research analyzing the paradigm of women designers.[21]

An examination of feminist research in the history of built environment shows that women's contributions are not limited to their participation in the design of buildings. Women architectural critics' rich history ranges from Charlotte Perkins Gilman's "economic, social, and architectural arguments for collective domestic life"[22] to Edith Wharton and Ogden Codman's views on division of labor in architecture toward the end of the nineteenth century.[23] In the twentieth century, by addressing housing, planning, and architectural design, women critics such as Catherine Bauer, Jane Jacobs, Sibyl Moholy-Nagy, and Ada Louise Huxtable played significant roles.[24] They each addressed architectural issues relevant both to the profession and to the general public. In fact, these women were ahead of their time in criticizing the Modern Movement at a time when their colleagues often promoted it uncritically.[25]

Just as feminism has sparked a new brand of scholarship in architecture, an increasing awareness of the role of race, and especially that of African Americans in architectural history, has begun to do so as well.[26] Toward the end of the twentieth century, the history of African Americans and their architecture was rediscovered. In fact, according to Brad Grant and Dennis Mann, longtime scholars of African American architects, African Americans have had a lengthy tradition in the building of this country beginning with architects like Joseph Francis Mangin, the principal designer of New York City's City Hall; Benjamin Banneker, who assisted Pierre Charles L'Enfant in the planning of Washington, DC; Julian Abele, who designed the Widener Library at Harvard University; and Paul Revere Williams, who designed Hollywood homes for a number of movie stars. Even today, architects like J. Max Bond, former Dean of the School of Architecture and Environmental Studies at City College of New York has been honored for his award-winning design of the Martin Luther King Jr. Center for Nonviolent Social Change in Atlanta (1984), and Donald Stull and David Lee, partners in their own firm in Boston, have been recognized for their many award-winning designs.[27]

Others have described the early architecture of pre-Civil War slave plantations, many of which were designed and built by African Americans. The pioneering role of Booker T. Washington in shaping Tuskegee University, one of the nation's first African American institutions of higher education, has also been recognized. A body of scholarly literature on these groundbreaking architects is now beginning to appear.[28]

The sample of gender and racial architectural research included here is far from complete. Nonetheless, it illustrates various attempts to integrate women and African Americans into architectural history. Such critiques prompt the reconsideration of the confinements of the canon. They raise the questions, what kind of picture do architectural history survey texts provide about our built environment? And how complete is that picture? What are the selection criteria used to build the canon? And who decides what is included—and what is excluded? Who have been the gatekeepers of the architectural profession, and who are the gatekeepers of architectural history?

Rethinking the Canon and Architectural History Textbooks

Historians of art and architecture have challenged the metanarrative or the canon presented through mainstream history texts. Drawing upon Pierre Bourdieu's social theory, Christopher B. Steiner suggested that the canon was "a *structuring* structure which is in a continuous process of reproducing itself, mediating its identity through market forces."[29] Steiner argued, "it is not... what is in and out of the canon that ought to be of concern to us, but rather the social structure of the canon itself that must be reconsidered."[30] Questioning the rationale behind the canon has probed the expansion of its premises to include new entries such as non-Western architecture in various ways.[31]

Table 1. *General survey textbooks covering architecture from prehistory to present*

No. of schools using book	Title	Author(s)	First edition	Second edition
7	Architecture, from Prehistory to Postmodernity	M. Trachtenberg and I. Hyman	1986	2002
7	A History of Architecture: Settings and Rituals	Spiro Kostof	1985	1995
5	Buildings across Time	M. Moffett, M. Fazio, and L. Wodehouse	2004	

Table 2. *Survey textbooks covering twentieth-century architecture and American architecture*

No. of schools using book	Title	Author(s)	First edition	Newer editions
5	Modern Architecture Since 1900	William J.R. Curtis	1982	1983, 1987, 1996
2	Modern Architecture: A Critical History	Kenneth Frampton	1980	1985, 1992, 2000 (reprint), 2004 (reprint)
2	American Architecture	Leland M. Roth	2001	

However, an important consideration is the nature of how these new entries are included. New inclusions, when tacked onto the existing grand narrative, are inevitably defined by the dominating discourse. A prominent survey textbook that has been both praised and criticized for its inclusiveness is Spiro Kostof's *A History of Architecture*. According to Zeynep Çelik, Kostof's book is "a remarkable example . . . which goes beyond mere 'inclusion' and pulls the non-Western material into the heart of the argument."[32] By contrast, drawing attention to the limitations of Kostof's book, Panayiota Pyla argued that addition of suppressed or alternative histories "constructs a false dichotomy between existing knowledge and new knowledge" for they "have the potential to revise our understanding of history at large."[33]

Perhaps the value of Kostof's book lies in how it serves as a seminal example of rethinking and challenging the structure of the Western canon. As the canon is restructured to include emerging ideas and tendencies, the principles that underlie its presence become stronger. According to Gülsüm Baydar, "when other architectures entered the grand narrative of architectural discipline (i.e., the canon) they found themselves always already inscribed by the premises of the latter."[34] Proponents of vernacular architecture, such as Dell Upton and Henry Glassie, suggested the replacement of the canonical approach with a more populist endeavor that portrayed a society—its sociopolitical agenda— through the study of ordinary everyday life.[35]

Debates on the status and operation of the canon open new paradigms through which architectural history may be re-evaluated. Meanwhile, teaching architectural history through the pedagogy of an accepted grand narrative remains standard practice. Moreover, architectural survey courses substantiate the only historical exposure a student is most likely to acquire in a professional program. In this respect, the visibility of "other" architectures and "other" people (women, African Americans, non-Westerners, etc.) in history textbooks demystifies the belief that no alternative histories exist.[36] Such visibility has not only the potential to provoke awareness of women's and other influences in the evolution of the built environment but also to spark critiques of the hegemonic discourses.

Research Methodology: Selection of Architectural History Textbooks

Acknowledging the capacity of major textbooks to reshape our understanding of architectural history, this study focused primarily on coverage of twentieth-century architecture—an era characterized by women's proliferation and dissemination in the field. To evaluate the extent to which research reflecting women's and African Americans' contribution to the built environment penetrated into the text, we analyzed architectural history textbooks published since 1985. In order to provide a chronological dimension to our study, we also compared both earlier and later editions of the same text, if available. We sought to understand if and how the grand narrative of architecture has changed. Have prior omissions or misattributions of women's work been corrected? How, if at all, have African Americans been portrayed in American architectural history texts?

Two genres of textbooks were targeted: 1. general survey books covering architecture from prehistory to the present and 2. twentieth-century architecture. In this respect, we build upon Karen Kingsley's 1988 essay on gender issues in teaching architectural history.[37] Almost two decades later, was Kingsley's description of architecture as a "woman-less history" still true? Were architectural history texts still, as Peggy McIntosh argued, "taught without any attention to the products, contributions, or experience of women?"[38]

We used two broad-reaching criteria to identify the architectural programs whose history textbooks were included in this research. 1. The school was one of the 113 institutions offering an NAAB-accredited undergraduate and/or graduate program. 2. On the basis of its history, reputation, and contribution to architectural education, the school could be considered a benchmark program, influencing the curricula of other programs around the world. We narrowed down the selection process in three ways. First, we drew upon a list of 13 schools that architectural historian Stanford Anderson identified as having "played a role in . . . producing the emerging voices in history of architecture" and shaping the debates on history, theory, and criticism.[39] Second, we reviewed three of the most recent volumes ranking architectural programs in the United States, *America's Best Architecture & Design Schools* (2005) and the *Almanac of Architecture & Design* (2002, 2004).[40] Practitioners and firms rate schools based on their ability to prepare students for professional practice. We included only those schools that appeared consistently in all three volumes. Third, we supplemented the prior two lists with a historically African American institution with a longstanding architecture program. Based on this selection process, we identified a total of twenty-one schools.

For the first phase of research, we contacted each of these twenty-one architecture programs with a request to name the textbooks used in their introductory architectural history survey courses. Faculty representatives who teach these courses at fifteen architectural programs responded. One school did not provide book titles for the introductory course; as a graduate program only, it relied only on theoretical texts for its courses on modern architecture. As a result, we obtained information from a total of fourteen schools.[41] A number of faculty members indicated their dissatisfaction with the scope of the textbooks that they assign. Four professors noted that they and their colleagues have previously used different architectural history survey books. One professor mentioned using supporting documents in addition to the textbook. Two faculty members indicated that they recently switched to textbooks that included greater coverage of non-Western traditions than was the case in their prior texts. Three professors used supplementary textbooks to address non-Western architecture. They assigned Dora P. Crouch and June G. Johnson, *Traditions in Architecture: Africa, America, Asia, and Oceania* (2001).[42] Two professors assigned Leland M. Roth, *Understanding Architecture: Its Elements, History, and Meaning* (1993).[43]

Our responses indicate a strong consistency among architectural history textbooks assigned at all 14 architectural programs. Not only did we find consistency across schools but also we found consistency over time; in fact, some textbooks were the same as those to which Kingsley referred.[44] Table 1 displays the results of our analysis, listing architecture history survey textbooks according to their genre and popularity. Note that some schools used multiple texts. For general architectural history survey courses, all schools studied assigned one of the following three books: Marvin Trachtenberg and Isabelle Hyman, *Architecture, from Prehistory to Postmodernity* (2002); Kostof, *A History of Architecture: Settings and Rituals* (1995); and Marian Moffett, Michael Fazio, and Lawrence Wodehouse, *Buildings Across Time* (2004).[45]

For the second phase of this research, we examined texts addressing twentieth-century architecture and American architecture. Faculty had mentioned some of these texts in their responses to our query. The text most often cited was that by William J. R. Curtis, *Modern Architecture Since 1900* (1996) (see Table 2).[46]

Analysis of General Survey Texts Covering Architecture from Prehistory to Present

One of the most commonly assigned introductory textbooks in architectural programs appears to be *Architecture, from Prehistory to Postmodernity* by Trachtenberg and Hyman. While an admirable volume that reflects a vast amount of historical research, as is no doubt true of all architectural history texts, this book exemplifies the traditional Eurocentric, monumental, patriarchal approach. The contributions of women creators, clients, and critics are largely overlooked. For example, in a discussion of the *École des Beaux Arts* in Paris, established in 1819, the authors state, "it was in theory completely open and democratic; anyone, French or foreign, between fifteen and thirty years of age, could take and pass the entrance exam."[47] But what about women? In fact, they were not allowed. The authors later mention Richard Morris Hunt, the first American at the *École des Beaux Arts* (1846–1852). Here would be an ideal opportunity to discuss the pioneering role of Julia Morgan. Bernard Maybeck encouraged her to pursue her studies in architecture after she received an engineering degree from the University of California, Berkeley, in 1894, passing on a rumor that the *École des Beaux Arts* might be ready to accept women. Yet, when Julia Morgan arrived in Paris to begin her studies in 1896, she was initially refused admission for two years because the *École des Beaux Arts* had never admitted a woman. Morgan was eventually admitted.[48]

The discussion of Frank Lloyd Wright overlooks Marion Mahony Griffin, who worked in his studio from 1895 to 1910 and played an active role both as a designer and in creating outstanding renderings of Wright's ideas. The same section could also include an entry on one of Wright's greatest masterpieces, the Dana Thomas House (1902–1904) in Springfield, Illinois, where client Susan Lawrence Dana (1862–1946) encouraged Wright to stretch his design talents in new directions. By contrast, a later section cites Edgar Kaufmann, the client for Fallingwater in Bear Run, Pennsylvania (1937).[49] In retrospect, if Kaufmann merits a brief mention, why exclude Dana? Both clients were unusually enlightened, allowing Wright to create some of his most creative residential designs.

Both 1986 and 2002 versions include a lengthy discussion on the Barcelona Pavilion (1929) and its textual qualities; yet, they fully dismiss Mies van der Rohe's long term collaboration with Lilly Reich on this and other projects of the interwar period.⁵⁰ Even in the 2002 edition of this text, women architects and designers, such as Eileen Gray and Charlotte Perriand, influential figures of Modern architecture, are omitted.

A four-page section focusing on Post-Modernism and Robert Venturi briefly mentions Denise Scott Brown: "In 1972, Venturi, together with his wife, Denise Scott Brown, an architect and planner, and the architect Steven Izenour, published a second assault on Modernism—*Learning from Las Vegas*. . . ."⁵¹ Yet, the authors fail to acknowledge her elsewhere. For example, "So crucial were Venturi's ideas to contemporary architecture that he might well be called the Viollet-le-Duc of Postmodernism. . . ."⁵² But what about Scott Brown? She herself stated, "We both design every inch of a building together."⁵³

To the authors' credit, the latter portion of the 2002 edition of this book includes new discussions of three female "star" architects, among them, Zaha Hadid.⁵⁴ Also mentioned is Elizabeth Plater-Zyberk, along with her husband, Andres Duany, in the context of the New Urbanism movement and Seaside, Florida.⁵⁵ Another woman featured is Gae Aulenti and the Musee d'Orsay in Paris, the adaptive reuse of the turn-of-the-century (originally built circa 1898–1900) train station before and after interior remodeling.⁵⁶

Broadening the paradigm from a focus purely on the monumental to include non-Western as well as vernacular architecture, Kostof's *A History of Architecture: Settings and Rituals* recognizes the contributions of Catharine Beecher and Harriet Beecher Stowe to nineteenth-century American residential architecture. Yet, the discussion of the 1893 World's Columbian Exposition in Chicago makes no mention of Sophia Hayden and her pioneering role in designing the Women's Building.⁵⁷ Given Kostof's location at the University of California, Berkeley, one might expect to see a description of the prolific work of Julia Morgan, who practiced in the San Francisco Bay Area. Yet, it cannot be found. Like Trachtenberg and Hyman, Kostof's discussion dismisses most contributions of women architects.

Nonetheless, the later edition of Kostof's classic text (revised by Greg Castillo), published posthumously, corrects some prior oversights and is more gender inclusive. For example, while Kostof's 1985 edition discusses *Learning from Las Vegas* (1972) and cites it as "one of Venturi's influential books"⁵⁸ without mentioning coauthors Denise Scott Brown and Steven Izenour, the 1995 edition acknowledges Scott Brown, drawing her into the discussion of Venturi's work.⁵⁹

Moffett, Fazio, and Wodehouse's *Buildings Across Time*, the newest of the volumes analyzed here, discusses nineteenth-century developments that include Richard Morris Hunt and the World's Columbian Exposition, but it overlooks the contribution of Sophia Hayden (1869–1953), the first woman to graduate in architecture from MIT and the designer of the Woman's Building (1893).⁶⁰ The discussion of twentieth century and Modernism addressing Charles Rennie Mackintosh omits the role of his wife, Margaret MacDonald (1864–1933), one that Macintosh, himself, identified as critical.⁶¹ In a letter that Macintosh wrote to his wife, he stated, "You must remember that in all my architectural efforts, you have been half, if not three-quarters of them."⁶² The authors' discussion of Gerrit Rietveld's Schroeder House (1924) as a quintessential De Stijl building omits the role of Truus Schroeder (1924), his female client, who, as Alice Friedman argued, served as collaborator in design or catalyst for architectural innovations.⁶³ Similarly, a section on Le Corbusier makes no mention of Charlotte Perriand.⁶⁴ The section on Ludwig Mies van der Rohe (1886–1969) includes a short mention of Lilly Reich (1885–1947) and her role in the Barcelona Pavilion (1929): she "shares credit with him for the interior design, particularly for the deep red velvet curtain that hung over the front glass wall."⁶⁵ In fact, her contributions to Mies van der Rohe' designs are minimized. As Mark Wigley has acknowledged, much of Reich's collaboration with Mies van der Rohe—"as is the case with almost all of the many such relationships in modern architecture that confuse the overdetermined opposition between the 'masculine' domain of structure and the 'feminine' domain of ornament—has been stricken from the apparently exhaustive accounts of the 'master.'"⁶⁶

Moffett, Fazio, and Wodehouse also discuss Edith Farnsworth and the Farnsworth House (1950–1952); however, no mention is made of the lengthy legal battle fought out in the courts and in the press between Mies van der Rohe and his client.⁶⁷ Their analysis of Modernism in the mid- and late twentieth century includes Alvar Aalto, Louis Kahn, and Robert Venturi and their reactions to earlier ideals of Modernism; yet, it omits any mention of their female collaborators.⁶⁸ This theme could be enriched by a discussion of women critics such as Jane Jacobs who reacted strongly against the modern movement.

To what extent is racial diversity included as a component of architectural history in these texts? It is fair to say that it is generally overlooked. In particular, the African American dimension of recent architectural history is ignored, giving students the impression that it does not even exist.

Analysis of Survey Textbooks Covering Twentieth-Century Architecture and American Architecture

In the domain of twentieth-century architecture, Curtis's *Modern Architecture since 1900* is a widely used textbook. Within the canonical premises, the 1996 edition includes "non-Western architects," such as Hasan Fathy and Sedad Hakki Eldem, as well as a few women.⁶⁹ Marion Mahony marginally enters the 1996 edition, relegated only to an illustration, with her 1912 competition rendering for the design of Australia's New Federal Capital. Yet, her role as a professional partner to her husband, Walter Burley Griffin, and her contribution to winning the Canberra competition entry, is totally overlooked.[70] No mention is made of Julia Morgan and her prolific architectural career. In his 1996 version, Curtis's extensive coverage of Le Corbusier and his influence on the International Style briefly mentions Charlotte Perriand, who had been omitted from the prior 1982 edition: "Working in collaboration with Charlotte Perriand, [Le Corbusier] developed an entire range of tubular steel furniture relying upon bicycle technology and fitted to the human body in sitting or reclining positions."[71] Curtis also recognizes architect and designer Eileen Gray for her "refined aesthetic for the interior" in somewhat greater length in the same paragraph.[72] Yet, one can argue that these two women had an even greater impact than that acknowledged in the text. For example, Gray's departure from the mainstream Modernist discourse on functionalism at the time may signal her as a forerunner of a later Modernist perspective. Gray's close consideration of everyday and domestic activities led her to design the first colored sheets and drawers with pivotal mechanisms.[73] Her work can be best understood at the intersection of interior content and the container or architectural shell. In this respect, she brought a fresh perspective to the plurality of Modernism and can be viewed as a figure ahead of her time.

Curtis's extensive examination of Mies van der Rohe's work excludes his important collaboration with Lilly Reich while in Germany. Understanding the changing nature of this collaboration sheds light on some of the differences between Mies van der Rohe's earlier pre–World War II work in Germany and his later postwar work in the United States. Another prolific collaboration excluded is that of Ray and Charles Eames. Curtis describes their classic 1945–1949 residence, in Santa Monica, California, as "Charles Eames's own house"; yet, he makes no mention at all of Ray Eames either as an architect or as a client/owner.[74] Other famous couples of midcentury modernism, such as Alison and Peter Smithson, and Jane Drew and Maxwell Fry, are given shared credit. Curtis includes voices of selected women critics of Modern architecture such as Denise Scott Brown in *Learning from Las Vegas*,[75] Jane Jacobs in *The Death and Life of Great American Cities*,[76] as well as Catherine Bauer's writings in praise of Dutch town planning.[77]

A careful examination of Curtis's text reveals an absence of African American architects and their role in shaping modern architecture since 1900. For example, no mention is made of such luminaries as Paul Revere Williams, known as "architect to the stars" because of his many Hollywood clients, or of Max Bond, architect of the Martin Luther King, Jr. Center for Nonviolent Social Change in Atlanta, Georgia.

Kenneth Frampton's *Modern Architecture: A Critical History* appears to be more sensitive to recognizing collaborations. Even in his early 1980 edition, Frampton refers to Gertrude Jekyll's "small but complex gardens"[78] when describing early country houses of Edward Lutyens, to Margaret Macdonald alongside Charles Rennie Mackintosh, and to Anne Tyng and Louis Kahn. Frampton's 1985 revision acknowledges Tyng's influence on Kahn, and their common fascination with the geometric forms of Buckminster Fuller, in the following passage: "It is clear from Kahn's subsequent career that this side of Fuller's thought exercised a strong hold over his development, and never more so than during the period of his association with Ann [sic] Tyng, who was an ardent follower of the Fuller line."[79] Frampton's 1985 revision briefly lists Eileen Gray and Charlotte Perriand in the context of the Parisian Neo-Cubist traditions of the 1930s but, unlike Curtis, provides no discussion of their work. Gray and Perriand are woven into the modern fabric regarding their elaborations of "French lightweight ferrovitreous constructions" along with Jean Ginsberg, Bruno Elkouken, "and above all Le Corbusier."[80] Similarly, the discussion of rational architecture and Ernst May's work briefly refers to Margarete Shutte-Lihotzky's design of the Frankfurt Kitchen. Although criticized for creating a severe working environment, Shutte-Lihotzky's kitchen design for the city of Frankfurt aimed to eliminate "household drudgery through rationalization."[81] In fact, the Frankfurt Kitchen has often been misattributed to Ernst May.[82]

Frampton's approach is more theoretical and perhaps more challenging for an undergraduate audience than the other textbooks covered here; accordingly, it is usually a recommended rather than a required text. Nevertheless, it portrays a commendable start to incorporate women architects and designers into the historical mainstream or the canonical premises. That said, as was the case for the Curtis text, a review of the Frampton monograph revealed no mention of African American architects or their work.

Leland Roth's *American Architecture: A History* makes a modest attempt to integrate women.[83] For example, a section on the architecture of the American city and suburb (1885–1915) includes a discussion of women and the American architectural profession. Contributions of Catharine Beecher, Mariana Griswold van Rensselaer, Louise Bethune, Minerva Parker Nichols, Sophia Hayden, Theodate Pope, and Julia Morgan are outlined here.[84] Marion Mahony is credited with "the splendid published perspective drawing" for Wright's plans of the third model house, published in the April 1907 issue of the *Ladies' Home Journal*.[85] In a discussion of responses to Modernism (1973–2000), Denise Scott Brown is credited for her collaborative work with Robert Venturi and John Rauch for such projects as the Fire Station No. 4 in Columbus, Indiana (1966), and for her partnership with Venturi on their competition for the Yale Mathematics Building (1968), which won first prize but was not built.[86]

Elsewhere, however, the Roth text falls short. For example, in a chapter on architecture in the age of energy and enterprise (1865–1885), a section discussing architectural education lists when architecture curricula were first offered at American colleges and universities: MIT, 1868; University of Illinois, 1870; and Cornell, 1871.[87] Here would be an opportunity to point out that few, if any women or persons of color attended these architecture schools until much later. In a chapter on nostalgia and the avant-garde (1915–1940), a section describing the architecture of the Southwest fails to mention Mary Colter and her extensive work for the Fred Harvey Company.[88] Nor does a subsequent chapter on the emergence of Modernism mention Elissa Aalto, Alvar Aalto's wife, although Aalto is given substantial coverage.[89] The section on preservation omits the role of women as preservationists and could include Jacqueline Kennedy who helped launch the preservation of Lafayette Square and the revitalization of Pennsylvania Avenue in Washington, DC, and Beverly Willis and her catalytic role in the adaptive reuse of historic Victorian structures on San Francisco's Union Street.[90] A subsequent section could also discuss the pioneering preservation work of Ann Beha. A search for African American architects and their work found only one: Joseph Mangin, who trained in France and designed New York City's City Hall (1802–1811).[91]

Conclusion

Recent historical research on women's contributions to the built environment has expanded the boundaries of architectural history. A myriad of books and articles have illuminated the limitations of the canonical core and urged us to rethink its scope from a feminist perspective. So, too, have recent publications stressed the contributions of African American architects. Yet, our study of architectural history texts indicates that such critical thinking continues to remain marginal to the grand narrative of architecture. Even in the most recent texts published in the twenty-first century, figures that other authors widely acknowledged as prolific female voices remain, at best, marginally covered in the canonical premises of the text or at worst, totally dismissed.[92] Most works on modern American architecture omit the work of African American architects altogether. While we recognize the enormous amount of research and depth of scholarship required to produce these volumes, and we understand the complexities confronted by each of these authors in determining what to include and exclude in their surveys, we challenge historians to reassess the next generation of architectural history texts.

Unfortunately, this void in today's leading architectural history survey texts continues to portray an almost exclusively white, male, "woman-less" history. Perhaps it is not quite the absolute womanless history described by Kingsley, yet overall not much has changed. Despite the fact that only recently have significant numbers of women been entering the architectural profession, the accomplishments of a few early leading women architects were acknowledged—up to a point—even during their lifetimes. For example, Henry-Russell Hitchcock and Philip Johnson included the interior designs of Lilly Reich and Charlotte Perriand, along with the architecture of Mies van der Rohe and Le Corbusier in *The International Style* (1932); it aimed to formulate a prescription of European Modernism for an American architectural audience.[93] Eileen Gray was considered a successful designer when she practiced in the first half of the twentieth century—before history left her out. Her furniture and interiors were published widely, and the prestigious Dutch journal *Wendingen* dedicated an issue to her work in 1924. Gray was rediscovered in the 1970s and elevated to star status. Subsequently, she was included in Sir Banister Fletcher's *A History of Architecture* (1987).[94]

In this respect, the continued dismissal or marginal coverage of these women and others in architectural history texts can be tied to prevailing attitudes dominating the construction of architectural history. Reich, Perriand, and even Gray constitute illustrious cases of women who have been largely absent from mainstream architectural texts because their work had been largely relegated to furniture and interior design, two professions emblematic of an inferior status by the standards of the canonical core of architecture. And even today, when numerous scholarly works have illuminated the spatial contributions of designers like Reich and Perriand, as well as their collaborative role with their respective "masters," both women remain distant to the grand narrative of architecture as rendered in history texts. The most widely used architectural textbooks examined here, whether covering world history or twentieth-century modern history, overlooked Reich's influence on Mies van der Rohe's early work. Discussions comparing Mies van der Rohe's earlier work in Europe and his later work in America, devoid of Reich's influence, bear testimony to the voids in the selection and evaluation processes that form canonical premises. Documenting such collaborations enables readers to better understand and assess the work of architects who have been elevated to star status. It also has potential to expose "the collaborative nature of modern architecture and the success of bringing different values to the design process."[95]

The almost total exclusion of African American architects in the texts analyzed here poses new challenges to authors revising these works and to scholars writing future architectural history surveys. One hopes for greater coverage of African American architects and their contributions especially in future surveys of twentieth-century architecture and American architecture, since that is when their most solid body of work began to emerge. The recent volume by Dreck Spurlock Wilson, *African American Architects: A Biographical Dictionary 1865–1945* is an excellent starting point, providing a wealth of information for historians who may be unfamiliar with this work.[96]

Furthermore, criteria for inclusion in future texts can be broadened to include historic significance as well as artistic merit. In this regard, the criteria for listing buildings on the National Register for Historic Places can serve as a useful model for future historians to consider, thus widening the gates of architectural history. Among the evaluation criteria for the National Register are buildings or structures:

1. that are associated with events that have made a significant contribution to the broad patterns of our history; and/or
2. that are associated with the lives of persons significant in our past; and/or
3. that embody the distinctive characteristics of type, period, or method of construction, or that represent the work of a master, or that possess high artistic values, or that represent a significant and distinguishable entity whose components may lack individual distinction; and/or
4. that have yielded, or may be likely to yield, information important in prehistory or history.[97]

Expanding the criteria for inclusion in such a manner would allow historians to integrate milestones in African American architectural history into the broader spectrum of American architectural history, for example, the role of Booker T. Washington and the founding of Tuskegee University in Tuskegee, Alabama; the contributions of Historically Black Colleges and Universities; the formation of the National Organization of Minority Architects; the jolting impact of Whitney Young's accusations of racism at the 1968 American Institute of Architects National Convention;[98] and, most recently, the 2004 opening of the National Underground Railroad Freedom Center in Cincinnati, Ohio, designed by the late Walter Blackburn, a grandson of slaves. Key issues of historical importance that could be discussed in future architectural history texts include the ways in which spaces define insiders and outsiders, space as a framework for constructing racial and ethnic identity, and the invisibility of racialized spaces.[99]

Textbooks provide a medium through which students and readers with an interest in architecture are exposed to the premises of architectural history. As a primary component of survey courses that must fulfill accreditation requirements of the NAAB, these texts play a major role in shaping how students formulate their conceptions of the built environment. For students who are not majoring in architecture, architectural history courses are likely to be their only exposure to the field. Faculty members at most schools included in this study supplement their mainstream textbooks with additional non-Western material. Yet, by doing so, and because history texts, for the most part, fail to fully integrate non-Western work, these suppressed histories still retain secondary status.

African Americans remain overlooked in architectural history texts. One cannot help but wonder if the NAAB had not required the non-Western component, would architectural courses have changed at all?

NAAB has not yet specifically acknowledged gender issues in architectural history as a criterion for accreditation. Thus, it is possible for students to graduate from an accredited architecture program without ever being exposed to women's contribution to the built environment. Because they remain relegated to elective courses and small-scale seminars—still rarities in most architectural programs—women's architectural history remains segregated from the "mainstream" history of architecture.[100]

If called upon during their graduation ceremonies, how many architecture students could name at least five African American architects and their work? Our guess is that at best, very few students at *any* school of architecture—with the exception of Historically Black Colleges and Universities—could do so. In this respect, architectural education is missing the mark. And in a profession where the number of African American students continues to remain astonishingly low, at less than five percent, it is all the more important that texts recognize their heritage and contributions.[101] It is up to authors of future NAAB student performance criteria as well as future architectural history texts to remedy these deficiencies. In order for change to occur, NAAB criteria regarding diversity, and gender and racial issues in particular, must be strengthened and more specific. A greater measure of accountability is needed to ensure that faculty teach and students learn about the importance of gender and racial diversity in architectural history. As we have already seen, changes in the NAAB criteria can translate into enhanced versions of architectural history, but one need not preclude the other.

The tendency of faculty members to select the same few books, as indicated here, underscores the power of the canon. While conserving what has been sanctioned as "great works of architecture," the void remains predominantly unnoticed. Architectural history textbooks play a critical role in shaping and reshaping architectural education. They bear an important responsibility in exposing the students to more diverse histories, and those that have only recently been uncovered. As Edward Said has argued, "society and culture have been the heterogeneous product of heterogeneous people in an enormous variety of cultures, tradition and situations."[102] In the architectural sphere, women and African Americans and their contributions to the mosaic of the built environment constitute a significant component of this heterogeneity. In sum, the premises of the canon must continue to be challenged.

Acknowledgments
We thank all faculty members who responded to our inquiries and enabled us to conduct this research.

Notes

1. Karen Kingsley, "Gender Issues in Teaching Architectural History," *Journal of Architectural Education* 41, no. 2 (Winter 1988): 21–25.
2. Panayiota Pyla, "Historicizing Pedagogy: A Critique of Kostof's A History of Architecture," *Journal of Architectural Education* 52, no.4 (May 1999): 223.
3. Until 2004, NAAB specified three levels of competence for accreditation purposes: 1. awareness, 2. understanding, and 3. ability. The 2004 NAAB Conditions for Accreditation now specify only 1. understanding, or 2. ability.
4. The National Architectural Accrediting Board, *The NAAB Conditions for Accreditation* (Washington, DC: NAAB, 2004), http://www.naab.org (accessed August 15, 2005).
5. The National Architectural Accrediting Board, *1998 Guide to Student Performance Criteria* (Washington, DC: NAAB, 1998).
6. Susana Torre, ed., *Women in American Architecture: A Historic and Contemporary Perspective* (New York: Whitney Library of Design, 1977).
7. See, for examples, Dolores Hayden, "What Would a Non-Sexist City Be Like? Speculations on Housing, Urban Design and Human Work," in *Gender, Space, Architecture*, eds. Jane Rendell, Barbara Penner, and Iain Borden (London: Routledge, 2000), 266–81; Matrix, *Making Space: Women and the Man-Made Environment* (London: Pluto Press, 1984); Leslie K. Weisman, "Women's Environmental Rights: A Manifesto," in *Making Room: Women and Architecture*, special issue, *Heresies 11* vol. 3, no. 3 (1981): 6–8; Leslie K. Weisman, *Discrimination by Design* (Urbana and Chicago, IL: University of Illinois Press, 1992).
8. Jane Rendell, "Introduction: Gender, Space, Architecture," in *Gender, Space, Architecture*, eds. Jane Rendell, Barbara Penner, and Iain Borden (London: Routledge, 2000), 232.
9. Rendell, "Introduction,", 232.
10. See Peter Adam, *Eileen Gray: Architect/Designer* (New York: H. N. Abrams, 1987); Sara Holmes Boutelle, *Julia Morgan Architect* (New York: Abbeville Press, 1988); Caroline Constant, *Eileen Gray* (London: Phaidon, 2000); Sonja Günther, *Lilly Reich, 1885–1947: Innenarchitektin, Designerin, Ausstellungsgestalterin* (Stuttgart, Germany: Deutsche Verlags-Anstalt, 1988); Mary McLeod, *Charlotte Perriand: An Art of Living* (New York: H. N. Abrams, 2003); Matilda McQuaid, *Lilly Reich Designer and Architect* (New York: Museum of Modern Art, 1996).
11. See Kathryn H. Anthony, *Designing for Diversity: Gender, Race and Ethnicity in the Architectural Profession* (Urbana and Chicago, IL: University of Illinois Press, 2001), 56–65.
12. Denise Scott Brown, "Room at the Top? Sexism and the Star System," in *Architecture: A Place for Women*, eds. Ellen P. Berkeley and Matilda McQuaid (Washington, DC: Smithsonian Institution Press, 1989), 237–246.
13. Gwendolyn Wright, "A Partnership: Catherine Bauer and William Wurster," in *An Everyday Modernism: The Houses of William Wurster*, ed. Marc Treib (Berkeley, CA: University of California Press, 1995), 188; cited in Beatriz Colomina, "Collaborations," *Journal of the Society of Architectural Historians* 58, no. 3 (September 1999): 467–468.
14. Alice T. Friedman, *Women and the Making of the Modern House: A Social and Architectural History* (New York: H. N. Abrams, 1998) see also Alice T. Friedman, "Architecture, Authority, and the Female Gaze: Planning and Representation in the Early Modern Country House," *Assemblage* 18 (1992): 40–61.
15. Kingsley, "Gender Issues," 24.
16. Dolores Hayden, *The Grand Domestic Revolution: A History of Feminist Designs for American Homes, Neighborhoods, and Cities* (Cambridge, MA: MIT Press, 1981).
17. Rendell, "Introduction," 227–228.
18. See, for example, Annmarie Adams, "The Eichler Home: Intention and Experience in Postwar Suburbia," *Gender, Class, and Shelter: Perspectives in Vernacular Architecture* V (1995), 164–178.
19. See, for examples, Cheryl Robertson, "From Cult to Profession: Domestic Women in Search of Equity," in *The Material Culture of Gender: The Gender of Material Culture*, eds. Katharine Martinez and Kenneth L. Ames (Winterthur, DE: Henry Francis du Pont Winterthur Museum, 1997). For an argument on the reception of interior designers, see Dana Arnold, *Reading Architectural History* (London: Routledge, 2002), 131–32. See also Dana Arnold, "Defining Femininity: Women and the Country House" in *The Georgian Country House: Architecture, Landscape and Society*, ed. Dana Arnold (Stroud, NY: Sutton, 1998), 79–100. There are numerous books on prolific women designers, such as Elsie de Wolfe, Dorothy Draper, and Candice Wheeler (as well as books and articles written by them). For a recent addition to this genre, see Penny Sparke, "Elsie de Wolfe and Her Female Clients, 1905–15: Gender, Class and the Professional Interior Decorator," in *Women's Places: Architecture and Design 1860–1960*, eds. Brenda Martin and Penny Sparke (New York: Routledge, 2003), chapter 3.
20. Isabelle Anscombe, *A Woman's Touch* (New York: Viking Penguin, 1984).
21. Pat Kirkham and Penny Sparke, "A Women's Place . . .? Part 1," in *Women Designers in the USA 1900–2000*, ed. Pat Kirkham (New Haven, CT: Yale University Press, 2000), 305–316.
22. Hayden, *The Grand Domestic Revolution*, 183.
23. Edith Wharton and Ogden Codman, *The Decoration of Houses* (London: B. J. Batsford, 1898).
24. See Anthony, *Designing for Diversity*, 65–67.
25. Suzanne Stephens, "Voices of Consequence: Four Architectural Critics," in *Women in American Architecture: A Historic and Contemporary Perspective*, ed. Susana Torre (New York: Whitney Library of Design, 1977), 136–143.
26. Literature on race in architecture, including the contributions of Native Americans, Asian Americans, and Latino/a Americans has also begun to emerge but it is outside the scope of this article.
27. Brad Grant and Dennis Mann, "Directory of African American Architects," http://blackarch.uc.edu/publications/introdir91.html (accessed April 24, 2005).
28. Several bibliographic sources on the historical contri-

butions of African American architects can be found in Anthony, *Designing for Diversity*, 2001, 81–91.
29. Christopher B. Steiner, "Can the Canon Burst?" *Art Bulletin* 78, no. 2 (June 1996): 217.
30. Steiner, "Canon," 213.
31. It should be noted that Edward Said, *Orientalism* (New York: Vintage Books, 1978) has been very influential in promoting the reassessments of the canon.
32. Zeynep Çelik, "Colonialism, Orientalism, and the Canon," *Art Bulletin* 78, no. 2 (June 1996): 202.
33. Pyla, "Historicizing Pedagogy," 223.
34. Gulsum Nalbantoglu Baydar, "The House of Architecture," *Proceedings of the 19th EAAE International Conference* (Ankara: Gazi University, 2001), 106.
35. See Dell Upton, "Architectural History or Landscape History?" *Journal of Architectural History* 44, no. 4 (1991): 195–99; Henry Glassie, "Vernacular Architecture," in *Material Culture* (Bloomington, IN: Indiana University Press, 1999), chapter 5.
36. Our use of the term demystification is inspired by Roland Barthes' discussion on the "myth." See Roland Barthes, *Mythologies*, trans. Annette Lavers (New York: Hill and Wang, 1972).
37. Kingsley developed recommendations to incorporate women into architectural education. She proposed that architectural history courses should render Lilly Reich, Charlotte Perriand, and Margaret MacDonald for their collaboration with Mies van der Rohe, Le Corbusier, and Charles R. Mackintosh, respectively, Julia Morgan for her prolific career and Catharine Beecher for her contribution to feminist domestic theory and nineteenth-century residential architecture. See Kingsley, "Gender Issues."
38. Kingsley, "Gender Issues," 22.
39. Stanford Anderson, "Architectural History in Schools of Architecture," *Journal of the Society of Architectural Historians* 58, no. 3 (September 1999): 285.
40. *America's Best Architecture & Design Schools* 6th ed. (Atlanta, GA: Design Futures Council, 2005); *Almanac of Architecture & Design* (Atlanta, GA: Greenway Communications, 2002 and 2004). All three publications are affiliated with *Design Intelligence*.
41. Information was obtained from Cornell University, Georgia Institute of Technology, Harvard University, Iowa State University, Massachusetts Institute of Technology, Tuskegee University, University of California, Berkeley, University of Cincinnati, University of Colorado, University of Illinois at Urbana-Champaign, University of Michigan, University of Pennsylvania, University of Texas at Austin, Syracuse University, and University of Virginia. We were unable to obtain many responses from faculty about which books were required for twentieth-century and American architecture. While some instructors provided this information, others noted that course offerings on these subjects varied—either no specific course was offered or else a variety of courses were offered. We noted books that were cited more than once by faculty who included this material.
42. Dora P. Crouch and June G. Johnson, *Traditions in Architecture: Africa, America, Asia, and Oceania* (New York: Oxford University Press, 2001).
43. Leland M. Roth, *Understanding Architecture: Its Elements, History, and Meaning* (New York: Icon Editions, 1993).
44. Kingsley, "Gender Issues."
45. Marvin Trachtenberg and Isabelle Hyman, *Architecture, from Prehistory to Postmodernity* (New York: H. N. Abrams, 2002); Spiro Kostof, *A History of Architecture: Settings and Rituals* (New York: Oxford University Press, 1995); Marian Moffett, Michael Fazio, and Lawrence Wodehouse, *Buildings Across Time* (New York: McGraw-Hill, 2004).
46. William J. R. Curtis, *Modern Architecture Since 1900* (Englewood Cliffs, NJ: Prentice-Hall, 1996).
47. Trachtenberg and Hyman, *Prehistory to Postmodernity* (2002), 428.
48. "Julia Morgan Biography, the Julia Morgan Collection," Special Collections, California Polytechnic State University, San Luis Obispo, http://www.lib.calpoly.edu/spec_coll/morgan/bio/bio.html (accessed February 25, 2005).
49. Trachtenberg and Hyman, *Prehistory to Postmodernity* (2002), 508.
50. Marvin Trachtenberg and Isabelle Hyman, *Architecture, from Prehistory to Postmodernity* (New York: H. N. Abrams, 1986), 531–34.
51. Trachtenberg and Hyman, *Prehistory to Postmodernity* (2002), 536.
52. Trachtenberg and Hyman, *Prehistory to Postmodernity* (2002), 536.
53. Jill Jordan Sieder, "A Building of Her Own." *US News and World Report*, October 14, 1996, 67.
54. Trachtenberg and Hyman, *Prehistory to Postmodernity* (2002), 562–563.
55. Trachtenberg and Hyman, *Prehistory to Postmodernity* (2002), 575.
56. Trachtenberg and Hyman, *Prehistory to Postmodernity* (2002), 578–579.
57. Kostof, *A History of Architecture* (1995), 670 (text) and 673 (photo).
58. Kostof, *A History of Architecture* (1985), 750.
59. "The bright young architecture and planning team of Robert Venturi (b. 1925) and Denise Scott Brown (b. 1931) relieved the tension by embracing Main Street as it was—cars, tinsel, and all. Their *Learning from Las Vegas* (1972) is a serious analysis of the form and meaning of the Strip—from supermarket parking lots, service stations, and billboards to the neon marquees of gambling casinos." Kostof, *A History of Architecture* (1995), 751.
60. Moffett, Fazio, and Wodehouse, *Buildings Across Time* (2004), 433–34. Note that some architectural history faculty indicated that they selected this book in large part because, compared to other texts, it pays greater attention to non-Western architecture such as indigenous architecture in the pre-Columbian Americas, Islamic architecture, the traditional architecture of China and Japan, and the architecture of ancient India and Southeast Asia.
61. Moffett, Fazio, and Wodehouse, *Buildings Across Time* (2004), 457–460.
62. Thomas Neat, *Part Seen, Part Imagined: Meaning and Symbolism in the Work of Charles Rennie Mackintosh and*

Margaret Macdonald (Edinburgh: Canongate Press, 1994), 18.

63. Alice T. Friedman, *Women and the Making of the Modern House* (New York: H. N. Abrams, 1997), Chapter 2; Alice T. Friedman, "Not a Muse: The Client's Role at the Rietveld Schroeder House," in *The Sex of Architecture*, eds. Diana Agrest, Patricia Conway, and Leslie Kanes Weisman (New York: H. N. Abrams, 1996), 217–232.
64. Moffett, Fazio, and Wodehouse, *Buildings Across Time* (2004), 522.
65. Moffett, Fazio, and Wodehouse, *Buildings Across Time* (2004), 517.
66. Mark Wigley, *White Walls, Designer Dresses* (Cambridge, MA: MIT Press, 1995), 151.
67. Moffett, Fazio, and Wodehouse, *Buildings Across Time* (2004), 522.
68. Moffett, Fazio, and Wodehouse, *Buildings Across Time* (2004), 533–542.
69. "Non-Western architect" is a problematic term that is beyond the scope of this study. Considering both Fathy and Eldem had "Western" education, can they be accounted as "non-Western" architects? For a discussion on Curtis's approach to non-Western architecture, see Sibel Bozdogan, "Architectural History in Professional Education: Reflections on Postcolonial Challenges to the Modern Survey," *Journal of Architectural Education* 52, no. 4 (1999): 207–215.
70. Curtis, *Modern Architecture* (1996), 299.
71. Curtis, *Modern Architecture* (1996), 265.
72. Curtis, *Modern Architecture* (1996), 265.
73. See Deborah Nevins, "Eileen Gray," *Making Room: Women and Architecture*, special issue, *Heresies 11* vol. 3, no. 3 (1981), 68–72; Karen A. Franck, "A Feminist Approach to Architecture," in *Architecture: A Place for Women*, eds. Ellen P. Berkeley and Matilda McQuaid, (Washington, DC: Smithsonian Institution Press, 1989), 202–211; for Eileen Gray's different approach and criticism of modern architecture, also see John Kurtich and Garret Eakin, *Interior Architecture* (New York: Van Nostrand Reinhold, 1993), 14–16.
74. Curtis, *Modern Architecture* (1996), 405. For the collaborative work of Ray and Charles Eames, see *The Work of Charles and Ray Eames: A Legacy of Invention*, ed. Diana Murphy (New York: H. N. Abrams, 1997). Pat Kirkham, *Charles and Ray Eames, Designers of the Twentieth Century* (Cambridge, MA: MIT Press, 1995).
75. Curtis, *Modern Architecture* (1996), 562.
76. Curtis, *Modern Architecture* (1996), 562.
77. Curtis, *Modern Architecture* (1996), 246.
78. Kenneth Frampton, *Modern Architecture: A Critical History* (London: Thames & Hudson, 2000), 50.
79. Frampton, *Modern Architecture*, 243–244.
80. Frampton, *Modern Architecture*, 334.
81. Susan R. Henderson, "A Revolution in the Women's Sphere: Grete Lihotzky and the Frankfurt Kitchen," in *Architecture and Feminism*, eds. Debra Coleman, Elizabeth Danze, and Carol Henderson (New York: Princeton Architectural Press, 1996), 245.
82. Such is the case in Curtis, *Modern Architecture* (1982). However, this was corrected in the 1996 edition.
83. Leland M. Roth, *American Architecture: A History* (Boulder, CO: Westview Press, 2001).
84. Roth, *American Architecture*, 266–267.
85. Roth, *American Architecture*, 308.
86. Roth, *American Architecture*, 487.
87. Roth, *American Architecture*, 211–212.
88. Roth, *American Architecture*, 348–349.
89. Roth, *American Architecture*, 454–455.
90. Roth, *American Architecture*, 468–471.
91. Roth, *American Architecture*, 127–128. [Editors' note: The historical record on Joseph-François Mangin, the designer of New York City Hall, does not describe him as either African American or a former slave.]
92. Trachtenberg and Hyman, *Prehistory to Postmodernity* (2002), and Moffett, Fazio, and Wodehouse, *Buildings Across Time* (2004).
93. Henry-Russell Hitchcock and Philip Johnson, *The International Style* (New York: W. W. Norton & Company, 1966, first published in 1932), 204, 127.
94. Lynne Walker, "Architecture and Reputation: Eileen Gray, Gender and Modernism," in *Women's Places: Architecture and Design 1860–1960*, eds. Brenda Martin and Penny Sparke (New York: Routledge, 2003), 86–111.
95. Kingsley, "Gender Issues," 23.
96. Dreck Spurlock Wilson, ed., *African American Architects: A Biographical Dictionary 1865–1945* (New York: Routledge, 2004). For a thorough account of the work of Paul Revere Williams, the most prominent African American architect of the first part of the twentieth century, see Karen Hudson, *Paul Revere Williams: A Legacy of Style* (New York: Rizzoli, 1993).
97. National Park Service, National Register of Historic Places. "Listing a Property in the National Register of Historic Places," http://www.cr.nps.gov/nr/listing.htm (accessed August 15, 2005).
98. "You are not a profession that has distinguished itself by your social and civic contributions to the cause of civil rights . . . . You are most distinguished by your thunderous silence and your complete irrelevance." Stephanie Stubbs, "Breaking through a Thunderous Silence," *American Institute of Architects Memo* (December 1992): 4.
99. These themes and others were the subject of a symposium on "Constructing Race: The Built Environment, Minoritization, and Racism in the United States," held at the University of Illinois at Urbana-Champaign, March 5–6, 2004. The symposium forms the basis of a forthcoming issue of *Landscape Journal* (Dianne Harris, ed.). [Editors' note: see Dianne Harris, ed. *Landscape Journal* 26, no. 1 (2007).]
100. The second author teaches such a seminar. This article is a collaborative outgrowth of that course. Several reference materials can be found on the following website: "Architecture/Gender & Women's Studies 424—Professor Anthony—Gender and Race in Contemporary Architecture," http://www2.arch.uiuc.edu/kanthony/arch424FA04/ (accessed August 15, 2005).
101. "Data Collection," *ArchVoices*, June 25, 2004, http://www.archvoices.org (accessed August 17, 2005).
102. Edward Said, "Politics of Knowledge," *Raritan: A Quarterly Review* 1, no. 1 (Summer 1991): 25.

From Model to Mashup: A Pedagogical Experiment in Thinking Historically About the Future

Ana Miljački
Massachusetts Institute of Technology

The fall 2009 option design studio at MIT—Ferry Slip Mashup—was the site of a pedagogical experiment in engaging the vast historical archive of disciplinary knowledge for the purposes of designing a ferry terminal on the Maine State Pier in Portland, Maine. While the first premise of the studio was that we needed to relearn how to think historically, its second premise was that we had to find an appropriately contemporary way to do that. And if the first premise pointed us to engaging the issue of precedent head on, the second ensured for our precedents the status of entries in a vast archive of architectural knowledge.

Critically Projective
The *Ferry Slip Mashup* studio began with a hypothesis that the recent abundance of crisis narratives in general, and in architecture competitions, studios, and publications specifically, was a symptom of the end of an era in which it was difficult to imagine alternatives to the logic of advanced global capitalism. That some form of outside to global capitalism could now begin to be grasped conceptually, however different any particular image of that post- or other world might be, has in part been reigniting architects' collective will to think prospectively and therefore also historically. For, the future, we are now reminded, can be imagined only when thinking historically. If the first premise of the studio was that we needed to relearn how to think historically (with or without the help of the global financial and ecological crises), then the second premise of the studio was that we had to find an appropriately contemporary way to do that.

In 2003, French historian of science and cultural theorist Bruno Latour invited his readers to take a mental test: If we thought that the time would come when we would be able to distinguish ends from means, facts from values and humans from non-humans—trusting that clarity was merely a question of progress—we could still consider ourselves modern.[1] If we hesitated at all when presented with this idea—Latour called us postmodern. But if we believed that the world is getting ever more entangled—we might have entered another paradigm, one that Latour insists on calling "non-modern." We don't need to give up the fact that modernism, as a period with a specific ethos, concept of time, and a specific idea of progress, actually occurred in order to accept the idea that we are now able to see and describe complex relationships between various agents, objects, histories, and processes.

A type of periodization is important here—to supplement Latour's experiment—even if we lack a convenient name for the contemporary. Terms such as Marc Augé's *supermodernity*, Hans Ibelings's *supermodernism*, Zygmunt Baumann's *fluid modernity*, or Latour's *non-modernity*, have all resulted from descriptions of an important difference between the contemporary and the modern (understood historically).[2] If modernism can be seen (following Baumann's description of "solid modernity") as having operated with the idea that progress and the trajectory of time would eventually deliver things to perfection, or to a perfectly rationally organized world—in distinction to modernism, the general consensus is that today we can no longer tap into the authority and certainty of modernism's "project."

From Model to Mashup
For a generation of architects and critics who "grew up" with sampling, with networks as fully internalized and lived protocols, knowing about the genome, contributing to and learning from Wikipedia, donating money to and SMSing with the Obama campaign—having a set of external, authoritative truths is not a precondition for action. Still, in order to intervene consciously (or even nearly consciously) in the world, as architects ultimately do, requires the production of (personal and/or collective) narratives that in some way mediate between the circumstances exterior to any given project and the design process. These narratives function as positioning devices, postulating the role of the architect and of the discipline of architecture in a complexly entangled world. Legitimating narratives have existed throughout the history of architecture, both as entire authoritative discourses (on style, on origins, on social responsibilities, on the nature of public space, on the function of cities, etc.) and as individual architects' interpretations of those discourses. But what distinguishes our most recent versions of these narratives from all earlier versions in architectural history is: that the narratives of architectural production are now fluid, multiple, and generally smaller; they are often adaptations of the best parts of a number of earlier stories; and they rely on and produce the need for research (wiki, archival, and field).

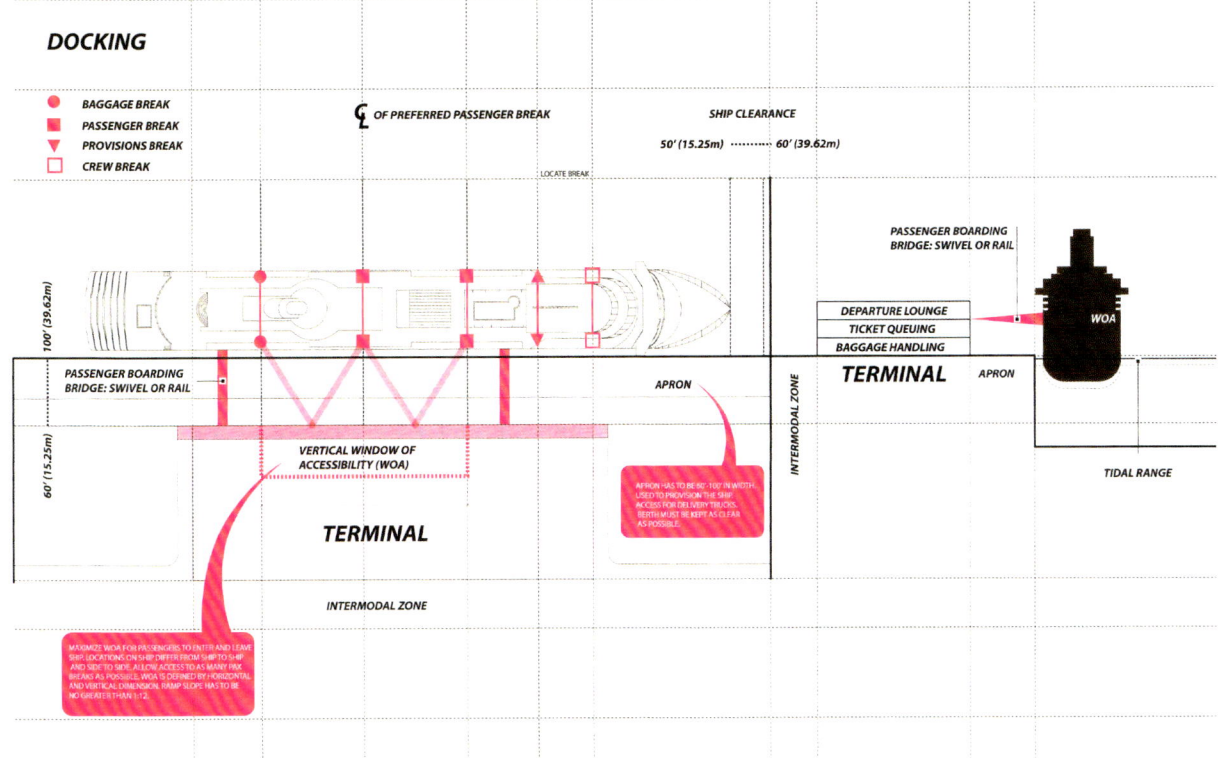

Figure 1. Study of the relationship between the cruise ship and the docking terminal contributed to the collective archive by Natsuki Maeda and Oliver Wuttig.

In a world in which new records are rare and remixes rule, within the music industry and everywhere else, we could decide to clear the slate and install an old type of authenticity, or criticality, or even disciplinarity, or we could invest in articulating why there is no going back to an older "clearer" trajectory. Today, even clarity itself has to be seen as a type of remix. Relying on this reading of our contemporary predicament in esthetic production in general and in architecture specifically, the main provocation of the studio was to place the mashup at the center of methodological investigations.

There are several definitions of mashup circulating in contemporary culture; the most important one for our studio discussions was the musical mashup, which of course entirely depends on the medium of music, but not without certain possible equivalences to architecture.[3] Musical mashup has its own history, starting with adaptations, remixes, sampling, but the most sophisticated contemporary versions of it rely on a deep musical understanding of the material used in combination with aesthetic ends that are in no way contained in the pre-existing musical material.[4] Mashup can draw material from two or many sources, and its origin is sometimes completely obliterated into a near glow of reference, while it is at other times present as a deliberate signifier of an era, an atmosphere, or a tune.[5] A possibly contentious issue of whether musical mashups rely on sophisticated processing of medium-specific information, or on real disciplinary knowledge—we leave to the theorists of music, but this studio's experiment with architectural mashup was premised on a critical evaluation of disciplinary knowledge.

Our studio's two main hypotheses on mashup were that working in this mode was not a question of intentions as much as it was an inevitable response to the status of knowledge in general and to the complexity of the contexts in which we operate as architects, and that mashup may be well suited to delivering an unprecedented (i.e., new) form of aesthetic experience and outcome. What used to be Modernism's (and Harold Bloom's) "anxiety of influence" has for the contemporary generation of architects positively (i.e., in the best case scenario) turned into an "ecstasy of influence," and in the mashup studio we wanted to have that ecstasy encounter the resistance of history.[6] Thinking historically was an important precondition for ensuring that the architectural mashup would become more than a second rate copy-paste project, in which decisions to retool a piece of architectural history were based on a shallow understanding of that history (thereby avoiding types of projects that litter contemporary architectural journals and students' go-to websites like ArchDaily). It was the ultimate hope of the studio that a willingness to operate self-consciously with disciplinary knowledge and a willingness to stake out (and update) political positions could lead to figuring new projects that are distinctly contemporary, while also grounded in long-term disciplinary issues. That is,

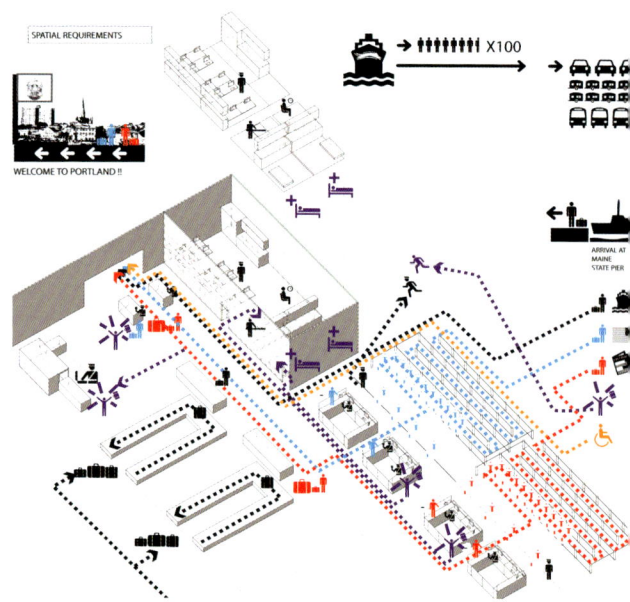

Figure 2. Excerpt from Ryan Maliszewski and Mishayla Greist's study of tourism in Portland, correlating seasonal changes and tourist offerings.

Figure 3. Immigration protocol and programmatic requirements, contributed to the collective archive by Chai Pattamasatayasonthi and Najiyah Edun.

if there were really going to be such a thing as ecstasy of influence (in opposition to mere consumption and emulation of trends) it would in large part come from a self-conscious conversation with disciplinary history and contemporary discourse.

In the long process of moving away from Modernism's "truths" and surviving Postmodernism's iconoclastic historicism, the status of a historical model in architectural pedagogy shifted as well. We rarely review a precedent these days with hopes of getting some form of an essential guideline from it, and even less often do we study precedents as blueprints of relationships or dimensions to be simply reproduced. In fact, a particular parti, a facade solution, an engagement with the developer logic, or with digital fabrication are all possible contemporary registers of architectural production and thinking and thus sources of historical material with particular lessons and lineages of questions worth building upon. Since we can now access and retool any type of knowledge (technical, disciplinary, cultural), learn from an enormous database of old errors and successes, and even conduct new tests (all the while collecting information on those tests), it has become more important than ever to articulate the lineages (even if these are merely simulated) to and through the historical archives. This is to say that raw data and vague extra-disciplinary inspiration were of no interest to us in studio; our precedents had to carry enough historical specificity with them to be understood in terms of particular circumstances and ideologies that made them possible, and ultimately comparable and connectable.

Moving from working with precedents as models to working with an archive of diverse types of architectural knowledge required a method for producing (or again, simulating) coherence, and for this we relied on one of the most archaic methods of synthesis: storytelling. Thus, through trial and error, editing and fine-tuning, students attempted to isolate stories; as if they were trajectories through the archive of the knowledge they needed (and wanted to have) in order to produce their designs. That is, the mashup brought with it pressures to consciously and intelligently store, sort, retrieve, and re-articulate architectural knowledge. Thus, our studio's archives were not merely repositories of searchable data. The studio's ambition for them tended toward Foucault's famous definition of an archive as actively organizing systems of enunciations with the historian or the archeologist as the ultimate "user" of that archive. In the roles of archivists and archeologists students were asked to consider, produce and use their archives on three different levels. One, the collective archive of all relevant facts and realities of the project described the real constraints of the project. Two, every student was responsible for a more monographic "deep dive," based around a single project. This method produced an archive that in its monographic nature most closely approached the status of the precedent. Three, the final, and most complex level of archiving involved finding historical threads around issues that students identified as particularly meaningful to explore given the constraints of the project, and given the issues

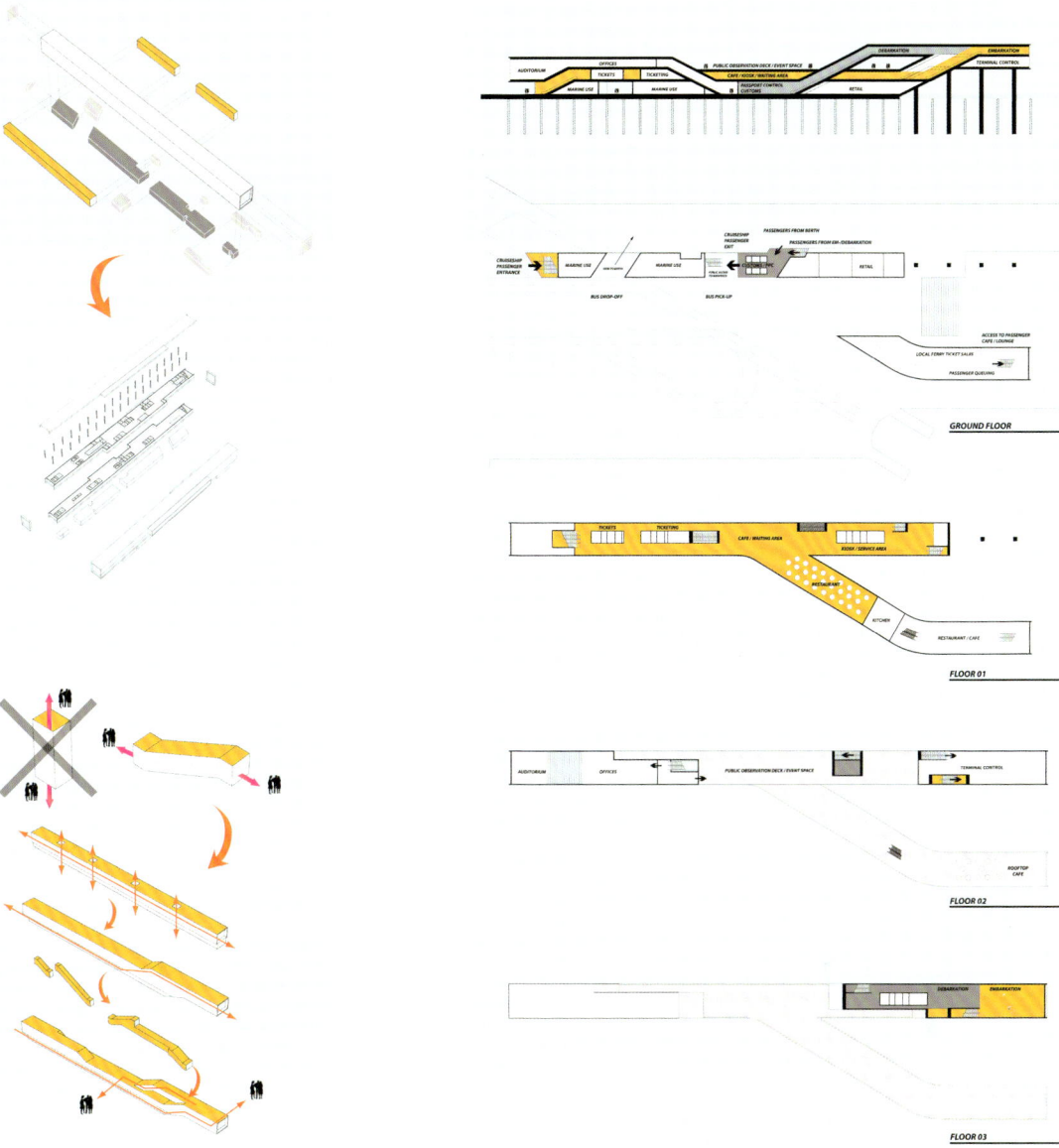

Figure 4. Wuttig's analysis of the 3XN ferry terminal DFDX in Copenhagen and a proposal for reworking its architecture through a single sectional shift.

Figure 5. Section and plans of the 3XN DFDX terminal newly adapted to fit the programmatic and site needs of the Maine State Pier in Portland by Wuttig.

coming out of their monographic deep dive and their projective ambitions for the discipline in general and their own design project in particular.

Maine State Pier: Open Source Archive
In order to ground our studio's highly self-conscious methodological investigations, we went to a medium-sized New England town known for its maritime tourism and its industrial past (with no Architecture—capital A—to speak of): Portland, Maine. Studio posited Portland, ME as American architecture's frontier. It is not exotic, just self-contentedly quaint, which has historically made it even less glamorous for academia

to consider than the "grey goo" of American exurbia. The city of Portland has had an RFP out for the reworking of the Maine State Pier for at least three years. Last year, the development company that won the bid lost its financial backing or, at least, lost its nerve. Consequently, the Maine State Pier planning and design conversations have continued (and have been made available in great detail for public scrutiny). The Maine State Pier is slated by the planning department and the city to take on passenger transport functions, with two other Portland piers scheduled to deal with fishing and freight separately. Once known as Canada's winter port, Portland is still an international port and point of entry,

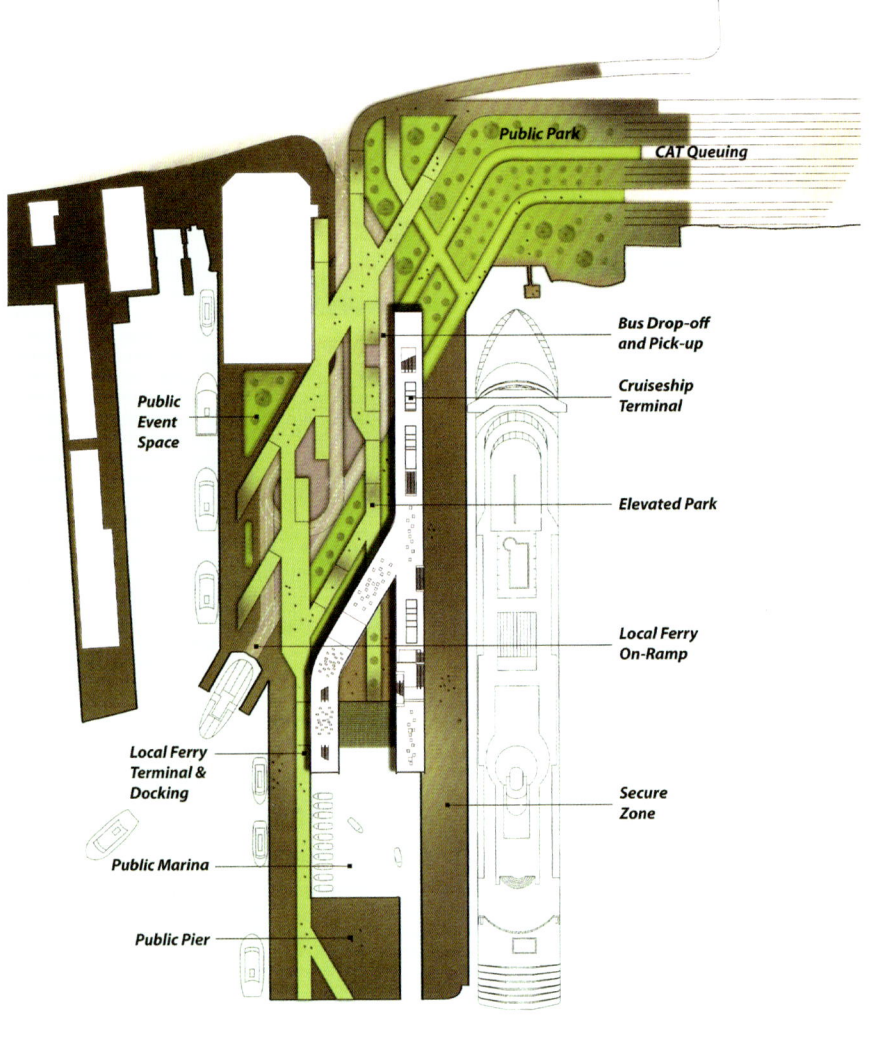

Figure 6. Larger site of the Maine State Pier reworked to fit the adapted 3XN project by Wuttig.

which means that on top of dealing with local islander transport, the Maine State Pier includes an international ferry terminal, along with its enlarged immigration facilities, post 9/11 security zone fences, and Homeland Security regulations. The Maine State Pier is an appropriately contemporary agglomeration of complex issues: various regulatory pressures, business plans, marine transportation logistics, structural dimensioning, infrastructural functioning, stimulus money, natural systems, seasonal cruise ship travel, public fishing needs, and symbolic dimensions of both local and, if not global, then at least international significance. Organized in teams students collectively measured, surveyed, and explained the site in an open-source mode of collaboration. This first attempt at producing an organized and highly pragmatic archive was broken down into six important issues: everything about the ships that ship in and out of Portland (Figure 1), a survey of Portland's tourism (Figure 2), the berthing and pier structures, the existing RFP (along with the hopes of the townspeople and previous gambles of the developers involved), Portland's sea levels and sea life, and homeland

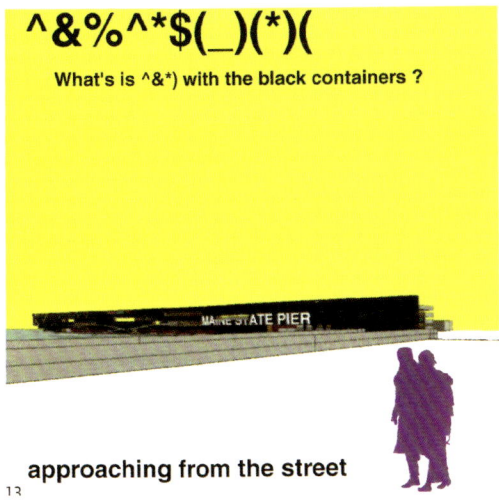

Figure 7–9. Excerpts from Pattamasatayasonthi's "tour" of the new Pier 57 reworked for the Maine State Pier, presented in the visual language that deliberately approximates LOT-EK's high contrast, vibrant renderings. These are not directly based on images LOT-EK produced for the Pier 57 project, but the reference is to be found in their larger body of work.

security regulations (Figure 3). The open source mode of this archive ensured that facts and constraints would inform every project without becoming the ground of a positivistic problem-solving frenzy.

Nip-Tuck: Learning from Adapting a Monographic Archive

Once everyone learned about the basic constraints and ambitions of the Maine State Pier project, we moved onto reviewing a series of more and less recent pier and transportation hub projects, adapting these specifically to the local constraints. Our Nip-Tuck exercise was the first step in testing what it might mean to produce within a lower (historically older) order of the mashup logic: adaptation. Without yet having to completely "own" the design outcome of this exercise, but instead being responsible for taking the projects and their representational and ideological specificity to their logical conclusions ensured that no "anxiety of influence" entered the equation of architectural production. Thus, it was through wearing someone else's hat that students were able to really comprehend the scale and demands of an architectural solution for the Maine State Pier, and they were able to begin to be critical of possible ideological postures they could inhabit in relation to this project and the production of architecture in general.

Oliver Wuttig adapted a recent project for a ferry terminal in Copenhagen by 3XN architects, and Chai Pattamasatayasonthi used a recently published LOT-EK project for Pier 57 in New York. Wuttig's analysis of the 3XN ferry terminal involved deep programmatic, structural and architectural logics that governed the long bar building of his precedent (Figure 4). His adaptation of it responded to the specific ship sizes and programmatic requirements of the Maine State pier site. In order to make the 3XN project work on and for this new site, Wuttig had to introduce a forking element into the bar building which allowed his bar to be on two different sides of the pier, responding to both international cruise ships and the local island ferry services (Figure 5). He also significantly reworked the ground of the Main State Pier in a manner that had very little to do with the 3XN proposal, thus opening up a line of inquiry for his own project (Figure 6). Pattamasatayasonthi's precedent came with too little architectural articulation to really study details of connection or circulation, but since he was dealing with a LOT-EK project he was able to rely on the firm's famous and often articulated position on reusing industrial objects for the production of a type of surreal estrangement. In order to adapt the LOT-EK pier for Portland, Pattamasatayasonthi relied on the stacking of containers as did LOT-EK, which were available in the local context, but he also began to consider what materials might produce an association with the state of Maine and could be repurposed for architectural applications, thus playing into the quaint and often automatic identification and self-identification of Maine with red lobsters and fishermen's buoys (Figures 7–9).

Figure 10. Pattamasatayasonthi's rendering of the contain based ferry terminal for Maine State Pier, introducing an anti LOT-[EK] emphasis on nasty weath[er] and thus actively beginn[ing] to change ownership of [the] project.

Figure 11. Site maneuve[rs] treating the Maine State Pier site as a found object, in the spirit of LOT-EK's repurposing of industrial objects, but at a rather different scale, and adjusting to the "nip-tuck" procedures already performed on the terminal building by Pattamasatayasonthi.

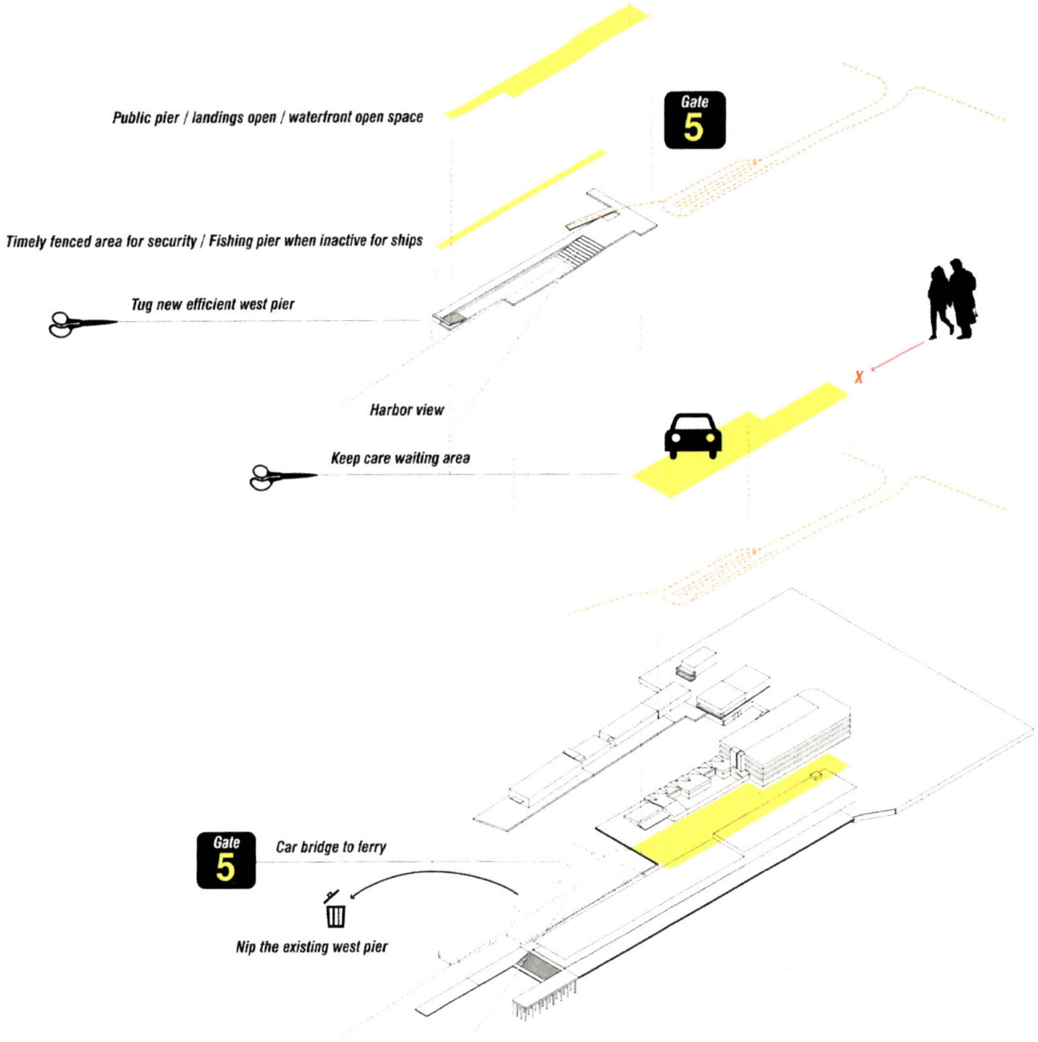

Public pier / landings open / waterfront open space

Gate 5

Timely fenced area for security / Fishing pier when inactive for ships

Tug new efficient west pier

Harbor view

Keep care waiting area

Gate 5

Car bridge to ferry

Nip the existing west pier

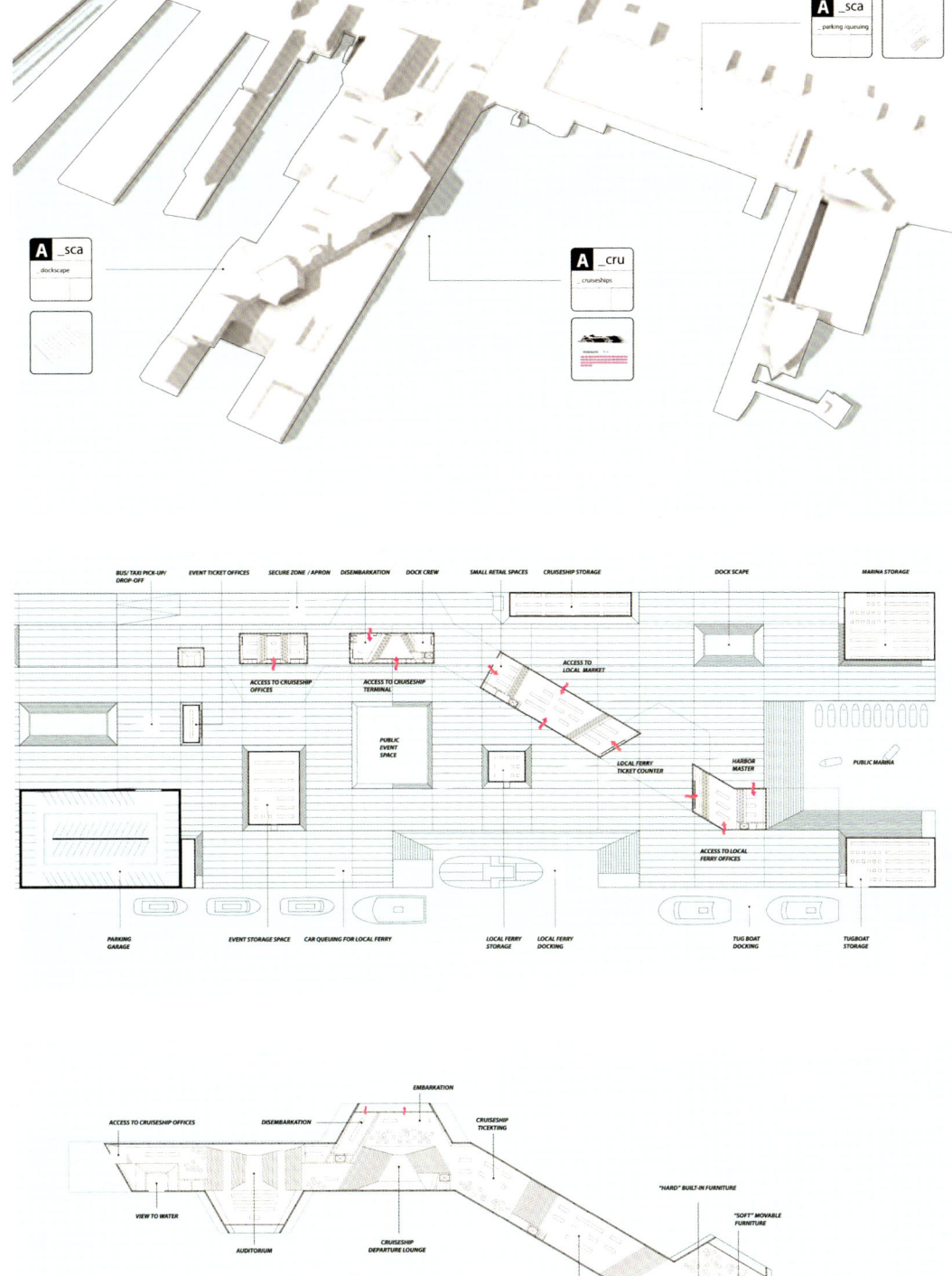

Figures 12–14. Site and plan work for Wuttig's final Ferry Terminal proposal. Influenced by his earlier "nip-tuck" exercise but now also consciously working with issues of conduit and scoop both in the architectural dimensions of the ferry terminal and the ground of the site.

Figures 15. Wuttig's final Maine State Pier rendering, showing the ground and the terminal scoops.

Figures 16-19. Maine State Pier presented from the point of view of a local Portland traveler, who arrives by car. Excerpt from Wuttig's final movie.

Figures 20. Pattamasatayasonthi's rendering of the final Maine State Pier proposal.

Figures 21. Plans and sections of Pattamasatayasonthi's final proposal.

Thus, LOT-EK's industrial vernacular (in Pattamasatayasonthi's analysis of their work) was made to approach the rhetoric of locality; it used the city, the developers, the shopkeepers in each case slightly differently in order to re-produce the citizen's and the tourist's expectations of this location. In Pattamasatayasonthi's case the discovery of this line of argument, through the adaptation of LOT-EK, would open a larger set of issues of "learning from" the Main street (in the Venturi and Scott Brown sense), and repurposing the image of the vernacular enough to estrange its image and logic without losing the reference to it and thus its rhetorical power in this context.

Ferry Slip: Personal Archives

The third version of the archive coincided with the final exercise in the design of the ferry terminal and pier for Portland. Although for many students the previous exercise based on a monographic precedent had great catalytic power for this final stage as well, students were asked to develop their own mashup archive (its content and logic of deployment) without relying on a single precedent, but instead by consciously constructing lineages and positions on specific issues they found relevant for the design of the ferry terminal and pier in Portland. They could draw from the two previous archives, and use their own tests on an equal footing

Figures 22–25. Stills from Pattamasatayasonthi's final movie in which stereotypical tourist photographs are backgrounded by the sound of a clicking camera presenting all the important programmatic and architectural aspects of his project.

with the historical and discursive material they wanted to be in conversation with. Thus, everyone's archive contained highly pragmatic nuggets on the construction of the pier in Portland, precedents framed through particular lenses or lineages of concerns and tests produced within the design process itself.

Including his previous studio exercises into final—personal—archive Wuttig developed a line of argument that posited a play between nearly opposing formal tools as a way to both deal with specific programmatic needs of the ferry terminal project and to produce a contemporary hybridity of intention and reading in the project (Figures 12–14). On the scale of the architectural proposal the pair of tools included the tube and the branching view scoops, and on the scale of the site he opposed the bar to the logic of the field. He used his own design versioning process to discover possible lineages in dealing with structure and form of the project in relation to his programmatic ambitions. It is only through trying out minimal solutions (of a kind of a modernist bar: Mies van der Rohe) in relationship to more expressive and stylized structural articulation (of more recent years: Jurgen Mayer) that he honed in on the tone of his own project. Discovering a kind of formal reversibility of the view or lighting scoops allowed him to produce variation and ultimately embed a type of interpretive ambiguity into the form of the project (Figure 15). Horizontal and vertical scoops, highly stylized formally, were sometimes placed instrumentally in relationship to the embarkation and debarkation of the ships, and other times their function was less strictly scripted via that more basic notion of efficacy. Chai Pattamasatayasonthi, on the other hand, already set on a track through interpreting LOT-EK's recycling of materials in a direction that the City of Portland, the local developers and tourists seemed to embrace (given their respective rhetoric about the city and about tourist attractions), understood that he was embarking on a project that had a number of possible lineages in retooling the popular and the vernacular. Most famous of his "precedents" (now understood in this new way, as entries in his archive) were Venturi and Scott Brown examples, but more recent work by Herzog and de Meuron, or even by the young U. S. firm MOS, pointed to a slightly different direction. What was common among them, at least to some extent, was their estrangement of the vernacular through a type of material or formal abstraction. But even this was not at the core of each of the positions that argued for "learning from" the vernacular. Pattamasatayasonthi chose not to go all the way toward a kind of commercialized proposal that perhaps most realistically embraced the economic logic of leasing space and allowing the shopkeepers and the ultimate operators of the pier to determine the final aesthetic outcome of it as well. But instead his project embraced the Maine Tourism Association's (and colloquial) rhetoric of "absolute Maine-ness" while offering a type of formal coherence and even freshness that is rarely the outcome of basic economic thinking employed by developers and city officials (Figures 20–21). Once the students were allowed to borrow and steal, and define their own trajectories via their research (as long as the agenda and the lineage of a certain architectural idea was clearly articulated), some of the usual anxieties about authorship (and influence) crept back into the discussion, which in part ensured that the final designs were creatively in excess of their controlled input material.

Storytelling: Divorcing the Method of Production from the Final Reception of the Projects

The final request of the studio was to produce a linear narrative, a movie, of the production of the project, its habitation or its architectural agenda, such that all of the previous highly conscious and didactic methodological operations would vanish when it came to the final reception of the project. Our goal was to separate the reception of the final architectural proposals from the highly didactically clear methodology used for their production. This was as much an experiment in navigating the archive and thinking through storytelling as it was a test for the usual mindset of the critics in an academic context. Most importantly, we were curious to see to what extent the mashup was able to stand on its own, both esthetically and discursively. The request to produce linear narratives separate from the archiving and retrieving of knowledge and even separate from possible positioning narratives pushed students to think through precedents in storytelling structures and genres, both in architecture and outside it. Oliver Wuttig showed his project through a standard modernist filmmaking technique, a Dziga Vertov type of "a day in the life of" narrative, but such that the same day repeated three times from the perspective of the cruise-ship traveler, a local Maine State Pier worker and a seagull (Figures 16–19). This narrative structure allowed him to show off the project literally from a number of different spatial perspectives while it also allowed him to humorously intertwine the protagonists across the three different "takes" of the pier. The atmospheric quality of the movie he made in a very direct sense undermined the didactic formal reading of the project favoring the architectural effects of his form over any type of explanatory narrative. Pattamasatayasonthi on the other hand extended his narrative of tourism. Structuring his presentation into a relentless series of touristy snapshots of his project including many of the affectations of tourist photography, the ultimate effect of his narrative technique was to literally project his architectural proposal into the status of an already existing tourist attraction (Figures 22–25). The final projects were critiqued in terms of their developmental logic, as well as separately from it, as proposals rich with embedded intelligence and ideologies the reading and misreading of which were both equally valuable for our studio's discussions.

In conclusion, it may be important to consider the reactions of numerous critics who participated in our studio discussions and reviews. Although the mashup studio invoked nausea for those who interpreted its contrivance as a repeat of the postmodernist narrative of *quotation*, it simultaneously managed to satisfy the latent avant-gardist hunger in others by proposing that something *new* and unrecognizable would eventually emerge from its experiments. The mashup studio proposed that, left without authoritative truths to rely on, but with greatly expanded expertise and concerns, the new generation of architects needed to relink (and even simulate links) to and rewrite the old political and cultural projects in architecture to fit their own time. That an older generation of critics thought they recognized projects (especially vastly different ones like oldness and newness) in the premise of the studio was proof (of sorts) that at least some connections and rewriting had begun.

Notes

1. Bruno Latour's invitation to perform this test was published in his text *Reassembling the Social—An Introduction to Actor-Network-Theory* (Oxford: Oxford University Press, 2005), but the spirit of this challenge can be found at the basis of a number of Latour's works in the 1990s and 2000s, and most famously, in Bruno Latour, *We Have Never Been Modern* (Cambridge, MA: Harvard University Press, 1993).
2. See Marc Augé, *Non-Places: Introduction to an Anthropology of Supermodernity* (London: Verso, 1995); Hans Ibelings, *Supermodernism: Architecture in the Age of Globalization* (Rotterdam: NAi, 1998) and more recently, Zygmunt Bauman, *Liquid Modernity* (Cambridge, MA: Polity, 2000).
3. See, for example, a book of texts edited together from a variety of fields, Stefan Sonvilla-Weiss, ed., *Mashup Cultures* (New York: Springer, 2010).
4. A recent *New York Times* article goes specifically into the issues surrounding the recent history of the musical mashup, Michiko Kakutani, "A Mash-Up Culture: Ten to Watch," *New York Times,* March 17, 2010.
5. In contemporary music the most famous example of a two-source mashup was D. J. Danger Mouse's *Grey Album* produced through a careful combination of the Beatles' *White Album* and Jay-Z's *Black Album*, while much of the recent work by Girl Talk is a more meandering concoction of a myriad sources.
6. See Harold Bloom, *Anxiety of Influence: A Theory of Poetry* (New York: Oxford University Press, 1973), as well as brilliant essays by Jonathan Lethem constructed out of borrowed or plagiarized pieces from a large number of sources, "The Ecstasy of Influence: A Plagiarism," *Harper's Magazine,* February, 2007.

Politics

228
1955
The Architect's Role in Urban Renewal
Catherine Bauer

230
1968
What Architectural Schools Expect from Sociology
Robert Gutman

232
1969
The Money Problem
Daniel Solomon

234
1988
Gender Issues in Teaching Architectural History
Karen Kingsley

240
1989
Black Architects: An Endangered Species
Robert Traynham Coles

243
1991
The Crisis of Interdisciplinary Historiography
Mark Jarzombek

249
1991
The Pruitt Igoe Myth
Katharine G. Bristol

258
1992
The Ecology Question
Richard Ingersoll

261
1993
Writing Multiculturalism into Architectural Curricula
Regina Davis

269
1995
Contesting the Public Realm
Margaret Crawford

275
2001
Bauhaus Hausfrau
Katarina Rüedi Ray

283
2003
Immanent Domain
Dana Cuff

292
2019
Images Doing Work
Anna Goodman and Maura Lucking

Politics

Igor Marjanović

> As we organize, lobby, march, and demonstrate against racist violence, we who are women of color must be willing to appeal for multiracial unity in the spirit of sister-ancestors. Like them, we must proclaim: We do not draw the color line. The only line we draw is one based on our political principles.
>
> —Angela Y. Davis

It was with a vocabulary that evoked the practice of architecture—including words such as *line* and *draw*—that the activist and philosopher Angela Y. Davis so vividly painted the deeply intertwined character of radical social and feminist agendas in the United States and globally. Suggesting that the liberation of one group is inseparable from the liberation of an entire society, Davis called for a constant engagement with politics in the broadest possible sense of the word and at every possible scale. In some ways this synthetic and expansive approach is mirrored in the ambitions of many authors represented in the *Journal of Architectural Education* (JAE). In many cases their engagement with *politics* follows the broad arc of architecture's intersections with the larger socioeconomic context. The fourteen articles presented in this section of the book demonstrate this arc. Initially understood primarily as an issue of state power and governance—in particular as they relate to urban policy—the notion of politics has been gradually expanded to encompass economics, identity politics, and other discourses.

Policy

It is perhaps befitting that this section of the book opens with the San Francisco Bay Area activist Catherine Bauer's essay "The Architect's Role in Urban Renewal" (1955), covering one of the most debated architectural topics of the twentieth century. Written in a socially progressive voice of its era, the article calls for more inclusive design processes, urging architects and planners to engage community members as they work on public housing and other projects. Following the ebbs and flows of national politics and economic trends, urban renewal was seen as a key arena for both design exploration and social action for architects in the early decades of the journal, the 1950s and the 1960s. Yet by the 1990s this notion of architects' agency was shattered by a generation of authors who were critical of architecture's messianic power and also aware of the real impact of politics and economy as the main drivers of success and failure in urban development.

In her historical reflection on the iconic Pruitt-Igoe housing project in St. Louis, Katherine Bristol (1991) exposes the project as a myth that "not only inflates the power of the architect to effect social change, but . . . masks the extent to which the profession is implicated, inextricably, in structures and practices that it is powerless to change." Bristol sees US public housing policy as deeply problematic, undermined by issues such as poor construction and maintenance as well as racism and social class, and she criticized architects who all too easily assumed the moral authority of social saviors, only to be excluded from key decisions and ultimately to achieve very little impact. Articles like this contributed to a realization that what was often seen as the domain of the profession was in fact an arena of economic and political struggle linked more closely to policy than to design and, relatedly, that a deep understanding of social and economic policy is essential to an architect's success in practice and social agency.

Situated as it is within a capitalist society, the JAE often engaged issues of economic policy, although more often from the angle of finance than that of economic inequality. Daniel Solomon's essay "The Money Problem" (1969)—perhaps one of the most telling and succinct titles in the journal's history—discusses a core studio project in which students produced abstract models and drawings to visualize profit on apartment rentals, boldly acknowledging the "capitalistic notion of environmental design as a system of payoffs."

Politicizing History and Identity

Yet as much as some of the "money" articles failed to politicize the economic system in which architects operate, other articles were highly effective in politicizing the very territory of the discipline itself. Mark Jarzombek (1991), for example, argued for the importance of historical knowledge in contemporary theoretical consciousness, cautioning against the tendency of architects to make unfounded theoretical associations based on loosely "borrowed" concepts from philosophy and literature. Rather than stemming from a genuine criticality founded on deep socioeconomic and cultural investigations, these associations often served merely to justify formal decisions. Essays like this politicize architectural history, presenting it not only as a survey of styles and movements but also as a dynamic field meant to expose the socioeconomic underpinnings of the otherwise seemingly neutral field of architectural design.

Nowhere else is this desire to politicize the discipline stronger than in a cluster of essays examining the identity formation of an architect. And under this umbrella the topic of gender identity emerges as a major arena for critical examination of the field, in particular its inclusivity, equity, and representation. Katerina Rüedi Ray's (2001) recasting of Bauhaus studio practices as a series of theatrical "repairs" that sought to address wounded masculinity after World War I expose design education as often deeply patriarchal, while Karen Kingsley's (1988) close examination of history textbooks and their inclusion (or more often their exclusion) of female voices stands as a powerful reminder that diligent historical research and data are powerful tools in curriculum decolonization. Such articles were also significant as they expanded the field of architecture to include feminist discourses. Indeed the plurality of voices and subjectivities becomes the main thread of politicization in articles after the 1990s and into the 2000s, suggesting the important role of the journal in recasting a new relationship between architecture's theoretical aspirations, scholarly pursuits, and activist agenda—all of which served as important topics from the early days of the journal.

The intersections of the activist agenda, scholarship, and design are particularly powerful in another cluster of essays that deal with race and racism in the United States. Regina Davis's 1993 article reports on a course that she cotaught with Ken Simmons, in which students were asked to write about the work of African American, Asian American, Latino, and Native American architects and artists. Offered in response to demands presented by the architecture students at the University of California, Berkeley—clearly in the aftermath of the widespread protests following the acquittal of the Los Angeles police officers who brutally beat Rodney King in 1991—this course and subsequent article were an example of the real impact of student advocacy on the curriculum. The on-going struggle for a socially just public space features prominently in the essays by Margaret Crawford (1995) and Dana Cuff (2003), signifying its continued relevance in the following decades and even today.

Social Action: Educators as Scholars, Practitioners, Entrepreneurs, and Advocates

Rather significantly, the last article in this volume deals with the representation of Black, brown, and white bodies of American students of architecture. Anna Goodman and Maura Lucking (2019) analyze period photographs from the Tuskegee Institute and Black Mountain College that show students engaged in various campus construction projects. With their bodies and gestures highly staged—and in particular with the gazes of African American students always tucked away—these images perpetuate social myths about race and identity as well as professional myths about the production of buildings and attention to detail, often at the expense of human individuality. With their rural context completely obscured and reduced to a mere natural backdrop, such images not only veil the social order of class but also fall short—like the field of architecture in general—in speaking about different social groups across the omnipresent urban/rural divide.

We are finalizing this volume in the age of Black Lives Matter and the immense social energy manifested in the protests following the murders of George Floyd, Breonna Taylor, and other victims of police violence. This reckoning with race and racism is perhaps telling of the need to examine social, political, and architectural issues in relationship to one another rather than in isolation. As architectural educators engage politics very broadly on the pages of JAE, they critically examine the social relationships between people and buildings, acting not only as teachers but also as scholars, practitioners, entrepreneurs, and advocates. Most often they reaffirm the immense diversity of our field itself, constantly straddling the boundaries between design, technology, and history. In the process they make a case for a socially responsible architecture, which, despite the imperfect nature of the institutions of architectural education and practice, remains a crucial concern for educators and students alike. Yet as Richard Ingersoll (1992) reminds us, architects should engage social responsibility thoughtfully and inclusively since "what previously might have been justified as social responsibility eventually reveals itself to be social control." This cautionary statement and the evolution of the architect's social engagement is clearly evident in the articles written by architectural educators over the last seventy-five years as they have constantly evolved, repositioned, and, perhaps most importantly, critically examined the larger purpose of what we do. In doing so, they demonstrate that "freedom is a constant struggle"—to quote the title of a recent book by Angela Y. Davis—and that teaching, scholarship, and academic service constitute a dynamic space of reckoning and indeed one of the last critical outlets for the entire discipline not only to generate new architectural proposals but also to participate in relevant political debates addressing issues that affect us all.

Note
Epigraph: Angela Y. Davis, *Women, Culture & Politics* (New York: Vintage / Random House, 1990), 11.

The Architect's Role in Urban Renewal

Catherine Bauer
University of California, Berkeley

Out of all the turmoil of the past twenty years we have made some bona fide progress in housing and city planning, We have a whole range of new tools, some of them very powerful tools indeed. And the tools have produced some good results, whether in terms of social and economic benefit, or civic efficiency.

But although many architects have been vitally interested in housing and city planning, and have made important contributions all along the way, it is curious that where we have the least progress in this whole field is at the visual, three-dimensional level. You can point to all kinds of improvements, but not really in the attractiveness and pleasantness of the physical environment we are creating. This is true whether you look at the results of the FHA formula, with its monstrous and monotonous expanse of suburban chicken-coops, or those of the public housing-insurance company formula, which seems to produce either railroad cars on a siding, or vast institutional buildings that look like veterans' hospitals. There are exceptions, of course, but they are rare.

The most powerful and important new tools for shaping human environment are (1) large-scale operations, and (2) public policy, but these seem to be very difficult tools for the housing and town designer to wield, and we have not yet learned how to use them to produce satisfactory physical results. One problem these tools have in common is that they tend to remove the designer from direct contact with his client, the ultimate user. He therefore does not have the kind of personal check that might automatically humanize the end product.

At the training level, there is one particular weakness which tends to inhibit progress in humanizing the design of housing and communities; too frequently we assume that there must be a single rational, logical solution, and that it is the experts' responsibility (with however much research) to find that one right solution and then impose it on the product, wholesale. And because of this faith in and desire for universal answers, we get too dogmatic—dogma about architectural style, for instance, which results in vast housing projects that are apparently viewed by their designers mainly as huge pieces of technocratic sculpture, abstract forms that have little to do with satisfying, pleasing or delighting the occupants, as places to live in. There are also dogmas about neighborhood design and community planning; you know them as well as I do, and they all tend toward super-standardization and dehumanization.

At the city planning level we also have dogma, not so much about the form of cities as about planning procedure. The planners, no matter how complicated the problem or uncertain the future, are expected to come up with a single plan before it is handed out to the public., If it does not go over with the public, *tant pis*. But it is an article of faith that there is one rational scheme for every city, which the experts must figure out by themselves.

The fallacy is that we are still in a highly experimental stage in housing and city planning, and in using all these shiny new tools for urban development. The experts don't, can't, and shouldn't know enough to make such big decisions on a wholesale basis all by themselves before they have any dealings with their client, the public.

And it seems to me that it is a major part of the experts' responsibility today to pose the alternatives for the public, so that the big decisions can be shared in by the ultimate users. But instead it is a sign of professional weakness if the architect or planner comes out of his drafting room to face the public without having first determined exactly what would be good for them.

You may feel the public is too dumb to participate. But if the citizens and consumers are unenlightened, it may be because we have never encouraged public argument about our problems. This is one of the most backward countries in the world from the viewpoint of public debate about the big issues in architectural design and city planning. Isn't it partly our own fault?

Consider two issues, at opposite ends of the pole: architectural style, and the pattern of urban development.

Last year there was a great hullaballoo about a series of articles that venomously attacked certain trends in modern architecture. To many of us there was a germ of truth here and there in those articles, but we could not admit it because of the mean and vicious spirit in which the articles were written. But if there had been a healthy kind of continuing public debate about the various conflicting dogmas apparent in modern architecture, this cheap effort to exploit the public ignorance would have been unimportant. The only reason it loomed so large was because it was the first time the issues had been raised in public.

At the other end of the scale, there is a similar lack of responsible effort to engage the public in discussion as to the ultimate shape and destiny of our cities. In many metropolitan areas we are likely to have millions of additional people in the next few decades. This means major alternatives with respect to centralization, decentralization, sub-centralization, size and self-sufficiency of local communities, etc. And there are all kinds of tools available to guide the pattern one way or the other. But even if the planners were ready and willing to face up to these alternatives (which they are not), how can they possibly make such big and basic human decisions all by themselves? Our first responsibility should be to explain the different possibilities to the public, in a form simple and dramatic enough so that the big issues are raised and can be debated. Only then can we begin to make sense with concrete schemes for suburban expansion or central redevelopment.

Perhaps the planners need more help from the architects on these big overall questions. I have come to respect the claims of architects that you are the visualizers. So it may be up to you to visualize the alternatives for future urban development in such a way that the public can make the big decisions properly. But never act as if there is just one answer for any city. And don't make all the compromises in advance: that's what makes city planning dull. Get out in front, and argue, from different viewpoints: Le Corbusier versus Frank Lloyd Wright versus Robert Moses versus Ebenezer Howard and Lewis Mumford. If we had more public controversy on the big issues, we'd have more real planning, and better architecture.

What Architectural Schools Expect from Sociology

Robert Gutman
Rutgers University

The curriculum reforms suggested by Professor Gutman result from a study directed toward three principal questions: How does architecture influence human behavior and social organization? How are the problems of the built environment viewed and influenced by the culture and social organization of the architectural profession and by the schools of architecture? How might sociology contribute to architectural practice and design education?

Material for this study was gathered principally through discussion, observation, and teaching in two schools of architecture—one in England, one in the United States—during 1965-66. Following are some of Professor Gutman's observations regarding the present use of sociology in architectural schools.

—The Editor

Courses in the Field of Sociology

One way in which English and American architectural students are given an acquaintance with the theories, the methods, the research findings, and also the ideology of sociologists is through lecture courses taught primarily by professional sociologists. These courses are of four kinds:

1. Courses in general sociology which survey the field, familiarize the student with issues and principles that claim the attention of scholars in the discipline, or otherwise provide an introduction to basic sociology. These courses are usually taken during the freshman or sophomore year in college, while the American student is fulfilling his liberal arts distribution requirement. Architectural education in England is founded on the tradition of the arts and crafts movement which in the last century encouraged the proliferation of many training centers outside the university structure. These schools offer little of what we recognize as general education and consequently students do not often have an opportunity to take any work in sociology. At Cambridge and the Bartlett and in the many other schools now developing within or becoming incorporated into the universities, courses in general sociology are available to undergraduates in much the same way as they are in this country.

2. Courses in subfields of sociology which deal with social institutions or communities that correspond to the types of buildings or built environments which the student will design when he becomes a practitioner. An example of a course on social institutions is one in the sociology of the family. Such a course typically discusses cultural variations in family structure among societies and within the same society: the functional needs of family life and anticipated changes in family structure over the next three or four decades. The sociology of the family is considered a relevant subject because a good part of the student's career may be taken up with the design of large housing schemes. Students interested in the design of schools, colleges, and universities sometimes study the sociology of education, etc.

Architectural students, with rare exceptions, do not exhibit great interest in the social organization of rural communities but many of them are enrolled in courses dealing with the sociology of cities, suburbs, and metropolitan regions. Urban sociology, or some course with another title which incorporates much of the subject matter of the field, is a *required* course now in several schools of architecture in this country, and therefore the sociological subject most frequently studied at present. The content of courses in urban sociology, it is assumed, will prove helpful in the design of particular building types such as houses; but its principal justification has to do with preparing students for work as urban designers and city planners.

3. Courses in subfields of sociology which focus on the unresolved organizational problems of American society or which concern themselves with the fundamental trends of modern society are likely to give rise to problems in the future. Student attention to courses of this kind reflects the continuing emphasis in the architectural tradition to make buildings which express or otherwise reflect the dominant trends of society.

Architects believe it is important to understand the principal future thrust of society and the general direction of social change. The architect then tries to adopt a stance toward design problems which signifies this direction. Many of the notions about building form associated with the modern movement can be read as an effort to encapsulate the principal themes of early 20th century society within a conceptual ideology regulating building design. Thus the ideas about building form advocated by Marinetti and Sant'Elia were regarded by them, and by their audience, as an expression of a civilization in which motorized means of transportation were transforming the fundamental social bases of urban life; or the design esthetic of Gropius or Mies, each in a different way, can be interpreted as an impulse to highlight the industrial basis of contemporary social structure.

One can easily imagine that in our setting the futurists, members of the German Werkbund or the followers of *de Stijl* would turn to courses in technology and culture, or industrial or urban sociology, as sources from which they could generate design theories.

A similar search for sociological knowledge relevant to the formulation of a design philosophy in our own time is represented by the interest of architectural students in sociology courses with subjects such as the culture of poverty, race relations, mass culture, communications, and sociological linguistics.

It is usually true of the three kinds of courses I have described so far that the student himself bears the burden of extracting their implications for design and building problems, or he does so with the help of other architectural students attending the course. This is so because, for the most part, these courses are not taught by sociologists who have much interest in or familiarity with the problems of the architectural tradition; often they are positively hostile to it.

The general sociology and the institution-oriented or problem-oriented courses are directed primarily to students who major in sociology; the architectural students enrolled usually form a minority of the class. Interestingly enough, I have found that extrapolating the significance of sociology for design problems is also a problem for students in English architectural schools, even though the sociology courses offered are taken almost exclusively by architectural students. According to what their directors and professors have told me, the difficulty arises because of the serious shortage of sociologists in England who are sympathetic to or familiar with the specific intellectual requirements of design education.

4. Sociology courses which attempt to fit the literature on the perspectives, theories, and research findings of sociology to issues raised within the framework of the architectural tradition, and to discuss these issues in the manner and in the sequence in which they arise for the architect during the course of the design process. This fourth kind of course, now being given in a few architectural schools, is directed at the needs of architectural students in particular. The content seems to be concentrated in the fields of town planning and housing sociology; except that in one English architectural school, there is a lecture course concerned with special professional problems of the architectural practitioner, taught from the perspective of the sociology of occupations. The courses dealing with housing sociology, as distinguished from courses in the sociology of town planning, are recent innovations. The instructors are equally divided between individuals formally trained as architects or planners who have schooled themselves in sociology and persons trained in sociology who have developed an interest in or knowledge of architecture.

Editors' note: Please note the "Editor" referred to in this note is the editor at the time of publication, Donlyn Lyndon. This article is an excerpt of the original.

Journal of Architectural Education, 23:4, 1969

The Money Problem

Daniel Solomon
University of California, Berkeley

A first-year introductory investigation of the interrelationship of physical and economic factors in diagrammatic models.

The course I developed was influenced by several factors including its relationship to the curriculum as it was last year and, of course, my own interests and what I felt I was able to do competently.

Unlike some first year design courses, Environmental Design 3 was not intended as an all-embracing introduction to the field of environmental design. It was part of a three-course package and its objectives were quite narrow. The other parts of the package were a visually oriented skills course and a very generalized introduction to the historical and political situation of the design professions. ED 3 was an introduction only to the technical and economic side of design. Its orientation was visual only in an indirect way, and sociological only by inference.

The nucleus of the course was a series of optimization problems designed to illustrate the impact of various preoccupations on physical things. Problems had titles such as: construction, structure, movement, money, etc., and I think the problem statements are more or less self explanatory. The money problem was given twice in slightly different forms and both times it began the quarter. "Money" was first because it established a context for the other problems; that is, a rather hard-nosed, capitalistic notion of environmental design as a system of payoffs. Light, air, and proximity to amenities had to be justified in terms of the optimization objective—profit after one year, profit after five years, or revenue per year. The rules of the problem were carefully adjusted so that different economic objectives resulted in quite different physical solutions.

The money problem was not intended to teach or even introduce real methods for determining an optimal development package. It was designed only to demonstrate in a quick, dramatic, and generalizable way the interrelationship of physical and economic factors in a design problem. Subsequent problems in the series, whether their objectives were the minimization of labor, material, time, or drawing, could be related to the view of the world presented in the money problem.

After giving the problem once, we determined that it might be given a secondary objective as well. As you know, various people have for years thrashed over the question of whether the teaching of basic skills such as drawing and model building should be built into prob-

lem solving exercises or whether they should be taught independently. I have always believed that basic skills taught in vacuo are a drag and that they can be integrated with problems which have other objectives without diluting either those objectives or the teaching of basic skills. On the contrary, by combining basic skills with design exercises one is able to get across some sense of why a particular skill exists, when it's used, and what its limitations are.

The money problem, we discovered, was a neat vehicle for teaching orthographic projection and some-

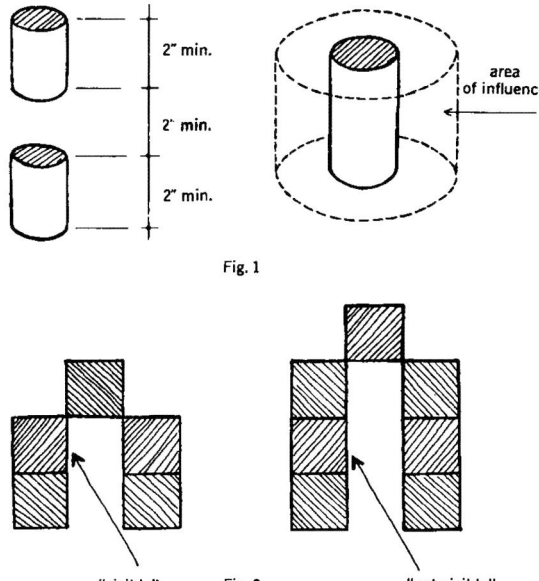

Fig. 1

"visible" Fig. 2 "not visible"

thing about the difference between pictorial drawing and diagramming. The second quarter (which was the second time we taught the course) we asked students not to build a three-dimensional model for the money problem but develop a solution using plans, sections, elevations, and isometrics. Some drawings had to show what the thing looked like, and others had to show certain abstract relationships such as the spheres of influence of the "amenity items"—balls and cylinders.

I felt that the money problem illustrated an important point in a clear way, although the process of actually getting the rules to work was a bit of a nightmare. If I were ever to give the problem again I would want to make it quicker—three or four days at the most.

The photographs show several of the first term's solutions and indicate certain constraints and variables. The maximum development envelope was a 7½-inch cube. Students did not have to fill it, they did not have to build at all. But they did have to examine the financial investment and return and justify their solution accordingly. Variations resulted, too, from the combinations of 1½-inch cubes, ¾-inch cubes, cylinders, or spheres, studied and then selected as optimums. Although drawings, not models, were called for winter term, this second go-around with the money problem was similar in rules and specifications. Criteria for evaluating solutions noted their amount of accumulated profit, completeness and clarity of drawings, clarity and correctness of tabulations, craftsmanship and graphics, and their adherence to rules.

The winter term problem statement went about as follows:

Problem One, Two Weeks. ED 3, Winter 1968. Using the rules and specifications described below, design an object which will produce a maximal accumulated profit after four years. All revenue will be from rental receipts earned by cubes 1½ inches on a side. They have a basic rent of $250 per month and cost $12,000 to build.

All cubes must be exposed on at least two sides. Exposures may be vertical or horizontal. A space may qualify as an exposure if its volume is equal to that of an adjacent cube. A single volume may serve as an exposure for more than one cube.

South facing cubes may increase their rent 10 percent. Cubes that face both south and west may increase their rent 15 percent. A cube is considered south facing only if it has an unobstructed view in that direction. The same holds true for south and west facing cubes.

Cubes within ½ inch of cylinders 1 inch in diameter may increase their rent 15 percent. Cubes within 2 inches of cylinders may increase their rent 5 percent. Cylinders cost $300 per inch and must be at least 2 inches long. No cylinder may be partially or totally on axis with another cylinder within 2 inches of it. A cylinder's influence occurs perpendicular to its axis only. (See Figure 1) Each separate cylinder costs $50 per month to maintain.

Cubes within 1½ inches of a sphere 1½ inches in diameter may increase their rent 20 percent. Spheres cost $1,000 each. Spheres must be at least 4½ inches apart. All dimensions are taken face to face.

Each cube should be numbered for purposes of tabulation, and all numbers should be visible from outside the structure. Numbers are considered visible if they can be viewed from an angle of not less than 30 degrees. (See Figure 2)

All rent bonuses are calculated against the basic rental rate of $250 per month.

Unit characteristics: (1½)3 cubes cost $12,000 and rent for $250; 1x2-inch (min.) cylinders cost $300 an inch and $50 a month to maintain; spheres, 1½-inch D, cost $1,000.

Bonuses are given for the following: 15 percent for a cylinder @ ½ inch, 5 percent for a cylinder @ 1½ inches, 20 percent for a sphere @ 1½ inches, 10 percent for south orientation and 15 percent for south-west orientation.

Gender Issues in Teaching Architectural History

Karen Kingsley
Tulane University

This essay looks at gender issues in the teaching of architectural history. It argues that when perspectives and materials from scholarship on women are brought into the traditional curriculum, our knowledge of both history and the process of architectural production are enlarged. Using Peggy McIntosh's successful model for curriculum revision in the liberal arts, the architectural history syllabus is evaluated and ideas are proposed that would lead to a more integrative curriculum. Bias and exclusion in some of the more popular recent texts in architectural history are examined and alternative readings are suggested. The issues raised are applicable, too, for rethinking teaching approaches and attitudes in the design studio.

Recently I have been researching the characteristics and perception of the American city as it is described in turn-of-the-century travel books written by middle-class European visitors. These travel books, designed both to inform and entertain, created the image of the American city for their audience. In reading these narrative accounts a number of significant issues emerged. One of these issues is that men and women seem to exhibit fundamental differences in their experience, perception, and interpretation of the built environment.

For example, male travel writers invariably focus on the organization of a city's landscape, on its streets, methods of transportation, and its monuments. Their cities, a collection of isolated and disparate parts, are almost unpeopled. In contrast, females characterize, interpret, and evoke the city through its relationship with nature (parks and open spaces) and through its people. The city's neighborhoods, its streets, and its buildings are unified through the human presence into a more organic and complex composition of place. The male, then, constructs and perpetuates one particular set of experiences and meanings; the female, another. The male experience focuses on public institutions and the individual buildings that represent those institutions, the female on the relationships embodied in the institutions. Two distinct visions of American cities are presented in these travel books. Encountering these differences led me to consider the reasons behind them.

Recent scholarship on women in such disciplines as anthropology and psychology substantiates these differences, emphasizing that men and women have different approaches to thinking and structuring experience, and different ways of organizing knowledge. For example, the Harvard University psychologist Carol Gilligan in her pioneer work, *In a Different Voice*, argues that men's and women's two disparate modes of analyzing experience affect their moral development and values and views of the world.[1] Gilligan extracts from her research on families to show that females have an affiliative relationship with their parents, while the male process of development is one of separation and thus greater emphasis on independence and autonomy. She maintains that females pay more attention to context in making judgments and place a greater value on relationships and interdependence. Thus, in general women and men are different in the way they think, in the way they connect with other people, and in their values. Her research shows that women understand the world in a more interconnected way. Scholars in a wide variety of fields, especially the social sciences, have continued to expand our knowledge of gender difference.[2]

The body of evidence regarding these fundamental differences in experience and interpretation makes imperative a serious reevaluation of our teaching programs to make them more gender inclusive. Architectural education lags far behind other disciplines in curriculum revision. Changes have been successfully achieved in such fields as literature and history and, more recently, in the sciences.[3] A recently published study by the Association of American Colleges stresses the urgency of curriculum revision.[4] The study focuses on the education of women for traditionally male fields and points out many problems within higher education including sex-role stereotyping, the quality of the campus environment, and gender biased curricula. Among its recommendations are significant changes in curriculum materials. Moreover, the increasing number of women entering the architectural profession and the radical changes taking place in work, social, and family patterns make the issue of a gender inclusive curriculum particularly pressing.

Florence Howe has emphasized that the possibilities for female and male students are defined more obviously within the liberal arts curriculum. Here women are presented with an interpretation of history in which they do not all appear, or in which their particular values are not given recognition.[5] On that basis, it seems especially fitting to discuss the placing of women and women's ideas and values specifically within the history/theory component of the curriculum.

Architectural history/theory syllabi invariably utilize the great monuments and/or great men approach, isolating and objectifying designer, group, and work. It is a male-centered curriculum from a male perspective.

It ignores the differences in the way women learn as well as women's contributions to the built environment. Inevitably this monumental approach is exclusive because it provides only a partial view of the making of our environment. Fortunately, there is now a growing body of new scholarship in the history of women which can enrich and expand our perspectives.

The curriculum research of Peggy McIntosh at the Wellesley College Center for Research on Women provides an appropriate model for transforming our teaching, and McIntosh's scheme is still the only comprehensive approach to curriculum change. McIntosh has identified five phases of change that occur when perspectives and materials from scholarship on women are brought into the traditional curriculum.[6] Although designed for the liberal arts disciplines these five phases offer a model for rethinking the history and theory of architecture courses. The history courses, in turn, can act as a catalyst for considering ways in which more integrative approaches can have impact on the teaching of studio-design classes. It is a model, too, that can be used to make our curricula more racially inclusive.

First, I will outline these five phases and then discuss each in greater depth as they pertain specifically to the history of architecture curriculum. Concurrently, I will comment on some of the most widely used history texts and suggest some alternative readings. In order of complexity the five phases are as follows: 1) the absence of women in the curriculum; 2) the inclusion of notable women as defined within traditional frameworks; 3) the definition of women as "problem" or "minority" in order to explain their absence; 4) the inclusion of less traditional sources and inclusion of women's realm of experience as subject of study; and finally 5) a synthesis of all four stages, or history reconsidered.[7] Architectural history is at phase one or two now.

The first of McIntosh's phases is what she calls "womanless" history. This is history taught without any attention to the products, contributions, or experience of women. It is the kind of history perpetuated in the latest contribution to history of architecture surveys: Marvin Trachtenberg and Isabelle Hyman's *Architecture: From Prehistory to Post-Modernism*.[8]

Trachtenberg and Hyman are both gender and racially exclusive. In their text they discuss only monuments, not industrial buildings nor smaller residential buildings. Yet even their descriptions of monuments are incomplete. For example, with any discussion of Mies van der Rohe's work of the 1920s and 1930s there should be recognition of Lilly Reich's collaboration with Mies. Curiously there is no mention of her at all. Trachtenberg and Hyman discuss Mies' passion for perfection of "structure, proportions and detail" and after a lengthy formal analysis of, for example, the Barcelona Pavilion conclude that it is ". . . a sumptuous variety of masterfully used materials . . . contrasting colors and textures of the materials . . . ."[9] Yet it was Reich who through her contributions in precisely these particulars of color and textures proved the "master" in the use of materials. The essence of Mies' work was the inclusiveness of his designs and Reich played a major role. So why did she disappear into the void?

Omission or, at best, minimal or superficial recognition of women architects or designers is not unique to Trachtenberg and Hyman. For example, Peter Blake in *The Master Builders* reduces Reich's contribution to one sentence: "Lilly Reich, the brilliant furniture designer who had collaborated with Mies on some of the exhibitions in the 1920s, was among those waiting for him."[10] Blake's book was first published in 1960 at the height of a time of monumentalization and heroization of both buildings and architects. Within such a patriarchal climate women inevitably were ignored.[11] What is more disturbing is that this neglect of women's contributions continues. A sampling of recent standard texts on either architecture or furniture design (a field in which women played a prominent role, as Charlotte Perriand and Eileen Gray attest) will show the neglect of or, at best, only partial recognition of women designers.

Once the neglect of women is recognized, the second phase of curriculum change begins with a search for the missing women according to traditional measures of excellence. The question posed at this stage is "Who are the great women?" Who should be included? Essentially, this phase consists of adding on to existing data within traditional frameworks. There are several ways to go about adding women to the curriculum and each has its own set of advantages and disadvantages.

One method is to devote a special lecture in, say, a semester of some thirty lectures to the work of women architects. A somewhat more sophisticated (or less simplistic) method is to include the work of a woman architect at the seemingly appropriate point. Among the designers who should be included are Lilly Reich, Charlotte Perriand, Margaret MacDonald Mackintosh, Julia Morgan (it is significant that San Simeon is still described first in terms of its client—William Randolph Hearst—and not by its architect, whereas such "palaces" as the Breakers or Biltmore are identified primarily by their architect Richard M. Hunt), Gertrude Jekyll, and Eleanor Raymond. As well, any discussion of the design and development of nineteenth-century residential architecture must include Catharine Beecher. Her role, along with her sister Harriet Beecher Stowe, in the redesign of the house and especially the kitchen, and in domestic ideology, is crucial to a proper appreciation of domestic planning of the era.

Yet few of these women make it into the history texts. Beecher is the most consistently recognized woman designer in the texts. For example, she features almost as large as Davis and Downing in Spiro Kostof's discussion of residential architecture in his *A History of Architecture: Settings and Rituals*.[12] Trachtenberg and Hyman, of course, by excluding vernacular architecture in their history of monuments, omit Beecher. She is accorded proper recognition in Leland Roth's collection of primary sources in his *America Builds* and the extract from Beecher's writing can be given as required class reading.[13] But Beecher may be the most visible because she is associated with domestic ideology and therefore exemplifies properly "feminine" virtues. Moreover, she did not consider herself an architect.

For twentieth-century history, Kenneth Frampton's *Modern Architecture: A Critical History* is the most gender inclusive history text.[14] He focuses on formal considerations and theoretical writings but does give recognition, although brief, to some women designers. He includes Jekyll, MacDonald, Reich, and Perriand. This recognition is one of the reasons I use it as the basic required text in my architectural survey class.[15]

Frampton comes close to "mainstreaming"—that is, weaving into his flow of history—women designers throughout his text. The crudity of the add-on method—devoting a separate chapter or section to women's work or issues—is typified by Paul Venable Turner's well-received book *Campus: An American Planning Tradition* on the development of American, primarily male, campus design.[16] In his preface, Turner talks about the campus as if it is a generic term. This is not borne out in the rest of the book. Turner's "campus" of title and text is gender and racially specific. His book essentially is about men's colleges and he minimizes both women's colleges as well as historically Black colleges. On page 133 Turner reveals his single lens vision when he introduces a section entitled "Coeducation and Women's Colleges."

In his little section on women's colleges, Turner notes the contradiction in the need for a large single building and the desire for a home-like atmosphere. But besides the many small parlors and drawing rooms for the "intimate and domestic" atmosphere that he mentions, of what does this home-like character consist? What are the specific formal qualities that give a domestic or "feminine" imagery to a large institutional building? Are we to construe the word "feminine" to mean home-like or as designating that a building has an appropriate scale? Even more interesting, why was it necessary to make women's colleges look home-like? Is that still necessary? Helen Lefkowitz Horowitz's study on women's colleges, *Alma Mater*, and her recent article on Scripps College and Cal Tech can provide some of those answers.[17]

But whether women architects are integrated throughout a text or appended in a separate section, and while both methods at least showcase women designers, new problems arise. Incomplete methods of integration have the unintended effect of distorting the historical picture, for they give a weight to women as professional architects disproportionate to their numbers and diminish their actual role and contributions. These systems make it appear that there were really far more women practicing architecture than in fact there were. Very few women have been—or are today for that matter—practicing architects or designers and those few who have been, are exceptions. This, then, is an issue in itself that must be addressed in order to understand properly the history of our built environment. It is not enough just to notice the women, or name them; it is their very absence from professional architectural practice that raises the larger issues.

At this point, one realizes that the "he" and "him" referred to through the history of architecture are gender specific terms, not generic terms. Where were the women? Why are there so few women architects? Not just great women architects, but architects at all? And why are the few who were architects, invisible? These are phase three questions.

What happened that Lilly Reich could be excluded from the text books? Is it because the recognition of her presence deemphasizes the isolation of Mies van der Rohe's talent? The work of Lilly Reich is important in itself, but examining Reich's work in relation to Mies also enlarges our knowledge of Mies van der Rohe. In addition, her work tells us something about the collaborative nature of modern architecture, and the success of bringing different values to the design process. This is just as true for countless other women designers who worked in collaboration with, or side by side with, men. While it is often difficult to disentangle exactly who did what in any given collaborative work, the recognition of the woman's contribution is invariably diminished and often lost.

For example, why are significant pieces of furniture (e.g., *grand comfort, basculant, chaise longue*) which Charlotte Perriand designed with Le Corbusier attributed only to him in virtually all the textbooks, when in the journals of the 1920s her name is written as large as his? Why is Gertrude Jekyll not mentioned along with Edwin Lutyens when his houses are discussed? Lutyens needed Jekyll's lush gardens to bring out his picturesque houses as Jane Brown has shown in her book *Gardens of a Golden Afternoon*.[18] He also needed Jekyll's encouragement and psychological support to realize his potential. This is equally true for Louis Kahn who was only able to realize his creative possibilities through his close personal and working relationship with Anne Tyng.[19] And Aino Marsio Aalto's support of and collaboration with Alvar Aalto—they worked jointly on a number of buildings, including the Paimio Sanatorium and the Villa Mairea—are rarely given proper recognition in texts or lectures.[20]

Why do we show Robert Delaunay's paintings of the Eiffel Tower to illustrate the relationship of art to architecture and to life in the early-twentieth century and not the designs of Sonia Delaunay which more directly speak of that integration of modern thought and design? Sonia Delaunay broke the boundaries between the fine and the applied arts by showing that abstract theories of form and color could be expressed in textiles, ceramics, and costume and clothing design. Where is Eleanor Raymond in a discussion of American Modernism, or Eileen Gray in European?

And at phase three the issue of the sexual division of labor can be addressed: that is, why, when men and women cooperate, do women usually design the so-called "feminine" things, like the gardens or the interiors? Why was the design of landscape not considered an unladylike activity? And why do we place less value on these aspects of the built environment?

All of these questions are intimately linked as well with the lack of opportunity for women to receive an architectural education. This issue can be examined in the context of teaching about the École des Beaux-Arts curriculum, especially as it was adopted in the United States in the late-nineteenth century. And, at that point, the Cambridge School of Architecture and Landscape Architecture, established by Henry Frost in 1917 for the education of women architects, can be introduced, which will elicit thoughts as to what an appropriate education for an architect should comprise.[21] The Cambridge School's curriculum combined architecture and landscape design. And within the architectural component of this curriculum, domestic design was emphasized. Frost's belief that women were particularly suited to domestic architecture was widespread. It was part of the recurring debate on women's capabilities for practicing architecture. At the turn of the century popular architecture journals evaluated negatively women's emotional and physical stamina for practicing architecture. The topic was revived after the First World War in a different guise. This time it was argued that women lacked imagination and artistic sensibility. This debate in general raises a crucial issue, though, that gets to the core of architectural education: the debate between design by rational principles and design by intuition, or what might also be called the scientific versus the artistic temperament.

In phase three, courses focused on women emerge: the "Women in . . ." and the "Women and . . ." courses; courses with such titles as "Women and the Built Environment" or "Women in the Arts." Clearly, courses such as these can be described as being at a primitive level in an ideal curriculum or world.[22] But I do think such courses are necessary and valuable, particularly in the South (where I teach) with its more entrenched conservative attitudes and suspicion of women who assume non-volunteer public roles. One special virtue in the separate course is that students, even those not taking the course, realize that there is an issue being addressed here even if they are hesitant to address it themselves. Becoming aware of the absence of women's contributions to architecture helps us to pose new questions. What was the process of selection in writing our history texts? Who wrote them? How well, in fact, do these texts tell us about our history, about our built environment?

So far, I have suggested some ideas that can be developed to bring us to phase four of curriculum transformation. Two possible and promising areas that could be explored further to integrate women into the curriculum are patronage and residential architecture.

Patronage is one area in architectural history that is treated in a very uneven manner, and it is one in which women had a large and profound impact on our built environment. Unfortunately, a great deal more research is needed. Yet what we do know can radically change the way we look at certain buildings. For example, the importance of Hampstead Garden Suburb is usually described in terms of the formal qualities of the houses and the layout of the streets. Architectural historians know that Barry Parker and Raymond Unwin along with Edwin Lutyens were the designers. But not generally known is that the Suburb's founder, Henrietta Barnett, saw it as an extension of her ideas as a social worker with the poor.[23] She conceived the suburb as an opportunity to meld the social classes and to improve culturally and spiritually the working class. And it was she who insisted on preserving the natural beauty of the landscape, recognizing the regenerative powers of contact with nature. These facts open up some very interesting questions. For example, how, in this or other cases, does the client of residential buildings perceive his or her architect and vice versa? What kind of people are we designing for? What is the structure of the family? How is that changing along with work patterns? What kinds of values and hopes do clients have? What groups or kinds of people are included or excluded from such suburbs as Hampstead Garden Suburb, or Oak Park, or Tuxedo Park, or Palos Verdes? And in what ways have the exclusions affected the shaping of our buildings, of our environment, and our attitudes? Such issues are rarely raised in history classes when talking about residential architecture, yet they have had profound effects on the nature of our society as well as on the history of architecture and they have far-reaching implications for the architectural profession. Shifting the primary center of analysis from artist to audience and from architect to client enlarges our perspective.

Many critical architectural ideas can be raised in an examination of residential architecture and it is one in which there is already a rich source of alternative information. Dolores Hayden's and Gwendolyn Wright's scholarship and publications are prime examples.[24] Both writers clarify relationships between house design, urban growth, cultural and economic factors, and family and work structures. For example, Gwendolyn Wright's chapter "The Minimal House" in her *Moralism and the Model Home* makes any study of Frank Lloyd Wright's residential architecture more comprehensive. For the same time period, the chapter "The Heyday of the Decorators" in Isabelle Anscombe's *A Woman's Touch* provides a fuller picture of the design of turn-of-the-century grand mansions by looking at the role of women interior designers and clients in the creation of this building type.[25] By disregarding women's roles in the formation and diffusion of culture, the complexity of that culture is reduced.

Phase four will only be reached when the curriculum has been enlarged to include women architects, when the correct attributions are made, and women's contributions given proper representation. Much of the necessary work to achieve that goal is now being done. Stage four is also the place where the inadequacy of the great men/great building model of history is glaringly clear. At this stage the adequacy of accepted conceptual structures can be challenged and new paradigms tested. We can question the validity of our current definitions of historical periods, of greatness. We can consider what new categories need to be added to the study of architectural history. We can ask what cultural factors work on the designer rather than how the designer works on the culture. And not only can we examine women's experience and contributions but also women's interpretation of that experience and those contributions.

Phase five signals the emergence of a new, fully integrated history where these questions no longer need to be asked. That history is still all speculative; nobody knows what it looks like. But, if a genuine transformation of the curriculum is still in the future, integrating women into the curriculum at the phase four level now enriches our understanding of the relationship between architecture and environment. The entire curriculum is enlarged by raising new thoughts about the theory and practice of architecture.

Acknowledgments
I thank Sandra J. Peacock, Beth Willinger, and Linda S. Flynn for their comments on this essay.

Notes

1. Carol Gilligan, *In a Different Voice: Psychological Theory and Women's Development* (Cambridge, MA: Harvard University Press, 1982).
2. Joan Tronto brings up to date the discussion on moral expression and gender differences, and reviews all the important literature; see Joan C. Tronto, "Beyond Gender Difference to a Theory of Care," *Signs* 12, no. 4 (Summer 1987): 644–86. Nancy M. Henley's review essay examines the controversies in new research on cognition and gender issues; see Nancy M. Henley, "Psychology and Gender," *Signs* 11, no. 1 (Autumn 1985): 101–119.
3. See, for example, Ellen Carol Dubois et al., *Feminist Scholarship Kindling in the Groves of Academe* (Urbana, IL: University of Illinois Press, 1985). For a thorough review of issues in art history see Tholio Gouma-Peterson and Patricio Mathews, "The Feminist Critique of Art History," *Art Bulletin* LXIX, no. 3 (September 1987): 326–357.
4. Julie Kuhn Ehrhart and Bernice R. Sandler, *Looking For More Than A Few Good Women in Traditionally Male Fields,* Project on the Status and Education of Women (Washington, D.C.: Association of American Colleges, 1987).
5. Florence Howe, "Feminist Scholarship—The Extent of the Revolution," *Liberal Education and the New Scholarship on Women: Issues and Constraints in Institutional Change,* A Report of the Wingspread Conference, Racine, Wisconsin, October 22–24, 1981 (Washington, D.C.: Association of American Colleges, n.d. (c. 1982)), 5–21, 9.
6. Peggy McIntosh, "The Study of Women: Processes of Personal and Curricula Revision," *The Forum for Liberal Education* 6, no. 5 (April 1984): 2–4.
7. It needs to be emphasized that it is not necessary to begin at phase one and move through the five in sequence, nor is it required to step in every one of them. Curriculum revision can be initiated at, for example, phase three.
8. Marvin Trachtenberg and Isabelle Hyman, *Architecture: From Prehistory to Post-Modernism* (New York: Harry N. Abrams, 1986).
9. Trachtenberg and Isabelle Hyman, 532-533.
10. Peter Blake, *The Master Builders* (New York: W.W. Norton & Co., 1976 (originally published 1960)), 226–227.
11. This issue of monumentalization and omission belongs to a larger debate, one begun in the 1960s by Robert Venturi in *Complexity and Contradiction in Architecture* (New York: The Museum of Modern Art, 1966).
12. Spiro Kostof, *A History of Architecture: Settings and Rituals* (New York: Oxford University Press, 1985), 664.
13. Leland Roth, ed., *America Builds: Source Documents in American Architecture and Planning* (New York: Harper and Row, 1983), 57–68.
14. Kenneth Frampton, *Modern Architecture: A Critical History* (London: Thames and Hudson, 1980 (revised 1985)).
15. For a critical review of some of the basic studies on twentieth century architecture see Natalie Kempen and Elizabeth G. Grossman, *Feminism and Methodology: Dynamics of Change in the History of Art and Architecture* Wellesley College Center for Research on Women, Working Paper no. 122 (Wellesley, MA: Wellesley College, 1983). This study also includes a bibliography covering the years 1960 to 1983 on women architects and issues relating to women and architecture.
16. Paul Venable Turner, *Campus: An American Planning Tradition* (Cambridge, MA: MIT Press, 1984), 133–140. The text is minimal, six of the eight pages are devoted to illustrations.
17. Helen Lefkowitz Horowitz, *Alma Mater: Design and Experience in the Women's Colleges from Their Nineteenth Century Beginnings to the 1930s* (New York: Alfred A. Knopf, 1984); and Helen Lefkowitz Horowitz, "Designing for the Genders: Curricula and Architecture at Scripps College and the California Institute of Technology," *Pacific Historical Review* LIV, no. 4 (November 1985): 439–461.
18. Jane Brown, *Gardens of a Golden Afternoon: The Story of a Partnership, Edwin Lutyens and Gertrude Jekyll* (London: A. Lone, 1982).
19. Alexandro Tyng, *Beginnings: Louis I. Kahn's Philosophy of Architecture* (New York: John Wiley & Sons, Inc., 1984), especially page 21.
20. Ulla Markelin et al., *Profiles: Pioneering Women Architects from Finland* (Helsinki: Museum of Finnish Architecture, 1983), 56–59. I thank William C. Miller for telling me about this catalog.
21. Gwendolyn Wright's essay on architectural education for women is appropriate reading for both history and studio courses. Gwendolyn Wright, "On the Fringe of the Profession: Women in American Architecture" in *The Architect*, ed. Spiro Kostof (New York: Oxford University Press, 1977), 280–308. Also, see Susanna Torre, *Women in American Architecture: A Historic and Contemporary Perspective* (New York: Watson-Guptill, 1977). For landscape architecture see Catherine M.

Howett, "Careers in Landscape Architecture: Recovering for Women What the 'Ladies Won and Lost,'" in *Feminist Visions: Toward a Transformation of the Liberal Arts Curriculum* Fowlkes, eds. Diana L. Fowlkes and Charlotte S. McClure (Tuscaloosa, AL: University of Alabama Press, 1984), 134–148, 207.

22. In McIntosh's schema this is the case but other scholars would argue otherwise. For example, Deborah Rosenfelt maintains that "the materials, ideas, theories, and perspective (of women's studies) cannot be 'mainstreamed' in a way that approximates the full complexity and scope of feminist scholarship," and that autonomous programs are essential. See Deborah Rosenfelt, "What Women's Studies Programs Do that Mainstreaming Can't," *Women's Studies International Forum* 7, no. 3 (1984): 168.

23. R. L. Reiss, "Henrietta Octavia Barnett and Hampstead Garden Suburb," *Town and Country Planning* 25 (July 1957): 277–282.

24. Of their publications the following are especially pertinent: Dolores Hayden, *The Grand Domestic Revolution: A History of Feminist Designs for American Homes, Neighborhoods, and Cities* (Cambridge, MA: MIT Press, 1981); Dolores Hayden, *Redesigning the American Dream: The Future of Housing, Work, and Family Life*n (New York: W.W. Norton, 1984); Gwendolyn Wright, *Building the Dream: A Social History of Housing in America* (New York: Pantheon, 1981); and Gwendolyn Wright, *Moralism and the Model Home: Domestic Architecture and Cultural Conflict in Chicago, 1873-1913* (Chicago: University of Chicago Press, 1980).

25. Isabelle Anscombe, *A Woman's Touch: Women in Design from 1860 to the Present Day* (New York: Viking Penguin, 1984).

Black Architects: An Endangered Species

Robert Traynham Coles
University of Kansas

In 1968, five years after I started my architectural practice, I attended the National Convention of the American Institute of Architects in Portland, Oregon—I was one of less than a half dozen black architects who attended this event out of almost 4,000 persons. It was here that the late Whitney M. Young, Jr., the Civil Rights Leader and executive director of the National Urban League, embarrassed the nation's architects by saying:

> You are not a profession that has distinguished itself by your social and civic contributions to the cause of civil rights, and I am sure this does not come to you as a shock. ...You are most distinguished by your thunderous silence and your complete irrelevance. ...You are employers, you are key people in the planning of our cities today. You share the responsibility for the mess we are in, in terms of the white noose around the central city. We didn't just suddenly get this situation. It was carefully planned.[1]

Only a month later in June of 1968 the Report of the Kerner Commission—named after the Illinois governor who headed the Commission to Study the Urban Riots in the United States which had swept Newark, Detroit and Los Angeles—reported to then President Lyndon B. Johnson that "this nation is moving toward two societies—one black, one white, separate and unequal."[2]

Last year, this nation celebrated the twentieth anniversary of both of those events. The anniversary of the Kerner Commission Report did not go by unnoticed, and most of the in-depth news reporting on the event indicated that it was a prophecy come true—that we had indeed moved toward two separate and unequal societies, in spite of all of the civil rights legislation and rhetoric to the contrary.

Our cities and our suburbs are perhaps more segregated than they were in 1968. Our urban public school systems are increasingly becoming more black, and the opposite is happening on our university campuses, where the black enrollment has dramatically shrunk in the last decade.

An article in *Architecture*, the journal of the American Institute of Architects, on "The Plight of Minority Architects," in April 1985, stated,

> Now, almost 20 years later, if Young were alive, he probably would be aghast, though not surprised, at the situation for minorities in the profession. Their numbers have not appreciably increased, and, given the current anti-affirmative action posture in this country, it seems highly probable that the situation will get worse before it gets better.[3]

Last May, the American Institute of Architects held their annual convention in New York City; and this time, over 10,000 persons attended the event—the largest in their history—but there was nary a word spoken about the twentieth anniversary of the remarks of Whitney Young, Jr. And even though the event was held in the city with the largest black population in the country, and one of the largest groups of black architectural firms, again not more than a score of black architects attended the event. In fact, the focal point of the A.I.A.'s minority thrust at the convention was an elaborate exhibit on "Women in Architecture."

Between 1968 and 1974, spurred on by the words of Whitney Young, A.I.A., the national architectural organization mounted a major thrust to increase the number of blacks in the profession. Black architects were encouraged to join the A.I.A. and were elevated to major positions in that organization. Four black architects were elected as A.I.A. vice presidents in the past twenty years; one was elected to the board of directors; an A.I.A. Minority Scholarship Program was established; and major educational programs were aimed at the elementary and secondary schools to identify potential minority architectural students. Universities opened their enrollment to an increasing number of black students and put in place support programs to ease their transition into integrated schools and an integrated profession.

Unfortunately, it all came to a screeching halt in the late seventies with the recession that swept the architectural profession. From 1974 to 1976, I served in the newly created post of deputy vice president for minority affairs, the highest staff position that a black has ever held in the national A.l.A., but because of the recession, my task was not to bring more blacks into the profession, but to develop new programs to keep those who already were in practice. The post was abolished after my term of office, perhaps a reflection of the organization's lack of commitment to an ongoing effort to increase the number of blacks in the profession.

With the conservative tenure of President Richard Nixon, who in 1973—in one of his first acts after taking office for the second time—put a moratorium on low and moderate income housing, one of the mainstays of black professionals, the pattern was set.

Fortunately for black architects, Nixon's secretary of transportation was William Coleman, a black Philadelphia lawyer who initiated the most effective Affirmative Action program in public works by mandating that fifteen percent of all federal funds for mass transit go to minority firms. As major new mass transit systems were built in Washington, Atlanta, Baltimore, and even Buffalo, black architects began to thrive again. However, President Ronald Reagan, elected in 1980, dismantled the remaining low and moderate income programs as well as drastically reducing funding for mass transportation projects in this country as resources were directed toward building up the defense establishment.

In January of this year, the United States Supreme Court set the direction for the future of affirmative action when it struck down as unconstitutional a minority subcontracting program implemented by the City of Richmond, Virginia. By a 6 to 3 majority, the court ruled that Richmond's Minority Business Utilization Plan, which required the city's prime construction contractors to set aside 30 percent of each contract to one or more minority firms, violated the Fourteenth Amendment's Equal Protection clause. A similar law was declared unconstitutional in Atlanta, which had one of the most effective Affirmative Action programs in the country.

In 1970, according to the Department of Labor, there were approximately 50,000 architects in the United States. Of that number, 2 percent or approximately 1,000 were black, perhaps 3 percent, or less than 1,500, were female; and the other 95 percent were white males. In the last two decades, the number of architects in the United States has doubled, including the number of females who are approaching 5,000, and the number of black architects has grown to only about 2,000. In 1984, there were approximately 107,000 architects in this country. Of that, 2.4 percent or 2,568 were black. I find it difficult to substantiate these statistics, based upon my own observations.

Minority enrollment in the schools of architecture which increased to almost ten percent in the late seventies has fallen under 5 percent, even though female enrollment has increased from 10 percent in 1970 to 25 percent to 33 percent in some of the universities. This decrease in black enrollment is of major concern and is in evidence everywhere.

When I first taught in Kansas in 1969, I met with a dozen black architectural students, and saw many other black students on campus. Twenty years later, I am told that there are ten black students out of 600 in the School of Architecture, although in my three visits, I have seen less than half that number. It is the same at Ohio State University where I spoke last fall, and even less at the University at Buffalo, New York State's only public School of Architecture.

Black architects are an endangered species because those who are practicing are cut off from the mainstream of society that controls the resources that are necessary for architecture, just as the black community is isolated from those resources. Their clients are not the IBM's, the G. M.'s, the G. E.'s. Those who are in practice have a special practice which is focused on public works because of the lack of access to private resources. These practices flourished briefly during the seventies and early eighties when blacks obtained political power in our urban centers and mandated that an increased percentage of their contracts go to black entrepreneurs. However, as public spending shrinks, as affirmative action programs are struck down, and as black political power diminishes in our urban centers, black architects will be even more severely threatened.

Because of the concentration of blacks in urban public schools with their low standards of excellence, those who might be expected to go into the profession are crippled before they reach secondary school.

This crisis is of historic proportions because it threatens the profession which in order to survive must begin to look like the society that it must serve, and that society is becoming increasingly minority. It is expected that Dallas, Houston, and Los Angeles all will have minority majorities by the year 2000. It threatens our nation as well, for we can ill afford not to maximize the human resources that we have. We need the best and the brightest to compete, regardless of race.

In February, I attended the first Annual Awards Banquet honoring African American architects hosted by Howard University in Washington, D.C. to celebrate the 78th anniversary of the founding of its School of Architecture, the first of nine black schools of architecture. Two-thirds of the approximately thirty African American fellows of the A.I.A. were in attendance and they had the opportunity to relate their experiences in architecture to an afternoon symposium that was videotaped. They recounted their struggle to become members of this elite profession, and their continuing struggles to remain in it. The most moving experience of all was when Dean Harry Robinson of Howard University's School of Architecture asked the African American architects at the banquet to stand up—and several hundred of them did, which represented a significant percentage of the black architects practicing in America. The event was summed up best by Cleveland architect Robert Madison, a Harvard graduate and African American Fellow who received the firm award for 35 years of service, who said, "What is significant this evening is that blacks are being honored for their professional achievements as opposed to their athletic prowess."

Black architects share the dream that the late Reverend Martin Luther King, Jr. had. In 1963, the year that I started my architectural practice, he said in his famous speech at the Lincoln Memorial in Washington, D.C.,

> "I still have a dream. It is a dream rooted in the American dream, that one day this nation will rise up and live out the true meaning of its creed: 'We hold these truths to be self-evident, that all men are created equal.'"

But, as Lawrence's own Langston Hughes, the poet laureate of Black America wrote,

> What happens to a
> dream deferred—
> Does it dry
> up and die, like a
> raisin in the sun?[4]

Black architects are indeed an endangered species.

Editors' note: also published as Robert Traynham Coles, "Black Architects, an Endangered Species," editorial, *Progressive Architecture Magazine* (July 1989): 7; originally given as a lecture at the University of Kansas, where Coles served as the 1989 Langston Hughes Distinguished Professor, Robert Traynham Coles, "The Practice of Architecture in a Post-Industrial City: The Profile of a Black Architect – An Endangered Species," University of Kansas Lecture, March 28, 1989, mentioned in Richard K. Dozier, "The Circle and the Square: Robert Traynham Coles, FAIA" in *Robert Traynham Coles: Architect*, exhibition catalog, Burchfield-Penney Art Center (Buffalo, NY: Buffalo State College, 1996), unpaginated.

Notes
1. Whitney M. Young, Jr., Speech at the 1968 AIA National Convention.
2. *Report of the National Advisory Commission on Civil Disorders,* Otto Kerner, chair (Washington, D.C: The National Criminal Justice Reference Service, 1968), 1.
3. Nora Richter Greer, "The Plight of Minority Architects" *Architecture* 74, no. 4 (April 1985): 58–61.
4. Langston Hughes, "Harlem," from *The Collected Poems of Langston Hughes* (New York: Knopf, 1994).

The Crisis of Interdisciplinary Histiography

Mark Jarzombek
Cornell University

I outline the discursive logic of the two principal ways architectural theory has been conceived: historiographic critique and interdisciplinary historiography. Post-Renaissance theory-making fell into a pattern I call historiographic critique, which centered around the humanist imperative to link historical knowledge, social criticism, and architectural practice. In the nineteenth century, historiographic critique became increasingly incapable of creating viable conceptions of the past and was replaced by interdisciplinary historiography. The advantages and disadvantages of interdisciplinary historiography can already be seen in the work of Ludwig Mies van der Rohe. He abolished narrow historicism in favor of consciously created dependencies between philosophy, history, and architectural theory drawn out over various times, cultures, languages, and academic disciplines. Unfortunately, the paradoxes inherent in the discursive logic of interdisciplinary historiography left it open to manipulations by intellectual formalists, in whose hands theory came to be treated as a discourse separate from its own historicity.

Syllables of Time

The "syllables of time," Augustine explained in his *Confessions*, determine the historical boundedness of human experience. One cannot escape the "presence of things past."[1] Only angels, according to Augustine's argument, exist in privileged exclusion, as they alone were not subject to time. Augustine's conception of "things past" went beyond then current notions of history as mythology, or as a litany of meritorious deeds and celebrated events. Though he was careful to warn of narcissism and "looking-glass phantasms," he felt that history was illuminated—indeed constituted—by a need in the present; in his words, history is "that which makes the past credible by means of the present."[2]

Western philosophy never unanimously embraced Augustine's position. René Descartes, for example was convinced that human rationality would ultimately push history into the realm of trivia; David Hume interpreted all human actions in the clean world of quasi-scientific analysis; Immanuel Kant envisioned history narrowly, as the actualization of reason towards its theoretical potential; and Rudolf Carnap imagined a rational and secular world liberated from what he perceived to be the interpretative ambiguities of the metaphysical speculations associated with history.

There have been others, however, who have accepted history as an agent in existence and who have partaken, for better and for worse, in the discourse of its readings. Since the Renaissance, architectural theorists have traditionally stood on this side of the debate, invariably interlocking an understanding of history with a definition of praxis. This was even true of some of the modernists, who may have rejected historical forms, but not historiographic thinking that makes knowledge of the past instrumental to acting in the present.

In recent years, underlying concepts about the nature and goals of theory have changed. Architectural theory seems increasingly to be envisioned not only in opposition to history, but also as immune from any historiographic knowledge that might temporalize theory and undermine its alleged commitment to the "present." In essence, philosophy *of* history has been replaced by philosophy *or* history; theory sees itself as allied with philosophy, and has left history for scholars, antiquarians, preservationists, and neoclassical architects. Newly created doctoral programs in the theory of architecture will certainly contribute to the division, with the result that we may see a troublesome separation of the discourse on the past from the discourse on the present.

To understand the roots of our predicament, I believe we have to understand a transformation that took place in the late nineteenth century in the structure of the discourse on architectural theory. Beginning with the Renaissance, most architectural theorizing followed the logic of what I shall call historiographic critique: the humanist imperative to link historical knowledge, architectural practice, and social criticism. By the nineteenth century, historiographic critique, no longer able to sustain workable definitions of practice, gave way to interdisciplinary historiography, which was based on the idea that philosophy, history, and theory can touch the same domain of praxis. But the very advantage of interdisciplinary historiography, freeing theory from its obsessions with history, was also its principal weakness. Theory could no longer contribute to a critical historiographic perspective of its own discourse.

Historiographic Critique

Nineteenth-century Idealist philosophy was characterized by its attempt to define praxis in terms of historical consciousness. *The Communist Manifesto* (1848) by Karl Marx and Friedrich Engels, for example, begins with the word *history* ("The history of all hitherto existing society is the history of class struggle") and then moves from a historical survey of capitalism, to the theory of communism, to a critique of other forms of political change, to a final defense of communism and its particular concept of "historical action," closing with the famous directive: "Workers of the world unite." The linkage of history, theory, and praxis stood in opposition to alternative definitions of culture that aimed to interpret humanity's efforts in ahistorical contexts of rationalism or empiricism. Marx and Engels presented a picture of theory in which to understand how to act one had to know not abstract principles of reason, science, or even moral philosophy, but how history activates itself in the present. This idea was succinctly defended by Augustine Thierry in 1835: "Human societies must know where they come from in order to see where they are going."[3]

The notion of an operative conception of the past was hardly a nineteenth-century invention, but rather one of the essential platforms of humanist politics. Perhaps the earliest example of a historically informed path to praxis is the infamous uprising of Cola di Rienzo in 1347 against the Roman papacy. Rienzo's revolt was more than a populist rejection of papal authority. With Petrarch admiringly exhorting him on, Cola took his idealization of ancient republican Rome out of the library and into the streets. Lamenting the decline of Rome, and hoping to restore its former glory, Cola inspired the populace to force the pope into exile and elevate himself to leadership. In his short-lived dictatorship, Cola donned Roman garb, staged spectacular cavalcades, and made grand titular claims in an attempt to imitate Roman emperors. Petrarch hailed him as a new Brutus.[4]

Cola's rule was a farce; he did not live up to the stature of his noble predecessors, nor were popes Clement VI and his successor Innocent VI about to relinquish power to an upstart without a fight. Nevertheless, he opened a Pandora's box. He released a type of power that was based not on authority, military might, or political convention, but rather on the manipulation of history to empower a political program. Interest in ancient Rome and classical culture, for Cola, was not a product of humanist antiquarianism, but was embedded in a metaphorical and critical apparatus that enabled broad links to be made between an absent classical past and contemporary political realities.

By the late fifteenth century, almost every ruler in Italy was engaged in programmatic efforts of "past-making" that linked the knowledge of history with the knowledge of praxis; Cosimo de Medici, for example, well aware that when society can be made to comprehend its historical construction (as fake or real as it might be) it is bound to fulfill itself in response to that knowledge, used artists and architects in a calculated effort to intertwine past and present.[5]

Renaissance architectural theorists were among the first to develop operative conceptions of the past. In fact, what distinguished Renaissance architectural theories from medieval ones is the assertion that the practice of architecture depends on a conception of the history of architecture. One of the first instances in architectural theory of this type of historiography *qua* critique can be found in the writings of Filarete, the mid-fifteenth-century architectural consultant to the Dukes of Milan. The construction of the mythical cities, "Sforzinda" and "Plusiapolis," that Filarete described in his treatise, could only begin once the fictive patron had comprehended his historiographically determined role in society. Filarete devised an elegant strategy to get the message across. He described how a golden book was unearthed on the building site; this book, when translated by a scholar, revealed the layout and meaning of an ancient Plusiapolis, which of course, legitimizes the construction of a new one. Here, as with all subsequent examples of historiographic critique, we find the necessary "translation" that collapses an alien but relevant past into the present. For Filarete, the implication was that patronal power was not defined by means of divine rights, military might, or hereditary claims, as one might expect, but rather by means of a privileged understanding of the historiographic interdependencies of past and present.

Leon Battista Alberti, convinced that contemporary practice had lost itself in the hopeless confusion of *varietà e varietà*, believed that the making of a corrective theory required first the creation of a historical proposition. Accordingly, he argued that architectural elements, such as columns, walls, apertures, and roofs, for example, were developed at the same time primitive society first began to differentiate public from private, and religious from secular. Subsequent developments in architecture paralleled society's own development towards increasingly complex forms. It was the failure on the part of contemporary architects to recognize the process as fundamentally historical that had induced them to explore the "infinite possibilities" now open to them, defy nature, and design "out of whim." The ideal Albertian architect—should he exist—while aware of *varietà* must struggle to keep society from moving too far away from its historically determined characteristics. That was the task of theory.

By the seventeenth century, the logic of historiographic critique was unmistakable. Its two primary principles were a focus on a single "correct" historical past (by the nineteenth century some variation on primitive, Roman, Greek, or Gothic architecture) and a fundamental belief in architecture as a medium of social change. Increasingly architectural theorists stood alone in their defense. The operative conception of the past, for example, was questioned by Francis Bacon, whose *New Atlantis* (1627) portrays a society in which no historical past haunts the system. Jean-Jacques Rousseau in his *Discours sur les Sciences et les Arts* (1750) rejected the contention that architecture could be an agent of beneficial change. At best, so he argued, it served to exemplify humankind's corrupt and over-civilized state.[6] As to the narrow historical focus necessary for historiographic critique, Giambattista Vico and Georg Friedrich Hegel elevated discussions of history to a plane far above the limiting obsessions of architectural historiographers.

With Marc-Antoine Laugier, architectural historiographic critique became a topos. Laugier's hut was intended, like Filarete's golden book, to collapse humankind's innocent primitive past back into the civilized world and make architecture—if not life in general— meaningful once again. But his conception of the past was so simplistic and naive-compared even with Rousseau's—that the historical vision underlying it could hardly be taken seriously by even his contemporary historians.

Historiographic critique, alienated from history, survived only as a discourse of mystification. In the early nineteenth century, it received a new breath of life in the works of Idealist philosophers, but in architecture it survived in spite of itself. It remained frozen in a narrow humanist time warp. W. N. Pugin's *Contrasts: or a Parallel Between the Noble Edifices of the Middle Ages and Corresponding Buildings of the Present Day; Shewing the Present Decay of Taste* (1836) stands at the end of the serviceability of historiographic critique. Architectural past-making, now generated almost in defiance of history, evolved into a rhetorical exercise that served only an idiosyncratic field of interests.

Interdisciplinary Historiography, Le Corbusier Versus Mies van der Rohe
In the nineteenth century, as architectural theory histories lost ground, the organization of the discourse on theory changed from one of individual theorists who synthesized history and critique, to one characterized by an ever more complex and disparate configuration of philosophers, historians, theorists, and practitioners. The new way in which theory came to be generated (and as a consequence the new way in which praxis was defined by theory) has rarely been taken into account in discussions on early modernism. The difference between Le Corbusier and Ludwig Mies van der Rohe is symptomatic of the change. Le Corbusier, though a high priest of modern architecture, had an approach to theory that belonged to the antiquated post-Renaissance tradition just discussed. In *Towards a New Architecture* (original French, 1922) he criticized contemporary architectural practice, as "an architecture no longer conscious of its own beginnings" and proceeded to generate a mythical historiography that included a "primitive man," Praxiteles and Michelangelo. Like Filarete and Laugier, Le Corbusier purposefully telescoped the past into the present. "Architecture can be found in the telephone and in the parthenon."[7] In accordance with other conventions of historiographic critique, Le Corbusier put architecture in the driver's seat of social change ending with the *de rigueur* call to reform. "Architecture or revolution."

Whereas Le Corbusier hoped to get one drunk on old wine disguised in a new bottle (and in this he was amazingly successful), Mies van der Rohe made a new potion altogether. The terms of Mies van der Rohe's thinking reflected an interdisciplinary approach to the definition of praxis. Unlike Le Corbusier, he did not construct a historiographic trajectory through time, but interwove his thoughts with ideas transferred and adapted to architecture from the academic fields of philosophy and history. This was largely due to his acquaintance with the philosopher Alois Riegl, who in turn introduced him to a range of other philosophers, such as Romano Guardini, and to a range of historians, including Heinrich Wölfflin. Mies van der Rohe was one of the first to recognize that architectural theorists, historians, and philosophers can affect the same domain of praxis. The works of the medievalist historians Karl Scheffler and Paul Ludwig Landsberg played an important role in Mies van der Rohe's thinking. not because the architecture of the Middle Ages needed to be revived, but because the neoplatonic concepts that underlay their work showed him a way to mediate his own interests in philosophy with his commitment to developing a theory suitable to modern architectural praxis.[8] Unlike Le Corbusier, who created a personal vision of architectural history, Mies van der Rohe developed methodological connections to the past, which enabled him to rely on ideas purposefully borrowed from and shared with historians and philosophers.

The Historian in the Interdisciplinary Realm
In historiographic critique, the "history" behind the definition of praxis was meant to be explicit; this was essential to its engagement with the world. In interdisciplinary historiography, there is no parallel situation as there is no single "text" behind praxis, but a multiplicity of texts and textual transformations. But among these texts, there is inevitably a history that brings philosophical inquiries into the domain of architecture. Because of the modernist ambivalence about history, however, the historian is pushed aside. Mies van der Rohe, for example, purposefully camouflaged his debt to architectural historians and was all too readily believed when he proclaimed: "The creative building artists want to have nothing, nothing whatever, to do with the aesthetic traditions of the past centuries. We leave this field without regret to the art historians."[9] It is in the work of Mies van der Rohe, consciously creating the illusion that the discourse of theory functioned on a level separate from history, that we perceive not only the beginning of complex discursive interactions between philosophy, history, and theory—what I call interdisciplinary historiography—but also the roots of our own predicament where theorists function very much like the historians they replaced, but without being called to task on it.

Despite the dependency of twentieth-century theory on history writings, the contribution of the historian became increasingly obscure. Robert Venturi's *Complexity and Contradiction in Architecture* (1966), for example, outlined a program that was a clear descendant of the late nineteenth-century ahistorical and asocial world view of Heinrich Wölfflin. Wölfflin, in turn, must be seen together with other neo-Kantians, such as Friedrich Herbart (*Schriften zur praktischen Philosophie*, 1808), Robert Zimmermann (*Allgemeine Aesthetik als Formwissenschaft*, 1865), and Wilhelm Dilthey (*Einleitung in die Geisteswissenschaften*, 1883). But Venturi, like Mies van der Rohe, placed the work of historians in the shadows, and made no attempt to scrutinize or question his thought in the intellectual tradition of Wölfflin, much less recognize its place in the nineteenth-century neo-Kantian disembodied moral worldview.

In the modern realm of architectural interdisciplinary historiography—where philosophical and historical texts are present but left invisible—there can be no precise moment of fruition, no absolute closure, and ultimately no privileging of praxis by virtue of a fully visible philosophical system, nor is there a privileging of a particular philosophy by means of a consciously programmed implementation of it in practice. Venturi's neo-Kantianism is bizarrely disconnected from the philosophical platform on which it stands. This is because each translation between philosophy, history, and theory alters the discourse in ways that leave a great deal of ambiguity as to where to find the "text" behind the discourse of practice.

In analyzing such connections between philosophy and praxis, one will find purposeful misreadings, accidental misunderstandings, blind oversights, oversimplifications, strained reasoning, ingenious connections, and bizarre misplacements. The patterns of contact between philosophy and praxis are, therefore, neither instantaneous nor necessarily logical. They do not necessarily build, nor do they necessarily simplify. Rather they unfold over time in ways that obscure their own conceptual, cultural, and textual origins. Wölfflin's thesis of "observationalism," privileging the observed object at the expense of contextual and cultural investigations, is now taken so much for granted in architectural schools that it is often mistaken for truth rather than a twentieth-century ideology based on a nineteenth-century philosophy.

Interdisciplinary historiography, as it affects architecture, is not dependent on singular authority, but on multiple layers of authorities stretched out over time, place, language, and culture. A text that demonstrates this is Sigfried Giedion's *Space, Time and Architecture* (1941). Though a defense of "modernism," it is in reality one of the last texts in an intellectual tradition that goes back at least to the eighteenth century, in particular, the philosophy of Giambattista Vico and Georg Friedrich Hegel. As with *Complexity and Contradiction*, we are dealing here with a unique type of historical problem, not merely a question of influence, linear progression, or cultural context. One should not naively think that Giedion read Vico and Hegel and was "influenced" by them. He engaged in a specific type of rewriting that involved purposeful borrowings, as well as purposeful and accidental misprisions. There is only space for the most cursory diagram to demonstrate the differences and similarities (see below).

The numerous connections and hybrid states—which this chart can only barely begin to reveal—are by no means easy to explain, especially when we look at the history of Hegelian thought. When Hegel published his philosophy of history in 1815, its impact began to be felt first in biblical and political studies. F. C. Baur attempted to challenge conventional histories of biblical interpretation by carrying out a thoroughgoing reconstruction of New Testament history, and in the 1850s, L. Feuerbach re-explored the development of western political systems using the tools of Hegelian philosophy. But Hegelianism was hardly the dominant philosophy of the mid-nineteenth century. In fact, it met so much resistance that it went underground for several decades following bitter attacks on its principles. Only toward the end of the nineteenth century did it reemerge, significantly altered, in the domain of aesthetics, for example, in the work of Eduard von Hartmann in the 1890s.

The impact of Hegelianism in 1940s architectural history is, therefore, extraordinarily belated. It came to architecture only after it had been tested, critiqued, reformulated, and modified in other realms, such as religion, politics, and art. Giedion certainly benefited from over a century of debate about the pitfalls and dangers that provided him with clues about where to camouflage his thoughts and where to hold forth. Nevertheless, *Space, Time and Architecture* is perhaps

Vico 1730			
PRIMITIVE CULTURE Period of infancy	CIVIL STATE Period of youth	SOCIETY BASED ON REASON AND JUSTICE Period of maturity	Breakdown of society

Hegel 1820			
PRIMITIVE CULTURE Period of infancy commanded from within: totalitarian ziggurat	GREECE 1st manifestation of the Spirit	ROME Civil laws social complexity Pantheon	GERMAN WORLD Revelation of the Spirit

Giedion 1940			
PRIMITIVE CULTURE Focus on inner world death: Egypt, dreams: Malta object in space: ziggurat	GREECE Development of exteriority Parthenon	ROME Civil laws development of interiority Pantheon	MODERN WORLD *Befreites Wohnen* Synthesis exteriority and inferiority; breakdown of nationalism; revelation of Moderism

the last full-scale attempt to imbue an exhausted song with new life. That, of course, did not diminish the book's impact. *Space, Time and Architecture* was assigned reading in many universities and by 1966 it had gone into its 16th printing. The rapid spread of modernism, simplified for the consumer market by such influential journals as *House and Home* and *Architectural Record*; can be attributed not simply to economic revival of the American postwar economy, but also to the institutionalization of Giedion's historiographic thesis. Can *Space, Time and Architecture* be considered a bizarre miscarriage of quasi-philosophical inquiry, or was it an almost natural outcome of the interdisciplinary imperative in architecture to compress an unwilling philosophy into a discourse on praxis?

It is ironic that the philosophy of Vico and Hegel began to find its architectural "praxis" 150 years after its initial formulation, and not in Germany but in the conservative atmosphere of postwar America, and not in music and painting, as Hegel might have hoped, but in the lowly realm of architecture. This does not mean that an architect practicing in the 1950s, according to Giedion's world view, was a Hegelian (much as Venturi cannot be held accountable for his post-neo-Kantian views), for the relationship between philosophy and architectural practice involved so many conceptual translations, from philosophy, to history of philosophy, to history of architecture, to theory of architecture, to the architect practitioner, that ultimately the philosophical basis on which praxis was founded was almost totally obscured. These mutations erased the past, recontextualized it, and blocked it from view.

The meta-history of architectural theory must recognize and accept the distorted and imperfect ways in which architectural thought manifests itself kaleidoscopically in society. This makes it impossible to assign a position of privilege to philosophy as the unilateral "text" of architectural theory. It is also impossible to ascribe any independence to the "discourse" on architectural theory.

The History that Haunts the Theory

Although interdisciplinary historiography abolished the precarious dependence on narrow historical centerings in favor of a complex set of philosophical-historical underpinnings, it was not a process of demystification. On the contrary, the newly formed relationships between philosophy, history, and architectural theory in the twentieth century ranged from the immediately comprehensible to the totally bizarre and from the still perceptible to the long-since obscured. Within the domain of the unusual "discourse"—based on submerged atavisms and perplexing continuities—philosophies and histories released meaning in overlapping time-delay fashion, even though they were no longer part of their own present polemic. They may have been dated, yet still had relevance after a decade or even a century. Their meanings changed through time—what was once progressive became reactionary, what was once meaningful in its newness was dangerous in its reincarnated and mutated form. What was once a narrow philosophical postulate became the avenue of mainstream praxis.

In conclusion, I believe that there are three lessons that interdisciplinary historiography teaches. The first is that philosophy cannot generate a praxis contemporaneous with it. The true impact of Jacques Derrida, for example, cannot possibly be felt in the domain of architecture for at least several decades, maybe centuries, until it has undergone a process of adjustment, infiltration, and contamination similar to that of Hegelian or Kantian ideas that began to touch architectural praxis over a century after their inception. Any theory that envisions a direct relationship between contemporary thought and contemporary praxis can only be a theory in the weakest and most trivial sense of the word.

The second lesson is that though twentieth-century theory attempts to exorcise the ghost of history, historians wound up playing determinative roles. The historian may be consciously directed toward influencing praxis, as with Giedion, or he or she may touch praxis only belatedly through the work of others, as with Wölfflin, whose writings underwent a process of academic legitimation in architecture only in the 1960s. Philosophy has never impacted architectural praxis directly. Theories that function on that assumption can only address the intellectually and culturally naïve.

The third lesson that interdisciplinary historiography teaches is that since philosophical texts lose visibility in the process of their dissemination, praxis becomes increasingly *unaware* of its genesis and philosophical dependencies. As a result theory, like old bones dressed in the garb of contemporaneity, cannot expose its true intellectual origins without simultaneously accepting its atavistic relationship to the present. This problem has given rise to the slow yet inevitable separation of theory from history. Theory now requires an audience that, on the one hand, serves to affirm and legitimize its independent discursive existence and that, on the other hand, functions as a smokescreen protecting it from its own historicity. Theories of architecture are today more historically determined than ever before, yet never have they been more incapable of addressing the syllables of time.

Notes

1. Augustine, *Confessions* (See Books 11 and 13), in *Fathers of the Church*, eds. Roy Joseph Deferrari, et al. (Washington, D.C.: Catholic University of America Press, 1953), Volume 5, 343–365.
2. Augustine, "Letter to Marcellinus" (4.15), in *A Select Library of the Nicene and Post-Nicene Fathers*, ed. Philip Schaff (New York: Scribner's Sons, 1892), 137.
3. Nelly Noémie Schargo, *History in the "Encyclopedie"* (New York: Octagon Books, 1970), 199.
4. "There are now three of the name of Brutus celebrated in history, the first who exiled the proud Tarquin; the second who slew Julius Caesar. The third Brutus, then,

is equal to both of these in that in his own person he has united the causes of the double glory which the other two divided between them." Peter Bondanella, *The Eternal City* (Chapel Hill, NC: The University of North Carolina Press, 1987), 33.

5. Janet Cox-Rearick, "Themes of Time and Rule at Poggio a Caiano: The Portico Frieze of Lorenzo il Magnifico," *Mitteilungen des Kunsthistorischen Institutes in Florenz* 26, Hft. 2 (1982): 167–210.
6. Jean-Jacques Rousseau, *Discours sur les Sciences et les Arts* (1750) in *Oeuvres Complètes,* eds. Bernard Graghebin and Marcel Raymond (Paris: Bibliothèque de la Pléiade, 1966), Volume 3, 22.
7. Le Corbusier, *Towards a New Architecture,* trans. Frederick Etchells (New York: Dover Publications, 1986), 15.
8. Fritz Neumeyer, *Mies van der Rohe: Das Kunstlose Wort* (Berlin: Siedler Verlag, 1986), 135–137. Mies van der Rohe, for example, has frequently been discussed as someone who did little in the way of reading. Neumeyer has fortunately dispelled that myth.
9. Neumeyer, *Mies van der Rohe*, 299.

The Pruitt-Igoe Myth

Katharine G. Bristol
University of California, Berkeley

This paper is an effort to debunk the myths associated with the demolition of the Pruitt-Igoe public housing project. In the seventeen years since its demise, this project has become a widely recognized symbol of architectural failure. Anyone remotely familiar with the recent history of American architecture knows to associate Pruitt-Igoe with the failure of High Modernism, and with the inadequacy of efforts to provide livable environments for the poor. It is this association of the project's demolition with the failure of modern architecture that constitutes the core of the Pruitt-Igoe myth. In place of the myth, this paper offers a brief history of Pruitt-Igoe that demonstrates how its construction and management were shaped by profoundly embedded economic and political conditions in postwar St. Louis. It then outlines how each successive retelling of the Pruitt-Igoe story in both the national and architectural press has added new distortions and misinterpretations of the original events. The paper concludes by offering an interpretation of the Pruitt-Igoe myth as mystification. By placing the responsibility for the failure of public housing on designers, the myth shifts attention from the Institutional or structural sources of public housing problems.

Few architectural images are more powerful than the spectacle of the Pruitt-Igoe public housing project crashing to the ground (Figure 1). Since the trial demolition of three of its buildings in 1972, Pruitt-Igoe has attained an iconic significance by virtue of its continuous use and reuse as a symbol within a series of debates in architecture, In these discussions there is virtual unanimity that the project's demise demonstrated an *architectural* failure. When Charles Jencks announced in 1977 that the demolition of Pruitt-Igoe represented the death of modern architecture, he invoked an interpretation of the project that has today gained widespread acceptance. Anyone remotely familiar with the recent history of American architecture automatically associates Pruitt-Igoe with the failure of High Modernism, and with the inadequacy of efforts to provide livable environments for the poor.

This version of the Pruitt-Igoe story is a myth. At the core of the myth is the idea that architectural design was responsible for the demise of Pruitt-Igoe. In the first section of this essay I debunk the myth by offering a brief history of Pruitt-Igoe from the perspective of its place within a larger history of urban redevelopment and housing policy. This history engages the profoundly embedded economic and political conditions that shaped the construction and management of Pruitt-Igoe. I then consider how the Pruitt-Igoe myth came to be created and disseminated, both by the national press and by architects and architecture critics, and how each successive retelling of the Pruitt-Igoe story has added new dimensions to the myth. I want to focus particular attention on one of the most important aspects of the myth: the alleged connection between the project's failure and the end of modern architecture. In the final section I argue for an interpretation of the Pruitt-Igoe myth as mystification. By placing the responsibility for the failure of public housing on designers, the myth shifts attention from the institutional or structural sources of public housing problems. Simultaneously it legitimates the architecture profession by implying that deeply embedded social problems are caused, and therefore solved, by architectural design.

The Pruitt-Igoe Story: Public Housing and Urban Redevelopment

Pruitt-Igoe was created under the United States Housing Act of 1949, which made funds directly available to cities for slum clearance, urban redevelopment, and public housing. Like many other cities in the postwar era, St. Louis was experiencing a massive shift of its predominantly white middle-class population towards the suburbs. At the same time, central city slums were expanding as poor households moved into units abandoned by those leaving the city.[1] Located in a ring immediately surrounding the central business district, these slums were racially segregated. Blacks occupied the area immediately north of downtown, while whites tended to live to the south. The black ghetto expanded particularly fast with the postwar influx of poor black population from the South. As the growing slums crept closer to the central business district, city officials and the local business community feared the accompanying decline in property values would threaten the economic health of downtown real estate. They responded by developing a comprehensive plan to redevelop the zone immediately surrounding the downtown business core.[2]

Using the urban redevelopment provisions of the 1949 Housing Act, St. Louis's Land Clearance and Redevelopment Authority planned to acquire and clear extensive tracts within the slums and to sell them at reduced cost to private developers. These redevelopment projects were slated to accommodate mainly middle-income housing and commercial development in an

Pruitt-Igoe demolition, courtesy Missouri Historical Society.

effort to lure the middle class back to the central city. At the same time, the St. Louis Housing Authority would clear land for the construction of public housing. These projects were intended to provide large numbers of low-rent units to the poor in order to stem ghetto expansion, and also to accommodate households displaced by redevelopment and other slum clearance projects.[3]

Pruitt-Igoe was one of these public housing projects. Located on a 57-acre site on the north side black ghetto, it was one of several tracts that had been targeted for slum clearance under the postwar redevelopment plan. In 1950 St. Louis received a federal commitment for 5,800 public housing units, about half of which were allocated by the St. Louis Housing Authority to Pruitt-Igoe. The 2,700-unit project would house 15,000 tenants at densities higher than the original slum dwellings. The high density resulted from housing and redevelopment officials' expectations that these projects would eventually come to house not only those displaced by slum clearance for Pruitt-Igoe, but also by demolition for redevelopment projects and for future public housing.

In 1950 the St. Louis Housing Authority commissioned the firm of Leinweber, Yamasaki & Hellmuth to design Pruitt-Igoe. The architects' task was constrained by the size and location of the site, the number of units, and the project density, all of which had been predetermined by the St. Louis Housing Authority. Their first design proposals called for a mixture of high-rise, mid-rise, and walk-up structures. Though this arrangement was acceptable to the local authority, it exceeded the federal government's maximum allowable cost per unit. At this point a field officer of the federal Public Housing Administration (P. H. A.) intervened and insisted on a scheme using 33 identical eleven-story elevator buildings (Figures 2 and 3). These design changes took place in the context of a strict economy and efficiency drive within the P. H. A. Political opposition to the public housing program was particularly intense in the conservative political climate of the early 1950s. In addition, the outbreak of the Korean War had created inflation and materials shortages, and the P. H. A. found itself in the position of having to justify public housing expenditures to an unsympathetic Congress.[5]

Despite the intense pressure for economical design, the architects devoted a great deal of attention to improving livability in the high-rise units. One of their strategies was to use two popular new design features: skip-stop elevators and glazed internal galleries (Figures 4 and 5). These were intended to create "individual neighborhoods" within each building. The galleries, located on every third floor, were conceived as "vertical hallways." Skip-stop elevators transported residents to the gallery level, from which they would walk to their apartments. Laundry and storage rooms also opened off the galleries. When Pruitt-Igoe was published in the *Architectural Forum* and *Architectural Record,* it was these specific design features that received the most attention.[6] The *Architectural Record* praised the skip-stop elevators and galleries as innovative compensations for the shortcomings of the high-rise housing form:

> Since all of these are, under federal legislation, combined low-rent housing and slum-clearance projects, located near the heart of the city, a high-rise, high-density solution was inescapable, and the problem was how to plan a high-rise project on a huge scale, and still provide, to the greatest extent possible under present legislation, communities with individual scale and character which would avoid the "project" atmosphere so often criticized.[7]

Aerial view of Pruitt-Igoe, courtesy of U.S. Geological Survey.

Even after the architects had switched to an all high-rise scheme, they faced continued pressure from the Public Housing Administration to keep costs to a bare minimum. In a 1975 study of the St. Louis Housing Authority's expenditures on Pruitt-Igoe, political scientist Eugene Meehan analyzed the extent to which these budget constraints affected the final design. In addition to the elimination of amenities, such as children's play areas, landscaping, and ground-floor bathrooms, the cost cutting targeted points of contact between the tenants and the living units. "The quality of the hardware was so poor that doorknobs and locks were broken on initial use. ... Window panes were blown from inadequate frames by wind pressure. In the kitchens, cabinets were made of the thinnest plywood possible."[8]

Pruitt-Igoe was completed in 1954. Though originally conceived as two segregated sections (Pruitt for blacks and Igoe for whites), a Supreme Court decision handed down that same year forced desegregation. Attempts at integration failed, however, and Pruitt-Igoe was an exclusively black project virtually from inception. Overall Pruitt-Igoe's first tenants appeared pleased with their new housing. Despite the relatively cheap construction quality, the units still represented a much higher level of amenity than the dilapidated units they had vacated or been forced to leave.

By 1958, however, conditions had begun to deteriorate. One of the first signals was a steadily declining occupancy rate. As Roger Montgomery has persuasively argued, St. Louis's housing officials failed to anticipate changing postwar demographic trends that dramatically affected the inner-city housing market and threatened the viability of public housing projects.[9] Pruitt-Igoe was conceived at a time when the demand for low-income housing units in the inner city had never been higher, due to widespread dislocation caused by slum clearance, urban renewal, and the federal highway program. However, by the time the project opened in 1954, this demand had tapered off. Slow overall metropolitan population growth and the overproduction of inexpensive suburban dwellings helped open up the previously tight inner-city rental market to blacks. Many chose to live in inexpensive private dwellings rather than in public housing. Pruitt-Igoe's occupancy rate peaked in 1957 at 91 percent and immediately began to decline.

This decline in occupancy directly impacted the St. Louis Housing Authority's ability to maintain the project, as Eugene Meehan has amply demonstrated.[10] Under the 1949 Housing Act, local housing authorities were expected to fund their operations and maintenance out of rents collected from tenants. In a period of rising costs and declining occupancy, the Housing Authority was placed in a cost-income squeeze that impeded its ability to conduct basic repairs. In addition, average tenant income was declining. The project came increasingly to be inhabited by the poorest segment of the black population: primarily female heads of households dependent on public assistance. These demographic shifts and economic pressures resulted in chronic neglect of maintenance and mechanical breakdowns. Elevators failed to work and vandalism went unrepaired. In a project increasingly inhabited by the poorest and most demoralized segment of the population, the vandalism came also to be accompanied by increasing rates of violent crime.

The ongoing problems of vandalism, violence, and fiscal instability prompted a number of efforts to salvage Pruitt-Igoe. In 1965 the first of several federal grants arrived to provide physical rejuvenation and the establishment of social programs to benefit the residents and to combat further rent arrearages. The programs had little effect: Occupancy rates continued to decline, crime rates climbed, and routine management

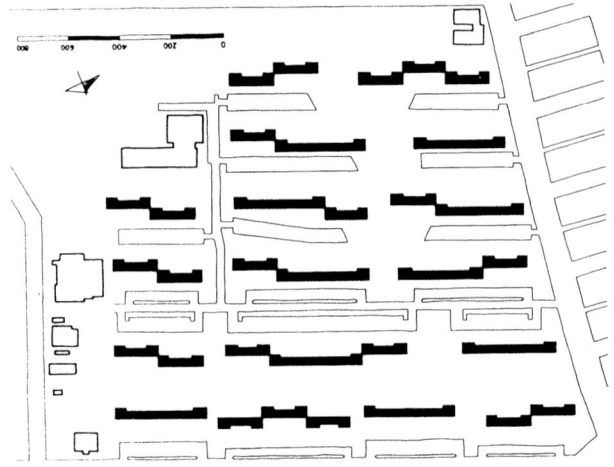

Site Plan, courtesy Roger Montgomery.

and maintenance were neglected. In 1969 Pruitt-Igoe tenants joined residents of two other St. Louis public housing projects in a massive nine-month rent strike. This further depleted the Housing Authority's limited financial reserves and aggravated the vacancy problem, prompting H. U. D. to consider closing the project.[11] In an effort to determine whether explosion or traditional headache-ball demolition would be cheaper, all the remaining tenants were moved to 11 buildings, and on March 16, 1972 a demolition experiment levelled three buildings in the center of the project. Despite some last-minute rehabilitation plans, in 1973 H. U. D. decided to demolish the rest of the project, and finally finished it off in 1976.

Rise of the Pruitt-Igoe Myth
Clearly there were a number of powerful social and economic factors at play in the rise and fall of Pruitt-Igoe. Yet for most architects the entire story can be reduced to a one-line explanation: The design was to blame. This interpretation gained its greatest acceptance in the aftermath of the project's demolition. The roots of the Pruitt-Igoe myth, however, go back to the first years of the project's history.

The deterioration of Pruitt-Igoe became evident only a few years after its completion in 1954, and the local press noted as early as 1960 that certain design features exacerbated the project's problems.[12] The skip-stop elevators and galleries, far from promoting community association, had proved to be opportune environments for violent crime. Forced to walk through the galleries to reach their apartments, residents were threatened and attacked by gangs, who used these spaces as hangouts. Residents were also frequently attacked in the elevators.

This connection between imputed design flaws and Pruitt-Igoe's deterioration first came to the attention of a wide audience of design professionals in 1965, when the growing notoriety of the project prompted *Architectural Forum* to publish a second article on Pruitt-Igoe. In "The Case History of a Failure," James Bailey retracted virtually all of *Forum's* earlier statements about the project, acknowledging that many of the features praised in their 1951 article had proved to be hazards, rather than improvements to the quality of life:

> The undersized elevators are brutally battered, and they reek of urine from children who misjudged the time it takes to reach their apartments. By stopping only on every third floor, the elevators offer convenient settings for crime. . . .The galleries are anything but cheerful social enclaves. The tenants call them "gauntlets" through which they must pass to reach their doors. . . .Heavy metal grilles now shield the windows, but they were installed too late to prevent three children from falling out. The steam pipes remain exposed both in the galleries and the apartments, frequently inflicting severe burns. The adjoining laundry rooms are unsafe and little used. . . .The storage rooms are also locked—and empty. They have been robbed of their contents so often that tenants refuse to use them.[13]

To his credit, Bailey tempered his criticism of the architecture by pointing out that the problems at Pruitt-Igoe went deeper than physical design. He mentioned, in particular, the absence of adult males as heads of households, the project's notoriety, and the deficient management and maintenance. Nonetheless, Bailey's article laid the foundation for a continuous rearticulation of the Pruitt-Igoe story throughout the late sixties and early seventies as the situation at Pruitt-Igoe continued to deteriorate.

The trial demolition of 1972 brought Pruitt-Igoe unprecedented attention in the architectural and the national press. *Architectural Forum, AIA Journal, Architecture Plus,* and *The Architect's Journal* all published articles on the failure of the supposedly innovative design features.[14] *Life, Time, The Washington Post,* and *The National Observer,* among others, reported on the demolition experiment and pointed to the architecture as one of the contributing causes.[15] These articles represent the first appearance of the Pruitt-Igoe myth. No longer confining their criticism to particular architectural features, such as the open galleries, the critics now began to relate the project's failure to flaws in the overall approach or design philosophy. The general theme that emerged was that the architects were insensitive to the needs of the lower class population and were trying to use the design to force a middle-class, white, lifestyle on Pruitt-Igoe residents. For example, an article in *Architecture Plus* argued that the design was simply inappropriate for the social structures of the

View of a Pruitt-Igoe building, courtesy Missouri Historical Society.

people who were going to live there. George Kassabaum, one of the project architects, was quoted as saying, "You had middle class whites like myself designing for an entirely different group."[16] The implication was that low-income urban blacks constituted a tenant group with special needs. They were not instilled with the middle class value of taking pride in the upkeep of their environment, and they also brought with them certain destructive behaviors. As the *Washington Post* put it, there was an "incompatibility between the high-rise structure and the large poor families who came to inhabit it, only a generation removed from the farm."[17]

This interpretation of the demise of Pruitt-Igoe received strong reinforcement when it appeared in Oscar Newman's *Defensible Space* in the same year as the trial demolition. This seminal text of the then emerging discipline of environment and behavior argued that there was a direct relationship between physical environments and human behavior. According to Newman, the widespread vandalism and violence at Pruitt-Igoe resulted from the presence of excessive "indefensible" public space.[18] Corridors were too long and not visible from the apartments. The residents did not feel that these spaces "belonged" to them and so made no effort to maintain or police them. The entryways, located in large, unprotected open plazas, did not allow tenants any control over who entered the buildings. Newman further argued that by designing public housing in such a way as to provide an appropriate amount of private, semi-private, and public space, architects could reduce violence and vandalism in the environment.

With all the attention being paid to the project's design in the early 1970s, a strong associative link was forged between architectural flaws and Pruitt-Igoe's deterioration. In 1965 James Bailey had taken care to point out that two of the major causes of the deterioration of Pruitt-Igoe were chronically inadequate maintenance and the increasing poverty of tenants. By 1972 these crucial elements of the story had been all but forgotten in the rush to condemn the architecture. It is the privileging of these design problems over the much more deeply embedded economic and social ones that constitutes the core of the Pruitt-Igoe myth.

The myth ignores the connection between Pruitt-Igoe's problems and the fiscal crisis of the St. Louis Housing Authority, or what Eugene Meehan has called the "programmed failure" of American public housing.[19] Political and social ambivalence to public housing had resulted in a token housing program burdened by impossible fiscal management constraints. The federal Public Housing Administration also impeded public housing efforts by insisting on unrealistically low construction costs. The myth also omits the subordination of public housing to postwar urban redevelopment programs. Federal dollars helped cities clear unsightly slums and assisted private interests in developing valuable inner city land. Public housing projects were confined to the unwanted sites in the heart of the slums, and developed at high densities to accommodate those displaced by the wholesale clearance of poor neighborhoods.

The myth also ignores the connection between social indifference to the poverty of inner city blacks and the decline of Pruitt-Igoe. In 1970 sociologist Lee Rainwater wrote *Behind Ghetto Walls,* based on the findings of a massive participant observer study conducted during the mid-1960s at Pruitt-Igoe.[20] Rainwater argued that the violence and vandalism that occurred at the project were an understandable response by its residents to poverty and racial discrimination. In his view architectural design was neither the cause nor the cure for these problems. Improved housing conditions and other efforts directed at changing the behavior of the poor were, in his opinion, useless if not accompanied by efforts to raise their income level.

This evidence directly contradicts the Pruitt-Igoe myth by demonstrating the significance of the political and economic sources of Pruitt-Igoe's decline. In addition, it reveals that the type of argument proposed in *Defensible Space* is a subtle form of blaming the victim.

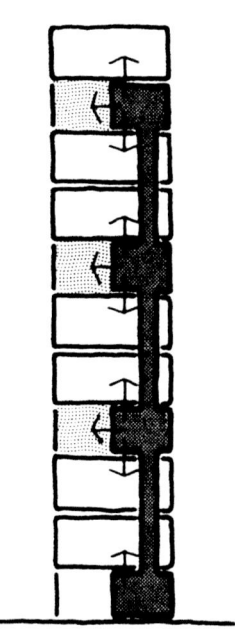

Diagrammatic section, courtesy Roger Montgomery.

The idea of defensible space is based on the assumption that certain "populations" unavoidably bring with them behavioral problems that have to be designed against. This kind of argument does not question why public housing projects tend to be plagued by violent crime in the first place. It naturalizes the presence of crime among low-income populations rather than seeing it as a product of institutionalized economic and racial oppression.

Pruitt-Igoe and the end of Modernism
Despite the extensive evidence of multiple social and economic causes of Pruitt-Igoe's deterioration, the Pruitt-Igoe myth has also become a truism of the environment and behavior literature. For example, John Pipkin's *Urban Social Space,* a standard social-factors textbook, uses Pruitt-Igoe as an example of indefensible space and of the lack of fit between high-rise buildings and lower class social structure.

In social terms, public housing has been a failure. Social structures have disintegrated in the desolate high-rise settings. ... Many projects are ripe for demolition. One of the most notorious... was Pruitt-Igoe. When built, it won an architectural prize, but ... it epitomized the ills of public housing.[21]

This passage is notable because it illustrates one particular example of how the Pruitt-Igoe myth has grown by incorporating misinformation. Though it is commonly accorded the epithet "award-winning," Pruitt-Igoe never won any kind of architectural prize. An earlier St. Louis housing project by the same team of architects, the John Cochran Garden Apartments, did win two architectural awards. At some point this prize seems to have been incorrectly attributed to Pruitt-Igoe. This strange memory lapse on the part of architects in their discussions of Pruitt-Igoe is extremely significant. Beginning in the mid-1970s, Pruitt-Igoe began increasingly to be used as an illustration of the argument that the International Style was responsible for the failure of Pruitt-Igoe. The fictitious prize is essential to this dimension of the myth, because it paints Pruitt-Igoe as the iconic modernist monument.

The association of Pruitt-Igoe's demise with the perceived failures of the Modern movement had begun as early as 1972. In the aftermath of the project's demolition, several writers suggested that insensitivity to residents' needs was typical of modern architecture. The *Architect's Journal* called the demolition of Pruitt-Igoe "the modern movement's most grandiloquent failure."[22] With the critique of Modernism emerging in the 1970s, it was not surprising that a number of critics and theorists, who can be loosely termed Postmodern, began to use the project in their writing to represent the Modern movement.

The first important appearance of Pruitt-Igoe in a critique of Modernism came in 1976 when Colin Rowe and Fred Koetter used the photograph of the demolition in their introduction to *Collage City*. This section of the book was devoted to a demonstration of the premise that the Modern movement's architectural and social revolution had backfired. Instead of furthering the development of a new society, the city of modern architecture, both as psychological construct and as physical model, had been rendered tragically ridiculous ... the city of Ludwig Hibersheimer and Le Corbusier, the city celebrated by CIAM and advertised by the Athens Charter, the former city of deliverance is everyday found increasingly inadequate.[23]

Though Rowe and Koetter do not refer to Pruitt-Igoe specifically, the implication of the photograph's inclusion is clear. Pruitt-Igoe is used as an example of this "city of modern architecture" whose revolution failed. It presents Pruitt-Igoe as a product of the ideas of Hibersheimer, Le Corbusier, and CIAM (*Congrès Internationaux d'Architecture Moderne*) and implicates the inadequacy of their ideas in the demolition of the project.

Only one year after the publication of *Collage City,* Charles Jencks further advanced this interpretation in *The Language of Post Modern Architecture*. In the introduction to his discussion of Postmodernism, Jencks asserted that the demolition of Pruitt-Igoe represents the death of modern architecture. Like Rowe and Koetter, he associated Pruitt-Igoe with the rationalist principles of CIAM, and particularly with the urban design principles of Le Corbusier. According to Jencks, even though the project was designed with the intention of instilling good behavior in the tenants, it was incapable of accommodating their social needs:

> Pruitt-Igoe was constructed according to the most progressive ideas of CIAM ... and it won an award from the American Institute of Architects when it was designed in 1951. It consisted of elegant slab blocks fourteen

storeys high, with rational "streets in the air" (which were safe from cars, but, as it turned out, not safe from crime); "sun, space and greenery," which Le Corbusier called the "three essential joys of urbanism" (instead of conventional streets, gardens and semi-private space, which he banished). It had a separation of pedestrian and vehicular traffic, the provision of play space, and local amenities such as laundries, crèches and gossip centers—all rational substitutes for traditional patterns.[24]

These uses of the Pruitt-Igoe symbol added significantly to the Pruitt-Igoe myth. Like the defensible space argument popularized by Oscar Newman, these accounts failed to locate Pruitt-Igoe in its historical context and thereby ignored evidence that economic crisis and racial discrimination played the largest role in the project's demise. Now, they added a set of ideas about the architects' intentions in designing the project. Both accounts presented the project as the canonical modernist monument (Jencks in particular perpetuating the mistaken idea that it was an award-winning design). They described the project as Modernist not only in formal terms, but in political and social terms as well, as reflecting an agenda for social engineering.

These uses of Pruitt-Igoe misrepresented the designers' intentions and the extent to which the architects controlled the project's design. As the summary of Pruitt-Igoe's history demonstrates, much of the project's design was determined by the St. Louis Housing Authority and the federal Public Housing Administration. The architects had no control over the project's isolated location, its excessive densities, the elimination of amenities, or the use of high-rise elevator buildings. Their task was limited to providing the form of the individual buildings and incorporating as much amenity as possible, given the restricted budget.

In carrying out this task, the architects did follow the formal conventions of modern architecture. Pruitt-Igoe was one of Leinweber, Yamasaki & Hellmuth's first major commissions, so it is certain that they wished to make an impression on their architectural peers. The glazed galleries combined with skip-stop elevators, the extensive open spaces between the slabs, and the minimalist surface treatment certainly reflected the prevailing interest in Modernism as elaborated by CIAM. However, the use of these formal conventions does not demonstrate that the architects had particular intentions for social reform. In fact, in published statements Minoru Yamasaki expressed doubt that the high-rise form would have a beneficial effect on public housing tenants.

These statements appeared in a series of articles in the *Journal of Housing* in which Yamasaki engaged in a debate with the progressive housing reformer Catherine Bauer.[25] Yamasaki defended high-rise design, not on its architectural merits, but as the best possible response to what he perceived as the social imperative of slum clearance and the economic necessity for urban redevelopment. Given the high cost of urban land occupied by slum housing, he argued, it is most economically efficient to acquire small parcels and build at high densities. Yet despite its economic advantages, Yamasaki was skeptical of the value of the high-rise as a form for mass housing: "the low building with low density is unquestionably more satisfactory than multi-story living. ... If I had no economic or social limitations, I'd solve all my problems with one-story buildings."[26] He defended high-rise design as the only way to respond to external economic and policy conditions.

In her defense of low-rise housing, Catherine Bauer suggested that the policy of clearing slums and then rehousing low-income populations in high-density central city projects is not necessarily the result of economic imperatives but a conscious choice on the part of policy-makers. High-density inner city projects are the result of making public housing subordinate to urban redevelopment schemes: If business interests and city officials were willing to locate projects on the urban periphery then the high-density, high-rise projects would be unnecessary. Bauer criticized Yamasaki less for his architectural views than for his politics; he was too willing to give in to prevailing profit-motivated redevelopment and housing policy.

In his statements in this debate, Yamasaki hardly fits the image of the radical social reformer depicted by the Pruitt-Igoe myth. His firm did indeed adopt particular design features in order to conform to the latest trends and was insensitive to the potential effects of those features. The architects also incorrectly assumed that the galleries would help promote community interaction in what was bound to be a harsh environment. Yet before making any of these decisions, they had agreed to work within the framework of the large-scale, high-rise, high-density project mandated by urban redevelopment practices. Rather than social reformers destroying the public housing program with their megalomaniac designs, the architects were essentially passive in their acceptance of the dominant practices of their society.

Despite its dubious authenticity or historical accuracy, the Pruitt-Igoe myth had achieved the status of architectural dogma by the late 1970s. The idea that Prutt-Igoe's failure resulted from the insensitivity of orthodox modernist design found a receptive audience and became an illustration for many Postmodern and anti-Modern texts. Peter Blake, in *Form Follows Fiasco: Why Modern Architecture Hasn't Worked,* echoed the assertion that Pruitt-Igoe followed *Ville-Radieuse* design ideas. As a result, he argued, there was "no way this depressing project could be made humanly habitable" and communities of high-rises are inherently doomed.[27] It also became a convenient symbol for Tom Wolfe to include in his attack on the importing of German-inspired 1930s architecture to the United States after World War II.[28] In *From Bauhaus to Our House* Wolfe repeated the by now generally accepted fiction that the project was an award winner, and then added a fabrication of his own, asserting that in 1971 a general meeting was held at which the residents called for blowing up the buildings.[29]

The Pruitt-Igoe Myth as Mystification
Why is the Pruitt-Igoe myth so powerful? There is clearly ample evidence that architectural design was but one, and probably the least important, of several factors in the demise of the project. Why then has the architecture community been so insistent that the failure of Pruitt-Igoe was its own fault?

At one level, the myth can be understood simply as a weapon in an ongoing conflict between different factions within the architecture profession. The two most central critiques of the design of Pruitt-Igoe have come from successor movements to High Modernism: Postmodernism, and environment and behavior. For proponents of these new approaches, such as Oscar Newman or Charles Jencks, Pruitt-Igoe provides a convenient embodiment of all the alleged failings of Modernism. However, though these successors are critical of the modernist approach to the design of public housing, they do not question the fundamental notion that it is at the level of *design* that public housing succeeds or fails. They attribute the problems of public housing to architectural failure, and propose as a solution a new approach to design. They do not in any significant way acknowledge the political-economic and social context for the failure of Pruitt-Igoe. This is because the myth is more than simply the result of debate within architectural culture: It serves at a much more profound level the interests of the architecture profession as a whole.

As we have seen in tracing the rise of the Pruitt-Igoe myth, the architects' version has consistently insisted on the primary significance of the project's overall design in its demise. This interpretation denies the existence of larger problems endemic to St. Louis's public housing program. By attributing more causal power to architecture than to flawed policies, crises in the local economy, or to class oppression and racism, the myth conceals the existence of contextual factors structuring the architects' decisions and fabricates a central role for architecture in the success or failure of public housing. It places the architect in the position of authority over providing low-income housing for the poor.

This presentation of the architect as the figure of authority in the history of Pruitt-Igoe is reinforced by linking the project's failure to the defects of High Modernism. The claim that Pruitt-Igoe failed because it was based on an agenda for social reform, derived from the ideas of Le Corbusier and the CIAM, not only presupposes that physical design is central to the success or failure of public housing, but also that the design was implemented to carry out the architects' social agenda. What this obscures is the architects' passivity in the face of a much larger agenda that has its roots not in radical social reform, but in the political economy of post-World War II St. Louis and in practices of racial segregation. Pruitt-Igoe was shaped by the strategies of ghetto containment and inner city revitalization—strategies that did not emanate from the architects, but rather from the system in which they practice. The Pruitt-Igoe myth therefore not only inflates the power of the architect to effect social change, but it masks the extent to which the profession is implicated, inextricably, in structures and practices that it is powerless to change.

Simultaneously with its function of promoting the power of the architect, the myth serves to disguise the actual purpose and implication of public housing by diverting the debate to the question of design. By continuing to promote architectural solutions to what are fundamentally problems of class and race, the myth conceals the complete inadequacy of contemporary public housing policy. It has quite usefully shifted the blame from the sources of housing policy and placed it on the design professions. By furthering this misconception, the myth disguises the causes of the failure of public housing, and also ensures the continued participation of the architecture profession in token and palliative efforts to address the problem of poverty in America. The myth is a mystification that benefits everyone involved, except those to whom public housing programs are supposedly directed.

Notes
1. St. Louis City Plan Commission, *Comprehensive City Plan* (St. Louis, 1947), 27–34; James Neal Primm, *Lion of the Valley* (Boulder, CO: Pruett, 1981), 472–473.
2. "Progressor Decay? St. Louis Must Choose: The Sordid Housing Story," *St. Louis Post-Dispatch* (March 3, 1950), Part Four in a Series.
3. For the role played by the public housing program in St. Louis redevelopment plans, see Roger Montgomery, "Pruitt-Igoe: Policy Failure or Societal Symptom," in *The Metropolitan Midwest: Policy Problems and Prospects for Change*, eds. Barry Checkoway and Carl V. Patton, (Urbana, IL: University of Illinois Press, 1985), 230–239; and Kate Bristol and Roger Montgomery, "The Ghost of Pruitt-Igoe" (paper delivered at the Annual Meeting of the Association of Collegiate Schools of Planning, Buffalo, NY, October 28, 1988). On the relationship of public housing to urban renewal more generally, see Mark Weiss, "The Origins and Legacy of Urban Renewal," in *Urban and Regional Planning in an Age of Austerity*, eds. Pierre Clavell, John Forester, and William W. Goldsmith, (New York: Pergamon Press, 1980); Richard O. Davies, *Housing Reform During the Truman Administration* (Columbia, MO: University of Missouri Press, 1966); and Arnold Hirsch, *Making the Second Ghetto: Race and Housing in Chicago, 1940–1966* (Cambridge: Cambridge University Press, 1983).
4. Eugene Meehan, *The Quality of Federal Policymaking: Programmed Failure in Public Housing* (Columbia, MO: University of Missouri Press, 1979), 71; James Bailey, "The Case History of a Failure," *Architectural Forum* 123 (December 1965): 23.
5. U. S. Public Housing Administration, *Annual Report* (Washington, D.C., 1951); Davies, *Housing Reform*, 126–132.

6. "Slum Surgery in St. Louis," *Architectural Forum* 94 (April 1951): 128–136; "Four Vast Housing Projects for St. Louis: Hellmuth, Obata and Kassabaum, Inc.," *Architectural Record* 120 (August 1956): 182–189.
7. "Four Vast Housing Projects for St. Louis," 185.
8. Meehan, *Quality,* 71.
9. Montgomery, "Pruitt-Igoe," 235–239.
10. Meehan, *Quality,* 60–63, 65–67, 74–83.
11. In 1965 the U.S. Public Housing Administration (P. H. A.) was incorporated into the newly created Department of Housing and Urban Development (H. U. D.).
12. "What's Wrong with High-Rise?," *St. Louis Post-Dispatch,* November 14, 1960.
13. Bailey, "Case History," 22–23.
14. "St. Louis Blues," *Architectural Forum* 136 (May 1972): 18; *Architect's Journal* (July 26, 1972); Wilbur Thompson, "Problems that Sprout in the Shadow of No Growth," *AIA Journal* 60 (December 1973); "The Experiment That Failed," *Architecture Plus* (October 1973).
15. "The Tragedy of Pruitt-Igoe," *Time* (December 27, 1971): 38; Jerome Curry, "Collapse of a Failure," *The National Observer* (May 20, 1972): 24: Andrew B. Wilson. "Demolition Marks Ultimate Failure of Pruitt-Igoe Project," *Washington Post* (August 27, 1973): 3.
16. "The Experiment That Failed," 18.
17. Wilson, "Demolition," 3.
18. Oscar Newman, *Defensible Space* (New York: Macmillan, 1972), 56–58, 66, 77, 83, 99, 101–108, 188, 207.
19. Meehan, *Quality,* 83–87, 194–198.
20. Lee Rainwater, *Behind Ghetto Walls: Black Families in a Federal Slum* (Chicago: Aldine Publishing, 1970), 9, 403.
21. Mark LaGory and John Pipkin, *Urban Social Space* (Belmont, CA: Wadsworth, 1981), 263.
22. *Architect's Journal*, 180.
23. Colin Rowe and Fred Koetter, *Collage City* (Cambridge, MA: MIT Press, 1976), 4, 6.
24. Charles Jencks, *The Language of Post-Modern Architecture* (New York: Rizzoli, 1977), 9–10.
25. Minoru Yamasaki, "High Buildings for Public Housing?" *Journal of Housing* 9 (1952): 226; Catherine Bauer, "Low Buildings? Catherine Bauer Questions Mr. Yamasaki's Arguments," *Journal of Housing* 9 (1952): 227.
26. Yamasaki, "High Buildings," 226.
27. Peter Blake, *Form Follows Fiasco: Why Modern Architecture Hasn't Worked* (Boston: Atlantic Monthly Press, 1977), 80–81.
28. Tom Wolfe, *From Bauhaus to Our House* (New York: Simon and Schuster, 1981), 73–74.
29. Actually in the late 1970s a local community redevelopment group that included former Pruitt-Igoe residents made a proposal to buy and renovate four of the buildings, but were turned down by H. U. D. Mary Comerio, "Pruitt-Igoe and Other Stories," *Journal of Architectural Education* 34 (Summer, 1981): 26–31.

The Ecology Question

Richard Ingersoll
Rice University

On March 2, 1991, the New York chapter of Architects, Designers, and Planners for Social Responsibility (ADPSR) held a forum at the New School for Social Research. ADPSR, which was founded ten years ago around the issue of stopping nuclear proliferation, is currently seeking to broaden and strengthen the criteria for "social responsibility" in the design fields. In this effort, the forum, coordinated by Susana Torre, invited twenty participants to make ten-minute position statements. I offer my intervention in the interests of further debate.

No matter how one feels about the validity of the reasons for the recent counter-invasion of Kuwait, I think we may all eventually agree that the stunning victory of the US-led coalition will be a Pyrrhic victory, specifically because of the "Ecology Question." As an intimation of a greater loss, consider the unveiling last February of the National Energy Security Act, which will reverse previous decisions against off-shore drilling and exploitation of wildlife reserves for fossil fuels and encourage the development of nuclear power plants but not favor solar or wind technologies; or consider the Department of the Interior's new transportation policy, which calls for a 40 percent increase in the highway budget, but only a 1.8 percent increase in the public transportation budget. These significant gains for the military-industrial lobbies, if enacted, will be our long-term loss as occupants of the biosphere.

Most designers today probably do not feel comfortable with a term like "social responsibility" in reference to the built environment—especially after the last decade of history, one would have to suspect it to be inherently contradictory. Looking at the roster of supporters for this New York chapter, the identity seems to be located somewhere between "socialite responsibility" and "socialist responsibility"—between the patronizing liberal and the grassroots radical. The happy median is that those who identify with the term "social responsibility" are essentially people of conscience, who believe in the possibility of justice for all people.

The crisis of the welfare state during the last twenty-five years, however, has brought ever more doubt to the matter of how to follow one's conscience. Michel Foucault, and other social philosophers of our times, have opened our eyes to the fact that most social institutions become tools of systematized repression, and thus what previously might have been justified as social responsibility eventually reveals itself to be social control. As much as I admire Foucault's critique, I am also disconcerted that the atmosphere of relativism that has followed it has often turned out to be less humane than what was being criticized. There were scattered instances of alternatives based on Foucault's theories that are excellent models of social reintegration: the Democratic Psychiatry movement in Italy in the 1970s, which shut down asylums and opened publicly funded centers for mental hygiene in the central cities, or the German Green Party, which practices a non-hierarchical organization, rotating its leaders, might serve as examples. But these are small tokens of resistance compared to the revenge that free enterprise has taken on public welfare.

The Postmodern condition can be characterized as a vacuum of conscience, in which such socially responsible notions as fair housing, full employment, or access to services are considered somewhat of an embarrassment. Commodity culture has been allowed to run wild and has substituted with ingenious spectacle—much of it provided by our professions—the values that originate in production and community. The Reagans and Thatchers made social Darwinism fashionable again, realizing that it was much more difficult for the disadvantaged to bite the invisible hand that feeds them than it was when the state was supplying the handouts. Social responsibility has been returned to private philanthropy, with the mandate that humanity should take care of its own. Meanwhile, the savings and loan embezzlers have taken care of their own, building million-dollar second homes and requiring the state to intervene with a $580 billion bailout, while the estimated 600,000 homeless have been left to take care of themselves in a society in which housing, employment, and services are well out of reach. This is only the most strident of a series of contrasts we are witnessing in the renewed acceptance of social Darwinism.

In these times of mounting bankruptcy, militarism, and destitution, it is becoming a little difficult to recognize ecology within the hierarchy of social problems, and this is encouraged by the fact that many ecology activists seem to be more dedicated to saving wildlife than saving people. Ecologists, who call for a transition from the dominant Western mentality of anthropocentrism to one of biocentrism, rarely take into account the immediate social injustices that also demand solidarity. The neo-Malthusians are thus able to interpret starvation in remote quarters as a natural process not to be interfered with, while never doubting the primacy of their own well-fed being.

There are others, however, who see the attempt to restore the ecological balance of the biosphere as having profound social relevance. In effect, the very means for exploiting and controlling the natural environment are no different than those that have exploited and controlled the social one. By calling it the "Ecology Question," I mean to make direct allusion to Engels's "The Housing Question." This latter served as one of the most powerful critiques of late nineteenth-century capitalism and was instrumental in mobilizing a consciousness of social responsibility among designers, predicated on fair and healthy housing for all. The famous social failures of public housing in our own times, which have alerted us to functionalist fallacies, should not blind us to the fact that the demand is still there. We can anticipate, however, that the ever-worsening environmental crisis will probably supersede matters such as housing, and in the near future the housing question will be absorbed into a greater ecology question. This will occur with the awareness that the costs of high entropy have become greater than the benefits from exploiting nonrenewable resources. The "Ecology Question" has the potential of generating one of the most effective critiques of late twentieth-century capitalism, especially since the demise of official Marxism in Eastern Europe and elsewhere.

Americans should rightly feel guilty for the statistic that has been often cited during the last twenty years: that 6 percent of the world's population consumes 35 percent of its resources. Unfortunately, individual sentiments of guilt have done little to alter collective accountability. What is even more astounding is that each new verification of the environmental crisis has contributed to a normalization of a Green Apocalypse. The ozone holes above Antarctica, first documented in 1985, the progress of global warming (1990 was the hottest year in the 100 years of climate records, and six years of the 1980s were the hottest on record before it), acid rain, and soil and water depletion—these, for some reason, have become the acceptable compensations for the high entropy way of life. The global consequences, which used to seem far off and uncertain, are now with us, and yet are treated with the same deference as the weather.

The three major contributors to the crisis, mechanized agriculture, unclean forms of industry, and rapid urbanization, are well known, and the expansion of all three has been exponential since the end of World War II. Urbanization, which is the particular responsibility of architects, designers, and planners, is arguably the most important of this deleterious triad and the most difficult to discipline because it is less a technological, or biological matter than an expressly social and cultural one. Roughly 70 percent of energy use in this country (which produces a quarter of the planet's greenhouse trace gases) can be attributed to the domain of urbanization: this includes transportation, heating, lighting and power, and the generation of that power itself.

The energy crisis of 1973-1974 mandated effective policies of conservation, including obligatory insulation and improved miles per gallon, and during the period of 1975-1985 there was a 35 percent energy savings. During the same period, however, the economy grew 35 percent, thus annulling any true environmental gains. If solar panels were ceremoniously installed on the Carter White House to dramatize openness to alternative energy, they were just as unceremoniously dismantled from the Reagan White House at the same time that the price of oil was lowered and federal funding for research on photovoltaics was cut from $150 million per year to $35 million.

Beyond the realm of government policies, the choices of individual designers make a difference, just as those of individual citizens make a difference. The choice of less wasteful processes, for example, is analogous to the consumer's choice to recycle. But to put the responsibility on to the individual's sense of guilt is again a practice of social Darwinism. Unless policy on the macro level is geared to reform, the reforms of the individual will be ineffectual. During the last fifteen years a trillion dollars have been spent on eliminating pollution, yet the costs are generally passed on to those who pay taxes, rather than to those who profit from pollution. As often as not the victims are being blamed. The policies have not come from a social conception of ecology, but from a mechanical one of cause and effect. The parallel with social housing should thus not be forgotten: when housing is conceived merely in technological or economic terms, it usually fails to fulfill its social brief. Ecology, just like the built environment, must be conceived in social terms if it is ever to aspire to justice.

There are a number of things that designers should do out of a sense of responsibility: from eliminating reliance on toxic materials to discouraging unnecessary resource use (for graphic designers this might mean an attack on superfluous packaging; for architects it might concern square footage). But unless the reliance on fossil fuels for transportation (half of the world's oil goes to vehicles) is curtailed, and an end is put to the wholesale exploitation of land surrounding cities for urbanization, any energy savings in design will be compromised. The form of urbanization thus becomes the highest design priority, and it implies a slightly different social organization as well. In practical terms existing and new urban settlements should be clustered into more densely packed nuclei that reintegrate a multiplicity of functions; they must be supported by efficient and accessible public transportation; they must preserve greenbelts and encourage urban farming; they must sponsor low technology amenities such as bicycle lanes—none of this can or will happen without the vision and expertise of designers and planners.

But it is unnecessarily optimistic to imagine what *could* happen, if we do not know *how* it will happen. And this is also why ecology concerns social responsibility:

the government, especially in the aftermath of the Gulf War, will never of its own accord be socially responsible about its energy policy. Only through activism, through communities of interest such as this, will a voice of reason be able to emerge. Recycling or making a passive solar design is only a drop in the bucket unless it is linked to a greater social process that can influence policy. As the audible consequences of the environmental crisis intensify—the gurgle of rising waters, the crinkle of crop failures, the gasps of mass starvation, the moans of environmental illnesses—the social responses, as in times of plague or war, will become negligent of human rights, and reason is less likely to be heard. Some sort of environmental dictatorship, what we could gingerly call ecofascism, might gain favor with promises of restoring the biosphere.

This last prospect probably sounds like a wildly paranoid political fantasy, a private nightmare that is somewhat irresponsible to invoke as evidence. Within the scheme of ecofascism we might foresee designers and planners forced to submit to a new ecological functionalism. As with the old functionalism, it will have benign intentions masking the potential for a new code of repression. My point is that while we might currently be justified in feeling some guilt and despair about the environmental crisis, we should also recognize that responsibility is located in the formation of the question. Can there be such a thing as ecological balance if it is not socially determined? Is not human consciousness the major component both of the cause of the imbalance and of its possible rectification? The "Ecology Question," if it is not proposed as a question of justice among humans, will risk in the short term to continue to be submerged, and thus in the long term will require drastic, and probably inhumane, palliatives. For designers and planners we should recognize that each act of design not only plays a part in the balance of the environment but also is dependent upon policy, and that a strategy at both levels that does not include the self-determination of communities and the social reintegration of life functions will contribute to repressive consequences analogous to those engendered by so many of the functionalist public housing projects. It is therefore imperative that we keep it a question and not a solution if we want it to be liberating, and that we continue to ask this question of ourselves, in our communities, and in our larger spheres of influence. The "Ecology Question" as a socially based priority asks that design and planning conceive of sustainability and social justice as reciprocal conditions—that saving the planet and saving the community become inseparable.

Writing Multiculturalism into Architectural Curricula

Regina Davis
University of California, Berkeley

In the spring of 1991 I taught a new writing course with another African American faculty member, Ken Simmons, in the Department of Architecture at the University of California at Berkeley. The purpose of the course was to write about African American, Asian American, Latino, and Native American architects and artists and their works. We created this course at the urgent request of African American architecture students who were angered by the omission of architects of color in our curriculum. This paper discusses the academic benefits and difficulties of teaching a multicultural writing course in an architecture school.

Participation of Minorities and Women in Architecture

Our class was taught in the context of relatively low participation by African Americans, Asian Americans, Chicana/Latino Americans, and Native Americans in architecture. Nationally, these groups represent 6.5 percent of practicing architects, 8.5 percent of full-time faculty teaching in architecture schools, and 16 percent of architecture graduates. African American and Latino American participation in architecture (4 percent) is slightly greater than in city planning (3 percent) but less than in civil engineering (7 percent).[1] The American Institute of Architects (AIA) reports that the combined membership of African American, Latino, Native American, and Asian American architects totals only 2,885 (6.5 percent) of the total 44,470 registered architects. Female architects represent 7 percent of the total registered AIA membership. However, both groups are growing at an annual rate of 10 percent while the rest of the membership growth is flat.[2] Although these numbers are relatively small, they represent thousands of architects and places unknown to many of us.

We taught our course at an architecture school with a faculty composition that represents the national statistical status quo. People of color represent 8 percent of the architecture faculty. There are three minorities—one Asian woman and two African American men—on the full-time architecture faculty of 40.

The National Architectural Accrediting Board (NAAB) reports that the 162 architecture faculty of color compose 8.5 percent of the total 1,893 full-time faculty. The 267 women compose 14 percent of the total full-time faculty.[3]

Nearly half of U. S. architecture schools have neither African American faculty nor African American administrators, although African American faculty make up 40 percent of architecture faculty of color.[4] Minority faculty recruitment is an intolerably subjective and slow process. At UC Berkeley, for example, minority faculty increased a mere 2 percent over the last ten years.[5]

The NAAB reports that in 1991, a total of 1,266 minority students graduated with degrees in architecture, making up 17 percent of the total graduates in that field. Female graduates comprised 27 percent of the 7,448 total graduates.[6] UC Berkeley was the top producer of minority graduates in architecture. A 1991 review of the architecture department at UC Berkeley challenged the department to deal with the diversity of its student body: "The student body is one of the most diverse to be found in an architectural program anywhere. The Department faces the challenge of addressing this diversity, and the various objectives these groups and their representatives bring to the issue of curriculum."[7] This is exactly the challenge that our course undertook.

Expansion of Multicultural and Architectural Curricula

Students are demanding multicultural education. Students of color are especially unwilling to accept an education that excludes an examination of their heritage, cultural contributions, and issues. Following three years of student initiatives for greater ethnic diversity within the curriculum, the University of California developed the American Cultures graduation requirement in 1991. The American Cultures requirement "is not an ethnic studies requirement, nor an adjusted Western Civilization requirement, nor a course on racism. It is a new approach that responds directly to the problem in numerous disciplines of how to present better the diversity of American experience to the diversity of American students whom we now educate," explains William Simmons, Director of the Center for the Teaching and Study of American Cultures. The requirement courses must all adhere to the same basic framework. According to Simmons, the courses:

1. Focus on important themes or issues in United States history, society, or culture.
2. Address major theoretical and analytical issues relevant to understanding race, culture, and ethnicity in American society.
3. Provide a framework and the intellectual tools to understand better one's own particular cultural/historical identity and that of others in their own terms.

4. Take substantial account of groups drawn from at least three of the following: African Americans, American Indians, Asian Americans, Chicano/Latino Americans, and European Americans. *No single group may be the focus* of the greater part of a course.
5. Are integrative and comparative in that each group is studied in the larger context of American society, history, or culture.[8]

Although our writing course preceded the University's development of most American Cultures requirement courses, the required framework of those courses illuminates the basic principles of our class.

In his 1992 award-winning *Journal of Architectural Education* article, "Biculturalism and Community: A Transformative Model for Design Education," Anthony Ward argues against the exclusion of histories of minorities in architecture:

> In design, our built history tends to be that of the dominant Eurocentric culture. The histories of minority cultures are rarely, if ever, valorized in the contested space of the urban landscape. This process of historical appropriation denies subordinate cultures a public expression and awareness of their own struggles, and of their important role as creators of history.[9]

Several architectural professors have recently set out to correct this exclusion of our histories in architecture. Out of 103 University of California research fellowships that were awarded to professors to create new American Cultures requirement courses, three were awarded to architecture faculty, all of whom are women and/or people of color. Courses on "Architecture, Housing, and Neighborhood Patterns for Different Subcultures"; "Architecture: Cultural Authenticity versus Political Authority"; and "Picture Identity" were taught by Professors Sara Ishikawa, Jill Stoner, and Lewis Watts, respectively.[10] Particularly useful and encouraging essays about teaching strategies to transform architectural curricula using multiculturalism were published in *Voices in Architectural Education*, which was edited by Thomas Dutton.[11] Essays by Professors Bradford C. Grant, Thomas Dutton, Anthony Ward, Jacqueline Leavitt, Karen Kingsley, and Alan Feigenberg outlined strategies to transform architecture courses to be inclusive of women and minorities. In *Intercultural Architecture*, Professor Kisho Kurokawa advanced a proposal for multicultural theory in architecture by creating a philosophical approach to understanding architecture that has multicultural fusion as its goal.[12]

To date, fewer than a dozen books by or about architects of color rival the number of architectural magazine articles that ask, "Why aren't there more minorities in architecture?" These books include Paul Williams' *The Small Home for Tomorrow* and *New Homes for Today*; Carter Wiseman's biography of well-published Chinese-American architect I. M. Pei; Genell Anderson's *Call of the Ancestors* on the philosophy of African influences on world architecture; Dell Upton's edited volume, *America's Architectural Roots: Ethnic Groups That Built America*; Peter Nabokov's *Native American Architecture*; and Jorge Rigau's *Puerto Rico: Turn of the Century Architecture in the Hispanic Caribbean, 1890-1930*.[13] Recent publications include George Cantor's *Historic Landmarks of Black America*; Jack Travis's *African American Architects in Current Practice*; and Bradford Grant and Dennis Mann's *Directory of African American Architects*.[14] These are good examples of the type of research that is needed to create more interpretive works. All of these books were published in the last three years except the two books by Paul Williams, which were written in the forties. Only three of the books (Wiseman, Anderson, and Nabokov) were available when the class was in session. The recent growth of architectural books and architectural courses with multicultural themes signals an important change in architectural research toward greater inclusion of minorities.

However, articles such as "Black Architects: An Endangered Species," "Invisible Architects: Minority Firms struggle to Achieve Recognition in a White-Dominated Profession," and "Black Architects up against a Brick Wall" typically address minority architects' woes but not their architectural contributions nor solutions to systemic discrimination in the profession.[15] The dearth of articles that address the merits of built works designed by architects of color is directly related to the complete lack of Asian, African American, Chicano, Latino, or Native American editors of major architectural journals. Considering the number of minority faculty, the books are too few, and many articles avoid critiquing the contributions of the architects of color that they introduce.

Our Class
Professor Ken Simmons and I developed the experimental writing course, Writing about Environmental Design: Third World Architects and Artists and Their Works, with three goals in mind: 1. broadening the curriculum to include the needs and interests of architecture students from many cultural backgrounds; 2. producing critical works on architects of color to fill the current intellectual void; and 3. providing multicultural role models against the backdrop of cultural invisibility experienced by students of color in architecture courses. The cultural backgrounds of the dozen students enrolled in the class were African American, Chinese American, Japanese American, Chicano, Japanese/African American, and White/African American. Our class included graduate and undergraduate students from the architecture, geography, and English departments. The three-unit course met for three hours weekly and covered multicultural aesthetics, research-

First Evangelical Missionary Baptist Church, Oakland, California. Photograph by Stacy Harris.

Canaan Christian Covenant Missionary Baptist Church, Oakland, California. Photograph by Stacy Harris.

ing architectural and ethnic sources, and writing critical essays about architects of color, their works, and their communities. Guest lecturers presented their ideas on multicultural aesthetics, and students presented their research to the class. Ultimately, we compiled the writings into a bound anthology for distribution to architecture libraries.

The students' first assignment was to write an in-class essay on why they are interested in the class. Students expressed specific hopes to explain why they had enrolled in the class. An undergraduate Chicano student wrote:

I am interested in this class because I saw an opportunity to write about minority architects. Many times we hear about how great Frank Lloyd Wright and his accomplishments are. It's great hearing about someone having so much creativity, but sometimes I get angry because I don't hear about what my people have accomplished.

An undergraduate Japanese/African American student commented, "It was embarrassing not being able to name one black architect before I came to UC Berkeley. With this class I hope to broaden my knowledge to include all minorities: Asian American, African American, Native American, and Chicano architects."

From this first assignment, our class found American "cultural experience" to be so important that we decided to study only American architects of color and their communities, not renowned nationals such as Hassan Fathy, Luis Barragán, and others who practice in their home countries. It is this American experience that students sought to uncover because it related to their own experiences and to their future as architects.

Adrian Wilson and Paul R. Williams, Nurses' Residence Building, Los Angeles County Hospital. Photograph by Bradford C. Grant.

Paul R. Williams, LAX Restaurant, Los Angeles. Julius Shulman, photographer. © J. Paul Getty Trust. Getty Research Institute, Los Angeles (2004.R.10).

The multicultural makeup of the class gave us the advantage of "epistemological privilege": the understanding of both our many "subcultures" and the dominant American culture, with each providing a critical perspective on the other.[16] Our knowledge of both minority and majority issues expanded our critical views.

From Eurocentric to Multicultural Aesthetics
The next step was to place architects of color in a context to gain a better understanding of the cultural aesthetics that influence their works. We selected the following readings to broaden the opportunity for discourse about multicultural aesthetics: *Black Culture and Black Consciousness* by Lawrence Levine; *Woman, Native, Other* by T. Minh-Ha Trinh, *Chicano Art* edited by Richard Griswold del Castillo and others, and *Native American Architecture* by Peter Nabokov.[17] In addition to the assigned readings, UC Berkeley African American Studies Professor Roy Thomas gave a guest lecture about the aesthetic development of African American art. Using examples from the film *Two Hundred Years of African American Art*, he outlined the five evolutionary stages of aesthetics in African American painting. The first of the five stages of this multicultural model was naive paintings that represented a crude and direct copying of European techniques and that portrayed only European images. The second stage involved refined European techniques and the confident portrayal of only European subjects by such artists as Henry O. Tanner. In the third stage, artists used European techniques to depict African images. The fourth stage was a clumsy merging of African techniques with Europe-

an techniques and the confident portrayal of African images. The final stage was the confident synthesis of both African and European techniques and images, represented by artists such as Charles White and Romare Bearden. Bearden's personal artistic development can be roughly traced in these stages.[18]

A Japanese American student adapted the multicultural model of aesthetic development presented by Professor Thomas to examine a Japanese American aesthetic. The student's final paper, "New Stone Gardens: Isamu Noguchi Develops a Japanese American Aesthetic," discusses the sculptor's several attempts to synthesize Eastern and Western aesthetics. Noguchi struggles to validate his Japanese American identity from his earliest clumsy juxtaposition of styles at the UNESCO Headquarters Garden in Paris to a successful synthesis of Eastern and Western aesthetics in his Chase Manhattan Bank Plaza in New York, which demonstrates a confident use of tradition and modern materials. A multicultural model opens a new way to understand the sculptural spaces created by Noguchi and has great potential for understanding the works of architects of color and others.[19] Architecture schools in the United States, with the many cultures they represent, could broaden their curricula with the study of an intercultural architecture.

Table 1 Registered Architects of the AIA by Ethnicity in California and in the United States, 1991

Ethnicity	No. in AIA (National)	%	No. in CCAIA (California)	%	State (% of National)
African American	380	1.1	53	1.0	13.9
Hispanic	785	1.9	151	3.3	19.2
Indian and Other	190	0.4	57	1.0	30.0
Asian	1530	3.6	575	9.9	37.6
Total Minority Members	2885	6.5	836	14.4	28.9
All Members	44,470		5791		13.0

The AIA, a trade organization of professional architects, generally represents 50 percent of all registered architects. For example, there are 771 African American architects nationwide, and 380, or 49 percent, are AIA members. In California, there are 110 registered African American architects, and 53, or 48 percent are AIA members.

Table 2 Full-Time Faculty in Architecture Schools by Ethnicity and Gender, 1991

All Faculty	Women	African American	Asian American	Latino	Native American
1893	267	64	49	47	2
100.0	14.0	3.3	2.5	2.5	0.1

Source: NAAB.

Table 3. Degree Completions in Architecture by Ethnicity and Gender, 1991

Degree Programs	Total	Women	Asian American	Latino	African American	Native American
Nonaccredited undergrad	2384	697	269	141	64	4
Accredited undergrad	3489	810	278	197	177	17
Master's	1575	499	105	69	37	8
Total	7448	2006	552	407	278	29
	100.0%	27.0%	7.0%	5.0%	4.0%	0.3%

Source: NAAB.

Research: If You Can't Find It, Think and Write It Down

We designed the third assignment as a team project to determine which resources were valuable in researching architects of color. For three weeks, the students evaluated university architectural libraries, ethnic-specific libraries, private museum collections, the American Institute of Architects' archives, the National Organization of Minority Architects' newly formed archives, historical societies' collections, building surveys and other resources including university faculty, professionals in private practice, and representatives of ethnic and business organizations.

The students found the small quantities of literature and the poor indexing of resources about architects of color to be inadequate and frustrating. Few interpretive works existed. Resources were unusually fragmented, and subject headings were not obvious for research of this nature. For example, there were headings for Japanese architects and Japanese architecture, but none for Japanese American architects or their works. Librarians and other scholars often told students that the proper way to research architects of color is by proper name, but architectural libraries rarely had any information on individual architects of color. One student summed up the class experience in a team research report: "I must admit I was discouraged to find that there are so few books about architects of color, but I was happy to find that our people are slowly being recognized in journals, film, and other source directories. One must approach this research by intuitively digging and searching for the smallest piece of information." In response to this frustrating situation, a geography Ph. D. student wrote an original bibliographic essay that annotates sources about African and African American building traditions, all-black towns and settlements, and African American art museums and historical societies.[20]

When the students began their individual research projects, these early disappointing findings led to a new attitude about research. They realized from the results of the team research projects that they must pursue original source material, the best form of research. Students began making intuitive guesses about possible sources. They developed their own criteria and wrote about their direct observation of the subjects. They made many calls to scholars, librarians, and relatives of subjects to gather information. They also developed questionnaires and conducted interviews. Though initially reluctant to use them, students eventually found oral resources to be invaluable. Students became more willing to analyze subjects without supportive interpretive works. They legitimized their subjects as important to research and claimed themselves to be experts when others did not yet exist. Their topics included murals in the San Francisco Bay area, storefront churches, the status of black architecture students, the twenty-year development of an organization for Chicano architecture students, a visionary artisan's search for environmentally sound architecture, and the works of Isamu Noguchi, I. M. Pei, Paul Williams, and McKissack, McKissack & Thompson.

Table 4. Top Degree Producers in Architecture, All Minority Groups, 1990–1991

Institution	Asian American	Hispanic	African American	Native American	Total
University of California, Berkeley, CA	69	25	9	3	106
University of Houston, TX	50	15	11	0	78
California Polytechnic, San Luis Obispo, CA	28	17	3	2	50
City University of New York, NY	12	28	9	0	49
University of Illinois, Champaign, IL	17	7	13	1	38
University of Texas, Arlington, TX	26	6	4	0	36
University of Miami, FL	30	1	3	0	34
Southern California Institute of Architecture, CA	8	7	2	15	32
Howard University, Washington, D.C.	1	0	30	0	31
California Polytechnic, Pomona, CA	13	15	1	2	31
University of Puerto Rico,	*	*	*	*	31

* Ethnic breakout not available.

The most valuable critical analysis of the students' writings occurred during the in-progress research presented to the class. These discussions allowed students to air frustrations, uncertainty of focus, and exciting discoveries. The open dialogue among the students and faculty about the presentations provided the opportunity to share information and critical viewpoints. Everyone presented their papers, evaluated other presentations, and revised their essays based on comments from in-class critiques. The knowledge gained during this process helped students to develop their many small findings into original essays.

For example, the class discussion of an in-progress work about storefront churches in African American communities resulted in a much improved analytical approach in a student's final paper. Because no published interpretive works existed about the thousands of storefront churches, the student relied on the few texts about traditional, primarily southern black churches and photographed thirty or more storefront churches in the San Francisco Bay Area. In an early presentation of his in-progress paper, he reviewed the literature of the traditional black church without an analysis of the storefront churches that he had directly observed. The pictures of the storefront churches he presented so intrigued the class that we focused our critical remarks on ways to interpret the storefront churches with the traditional black churches for possible influences. With new insights, the student wrote his final essay on the comparative features of the storefront churches and the influences of the traditional black church evidenced in them, including adaptations to commercial settings, uses of religious symbols, facade and fenestration configurations, and interior elements.[21]

Another student researched and wrote a critical analysis of the leadership and buildings by the eighty-five-year-old family-owned African American architectural firm in Tennessee, today known as McKissack, McKissack & Thompson (MM&T). Her original research on MM&T was especially challenging and well developed. Articles had been written about this family and its business history, but there was little critique of the more than four thousand buildings that MM&T has designed and built, including the Tuskegee Air Force Base, Universal Life Insurance Company's main headquarters in Memphis, and numerous schools, homes, churches, office buildings, hospitals, and university buildings. Nor was there much discussion of the special problems that the female executive management met while orchestrating an architectural firm's dramatic development which included securing the award of a $50-million contract and successfully suing the City of Nashville for excluding black architects from the city's airport expansion project. The student pursued many resources in her original research, including interviews with the management of MM&T, historical and contemporary photographic materials of MM&T buildings, articles from ethnic and business magazines about the architectural firm, and company-produced brochures. The edited interview with Leatrice McKissack and the analysis of several buildings designed by the firm were brought together in an illuminating essay.[22]

A Japanese/African American student remarked on his future as an architect in his final paper, "Paul Revere Williams: Innovator, Achiever, Architect": "As minority students in a field whose minority makeup is not too unlike that of a half a century ago, we often look to exceptional individuals that are like us for inspiration and recognition. Paul Williams is such a person, especially for the young, black, aspiring architect. His endurance in the environment of decades ago leads me to believe I can at least accomplish the same feat of endurance in today's tamer environment."

Paul Williams overcame racial prejudice to become a highly successful architect. During his prolific fifty-eight-year career, he designed more than two thousand homes, including several mansions designed for Hollywood stars, and hundreds of public buildings, including offices, restaurants, hotels, hospitals, churches, public housing, and an airport terminal. Williams's strong personal drive, exceptional communication skills, and design innovations made him one of Los Angeles's top architects. He ignored the discouragement of his high school teacher to avoid this field because success would depend on his ability to convince white clients to "cross the color line." He taught himself to draw upside down so that he could avoid standing next to his white clients and would appear to know his "place as a Negro." He produced sets of drawings in 22 hours while white architects insisted on two weeks to do the same job. Williams's innovations in small house design and his two subsequent books on the subject helped establish him as a design specialist of smaller homes for new couples and young families. Williams was hated by some blacks and embraced by some whites for his controversial remarks in the national press about "ignorant" slaves and the "fair treatment" blacks received from whites under the Jim Crow laws.[23]

As the students looked to role models to discern what their own future roles as architects might be, they uncovered design innovations, survival skills, consistent service to an underserved public, and new creations of intercultural aesthetics. Students analyzed the careers of professional architects and artists to construct a path of development for themselves in an environment that does not usually discuss such role models. A Chinese American architecture student who wrote about I. M. Pei commented in a class evaluation interview: "I learned from this class that architects of color have already done more than society leads us to believe. So, I know I can do even more now."

We compiled the results of the students' enthusiastic efforts to research the largely undocumented contributions of American architects of color in an unpublished anthology. The anthology includes an introduction, original essays, photographs, annotated bibliographies, brief biographical statements on the authors, and an appendix of additional research sources. After much discussion about the processes employed in research and writing, the students decided to call the anthology, *Looking Beneath the Surface: Discovering Third World Architects and Artists and Their Works*.[24] The bound anthology was the important final stage of the process. Students informally presented their work to a larger audience of friends and peers at a book-signing party held in the lobby of Wurster Hall. The class distributed the anthology to many of the traditional architectural research sources that struggled to help us earlier in the semester. We had hoped that others would find it useful in their efforts to write about architects of color and building traditions in communities of color. We continue to receive requests for the anthology from scholars and architectural libraries.

Summary and Conclusions

Writing multiculturalism into architecture curricula requires several changes. First, the course must integrate the classroom with the outside world. We drew on the knowledge, connections, and records of the larger community of architectural professionals and leaders from professional and business organizations. Scholars from other architecture schools, from other university departments, such as Ethnic Studies, and from national ethnic and architectural archives were able to share in the educational responsibilities of these students. In turn, students were able to establish scholarly relationships beyond the duration and scope of the class.

Second and related to the above issue is the use of a pedagogy that allows students to develop their own sense of value and learning initiatives. Rather than simply being recipients of research findings by other scholars, the students produced information that is not readily available within our profession. The students have pursued their interests in their research in impressive ways. Some decided to continue their research using the anthology to develop possible thesis projects. A Japanese American student went on to be a writer and translator for *Global Architecture* in Japan. An African American student went on to organize an annual symposium on African American architecture and environmental issues and to produce a publication based on the symposium. Other students from the class recently won a university grant to publish an architectural newsletter.

Third, as teachers we must be willing to be helpful guides to students' own learning initiatives, rather than lecturers on our own narrow, specialized interests. Our students, who were primarily motivated by their personal learning issues and who received broad guidance from us, produced results that were remarkable for their diversity, depth, and originality. The teachers did not have dominant roles in the class, but rather participatory roles, critical voices equal to other critical voices. Some students believed that we should provide more outside lecturers. Although lecturers on these topics were rare but happy finds, they also encouraged a business-as-usual attitude in which students could become spectators rather than producers of self-initiated research. The role of student-as spectator gave way to responsible participants in the class, who carried their new attitude outside the class to converse with other professional scholars. Other professors who address similar subjects concur that a transformative model in which students take responsibility for teaching each other is needed.

Fourth, architectural education must seek to engender social awareness and identification with a broadly understood social good. Students who are knowledgeable about the experiences of other American cultures are better prepared to participate creatively in our changing profession and society.[25]

Fifth, more of us must take up needed research into the treatment of architects of color and related subjects. To do so will require improvements in the research tools, research sources, and publications. The provision of electronic access from academic architectural libraries to national and private architectural archives that house much of this material would vastly improve access to research information. Also, subject headings must change to allow more direct access to existing information on architects of color. In the meantime, the continued publication of current bibliographies and directories on these subjects will aid preliminary research efforts.

Finally, these suggestions must be employed simultaneously to write multiculturalism into architecture curricula. Our modest teaching effort is offered as an example of the difference one course can make. Each of us has a unique role to play in augmenting our students' understanding of the diversity of professional experience. Ultimately, architectural scholarship that fully includes all American cultures will attract more students of color to our profession.

Editors' note: Students' quotations were not attributed in the original.

Notes

1. Sylvia Lewis, "Breaking through the Glass Ceiling," *APA Planning* 57 (July 1991): 13.
2. AIA Minority Resources Committee (MRC) "Minority Membership Statistics," *MRC Report* (Winter 1991), back cover.
3. NAAB, annual reports, "Statistical Information," Washington, D.C. (September 1991).
4. Raymond Dalton, *Admission, Retention, and Support Services of African-American Architecture Students: A National Survey*, Ph. D. Dissertation, Purdue University (Ann Arbor, MI: UMI Dissertation Information Service, 1990), 3, 8.
5. Kim Moy, "Faculty Diversity Comes Slowly," *The Daily Californian* 27, no. 180 (November 27, 1991): 1.
6. NAAB, annual reports.
7. Robert Bea, Robert Beckley, Adèle Santos, et al. of the Ad Hoc Committee of the Graduate Council, University of California, Berkeley, *A Review of the Department of Architecture: Academic Years 1990–1992*, App. A: "Summary of Outside Reviewers' Reports," (unpublished), 3.
8. William Simmons, "American Cultures at the University of California, Berkeley," Brochure (May 1992), 1.
9. Anthony Ward, "Biculturalism and Community: A Transformative Model for Design Education," *Journal of Architectural Education* 44, no. 2 (February 1991): 93.
10. Simmons, "American Cultures,'" 2.
11. Thomas Dutton, ed., *Voices in Architectural Education: Cultural Politics and Pedagogy* (New York: Bergin & Garvey, 1991), 149–278.
12. Kisho Kurokawa, *Intercultural Architecture: The Philosophy of Symbiosis* (Washington, D.C.: American Institute of Architects Press, 1991).
13. Paul Williams, *The Small Home of Tomorrow*. (Hollywood, CA: Murray and Gee, 1945); Paul Williams, *New Homes for Today* (Hollywood, CA: Murray and Gee, 1946); Carter Wiseman, *I. M. Pei* (New York: Random House, 1990); Genell Anderson, *The Call of the Ancestors* (Washington, D.C.: AMAR Publications, 1991); Dell Upton, ed., *America's Architectural Roots: Ethnic Groups That Built America* (Washington, D.C.: National Trust for Historic Preservation, 1986); Peter Nabokov, *Native American Architecture* (New York: Oxford University Press, 1989); Jorge Rigau, *Puerto Rico 1900: Turn-of-the-Century Architecture in the Hispanic Caribbean 1890-1930* (New York: Rizzoli, 1992).
14. George Cantor, *Historic Landmarks of Black America* (Detroit: Gale Research, 1991); Jack Travis, ed., *African American Architects in Current Practice* (New York: Princeton Architectural Press, 1991); Bradford C. Grant and Dennis Mann, *Directory of African American Architects* (Cincinnati, OH: Center for the Study of the Practice of Architecture of the University of Cincinnati, 1991).
15. Robert Traynham Coles, "Black Architects, an Endangered Species," editorial, *Progressive Architecture Magazine* (July 1989): 7 [Editors' note: Also published in the *Journal of Architectural Education*, including republication in this volume; see Robert Traynham Coles, "Black Architects: An Endangered Species," *Journal of Architectural Education* 43, no. 1 (Autumn 1989): 60–62]; Jane Kay, "Invisible Architects: Minority Firms Struggle to Achieve Recognition in a White-Dominated Profession," *Architecture* (April 1991): 106; Roberto Rodriguez, "Black Architects up against a Brick Wall," *Black Issues in Higher Education* (December 5, 1991): 18; also see Bradley Inman, "Hispanic Contribution to City's Architecture Often Overlooked," *San Francisco Examiner*, May 10, 1992, F-1; Eve Kahn, "Renewed Hope for Black Architects" *New York Times*, April 9, 1992, B-1; Paul Williams, "Blacks Who Overcame the Odds," *Ebony Magazine* (November 1986): 148. This abridgment from the autobiographical "I Am a Negro" essay in *American Magazine* (1937) selectively edits quotes likely to be offensive to contemporary African Americans.
16. See Ward, "Biculturalism and Community," 94–95, for a discussion about the impact of cultural experience ("epistemological privilege") on pedagogy.
17. Lawrence Levine, *Black Culture and Black Consciousness: Afro-American Folk Thought from Slavery to Freedom* (New York: Oxford University Press, 1977); T. Minh-Ha Trinh, *Woman, Native, Other: Writing Postcoloniality and Feminism* (Bloomington, IN; Indiana University Press, 1989); Richard Griswold del Castillo, Teresa McKenna, and Yvonne Yarbro-Bejarano, eds., *Chicano Art: Resistance and Affirmation, 1965-1985* (Los Angeles, CA: Wright Gallery, University of California, 1991); Nabokov, *Native American Architecture*.
18. Mary Schmidt Campbell, "History and the Art of Romare Bearden," in *Memory and Metaphor: The Art of Romare Bearden 1940-1987*, eds. Romare Bearden, Mary Schmidt Campbell, Sharon F. Patton, Studio Museum in Harlem (New York: Oxford University Press, 1991), 7–17.
19. Takashi Yanai, "New Stone Gardens: Isamu Noguchi Develops a Japanese-American Aesthetic," in *Looking Beneath the Surface: Discovering Third World Architects and Artists and Their Works*, eds. Regina Davis and Ken Simmons (unpublished anthology, University of California, Berkeley, 1991), 9–21. This unpublished anthology of student works was compiled from "Writing about Third World Architects and Artists and Their Works," offered by Regina Davis and Ken Simmons at the College of Environmental Design of the University of California, Berkeley in Spring 1991.
20. David Organ, "The Study of African American Architects, Artists and Urban Designers in the New World," in *Looking Beneath the Surface*, ed. Davis and Simmons, 177–92.
21. Stacy Harris, "The Storefront Church: Aesthetics and Functionalism in the Black Community," in *Looking Beneath the Surface*, eds. Davis and Simmons, 132–58.
22. Carol Corr, "The Architecture of McKissack, McKissack & Thompson," in *Looking Beneath the Surface*, eds. Davis and Simmons, 71–83.
23. David Y. Garnett, "Paul Revere Williams: Innovator, Achiever, Architect" in *Looking Beneath the Surface*, eds. Davis and Simmons, 44–70.
24. Davis and Simmons, eds., *Looking Beneath the Surface*.
25. David Norton, "Afterword: A Philosophical Appraisal," in *Education for Creative Living: Ideas and Proposals of Tsunesaburo Makiguchi*, ed. Dayle Bethel (Ames, IA: Iowa State University Press, 1989): 203–214.

Contesting the Public Realm:
Struggles Over Public Space in Los Angeles

Margaret Crawford
Southern California Institute of Architecture

This article, in response to architectural "narratives of loss" lamenting the disappearance of public space, argues that urban residents are constantly remaking public space and redefining the public sphere through their lived experience. Following Nancy Fraser, this article questions the insistence on a unified public, the desire for fixed categories, and the rigid concepts of public and private space that characterize the bourgeois public sphere and proposes contestation, competing "counter-publics," and the blurring of private and public as equally significant aspects of the public sphere. In Los Angeles, the struggles of two "counter-publics," street vendors and the homeless, over use of the streets and public places reveal the emergence of another discourse of public space, suggesting new forms of "insurgent citizenship" and offering new political arenas.

Today, many discussions of the public sphere and public space are dominated by a narrative of loss. From the political philosopher Jurgen Habermas's description of a public sphere overwhelmed by consumerism, the media, and the intrusion of the state into private life, to Richard Sennett's lament for "the fall of public man," to urban critics Michael Sorkin's and Mike Davis's announcements of "the end of public space" and the "destruction of any truly democratic urban spaces," claims that once vital sites of democracy have all but disappeared are widespread.[1] These narratives of loss contrast the current debasement of the public sphere with golden ages and golden sites: the Greek agora, the coffeehouses of early modern Paris and London, the New England town square, where, allegedly, cohesive public discourse once thrived. This narrative inevitably climaxes in what these critics see as our current crisis of collective life, which places the very identities and institutions of citizenship and democracy in peril.

I argue that this perceived loss is primarily perceptual, derived from extremely narrow and normative definitions of both public and space. In fact, the meaning of concepts such as public, space, democracy, and citizenship are continually being redefined in practice through lived experience. By eliminating the insistence on unity, the desire for fixed categories of time and space, and the rigid concepts of public and private that underlie these narratives of loss, we can begin to recognize a multiplicity of simultaneous public interactions that are restructuring urban space, producing new forms of insurgent citizenship, and revealing new political arenas for democratic action.

In her important article, "Rethinking the Public Sphere," Nancy Fraser identifies some significant theoretical and political limitations contained in the arguments about these disappearances of the public sphere.[2] While acknowledging the importance of Habermas's influential concept of the public sphere as an arena of discursive relations conceptually independent of both the state and the economy, she questions many of its underlying assumptions. Habermas's account of "the liberal model of the bourgeois public sphere" links its emergence in early modern Europe with the development of nation-states in which democracy was realized through universal rights and electoral politics.

This version of the history of the public sphere emphasizes unity and equality as ideal conditions. The public sphere is depicted as a "space of democracy" that all citizens have the right to inhabit and where all public discourse takes place. Here, social and economic inequalities are temporarily put aside in the interest of determining a "common good." Discussion about matters of common interests is achieved through rational, disinterested, and virtuous public debate. However, like the often-cited ideal of Athenian democracy and the agora, this model is structured around significant exclusions. In Athens, access was theoretically open to all citizens, but in practice this excluded the majority of the population—women and slaves—who were not "citizens." Similarly, the modern bourgeois public sphere began by excluding women and workers. Women's interests were presumed to be private and therefore part of the domestic sphere, and workers' concerns were presumed to be economic and thus excluded as self-interested. Moreover, the requirements for rational deliberation and a rhetoric of disinterest privileged middle-class and masculine modes of public speech and behavior by defining them as universal norms.[3]

Recent revisionist history has contradicted this account, demonstrating that non-liberal, non-bourgeois publics also emerged, producing competing definitions and spheres of public activity in a multiplicity of public arenas. In nineteenth- and twentieth-century America, for example, middle-class women organized themselves into a variety of exclusively female voluntary organizations that undertook philanthropic and

Pershing Square in downtown Los Angeles, redesigned by Ricardo Legorreta.

reform activities based on private ideals of domesticity and motherhood. Less privileged women found access to public life through work and public roles that addressed both domestic and economic issues. Working-class men also founded their own public organizations, often structured around workplace or ethnic identities, such as unions, lodges, and political organizations. If we broaden the definition of public from a singular entity to include these "counterpublics," a very different picture of the public sphere is revealed, one based on contestation, rather than unity, and created through competing interests and violent demands as much as by reasoned debate. Demonstrations, strikes, and riots, as well as struggles over issues such as temperance or suffrage, propose alternative public spheres, arenas where multiple publics with inevitably competing concerns struggle and where conflict takes many forms.

In the bourgeois public sphere, public citizenship is primarily defined in relation to the state, addressing issues and concerns dealt with through political debate and electoral politics framed within clear categories of discourse. This assumes a liberal notion of citizenship based on abstract universal liberties, with democracy guaranteed by the electoral and juridical institutions of the state. Fraser instead argues that democracy itself is a complex and contested idea that can assume a multiplicity of meanings and forms. These often violate the strict lines between public and private on which the liberal bourgeois concept of the public sphere insists. In contrast, counterpublics of women, immigrants, and workers have historically not only defended established civil rights, but also demanded new rights based on differentiated roles originating in the domestic or economic spheres.

These constantly changing demands continually redraw the boundaries between public and private. Two current efforts to redefine public and private behavior demonstrate both the intensity and the complexity of these struggles. On one side, feminists are attempting to transform domestic violence from a matter of strictly private or domestic concern, dealt with within the family or through specialized institutions of family law or social work, into a matter of public concern and legal control. On the other side, the religious right is attempting to transform abortion from a private decision about one's own body into a public act regulated by civil law. While pursuing conventional remediation through legal or legislative means and attempting, through public debate, to mobilize public opinion, both groups also adopt less conventional methods that further blur the line between public and private. Feminist activists have attempted to create an alternative domestic sphere to the family by creating shelters and other communal living arrangements for battered women. Antiabortion demonstrators have abandoned rational discourse in favor of direct action and civil disobedience.

Rethinking Public Space

How can Fraser's ideas of multiple publics, contestation, and the redefinition of public and private be extended and applied to the physical realm of public space without losing their connection with larger issues of democracy and citizenship? First of all, they suggest that no single physical space can represent a completely inclusive "space of democracy." Like Habermas's idealized bourgeois public sphere, the physical spaces often idealized by architects—the agora, the forum, the piazza, or the town square—were similarly constituted by exclusion.[5] Thus, instead of a single "public" occupying an exemplary public space, the multiple and counterpublics that Fraser identifies necessarily produce multiple sites of public expression, creating and using spaces that are partial and selective, responsive to limited segments of the population and to a limited number of the multiple public roles individuals play in urban society. Rather than being fixed in time and space, these public spaces are constantly changing, as users reorganize and reinterpret physical space. Unlike normative public spaces, which simply reproduce the existing ideology, these spaces, often sites of struggle and contestation, help to overturn it. The public activities that occur here suggest that urban politics and urban space can be restructured from the bottom up as well as from the top down.

The narrative of lost public space presents Los Angeles as particularly compelling evidence for the disappearance of public life. Most critics agree that the city's low-density development and widespread dependence on the automobile have eliminated street life and public interaction. The city's traditional public spaces support the argument that public space and public life in the city are either commodified, bankrupt, or nonexistent. For example, over the last thirty years, Pershing Square, historically the central focus of the downtown business district, has lost any public meaning. Mexican architect Ricardo Legorreta's recent redesign, featuring

The *Los Angeles Times*'s coverage of struggles over public parks in Santa Monica.

brightly colored walkways, plazas, and seating areas above underground parking and a subway station, has failed to reinstate its public function. Although still physically recognizable as a traditional public square, it is usually unoccupied, except for a few hours at lunch time, and its emptiness visibly demonstrates the city's impoverished public life.

In contrast, the sidewalks of Citywalk are always jammed with people. Operated by MCA, Inc., and Universal Studios, this complex of movie theaters, shops, and restaurants was designed as a simulation of a public street, a collage of Los Angeles's most attractive urban elements supervised by mall designer Jon Jerde. Citywalk's popular appeal, however, owes as much to its crime-free image as to its architectural spectacle. The management of this privately owned space has the right to exclude anyone they deem undesirable, in addition to those groups of the public already discouraged by its suburban location, six dollar parking fee, and heavily policed spaces. To many architectural and urban critics, Citywalk's success demonstrates the total absorption of public life by private enterprise.[4]

However, Fraser's redefined public sphere allows us to identify other sites of public expression that propose an alternative conception of public space. The civil unrest of April 1992, for example, can be interpreted as a spontaneous and undefined moment of public expression, an explosion of multiple and competing demands (some highly specific, others barely articulated) on the streets and sidewalks of Los Angeles. These events unleashed a complex outpouring of public concerns, involving a number of different ethnic and social groups. African Americans, many of whom called the uprising the "justice riots," attacked the inadequacy of urban politics to redress the juridical inequality demonstrated by the Rodney King and Latasha Harlins verdicts. To many, this constituted a denial of fundamental rights of citizenship. Liberal concepts of universally defined civil rights failed to address the visible racism of the police department and the court system, allowing them to avoid public responsibility to more specifically defined ethnic and social groups.

The riots also dramatized economic issues: poverty and the lack of jobs, exacerbated by the recession and the long-term effects of deindustrialization. This was expressed through highly selective patterns of looting and burning that largely spared residences while attacking commercial property; 74 percent of damaged buildings were retail stores and restaurants.[5] Despite public perception, the riots were multicultural. Thirty-four percent of those arrested were black, 51 percent were Hispanic, mostly recent immigrants. Also economically marginalized and exploited, they protested their economic exclusion and political and social disenfranchisement. The riot also pitted immigrants against one another. Korean-owned stores were the focus of much of the burning and looting, serving as targets for pent-up frustration about the lack of economic self-determination in low-income neighborhoods. Briefly, streets, sidewalks, parking lots, swap meets, and mini-malls became sites of protest and rage: new zones of public expression.

The violent dissatisfaction revealed by the unrest makes it imperative to look more closely at the lived experience of different groups in the riot areas and to acknowledge their use of everyday space as a site of public discourse. Looking around the city, we can discover innumerable places where new social and economic practices reappropriate and restructure urban space. Arenas for struggle over the meaning of social participation, these new public spaces are continually in flux, producing constantly changing meanings. Streets, sidewalks, vacant lots, parks, and other places of the city, reclaimed by immigrant groups, the poor, and the homeless, have become sites where public debates about the meaning of democracy, the nature of economic participation, and the public assertion of identity are acted out on a daily basis. Without claiming that they represent a totality of public space, in their manifold forms these public activities collectively construct and reveal an alternative logic of public life.

Street Vendors

No longer deserted, Los Angeles's streets, sidewalks, and vacant lots are increasingly populated by street vendors. Existing on the margins of the formal economy, their informal commerce supplements income, rather than constituting an occupation, or else supports only the most marginal of existences. Although all types of street vendors openly occupy space all over the city, street vending remains illegal. Current discussions about centralizing vendors in designated locations acknowledge the existing reality of widespread vending but attempt to restrict one of the main advantages of vending: its flexibility to respond to changes in activity and demand. Street vending constitutes a complex and diverse economy of microcommerce, recycling,

Street vendor selling papaya on Sixth Street in Los Angeles.

Vendors along La Brea Avenue in Baldwin Hills.

and household production. The innumerable variety of vendors publicly articulates the multiple social and economic narratives of urban life in Los Angeles. In the process of pursuing their trade, vendors blur established understandings of public and private in complex and paradoxical ways.

Dramas of immigration are played out daily on the streets of Los Angeles, increasingly exposing to the consciousness of the city stories both heroic and horrifying. For example, the ubiquitous orange vendors, working on street dividers all over the city, are almost always undocumented immigrants. Working for the "coyotes"' who brought them across the border, they sell the fruit the coyotes supply to pay off the cost of their illegal crossing. Along streets in the Zona Centroamericana, other immigrants use vending as a means of economic mobility. For many self-employed vendors, their vending carts provide an alternative to sweatshop labor and may eventually lead to a stall at a swap meet or even a small store. Lined up along sidewalks, wearing aprons, female vendors extend the domestic economy into urban space, selling tropical fruits, tamales, or nuts that they have prepared or packaged in their own kitchens. Defending the right to sell on the street has become a political issue to many immigrant vendors, many of whom are undocumented, therefore doubly illegal. The organization of *Vendadores Ambulates* represents the interests of more than eight hundred vendors to the city government. Other vendors recently demonstrated against police harassment, chanting, "Somos vendedores, no criminales" (We are vendors, not criminals).[6] Defending their livelihood, vendors are becoming a political as well as an economic presence in the city.

In other parts of the city, vending takes different forms. In Baldwin Hills, a middle-class African-American neighborhood, a parking lot between a gas station and a supermarket has become a scene of intense, if fluctuating, social and commercial activity. On most days, a van parks in the lot, offering car detailing services. The operators, two local men who are now retired, set out chairs, providing a social magnet for neighborhood men who pass by. On weekends, a portable barbecue is set up nearby, selling "home-cooked" ribs and links. On holidays and weekends, a group of middle-aged women joins them, setting up tables to sell homemade crafts and gifts. Mostly grandmothers who work at home, their products represent both hobbies and an income supplement. Replicating the domestic order of the surrounding neighborhoods and expanding the private roles of grandparents into the public realm, their local activities provide a focus for the community that is also accessible to anyone driving by. Simultaneously local and public, the activities in this parking lot strengthen the neighborhood while they visibly represent its culture to outsiders.

The Homeless

No group challenges the limits of the concept of "public" more than the homeless. Even the designated social category of homelessness can be seen as a method of removing a group of people from the larger collectivity of the public by collapsing various life situations, such as joblessness, disability, or extreme poverty, into a generic category. For many homeless people, minimal boundaries exist between public space and the spheres of domestic and economic life. Occupying parks, streets, sidewalks, and the lawns of public buildings, they claim the space necessary for their own personal and economic survival. This forces them to live at least part of their private lives on the street and in other public places. It is often impossible for them to secure domestic privileges that are taken for granted, such as bedrooms, closets, and private bathrooms. Their private use of public space tests democracy's promise of universal access in a very literal fashion.

For the homeless, streets and sidewalks also function as important economic spaces. Although most homeless people work, they do not earn enough money to afford shelter. Instead, public spaces become their primary venue for seeking work and acquiring money. Waiting for day-labor jobs, posting bills, recycling cans and bottles, or collecting and reselling refuse or castoffs, homeless men and women claim their rights to be economic actors.[7] Using cardboard signs to explain their circumstances, they assert their identities as unique individuals in need of a job or money. Even panhandling can be understood as an economic transaction, encouraging individuals to evaluate requests for a certain amount of money or a specific need on the basis of their own judgment or financial situation.

Yet even these minimal social and economic rights are under attack. If Pershing Square, with its hard surfaces and intense security, was explicitly designed to repel the homeless, far more intense struggles over public space are taking place in Santa Monica. Intent on criminalizing the daily activities of the homeless, the city council is incrementally redefining the nature of public space while gradually expelling the homeless from the city. After a ban on sleeping in public parks proved unenforceable, the city closed all parks from midnight to 6 a.m. Even in daytime, the presence of homeless people in city parks has become a point of tension, with some parents demanding that homeless people be evicted from parks with playgrounds and sports facilities. Other anti-homeless measures include eliminating food programs in city parks and preventing the expansion of social service agencies. Local merchants are also attempting to eradicate panhandling; they have initiated a campaign to urge pedestrians not to give money directly to panhandlers but instead to put donations into a bronze dolphin, to be distributed to approved social service agencies.[8] For these people, the definition of a "public" place has become a space without homeless people. Homelessness is perhaps the ultimate determination of citizenship. Defined as undesirables, the homeless are not just evicted from public parks, they are stripped of "the right to have rights."[9] In Santa Monica, the right to public space has become conditional, based on official residence, appearance, or adherence to a set of values that defines "proper" use.

New Forms of Insurgent Citizenship
These struggles define what anthropologist James Holston has called "spaces of insurgent citizenship."[10] These emergent sites of citizenship accompany the processes of change that are transforming societies locally and worldwide. In cities such as Los Angeles, migration, industrial restructuring, and other economic changes increase social reterritorialization. When they appear in the city, residents with new histories, cultures, and demands inevitably disrupt the normative categories of social life and urban space. In the course of expressing the specific needs of everyday life, they dramatize the large-scale public issues of economic change and migration. Their urban experiences, the focus of their struggle to redefine the conditions of belonging to society, reshape cities like Los Angeles. As new and more complex kinds of ethnic diversity come to dominate the city, these multiple experiences increasingly define a new basis for understanding citizenship.

The homeless and the street vendors, demanding access to public space, are just two of many social groups articulating new demands. The demands of the urban poor for "rights to the city" and of women and ethnic and racial minorities to "rights to difference" constitute new kinds of rights, based on the needs of lived experience outside of the normative and institutional definitions of the state and its legal codes. These rights emerge from the social dramas acted out in the new collective and personal spaces of the city; they concern people largely excluded from the resources of the state; and they are based on social demands that are not constitutionally defined but that people increasingly perceive as entitlements of citizenship. Expanding the definition of urban political activity to include these new social bases can produce new forms of self-rule, which in turn can lead to new social movements that challenge existing formulations of democracy.

Holston warns that, while the city is an arena for the self-creation of these new citizens, it is also a war zone. The dominant classes have met the advances of these new citizens with new strategies of segregation, privatization, and fortification. The war zone includes gang-devastated neighborhoods, corporate fortresses, and suburban enclaves. Just as the local and the urban appear as crucial sites for articulating new social identities, they also engender exclusion and violent reaction. The public sites where such struggles occur serve as evidence of an emerging order, not yet fully comprehensible. Here differences between the domestic and the economic, the private and the public are blurring. Change, multiplicity, and contestation—rather than constituting the failure of public space may in fact define its very nature. The emergence of these new public spaces and activities in Los Angeles, shaped by lived experience more than built space, raises complex political questions about the meaning of economic participation and citizenship in our cities. By recognizing these struggles as the germ of an alternative development of democracy, we can begin to frame a new discourse of public space—one no longer preoccupied with loss, but filled with possibilities.

Notes
1. Jürgen Habermas, *The Structural Transformation of the Public Sphere: An Inquiry into a Category of Bourgeois Society* (Cambridge, MA: MIT Press, 1989); Richard Sennett, *The Fall of Public Man* (New York: Vintage Books, 1974); Michael Sorkin, "Introduction," in Michael Sorkin, ed. *Variations on a Theme Park: The New American City and the End of Public* Space (New York: Hill and Wang, 1992), xi–xv; and Mike Davis, "Fortress Los Angeles: The Militarization of Urban Space," in Michael Sorkin, ed. *Variations on a Theme Park*, 154–180.

2. Nancy Fraser, "Rethinking the Public Sphere: A Contribution to the Critique of Actually Existing Democracy," in Bruce Robbins, ed., *The Phantom Public Sphere* (Minneapolis, MN: University of Minnesota Press, 1993).
3. Fraser, "Rethinking the Public Sphere," 4–6.
4. David Wharton, "A Walk on the Mild Side," *Los Angeles Times*, May 27, 1994, Valley Edition, 10; Norman Klein, "A Glittery Bit of Urban Make-believe," *Los Angeles Times*, July 18, 1993, B17; Leon Whiteson, "Dream Street," *Los Angeles Times*, October 31, 1993, K1; and Charles Jencks, *Heteropolis* (London: Academy Editions, 1993), 46–51.
5. Frank Clifford, "Rich-Poor Gulf Widens in State," *Los Angeles Times*, May 11, 1992, A1; "The Path to Fury," *Los Angeles Times*, May 11, 1992, T1–T10; and Mike Davis, "In L.A., Burning All Illusions," *The Nation*, June 1, 1992, 743.
6. Robert Lopez, "Vendors Protest against LAPD," *Los Angeles Times*, August 2, 1994, B3.
7. For an excellent overview of homelessness in Los Angeles, see Jennifer Wolch and Michael Dear, *Malign Neglect: Homelessness in an American City* (San Francisco, CA: Jossey-Bass, 1993).
8. Nancy Hill-Holzman, "Brother, Keep Your Dime," *Los Angeles Times*, July 11, 1992, J1; Nancy Hill-Holzman, "A Lightning Rod for Anger over Homeless," *Los Angeles Times*, November 10, 1991, J1; and Jeff Kramer, "City Wants to Shut Palisades Park at Night," *Los Angeles Times*, June 10, 1993, B1.
9. Rosalyn Deutsche, "Art and Public Space: Questions of Democracy," *Social Text* 33 (Fall 1992): 37–39.
10. James Holston, "Spaces of Insurgent Citizenship," *Planning Theory* 13 (Summer 1995): 30–50.

Bauhaus Hausfrau: Gender Formation in Design Education

Katarina Rüedi Ray
University of Illinois at Chicago

This essay examines the crisis of masculinity at the Bauhaus and links it to a broader crisis in patriarchy after the First World War. Bauhaus reminiscences and depictions of Bauhaus students and buildings in the catalog of the 1938 MoMA Bauhaus exhibition show a re-enactment of war trauma in Bauhaus theatre and festivals. These and other experiments led to radical and subsequently conservative revisions of masculine identity. The paper suggests that the construction of a new disciplinary identity through institutional and media reproduction rather than its economically limited innovations in mass production forms the real legacy of the Bauhaus for the twentieth century. The essay draws heavily on personal statements by Bauhaus students and masters, and juxtaposes these with theoretical analyses of masculine formation. This technique at least in part allows for the theorists and historical subjects to speak for themselves.

Prologue: The Dominant Fiction

> *Through fantasy then, "we learn 'how to desire.'"*
>
> —Kaja Silverman[1]

For psychoanalytic theory from Sigmund Freud onward, human identity and desire are built on a void, or lack, which is initiated at the moment an infant consciously separates from its mother. Described by Jacques Lacan as the mirror or imaginary stage of identity formation, this is the moment when desire and lack are born, and for the male they function together in a second phase: when the male enters the Oedipal or symbolic stage, becomes aware of gender difference, separates from the mother again, and begins his association with the authority of patriarchy. The male expresses this double lack by projecting it both as a cultural and personal lack onto the female, assigning her world to a lower standing, consequently expecting her to be weak, unstable, and obedient and to hold multiple identities. Kaja Silverman links these psychoanalytic theories to Louis Althusser's theory of ideology. Patriarchy, she defines as a "dominant fiction" the principal unconscious belief system that regulates cultural reproduction. The dominant fiction is the ideological reality through which we live out and reproduce, both symbolically and practically, gender, class, race, and other differentiations. The system of those differentiations is the product of middle-class white men, and its beginning can be found in the institution of the family. Silverman's term *dominant fiction* allows her to emphasize the role of power in ensuring unconscious consent (dominant) as well as the role of fantasy (fiction) in maintaining the social order.

Reminiscences of Bauhaus students and masters demonstrate that Lacan's and Silverman's theories can elegantly explain the transitions in identity formation at this important model for twentieth century design education and that the crisis and subsequent victory of patriarchy at the Bauhaus provide important lessons for identity formation in design education.

Part One: War and Identity

> *There stands a man, a man*
> *As firm as any oak tree, oak tree,*
> *Maybe he has lived through many a tempest, tempest, tempest,*
> *Maybe by tomorrow he will be a corpse,*
> *Like so many brothers before him, him, him.*
>
> —Song composed by Bauhaus students for Lyonel Feininger's feast day[2]

Throughout Europe, the huge losses of what came to be called the Great War had a major impact on the collective unconscious. Germany was the greatest loser, with enormous casualties, reduced territory, and economic and social problems far worse than those of the victors. The crisis of its dominant fiction was extreme, spanning from social identity to architecture. Architectural forms associated with the old social order were rejected. Bruno Taut wrote,

> It was not possible to make use of any prewar traditions, for that period was perforce regarded as the cause of the misfortunes of the past, and because every achievement of those days seemed more or less to hang together with the origins of the war.[3]

Not only was the traditional social order in crisis, but human identity—and with it artistic and architectural identity—was seen to be in a similar state of profound uncertainty. War had ravaged not only the economy but also the collective psyche. Walter Gropius, himself a casualty of war (having been injured and abandoned for several days in a bombed and ruined building), later wrote,

Today's artist lives in an era of dissolution, without guidance. He stands alone. The old forms are in ruins, the benumbed world is shaken up, the old human spirit is invalidated and in flux toward a new form. We float in space and cannot yet perceive the new order.[4]

The *Arbeitsrat für Kunst*, under whose auspices this passage was written, was one of the radical new cultural collectives that looked to a new and utopian future. The creation of a new kind of human being was seen as the solution to social and cultural crisis. Gropius continued: "First man must be constructed; only then can the artist make him fine new clothing. The contemporary being must begin anew, to rejuvenate himself, to achieve a new humanity, a universal life-form of the people."[5]

Bauhaus students responded similarly. Magdalena Droste writes that many "arrived direct from active service, hoping for the chance to make a fresh start and give meaning to their lives."[6] T. Lux Feininger observed, "Almost all have been in the army, it is a new type, a new generation . . . these young people are not babies."[7] The transformation of the new arrivals began by reenacting wartime trauma. Herbert Bayer's description of the (partly fictional) Bauhaus entrance exam resembles that of a battlefield:

> When I saw the first Bauhaus proclamation, ornamented with Feininger's woodcut, I made inquiries as to what the Bauhaus really was. I was told that "during the entrance examinations every applicant is locked up in a dark room. Thunder and lightning are let loose upon him to get him in a state of agitation. His being admitted depends on how well he describes his reactions." This report, although it exaggerated the actual facts, fired my enthusiasm.[8]

Uniforms, gestures, songs, and anthems evoking military experience also formed part of corporate identity at the school. Tut Schlemmer wrote, "A Bauhaus garment was designed, the Bauhaus whistle and the Bauhaus salute were invented."[9] The Bauhaus song composed and sung by students for Lyonel Feininger's feast day quoted at the beginning of this section echoes the melancholy legacy of war.

Worship of physical obedience flourished. Ritualized mystical doctrines—in particular Mazdaznan, an ancient Persian religion related to Zoroastrism introduced to the Bauhaus by Introductory Workshop master Johannes Itten—provided students and masters with rigid rules of dress, movement, and diet. Itten inspired students to adopt monastic dress and coiffure. Lothar Schreyer wrote, "When one day Itten declared that long hair was a sign of sin, his most enthusiastic disciples shaved their heads completely. And thus we went around Weimar."[10]

Students also established control over identity by constructing precise rules for "reading" the body. Paul Citroen, a student, wrote proudly:

> When we shook someone's hand we could tell more about him from the handshake, the dryness or dampness of his skin, and other signs, than he would find comfortable. His vocal pitch, his complexion, his walk, every one of his involuntary gestures gave him away. We thought we could see through any person, because our method gave us advantage over the unsuspecting.[11]

Itten's teaching consciously used educational ritual to link (a lack of) bodily control to the production of new identities and beliefs. In the introductory course, he asked students to draw the war and directed the highest praise to an abstract drawing by a student who had never been a soldier. The condemned majority accepted this with admiration. The students' willingness to accept this revealed their acknowledgment of their bodies and minds as institutionalized objects.

Perhaps the most extreme example was a bizarre ritual instituted by Itten and here described by Citroen:

> There was, among other things, a little needle machine with which we were to puncture our skins. Then the body would be rubbed with the same sharp oil which had served as a laxative. A few days later all the pinpoints would break out in scabs and pustules—the oil had drawn the wastes and impurities of the deeper skin layers to the surface. Now we were ready to be bandaged. But we must work hard, sweat, and then, with continued fasting, the ulcerations would dry out. At any rate, that's what the book said. In actuality the puncturing didn't go according to plan or desire, and for months afterward we would be tormented with itching.[12]

Such extremes of self-denial were clearly masochistic in nature. They rewarded both pain and obedience with precious praise and a sense of social belonging. At the same time, displacing fears of the disintegration of identity onto physical actions of the body, they made these fears controllable. Unusually, masochistic fantasy created a fiction of power through which Itten's Bauhaus initiates could become superior to other students. Citroen continues:

> Great demands were made on our self-denial, and if we occasionally sinned when conditions were too hard or hunger or thirst

too great, on the whole we felt happy and privileged to have the firm support of our doctrine, to know the right way so that we did not, like the others, collapse in the general chaos.[13]

A far more important area of collective identity formation, involving many more students, consisted of Bauhaus festivals and theater. Festivals in particular, because all students and masters participated, commanded great enthusiasm. Felix Klee wrote:

> My dear friend, you have no idea how important festivals were at the Bauhaus—often far more important than the classes. They made the contact between master, journeyman and apprentice far closer. The masters radiated their influence on the students in the most positive way. They could develop all the more freely because they had enough time and were not hindered in their personal development by an overly rigid schedule. And there was a reciprocal action by the students on the teachers. One could call it a living "give and take" such as I have never again come across to such an extent.[14]

There were many kinds of festivals, including the kite, the lantern, and the metallic festivals. A festival was even held to celebrate Walter Gropius's birthday. Students created special costumes, invented dances, built installations, and made surreal presents for the masters. Klee wrote about the Yuletide festival:

> With great hue and cry a student dressed as an angel dragged a closed wash-basket to the door, tore it open, and practically threw the presents into our midst. There were large and small packages with names on them. We unwrapped one in high expectation, and there was another, a smaller package with another name on it. Each package was handed around until finally the very last one produced the gift itself. The Schlemmers had just had two daughters, Karin and Jaina, born in the coachhouse of the Belvedere Palace. That night Oskar received thirteen more daughters with marvellous imaginary names.[15]

Festivals were powerful in constructing collective identity precisely because they were non-curricular. They were true fantasies; through the "living 'give and take'" masters and students "could develop all the more freely" because they were not consciously constrained by an "overly rigid" identity implicit in the concept of a standard curriculum. Bauhäusler participated enthusiastically in such rehearsals of identity and through them learned to desire and enact multiple identities.

Through the Bauhaus theater, in contrast, Bauhäusler learned to desire a more "overly rigid" identity. The theater was central to the formation of a singular identity at the school and acted as the principal instrument for forming its dominant fiction. It was important enough to be singled out just before the conclusion to Walter Gropius's seminal 1923 essay "The Theory and Organization of the Bauhaus," as the embodiment of a "higher unity" parallel only to that of architecture.[16]

In the catalog to the 1938 Bauhaus exhibition at the Museum of Modern Art in New York, which is today still one of the most widely read Bauhaus publications, Schlemmer's description of the stage workshop at Dessau formed one of the longest texts after Gropius's 1923 essay.[17] The choice of figures from Schlemmer's Triadic Ballet for the front cover of the catalog underlined the Bauhaus's interest in reinventing not only objects but also human beings, actions, and spaces:

> If we go so far as to break the narrow confines of the stage and extend the drama to include the building itself, not only the interior but the building as an architectural whole—an idea which has especial fascination in view of the new Bauhaus building—we might demonstrate to a hitherto unknown extent the validity of the space-stage, as an idea.[18]

Whereas the Bauhaus craft workshops created a new identity for products, encompassing production (industry) and consumption (advertising), the theater designed a new identity for their producers and consumers. Teaching in the theater workshop recognized that the new ideology had to extend beyond the curriculum to reconstruct spatial and social behavior and that this had to take place through fantasy (theater) before it could take place in reality (architecture). Students took the theater workshop before the architecture course, in the second and third years of the curriculum, and, in any case, the architecture course did not begin until 1927. The theater therefore formed the first real Bauhaus experiments with space and program, and the spatial and figurative dream imagery of the theater workshop came before the constructional and programmatic invention of the building department. Theater was the foundation for architecture; fantasy anticipated reality; identity formation preceded the formation of the physical environment.

The theater connected the design of objects and space to that of the body, as a *Gesamtkunstwerk*. It was a legitimate, institutional extension of Bauhaus design principles to the human body itself. It formed the clearest, most consciously articulated mirror-image that the Bauhaus community offered up to itself. In allowing the body of the student to act and be acted upon by the institution, the Bauhaus theater also dissolved the division between the collective and the individual through which institutional life distinguishes itself from personal life. Silverman writes that, "In order for ideology to command belief, it must extend itself into the deepest reaches of the subject's identity and unconscious desire."[19] The theater allowed the transmission and incorporation of Bauhaus beliefs at the most profound level; by recruiting from the multiple experiments of the festivals, it made their "living 'give and take'" one-dimensional and thus formed a singular ideology of identity.

The body in Bauhaus theater had a specific identity. Whereas in traditional Western theater the figure had remained an instrument for representing naturalistic illusion, the Bauhaus theater exposed the body as a theatrical automaton—a focus for the assembly of form, light, movement and, only later, speech. This sensibility laid the ground for the mechanization of the actor's body. Costumes during the Schlemmer period were derived from abstract, geometric studies, inspired by mechanical parts.

Either specific references to gender were erased, or references to both genders were often combined in the same figure. The actions of the human figure were largely confined to silent performance and pantomime; words were a separate element to be juxtaposed later. Schlemmer wrote:

> Let us consider plays consisting only in the movements of form, colors and lights. If the movement is purely mechanical, involving no human being but the man at the switchboard, the whole conception would have the precision of a vast automaton.[20]

The actor's appearance and gestures were transformed into mechanized, abstracted, and neutral form.

The visibility of the principle of mechanization and abstraction in the Bauhaus theater resonates with Silverman's understanding of the construction of identity during the imaginary phase:

> At its deepest level—i.e., at the point at which it falls most fully under the influence of the primary process—the fantasmatic is "characterized by the absence of subjectivization," and "all distinction between subject and object [is] lost." The subject has no fixed locus, and can consequently take up residence anywhere, even at the site of the fantasy's verb or action.[21]

The representation of lack—the absence of subjective experience of the self—was achieved by the mechanization of the actor's appearance and gestures. In the Bauhaus theater, the multiple identities and gender differences explored in the festivals began to be lost.

Silverman claims that fantasy privileges and eroticizes specific classes and genders of people and, more importantly, specific social practices. In the Bauhaus theater, an apparently gender free but in fact male directed identity became the dominant fiction, and in turn fed the seemingly gender free yet similarly male taught designs of almost all the craft workshops. The gender neutral model of identity reinforced masculine cultural and economic authority at the school. It represented the restoration of patriarchal order from within while, more powerfully, it was being restored from without.

Part Two: Gender and Transgression

> *Many Weimaraners called us Bauhausler, and it sounded like convict—it had the taste of horror and fear.*
>
> —Lothar Schreyer[22]

By 1924, Bauhaus students and staff had become the focus of strong local criticism at Weimar. The popular press, politicians, leading cultural figures, and employees of the old Academy rejected Bauhaus teaching and united to remove the Bauhaus from the city. *Weimaraners* fetishistically projected their own fear of social disintegration onto the Bauhaus community. Barbara Miller Lane cites a local journalist who feared that the "subjectivism of instruction at the Bauhaus . . . only releases instincts which lead to chaos."[23]

The threat to gender boundaries figured particularly powerfully. Most students had rejected conventions of dress and appearance. Tut Schlemmer wrote, "At first people let themselves go. Boys had long hair, girls short skirts. No collars or stockings were worn, which was shocking and extravagant then . . ."[24] Masters too played with gender identities. Oskar Schlemmer used the Bauhaus festivals to reverse gender roles. Felix Klee wrote that, "On the stage at the Ilmschlösschen Schlemmer had set up two sets featuring headless characters. The boys took the women's parts and vice versa."[25]

Weimaraners saw this gender play as promiscuity. The *Weimarische Zeitung* claimed in 1924 that licentiousness was rife at the Bauhaus; one student had become pregnant and another had had an affair with a master. The article warned that "people must be prevented from sending their sons and daughters there."[26] Some of the claims were true; Gropius—while still married to Alma Mahler and seeing his mistress Lily Hildebrandt—had a brief sexual relationship with a student who was a war widow. Along with the dominant fiction, the war had also loosened sexual propriety; it gave women and men a greater sense of sexual independence.

However, *Weimaraners*' rejection of the Bauhaus as a hotbed of sexual depravity linked sexual morality to political morality, correctly aligning a loosened sexual order with a threat to the political order. The article continued: "And the consequence of all this [Communism] which can be seen in the life of the Bauhaus community!!! . . . We don't need to name individual cases in which [immorality] . . . is publicly celebrated by the students."²⁷ Finally, sexual transgression was linked to a threat to sanity. A Weimar publication, according to Miller Lane, "listed instances of immoral behavior among students and faculty . . . and it described cases of insanity among the students caused, it said, by the teaching methods of the school."²⁸

Weimaraners contained the threat of the Bauhaus to their dominant fiction by dismissing the Bauhaus as a "foreign" body— sexually licentious and mad— which are terms historically reserved for women who stray outside the Oedipal order. Such views reinforced emerging internal frictions and led to a swift return to traditional gender relations within the school.

Part Three: The Law-of-the-Father

> *gropius wore black trousers, white shirt, slim black bow tie*
> *and a short, natural-colored leather jacket*
> *which squeaked with each movement*
> *his short moustache, trim figure and swift movements*
> *gave him the air of a soldier*
> *(which in fact he had been until recently).*
> *gropius' manner of dress was in contrast*
> *to the generally fantastic individualistic appearances*
> *around the bauhaus.*
> *it was a statement of his opinion*
> *that the new artist need not oppose his society*
> *by wearing dress that, to begin with,*
> *would set him apart from the world he lives in*
>
> —Herbert Bayer²⁹

The return to tradition was gradual but irreversible. The androgyny of the theater was but one manifestation. From 1923 onward, with the growing focus at the school on standardization, mass production, and collaboration with industry, Gropius affirmed that the artist of today should wear conventional clothing— which was understood, of course, as male clothing.

Patriarchal values had been present at the school from the beginning. The veneration of father figures began already with Itten. Paul Citroen wrote:

> Itten exuded a special radiance. One could almost call it holiness. We were inclined to approach him only in whispers; our reverence was overwhelming, and we were completely enchanted and happy when he associated with us pleasantly and without restraint.³⁰

Gropius also became a figure of worship, not only during his leadership but thereafter. It was Gropius, not Meyer or Mies van der Rohe, who was credited with Bauhaus successes and became its symbolic figurehead. The catalog of the 1938 Bauhaus exhibition at the Museum of Modern Art in New York, which has become the most influential and widely disseminated document of the Bauhaus, embodies this perfectly. Gropius's first appearance on page 14 represents and heightens his status as originator and author of the Bauhaus (his signature features on the page as the sign of authorship) and as patriarch (his large photograph towers above a small photo of his wife that has shadows on two sides as if to suggest it is a painted canvas, an element of artifice). Further proof of his productive capacity is contained in his curriculum vitae on the same page and, more significantly, in the buildings pictured on the opposite page. His photograph and buildings precede even his famous 1919 Bauhaus manifesto on the next spread of the catalog. This spread is tellingly followed on page 19 by photographs of "the family"— twelve male Bauhaus masters—also accompanied by signatures. Only then does his essay on the organization of the Bauhaus follow.

Women were not accorded such treatment. Documentation of female students and teachers at the Bauhaus is limited and needs further research. References to students appear in a few meetings of the Council of Masters and occasionally in speeches. Although the 1938 catalog claimed that one-third of Bauhaus students were female, this is difficult to discern from the photographs and names of the authors of work shown, which are overwhelmingly male. Gunta Stadler-Stölzl, who ran the weaving workshop where almost all of the female students worked, is the only workshop mistress included in the biographical section, probably because it made the greatest profits for the Bauhaus business. Marianne Brandt, who ran the commercially successful metal workshop, is not included.

Women at the Bauhaus faced obstacles when they tried traditionally male areas of work. Brandt later wrote of her entry into the metal workshop:

> At first I was not accepted with pleasure— there was no place for a woman in a metal workshop, they felt. They admitted this to me later on and meanwhile expressed their displeasure by giving me all sorts of dull, dreary work. How many little hemispheres did I most patiently hammer out of brittle new silver, thinking that was the way it had to be and all beginnings are hard. Later things settled down, and we got along well together.³¹

Weimar legislation had given women equality of access to study. In 1920, therefore, seventy-eight male and fifty-nine female students were at the Bauhaus, whereas

Gropius had originally anticipated one hundred men but only fifty women. As the two genders continued to apply in equal numbers, the entry of women students at the Bauhaus was restricted, first via higher fees (180 marks for women and 150 marks for men) and second, in a 1920 decision by Gropius and the Council of Masters, via differential admission: "Selection should be more rigorous right from the start, particularly in the case of the female sex, already over-represented in terms of numbers."[32] Nevertheless, female students were grateful. Käthe Brachmann, a student, wrote in the Bauhaus student magazine *Der Austausch* in 1919: "So we women, too, came to this school because we, every one of us, found work to do here, which we durst not neglect! May no one begrudge us this work! Thanks to those who already accord it to us!"[33]

Droste noted Gropius's reluctance to conduct any "unnecessary experiments" (a euphemism for rejecting equal access to female students) and his recommendations that women should be sent directly from the introductory course to the weaving workshop, with pottery and bookbinding as possible alternatives. She also noted the passive, Pre-Raphaelite poses that the students of the weaving workshop were expected to adopt when being photographed. In particular, she identified the fear of the feminization of architecture at the Bauhaus: "Much of the art then being produced by women was dismissed by men as 'feminine' or 'handicrafts.' The men were afraid of too strong an 'arty-crafty' tendency and saw the goal of the Bauhaus – architecture – endangered." She added that "no women were to be admitted to study architecture" at the Bauhaus. Indeed, the building department had no female students at all.[34]

The construction of sexual difference at the Bauhaus was overt in admissions policies and academic progress, but it was far more deeply embedded in the very legitimation of artistic ability. Gropius, in a crucial statement as part of his first address to the school, made it absolutely clear that the experiences of male students made them better artists than female students:

> the awakening of the whole man through trauma, lack, terror, hard life experiences or love leads to authentic artistic expression. Dearest ladies, I do not underestimate the human achievement of those who remained at home during the war, but I believe that the lived experience of death to be all-powerful.[35]

This was direct recognition that the experience of suffering, and war trauma in particular, was for Gropius the driving force of artistic creativity and an exclusively masculine right and privilege. The importance of Gropius's statement lay in his recognition that trauma and lack are not essentially female experiences, but that their cultural value has been historically constructed by men and accepted by women. The traditional association of lack and trauma with weakness and femininity meant that, at the Bauhaus, male students could adopt their artistic representation only if they were revalued to carry high cultural status through their association with integrity (the awakening of the whole man), essentialism (authentic artistic expression), and the exclusively masculine experience of war.

Conclusion: Gender Indifference

> *The male subject's aspirations to mastery and sufficiency are undermined from many directions—by the Law of Language, which founds subjectivity on a void; by the castration crisis; by sexual, economic and racial oppression; and by the traumatically unassimilable nature of certain historical events.*
>
> —Kaja Silverman[36]

The story of identity formation at the Bauhaus is of resistance and return to the dominant fiction of patriarchy. Resistance to the "dominant" in the dominant fiction can take many forms. Silverman cites the identification with masochism, blackness, or femininity in Rainer Werner Fassbinder's films as examples of a "mechanism for eroticizing lack and subordination." She identifies feminine masochism in particular as providing an important challenge to the dominant fiction: "the male subject . . . cannot avow feminine masochism without calling into question his identification with the masculine position."[37]

The rituals of Mazdaznan introduced by Johannes Itten and elaborated by Bauhaus students like Paul Citroen clearly followed this model. More importantly, the dominant fiction, politically constructed and sustained in the broadest social sense, can be threatened by events originating far beyond the individual or the family, and this provides a further source of resistance. Silverman focuses on historically traumatic events that periodically threaten the stability of the dominant fiction:

> By "historical trauma" I mean a historically precipitated but psychoanalytically specific disruption, with ramifications far beyond the individual psyche. To state the case more precisely, I mean any historical event, whether socially engineered or of natural occurrence, which brings a large group of male subjects into such an intimate relation with lack that they are at least for the moment unable to sustain an imaginary relation with the phallus, and so withdraw their belief from the dominant fiction. Suddenly the latter is radically de-realised, and the social formation finds itself without a mechanism for achieving consensus.[38]

Her analysis of periods of historical trauma suggests that these are moments of a profound crisis of masculinity; the self-image of society shatters, with a commensurate loss of self-recognition by those in power: "at those historical moments when the prototypical male subject is unable to recognize 'himself' within its conjuration of masculine sufficiency our society suffers from a profound sense of 'ideological fatigue.'"[39]

Silverman identifies war as a key historical trauma that profoundly destabilizes the dominant fiction, shattering the mirror that patriarchal society normally holds up to itself and in which it uncritically views itself. Instead, the collective experience of death and the dissolution of inherited social order creates a collective crisis of masculinity. By confronting society with a repeated external manifestation of lack, war loosens the sign systems that normally bind society together. For the male in particular, war trauma connects the conscious experience of social crisis to the unconscious original double experience of lack. Silverman uses the example of post-World War II Hollywood films to show male characters acting out lack and a massive loss of faith in masculinity through visible physical war injuries and uncharacteristic self-doubt in relation to female characters.

The story of identity formation at the Bauhaus shows the powerful role played by the profound collapse of the dominant fiction in Weimar Germany. The traumatic experiences of war itself, the humiliation of defeat, and the real economic and physical hardships created by the reparations agreements imposed by the victorious Allies all contributed to the crisis of the imperial model of patriarchy.

The response of the Bauhaus to the trauma of war was to dissolve and then reconstruct personal identity through fantasy. In the first, utopian version, lack as pleasure was institutionalized and the construction of identity at the Bauhaus was "feminized." However, Gropius, as an ex-soldier, insisted that war and its associated release of creativity were exclusively masculine experiences. This contradiction between feminine and masculine identities caused internal and external political frictions and was resolved only by the invention of a new and permanent "neuter" model of identity that is still associated with the universal subject of the modernist designer today. Incorporating quasi-military ritual and bodily iconography symbolically promising sexual equality but politically, socially, and economically reinforcing the superiority of men over women, this was a patriarchal model of identity. Women may have worn short skirts, but as students they were trapped within the patriarchal division of labor. This privileged the male through excluding women's experiences (their lack of lack) and women's participation in classes (through higher fees, lower quotas, and placement in traditional workshops like weaving and pottery). Symbolically (and safely) representing masculine lack as plenitude—as universal, stable, powerful, and gender neutral (rather than as differentiated, volatile, weak, and feminine), the new belief system removed the threat to masculine stability beyond criticism and transformation. Gender difference at the Bauhaus was ultimately sublimated into a neutralized "indifference." It is ironic that the most widely known Bauhaus publication, *Das Bauhaus* by Hans Maria Wingler, has as its cover the well-known painting by Oskar Schlemmer, based on a Feininger photograph of female students from the weaving workshop, yet the entire book makes almost no reference to gender.

This rereading of the Bauhaus suggests that the construction of a new disciplinary identity through corporeal and image-based fantasy as well as its innovation in design and mass production significantly adds to the Bauhaus legacy for the twentieth century. Identity formation is a crucial but usually unacknowledged part of education. Yet education relies on the creation of a group identity that unconsciously unites and elevates the educated group and provides it with a cultural status, which is often inaccessible to other groups precisely because it is learned unconsciously. The importance of education thus lies as much in its reproduction and transformation of the identity of students as in the reproduction and transformation of knowledge, as Pierre Bourdieu has identified so eloquently in his writings. In design education, human identity can become the subject of design as much as a design object itself.

Festivals, theater, and other curricular and extracurricular rituals at the Bauhaus explicitly acknowledged the importance of identity formation in education, yet—perhaps because it holds such powerful utopian potential, fantasy, and, in particular, its harnessing of the collective body and space—is not well studied or understood. It is seldom embraced for its potential to change human relations. I propose that the repression of the fantasy-filled, multiple, non-patriarchal identities (that the Bauhaus showed so clearly as forming the basis of the creative process) lies behind the continuing pernicious gender and race imbalances within the architectural profession. The profession is sexist and racist precisely because it is so frightened of the feminine fantasy that lies at the heart of its masculinity. At the Bauhaus, which still stands as a model of architectural education for many design and architecture professionals today, masculine behavior for a time acknowledged this condition, experimenting with the disintegration of the self, gender confusion, and multiple identities using images, space, clothing, and the body itself.

This lesson of the Bauhaus extends beyond the school and its impact on design education. Silverman's model of the dominant fiction, spanning the personal and the political, the visual and the verbal, the contemporary and the historical, recognizes the importance of institutions and, in particular, body imagery in the formation of collective identity. Her work has far reaching implications for the study of institutions because it identifies mechanisms through which large, seemingly impersonal social structures act on and are acted upon by specific individuals to produce and reproduce the collective unconscious. Silverman affirms corporeal and image based fantasies as powerful institutional instruments, and identifies fantasy as a powerful potential source of resistance to the dominant fiction.

This identification of the role of corporeal fantasy as the bedrock in the formation of institutional beliefs implies that study of cultural institutions such as schools, professional organizations, and organs of publication and exhibition, particularly at times of major social upheaval, forms a fruitful point for the analysis of critical and utopian changes in culture, architecture, and design. Such work might identify the moments of friction within dominant modes of representation, the dialectic within dream images, the points of resistance within politics and the economy, the misrecognition within the ideological mirror, the ruptures in the integrity of the professional and the cracks in the masculine fiction. This may lead to a critical and fantasy filled reevaluation of identity formation in the cultural institutions, including that of architecture. This then is the broad, positive, and unfulfilled legacy of the Bauhaus. Bauhaus Hausfraus may lead us to Bauhaus Dream-House.

Acknowledgments
I would like to thank the Kingston University School of Architecture Development Fund and the University of Illinois at Chicago Office for the Vice-Chancellor for Research for support given for this research.

Notes
1. Kaja Silverman, *Male Subjectivity at the Margins* (London: Routledge, 1992), 6, quoting Slavoj Žižek, *The Sublime Object of Ideology* (London: Verso, 1989), 118.
2. Eckhard Neumann, ed., *Bauhaus and Bauhaus People*, E. Richter and A. Lorman, trans. (New York: Van Nostrand Reinhold, 1993), 158.
3. Bruno Taut, *Modern Architecture* (London: The Studio Limited, 1929), 92–93.
4. Walter Gropius, *Ja! Stimmen des Arbeitsrates für Kunst*, 1919, Bauhaus Archive, file 69.
5. Gropius, *Arbeitsrates für Kunst*.
6. Magdalena Droste, *Bauhaus 1919–1933* (Cologne: Benedikt Taschen, 1993), 2.
7. T. Lux Feininger in Neumann, *Bauhaus*, 186.
8. Herbert Bayer, Walter Gropius, and Ise Gropius, *Bauhaus 1919–1928* (New York: The Museum of Modern Art, 1975), 18.
9. Tut Schlemmer in Neumann, *Bauhaus*, 162.
10. Lothar Schreyer in Neumann, *Bauhaus*, 74.
11. Paul Citroen in Neumann, *Bauhaus*, 49.
12. Citroen in Neumann, *Bauhaus*, 51–52.
13. Citroen in Neumann, *Bauhaus*, 48.
14. Felix Klee in Neumann, *Bauhaus*, 44.
15. Klee in Neumann, *Bauhaus*, 43–44.
16. Bayer, Gropius, and Gropius, *Bauhaus 1919–1928*, 29.
17. Bayer, Gropius, and Gropius, *Bauhaus 1919–1928*, 162–164.
18. Bayer, Gropius, and Gropius, *Bauhaus 1919–1928*, 162 (Schlemmer's italics).
19. Silverman, *Male Subjectivity*, 16.
20. Bayer, Gropius, and Gropius, *Bauhaus 1919–1928*, 162.
21. Silverman, *Male Subjectivity*, 5.
22. Lothar Schreyer in Neumann, *Bauhaus 1919–1928*, 74.
23. Barbara Miller Lane, *Architecture and Politics in Germany 1918–1945* (Cambridge, MA: Harvard University Press, 1968), 82.
24. Tut Schlemmer in Neumann, *Bauhaus*, 164.
25. Felix Klee in Neumann, *Bauhaus*, 43.
26. *Weimarische Zeitung*, June 13, 1924.
27. *Weimarische Zeitung*, 13 June 13, 1924.
28. Miller Lane, *Architecture*, 81.
29. Herbert Bayer in Neumann, *Bauhaus*, 142.
30. Paul Citroen in Neumann, *Bauhaus*, 47.
31. Marianne Brandt in Neumann, *Bauhaus*, 106.
32. Walter Gropius, minutes of the meeting of the Council of Masters, September 1920, Bauhaus Archive Berlin, file Meisterrat.
33. Howard Dearstyne, *Inside the Bauhaus* (New York: Rizzoli, 1986), 49.
34. Droste, *Bauhaus 1919–1933*, 40. [Editors' note: After the publication of the original essay, Rüedi Ray has noted that research by other Bauhaus scholars has brought to light that some women students were accepted into the Bauhaus building department.]
35. Walter Gropius, first lecture to the Bauhaus, April 1919, 3, Bauhaus Archive Berlin, file 18, my translation.
36. Silverman, *Male Subjectivity*, 52.
37. Silverman, *Male Subjectivity*, 189.
38. Silverman, *Male Subjectivity*, 55.
39. Silverman, *Male Subjectivity*, 16.

Immanent Domain: Pervasive Computing and the Public Realm

Dana Cuff
University of California, Los Angeles

A wave of emergent digital technology holds vast implications for the public sphere. Indeed, these new forms of mobile and ubiquitous systems, called pervasive computing, *challenge some of our fundamental ideas about subjectivity, visibility, space, and the distinction between public and private. Together, these challenges reformulate our conception of the civic realm. From cell phones to wireless local area networks, smart buildings to embedded vehicular computers, an invisible web of digital technology already lies across the visible world creating new space for work, data, advertisement, investigation, communication, intimacy, and danger. This generation of computers is so well integrated with the environment that it will be difficult to distinguish between the two, which represents a profound transformation for everyday life.*

> Machines that fit the human environment instead of forcing humans to enter theirs will make using a computer as refreshing as taking a walk in the woods.
>
> —Mark Weiser

Figure 1. Surveillance, voyeurism, and exhibitionism collide.

Introduction

In 1991, the late Mark Weiser wrote a prescient essay for *Scientific American* foretelling the age of ubiquitous computing that he described as "embodied virtuality," in contrast to then cutting edge virtual reality.[1] It is this very distinction that motivates the present essay. For architects and urbanists, there can be no more significant revolution in digital technology than the spatial embodiment of computers embedded everywhere.

This essay makes the argument that, although embodied virtuality has emerged from clear historic precedent and origins, it raises four distinct implications that hold the potential to change our ideas about space and spatial practices. First, our environment is enacted and given life, not in the sense that robots are actuated, but the entirety of the physical environment is re-created as a potential source of coordinated, interdependent actions and reactions. Whether this enacted environment is actual or imagined, as Foucault argued in the case of the panopticon, it reformulates our notions of power and, moreover, our relationship to the world around us. Second, visibility both literal and metaphorical is transformed. What was solid and opaque becomes transparent, yet what makes the hidden accessible is itself invisible. Third, further erosion of the concepts of public and private force their reconsideration. In particular, questions of surveillance, control, and exhibitionism render the distinction between public and private anew. Fourth, heightened security and surveillance possibilities hold the potential to restructure civility, or public life as we know it. In Britain, in the four years following terrorist attacks in London, there was a fifty-fold increase in surveillance networks. Post-9/11 America is experiencing a similar expansion, with even more sophisticated systems and little debate about the "Orwellian potential."[2] The consequences for the public sphere are paradoxical given the intrinsic nature of information technology to bite back, to be turned and used in ways opposed to its original intent (see Figure 1).

This essay introduces topics for debate, essentially asking more questions than it answers. The four-part argument for a transformed public sphere raises provocative issues for architects and urbanists. Just as the panopticon spatially embodied a complex cultural order in the eighteenth-century prison, so will embodied virtuality stand as the spatial manifestation of the

Figure 2. This image portrays a post-9/11 proposal to reduce traffic in lower Manhattan via remote surveillance that monitors the number of people per car to assess variable fees. The fewer passengers, the more it costs to drive on the streets.

twenty-first century. We are only just beginning to realize the forms that pervasive computing will assume. Consider Spielberg's 2002 sci-fi movie *Minority Report*, in which futuristic biometric scanners can identify shoppers and emit a siren song of personalized consumer preferences as they pass through the mall. This portrays a near future, and it is at this generative phase of development that architects and urbanists must engage pervasive technologies. Although pervasive computing applications within the private sector, like advertising, may have a deep effect on society, I wish to explore ways that the technology is applied within and by the public sector, in particular, by the state.

Although there are clear technological precedents for the emergent, pervasive technologies, they can be distinguished from past developments by the fact that this new technology can be both everywhere and nowhere (unlike the automobile that is mobile but locatable); that it acts intelligently yet fallibly, and its failure is complex (versus the thermostat, which is responsive but singular and unintelligent); and that intelligent systems operate spatially, yet they are invisible (unlike robots). For utopians like Weiser, these distinctions suggest that an environment embedded with intelligent computing can be nuanced in compelling and even more natural ways, "as refreshing as taking a walk in the woods." Embedded networks, however, are just as likely to spark dystopic views, as have all preceding technological breakthroughs. Now, as pervasive computing grows, there is a certain urgency to its critical review by all those concerned with the public sphere.

Cyburgs, the Enacted Environment

To be an agent, one must be somewhere.

—Robert Sack (1988)[3]

The term *public sphere* is necessary to a discussion of embedded networks because it implies not only physical space but also the metaphorical space of public discourse, social norms, interaction, and social sentiment. I want to make a strong distinction between what has been called *cyberspace* from what I will call the *cyburg*. Cyberspace is defined as having no physicality, no matter, and no Cartesian duality because there is only the mind, and communication is the only transaction. ("Ours is a world that is both everywhere and nowhere, but it is not where bodies live."[4]) If cyberspace is dematerialized space, the cyburg is spatially embodied computing, or an environment saturated with computing capability. It is the imminent stage of digital media that places computation in all things around us, from our own skin and bodies (biotechnology and nanotech medication), to our clothing, to our cars, our streets, our homes, and our wildernesses. The cyburg is the opposite of Christine Boyer's cybercity and may indeed functionally sidestep all the dystopian visions of disembodied, disengaged, socially remote cyberlife.[5]

No longer residing in the abstract space of the Internet, digital communicating, processing, and sensing increasingly actuate the world around us. Ironically, as computing becomes more pervasive, we will exist simultaneously within both cyberspace and cyburg space. This dual existence characterizes a new postmodern space. Our own agency is enhanced by the cyburg, for we can know and act in more powerful ways. Complementing our empowerment is the newly enacted environment. Not only do the walls have ears, but networks of eyes, brains, and data banks to use for purposeful action. Although we are reluctant to attribute agency to objects in our surroundings, it is a stance that won't survive long. These embedded systems can be said to have intelligence insofar as they link diverse databases and change their response according to new information as well as the consequences of their own actions.

Baudrillard, in an essay on consumer society, says that the ecology of the human species has fundamentally mutated from a life surrounded by other human beings, to a life surrounded by objects:

> The concepts of "environment" and "ambiance" have undoubtedly become fashionable only since we have come to live in less proximity to other human beings, less in their presence and discourse, and more under the silent gaze of deceptive and obedient objects which continuously repeat the same

discourse, that of our stupefied (medusée) power, of our potential affluence and of our absence from one another.[6]

This could fundamentally mutate once again, as our objects/environment are no longer silent but active, nor are they obedient but indirectly willful.

New capabilities of pervasive computing systems will expedite the restructuring of everyday life because they permit what we considered the context to become a bona fide agent in the public arena. This is the opposite of early projections about electronic technology. In 1964, Marshall McLuhan wrote "The telephone: speech without walls. The phonograph: music hall without walls. The photograph: museum without walls. The electric light: space without walls. The movie, radio and TV: classroom without walls. Man the food-gatherer reappears incongruously as information-gatherer. In this role, electronic man is no less a nomad than his Paleolithic ancestors."[7] Instead, speech is issued by the walls, and the museum's walls present visitors its works of art according to their particular viewing habits, or any of myriad curatorial themes. Street lights monitor as well as regulate traffic by assessing variable fees and suggesting less-crowded routes (see Figure 2); public park sensors scan for unusual behavior and known criminals, reporting each to the authorities; smart glass becomes more obscure and reflective during the hottest part of the day; stores can identify your vehicle and send drive-by messages tailored to your past consumer behavior. These new levels of information, security, conservation, and access are balanced by heightened possibilities of intrusion, tracking, classification, and exclusion.

Thus, our urban environment can be qualitatively transformed so that it occupies a new status and role in everyday life. We can be complicit with the sidewalks, rejected or embraced by a park, bombarded in the streets with advertisements.[8] Marshall McLuhan, sometimes called the "oracle of the electronic age," argued that the content or message was not just distorted but defined by the media. Had he lived to see pervasive computing, his thesis might have extended to question the boundary between space and subject, between the advertisement, the object being advertised, and the reception of that ad. Even if we are less technological determinists than McLuhan, his analysis sets the stage for embedded virtuality.[9]

Invisibility and Exposure

Pervasive computing enhances what we can know, where we can know it, and how immediate it will be. As when Muybridge showed stop-frame action in his time-sequence photographs, infrared sensors, micro sensors, and processors can network together to build a dynamic portrayal of what otherwise could not be known. Doctors can track the real-time progress of an ingested medication or see the internal anatomical details of a surgery patient; firefighters can get critical information about the fire as it rages and their rescue efforts; the migration of endangered whales can be closely monitored.

"Visualization technologies" provide access into what was opaque, knowledge where there was previously ignorance, bringing close what had been remote—all these capabilities of pervasive computing transform our ideas about space. Now that police equipped with increasingly common thermal imaging technology (and a search warrant) can drive past a house and "peer through" the walls, our ideas about not only privacy, but the walls themselves must change.[10] Even stranger is the use of the same imaging to see where a person has been—sensors of the past tense (see Figure 3). This new technology goes beyond the often mentioned collapse of distance promulgated by fax, telephone, or overnight delivery. It also represents the possibility of new knowledge that will enhance safety, inform action, and provide perspective. Publicly accessible monitors that display moment-by-moment readings of everything from water quality to activity in the public square to traffic patterns can provide a type of information previously unavailable and potentially community enhancing. Pervasive computing can open up the workings of an otherwise inaccessible mystery, whether that be the performance of a building's structure in an earthquake or the nanny's behavior while mom and dad are at work. There is an irony here: it is invisible, miniaturized sensors that make formerly inaccessible realms visible.

That irony of pervasive computing is related to long-standing critical inquiry into the relationship of seeing and being seen. For example, Roland Barthes characterized the mythical status of the Eiffel Tower explicitly in these terms: because it "transgresses this separation, this habitual divorce of *seeing* and *being seen*; it achieves a sovereign circulation between the two functions; it is a complete object which has, if one may say so, both sexes of sight."[11] As such, it attracts meaning like a lightning rod. The digitally embedded city, strewn with sensors, pervasively monitored and actuated, is fundamentally the opposite of the Eiffel Tower. De-monumentalized, the seeing transpires with a spatial disconnect—not from a distance, but from somewhere else. The possibility of being seen, on the other hand, is everywhere. But, without the identifiable point of observation (the top of the Eiffel Tower, the center of the panopticon), surveillance becomes pernicious—potentially everywhere, by any agency, for unknown purposes. Embedded systems create the opposite of monument, the opposite of geographic centeredness, the opposite of subjectivity and objectivity. Consider the extensive implementation of closed circuit TV in London as well as other cities in Great Britain. Journalist Jeffrey Rosen found that the cameras, intended to reduce terrorism, were primarily used to watch hookers, girls in tight T-shirts, and young men of color.

Expected to protect society, bored security guards become voyeurs, reasserting their own discriminatory stereotypes and sending a chill over public behavior.[12]

In privacy debates, some take the position that signage to the effect of "camera surveillance in operation" must be required. But how far should the signage go? It could also post: "by the London Police," "your facial features will be scrambled," or "connected to Interpol database." Such signage under our current assumptions of the city is the public space equivalent of Duchamps's "Ceci n'est pas une pipe." Being watched for unclear purposes by uncertain authority contradicts basic notions of public space.[13] The uncertainty goes hand in hand with nanotechnologies, with embeddedness, with surveillance, and even closed-circuit TV. Unlike Maupassant who could choose to dine in the Eiffel Tower to both escape its presence and reverse its relation to the city, the surveillance state is intrinsically omnipresent. There is no escape except perhaps to exhibitionism.

Private and Public
Exhibitionism, the tendency to show off something that is generally held to be private, is part of modernity and has long had its spatial component. When Napoleon III and Georges Eugene Haussmann opened the great boulevards of Paris in the mid-nineteenth century, cutting swaths through working-class neighborhoods to link axial monuments, they also ushered in modern urban life. Baudelaire wrote about this new unified city space, a space of human activity and physical connectedness. Wide sidewalks, streets lined with trees, cafes, and multitudes of citizens from across Paris came to characterize the city. A new public realm was made, and with it came a new definition of the sixteenth-century dialectic between public and private. By some accounts, these highly public gestures created the frame for a kind of anonymity, so that the street both concealed and exposed its drama simultaneously. Marshall Berman, in his analysis of modernity, says, "For lovers, . . . [Haussmann's Parisian] boulevards created a new primal scene: a space where they could be private in public, intimately together without being physically alone."[14]

Haussmann's boulevards shaped the modern city, opening intimacy to publicity across Paris, but they also promoted state control of the physical whole and the populace. A parallel transformation is occurring in our own decade: the reformulation of public and private urban life resulting from a sophisticated, digital connectivity. Even now, wireless networks available to cell phones and a variety of handheld devices enable people in public space to engage in a new primal scene: a space where they can be private in public, but, unlike Haussmann's Paris, intimately involved with *no one* intimate present, surrounded only by the company of strangers. Wireless internet already exists at offices, airports, and college campuses, and more recently commercial establishments like Starbucks are instituting their own networks available to customers for a fee. The results are paradoxical: greater connectivity coupled with increased isolation, intimacy paired with distance, privacy with publicity. Although the multiple effects of pervasive computing will take time to comprehend, new displays of intimacy and their dismal shadow, terrorism, are enabled by transformations of visibility, privacy, and publicity.

Some of the effects of pervasive computing are clearly extensions of those wrought by the telephone and the automobile, heightening individual privacy in the city, collapsing spatial distance, and restructuring physical space. But some consequences are unique to the electronic age. Perhaps the most profound effect concerns the realms of public and private, traditionally separated by semi-public/semi-private zones. This continuum has served to describe regions of social life and space for centuries. Public life, public space, and public man have stood for a certain notion of civility where chance interactions among strangers produce a societal tolerance. Many technological advances and social transformations have been accused of weakening the public sphere, including the automobile and the concomitant suburbs, the air conditioner, and the elevator and resultant skyscraper. However, only the most recent technological innovations threaten to dissolve the public-private continuum all together. This is possible when what was once considered private is integrated and exposed in public—our intimacies (for example, cameras that watch bedrooms and bathrooms on reality TV) and our secrets (such as medical, legal, and financial databases linked to a national identity card).

In *The Fall of Public Man*, sociologist Richard Sennett decries the crisis of public culture, arguing that public life had succumbed to an ideology of intimacy and personality, in turn sparking the transmutation of political into psychological order. If we agree with Sennett, then the eroded boundaries between public and private are merely further dissolved by the advent of embodied virtuality. But, whereas Sennett saw public man in a free fall, it may be that pervasive computing in some sense restores his notion "that people grow only by processes of encountering the unknown."[15] Might the continuous representation of the unfamiliar, the unseen, and the remote counteract isolationism and withdrawal from public life? Similar to the way that Jacob Riis's photographs of the slums at the turn of the century showed "how the other half lives," there are ways that remote sensing could expose previously hidden worlds. To adopt the view that the private is public requires the replacement of Sennett's public man with a subject no longer bound by conventional public-private distinctions.

Privacy, at the other end of the traditional polarity, has been defined as the achievement of desired levels of boundary control and access.[16] Thus, I have privacy if I can keep unwanted visitors from my home or resist intrusions while engrossed in a book. Indeed, privacy has been formulated as the central concept integrating

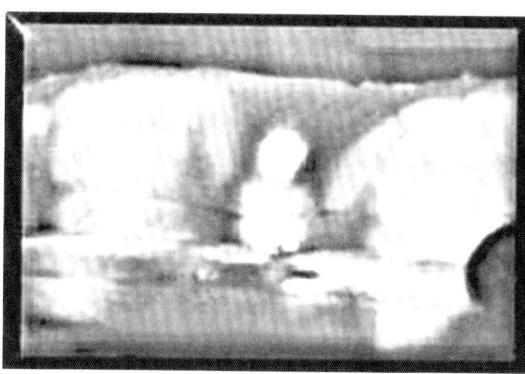

Figure 3. Traces of the people on the couch (Figure 3a) remain in the thermal image (Figure 3b), so that we can now record not only aspects of the invisible, but the past.

socio-spatial behavior. This notion of privacy hinges on individual subjectivity: my desired levels of access, my boundaries. It seems obvious to anyone experiencing "cell yell" (private cell phone conversations audibly broadcast to proximate strangers) that boundaries are difficult to establish, but it may be less obvious that these boundaries are corroding. The continuum model, from private to semi-public to public, might instead be replaced by a nested metaphor in which publicity has infected privacy in every conceivable context, and vice versa. Moreover, embedded networks undermine the pretense that we control our environment or our boundaries within it—a pretense that is fundamental to the construct of privacy.

The usurpation of privacy by means of technology is a modern phenomenon but not a new one. Indeed, the concerns about pervasive computing's intrusion into everyday routines were echoed in Rudofsky's 1955 book on American domesticity and an unnervingly diminished solitude in daily life. He worried about media technologies replacing conversation with mere listening:

> The latest invention in the art of listening introduces a prankish element into what is left of social intercourse. The pocket recorder, a gadget heralded as "of unparalleled usefulness," can be counted upon to remove the last dregs of privacy from our lives. Originally designed for military and diplomatic secret service, it enables everyone to strike out a line of one's own murky practices; . . . "Just stick it in a pocket and pin a tiny mike under your lapel (or wear the facsimile wristwatch mike!)—[the joyous exclamation point is theirs, not mine]— and you can record the words of anything within about twenty feet; you simply put your hand in your pocket and flick a silent switch." What, one may ask, makes the promoters of the new furtiveness so sure that we shall keep on talking?[17]

He goes on to imagine counter spying techniques, like scattering "anti-acoustic confetti" all over our houses. Sounding like an inversion of the "smart dust" being developed for military purposes, Rudofsky's concerns may have been technologically prescient but socially off base. Legal privacy standards maintain social norms, but, at the same time, social norms evolve so that "the last dregs of privacy" are redefined. Perhaps the increasing numbers of surveillance cameras will have no more chilling effect on social life than did the tape recorder. But, on the other hand, one could say Rudofsky's worry was merely misplaced: Walkmans, not secret listening devices, are the pocket recorder's greatest blow to social intercourse.

If our awareness of the new social roles for wireless technologies was growing before September 11, 2001, it became our collective nightmare as last, loving calls were made from cell phones at the top of the World Trade Center and from within the fourth airliner before it crashed in Pennsylvania. As it turned out, terrorists too were linked by cellular technologies that suited their mobile, network-structured organization. In the wake of 9/11, a surveillance society lurks. We can look again at the case of Great Britain: after terrorist attacks in London in the early 1990s, installation of closed-circuit cameras to surveil city streets and squares increased dramatically. In 1994, 79 city centers had surveillance systems; there were 440 such systems by 1998; and by 2001 there were more than 2.5 million surveillance cameras across Britain. There, the average citizen is photographed three hundred times each day.[18] By contrast, the average American was photographed seven times a day in 2001 by surveillance cameras. Since 9/11, there has been a proliferation of surveillance systems like the one hundred cameras proposed for Times Square, and three hundred for Los Angeles International Airport.

The effect of ubiquitous surveillance cannot yet be known, but it is clear that security interests of the state have negative consequences for individual privacy. The

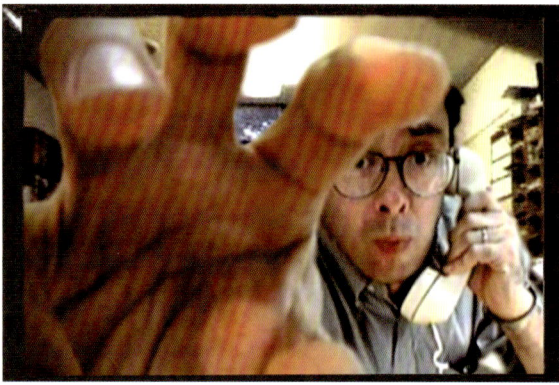

Figure 4. Diller + Scofidio's first web art project, for the Dia Foundation, investigates live office webcams.

Patriot Act, signed into law just one month after 9/11, expedites counterterrorism efforts by easing restrictions on electronic surveillance. Our online activities are more likely to be monitored, and data is easier to collect from Internet service providers in what is often called "domestic spying." In Washington, D.C., police activated a "command center" after 9/11 to monitor in integrated ways criminal databases and surveillance cameras that operate in "shopping areas, streets, monuments, and other public places in the U.S. capitol."[19] Proposals for a "smart" national identity card resurface regularly, with computer chips to identify the user, limit access, and track the user's criminal history, location, travel speed, and financial transactions, for starters.

We can be certain that privacy will not be the only terrain in which social impacts will result. Sociologist Anthony Giddens describes the "disembedding" mechanisms of modernity. By this he means those mechanisms that break apart social relations across space and time and that remove local control of resources, services, information, and even the mechanisms themselves. Pervasive computing used as a tool of surveillance is a disembedding, abstract mechanism, because the sensors, processors, and actuators are anonymous. Thus, although any abstract system requires trust of the anonymous (such as that nuclear reactors are built well enough to withstand terrorist attacks), that trust is intertwined with intrinsic doubt. The streets are surveilled by the police, yet we know that the police are not always trustworthy and that surveillance systems can be hacked. The pervasiveness of the systems is astounding: as early as 1998, a map of "every camera, public or private, which records people in public space" in Manhattan documented 2,397 such cameras.[20]

It may be the urban designer's task to create physical space or new forms of visibility to restore social bonds. In their project entitled "Refresh," architects Diller + Scofidio created a project from a dozen office webcams (see Figure 4). In considering why these cameras exist, the architects say.

The live cam phenomenon can be thought of as a public service, or a mode of passive advertisement, or it may be a new type of exhibitionism, or self-disciplinary device. The desire to connect to others in real time may be driven by a response to the "loss" of the public realm. But however varied the motives, live cam views always seem casual and lacking dramatic interest and content; they appear unmediated. Despite this apparent innocence, cameras are willfully positioned, their field of vision is carefully considered, and behavior within that field cannot help but anticipate the looming presence of the global viewer.[21]

In such applications reside possibilities for critique and modification of pervasive surveillance. And the critique emanating from the arts can spark debate that contributes to evolving social norms. Consider Lars Spuybroek's D-Tower project for Doetinchem in the Netherlands. The whimsical multimedia project includes a web site that surveys participating townspeople's emotions on a monthly basis, and those emotions are in turn displayed in differing colored surfaces of the tower: when it is deep red, passersby know the town is feeling more love and happiness than hate and fear (see Figure 5).

Public Life

The preceding examples hint at possible ways that pervasive computing will nudge a newly defined public life into existence. It will be part of the historical trajectory of technology's socio-spatial implications for public life, as is the development of plate glass with the resultant shop window, and the television with the interiorization of residential space. In "A Manifesto for Cyborgs" (cybernetic organisms, like us), Donna Haraway argues that digital capabilities will transform everyday life: "No longer structured by the polarity of public and private, the cyborg defines a technological polis based partly on a revolution of social relations in the *oikos*, the household."[22] Just as Haraway sees the restructuring of the previously private household, there are parallels in the public sphere where common ground grows more individuated and privatized because of wireless technology. And public space can incorporate, even publicize, that which was remote and inaccessible: a town broadcasts its emotions, or a school projects the children's collaborative art project as it develops or webcasts their music lesson.

Foucault's analysis of the panopticon captured a formal-social symbiosis, whereby a spatial model arose to typify and exemplify a complex nexus in cultural history. Koolhaas's description of the skyscraper as proximate stacking of unrelated lives captured the essence of the twentieth century. The immanent equivalent is the city of embodied virtuality: the cyburg for cyborgs.

The embedding of tiny computers and their networks into the city brings promise and uncertainty. Creating a realm of dispersed displacement, surveillance aims toward a particular space or spaces. It—and we know not what or who it is—observes us and our actions, emotions, histories, and reactions. These observations may be known to us (screening for passenger-carried weapons at airports), uncertain to us (visible cameras linked to unknown processors, such as face recognition systems and criminal databases), or opaque to us (cyber-interceptions of potential terrorist communications). Thus, the actuated environment, our actuated surroundings, can now "manage" not only that which is capable of being seen and known, but also that which is not capable of being seen, and about which we remain ignorant.

In a realm of dispersed displacement, discourse about centers and margins becomes irrelevant. For lovers walking hand in hand while speaking simultaneously by cell phone to their respective spouses, spatial dislocation is crucial and unquestioned. In this they remain secure. But they cannot be certain even about the immediate other: with whom is she speaking? Is she with me, or is she elsewhere? In this context, the other is not just distracted; neither is she absent. Instead, she is both present and absent in a way that was not possible prior to wireless technologies whereby everywhere is connected. There is no spatial logic nor spatial guarantees for intimacy. Publicity likewise embodies uncertainty. Public life is spatially located but also displaced and dispersed, requiring new logics and new physical forms.

Conclusion

The age of pervasive computing is immanent; its implications for architecture and for the city are just beginning to emerge. It is clear that ubiquitous and mobile systems will alter fundamental ideas about public and private, civic life, invisibility, and environmental agency. Each of these terrains is situated within the domain of design, giving rise to new architectural concerns. The existing literature projects consequences with either a utopian tone (as with Weiser's seminal article of 1991 and William Mitchell's *e-topia*) or a dystopian view (such as Rosen's essay on British CCTV).[23] Instead, in this preliminary exploration of issues, I have tried to present a double view, utopian and dystopian, equally aware of the promise and uncertainty that lies within embedded networks. Under such circumstances, the architect's goal must be to embed civility in a pervasively computerized public realm.

If the "public geography of a city is civility institutionalized" and if civility is, as Sennett puts it, "treating others as though they were strangers and forging a social bond upon that social distance," then the designer must invent means to embed the possibility of civility into both new pervasive technologies and new urban geographies.[24] What does it mean to embed civility in

Figure 5. D-Tower (a tower, a questionnaire, and a website) for the city of Doetinchem. Project by Lars Spuybroek of NOX studio in Rotterdam, in collaboration with artist Q. S. Seafijn, 1998–2003.

the public sphere? I would offer three linked guiding principles—information, choice, and control—which architects must find ways to embody in physical form. The first goal is to provide useful information about the embedded networks so that the public maintains an awareness about otherwise imperceptible systems. Information then contributes to people's ability to make choices about their public lives, and simultaneously returns to them a degree of control. A parallel from the 1960s and early 1970s: the Vietnam War protests and "love-ins" that rejuvenated life in urban America's public sphere were catalyzed by television broadcasting. Anti-surveillance web camera performances in public settings are a similar phenomenon. Until awareness of pervasive computing is heightened, the lack of public debate restricts architecture's full participation in the project to embed civility.

Nevertheless, the simultaneous existence of cyberspace and cyburg space creates a socio-spatial-digital arena like none before. Its origins are inherently modern: the modern world of contradiction and display, and where, as Marx famously put it, "all that is solid melts into air, all that is holy is profaned." In Giddens' conception of the late-modern condition of increasingly abstract systems, he cites intensifying conditions of risk and danger. Within his array of risks, one component is the created environment or socialized nature. This is "the infusion of human knowledge into the material environment." Giddens identifies rightly "the altered character of the relation between human beings and the physical environment."[25] What I have

Figure 6. Digital House. Project by Hariri and Hariri, 1998. Both interior and exterior walls are liquid crystal displays in this demonstration of new electronic technology for *House Beautiful* magazine.

Figure 7. Spuybroek's water pavilion for the Ministry of Water Management and the Destra Expo (1994–1997) in the Netherlands. The building incorporated digital sensors to activate light, sound, and projections according to the visitors' movements through the space.

called the *enacted environment*, Weiser's embodied virtuality, is knowledge extended such that the material environment is infused also with intelligent action and reaction, data gathering, surveillance, and networked information. The intensity of risk increases substantially, but so can the intensity of experience.

Giddens concludes his exegesis of modernity with the ways it might be engaged, which parallel the ways an era of embodied virtuality could be engaged: pragmatic acceptance, sustained optimism, cynical pessimism, and radical engagement. The last is the domain architects and urbanists must inhabit when designing to provide information, choice, and control. Radical engagement, or what Giddens at one point calls utopian realism, is indeed the ken of designers who use their expertise to reveal, contradict, play with, or intervene in pervasive computing. As a first step, designers are projecting information on surfaces that were formerly static (see Figure 6). Works are increasingly interactive and customized (see Figure 7). Here, the opportunities for informed choice and control can grow in complexity, sophistication, and diversity over the coming decade. The immanent domain of a newly public realm depends upon it.

Notes

1. Mark Weiser, "The Computer for the 21st Century," *Scientific American* 265, no. 3, (September 1991): 94–104.
2. See David A. Fahrenthold and David Nakamura, "Council Attacks D.C. Surveillance Cameras," *Washington Post*, November 8, 2002, B01. There is a growing literature and spreading activist movement against the recent, rapid expansion of video surveillance systems. Two web sites documenting activist projects are from the New York Civil Liberties Union ("NYC Surveillance Camera Project," www.mediaeater.com/cameras/) and from Washington DC's Electronic Privacy Information Center (www.epic.org/privacy/surveillance/).
3. Robert Sack, "Consumer's World: Place as Context," *Annals of the Association of American Geographers* 78 (1998), 642. [Editors' note: Robert Sack is quoted in Anthony Giddens, *The Consequences of Modernity* (Stanford, CA: Stanford University Press, 1990), 117.]
4. From John Perry Barlow, "A Declaration of the Independence of Cyberspace," 1996, Electronic Frontier Foundation. Barlow first applied sci-fi writer William Gibson's term *cyberspace* to the digital social space enabled by the Internet. See https://www.eff.org/cyberspace-independence.
5. *Cyberspace* was first coined by science fiction writer William Gibson, then taken up in architecture by writers like Michael Benedikt in *Cyberspace: First Steps* (Cambridge, MA: MIT Press, 1991) and Christine Boyer in *Cybercities* (New York: Princeton Architectural Press, 1996). [Editors' note: William Gibson coined *cyberspace* in the short story, "Burning Chrome," published in *Omni* in July 1982.]
6. Jean Baudrillard, *Selected Writings*, ed. Mark Poster (Stanford, CA: Stanford University Press, 1988), 29.
7. Marshall McLuhan, *Understanding Media: The Extensions of Man* (Cambridge, MA: MIT Press, 1998), 283.
8. The formal likenesses between physical urban infrastructure—the sidewalks, streets, systems of parks, sewers, and electrical grids—and pervasive computing networks facilitate each one's absorption of the other.
9. McLuhan also recognized the connection between space, society, and technology. In his discourse on the book he says, "Printing, a ditto device, confirmed and extended the new visual stress. It created the portable book, which men could read in privacy and isolation from others." Marshall McLuhan, *The Medium Is the Massage* (New York: Random House, 1967), 50.
10. Regarding search warrants, see Linda Greenhouse on the Supreme Court decision regarding privacy and thermal imaging searches. "Justices Say Warrant Is Required in High-Tech Searches of Homes," *New York Times*, June 12, 2001.

11. Roland Barthes, *The Eiffel Tower and Other Mythologies*, trans. Richard Howe (New York: Hill and Wang, 1979), 5. These are Barthes' italics.
12. Jeffrey Rosen's informative essay was published just after 9/11. Jeffrey Rosen, "A Watchful State," *New York Times Magazine*, October 7, 2001: 38–43, 85, 92–93.
13. For a comprehensive and articulate discussion of the changing notions of public space, see Anastasia Loukaitou-Sideris and Tridib Banerjee, *Urban Design Downtown* (Berkeley, CA: University of California Press, 1998).
14. Marshall Berman, *All That Is Solid Melts Into Air* (New York: Penguin, 1982), 152.
15. This is the concept of public life constructed by Richard Sennett in his seminal book, *The Fall of Public Man* (New York: Alfred A. Knopf, 1977), 295.
16. Irwin Altman offered this classic definition of privacy in *The Environment and Social Behavior* (Monterey, CA: Brooks/Cole, 1975).
17. Bernard Rudofsky, *Behind the Picture Window* (New York: Oxford University Press, 1955), 196.
18. Jeffrey Rosen, "A Watchful State."
19. Reuters, "Washington Plans Unprecedented Camera Network," New York, February 13, 2002.
20. See New York Civil Liberties Union, "NYC Surveillance Camera Project," www.mediaeater.com/cameras.
21. See Diller + Scofidio, "Refresh," Dia Center for the Arts, New York, October 1, 1998, https://diaart.org/exhibition/exhibitions-projects/diller-scofidio-refresh-web-project.
22. Donna Haraway, "A Manifesto for Cyborgs: Science, Technology and Socialist Feminism in the 1980s," *Socialist Review* (80) 15, no. 2 (1985): 67.
23. William Mitchell's *e-topia* argues that digital technology will transform the city in myriad positive ways. William Mitchell, *e-topia: "Urban Life, Jim—But Not As We Know It"* (Cambridge, MA: MIT Press, 2000); Weiser, "The Computer"; Rosen, "A Watchful State."
24. Sennett, *The Fall of Public Man*, 264.
25. These two quotes are taken from Anthony Giddens, *The Consequences of Modernity* (Stanford, CA: Stanford University Press, 1990), 124, 127.

Images Doing Work: Construction Photography at the Tuskegee Institute and Black Mountain College

Anna Goodman
Portland State University

Maura Lucking
University of California, Los Angeles

Class and race have historically impacted and continue to shape our perception of what is and who should engage in architectural "work." Much current writing on architectural labor—be it the critical assessments of The Architecture Lobby, advocacy for design-build programs, or discourses on digital crafts—finds it difficult to maintain distinctions between knowledge work and more traditional configurations of labor. These two forms of work are, in fact, produced within particular historical contexts and defined by their relation to each other and to references outside the architectural field. While new technologies and configurations of capitalism have remade architectural labor on a broad scale, competing definitions of architectural practice and variation among architectural workers predate these contemporary concerns. In the paired essays that follow, we examine two case studies that made significant use of students' manual labor on campus construction projects: the Tuskegee Institute and Black Mountain College. In these analyses, we demonstrate that student labor—whether organized toward building vocational skills or individual character—is always deeply linked to more fundamental understandings of American citizenship.

While their particulars are very different (one taking on African American industrial education as a method of racial uplift and the other Americanizing the intellectual project of the European avant-garde), Tuskegee and Black Mountain share important geographical, political, and aesthetic concerns. First, each speaks to the way manual labor, performed against the backdrop of the rural South, struck a chord in the American cultural imaginary during that historical period. Second, both depended on financial support outside their immediate communities. This required them to formulate strategic aesthetic practices of self-representation that spoke to the taste cultures of their respective audiences. It also required them to address these audiences' racial and class expectations: on the one hand, naturalizing African American industriousness as an artisanal practice; on the other, safeguarding the special status of the artist-intellectual.

Our analyses depart from a close reading of each school's construction photographs to consider these underlying operations. While photography has been long recognized as a generative and documentary component of architectural design, it is less often used to consider the discursive formations that surround architectural labor. The two essays below expose the constructed nature of such scenes to de-romanticize images of "building architecture." In these examples, the public circulation of images depicting educational student labor do their own critical work—exposing and making palatable certain social issues while concealing others. The essays stress how the schools tapped into historically specific cultural associations by employing stylized aesthetic sensibilities. In both cases, imagery of building helped bridge the rural-urban divide and resolve potentially troubling identity politics. For contemporary scholars and practitioners, the essays warn against collapsing the experience and significance of all laboring bodies. Instead, to address the unequal foundation of the architectural profession, we must recognize that labor and its representation are not neutral, nor are their advantages evenly distributed.

Tuskegee Institute: Racial Uplift, "Erected by Students"

Maura Lucking
The construction site is rarely considered under the iconographic category of the rural idyll. Yet, for several decades at the turn of the twentieth century, this is precisely how the campus of the Tuskegee Institute was represented and broadly understood. As one of the earliest (and most famous) black-led institutions of higher learning founded in the years following the Civil War, Tuskegee administrators leveraged photography as an important rhetorical tool to display the potential for racial uplift and self-help within black communities, as well as the instrumentality of the school's industrial curriculum to achieve that ambition. In such a loaded transitional moment in American race relations, the distribution of seemingly staid tableaux of well-mannered students and charismatic portraits of school principal Booker T. Washington endeavored to remake the visual culture of black life for a diverse national audience.[1] Photographs of construction were particularly exemplary within this aesthetic project for the way they

Figure 1. Tuskegee students amongst the brick formwork of Milbank Hall, 1909. Photographer unknown, likely Charles D. Robinson. Courtesy Tuskegee University Archives, Public Domain.

drew together the pedagogy, politics, and, somewhat counterintuitively, pastoral aesthetics of Tuskegee's campus in the rural Alabama Black Belt.

Building projects connected the school's disparate modalities of learning, reflecting Washington's aphorism that "head, heart, and hand" ought to work together through industrial education to elevate the black community out of poverty.[2] The same students who studied architecture in the drafting room might learn carpentry in the workshop and subsequently frame the roof of the newest classroom building. From 1881 until the late 1920s, students spent one or two days per week working on building, infrastructure, agriculture, and maintenance projects on campus to defray school expenses and academic tuition.[3] The practice nominally contributed to the school's development, although numerous accounts reported the increased cost and decreased quality of using student labor.[4] Borrowing from global models of manual education, Tuskegee also participated in the gospel of work that characterized social and design reform movements, wherein figures from Thomas Carlyle to William Morris elevated any "vocation" to a spiritual calling.[5] These references, and their institution through photographic representations, provided a modern ideological update for the forced labor practices that had long underpinned America's institutions during slavery. Despite obvious continuities with enslaved black builders and the near-simultaneous appearance of convict camps of incarcerated black men across the South that replaced slave labor, for a brief historical moment building construction socially reproduced labor as industrial learning: not a job site, but the classroom expanded to the scale of the campus itself.[6]

Images showing construction labor on Tuskegee buildings were widely published in promotional materials, African American and mainstream newspapers, and Washington's own popular autobiographies, with prints tucked surreptitiously into correspondence with big-ticket donors (Figure 1). Despite differing camera styles, a remarkably similar aesthetic language emerged through the innumerable images of students at work. Photographs were typically made at the scale of the building rather than the individual laborer, often rendering students ant-like along a crenelated roofline. This operation seemingly placed the focus on campus improvements that might be used to procure funding for continued development. While, in general, documentation of new building sites had become de rigueur (celebrating the modernity of these urban endeavors with rhythmic grids of exposed steel beams, rivets, and formwork), Tuskegee's construction photographs evoke a different temporality altogether.

The artisanal skills of carpentry and brickmaking were invariably foregrounded over the standard fare of architectural modernization. This imagery aligns with the prevalent critique that the Tuskegee program failed to competitively prepare students for the workforce, yet specification lists show that Tuskegee's large academic buildings were quite industrial, despite their historical styling, featuring concrete block foundations, hybrid steel masonry, and Celotex fireproofing.[7] Alumnus William Sydney Pittman, later an instructor of architectural drawing, even advertised steel construction as his specialty, suggesting its presence in the curriculum.[8] This disconnect between practice and representation suggests that such images were less concerned with signifying advances in industrial technologies and more with physically and administratively disciplining student bodies through a historically legible set of artisanal practices. The handcrafted and often imperfectly finished buildings were themselves imagined, then, as a reforming heuristic or object lesson. Evinced by the oft-repeated caption, "Erected by students," student labor marked the buildings rather than the other way around.

The anonymous students are depicted as hard-working, cooperative in their labor, and out of time in a manner simultaneously nostalgic and primitivizing. Their presence on one pitched roofline after another evokes an early American barn raising, which relied on unpaid labor to support the wellbeing of highly interdependent rural communities. Pastoral themes had seen a revival at the end of the nineteenth century in reaction to industrialization and shifting demographics in American cities.[9] Like the Hudson River School, who painted yeoman farms that no longer existed, a 1926 photograph depicts Tuskegee as a sylvan wonderland (Figure 2), despite the more than one hundred buildings, twenty thousand acres, and a football stadium that would have characterized the campus.[10] This industrious pastoralism characterized African Americans as skilled rather than unskilled workers elevated by the moral purity and proto-capitalism of unalienated labor, not unlike those under the rhetoric of the Arts and Crafts movement. Indeed, Washington often spoke about the need for simple and modest construction, appropriate to the needs and social station of black Southerners less than a generation after the end of slavery: uplift, but not too much.

To that end, the celebrated photographer Frances Benjamin Johnston was hired to photograph the school on several occasions. Johnston had the independent means and progressive outlook to work fluidly between reportage and society portraiture, which meant that her photographs of Tuskegee and other Southern industrial schools were guaranteed a positive reception among donors. Her images of Tuskegee are distinctive from that of other photographers for their evocative historical references to portraiture rather than landscape; their dramatically staged and somewhat wooden tableaux position student bodies like Golden Age courtiers within and among the objects signifying their rank and occupation (Figure 3). Scholars have argued that, despite this decorum, the photographs deny the subjectivity of the young black men they depict, both in their visual uniformity and averted eyes.[11] The latter, in particular, leads to an impenetrability unlike the conventions of social documentary photography coalescing at the time, which largely insisted on the assertiveness of an individual sitter as a marker of a kind of universal humanity, regardless of class. Nor do they provide the access to

Figure 2. Students workers constructing the roof of Sage Hall, 1926. Photographer unknown, likely A. P. Bedou. Courtesy Tuskegee University Archives.

a contemplative inner life that characterized realist painting, the other dominant representational genre depicting workers, if not as individuals then at least as discernable types. Rather than reading Johnston's compositions as solely her unknowing resistance to dignifying black subjects, it is also possible to recognize the unique burden of this aesthetic project for school administrators. Responsible for advertising not only an educational experience but also a labor force and an entire race, the distributed human and object systems of artisanal labor constructed by these photographs offered an appeal to respectability politics only possible on a collective level.

If such a reading demonstrates how these images courted a white audience by embracing the equivocation of the laboring body between dignity and tractability, a closer analysis of Johnston's 1902 photograph of students constructing the roof of an academic building demonstrates the complex, multidirectional nature of social position at Tuskegee in ways that might not have been immediately visible to outsiders (Figure 3). In the foreground, two instructors confer over an unfurled blueprint, mimicking the traditional division of labor (and class distinction) between architect and construction manager. Smart in a suit coat and bowler hat, the former gestures to a point on the plan; his companion, matching the students behind him in rumpled shirtsleeves, reads right along. While the architect has reached the limit of his sphere of influence, the worker

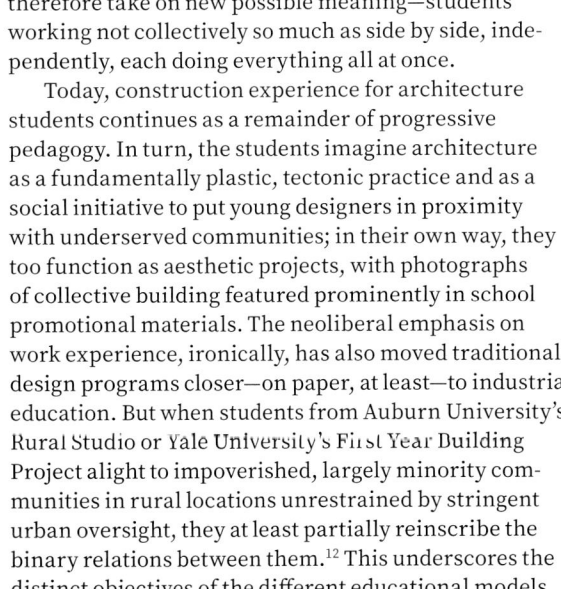

Figure 3. Instructors reference a blueprint while students work at the construction of the pitched roof frame of the Collis P. Huntington Memorial Hall, 1909. Photographer Frances Benjamin Johnston. Library of Congress, Prints & Photographs Division, Public Domain.

has a multilateral purview over both the rarified world of drawing and the fulsome embodied tradition of the construction site. The surrounding students would have been trained in both spaces. This dualism was essential not only for unlocking the potential upward mobility of white-collar work but also for perpetuating the realities of anti-black discrimination in the Jim Crow workplace: architectural training notwithstanding, most would still need to find work, at least intermittently, in the trades. Their strange poses in Johnston's long exposure therefore take on new possible meaning—students working not collectively so much as side by side, independently, each doing everything all at once.

Today, construction experience for architecture students continues as a remainder of progressive pedagogy. In turn, the students imagine architecture as a fundamentally plastic, tectonic practice and as a social initiative to put young designers in proximity with underserved communities; in their own way, they too function as aesthetic projects, with photographs of collective building featured prominently in school promotional materials. The neoliberal emphasis on work experience, ironically, has also moved traditional design programs closer—on paper, at least—to industrial education. But when students from Auburn University's Rural Studio or Yale University's First Year Building Project alight to impoverished, largely minority communities in rural locations unrestrained by stringent urban oversight, they at least partially reinscribe the binary relations between them.[12] This underscores the distinct objectives of the different educational models that have been historicized under the rubric of the "design-build." Students in the aforementioned programs do not work on job sites to master construction techniques but, rather, to become better architect-managers capable of anticipating problems of materiality and labor, even in the design phase. By contrast, many historically black colleges and universities continue to offer degrees in facilities planning and construction science alongside architecture. While they no longer need to court white philanthropic investment through picturesque aesthetics, their own professional fluidity attests to the unmistakable persistence of racial inequity in contemporary architectural practice.

Amid the Great Migration, Tuskegee educators still imagined the New South as a viable future for black-led modernization—a productive pastoral landscape—rather than simply as a rustic escape. An unusual image of a single student (Figure 4), who by the 1920s was as likely to come from a northern city as from a local town, conceals the young man's face in shadow, his body unified in a linear composition with two-by-fours, slat fencing, and the unfocused horizon. It is his individuated labor, not his individual self, that is made visible, naturalized within a pedagogical and material landscape. This picture troubles received assumptions about the ways that the rural-urban divide emerged following late nineteenth century industrialization, both along economic and racial lines, and the ongoing ramifications of those changes. Would rural building projects have become so appealing to late twentieth-century architectural educators were it not for the uneven distribution of resources between the two locales? How do we talk about practices that aim to ameliorate and simultaneously exploit this structural inequity? While the recognition of manual labor as a form of architectural knowledge is

Figure 4. Student worker at Sage Hall, 1926. Photographer unknown, likely A. P. Bedou. Courtesy Tuskegee University Archives.

a valiant interest, it is important to remember through programs such as those at Tuskegee that performativity by itself should not be mistaken for criticality. Sometimes, making something visible is not enough.

Black Mountain College: The Aesthetics of Individual and Community Work

Anna Goodman

Photography has long been a potent tool of the aesthetic avant-garde. Its ability to be both image-object and a proxy for experience has made it a key medium for expressing and interpreting technological and social change. At Black Mountain College (a school based on the pursuit of experience but most celebrated for its artistic output), construction photography offered a means of not only projecting the isolated community to the outside world but also addressing questions of individual and collective citizenship in a moment of national crisis.

Black Mountain was an experimental liberal arts college that operated in rural North Carolina from 1933 to 1956. Despite its short life, Black Mountain substantially impacted twentieth-century art, design, and education in the US. The college was the long-time home of Anni and Josef Albers and was frequently visited by other Bauhaus émigrés and important American artists, writers, and designers.[13] Dominant narratives surrounding the college's contributions to the aesthetic avant-garde (and, later, its role as a precedent for design-build education) have obscured the deeper contexts of the college's relationship to questions of independence and intellectual freedom.[14]

The school's identity was, from the beginning, closely tied to reformer John Dewey's educational philosophy. This partially arose from the significance of Black Mountain's work program, which required all students to support the college by working in the kitchens, on the farms, and on building programs. For Dewey, progressive education meant not only "learning by doing" but more importantly fostering students' individual development.[15] This individualized focus, he argued, would not produce individualism but would instead prepare students to reflect on society's contradictions and to alter its trajectory toward greater aims. Though it became famous as the training ground for several important twentieth-century artists, this was not the college's initial agenda. As one of Black Mountain's founders, John Rice, wrote in his biography, "The center of the curriculum, we said, would be art. The democratic man, we said, must be an artist. The integrity, we said, of the democratic man was the integrity of the artist, an integrity of relationship."[16] He went on, "The artist, we said, was not a competitor. He competed only with himself. His struggle was inside, not against his fellows, but against his own ignorance and clumsiness."[17] Per Dewey's teachings and against the negative individualism noted in Tocquevillian critiques of American democracy, the school used work to mediate individual development and societal commitments.[18] The images that document the school's building program illustrate how "work" at Black Mountain had a double meaning: the work of one's individual development as a scholar or artist and "community work." The former involved freedom from intellectual constraint or habit, while the latter referred to physical labor done in the service

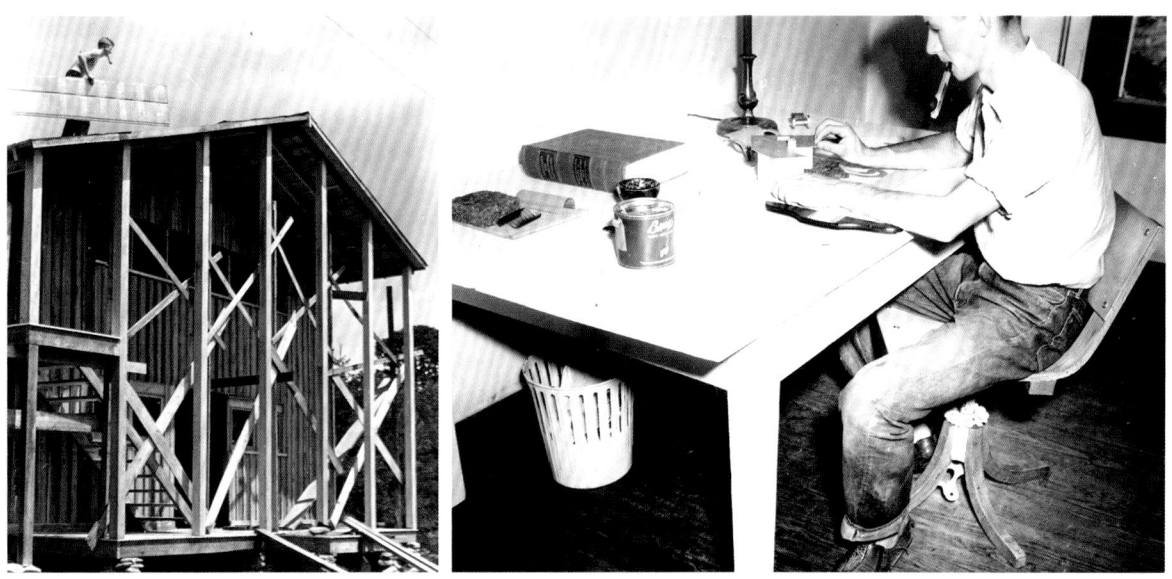

Figure 5. Robert Bliss on the roof of the Service Building, fall 1940 and Bliss with model of low-cost housing. Courtesy of the Western Regional Archives, State Archives of North Carolina.

of the whole community. Take, for example, images of Robert Bliss constructing the Service Building—living quarters for the school's African American staff. Here, he is set off by his characteristic pipe (Figure 5). In the photos, we also see Bliss bare-chested in the midst of the construction process or in his study with a model designed for one of the architectural program's low-cost housing courses. He moves fluidly between intellectual and physical labor, collective and individual production, all while remaining steadfastly himself.[19]

When the school was forced to move from its original campus in 1940, the building aspect of the work program became especially important to convey to a wider audience the principles that underlaid the Black Mountain mission. Buildings designed by modernist architect A. Lawrence Kocher for the school's new Lake Eden campus used a combination of locally harvested and advanced prefabricated materials. Notably, prefabrication allowed their construction with mostly unskilled labor, enabling student participation while pushing the boundaries of existing technology.[20]

To attract the attention of the press and the support of New York's artistic elite, who in turn brought desperately needed donations, college leaders realized that building projects had to be perceived as part of the aesthetic avant-garde. Yet, on the ground, the school relied on local connections—to both Asheville citizens and institutions such as the Asheville Farm School—to navigate the challenges of both farming and on-site construction management.[21] The school's continued existence rested on the successful combination and purposeful contrast between these modes of working, and the resultant aesthetic references reflected this delicate balance—the modernist avant-garde and an American pastoral ideal.

This became ever more important as the rejection of academic hierarchy of the 1920s became, in the late 1930s, a nationalistic project linked to the war effort. Materials from Black Mountain's summer work camps showed a strong and resourceful (white) youth willing to get their hands dirty for the sake of the nation (Figure 6). When we see these youths working farm equipment or digging trenches, one would never mistake them for the anonymous workers of any other farm or building site in North Carolina. In the upper left photo, the young men are shirtless and hatless, enjoying the hot sun on their backs. Compositionally, they are suspended between the lush hills and the corrugated metal façade of the Studies Building—literally straddling their role as laborers and future professionals. In the bottom two spreads, we see young women in traditionally male roles, easily laying bricks or assembling trusses. In 1941 in the rural South, the subversion of traditional gender roles signaled a liberal philosophy while suggesting a democratic alternative to images of youth in fascist and communist propaganda.

The students' bodies are on display, communicating youth, health, and positive character traits (optimism, pleasure in a job well done, and cooperation). While these images took aesthetic cues from Depression-era propaganda art—including posters produced by the Works Progress Administration—and contemporaneous Social Realist photography that emphasized the struggle and nobility of rural workers, the photos also distinguish Black Mountain College students as exceptional workers. Rather than downturned heads covered in wide-brimmed hats, we see their fresh upturned faces as an indication that their higher-education trajectory will ensure that their status as laborers is only temporary. Deftly navigating cutting edge intellectual and artistic terrains while drawing moral authority from

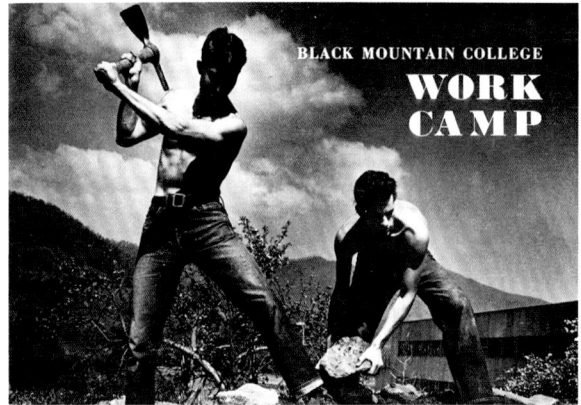

Figure 6. Work Camp Brochure, summer 1941. Work camps occurred in the summers during the early 1940s. Students from other universities paid to live with and learn from Black Mountain and visiting faculty while contributing to farm and building projects. The camps brought funds and supported student recruitment. Courtesy of the Western Regional Archives, State Archives of North Carolina.

the rural ideal, their labor elevates them farther from the traditionally constraining identity of laborers into special creative producers.

To this point, a dimension of "playacting" had always been part of the Black Mountain experience. In the 1930s, Robert Wunsch ran the school's theater program, involving the entire campus in the design, staging, and production of modern and classical plays. Wunsch felt his teaching methods helped students question their identities. He would, for example, place wealthy students in the role of "poverty-ground tenant or worker; the poor girl the part of the miserable rich woman."[22] Part of the agenda of this performance was to help students build empathy for a wider scope of human experience. Yet these experiments also allowed a safe terrain for students to play out social scenarios. They leveraged artistic freedom within a self-selected community yet remained outside the actual economic and racial relations that troubled the region and nation during this period. While described as "the very grassroots of democracy," it was a place of exception that was accessible only to those whose class and race allowed a fluid relationship between intellectual, artistic, and physical labor.

As young, mostly middle- and upper-class, students at Black Mountain engaged in construction and farm labor, the documentation of their practices reflects the foundational art training students were receiving at the hands of Bauhaus masters. In a series of photographs of students applying corrugated aluminum siding to the Studies Building façade—likely taken by a student photographer in one of Beaumont Newhall's courses—we see the play of positive and negative space, the appreciation of the human form in motion, and the compositional experimentation characteristic of Black Mountain's artistic sensibility (Figure 7). The images demonstrate a sensibility reminiscent of Bauhaus theater, with its intentional naiveté and return to elemental forms.[23] Students' double role—as actors within an artistic tableau *and* as workers temporarily transcending their class position—captures how the performance of labor threaded through every aspect of life at Black Mountain.

Despite the school's initial insistence that its mission was in the democratic rather than artistic sphere, the work program and its blending with aesthetic practices prefigured later Black Mountain artists, including John Cage and Merce Cunningham, who pursued more ephemeral and ultimately more self-referential artistic approaches.[24] These practices had little place for either collective building or pastoral sensibilities. Instead,

Figure 7. Construction of the Studies Building, collage of images glued to one sheet, 1940-41. Courtesy of the Western Regional Archives, State Archives of North Carolina.

freedom from restraint and the promotion of individual creative capacities usurped collective responsibility.

Today, design-build programs still grapple with these two worlds—one that focuses on the development of skills and understanding for the individual student, another that enfolds broader social worlds. The rural remains a favored terrain for experimentation, be it in Dalhousie University's Ghost Laboratory or the University of Utah's DesignBuildBLUFF.[25] Black Mountain should be seen as a reference for these contemporary practices but not as a precedent or point of origin. It should be studied for the way its success was predicated on a confrontation between two notions of work—one disciplinary and individual, the other grappling with collaboration and cross-class exchange. Like Black Mountain, the aesthetic output of many contemporary design-build programs melds avant-garde material experimentation with rural romanticism. Ultimately, it is essential to acknowledge that this combination is strategic. By linking to a deep cultural association with the moral value of rural labor and at the same time insisting on the special status of student workers, these practices rehearse a larger story of class and self-formation that has been at play for a century. Today, as in the 1940s, tensions around class-based politics, the organization of labor, and intellectual elitism animate debates on the meaning of American citizenship. How then are architectural educators using their command of images and institutions to define their allegiances?

Notes

1. See Michael Bieze, *Booker T. Washington and the Art of Self-Representation* (New York: Peter Lang, 2008); and Shawn Michelle Smith, *Photography on the Color Line: W. E. B. Du Bois, Race, and Visual Culture* (Durham, NC: Duke University Press, 2004).
2. Booker T. Washington, "The Atlanta Exposition Address," in *Up from Slavery: An Autobiography* (New York: Doubleday, 1901), 221.
3. By 1890, tuition was covered through a state appropriation, and board was eight dollars per month. *Twenty-First Annual Catalogue of the Tuskegee Normal and Industrial Institute, Tuskegee Alabama, 1890–1901* (Tuskegee, AL: Institute Press, 1890).
4. W. E. B. Du Bois, "Tuskegee Normal and Industrial Institute, Ala. (1901–1902)," in *The Negro Artisan: A Social Study* (Atlanta, GA: Atlanta University Press, 1902), 44.
5. See Walter E. Houghton, "Work," in *The Victorian Frame of Mind, 1830–1870* (New Haven, CT: Yale University Press, 1957), 242–62.
6. See Ronald Lewis and James E. Newton, eds., *The Other Slaves: Mechanics, Artisans, and Craftsmen* (Boston, MA: G. K. Hall, 1978); and Alex Lichtenstein, *Twice the Work of Free Labor: The Political Economy of Convict Labor in the New South* (London: Verso, 1996).
7. Ellen Weiss, *Robert Taylor and Tuskegee: An African American Architect Designs for Booker T. Washington* (Montgomery, AL: New South Books, 2012), 96.
8. "W. Sidney Pittman, Architect," *Tuskegee Student*, April 28, 1906.
9. Sarah Burns, *Pastoral Inventions: Rural Life in Nineteenth Century American Life* (Philadelphia, PA: Temple University Press, 1989).
10. *Thirty-Fourth Annual Catalog: The Tuskegee Normal and Industrial Institute* (Tuskegee, AL: Institute Press, 1915).
11. Judith Freyer Davidov, *Women's Camera Work: Self/Body/Other in American Visual Culture* (Durham, NC: Duke University Press, 1998).
12. Early Yale projects took place in Appalachia and rural New England through the 1970s; the last several decades have returned largely to the area around New Haven proper. On the two programs and their representational techniques, see Richard W. Hayes, *The Yale Building Project: The First 40 Years* (New Haven, CT: Yale University Press, 2007); and Anna Goodman, "The Paradox of Representation and Practice in the Auburn

University Rural Studio," *Traditional Dwellings and Settlements Review* 25, no. 2 (Spring 2014): 39–52.

13. Walter Gropius and Marcel Breuer designed a never-constructed masterplan for the campus, and it was the site of Buckminster Fuller's first (unsuccessful) dome experiments. To learn more about Black Mountain's influence, see Vincent Katz, Martin Brody, and Museo Nacional Centro de Arte Reina Sofía, *Black Mountain College: Experiment in Art* (Cambridge, MA: MIT Press, 2003); Helen Anne Molesworth, ed., *Leap Before You Look: Black Mountain College, 1933–1957* (Boston, MA: Institute of Contemporary Art, 2015); and Eva Díaz, *The Experimenters: Chance and Design at Black Mountain College* (Chicago, IL: University of Chicago Press, 2015).
14. See, for example, Tolya Stonorov, ed., *The Design-Build Studio: Crafting Meaningful Work in Architecture Education* (New York: Routledge, 2018), 10; and Lauren Bellard, "The Design-Build Program at Lake Eden," in Molesworth, *Leap Before You Look*, 132–141.
15. Dewey famously wrote that Black Mountain College was "the very grassroot of democracy," a statement heavily quoted in publicity material accompanied by images of the work program (see Figure 2). John Dewey to Theodore Dreier, July 18, 1940, quoted in Jonathan Fisher, "The Life and Work of Progressive Higher Education: Towards a History of Black Mountain College, 1933–1949," *Black Mountain Studies Journal* 6 (Summer 2014): 1. For more on Dewey's educational philosophy, see John Dewey, *Experience and Nature*, Lectures upon the Paul Carus Foundation (New York: W. W. Norton, 1929); and Larry A. Hickman and Giuseppe Spadafora, eds., *John Dewey's Educational Philosophy in International Perspective: A New Democracy for the Twenty-First Century*, (Carbondale, IL: Southern Illinois University Press, 2009).
16. John Andrew Rice, *I Came Out of the Eighteenth Century* (London: Harper and Brothers, 1942), 328.
17. Rice, *I Came Out*, 329.
18. Alexis de Tocqueville, *Democracy in America*, ed. J. P. Mayer, trans. George Lawrence (Garden City, NY: Doubleday, Anchor Books, 1969).
19. Notably, Bliss later served as chairman of the University of Utah's School of Architecture, founding University of Utah's Graduate School of Architecture.
20. For more on Kocher's role in Black Mountain's design-build efforts, see Anna Goodman, "Making Prefabrication American: the Work of A. Lawrence Kocher," *Journal of Architectural Education* 71, no. 1 (2017): 22–33.
21. David Silver has written extensively online about the connections between Black Mountain and surrounding agricultural resources. David Silver, "Building Autonomy. Creating Community: the Farm and Work Program at Black Mountain College," in Molesworth, *Leap Before You Look*, 120–131.
22. Bob Wunsch quoted in Louis Adamic, *My America, 1928–1938* (New York: Harper, 1938).
23. The connection was not incidental with faculty member Xanti Schawinsky and others applying Bauhaus methods to theater productions at Black Mountain. See Xanti Schawinsky, "From the Bauhaus to Black Mountain," *The Drama Review: TDR* 15, no. 3 (Summer 1971): 30–44.
24. Eva Díaz compares earlier Bauhaus experiments with this later period in "John Cage's Chance Protocols," in Díaz, *The Experimenters*, 53–100.
25. For more on these programs, see Shundana Yusaf and Jose Galarza, "Taking the Pulse of Bluff," *Dialectic* III (Spring 2015): 75–105; and Brian MacKay-Lyons, *Local Architecture: Building Place, Craft, and Community*, ed. Robert McCarter (New York: Princeton Architectural Press, 2014).

Index

All page numbers appearing in italic type refer to figures, images, and tables and their captions. Page numbers followed by an "n" indicate an endnote.

A

Aalto, Aino Marsio: and Alvar Aalto, 201; Paimio Sanatorium (1933), 236; Villa Mairea (1940), 236
Aalto, Alvar: and Aino Marsio Aalto, 201; and Elissa Mäkiniemi Aalto, 207; mentioned, 205; Paimio Sanatorium (1933), 236; Villa Mairea (1940), 236
Aalto, Elissa Mäkiniemi: and Alvar Aalto, 207
Abele, Julian: Harvard Widener Library (1915), 202
ACSA (Association of Collegiate Schools of Architecture), 13, 14, 15, 26, 132, 184, 186
activism, 226, 240, 258, 260, 270. *See also* protest
adaptations, 66, 105–6, 109–12, 212–23
ADPSR (Architects, Designers, and Planners for Social Responsibility), 258
aesthetics, 31, 55, 138, 246, 264
Affirmative Action, 240–41
African American Architects (Wilson), 207
African American Architects in Current Practice (Travis), 262
African-American spatial paradigm, 62–74
Agra, IN: Taj Mahal, 35
Agrest and Gandelsonas partnership, 57, 60
AIA (American Institute of Architects), College of Fellows, 75; Department of Education and Research, 90–91, 94; lack of diversity within, 208, 240, 261; mentioned, 22, 25, 85, 150, 152, 254; and research, 26–29, 84, *89*, 265; *Statement on Architectural Research* (1956), 89; Teachers Conference, 15
AIA Journal, 252
air conditioning, 116, 123, 151, 286. *See also* technology
Albany, NY, systems monitoring in, 115
Albers, Anni and Josef, 296
Alberti, Leon Battista: *De Re Aedificatoria,* 173; on form, 34, 244; mentioned, 180
Alexander, Christopher: mentioned, 132, 155; *Notes on the Synthesis of Form* (1964), 152
allegory, 60–61
Allen, Barbara, 17
Alma Mater (Horowitz), 236
America Builds (Roth), 236
American Architecture (Roth), *203,* 206–7
American Houses, Inc., 86–87
American Institute of Architects (AIA): College of Fellows, 75; Department of Education and Research, 90–91, 94; lack of diversity within, 208, 240, 261; mentioned, 22, 25, 85, 150, 152, 254; and research, 26–29, 84, *89,* 265; *Statement on Architectural Research* (1956), 89; Teachers Conference, 15
American Institute of Planners, 111
American Society for Testing and Materials, 25, 26
America's Architectural Roots (Upton), 262
Anderson, Genell: *Call of the Ancestors* (1991), 262
Anderson, Lawrence: "Environmental Design Umbrella, The" (1967), 132, 150–51
Anderson, Stanford, 204

Andrews University, 184
Anscombe, Isabelle: *Woman's Touch, A* (1984), 202, 237
Anthony, Kathryn H.: "Private Reactions to Public Criticism" (1987), 133, 182–92; with Metlem Ö. Gürel: "Canon and the Void, The" (2006), 133, 200–211
anthropomorphism, 66–67
apprenticeships, 132, 144, 275–82
Arbeitsrat für Kunst (Gropius), 276
Arbona, Javier: Domestic Encounters exercise, 197; "Studio Screen" installation (n.d.), *194,* 195–96
Archigram Group: *Instant City* (1969), 81
Architect at Mid-Century, The (Bannister), 89, 150
Architects, Designers, and Planners for Social Responsibility (ADPSR), 258
Architect's Journal, The, 252, 254
"Architect's Role in Urban Renewal, The" (Bauer), 226, 228–29
Architectural Association School of Architecture, 135, 137
Architectural Digest, 55
"Architectural Education and Behavioral Science" (Winslow), 22, 37–38
Architectural Forum, 250, 252
Architectural League of New York, 201
Architectural Record, 86, 183, 247, 250
Architecture, 240
Architecture and the Crisis of Modern Science (Pérez-Gómez), 56
Architecture and Utopia (Tafuri), 55
"Architecture as Drawing" (Pérez-Gómez), 132, 173–79
Architecture: from Prehistory to Postmodernism (Trachtenberg and Hyman), *203,* 204–5, 235
Architecture Intermundium, 181
Architecture Plus, 252
Architettura Civile (Guarini), *176*
Architettura et Prospettiva (Serlio), *173, 174*
Argonne National Laboratories Support Facility (Jahn and C. F. Murphy Associates), 54
Argyris, Chris, 183
ARL (Michigan Architectural Research Laboratory), 93
Arnhem, NL: Sonsbeek Sculpture Pavilion (Eyck), *120*
artificial intelligence, 132, 158–61, 284
Arup, Ove, 135
Association of American Colleges, 234
Association of Collegiate Schools of Architecture (ACSA), 13, 14, 15, 26, 132, 184, 186
Athens, GR: Parthenon (Iktinos and Kallikrates), 34, 35
Atlanta, GA: and Affirmative Action, 241; Martin Luther King, Jr. Center for Nonviolent Social Change (1984), 202, 206; mentioned, 23
Attwood, Charles W., 93–94
Auburn University, 184, 295
Augustine of Hippo, 243
Aulenti, Gae: Musee d'Orsay (1980-87), 205

B

Bacon, Francis, *110,* 244
Bacon, Roger, 25
Bailey, James: "Case History of a Failure, The" (1965), 252, 253
Baker, Houston, Jr., 65
Ball State University, 184

Banham, Reyner: *Los Angeles: Architecture of Four Ecologies* (1971), 81; mentioned, 123
Banneker, Benjamin, 202
Bannister, Turpin: *Architect at Mid-Century, The* (1954), 89; and JAE, 13, 22, 85; "Research Heritage of the Architectural Profession, The" (1947), 80
Barbaro, Daniele: *La Pratica della Perspettiva* (1569), 174
Barcelona, ES: Barcelona Pavilion (Mies van der Rohe), 204, 205, 235
Barnett, Henrietta, 237
Barthes, Roland, 56, 285
Bataille, George, 122
Batey and Mack partnership, 57
Baudrillard, Jean, 284–85
Bauer, Catherine: "Architect's Role in Urban Renewal, The" (1955), 226, 228–29; debate with Minoru Yamasaki, 255; mentioned, 14, 91, 202, 206; and William W. Wurster, 201
Bauhaus 1919-1928 (Bayer, Gropius, and Gropius), 276, 277, 279
"Bauhaus Hausfrau: Gender Formation in Design Education" (Rüedi Ray), 227, 275–82
Baur, F. C., 246
Baydar, Gülsüm, 203
Bayer, Herbert: with Walter Gropius and Ise Gropius: *Bauhaus 1919-1928* (1975), 276, 277, 279; "Theory and Organization of the Bauhaus, The," 277
Bearden, Romare, 63, 65, 265
Beauty, 138
Beck, Ulrich, 124, 126
Beecher, Catharine, 202, 205, 206, 235–36
Beecher, Harriet. *See* Stowe, Harriet Beecher
Beha, Ann, 207
behavioral science, 22, 37–38, 84
Behind Ghetto Walls (Rainwater), 253
Behind the Picture Window (Rudofsky), 287
Bell, David, 16
Bennet, Wells, 93
Berlin, DE: mentioned, 81, 141; Technical University of Berlin, 151
Berman, Marshall, 286
Bethune, Louise, 206
Bibiena, Ferdinando Galli, 174
"Biculturalism and Community" (Ward), 262
Bilkent University, 200
"Black Architects: An Endangered Species" (Coles), 240–42, 262
Black Culture and Black Consciousness (Levine), 264
Black Lives Matter, 227
Black Mountain College, 227, 292–300
Black music, 64–65, 72n26
Blackburn, Walter: National Underground Railroad Freedom Center (2004), 208
Blackmar, Elizabeth: "Urban Landscape, The" (1976), 99, 109–12
Blake, Peter: *Form Follows Fiasco* (1977), 255; *Master Builders, The* (1960), 235
Bliss, Robert, 297, *297*
Bloomer, Jennifer: "Hold It (Meditations Upon a Gorgonzola Cheese)" (1987), 23, 60–61
Bloomer, Kent, 15

Bond, J. Max: Martin Luther King, Jr. Center for Nonviolent Social Change (1984), 202, 206
Boston, MA: streetcar system, 110–11; Stull and Lee partnership, 202
Botta, Mario, 57
Boullée, Étienne-Louis, 54, 176, 178
"Boundary Studies" (Chi), 132, 193–99
Boyle, Robert, 25
Brachmann, Käthe, 280
Brandt, Marianne, 279
Braudel, Fernand, 124
Bristol, Katherine: "Pruitt-Igoe Myth, The" (1991), 226, 249–57
Brown, Jane: *Gardens of a Golden Afternoon* (1982), 236
Building Construction Research Board, 27
building materials: and building industry, 86, *89*; and ecology, 124; researching of, 25, 27, 28, 90–91; reuse of, 68, *69*
Building Officials Conference of America, 27
Building Research Advisory Board, 90
Buildings Across Time (Moffett, Fazio, and Wodehouse), *203*, 204, 205
built environment, 15, 42–43, 62, 65, 69, 98, 107, 200–211, 230, 234–238, 258–259
Burckhardt, Jacob: *Reflections on History,* 135
Bureau of Standards, 25, 26
Burton, Arthur E.: "Full Scale Prototype Structures" (1960), 133, 141–43
Bush, Vannevar: mentioned, 91; on research, 25; *Science the Endless Frontier* (1945), 87

C
Cacciari, Massimo, 56
California Polytechnic State University, San Luis Obispo, 184
Call of the Ancestors (Anderson), 262
Cal-Oregon Experiment, 132, 152–57
Cambridge School of Architecture and Landscape Architecture, 237
Campus: An American Planning Tradition (Turner), 236
Canberra, AUS: New Federal Capital (Griffin), 205–6
canon, 54, 134–35, 200–211
"Canon and the Void, The" (Anthony and Gürel), 133, 200–211
Cantor, George: *Historic Landmarks of Black America* (1991), 262
"Case History of a Failure, The" (Bailey), 252, 253
Castillo, Greg, 205
Cathedral of Paris (Notre-Dame), 34
Caudill Rowlett Scott (CRS), 132, 168–69
Caudill, William W.: founding member of Caudill Rowlett Scott (CRS), 87; mentioned, 94n15, 95n19-21, n30, n33; and research approaches, 86, 89, 91, 93; at Texas A&M University, *87* CED (College of Environmental Design), UC Berkeley, 91–92
Çelik, Zeynep, 203
Certeau, Michel de: mentioned, 66; *Practice of Everyday Life, The* (1984), 63–64, 72n16–17
Chartres Cathedral, 35
Chase Manhattan Bank Plaza (Noguchi), 265

Chesapeake Bay, MD: Loblolly House (KieranTimberlake), 77, *78,* 79
Chi, Lily: "Boundary Studies" (1999), 132, 193–99; mentioned, 17
Chicago, IL: 1893 World's Columbian Exposition, 205; Hip Hop Park, 23, 65–68, *67, 68, 69;* mentioned, 121
Chicano Art (Griswold del Castillo, McKenna, and Yarbro-Bejarano), 264
Church of S. Lorenzo (Guarini), *176*
churches, storefront, *263,* 265–66
CIAM (Congrès Internationaux d'Architecture Moderne), 254–55
Cincinnati, OH: National Underground Railroad Freedom Center (Blackburn), 208
Citroen, Paul, 276, 279, 280
City College of New York, 202
city planning, 51, 106, 177, 228–9; compared to other disciplines, 84, 89, 151; demographics of, 261; historical development of, 111, 112n15. See also urban planning
Clarke, Dave, 15
clients: and architects, 144, 204, 237; and collaboration, 201–2, 205, 228; differ from juries, 186–87; and ideas, 80; interactions with, 132, 168–69, 205
climate change, 99, 259
Codman, Ogden, 202
Colberg, Eugene: "Studio Screen" installation (n.d.), *195,* 196–97
Coleman, William, 240
Coles, Robert Traynham: "Black Architects: An Endangered Species" (1989), 240–42, 262
collaborations: among professionals, 85, 90, 201–2, 204–5, 235, 236; with clients, 201–2, 205, 228; organizational, 27, 29; with schools, 93
Collage City (Rowe and Koetter), 254
College of Environmental Design (CED), UC Berkeley, 91–92
Colter, Mary, 207
Columbia University, 80
Columbus, IN: Fire Station No. 4 (Venturi, Rauch and Scott Brown), 206
Commencement Address (Eyck), 99, 119–21
Communications Primer, A (Eames, C. and R.), 80, *81*
Communist Manifesto, The (Marx and Engels), 243–44
Como, ITA: Giuliani Frigerio apartments (Terragni), 58
"Compelling Yet Unreliable Theories of Sustainability" (Moe), 99, 122–29
Complexity and Contradiction in Architecture (Venturi), 54, 81, 245–46
computing, 158–61, 283–91
Concepts of Space (Jammer), 136
concrete, 141–43
Condit, Carl, 111
Congrès Internationaux d'Architecture Moderne (CIAM), 254–55
conservation, energy, 115, 122–23, 259
Construction Industry Advisory Council, 27
"Contesting the Public Realm" (Crawford), 227, 269–74
Cooper Union, The, 170
Copenhagen, DK: 3XN Ferry Terminal DFDX, *215,* 217
Cornell University, 193, 207, 243

Cranbrook Academy of Art, 15, 184
Crawford, Margaret: "Contesting the Public Realm" (1995), 227, 269–74
creative process, 30–32, 40, 139–40, 187
crime, 107–8, 251–54
"Crisis of Interdisciplinary Historiography, The" (Jarzombek), 226, 243–47
criticism, 30–32, 81–82, 152–57, 182–92
Crouch, Dora P. and June G. Johnson: *Traditions in Architecture* (2001), 204
Cuff, Dana: "Immanent Domain: Pervasive Computing and the Public Realm" (2003), 227, 283–91
Curious Perspective (Niceron), *175*
curriculum change, 75, 134–37, 182–92, 235–38, 261–68
Curtis, William J. R.: *Modern Architecture Since 1900* (1982), *203,* 204, 205–6

D

Dal Co, Francesco, 56
Dalhousie University, 299
Dana, Susan Lawrence, 204
Dana Thomas House (Wright), 204
Davis, Angela Y., 226, 227
Davis, Mike, 269
Davis, Regina: with Ken Simmons: *Looking Beneath the Surface* (1991), 267; mentioned, 16; "Writing Multiculturalism into Architectural Curricula" (1993), 227, 261–68
De Re Aedificatoria (Alberti), 173
Deamer, Peggy, 16
Death and Life of Great American Cities (Jacobs), 206
"Death of the Beaux-Arts, The" (Milne and Rusch), 132, 152–57
Defensible Space (Newman), 98, 107–8, 253, 254
Delaunay, Robert, 236
Delaunay, Sonia, 236
Delaware River basin, 105–6
Deleuze, Gilles, 61, 123
Delirious New York (Koolhaas), 81, 83
demolition, 249–57, *250*
Der Austausch, 280
Derrida, Jacques, 57, 247
Descriptive Geometry (Robertson), *177*
Desgodetz, Antoine: *Les edifices antiques de Rome* (1682), *177*
design: and drawing, 173–79; and economics, *232, 232*–33, *233;* and research, 39–44, 45–50, 75, *75,* 80–83, 84–95
design, civic, 100–102, 107–8. See also urban design
design exercises, 170–72, 193–99, 212–23, 232–33
design juries, 182–92, *184, 185, 186, 187*
design-build programs, 141–43, 292–300
Destra Expo water pavilion (Spuybroek), *290*
Dewey, John, 296
diagramming, 122–29, 154–55, *156*
Diamond, Henry, 55
Diller, Elizabeth, 201
Diller + Scofidio partnership, 288, *288*
Dilthey, Wilhelm, 246
Dimcheff, Luben: "Domestic Encounters" exercise (n.d.), 197; "Studio Screen" 2 installation (n.d.), *194, 195,* 196

Directory of African American Architects (Grant and Mann), 262
discrimination, 65–66, 119–21, 240–41, 249–57, 279–80
diversity: cultural, 261–68; lack of, 133, 200–211, 234–39; racial, 62–74, 240–42
Dodds, George, 17, 84
Doetinchem, NL: D-Tower project (Spuybroek), 288, *289*
Domestic Encounters design exercise, *196,* 197–98
Downsview Park Competition, Toronto, *125,* 127
drawing, 132, 170, 173–79. *See also* sketching
Drew, Jane: *Architects' Year Book,* vol. 1 (1945), 22; and Maxwell Fry, 206
Droste, Magdalena: on Bauhaus students, 276; on discrimination, 280
D-Tower project (Spuybroek), 288, *289*
Duany, Andres, 205
Durand, Jean-Nicolas-Louis: and descriptive geometry, 174, 175; mentioned, 176, 177; *Précis de Leçons d'Architecture* (1819), 175, *178*
Dutton, Thomas: *Voices in Architectural Education* (1991), 262

E

Eames, Charles and Ray: *Communications Primer, A* (1953), 80, *81*; mentioned, 23, 82, 201, 206; *Powers of Ten* (1968), 80, 83
eclecticism, 87, 134–35
École des Beaux Arts, 14, 174–75, 204
École Polytechnique, 174
"Ecology of the City" (McHarg), 98, 105–6
"Ecology Question, The" (Ingersoll), 227, 258–60
economics, 122–29, 232–33, 249–57, 269–74
ecosystems, 105–6, 119–21, 258–60
Edmunds, James R., Jr., 27
EDRA (Environmental Design Research Association), 98
Ehrenkrantz, Ezra, 92
Eiffel Tower (Sauvestre), 285
Eisenman, Peter: and decomposition, 57–58; "Formal Basis of Modern Architecture, The" (1963), 81; mentioned, 59n10, 60, 61; Visual Arts Center at The Ohio State University (1983), 58
Eldem, Sedad Hakki, 205
Elkouken, Bruno, 206
Ellis, W. Russell: mentioned, 14; "Review: *Defensible Space* by Oscar Newman" (1974), 98, 107–8
Elmer, Portia: "Body-Masque" construction (n.d.), *193,* 194
Empson, William: *Seven Types of Ambiguity,* 60
energy use, *113,* 113–18, *114, 115,* 122–23, 258–60
Engels, Friedrich: *Housing Question, The* (1872), 259; with Karl Marx: *Communist Manifesto, The* (1948), 243–44
engineering, 84–95, 134–37, 141–43, 150–51
environmental design, 98, 100–102, 119–21, 150–51, 232–33
Environmental Design Research Association (EDRA), 98
"Environmental Design Umbrella, The" (Anderson), 132, 150–51
Environmental Experience Stipends Program, 15
Erdman, Jori, 84
Estes, Charles: "Gaming at CRS" (1979), 132, 168–69
Evolving Architect, The, 13, 14
exercises, design, 170–72, 193–99, 212–23, 232–33
Eyck, Aldo van: Commencement Address (1979), 99, 119–21; Sonsbeek Sculpture Pavilion (1966), *120*

F

Fall of Public Man, The (Sennett), 286, 289
Fallingwater (Wright), 204
Farish, W., 25
Farnsworth, Edith, 205
Fathy, Hasan, 205, 263
Fazio, Michael, Marian Moffett, and Lawrence Wodehouse: *Buildings Across Time* (2004), *203,* 204, 205
Feigenberg, Alan, 262
Fein, Albert, 111
Feininger, Lyonel, 275, 276
Feininger, T. Lux, 276
Feuerbach, L., 246
Filarete: and historiographic interdependencies, 244; mentioned, 245; *Tratatto di Architettura II* (c. 1462), 174
Finnegans Wake (Joyce), 61
Fire Station No. 4 (Venturi, Rauch and Scott Brown), 206
Fitch, James Marston, 122
Fletcher, Banister: *History of Architecture on the Comparative Method, A* (1896), 134, 200, 207
Ford Foundation, 92
Form Follows Fiasco (Blake), 255
"Formal Basis of Modern Architecture, The" (Eisenman), 81
Fort-Brescia, Bernardo, 55, 201
Foster, Hal, 82
Foucault, Michel Paul, 63, 71n15, 258
Frampton, Kenneth: *Modern Architecture* (1980), *203,* 206, 236
Fraser, Nancy: "Rethinking the Public Sphere" (1993), 269–70, 271
Fred Harvey Company, 207
Friedman, Alice T.: mentioned, 205; *Women and the Making of the Modern House* (1998), 202
From Bauhaus to Our House (Wolfe), 55, 255–56
"From Model to Mashup" (Miljački), 132, 212–23
Frost, Henry, 237
Fry, Maxwell, 206
"Full Scale Prototype Structures" (Burton), 133, 141–43
Fuller, Buckminster, 206
functionalism, 119–21, 175, 179n22

G

Galveston, TX: "Action Plan for The Strand" (Venturi, Rauch, and Scott Brown), *52*
"Gaming at CRS" (Estes), 132, 168–69, *169*
Garden of the Generaliffe, 35
Gardens of a Golden Afternoon (Brown), 236
gender identity, 62, 71n4, 275–82
"Gender Issues in Teaching Architectural History" (Kingsley), 227, 234–39
Georgia Institute of Technology, 60
Ghirardo, Diane: JAE executive editor, 16; "Past or Post Modern in Architectural Fashion" (1986), 23, 54–59
Giddens, Anthony, 288, 289–90

Giedion, Sigfried: "History and the Architect" (1957), 133, 134–37; mentioned, 14; *Space, Time and Architecture* (1941), 246–47
Gilligan, Carol: *In a Different Voice* (1982), 234
Gilman, Charlotte Perkins, 202
Ginsberg, Jean, 206
Ginzburg, Moisei, 70
Giuliani Frigerio apartments (Terragni), 58
Glassie, Henry, 203
Goodman, Anna and Maura Lucking: "Images Doing Work" (2019), 227, 292–300
Goodman, Robert, 108
Graham Foundation, The, 81
Grand Domestic Revolution, The (Hayden), 202, 237
Grant, Bradford C.: with Dennis Mann: *Directory of African American Architects* (1991), 262; mentioned, 202; photographs by, *264*
Grant, George, 126
Graves, Michael: mentioned, 54, 59n10, 60; Portland Public Office Building (1982), 55
Gray, Eileen: designs of, 206, 207; mentioned, 201, 205, 236
Griffin, Marion Mahony: and Frank Lloyd Wright studio, 204; mentioned, 201; New Federal Capital (1912), 205–6
Griffin, Walter Burley, 201, 205
Griswold del Castillo, Richard, Teresa McKenna, and Yvonne Yarbro-Bejarano: *Chicano Art* (1991), 264
Gropius, Ise: with Herbert Bayer and Walter Gropius: *Bauhaus 1919-1928* (1975), 276, 277, 279; "Theory and Organization of the Bauhaus, The" (1923), 277
Gropius, Walter Adolph: *Arbeitsrat für Kunst* (1919), 275–76; on architecture, 135, 138; and discrimination, 280, 281; with Herbert Bayer and Ise Gropius: *Bauhaus 1919-1928* (1975), 276, 277, 279; "Theory and Organization of the Bauhaus, The" (1923), 277; mentioned, 54, 80, 230; and sexual independence, 278
Growth and Form, On (Thompson), 127
Guardini, Romano, 245
Guarini, Guarino: *Church of S. Lorenzo* in *Architettura Civile* (1737), *176*
Gürel, Metlem Ö. and Kathryn H. Anthony: "Canon and the Void, The" (2006), 133, 200–211

H

Habermas, Jurgen, 269, 270
Habraken, John: "Notes of a Traveler" (1979), 23, 39–44
Hadid, Zaha, 205
Halsband, Frances, 201
Hampstead Garden Suburb, 237
Haraway, Donna: "Manifesto for Cyborgs, A" (1985), 288
Harper's Magazine, 111
Harvard University: alumnus Robert. Madison, 241; Graduate School of Design, 151; mentioned, 30, 84, 109, 134; *Project on the City*, 80, *82*, 83n1; psychologist, 234; Widener Library (Abele), 202
Harvey, David, 127
Hassid, Sarni, 183
Haussmann, Georges Eugene, 286
Hayden, Dolores: *Grand Domestic Revolution, The* (1981), 202, 237

Hayden, Sophia: designs at 1893 World's Columbian Exposition, 205; mentioned, 206
Hegel, Georg Friedrich, 244, 246–47
Hejduk, John, 58, 177
Herbart, Friedrich, 245–46
hierarchy of importance, 172
Hildebrandt, Lily, 278
hip hop architecture, 62–74
Hip Hop Park, 65–67, *67, 68, 69*
Historic Landmarks of Black America (Cantor), 262
historical trauma, 275–82
Historically Black Colleges and Universities, 208, 236, 295
history, study of, 134–37, 173–79, 200–211, 243–47
"History and the Architect" (Giedion), 133, 134–37
History of Architecture, A (Kostof), 200, 203, *203,* 204, 205, 235
History of Architecture on the Comparative Method (Fletcher), 134, 200, 207
Hitchcock, Henry-Russell and Philip Johnson: *International Style, The* (1932), 54, 207
"Hold It (Meditations Upon a Gorgonzola Cheese)" (Bloomer), 23, 60–61
Holl, Steven, 57
Hollein, Hans, 23
Hollywood, CA and Paul Revere Williams, 202, 206, 266
Holston, James, 273
Home Planners Institutes, 93
homelessness, 258, 272–73
Horowitz, Helen Lefkowitz: *Alma Mater* (1984), 236
House and Home, 247
House Done in the Intention of the Villa Madama (Tigerman), 54
House of Seagram, 33, 35
housing: and government funding, 240–41; history of, 103–4, 202; and physical appearances, 49, 91, 101; policies, 226, 228–29; public: high-rise, 249–57, *250, 251, 252, 253, 254,* 259; specialized, *264*; and research, 86, 93; and technology, 287, 290, *290*
Housing Question, The (Engels), 259
Houston Home and Garden, 55
"How Become an Architect?" (Neutra), 132, 144
Howard University, 241
Howe, Florence, 234
HUD (U.S. Dept. of Housing and Urban Development), 81, 249–57
Hudnut, Joseph: "Humanism and the Teaching of Architecture" (1961), 22, 33–36
Hugo, Victor, 57, 59
humanism, 33–36, 120–21, 138
"Humanism and the Teaching of Architecture" (Hudnut), 22, 33–36
Hutchins, Robert M., 140
Huxtable, Ada Louise, 202
Hyman, Isabelle and Marvin Trachtenberg: *Architecture: from Prehistory to Postmodernism* (1986), *203,* 204–5, 235

I

I. M. Pei (Wiseman), 262
"Images Doing Work" (Goodman and Lucking), 227, 292–300

"Immanent Domain: Pervasive Computing and the Public Realm" (Cuff), 227, 283–91
In a Different Voice (Gilligan), 234
Ingersoll, Richard: "Ecology Question, The" (1992), 227, 258–60
Instant City (Archigram Group), 81
Institute of Architecture and Urban Studies, 81
Intercultural Architecture (Kurokawa), 262
interdisciplinary study, 45–50, 132, 150–51, 243–47
interiors, 75–79, 101, 103, 202, 206, 207, 235
International Style, 87, 134, 206, 254
International Style, The (Hitchcock and Johnson), 54, 207
International Visual Literacy Association, 163
Iowa State University, 141, 142, 143
"Is There Research in the Studio?" (Varnelis), 23, 80–83
Ishikawa, Sara, 262
Issacs, Reginald, 84
Itten, Johannes, 276, 279, 280
Izenour, Steven: *Learning from Las Vegas* (1972), 80–81, *82,* 83, 205

J
Jackson, John B.: mentioned, 99; "Purpose of the City, The" (1962), 98, 103–4
Jacobs, Jane: critic of Modernism, 205; *Death and Life of Great American Cities* (1961), 206; mentioned, 202
Jahn, Helmut and C. F. Murphy Associates: Argonne National Laboratories Support Facility (1979), 54
James, William, 36
Jammer, Max: *Concepts of Space* (1954), 136
Jarzombek, Mark: "Crisis of Interdisciplinary Historiography, The" (1991), 226, 243–47
Jeanneret, Charles-Édouard. *See* Le Corbusier
Jekyll, Gertrude: and Edward Lutyens, 201, 236; garden designs, 206; mentioned, 235
Jencks, Charles: *Language of Post Modern Architecture, The* (1977), 254; mentioned, 23, 60, 256; on Post Modernism, 54; on Pruitt-Igoe, 249, 254–55
Jerde, Jon, 271
John Cochran Garden Apartments (Leinweber, Yamasaki & Hellmuth), 254
Johnson, June G. and Dora P. Crouch: *Traditions in Architecture* (2001), 204
Johnson, Philip and Henry-Russell Hitchock: *International Style, The* (1932), 54, 207
Johnston, Frances Benjamin: *Instructors Reference a Blueprint* (1909), *295;* photography of, 294–95
Journal of Architectural Education (JAE): first issue of, 22, 80; historical overview, *13,* 13–18, *14, 15, 16, 17, 18;* interview, 152–57; mentioned, 94; and pedagogy, 132; and politics, 226–27; and research, 22–24, 80, 84–85, 94, 183; and sustainability, 99
Journal of Housing, 255
Journal of the Society of Architectural Historians, 13
Joyce, James: *Finnegans Wake* (1939), 61
juries, design, 182–92, *184, 185, 186, 187*

K
Kahn, Louis I.: mentioned, 201, 205, 206, 236; "Poetics" (1973), 162
Kassabaum, George, 253

Kennedy, Jacqueline, 207
Kieran, Stephen: with James Timberlake: Sculpture Building, Yale University (2008), 77, *78;* "Research in Design" (2007), 23–24, 75–79
Kilgore, Harley, 87
King, Chris: "Body-Masque" construction (n.d.), *193,* 195; "Studio Screen" excercise (n.d.), *194,* 195–96; Urban Encounters exercise, 198
Kingsley, Karen: "Gender Issues in Teaching Architectural History" (1988), 203, 210n37, 227, 234–39; mentioned, 16, 204, 207, 262
Kirkham, Pat: *Women Designers in the USA 1900–2000* (2000), 202
Klee, Felix, 277, 278
Klee, Paul, 135
Kliment, Robert, 201
Kocher, A. Lawrence, 297
Koetter, Fred and Colin Rowe: *Collage City* (1976), 254
Koolhaas, Rem: *Delirious New York* (1978), 81, 83; *Project on the City* (1996-2000), 80, 82, *82,* 83n1
Kostof, Spiro: *History of Architecture, A* (1985), 200, 203, *203,* 204, 205, 235
Kulper, Amy, 17
Kurokawa, Kisho: *Intercultural Architecture* (1991), 262
Kwinter, Sanford, 127

L
La Gory, Mark and John Pipkin: *Urban Social Space* (1981), 254
La Pratica della Perspettiva (Barbaro), 174
Ladies' Home Journal, 206
Lagos, NG, 80, 83n1
Laing, R. D., 183
Landsberg, Paul Ludwig, 245
Landscape, 33
landscapes: epigenetic, *124,* 127; styles of, 103–4; urban, 105–6, 109–12, 163–67
Language of Post Modern Architecture, The (Jencks), 254
Larson, C. Theodore, 93
Larson, Magali Sarfatti, 85
Las Vegas, NV: mentioned, 22, 23; study of, *45,* 45–50, *48* (*See also Learning from Las Vegas*)
Late Roman Arts and Crafts (Riegl), 136
Latour, Bruno, 212, 223n1
Laugier, Marc-Antoine, 245
Le Corbusier: and Charlotte Perriand, 201, 205, 206, 236; mentioned, 54, 80, 207, 229; Plan Voisin (1925), 55; and Pruitt-Igoe design principles, 254–55; Radiant City (1930), 55; *Towards a New Architecture* (1982), 70, 245
Learning from Las Vegas (Izenour, Scott Brown, Venturi), 80–81, *82,* 83, 205, 206. *See also* Las Vegas, NV
Leavitt, Jacqueline, 262
Ledoux, Claude Nicolas, 176, 178
Lee, David, 202
Lefaivre, Liane, 126
Lefebvre, Henri: mentioned, 70; *Production of Space, The* (1995), 63–64; and social space, 71n14
Legorreta, Ricardo: Pershing Square redesign (1993), *270,* 270–71, 273
Leinweber, Yamasaki & Hellmuth, 249–57, *250*

Lemont, IL: Argonne National Laboratories Support Facility (Jahn and C. F. Murphy Associates), 54
L'Enfant, Pierre Charles, 202
Les edifices antiques de Rome (Desgodetz), *177*
Levine, Lawrence: *Black Culture and Black Consciousness* (1977), 264
Levine Hall, University of Pennsylvania (KieranTimberlake), *76,* 76–77, *77*
Levittown, NJ, 91
Levittown, PA, 45–50, *46, 47*
Libeskind, Daniel: mentioned, 57, 58; *Micromegas* (1979), *177*; "Open Letter to Architectural Educators and Students of Architecture, An" (1987), 132, 180–81
Life, 252
lighting, 116–17, 147
Lipsitz, George: *Time Passages* (1990), 62, 71n5
literacy, visual, 163–67
Lobel, Josh: "Urban Encounters" exercise (n.d.), *197,* 198, 199n2
Loblolly House (KieranTimberlake), 77, *78,* 79
Locke, John, 63, 71n12
Lockwood, Charles, 111
Log, 82
London, UK: Hampstead Garden Suburb, 237; mentioned, 269; surveillance in, 283, 285–86, *287*; working class neighborhoods, 80, 83
London Architectural Association School, 135, 137
Looking Beneath the Surface (Davis and Simmons), 267
Loos, Adolf, 30, 32n1
Los Angeles, CA: airport surveillance, 287; Baldwin Hills, 272; CityWalk (Jerde), 271; Pershing Square redesign (Legorreta), *270,* 270–71, 273; and segregation, *271,* 273; and street vendors, 271–72, *272*; Theme Building (Williams), *264*
Los Angeles: Architecture of Four Ecologies (Banham), 81
Louisiana State University, 184
Lubove, Roy, 111
Lucking, Maura and Anna Goodman: "Images Doing Work" (2019), 227, 292–300
Lutyens, Edwin: and Gertrude Jekyll, 201, 206, 236; and Hampstead Garden Suburb, 237
Lynch, Kevin: "New Look at Civic Design, A" (1955), 98, 100–102

M
MacDonald, Margaret: and Charles Rennie Mackintosh, 201, 205, 206; mentioned, 235, 236
machine learning, 132, 158–61
Mack, Jordi: "Studio Screen" installation (n.d.), *195,* 196–97
Mackintosh, Charles Rennie: and Margaret MacDonald, 201, 205, 206
Mackintosh, Margaret MacDonald: and Charles Rennie Mackintosh, 201, 205, 206; mentioned, 235, 236
Madison, Robert, 241
Mahler, Alma, 278
Mahony, Marion: and Frank Lloyd Wright studio, 204; New Federal Capital (1912), 205–6; and Walter Burley Griffin, 201
Maner, Selin: "Domestic Encounters" exercise (n.d.), *196,* 197; "Studio Screen" 2 installation (n.d.), *194, 195,* 196

Mangin, Joseph Francis: New York City Hall (1802-11), 202, 207
Manheim, Ernest, 37
"Manifesto for Cyborgs, A" (Haraway), 288
Mann, Dennis: with Bradford C. Grant: *Directory of African American Architects* (1991), 262; mentioned, 202
marginalization, 65, 70, 74n39
Marjanović, Igor: introductions by, 13–18, 22–24, 226–27
Marsio-Aalto, Aino: mentioned, 201; Paimio Sanatorium (1933), 236; Villa Mairea (1940), 236
Martin Luther King, Jr. Center for Nonviolent Social Change (Bond), 202, 206
Marx, Karl and Friedrich Engels: *Communist Manifesto, The* (1948), 243–44
Massachusetts Institute of Technology: alumna Sophia Hayden, 205; Building Design Conference, 153; city studies, 101; design studio at, 212–23; establishment of architecture curricula, 207; mentioned, 33, 39, 100, 150, 158, 212; and student juries, 185
Master Builders, The (Blake), 235
McCurry, Margaret, 201
McHarg, Ian: "Ecology of the City" (1962), 98, 105–6; mentioned, 55
McIntosh, Peggy, 203, 235
McKenna, Teresa, Richard Griswold del Castillo, and Yvonne Yarbro-Bejarano: *Chicano Art* (1991), 264
McKissack, McKissack & Thompson (MM&T): mentioned, 265; Tuskegee Air Force Base (1942), 266; Universal Life Insurance Company Headquarters (1949), 266
McLaughlin, Robert, 85, 86–87
McLuhan, Marshall, 285, 290n9
meaning, 52, 54–59, 72n16, 163–67, 173–79
mechanical systems, 113–18
Meehan, Eugene, 251, 253
Memphis, TN: Universal Life Insurance Company Headquarters (MM&T), 266
"Messages in the Interstices" (Treib), 163–67
Metropolitan Home, 55
Michigan Architectural Research Laboratory (ARL), 93
Micromegas (Libeskind), 177
Mies van der Rohe, Ludwig: on architectural principles, 139; Barcelona Pavilion (1929), 204, 235; in history, 33–35; interdisciplinary approach of, 245; and Lilly Reich, 201, 204–5, 206, 207, 236; mentioned, 54, 153, 230, 279
Miljački, Ana: "From Model to Mashup" (2011), 132, 212–23
Mill Run, PA: Fallingwater (Wright), 204
Miller Lane, Barbara, 278, 279
Milne, Murray A. and Charles W. Rusch: "Death of the Beaux-Arts, The" (1968), 132, 152–57
Minneapolis, MN, *53*
MM&T (McKissack, McKissack & Thompson): mentioned, 265; Tuskegee Air Force Base (1942), 266; Universal Life Insurance Company Headquarters (1949), 266
mobility, social, 109–12
models, 141–43, *170,* 170–72, *171,* 193–99, 212–23
Modern Architecture (Frampton), *203,* 206, 236

Modern Architecture Since 1900 (Curtis), *203,* 204, 205–6
Modernism, 54–59, 87, 200–212, 249–56
Moe, Kiel: "Compelling Yet Unreliable Theories of Sustainability" (2007), 99, 122–29
Moffett, Marian, Michael Fazio, and Lawrence Wodehouse: *Buildings Across Time* (2004), *203,* 204, 205
Moholy-Nagy, Sibyl, 202
"Money Problem, The" (Solomon), 226, 232–33
Monge, Gaspard, 174, 175
monitoring of systems, 75–79, 113–18
Moore, Charles: Piazza d'Italia (1978), 55
Moralism and the Modern Home (Wright), 237
Morgan, Julia: and the École des Beaux Arts, 204; Hearst Castle (1919-47), 235; mentioned, 201, 205, 206
Mowitt, John: "Sound of Music" (1977), 62–63, 64, 71n9
multiculturalism, 261–68, 271
Mumford, Lewis, 126, 229
Musee d'Orsay (Aulenti), 205
music, 62–74, 212–23

N

NAAB (National Architectural Accrediting Board), 200–201, 208, 261
Nabokov, Peter: *Native American Architecture* (1989), 262, 264
Nashville, TN, 266
National Academy of Sciences, 90
National Architectural Accrediting Board (NAAB), 200–201, 208, 261
National Endowment for the Arts, 81
National Housing Agency, 93
National Observer, 252
National Organization of Minority Architects (NOMA), 208
National Register for Historic Places, 208
National Research Council on Industrial Research Laboratories of the United States, 27
National Science Foundation Act of 1946, 27
National Underground Railroad Freedom Center (Blackburn), 208
National Urban League, 240
Native American Architecture (Nabokov), 262, 264
Negroponte, Nicholas: "Toward a Theory of Architecture Machines" (1969), 132, 158–61
Nervi, Luigi, 135, 141
Neutra, Richard J.: "How Become an Architect?" (1960), 132, 144
Neveu, Marc J: introductions by, 11, 13–18, 132–33; mentioned, 17
New Federal Capital (Griffin), 205–6
New Homes for Today (Williams), 262
New Jersey Institute of Technology: Commencement Address (Eyck), 119–21
"New Look at Civic Design, A" (Lynch), 98, 100–102
New Orleans, LA: Piazza d'Italia (Moore), 55
New York City, NY: AIA convention in, 240; Chase Manhattan Bank Plaza (Noguchi), 265; City Hall (Mangin), 202, 207; and high-rise office buildings, 113–15; mentioned, 81, 83, 111, 121; *New York Times* Headquarters (Piano), 126; Pier 57, 217; RCA Building (Hood), 35

New York Times Headquarters (Piano), 126
Newman, Oscar: *Defensible Space* (1972), 98, 107–8, 253, 254
Newsweek, 55
Niceron, Jean-François: *Curious Perspective* (1638), *175*
Nichols, Minerva Parker, 206
Noble, David, 126
Noguchi, Isamu: Chase Manhattan Bank Plaza (1961-64), 265; UNESCO Headquarters Garden (1959), 265
NOMA (National Organization of Minority Architects), 208
Noormarkku, FI: Villa Mairea (Aalto), 236
Northeastern University, 122
"Notes of a Traveler" (Habraken), 23, 39–44
Notes on the Synthesis of Form (Alexander), 152
Notre-Dame (Cathedral of Paris), 34

O

"Objectives of Architectural Education" (Rapson), 132, 138–40
"Observations on Energy Use in Buildings" (Stein), 98, 113–18
Ohio State University, The: Visual Arts Center (Eisenman), 58
Olgyay, Victor, 122
Olmsted, Frederick Law, 111
O'Neil, C. Shayne, 16
"Open Letter to Architectural Educators and Students of Architecture, An" (Libeskind), 132, 180–81
Oppositions, 55, 81
Owings, Nathaniel, 55

P

Paimio, FI: Paimio Sanatorium (Aalto), 236
Paimio Sanatorium (Aalto), 236
Papademetriou, Peter, 16
Paris, FR: École des Beaux Arts, 14, 174–75, 204; Eiffel Tower (Sauvestre), 285; mentioned, 269; Musee d'Orsay (Aulenti), 205; Notre-Dame cathedral, 34; Plan Voisin (Le Corbusier), 55; and public spaces, 286; and suburbs, 104; UNESCO Headquarters Garden (Noguchi), 265
Parker, Barry, 237
Parthenon, 34, 35
"Partnership, A" (Wright), 201
"Past or Post Modern in Architectural Fashion" (Ghirardo), 23, 54–59
patents, 87
patriarchy, 200–211, 227, 234–38, 275–81
Pattamasatayasonthi, Chai, 217, *221,* 221–23, *222*
Pearl River Delta, 80, 83n1
Pei, I. M., 265
Pérez-Gómez, Alberto: *Architecture and the Crisis of Modern Science* (1983), 56–57; "Architecture as Drawing" (1982), 132, 173–79; mentioned, 58
"Perimeter Projects, The" (Segrest), 60
Perkins, Holmes, 47, 101
Perriand, Charlotte: furniture design, 206, 236; interior design, 207; and Le Corbusier, 201, 205; mentioned, 235
perspective, *174,* 174–75, *175*
Petit Trianon (Gabriel), 35

philanthropy, 258, 269–70, 295
philosophy, 31, 226, 243–47
photography, 45–50, 80–83, 283–290, 292–300
Piano, Renzo: *New York Times* Headquarters (2003-7), 126
Piazza d'Italia (Moore), 55
Pickens, Buford, 14
Pierce, M. Scheffel and Stuart W. Rose: "Television as a Design Tool" (1967), 132, 145–49
Pierce, Melusina Fay, 202
Pipkin, John and Mark La Gory: *Urban Social Space* (1981), 254
Piranesi, Giovanni Battista, 57, 176, 178
Pittman, William Sydney, 293–94
Plan Voisin (Le Corbusier), 55
Plater-Zyberk, Elizabeth, 205
"Poetics" (Kahn), 162
Poncelet, Victor, 175
Pope, Theodate, 206
Portland, ME: Maine State Pier Project, 212–23; exercises by Pattamasatayasonthi, *217, 218, 221, 222*; exercises by Wuttig, *215, 216, 219, 220*
Portland, OR: Portland Public Office Building (Graves), 55
Portland State University, 292
Portoghesi, Paolo, 54
Post Modernism, 54–59, 254, 258
"Postwar Legacy of Architectural Research, The" (Sachs), 22, 84–95
poverty, 230–31, 249–57
Powers of Ten (Eames Office), 80, 83
Practice of Everyday Life, The (Certeau), 63–64, 72n16–17
Praxis, 82
Précis de Leçons d'Architecture (Durand), 175, *178*
prefabrication, 87, 91, 93
Principles of the Science of Art (Schmarsow), 136
privacy, 196–97, 285–88
"Private Reactions to Public Criticism" (Anthony), 133, 182–92
Producers Council, 90
Production of Space, The (Lefebvre), 63–64
Progressive Architecture, 55
Project on the City (Koolhaas), 80, 82, *82,* 83n1
protest, 227, 240, 271, 274n6, 289. See also activism
prototypes, 141–43, 171–72
"Pruitt-Igoe Myth, The" (Bristol), 226, 249–57
public housing: Pruitt-Igoe, 249–57, *250, 251, 252, 253, 254*; and social responsibility, 258–60; and urban renewal, 228–29
Public Housing Administration, 250
public space, 107–8, 269–74, 283–91
Puerto Rico: Turn of the Century Architecture (Rigau), 262
Pugin, W. N., 245
"Purpose of the City, The" (Jackson), 98, 103–4
Pyla, Panayiota, 203

R
racism, 200–211, 240–42, 249–57, 271, 281, 292–300
Radiant City (Le Corbusier), 55
Rainwater, Lee: *Behind Ghetto Walls* (1970), 253
"(W)rapped Space: The Architecture of Hip Hop" (Wilkins), 23, 62–74

Rapson, Ralph: "Objectives of Architectural Education" (1959), 132, 138–40
Rauch, John and Robert Venturi: with Denise Scott Brown: "Action Plan for The Strand," *52*; Yale Mathematics Building design (1968), 206
Raymond, Eleanor, 235, 236
RCA Building (Hood), 35
recreation, urban, 62–74, 111
recycling, 124, 128n20, 260
redevelopment, urban: Pruitt-Igoe project, 249–57, *250, 251, 252, 253, 254*; and renewal, 226, 228–29
Reflections on History (Burckhardt), 135
Regionalism, 126
Reich, Lilly: Barcelona Pavilion (1929), 204–5, 235; and collaboration, 236; and Mies van der Rohe, 201, 206, 207
Reilly, William K., 55
Renaissance, 33, 80, *173,* 173–79, *174,* 244
Renaissance and Baroque (Wölfflin), 136
Rendell, Jane, 201
renewal, urban. See redevelopment, urban
Rensselaer, Mariana Griswold van, 206
research: applied, 25–29, 45; definitions of, 25, 84–85, 87; and design, 39–44, 75, *75,* 93, 212–13; pure, 25–29, 265–67; and science, 26, 84–95, *86*; social, 37, 200–211; and studios, 80–83
"Research and Criticism in Architecture" (Sekler), 22, 30–32
"Research Heritage of the Architectural Profession, The" (Bannister), 80, 85
"Research in Design" (Kieran), 23–24, 75–79
responsibility, social, 100–103, 228–29, 258–60
"Rethinking the Public Sphere" (Fraser), 269, 270
Rice University, 258
Richmond, VA: Minority Business Utilization Plan, 241
Riegl, Alois: *Late Roman Arts and Crafts* (1901, 1927), 136; mentioned, 245
Rienzo, Cola di, 244
Rietveld, Gerrit: Schröder House (1924), 205
Rigau, Jorge: *Puerto Rico: Turn of the Century Architecture* (1992), 262
Robertson, Jaquelin, 59
Robertson, R. G.: *Descriptive Geometry* (1966), *177*
Rolfe, Walter T., 13, 14
Rome, IT: architectural drawings, *173, 177*; and Cola di Rienzo, 244; map of, 49, *49*; mentioned, 33, 121; *Project on the City,* 80, 83n1; rebirth of, 103
Rose, Stuart W. and M. Scheffel Pierce: "Television as a Design Tool" (1967), 132, 145–49
Rosen, Jeffrey, 285, 289
Rossi, Aldo: *Scientific Autobiography* (1981), 57
Roth, Leland M.: *America Builds* (1983), 236; *American Architecture* (2001), *203,* 206–7; *Understanding Architecture* (1993), 204
Rousseau, Jean-Jacques, 244–45
Roussel, Raymond, 61
Rowe, Colin: with Fred Koetter: *Collage City* (1976), 254; mentioned, 81
Royal Institute of British Architects, 26
Royal Institute of Technology Sweden, 184
Ruckleshaus, William, 55

Rudofsky, Bernard: *Behind the Picture Window* (1955), 287
Rudolph, Paul, 33
Rüedi Ray, Katerina: "Bauhaus Hausfrau: Gender Formation in Design Education" (2001), 227, 275–82
Rumford, Count (Benjamin Thompson), 25
Rupnik, Ivan, 17
Rusch, Charles W. and Murray A. Milne: "Death of the Beaux-Arts, The" (1968), 132, 152–57
Rutgers University, 230

S

Saarinen, Eero, 33, 35
Sachs, Avigail: "Postwar Legacy of Architectural Research, The" (2009), 22, 84–95
Said, Edward, 208
San Francisco, CA: and Catherine Bauer, 226; Julia Morgan in, 205; murals, 265; storefront churches, 266; Union Street structures, 207
Santa Monica, CA: Charles and Ray Eames House, 206; public spaces, *271, 273*
Sauvestre, Stephen: Eiffel Tower (1889), 285
scarcity, 105–6, 113–18, 119, 122, 258–60
Scheffler, Karl, 245
Scheu, Lelia: "Body-Masque" construction (n.d.), *193,* 195
Schlemmer, Helena "Tut," 276, 277, 278
Schlemmer, Oskar, 277, 278, 281
Schmarsow, August: *Principles of the Science of Art* (1905), 136
Schön, Donald, 183
Schreyer, Lothar, 276, 278
Schroeder, Truus, 205
Schroeder House (Rietveld), 205
Science the Endless Frontier (Bush), 87
Scientific American, 283
Scientific Autobiography (Rossi), 57
Scofidio, Ricardo: and Elizabeth Diller, 201, 288, *288*; with Tod Williams: "Typology and Primary Events" (1982), 132, 170–72
Scott, Mel, 111
Scott Brown, Denise: Fire Station No. 4 (1966), 206; *Learning from Las Vegas* (1972), 22, 80–81, *82,* 83, 205, 206; mentioned, 55, 201; "On Formal Analysis as Design Research" (1979), 22–23, 45–50; "With People in Mind" (1981), 23, 51–53; Yale Mathematics Building design (1968), 206
Scully, Vincent, 81
Sculpture Building, Yale University (KieranTimberlake), 77, *78*
seeing, 43, 100–102, 163–67. *See also* surveillance
Segrest, Robert: "Perimeter Projects, The" (1984), 60
Sekler, Eduard: "Research and Criticism in Architecture" (1957), 22, 30–32
Selfridge, Oliver, 160
Sennett, Richard: *Fall of Public Man, The* (1977), 269, 286, 289
Serlio, Sebastiano: *Architettura et Prospettiva* (1519), *173, 174*
Seven Types of Ambiguity (Empson), 60
sexism, 200–211, 234–38, 275–82
sexuality, 62, 71n4, 278–82
Shutte-Lihotzky, Margarete, 206

Silverman, Kaja, 275, 278, 280, 281–82
Simmons, Ken: and multiculturalism, 227, 262; with Regina Davis: *Looking Beneath the Surface* (1991), 267, 268n19
Simmons, William, 261
sketching, 43, 47, 146. *See also* drawing
Skillern, John: "Domestic Encounters" exercise (n.d.), *196,* 197
Sky Lab at Texas A&M University, *87,* 89
Small Home of Tomorrow, The (Williams), 262
Smithson, Alison and Peter: mentioned, 23, 201, 206; research process, 80–81, 82, *82,* 83
Soane and Borromini, 61
social responsibility, 100–103, 228–29, 258–60
Sociological Abstracts, 37
sociology, 37–38, 50, 51–53, 230–31
solar energy, 77, 117, *123,* 128n14, 258–60
Solomon, Daniel: "Money Problem, The" (1969), 226, 232–33
Sonsbeek Sculpture Pavilion (Eyck), *120*
Sorkin, Michael, 269
"Sound of Music in the Era of its Electronic Reproducibility, The" (Mowitt), 62–63, 71n9
Southern California Institute of Architecture, 269
space, conceptions of, 136–37, 145–49, 168–69, 269–74
Space, Time and Architecture (Giedion), 246–47
space/music relationship, 62–74, 212–23
Sparke, Penny, 202
spatial practices, 23, 63–74, 109–12, 145–49, 193–99, 277–78, 283–90
Spear, Laurinda, 201
specialization, 39–44, 110, 138–40, 150–51, 267
Speer, Albert, 16
Springfield, IL: Dana Thomas House (Wright), 204
Spuybroek, Lars: Destra Expo water pavilion (1994-97), 288, *290*; D-Tower project (2001-3), 288, *289*
St. Louis, MO: John Cochran Garden Apartments (Leinweber, Yamasaki & Hellmuth), 254; Pruitt-Igoe public housing project (Leinweber, Yamasaki & Hellmuth), 249–57, *250, 251, 252, 253,* 254
Stadler-Stölzl, Gunta, 279
Statement on Architectural Research (AIA), 89
Stein, Richard G.: "Observations on Energy Use in Buildings" (1977), 98, 113–18
Stern, Robert A. M., 23, 54, 55, 59n10
Stevens, Sara: introductions by, 13–18, 22–24, 98–99
Stirling and Wilford partnership, 57
Stoner, Jill, 262
storefront churches, *263,* 265–66
storytelling, 72n19, 214, 223
Stowe, Harriet Beecher, 202, 205, 235
street vendors, 68, 103, 271–72, *272*
stress, emotional, 42, 106, 119–21, 187–90
structure: and cultural specificity, 65–68; and prototypes, 142–44; and technical knowledge, 113–18, 135, 138–40, 150–51
students: at the Bauhaus, 275–82; and design exercises, 170–72, 193–99, 212–223, 232–33; and educational objectives, 119–21, 138–40, 142, 144, 180–81; and juries, 182–91; and manual labor: at Black Mountain College, 296–99, *297, 298, 299*; at Tuskegee Institute, 292–96, *293, 294, 295, 296*; and research, 102, 265–67

Studio Screen design exercise, *194, 195,* 195–97
Stull, Donald, 202
Sullivan, Louis, 164
surveillance, 107–8, *283,* 283–91, *284, 288*. *See also* seeing
survey. *See* textbook
sustainability, 99, 122–29, 258–60
Suttles, Gerald, 108
symbiosis, 105–6
symbols and symbolization, 15, 46, 48, 65–67, 163–67, *164, 165, 166, 167*

T

Tafuri, Manfredo: *Architecture and Utopia* (1973), 56; mentioned, 57; *Theories and History of Architecture* (1976), 56
Taj Mahal, 35
TAMU (Texas A&M University): Sky Lab and Wind Lab, *87*
Tanner, Henry O., 264
Taube, Mortimer, 160
Taut, Bruno, 275
Taylor, Walter A.: "Architect Looks at Research, The" (1947), 22, 25–29, 85, 89–90
Technical University of Berlin, 151
technology, 119–21, 123, 126, 158–61, 283–91. *See also* air conditioning
TEES (Texas Engineering Experiment Station), *87,* 89
"Television as a Design Tool" (Rose and Pierce), 132, 145–49
Terragni, Giuseppe: Giuliani Frigerio apartments (1939), 58
terrorism, 283–91
Texas A&M University (TAMU): Sky Lab and Wind Lab, *87,* 89
Texas Engineering Experiment Station (TEES), *87,* 89
Texas Homes, 55
textbooks, 200–11, *203,* 234–38
theater, 67–68, 277–78, 298
Theme Building (Williams), *264*
Theories and History of Architecture (Tafuri), 56
"Theory and Organization of the Bauhaus, The" (Bayer, Gropius and Gropius), 277
thermal images, *285, 287*
Thierry, Augustine, 244
Thomas, Roy, 264, 265
Thompson, Benjamin (Count Rumford), 25
Thompson, D'Arcy: *Growth and Form, On* (1951), 127
Tigerman, Stanley: House Done in the Intention of the Villa Madama (1980), 54; and Margaret McCurry, 201; mentioned, 23
Timberlake, James: with Stephen Kieran: Sculpture Building, Yale University (2008), 77, *78*; teaching, 75
Time (magazine), 252
Time Passages (Lipsitz), 62, 71n5
Toronto, ON: Downsview Park Competition, *125,* 127
Torre, Susana: mentioned, 258; *Women in American Architecture* (1977), 201
"Toward a Theory of Architecture Machines" (Negroponte), 132, 158–61
Towards a New Architecture (Le Corbusier), 70, 245
Trachtenberg, Alan, 111

Trachtenberg, Marvin: with Isabelle Hyman: *Architecture: from Prehistory to Postmodernism* (1986), *203,* 204–5, 235
Traditions in Architecture (Crouch and Johnson), 204
Tratatto di Architettura II (Filarete), 174
trauma, historical, 275–82
Travis, Jack: *African American Architects in Current Practice* (1991), 262
Treib, Marc: "Messages in the Interstices" (1976), 163–67
Trinh, T. Minh-Ha: *Woman, Native, Other* (1989), 264
Tschumi, Bernard, 61
Tsien, Billie, 201
Tulane University, 184, 234
Turin, IT: *Church of S. Lorenzo* (Guarini), *176*
Turner, Frederick, 60
Turner, Paul Venable: *Campus: An American Planning Tradition* (1984), 236
Tuskegee Air Force Base (MM&T), 266
Tuskegee Institute, 68, 292–300
Tuskegee University, 202, 208
Two Hundred Years of African American Art, 264–65
Tyng, Anne: and geometric forms, 206; and Louis Kahn, 201, 236
typology, 81, 132, 170–172
"Typology and Primary Events" (Williams and Scofidio), 132, 170–72

U

Understanding Architecture (Roth), 204
Underwriters' Laboratories, 25, 26
UNESCO Headquarters Garden (Noguchi), 265
Ungers, O. M., 81
Unistrut building system, *93,* 93–94
Universal Life Insurance Company Headquarters (MM&T), 266
University of California, Berkeley: College of Environmental Design (CED), 91–92; and design juries, 184; mentioned, 84, 107, 163, 228, 232, 249, 261; research policy development, 92; and Spiro Kostof, 205; Wurster Hall, *90,* 92
University of California, Los Angeles, 283, 292
University of Houston, 173
University of Illinois, Chicago, 275
University of Illinois, Urbana–Champaign, 182, 184, 200, 207
University of Kansas, 240
University of Limerick, 80
University of Manitoba, 184
University of Miami, 185
University of Michigan, Ann Arbor: archives, 84; Michigan Architectural Research Laboratory (ARL), 93
University of Minnesota, 62, 138
University of Nebraska, 145, 146
University of Oregon, 185
University of Pennsylvania: Levine Hall (KieranTimberlake), *76,* 76–77, *77*; mentioned, 105
University of South Carolina, 37
University of Southern California, 54
University of Utah, 299
University of Washington, 185

Unwin, Raymond, 237
Upton, Dell: *America's Architectural Roots* (1986), 262; mentioned, 203
urban design, 42–43, 51–53, 62–74, 109, *109,* 151. *See also* design, civic
Urban Encounters design exercise, *197, 198*
urban history, 103–4, 109–12, 163–67
"Urban Landscape, The" (Blackmar), 99, 109–12
urban planning, 46, 51, 64, 80–81, 111, 150, 182
urban redevelopment. *See* redevelopment, urban
Urban Social Space (La Gory and Pipkin), 254
U.S. Chamber of Commerce, 27
U.S. Dept. of Housing and Urban Development (HUD), 81, 249–57
Utrecht, NL: Schroeder House (Rietveld), 205

V

Vance, James, 110
Vanity Fair, 55, 59n10
Varnelis, Kazys: "Is There Research in the Studio?" (2007), 23, 80–83
Venturi, Robert: *Complexity and Contradiction in Architecture* (1966), 54, 81, 245–46; with John Rauch and Denise Scott Brown: "Action Plan for The Strand," *52*; Fire Station No. 4 (1966), 206; *Learning from Las Vegas* (1972), 80–81, *82,* 83, 205, 206; Yale Mathematics Building design (1968), 206; mentioned, 52, 53, 60, 201
Versailles, FR: Petit Trianon (Gabriel), 35
Vico, Giambattista, 244, 246, 247
victim-blaming, 251–52, 259
Villa Mairea (Aalto), 236
Visual Arts Center at The Ohio State University (Eisenman), 58
visual literacy, 163–67
Vitruvius, 173, 174
Voices in Architectural Education (Dutton), 262

W

Waddington, C. H., *124,* 127
War Production Board, *92,* 93
war trauma, 275–82
Ward, Anthony: "Biculturalism and Community" (1992), 262
Ward, David, 110
Warner, Sam Bass, 110
Washington, Booker T., 202, 208, 292–94
Washington, DC, 202, 207
Washington Post, 252
Washington State University, 185
Watts, Lewis, 262
webcams, 288, *288*
Weiser, Mark, 283, 284, 289, 290
Wells-Bowie, Laverne, 68
Wendingen, 207
Wharton, Edith, 202
White, Charles, 265
Widener Library at Harvard (Abele), 202
Wigley, Mark, 205
Wilkins, Craig: "(W)rapped Space: The Architecture of Hip Hop" (2000), 23, 62–74
Williams, Paul Revere: and Hollywood, CA projects, 202, 206, 266; mentioned, 265; *New Homes for Today* (1946), 262; *Small Home of Tomorrow, The* (1945), 262; Theme Building (1961), *264*
Williams, Tod: mentioned, 201; with Ricardo Scofidio: "Typology and Primary Events" (1982), 132, 170–72
Willis, Beverly, 207
Wilson, Dreck Spurlock: *African American Architects* (2004), 207
Wind Lab at Texas A&M University, *87,* 89
Winslow, Carleton Monroe, Jr.: "Architectural Education and Behavioral Science" (1963), 22, 37–38
wireless technology, 286, 288–89
Wiseman, Carter: *I. M. Pei* (1990), 262
Wittkower, Rudolf, 35
Wodehouse, Lawrence, Marian Moffet, and Michael Fazio: *Buildings Across Time* (2004), *203, 204, 205*
Wolf, Leonard, 142
Wolfe, Tom: *From Bauhaus to Our House* (1981), 55, 255–56
Wölfflin, Heinrich: influence of, 245–46; mentioned, 247; *Renaissance and Baroque* (1888), 136
Woman, Native, Other (Trinh), 264
Woman's Touch, A (Anscombe), 202, 237
Women and the Making of the Modern House (Friedman), 202
Women Designers in the USA 1900–2000 (Kirkham), 202
Women in American Architecture (Torre), 201
World's Columbian Exposition (1893), 205
"(W)rapped Space: The Architecture of Hip Hop" (Wilkins), 23, 62–74
Wright, Frank Lloyd: Dana Thomas House (1902-4), 204; on disciples, 58; Fallingwater (1937), 204
Wright, Gwendolyn: mentioned, 202; *Moralism and the Modern Home* (1980), 237; "Partnership, A" (1995), 201
"Writing Multiculturalism into Architectural Curricula" (Davis), 227, 261–68
Wunsch, Robert, 298
Wurster, William W.: and Catherine Bauer, 201; mentioned, 14, 84; at UC, Berkeley, 91–93
Wurster Hall, UC Berkeley, *90, 92,* 267
Wuttig, Oliver, *213, 215, 217, 219, 220,* 222–23

Y

Yale University: Mathematics Building design (Venturi and Rauch), 206; mentioned, 35, 45, 52, 152, 185, 295; Sculpture Building (KieranTimberlake), 77, *78*
Yamasaki, Minoru, 255
Yarbro-Bejarano, Yvonne, Richard Griswold del Castillo, and Teresa McKenna: *Chicano Art* (1991), 264
Young, Whitney M., Jr., 240
Young Electric Sign Co., 48
Youtz Nine Unit House, *92*
Youtz, Phillip, 94

Z

Zimmermann, Robert, 246